Voices of the
U.S. Latino Experience

Voices of the U.S. Latino Experience

VOLUME 1

Edited by Rodolfo F. Acuña and Guadalupe Compeán

GREENWOOD PRESS
Westport, Connecticut • London

Library of Congress Cataloging-in-Publication Data

Voices of the U.S. Latino experience / edited by Rodolfo F. Acuña and Guadalupe Compeán.
    p. cm.
    Includes bibliographical references and index.
    ISBN 978–0–313–34020–8 (set : alk. paper)—ISBN 978–0–313–34021–5 (v. 1 : alk. paper)—ISBN 978–0–313–34022–2 (v. 2 : alk. paper)—ISBN 978–0–313–34023–9 (v. 3 : alk. paper)
    1. Hispanic Americans—History—Sources. I. Acuña, Rodolfo. II. Compeán, Guadalupe.
E184.S75V65 2008
973'.0468—dc22   2007046170

British Library Cataloguing in Publication Data is available.

Library of Congress Catalog Card Number: 2007046170
ISBN: 978–0–313–34020–8 (set)
      978–0–313–34021–5 (vol. 1)
      978–0–313–34022–2 (vol. 2)
      978–0–313–34023–9 (vol. 3)

First published in 2008

Greenwood Press, 88 Post Road West, Westport, CT 06881
An imprint of Greenwood Publishing Group, Inc.
www.greenwood.com

Printed in the United States of America

The paper used in this book complies with the
Permanent Paper Standard issued by the National
Information Standards Organization (Z39.48–1984).

10 9 8 7 6 5 4 3 2 1

To Our Angela and Her Shadow

Contents

VOLUME 3

Part XVIII Latinos in the 1960s   749

Documents by Group

CARIBBEANS

CENTRAL AMERICANS

CENTRAL AMERICANS IN THE UNITED STATES

DOMINICAN AMERICANS

MEXICAN AMERICANS/TEJANOS/CHICANOS

MEXICANS

PUERTO RICANS

SOUTH AMERICANS

Introduction

The wealth of documents in *Voices of the U.S. Latino Experience* were selected to help students and other interested readers better understand the diverse role of Latinos in U.S. history and today. *Voices of the U.S. Latino Experience* seeks to provide primary and secondary documents that shed light on relations between Latinos and other ethnic groups. The Latinos include Mexican Americans, Puerto Ricans, Cuban Americans, Dominican Americans, and Central American immigrants. Although the primary focus is Latinos in the United States, contextual documents concerning events in Spain, Mexico, Puerto Rico, Cuba and the Caribbean, and Central and South America are included as well. Sources include letters, memoirs, speeches, articles, essays, interviews, treaties, government reports, testimony, oral histories, and other documents of historical importance. The voices include whites and African Americans as well as Latinos, prominent and obscure, and Euro-Americans as well as people outside the United States. Each of the 423 documents has a short introduction to briefly place it in context and explain its significance.

The collection is divided into 21 sections that each cover a particular timespan, with an overarching theme for the period. Generally, the order of "appearance" of a Latino group in the documents is determined by how many Latin Americans from a specific nation resided in the United States at the given time in history in which the document was produced. The collection does not provide documents for each of the more than 20 Latin American nations equally as it would if it were documenting the history of Latin America. Instead, we have selected documents according to the intensity of the contact between the United States and the particular Latin American nation.

The bulk of the documents in this collection concerns Mexicans and Mexican Americans because Mexicans are the closest physically to the United States and have the longest history of contact and migration. At the time of this writing, Mexico's population is approximately 114 million people, making it the largest Spanish-speaking nation in the world. Of the Latin American countries, it is only second in land size to Brazil. Mexican migration to the United States has been a constant factor, and Mexican Americans are the largest Latino group in the United States.

The documents begin in 1648 and end in 2007. The real starting point for this collection, however, is during the 1800s because it was at this time that the borders between the United States and Latin America were formed. The various treaties set the boundaries between the United States and the new emerging Latin American nationalities, which had in part been formed by 300 years of Spanish colonialism. It was during these years that disparate cuisines, language intonations, and histories were formed. Inspired in part by the French Revolution (1789), most Latin American entities became independent from Spain by 1821. The Great Liberator, Simón Bolívar, had a vision of a united Latin America—but the differences and the distances prevented the formation of such a union.

Slowly, the United States exceeded its borders, encroaching on the lands of the Native American and then neighboring nations. At this point, the question of slavery takes on relevance. Voices within Latin America called for the abolition of slavery from their own nations during their wars for independence. At the same time, slavery was the engine that drove U.S. expansion at the frantic pace it enjoyed. After the United States annexed the Louisiana Territory in 1803, it looked south to what is today Mexico, and in 1819 after it took Florida into its borders, slave interests looked to Cuba.

By the 1820s, the religious notion of Manifest Destiny was expressed in the form of the Monroe Doctrine (1823) that essentially proclaimed that the Americas were for Americans. Slave interests moved into what is today Texas. The documents show that nativism was not a recent phenomenon but had been in motion even before 1803. These documents also show the formation of the Mexican nation (the formation of the Mexican nationality would take time). The purpose of the documents representing this period is to have the reader explore how Euro-Americans got to Texas, why they went there, and the interaction between Euro-Americans and Mexicans during this time period.

Two wars were fought with Mexico (1836, 1846–1848); these events, along with the Gadsden Purchase (1853), created 2,000 miles of border dividing the United States and Mexico. The Texas filibuster (1836) and the Mexican-American War (1846–1848) left indelible scars. Mexico lost half its land and great rivers like the Rio Grande, Colorado, and Gila. There are numerous books on this topic—both in English and Spanish—that will help the reader understand the documents, as they address the causes of the wars and the lives of those who had been left behind as the borders changed. (See the suggested reading list at the end of this introduction.) Without a doubt, the Treaty of Guadalupe Hidalgo (1848) is one of the most important primary documents in the history of people of Mexican origin in the United States. This important treaty affected their property and civil rights. Our collection explores the treaty.

Documents from the period after 1848 deal with Euro-American and Mexican relations on the border. The largest mass of Spanish-speaking people was along the 2,000-mile U.S. border as Mexican origin people crossed at will. There were Latinos other than Mexicans in the Southwest; however, they generally were assimilated into the Mexican community. As a group, they described themselves as Hispanos, referring to a common language and culture. They, however, maintained their individuality. Treaties, boundary commissions, and racism are important elements of this dialectic once the border crosses over and incorporates people of Mexican and Indian extraction.

Newspapers were an important part of the Mexican experience, as was racial conflict. It has been estimated that at least 132 Spanish-language or bilingual newspapers were published between 1848 and 1900 in the southwestern United States. In many ways, the documents in this collection show the other side—the English-language side. The Mexican voices include María Amparo Ruiz de Burton, the first Mexican woman to write novels in English.

In the nineteenth century, we took into account that Mexicans living in various places along the border formed slightly different identities. In Texas, Mexicans were called Tejanos, and because of their physical proximity to the heart of Mexico, incorporated the norteño, or northern Mexican, culture. Those living in Browns-ville, Texas, were less than 1,000 miles from Mexico City, almost half the distance to Los Angeles, California. With this in mind, we selected representative documents from Texas, New Mexico, Arizona, and California. There are excellent histories available which set a contextual framework for the limited space given to this period of history that some Chicano historians have characterized as a colonial period for the new, emerging Mexican American nationality.

The next Latino nationalities in contact with the Euro-American people were the Cubans and Puerto Ricans. The Cuban presence was felt by the 1850s in the aftermath of the Mexican-American War. Cuba was 90 miles south of Florida. De-spite its proximity to the United States, the Cuban experience differed from the Mexican experience; it was a lot easier to walk across a line than to swim across a sea. Puerto Rico was a thousand miles from Florida, and distance definitely was a barrier to mass migration. These two Caribbean islands did not gain independence until the turn of the century. Nevertheless, they inherited the negative feelings Euro-Americans had toward Mexicans and Spaniards.

Many Euro-Americans—especially Southerners—believed it was just a matter of time before the United States acquired these fertile islands run by "corrupt" Spaniards that were off the coast of Florida. In 1850, Cuba had a white population of 565,560; it also had 204,570 free Africans, and 436,400 African slaves. The Puerto Rican popula-tion was not as large as the Cuban population but was concentrated in a much smaller space. In 1847, Puerto Rico had a population of 628,000; of these, there were 329,000 mixed bloods, 258,000 free Africans, and 32,000 slaves. Because Cuba was closer to the U.S. mainland, Cuban migration was within reach, access was easier. However, the immobile nature of its population prevented a sizeable out-migration at this time.

As aspirations for an interocean canal grew in the United States, these islands became strategically important to Euro-American interests. The fact that Central America is an isthmus containing the shortest point between the two oceans, made it vital to the interests of the United States. Central American market resources such as coffee and bananas also attracted Euro-American adventurers and investors who wanted to seize the land for the United States. Because of trade between the two sides of the hemisphere, especially after the 1849 California Gold Rush, interest in an interocean canal increased, and Cuba and then Puerto Rico became gateways to the isthmus of Central America.

The documents tell of the rivalry between the United States and Great Britain around this time. The United States thought that it was "America's" canal, and that the region belonged to the chosen. This set the stage for U.S. filibustering expedi-tions—often with Euro-American sponsors—that left U.S. soil in an effort to re-annex what they considered U.S. soil and to expand slavery. Tennessean William Walker (1824–1860) led expeditions into Baja California and temporarily seized control of Nicaragua in 1857. Throughout this period, U.S. newspapers and journals discussed the Cuban Question and how democracy should be taken to the island; the documents address this question.

We focus on José Martí, who spent two decades in exile in the United States. He began his exile in this country full of hope for the independence of Cuba from

Spain, but racism and political realities embittered him. With few exceptions, we have purposefully stayed away from strictly literary works and concentrated on those that captured the historical moment. For example, Cuban cigar makers were not the only cigar makers in the United States, but they were the best. The Cuban cigar industry began a presence in Key West in 1831. After this point, there was a steady influx of Cuban cigar makers. The stream of Cubans quickened after 1868 and there were over 80 cigar factories by 1883. These factories employed almost 2,703 Cuban cigar workers. Primary source documents show how they founded the first trade unions in the U.S. South, and were politically conscious. In 1864, Cuban cigar makers introduced *lectores*, readers, who would read literary and political works to the cigar makers as they rolled cigars. They educated the workers through their readings. By the 1880s, cigar makers were closely associated with the Cuban independence movement. During this period, Cuba over shadowed Puerto Rico, not because the latter did not have its share of intellectuals—as mentioned, its population numbers rivaled those of Cuba—but because of Puerto Rico's distance from the U.S. mainland.

The U.S. imperial desire to fold Cuba and Puerto Rico within its borders never let up; however, the Civil War took some of the steam out of the movement. In the 1860s, the independence movements in both of these nations (1868–1897) accelerated. All of this set the stage for the Spanish-American War (1898). Cubans and Puerto Ricans had warred with Spain for thirty years to achieve independence without much help from the outside world. Unlike the experience of the 13 colonies that would later become the United States of America, in which other nations helped the rebels, the Latin American nations did it mostly on their own. In the case of Cuba and Puerto Rico, the United States stepped in late in the game. It then, independently concluded a treaty with Spain that ceded Puerto Rico, the Philippines, and other territories to the United States.

The documents deal with the forging of an imperialist U.S. mentality—an attitude that would lead to Latin Americans labeling the United States the Colossus of the North—an image that was confirmed during the first three decades of the twentieth century with its treatment of the Caribbean and Central America. At the conclusion of the Spanish-American War, Puerto Ricans were forcefully annexed to the United States, and life for Puerto Ricans worsened with the U.S. occupation. The tenuousness of the relation reinforced Puerto Rican nationalism. The war transformed the Puerto Rican economy and accelerated the diaspora of Puerto Rican workers throughout the region and to parts of the United States. Readers are also introduced to Puerto Ricans who are not normally portrayed in texts.

In 1898, Cuba did not become part of the United States because there were antiimperialist voices within the country that were paying attention to the question of expansion. Nevertheless, President Theodore Roosevelt built a web that included the Caribbean and Central American in what we will call the U.S. sphere of influence and a policy to defend "America's" canal in Panama at all costs.

The parallel history of Mexicans within the United States takes a different twist. They had been a nationality with a nation within a nation for over a half century. Identities of the individual U.S. Latino nationalities have changed with time of residence in the United States. Their separate national identities had been forged through centuries of civilization building and European colonialism. In the United States, these identities changed as they clashed with the white Anglo-Saxon

Protestants (WASP) ideal of Euro-Americans. Historically, they fought for equality under the U.S. Constitution.

Civil rights are the protections and privileges of personal power given to all citizens by law. But these rights are a "catch-22," a paradox in a law, regulation, or practice. For instance, one is a victim regardless of the choice he makes. Like searching for a job. A catch-22 develops when one cannot get a job without work experience, but one cannot gain experience without a job. Catch-22 is the chicken-or-the-egg dilemma. Personal power is based on education, but you cannot get an education without money, and you cannot get money without an education. Hence, civil rights are meant to resolve the paradox, which they seldom do.

Throughout their history in the United States, Mexican Americans and Puerto Ricans fought for civil rights, and as their populations grew they won the entitlements and guarantees that all Latinos now have and enjoy under the law. One of the first court cases was brought by Ricardo Rodríguez, a native of Mexico who had lived in Texas for 10 years. He petitioned to become a naturalized U.S. citizen in 1897, but was denied. The catch-22 was that only white people could become citizens; Mexicans were not considered white, so they could not be citizens. The dilemma was resolved by blurring the racial status of Mexicans because the Treaty of Guadalupe Hidalgo inferred that they were white—that is, the treaty made Mexicans neither Indians or Asians because they could be citizens. Time and time again the catch-22 was not resolved but short-circuited to be used to the disadvantage of Latinos.

Meanwhile, in the 1880s the Mexican Central Railroad linked Mexico with the United States, facilitating and determining the movement of huge numbers of workers from Mexico's interior to build the American Southwest. Industrialization demanded large work forces of unskilled workers. This migration accelerated at the turn of the century, which also saw large waves of Mexicans pulled into the United States by the dramatic expansion of U.S. mines, farms, railroads, and cities. U.S. economic expansion in Mexico accelerated the demise of small subsistence farms and the uprooting of thousands of small farmers and peasants. Moreover, Mexico's population had recovered to about 15 million during the first decade of the 20th century, and hence served as a large reserve labor pool for the United States. This labor pool was essential to the growth of the U.S. economy as Euro-Americans excluded the Chinese and other Asians from the workforce and limited the immigration of Central and Southern Europeans.

The history of immigration greatly affects the migration of Mexicans to the United States as the exclusion of the Chinese and then the limiting of European immigration created a demand for Mexican labor. The year 1910 brought changes with the Mexican Revolution, accelerating migration to the United States. Because of the proximity of Mexico, the populations on both sides of the border reacted to events north and south of the border. Hence, the Mexican Revolution played a huge role in the formation of stereotypes such as the violent Mexican outlaw and the need for the Texas Rangers. Later, World War I acts as a key event in forming a Mexican American identity.

The formation of the Puerto Rican identity differed from that of the Mexican during the 1910s. Readers cannot limit themselves to what is happening on the U.S. mainland but must also take into account the island of Puerto Rico, which is, after all, part of the United States. The Jones-Shafroth Act (1917) made Puerto Ricans citizens—consequently, they were eligible for the military draft.

Other Latino voices were present. During the 1920s, U.S. intervention in the Caribbean and Central American increased. The documents of this period provide a valuable context for future migration and understanding the Latino stereotype. Unlike the formation of a Latino consciousness, the making of the Central American identity was well under way; since the 1820s there were efforts to form a unified nation (they had a common language, contiguous space, and shared history). This effort was accelerated in face of U.S. intervention. At this point, aside from the Mexican voices, only the Puerto Ricans and the Cubans were loud enough to be heard in the United States. As mentioned, Cuban exiles and workers had been trickling into the United States for some time. According to the 1910 Census the number of Cubans in the United States was officially over 15,000. Their numbers were concentrated in Florida and New York.

During this period, Puerto Rican workers continued to migrate to Arizona and other parts of the United States, but New York was clearly their largest homeland after the island. Puerto Ricans in the United States numbered only 12,000 in 1920; by 1930 the number had climbed to 53,000. The documents show the Puerto Rican diaspora, their relationship to the island, and their formation of *colonias* in the United States.

During the 1920s, a second-generation middle class and labor organizations emerged among Mexican Americans. By this time, the profile of the group was shifting from a rural to an urban one. Prior to this time, mutual aid societies were the most popular form of organization. As with Puerto Rican and other Latino nationalities, first-generation societies concentrated on homeland issues. The 1920s saw a transformation of these groups that formed second-generation associations to deal more with local issues and obtaining equality under the law than with concerns about the homeland. The link between population and power became more evident as more groups took to the courts to protect their civil rights.

Between 1910 and 1920, at least 219,000 Mexican immigrants entered the United States. (The actual figure was probably closer to one million.) This doubled the population of Mexican origin in Arizona, New Mexico, and Texas. In California, it quadrupled. The best estimate is that there were between 1.5 and 2 million people of Mexican origin in the United States by 1930. Some would say that the number was closer to 3 million. The growing Mexican presence produced an intense nativist reaction with segregated schools jumping by at least 50 percent. This was all done under the guise of Americanization. We have included documents on this process to help the reader understand the transformation that was taking place during the 1920s, as the second and third generations of Mexican Americans increased in visibility and importance. Who were the voices that advocated for the working Mexicans and Mexican Americans and their families? How did identity change during these years? What were the newspapers saying? Did they differ from what is being said today?

Within this historical argument, we consider the Immigration Acts of 1921 and 1924. These acts are cornerstones in the history of all Latinos with the exception of the Puerto Ricans who were U.S. citizens as of 1917. The early twentieth century began a period of social engineering where the immigration policy of the United States was designed to maintain a nation that was not only white but as northern European as possible. Mexicans were excluded from the quotas because they were crucial to U.S. agriculture and Latin Americans were not subjected to immigration quotas because they simply lived too far away to come here in significant numbers. During this period, Mexicans individuals and organizations filed successful desegregation suits.

This section of documents has more documents than preceding decades. This is because of the size of the Mexican population is much larger, much more stable, and much more urban than in previous years. Greater numbers mean more organizations, more people studying the group, more literacy, and more awareness. A significant number of Mexican Americans served during World War I; they returned home with a much different attitude toward their rights. The 1920s ended, almost symbolically, with the 1929 formation of the League of United Latin American Citizens (LULAC), a middle-class, citizens-only organization that was the premier Mexican American Civil Rights organization of the time.

The next period our documents cover is the Great Depression, which began in 1929 and lasted throughout most of the 1930s. The Depression devastated Puerto Rico as the remaining small farmers were almost wiped out. But also important is that Pan American Airlines began its first flights to Miami, Florida, from the island—partially overcoming the 1,000-mile gap between Puerto Rico and the mainland. Meanwhile, Florida continued to house a large Cuban population, many of whom were Afro-Cubans. The cigar industry declined in the Great Depression, and an unsuccessful 1931 strike devastated the union. The decade accelerated a migration of Afro-Cubans back to Cuba and to the U.S. Northeast. Fifty percent of Florida's Afro-Cuban population left Florida in the 1930s. Job opportunities seemed better in Cuba or the North. Fifty percent of the Afro-Cuban community left Tampa from 1930 and 1940, leaving older members trying to keep the community together.

Militancy remained high in Puerto Rico as the needle workers, mostly women, struck for better wages. New Deal acts such as the National Recovery Administration (NRA) bypassed the island, worsening an already dire economic situation. The decade also saw the rise of the Puerto Rican Nationalist Party as misery on the island grew. Throughout the Caribbean, sugar prices fell drastically, and workers were without a source of income. In turn, the lack of income increased political discontent. On March 21, 1937, at Ponce, Puerto Rico, as some 100 demonstrators were wounded, 19 killed, including 17 men, a woman, and a seven-year-old girl. The documents on Puerto Rico from this era are key because they set the stage for the mass migration to the mainland that accelerated in 1945.

The Great Depression also had a huge impact on the segment of the population of Mexican origin in the United States. Between 600,000 and a million Mexicans who were repatriated (deported) largely to save money during the Depression. The documents included encapsulate this period. What was life like for the people? Because of the size of the group, more interviews and oral histories were recorded than in previous years, and attention was paid to this group.

At this time, Mexicans were also migrating within the United States and beginning to live outside the Southwest. The Midwest had a sizeable Mexican population in the 1930s. Chicago had as many as 25,000 Mexicans in 1930. However, as in every aspect of Mexican life, repatriation drives affected the Mexican community in the Midwest with its community shrinking to 16,000 by the end of the decade.

Los Angeles rivaled San Antonio, Texas, as the Mecca of Mexicans in the United States. In both states, Mexicans battled school segregation. In California, the notorious Bliss bill attempted to codify Mexican inferiority in the schools. During this period gigantic strikes took place in agriculture and the cities. Larger numbers of Mexican women worked in factories than ever before and their militancy increased. The purpose of the documents on this timespan is to widen the readers' appreciation for the period. These documents put a face on the people through interviews and other accounts—devoting space to heroes such as Emma Tenayuca and Luis Moreno, a Guatemalan who organized Mexican women.

An estimated 400,000 Mexican Americans and 53,000 Puerto Ricans fought in World War II. The war was a turning point in the history of these people who were impacted by the antiracism rhetoric of the war as well as forces that pulled them into the United States mainland in greater numbers than ever before. They were greatly impacted and changed by the experience. As in previous sections, the documents from the war years are meant to complement existing texts.

The war changed the world views of an entire generation. The war brought changes in Latino groups as well as with Mexican Americans. Many Latino soldiers returned home to encounter the same racism they had left before going to war. In the case of Puerto Ricans, many had been transported to the mainland and taken across oceans to Africa, Europe, and Asia. The war brought an increased awareness of the strategic value of Puerto Rico and Latin America, as technological breakthroughs in aviation made travel cheaper and safer than before.

The Cold War that followed World War II fueled the sense that the United States had to keep its sovereign power over the island for national security reasons. The number of military personnel and bases increased in Puerto Rico. A postwar economic boom led to more industrialization and modernization programs. This caused a mass migration of Puerto Ricans to the mainland.

Other changes were taking place as Puerto Ricans swept into Chicago. African Americans drew analogies between the Third World status of the island of Puerto Rico and themselves. The status of Puerto Rican women also changed. Cubans were recruited to play baseball during World War II. However, even in sports, the color line was enforced. The major leagues failed to recruit the first Puerto Rican baseball star Peruchín Cepeda, an infielder. He was African and not eligible to play U.S. baseball. His son, Orlando Cepeda, was later inducted into the Baseball Hall of Fame.

Cuban migration quickened after the war, as U.S.-sponsored dictators increased political dissent among dissatisfied compatriots. Cubans' favorite destination was Miami. The postwar documents tell not only how people lived in New York but also the reaction to Puerto Rican immigration. Many Puerto Ricans were brought over on labor contracts. Disillusionment gripped many Puerto Ricans and some refused military service. Still, approximately 60,000 Puerto Ricans served in Korea. Meanwhile, tensions built on the island as the Nationalists gained strength. The fact that poverty increased and the U.S. presence grew on the island solidified opposition. In 1950, Nationalists led an assault on Blair House in Washington, D.C., where President Harry Truman was temporarily being housed. Four years later, the Nationalists led an attack on Congress. They were labeled *terrorist* instead of *nationalist*. The surge in Puerto Rican nationalism accompanied the rise of nationalist, populist, and anticolonial movements throughout Latin America.

The fear of Soviet-Communist involvement in the hemisphere renewed calls for adherence to the Monroe Doctrine and saw increased U.S. support of right-wing dictatorships. Four years after the attack on Blair House, the Central Intelligence Agency (CIA) directed the overthrow of the constitutionally elected Guatemalan government. In 1958, the United States sent troops to Panama after flag protests. The decade ended with the success of Fidel Castro in Cuba and his triumphant march into Havana.

World War II also brought changes for the 350,000 to 400,000 Mexican Americans who served in the armed forces. The war created labor shortages and thus created opportunity for those who remained behind. Women were pressed into service in the labor force. Mexican Americans won 17 Medals of Honor during the war. Many returned from the frontlines determined to demand first-class citizenship and their rights as Americans. Cases such as the Sleepy Lagoon case (1942) increased awareness of racial injustices. New organizations such as the American G.I. Forum and the Community Service Organization (CSO) evolved in response to inequality. They joined older Mexican American organizations in the courts. Issues such as the Bracero Program, immigration, and the protection of the rights of the foreign born rivaled questions such as police abuse, land use problems, and inferior education.

The documents for the period 1945–1960 reflect the quest to resolve the catch-22 dilemma. When Pvt. Felix Longoria's body was brought home to Three Rivers, Texas, in the proverbial pine box, his family expected a hero's welcome. Instead, the mortuary refused to accept his body because he was a Mexican American. Even Three Rivers' cemetery was segregated. Hector García's American G.I. Forum swelled with new members who vowed, *never again*. The G.I. Forum along with LULAC and La Alianza brought suits to ensure protection of Mexican American rights. The year before, in *Méndez v. Westminster*, the 9th Circuit Federal Court in California found that Mexican students were entitled to equal protection. The case had been filed by Gonzalo Méndez, Thomas Estrada, William Guzmán, Frank Palomino, and Lorenzo Ramírez in 1945. Gonzalo Méndez was of Mexican extraction and his wife Felicitas was Puerto Rican. They challenged the state's right to put their children in segregated classrooms and won.

After the war, more Mexican Americans also participated in the political process by registering in their communities to vote. Edward R. Roybal was elected to the Los Angeles City Council in 1949, and four years later Henry B. González was elected to the San Antonio, Texas, City Council. Many Mexican American activists were Red-baited, called Communist, for insisting on equal rights. This reaction intensified as the United States entered the Korean War only five years after the World War II. As in World War II, Mexican Americans served beyond their proportion in the population. The corresponding documents reflect on the growing concern over immigration and the role of the Mexican American community to protect the rights of the foreign born. They closed out the decade a more aware and involved community.

The 1960s were driven by a global decline in colonialism, the baby boom, the African American civil rights movement, and the Vietnam War. There had been a surge in the Puerto Rican population on the mainland during the previous decades. After triumph of Fidel Castro in the Cuban Revolution, the number of Cubans, mostly in the Miami, Florida, area, increased dramatically. In 1959, the number of Cubans in the United States was estimated at 124,000. After this point, many of the wealthier Cubans fled the island to protect their assets. During the 1960s, about 215,000 Cubans moved to the United States.

Economic problems and political turmoil in the Dominican Republic also led to a vast migration of Dominicans to the United States. Throughout the century, the United States had sought stability in the region by supporting dictators. The United States worsened the situation by invading the Dominican Republic and preventing constitutionally elected president Juan Bosch from taking office.

The Puerto Rican community began to look less to Puerto Rico and more to the huge problems that they had in the United States. During the sixties, a youth generation emerged that was in tune with contemporary politics. Still highly nationalistic, they wanted to improve poor housing, education, health care, and end poverty. Territorial, the barrios were their homes. They fought for rights in the 1960s. They saw life with more urgency than their parents, wanting to end the colonization of Puerto Ricans; they were "colonial immigrants."

The 1960 census counted 892,513 Puerto Ricans in the mainland United States. Almost 72 percent, 642,622, lived in New York; 55,351 in New Jersey; and 36,081 in Illinois. The rest were scattered throughout the country. During the preceding decade, migration had quickened an average of 45,000 annually migrating to the United States. Migration slowed in the 1960s in response to temporary improvements and jobs created by Operation Bootstrap, which had been started in 1948 to industrialize the island. The annual migration of Puerto Ricans was cut by over half. However, the natural increase offset this decrease.

Puerto Ricans had a large youth population. As mentioned, after New York and New Jersey, it was Chicago, Illinois, that had the largest concentration of Puerto Ricans. Like other immigrant youth, Puerto Ricans were well aware of their disparate treatment at the hands of police. Chicago lacked the organizational infrastructure of older barrios such as those in New York, and was the scene of the first Puerto Rican protests in the United States. This uprising began on Division Street after a parade and was in response to the police shooting of a young Puerto Rican man. Chicago was also the birthplace of the Young Lords, a youth gang that evolved into a political and human rights organization. Documents from this period concentrate heavily on the Young Lords.

U.S. Cubans remained obsessed with what was happening in Cuba. Because the first wave of immigrants was an educated portion of the middle class, Cuban Americans acquired political power, whereas Puerto Ricans remained marginal. The Borinquen (as the island of Puerto Rico was called by the Taíno Indians native to the island) community was involved in protesting the Vietnam War and demanding civil rights for the community. There were still cries for self-determination for the island but the struggle for equality in the States took some of the steam from that movement—although not entirely. For example, there was uproar about reports of the mass sterilizations of Puerto Rican women on the island by mainland employers as a hiring practice. Nationalism continued, mingling with the Socialist ideas of the day.

By the 1970s, the Young Lords and other leftist groups were on the decline After being heavily infiltrated by police and federal agents. Both at home and abroad, the U.S. government became more proactive in fighting "communism." In 1973, the CIA participated in the overthrow of Chilean President Salvador Allende. This sent ripples throughout Latin America and led to the immigration of a small number of Chilean political refugees.

Changes were also taking place in Central America that would influence the composition of the Latino in the United States. Since the 1960s, the Catholic

Church through *comunidades de base*, base communities, had been politicizing Central Americans. As they grew more militant, the military and local elites clamped down on the dissidents. In El Salvador, the military assassinated a Jesuit priest in 1977. The opposition grew, and, in 1979, rebels overthrew Nicaraguan dictator Anastasio Somoza, who moved to Miami, Florida.

In 1960, there were officially about 3.5 million U.S. residents of Mexican origin in the Southwest (actual numbers were surely much larger). The largest concentrations were in California and Texas, with about 1.5 million Mexicans apiece. Just fewer than 55 percent were native born and their median age was 19.6 compared to 30.4 for Euro-Americans. The median age had fallen by a year in both cases. Migration from Mexico quickened during the decade as Mexico's population from 1940 to 1970 increased by 250 percent—growing at an average of 3.4 percent per year from 1960 to 1970. Mexico's population zoomed from 27.4 million in 1950 to 37.1 million in 1960, to 51.2 million in 1970.

Like Puerto Rican youth, Chicano youth were nationalistic and wanted to end the exploitation of Mexicans in the United States. As a group, young Chicanos were exposed to civil rights violations and the horrors of the Vietnam War. Activist groups like the Black Berets and the Brown Berets were part of this formation that included Chicano students. Their rhetoric took on cultural symbols and they reacted vigorously to racism. Aztlán, the legendary birthplace of the Aztecs, became a symbol to show that they were not foreigners in the United States, but that they were native to the land with ties to a culture that predated the original 13 colonies. They adopted the name *Chicano* and increasingly militant tactics invigorated the social movements of the time by giving hope that their catch-22 dilemma could be resolved.

Not all Mexican-origin activity was led by youth. Organizations such as LULAC and the G.I. Forum struggled within the mainstream for equal protection, bilingual education, and economic equality. Through the pressure and influence of youth they became more militant during this period. Within U.S. society, civil rights and the war in Vietnam had an impact. In response, Mexican Americans formed new organizations such as the Mexican American Legal Defense and Education Fund (MALDEF) to litigate their rights.

The sixties brought a growing awareness of inequities as organizations evolved to take advantage of the recognition of Chicanos as an entitled group. Both Puerto Ricans and Mexican Americans were influenced by nationalism, socialism, and anticolonial theories. This brought about a question, not only of equality of race, but of gender. For Chicanos, these events reached a climax at the Chicano Moratorium of 1970, after which three people involved in a peaceful rally were killed, including journalist Rubén Salazar. For Puerto Ricans, there are the Puerto Rican nationalist uprisings of the 1970s.

With more Chicanos making it to the universities in the 1970s, there was more seepage into the middle class. With this phenomenon, there was greater participation in mainstream politics, and larger numbers defected to so-called movement politics. In the Mexican-origin community, the first casualty was the term *Chicano* that defined movement politics as a mission to raise access to education, political participation, and economic opportunity to the working class. Broad sectors of the Mexican community turned to Hispanic and even Latino politics as a method of muting nationalism. It was as subtle as President Richard Nixon shifting the funds of antipoverty groups from job training to the Small Business Administration. The marketplace and the media also played a role by hyping the label *Hispanic*, which was easier than *Chicano* to sell to the middle class and the public. With politicos it created a larger voting bloc.

The 1970s also brought increased numbers of Mexican immigrants who did not accept the Chicano identity, in large part because it was not defined for them. The immigrant did not have the same historical memory or sense as the Mexican Americans or Chicanos had, and the schools substituted the illusion of inclusion for the reality that they were not Hispanics or Latinos. This sifted the focus from the struggle, protections, and entitlements under the law won by the Mexican American and Chicano generations. Subtly, there was the illusion that the catch-22 dilemma could be solved for all Latinos through political brokers and more professionals.

Meanwhile, events south of the border increased immigration. The Immigration Act of 1965 brought large numbers of Asians and Middle Easterners to the country as its policy shifted from national origins to family preferences. In reality, Latin Americans were discriminated against since historically the United States had sold the myth that the peoples of the Americas were members of the same family. This part of the family was not subject to immigration quotas until 1965.

Shaken by the fall of U.S.-friendly Nicaraguan dictator Anastasio Somoza, the United States stepped up its involvement in Central America. The United States carried on a war to overthrow the leftist Sandinistas and gave massive military aid to the right-wing governments of El Salvador, Guatemala, and Honduras, as well as continuing its economic boycott and political subversion of Cuba. Civil wars pushed millions of Central American Latinos north. The documents covering these topics appear in the section covering the 1980s as more than a million Central Americans immigrated to the United States during the decade.

With the arrival of such large numbers of Central Americans and critical numbers of South Americans, identity became more problematic, and the hegemony of Mexicans, Puerto Ricans, and Cuban Americans was challenged. Even before this time, Mexicans had moved in substantial numbers to the Midwest and Northwest. In Chicago, they lived in close proximity to Puerto Ricans. Over a million Mexicans migrated to the United States in the 1970s; this migration did not slow down in the next two decades as they were joined by millions of other Latin Americans. For the first time, they shared a common space, which was one of the requisites for sharing a nationality. This raised the question of a Latino identity, which will be resolved in the future through intellectual discourse and life experiences.

Within the documents presented for this time period, there is more crossover than previous decades. Puerto Ricans and Mexicans continued to share certain characteristics. Both groups began to gain political positions and patronage. There was a shift from idealism to ethnic politics where members of both groups gained political positions (not power). Core issues remained unresolved because of this lack of power and inability to shift their party's paradigm. Puerto Ricans and Mexicans gained tremendously by the increased numbers of other Latin Americans whose numbers collectively added to their national presence.

By the 1990s, the new Latino immigrants were forming their own distinct identities. Although the so-called Latino populations became more diverse—they spread to the U.S. South and East Coast. Mexican populations in New York City increased from around 62,000 in 1990 to more than 400,000 by many estimates at the turn of the century. There, they share space with Puerto Ricans and other Latinos. Growth in numbers and lawsuits by MALDEF, as well as the Puerto Rican Legal Defense and Education Fund, has increased the number of Latino elected officials immeasurably.

In 2002, there were 37.4 million Latinos in the United States population: 66.9 percent were of Mexican origin, 14.3 percent were Central and South American, 8.6 percent were Puerto Rican, 3.7 percent were Cuban, and the remaining 6.5 percent were of other Hispanic origins. Because many of these communities lived in close proximity, sharing the same economic class, intermarriage was taking place. In Los Angeles, for example, many college students are half Mexican and half Salvadoran. Both have large populations. Intermarriage is widespread among U.S.-born Mexican Americans. Census 2000 showed that almost half (48 percent) of Mexican American marriages involved a non-Mexican spouse. The Census data also showed that intermarriage is a fundamental as to whether the children of Mexican Americans retain their ethnic identification. With two U.S.-born Mexicans or between a U.S.-born Mexican and a Mexican immigrant, the child's Mexican identification is almost assured. Other Latino groups follow a similar trend.

It is hoped that these documents will help Latinos become more introspective. Documents on the Puerto Rican, Cuban, and Mexican experiences are fairly accessible, as shown in the suggested reading list at the end of this introduction. However, documents on the other Latinos' U.S. experience are sparse—the Dominicans being the exception. Collecting these data will be difficult, and is made even more nebulous by the Latino categorization.

Another challenge for new Latino groups in establishing their history in the United States through documents is that most of these groups have come to the United States after 1980. Although a corpus of knowledge exists about their experiences in Latin America, there are few studies on their U.S. experience. In this initial stage, newspapers and anthologies are important in forging a sense of the fields of study. But these groups are challenged by copyright laws that protect documents published after 1923. It is here that these groups must take the example of the Dominican Americans. We have included a number of websites in the suggested reading list that follows, to facilitate the document gathering process.

Two previous sections will help the reader find documents of interest: the table of contents lists each document by author, title, and (where known) year, and the list of documents by group forms an index arranged by geopolitical group. To further assist the reader in putting all of these documents into context, a suggested reading list completes this introduction, and the next section provides a timeline of U.S. Latino history.

SUGGESTED READING

Acuña, Rodolfo. *Anything but Mexican: Chicanos in Contemporary Los Angeles*. New York: Verso, 1996.
———. *Community under Siege: Chicanos East of the Los Angeles River*. Los Angeles: Mexican American Studies Resource Center, UCLA, 1984.
———. *Corridors of Migration: The Odyssey of Mexican Laborers, 1600–1933*. Tucson: University of Arizona Press, 2007.
———. *Occupied America: A History of Chicanos*. 5th ed. New York: Longman, 2004.
———. *Sometimes There Is No Other Side: Chicanos and the Myth of Equality*. Notre Dame, IN: University of Notre Dame Press, 1998.

Appel, John C. "The Unionization of Florida Cigarmakers and the Coming of the War with Spain." *Hispanic American Historical Review* 36, no. 1 (1956): 38–49.

Aranda, José, Jr., ed. *Recovering the U.S. Hispanic Literary Heritage*. Vol. 4. Houston: Arte Público Press, 2002.

Balderama, Francisco E., and Raymond Rodriguez. *Decade of Betrayal: Mexican Repatriation in the 1930s*. Albuquerque: University of New Mexico Press, 1994.

Bancroft, Hubert Howe. *History of Arizona and New Mexico, 1530–1888*. Albuquerque, NM: Horn & Wallace, 1962.

Carroll, Patrick. *Felix Longoria's Wake: Bereavement, Racism, and the Rise of Mexican American Activism*. Austin: University of Texas Press, 2003.

Craig, Jenkins J. "Push/Pull in Recent Mexican Migration to the United States." *International Migration Review* 11, no. 2 (1977): 178–89.

Cruz, Jose E. *Identity and Power: Puerto Rican Politics and the Challenge of Ethnicity*. Philadelphia: Temple University Press, 1998.

Deutsch, Sarah. *No Separate Refuge: Culture, Class, and Gender on an Anglo-Hispanic Frontier in the American Southwest*. New York: Oxford University Press, 1987.

Eisenhower. John S. D. *So Far from God: The U.S. War with Mexico, 1846–1848*. Norman: University of Oklahoma Press, 2000.

Ferrer, Ada. *Insurgent Cuba: Race, Nation, and Revolution, 1868–1898*. Chapel Hill: University of North Carolina Press, 1999.

Flores, John, ed. *Divided Arrival: Narratives of the Puerto Rican Migration, 1920–1950*. 2nd ed. New York: Centro Estudios Puertotiqueños, Hunter College, City University of New York, 1998.

Galarza, Ernesto. *Merchants of Labor: The Mexican Bracero Story, an Account of the Managed Migration of Mexican Farm Workers in California, 1942–1962*. Charlotte, NC: McNally & Loftin, 1964.

Gamio, Manuel. *The Life Story of the Mexican Immigrant: Autobiographic Documents*. New York: Dover Publications, 1972.

———. *Mexican Immigration to the United States: A Study of Human Migration and Adjustment*. New York: Dover Publications, 1971.

Garcia, Juan G. *Mexicans in the Midwest, 1900–1932*. Tucson: University of Arizona Press, 1996.

Gómez Quiñones, Juan. "Critique on the National Question, Self-Determination, and Nationalism." *Latin American Perspectives* 9, no. 2 (1982): 62–83.

———. *Mexican Students for La Raza: The Chicano Student Movement in California, 1967–1977*. Santa Barbara, CA: Editorial La Causa, 1978.

———. *Sembradores: Ricardo Flores Magon y el Partido Liberal Mexicano, a Eulogy and Critique*. Los Angeles: UCLA, 1979.

González, Juan. *Harvest of Empire: A History of Latinos in America*. New York: Penguin, 2001.

Grebler, Leo, Joan E. Moore, and Ralph C. Guzman. *The Mexican American People: The Nation's Second Largest Minority*. New York: Free Press, 1970.

Griswold Del Castillo, Richard. *The Treaty of Guadalupe Hidalgo: A Legacy of Conflict*. Norman: University of Oklahoma Press, 1992.

Gutiérrez, David G., ed. *The Columbia History of Latinos in the United States since 1960*. New York: Columbia University Press, 2004.

Haas, Lisbeth. *Conquests and Historical Identities in California, 1769–1936*. Berkeley: University of California Press, 1995.

Handbook of Texas Online. Available at: http://www.tsha.utexas.edu/handbook/online/articles/MM/qdm2.html.

Hardy, Osgood. "The Revolution and the Railroads of Mexico." *Pacific Historical Review* 3, no. 3 (1934): 249–69.

Harper, Paula. "Cuba Connections: Key West. Tampa. Miami, 1870 to 1945." *Journal of Decorative and Propaganda Arts* 22, Cuba issue (1996): 278–91.

Harrison, Brady. *Agent of Empire: William Walker and the Imperial Self in American Literature.* Athens: University of Georgia Press, 2004.

Hernández, José M. "Cuba in 1898." In *The World of 1898: The Spanish-American War.* Washington, DC: Hispanic Division, Library of Congress. Available at: http://www.loc.gov/rr/hispanic/1898/hernandez.html.

Lafeber, Walter. *Inevitable Revolutions: The United States in Central America.* New York: W. W. Norton, 1993.

Long, Jeff. *Duel of Eagles: The Mexican and U.S. Fight for the Alamo.* New York: William Morrow, 1990.

Maree Bachelis, Faren. *The Central Americans.* New York: Chelsea House, 1990.

Mathews, Thomas. *Puerto Rican Politics and the New Deal.* Gainesville: University of Florida Press, 1960.

Matovina, Timothy M. *The Alamo Remembered: Tejano Accounts and Perspectives.* Austin: University of Texas Press, 1995.

May, Robert E. *Manifest Destiny's Underworld: Filibustering in Antebellum America.* Chapel Hill: University of North Carolina Press, 2004.

———. *The Southern Dream of a Caribbean Empire, 1854–1861.* Baton Rouge: Louisiana State University Press, 1973.

McWilliams, Carey. *North from Mexico: The Spanish-Speaking People of the United States.* Westport, CT: Greenwood Press, 1968.

Meléndez, Miguel, and José Torres. *We Took the Streets: Fighting for Latino Rights with the Young Lords.* New Brunswick, NJ: Rutgers University Press, 2005.

Menchaca, Martha. *Recovering History, Constructing Race: The Indian, Black, and White Roots of Mexican Americans.* Austin: University of Texas Press, 2001.

Montejano, David. *Anglos and Mexicans in the Making of Texas, 1836–1986.* Austin: University of Texas Press, 1987.

Moya Pons, Frank. *The Dominican Republic: A National History.* 2nd revised ed. Princeton, NJ: Markus Wiener Publishers, 1998.

Nodin Valdes, Dennis. *Al Norte: Agricultural Workers in the Great Lakes Region, 1917–1970.* Austin: University of Texas Press, 1991.

Oboler, Suzanne, and Deena J. Gonzalez, eds. *The Oxford Encyclopedia of Latinos and Latinas in the United States.* New York: Oxford University Press, 2005.

Paredes, Américo. *"With His Pistol in His Hand": A Border Ballad and Its Hero.* Austin: University of Texas Press, 1970.

Park, Joseph F. "At Clifton: 1903 Clifton-Morenci Strike." *Journal of Arizona History* 18 (Summer 1977): 119–48.

Pérez Brignoli, Héctor. *A Brief History of Central America.* Berkeley: University of California Press, 1989.

Pitt, Leonard. *Decline of the Californios.* Berkeley: University of California Press, 1966.

Poniatowska, Elena, and David Dorado Romo. *Las Soldaderas: Women of the Mexican Revolution.* El Paso, TX: Cinco Puntos Press, 2006.

Ramos, Henry A. J. *A People Forgotten, a Dream Pursued: The History of the American G.I. Forum, 1948–1972.* N.p.: American G.I. Forum of the United States, 1983.

Reisler, Mark. *By the Sweat of Their Brow: Mexican Immigrant Labor in the United States, 1900–1940.* Reprint ed. Westport, CT: Greenwood Press, 1976.

Rivas-Rodríguez, Maggie. *Mexican Americans and World War II.* Austin: University of Texas Press, 2005.

Robinson, Cecil. *With the Ears of Strangers: The Mexican in American Literature.* Tucson: University of Arizona Press, 1963.

Rodríguez, Clara E. *Changing Race: Latinos, the Census, and the History of Ethnicity in the United States.* New York: New York University Press, 2000.

———. *Puerto Ricans Born in the USA.* Boulder, CO: Westview Press, 1989.

Romo, David Dorado. *Ringside Seat to a Revolution: An Underground Cultural History of El Paso and Juarez, 1893–1923.* El Paso, TX: Cinco Puntos Press, 2005.

Rosales, Francisco Arturo. *Chicano! The History of the Mexican American Civil Rights Movement.* Houston: Arte Publico Press, 1997.

———, ed. *Testimonio: A Documentary History of the Mexican American Struggle for Civil Rights.* Houston: Arte Publico Press, 2000.

Rubens, Horatio S. *Liberty: The Story of Cuba.* New York: Arno Press, 1970.

Sánchez, George J. *Becoming Mexican American: Ethnicity, Culture, and Identity in Chicano Los Angeles, 1900–1945.* New York: Oxford University Press, 1995.

San Miguel, Guadalupe. *"Let All of Them Take Heed": Mexican Americans and the Campaign for Educational Equality in Texas, 1910–1981.* Austin: University of Texas Press, 1988.

Shorris, Earl. *Latinos: A Biography of the People.* New York: W. W. Norton, 2001.

Sobarzo, Alejandro. *Deber y Consciencia: Nicolás Trist, el Negociador Norteamericano en la Guerra del 47.* México City: Fondo de Cultura Económica, 1996.

Sons of DeWitt Colony, Texas. Available at: http://www.tamu.edu/ccbn/dewitt/dewitt.htm.

Tenayuca, Emma, and Homer Brooks. "The Mexican Question in the Southwest." *Political Affairs* (March 1939): 257–68.

Thelen, David, ed. *Rethinking History and the Nation State: Mexico and the United States.* A special online issue of the *Journal of American History* (September 1999). Available at: http://www.indiana.edu/~jah/mexico.

Tijerina, Andres. *Tejanos under the Mexican Flag, 1821–1836.* College Station: Texas A&M University Press, 1994.

Vélez-Ibañez, Carlos G. *Border Visions: Mexican Cultures of the Southwest United States.* Tucson: University of Arizona Press, 1996.

Wagenheim, Olga Jiménez de, and Kal Wagenheim, eds. *The Puerto Ricans: A Documentary History.* Princeton, NJ: Markus Wiener Publishers, 2002.

Webb, Walter Prescott. *The Texas Rangers: A Century of Frontier Defense.* Austin: University of Texas Press, 1965.

Zavella, Patricia. *Women's Work and Chicano Families: Cannery Workers of the Santa Clara Valley.* Ithaca, NY: Cornell University Press, 1987.

Timeline of U.S. Latino History

1803   The Louisiana Purchase makes New Spain (Colonial Mexico) the neighbor of the United States and U.S. exploration of the area west of the Mississippi begins.

1810   In Mexico, Fr. Miguel Hidalgo issues the call for Mexican independence, beginning 11 years of warfare.

1819   Simón Bolívar, the great Latin American liberator, addresses the Congress of Angostura and expresses his vision of one Latin America strong enough to resist the encroachments of Europe and the United States.

Adams-Onís Treaty of 1819, in which Spain cedes Florida to the United States, is signed after years of border wars.

1821   Treaty of Córdova, in which Mexico gains independence from Spain, is signed on August 24.

A Congress of Central America declares independence from Spain on September 15.

Texas Gov. Antonio María Martínez authorizes Euro-American Stephen Austin to colonize 300 families in Texas. The Spanish originally made this grant to his father, Moses Austin, who died before completing the contract. Meanwhile, Texas, while still part of Mexico, gets its independence from Spain.

1823   In his December 2 speech to a joint session of Congress, U.S. President James Monroe declares that further European colonization in the Americas will not be permitted. The Monroe Doctrine serves as the justification for U.S. intervention in the hemisphere to this day.

1824   Mexico's Congress abolishes slave trade in Mexico.

1829   Mexican President Vicente Guerrero abolishes slavery.

1832   Former U.S. congressman Sam Houston arrives in Texas.

1836   White Texans and Mexican elites declare the independence of Texas on March 2.

Treaty of Velasco between Mexican President Antonio López de Santa Anna and Texas dissidents is signed on May 14 but never ratified by Mexico's Congress.

1845   President James Polk's December 2nd State of the Union Address blames Mexico for tensions between the two countries and makes public Polk's commitment to the expansion of the United States through the annexation of Texas, the Oregon territory, and the purchase of California.

1846   The Mexican-American War begins.

1848   Treaty of Guadalupe Hidalgo forces Mexico to cede 52 percent of its territory to the United States. In return, the United States pays Mexico $15 million. Article V of the treaty establishes the boundary between both countries, pending a survey. The controversy over this treaty continues to the present.

Nearly 600 Mexicans are lynched in the Southwest from this year to 1928.

1849   Survey efforts to establish the border between Mexico and the United States as required by Article V of the Treaty of Guadalupe Hidalgo begin in San Diego.

1850   Clayton-Bulwer Treaty is signed by the United States and Great Britain, both rivals in colonizing Central America and particularly concerned over a proposed isthmian canal. Both agree not to attempt to gain exclusive control over the canal or Nicaragua, Costa Rica, the Mosquito Coast, or any part of Central America.

1853   U.S. Senator Pierre Soulé's January 25 speech, "The Cuban Question," heats up the rhetoric to take Cuba from Spain. Soulé and other expansionists are supported by southern interests.

The Gadsden Purchase is made on December 30 after heavy-handed U.S. tactics and threats that if not allowed to purchase southern Arizona and parts of New Mexico from Mexico, the United States will take this land. For $10 million, Mexican authorities cede 45,000 square miles of land—including the Mesilla Valley as well as use of the Gila River—to the United States.

1854   The Ostend Manifesto, a secret document written by U.S. diplomats instructing Senator Pierre Soulé to try to buy Cuba from Spain, is signed on October 18.

1856   Filibusterer William Walker overthrows the government of Nicaragua, gaining a foothold for slave interests.

1859   In South Texas, Juan Cortina rebels and is chased by the Texas Rangers, the U.S. Army, and local authorities for the next 15 years.

1868   On September 23, between 600 to 1000 men, mostly Puerto Rican–born, demand Puerto Rico's independence from Spain but their revolt fails.

The unsuccessful Ten Years War begins and is fought under the leadership of attorney Carlos Manuel de Céspedes, who issues the Grito de Yara proclaiming Cuban independence.

1875   Report of the Mexican Commission on the Northern Frontier Question is issued.

California social bandit Tiburcio Vásquez is executed for murder and his alleged outlaw activities.

Cuban cigarmakers strike in Florida for better work conditions and higher wages.

1876   *La Ondina del Plata,* an Argentine journal, publishes an article by María Eugenia Echenique on the emancipation of women. Echenique was among a group of feminist writers who were read throughout the Americas.

1877   Salt War over Euro-American monopoly of salt deposits near El Paso leads to Mexican American opposition and one of the largest white vigilante actions against Mexicans in Southwest history.

1880   Mexican Central Railroad links Mexico City to El Paso, accelerating migration to the United States.

1882   U.S. passage of Chinese Exclusion Act keeps Chinese from entering the United States for the next 10 years and is the first serious immigration ban in U.S. history. It was renewed in 1892 and again in 1902, when Congress moved to make the ban permanent. It remained in effect until 1965.

1890   Manifesto of the Las Vegas, New Mexico White Caps (*Las Gorras Blancas*) declares war on land encroachers who monopolize the land and water.

1894   The Alianza Hispano Americana, a mutual aid society, was founded by Tucson, Arizona, elites in response to the growing nativism against Mexicans. By 1932, this group boasted 11,000 members and was active in civil rights litigation.

1895   José Martí, Cuban poet and martyr for Cuban independence, leads the second Cuban War of Independence.

   Border wars between Mexico and the United States intensify. Mexican American Victor Ochoa at El Paso is sentenced for violation of Neutrality Laws and leading revolutionary bands into Mexico.

1897   *In re Ricardo Rodríguez* holds that the Treaty of Guadalupe Hidalgo considered Mexicans eligible for citizenship and entitled to full rights under the U.S. Constitution.

1898   Spanish-American War between Spain and the United States begins while Cubans are already fighting for their independence.

   The Teller Amendment to the U.S. resolution of war with Spain stating that the United States claims it has no "intention to exercise sovereignty, jurisdiction, or control" over Cuba and resolves "to leave the government and control of the island to its people," passes in Congress.

   Treaty of Paris between the United States and Spain is signed. It excludes Puerto Ricans seeking independence from the bargaining table. The U.S. occupation of Puerto Rico begins.

1899   "The White Man's Burden," by English poet Rudyard Kipling is published. It reinforces the concept that the United States is the custodian of Western civilization in the world, taking its blessings to less civilized peoples.

1900   U.S. Congress passes the Foraker Act that establishes the governing structure of Puerto Rico.

1901   Gregorio Cortez, a poor Mexican farm hand who shoots a sheriff who had shot his brother eludes Texas Rangers and law enforcement during a massive 10-day manhunt. He is immortalized in *corridos* (ballads) that tell of his bravery and vicariously identify with his success against the hated Texas Rangers.

1902   A revolution gives Panama independence from Colombia. Shortly afterward, Panama signs a treaty giving the United States the right to build a canal across the Panamanian isthmus.

1903   The Platt Amendment is signed and makes Cuba a U.S. protectorate.

         Clifton-Morenci Strike pits 2,000 miners against the territorial militia, federal troops, and the Arizona Rangers.

1904   "To Roosevelt," a poem by Nicaraguan Rubén Darío to Theodore Roosevelt, expresses anger at U.S. intervention and high handiness in Latin America.

1910   The Mexican Revolution pushes over 10 percent of Mexico's population to emigrate to the United States over the next decade.

1911   Primer Congreso Mexicanista, Verificado en Laredo, Texas, a congress of mutual aid societies, meets to discuss recent lynchings and violations of civil rights.

1912   New Mexico and Arizona are granted U.S. statehood due to an increase in their white population.

1914   The United States sends troops to Vera Cruz, Mexico, occupying it for six months over an incident that occurred when U.S. Marines were sent to this Mexican port under the pretext of preventing a German steamer from importing arms to Mexico. U.S. steamers bombard the port.

1915   Plan de San Diego calls for the uprising of people of color, the division of the United States among them, and the killing of white men.

1916   Gen. John Pershing leads an expedition into Mexico to hunt for Mexican revolutionary hero Pancho Villa, who had invaded Columbus, New Mexico, earlier that year.

1917   The Literacy Act requires immigrants pass a literacy test that keeps most Europeans from coming to the United States and increases U.S. demand for Mexican laborers.

         Carmelita Torres, a 17-year-old Mexican maid, refuses to take a gas bath while crossing the border to work in El Paso. Her actions begin a riot as other Mexican women refuse to submit to this indignity.

         The Jones-Shafroth Act (also known as the Jones Act for Puerto Rico or the 1917 amendments to the "Organic Act of Puerto Rico") amends the Foraker Act to confer citizenship on Puerto Ricans.

         Nearly 1,200 striking copper miners in Bisbee, Arizona, mostly Mexican, are rounded up, put on cattle cars, and dumped in the middle of the New

Mexican desert under the pretext that they were members of the radical Industrial Workers of the World and thus unpatriotic.

1918   Puerto Ricans, as U.S. citizens, are consequently subject to the military draft.

Large numbers of Mexican Americans serve in U.S. armed forces.

1920s   U.S. intervention in Central America and the Caribbean affairs increases.

Americanization rises as almost 50 percent of U.S. public schools with Mexican American students are segregated during the decade.

1920   Mexican American sociologist Ernestine M. Alvarado makes a plea for mutual understanding among Mexican Americans and other Americans.

Protestant organizations challenge Catholic Church hegemony among Mexicans.

1921   The Immigration Act sets quotas for Europeans, excludes Asians, and denaturalizes U.S.-born women who marry noncitizens.

Economic recession prompts the deportation or repatriation to Mexico of thousands of Mexican workers.

1924   The Immigration Act of 1924 sets the policy of national origins, continues the exclusion of Asians, and reduces the number of immigrants by using the quota percentage from the 1890 Census instead of the 1910 Census. It supercedes the 1921 Immigration Act.

1925   *Adolfo Romo v Tempe School District*, the first U.S. desegregation case, is tried.

1927   Confederación de Uniones Obreras Mexicanas (Federation of Mexican Workers Union), CUOM, is founded in Los Angeles.

1928   Imperial Valley Worker's Union goes on strike in California.

1929   The League of United Latin American Citizens (LULAC) is organized in Texas.

Puerto Rican Luis Muñoz Marín rises to leadership, challenging the existing political parties. He would become the first democratically elected governor of the island in 1949.

The Great Depression begins.

Repatriation of between 600,000 and a million Mexicans, over 60 percent born in the United States, occurs between this year and 1936.

1930   *Independent School Dist. v. Salvatierra* (Texas), a discrimination case, is filed by the League of United Latin American Citizens. The appeal is dismissed and allows the school district to continue segregating migrant children because they start school late in the year. This policy only applies to Mexican Americans and not white migrant children.

The Lemon Grove segregation case in which Mexican American children were placed in a separate school in Lemon Grove, California, results in one of the first successful school desegregation court decisions in the history of the United States.

U.S. economist Victor S. Clark's *Study of Puerto Rico* gives a political, social, and economic portrait of the island and the conditions that were driving Puerto Rican emigration to the United States.

1933   Cotton pickers in California's San Joaquin Valley, 80 percent of whom are Mexican, take part in the largest agriculture strike in California history up to this date. Growers, assisted by police, shoot three strikers down in cold blood, starve nine infants to death, and beat and wound countless workers. The strike is broken by government intervention.

1935   The *Chicago Defender* comments on disturbance in the Puerto Rican section of Harlem, blaming uneven appropriation of relief to Harlem as compared to other parts of New York, unemployment, and poor housing conditions.

1936   Pedro Alibizu Campos, head of the Nationalist Party calling for independence for Puerto Rico, is convicted of trying to overthrow the U.S. government after widespread demonstrations the year before led to the killing of four nationalists and the attempted assassination of the U.S.-appointed governor of Puerto Rico.

1938   San Antonio pecan shellers, mostly Mexican women, numbering about 12,000, go on strike. During the three-month strike, shellers confront management and the San Antonio political establishment.

In Ponce, Puerto Rico, on July 25, police fire on demonstrators calling for the independence of Puerto Rico and protesting the arrest of nationalist leaders. Seventeen are killed.

1941   World War II begins. It brings huge changes to the hemisphere and to Latino groups in the United States.

U.S. President Franklin D. Roosevelt signs Executive Order 8802, June 25, which calls for equal employment opportunities for minorities in an attempt to quiet African American charges of racism and blacks' threat to oppose the draft.

1942   Nearly two dozen Mexican youths are put on trial in the Sleepy Lagoon case. They are accused of causing the death of José Díaz, a Mexican American youth, in Los Angeles, California, and convicted on murder and lesser chargers in an emotionally charged trial. The case is sent back for a retrial on appeal.

The *Bracero* program (1942–1964) allows Mexican nationals to take temporary agricultural work in the United States. More than 4.5 million Mexican nationals are legally contracted under this program.

1943   The Zoot Suit Riots take place in Los Angeles. Cheered on by the police and the media, servicemen beat Mexican youths during the course of a week.

1947   *Westminster School District of Orange County et al. v. Mendez et al.* desegregates the Orange County, California, school district and ends de jure segregation of Mexican children.

1948   The body of U.S. Army Pvt. Felix Longoria is returned to Three Rivers, Texas. The town mortuary refuses to provide services because he is a Mexican American. Uproar swells the ranks of Hector García's American G.I. Forum. Longoria is buried at Arlington National Cemetery.

Puerto Rico's Gov. Luis Muñoz Marin institutes Operation Bootstrap to relieve the island's unemployment problem. As part of the program, tax exemptions are given to U.S. industry to exploit cheap labor.

1949   Helped by a massive voter registration drive spearheaded by the Community Service Organization (CSO), Edward R. Roybal is elected to the Los Angeles City Council. He is the first Mexican American since 1887 to win a seat on the Los Angeles City Council.

1950   Approximately 40,000 Puerto Ricans migrate to the mainland United States in this year.

Puerto Rican nationalist uprisings produce armed attacks in Puerto Rico led by Blanca Canales. At Blair House in Washington D.C., Puerto Rican nationalists attempt to assassinate U.S. President Harry Truman.

1952   Walter-McCarran Act passes, making it so anyone accused of voicing the wrong political opinions (i.e., communism) could be denied entry into the United States. Those already working in the United States, visiting, or seeking citizenship, could be deported. Naturalized citizens could be denaturalized and deported.

1953   Operation Wetback initiates massive sweeps of undocumented Mexican workers in the United States that continue until 1955 and result in the deportation of a million Mexicans a year.

1954   Puerto Rican Lolita Lebrón and other Puerto Rican nationalists stage and take part in a shootout in the rotunda of the U.S. Congress in Washington, D.C., wounding five congressmen.

Hernandez v. Texas, a landmark U.S. Supreme Court case, upholds that Mexican Americans and all other racial groups in the United States have equal protection under the 14th Amendment of the U.S. Constitution. A Mexican had not been on a jury for over 25 years.

Guatemalan President Jacobo Arbenz is overthrown by a CIA-sponsored coup. Military dictators seize control and kill more than 200,000 Guatemalans to date. Guatemalan migration to the United States accelerates.

1959   Cuban leader Fidel Castro delivers "The Revolution Begins Now" speech signaling that the Cuban Revolution would not be sold out as it had in 1898 when Cuban leaders did not oppose U.S. intervention.

The first wave of Cuban immigration due to the revolution begins after tyrannical Cuban dictator Fulgencio Batista is overthrown and many of his supporters leave the island—most migrating to the United States.

The Mexican American Political Association (MAPA) is organized in California.

1960   Viva Kennedy political clubs are established to attract Hispanics to vote for John F. Kennedy for U.S. president.

1961   Puerto Rican Antonia Pantoja organizes Aspira in New York City. The group is dedicated to empowering the Puerto Rican community.

Mexican American activist Henry B. González wins election to Congress from Texas.

1962   Farmworker leader César Chávez, along with Dolores Huerta and others, form the National Farm Workers Association (NFWA).

New Mexico preacher Reies López Tijerina drafts the first plan of the Alianza Federal de Mercedes to recover Spanish and Mexican land grants from the United States.

1963   Crystal City, Texas, revolts lead to Mexican American majority elected to the city council, led by Juan Cornejo, a local Teamsters Union business agent.

1965   New York City's Puerto Rican population exceeds 1 million, an increase from 700,000 in 1955 and 13,000 in 1945.

The Agricultural Workers Organizing Committee (AWOC), a mostly Filipino union, strikes at Delano, California. They are joined by César Chávez and the NFWA.

U.S. Marines invade Santo Domingo to establish firm grip on the island. Working-class Dominican migration to the United States increases.

Puerto Rican nationalist Pedro Albizu Campos dies.

The Immigration Act of 1965 passes. This legislation changes U.S. immigration policy from national origins to family preferences. For the first time, Latin Americans are placed on a quota.

Voting Rights Act abolishes the poll tax on voting and ends de jure (not de facto) gerrymandering.

In a speech to the graduating class at Howard University, President Lyndon B. Johnson frames the concept underlying affirmative action.

1966   The Crusade for Justice is founded by boxer, poet, and activist Rodolfo "Corky" Gonzales.

1967   The Mexican American Youth Organization (MAYO) is founded at St. Mary's College in San Antonio, Texas.

1968   In Chicago, José "Cha Cha" Jiménez reorganizes the Young Lords, a Puerto Rican street gang, into a political and human rights organization.

The Los Angeles public school Blowouts demand equal education for Mexican Americans as students and some faculty walk out of class in a coordinated protest.

The Tlatelolco Massacre of Mexican students in Mexico City causes outrage among Chicano students in the United States.

The Mexican American Legal Defense and Educational Fund (MALDEF) is founded to pursue civil rights cases.

La Hermandad Mexicana Nacional (Mexican National Brotherhood) founded in the early 1950s is organized in Los Angeles by Bert Corona and Soledad "Chole" Alatorre to organize undocumented immigrants.

The National Council of La Raza (NCLR) is founded to organize disparate Latino organizations under one umbrella.

Bilingual Education Act, or Title VII, of the Elementary and Secondary Education Act (ESEA) encourages instruction in English and multicultural awareness. It gives school districts the opportunity to provide bilingual education programs without violating segregation laws. It provides funding and resources.

1969 Denver Youth Conferences adopt a Chicano identity and the Plan Espiritual de Aztlán.

Plan of Santa Barbara begins movement for Chicano Studies in public colleges and universities and the Movimiento Estudiantil Chicano/a de Aztlán (MEChA) is founded.

1970 Texas activist José Angel Gutiérrez and MAYO volunteers take control of the Crystal City, Texas, Board of Education.

La Raza Unida Party (LRUP), a Chicano political party is established on January 17, 1970 at Campestre Hall in Crystal City, Texas.

On August 29, some 30,000 Chicanos demonstrate against the Vietnam War at Laguna Park in Los Angeles. A police riot kills three, among them journalist Rubén Salazar who is shot in the head with a tear gas projectile at close range while seated at the Silver Dollar Bar.

Cisneros v. Corpus Christi Independent School District is the first case to extend U.S. Supreme Court's *Brown v. the Board of Education* decision (1954) to Mexican Americans. It recognizes them as a minority group that could be and was frequently discriminated against.

The conspiracy case against Salvador B. Castro, a Los Angles teacher who led the Los Angeles School Blowout (1968) is dismissed.

1973 The government of Chilean President Salvador Allende is overthrown with the support of the U.S. Central Intelligence Agency.

1974 The Chicana Research and Learning Center, the first research and service project in the nation founded and run by and for Mexican American women, is founded at the University Methodist Student Center in Austin, Texas.

Lau v. Nichols case determines that students not receiving special help in school due to their inability to speak English are entitled to this assistance under Title VI of the Civil Rights Act of 1964 that banned educational discrimination on the basis of national origin.

Communities Organized for Public Service (COPS), an affiliate of the Industrial Areas Foundation (IAF), is founded in San Antonio, Texas, to organize grassroots support in the west and south sides of the city.

1978   *University of California Regents v. Bakke* imposes limitations on affirmative action by claiming that affirmative action was unfair if it led to reverse discrimination. This has resulted in continual litigation led by Mexican American and Puerto Rican organizations.

1979   The overthrow of Nicaraguan dictator Anastasio Somoza starts civil wars throughout Central America and marks the beginning of mass migrations to the United States.

1980s   Continued violence in Central America drives immigration to the United States.

1980   Roughly 125,000 people are allowed to leave Cuba from the port of Mariel. Called *Marielitos*, most head for the United States.

1986   Initiative Proposition 63, English as the Official Language of California, is passed with the support of nativist organizations.

Immigration Reform and Control Act of 1986 gives amnesty to undocumented Latinos.

1990   Janitors in the Century City (Los Angeles) high-rise commercial office area stage a three-week general strike for improved wages and benefits. Los Angeles police officers attack a group of 400 nonviolent demonstrators, injuring two dozen janitors and causing at least two miscarriages.

1992   The Salvadoran Peace Accords are signed, ending that country's civil war and setting up a mechanism for elections.

1993   United Farm Worker President César Chávez dies in Yuma, Arizona, on April 23.

1994   The North American Free Trade Agreement (NAFTA) between the United States, Canada, and Mexico is implemented. It encourages the privatization of Mexico and the further demise of the subsistence farm, leading to a massive migration of peasants to Mexican cities and the United States.

Proposition 187, which denies illegal immigrants social services, health care, and public services, is overwhelmingly passed by California voters, penalizing undocumented residents.

1996   Mexican American union leader Miguel Contreras is elected executive secretary–treasurer of the Los Angeles Federation of Labor.

Proposition 209 amends the California Constitution to supposedly prohibit public institutions from discriminating on the basis of race, sex, or ethnicity. This is prompted by the California Civil Rights Initiative Campaign, which was designed to eliminate affirmative action. As a consequence, the number of African Americans college and university students in the state fell: at UCLA in 2006 there were only 100 first-year African American students admitted, down from 488 in 1996.

1998   Proposition 22, English for the Children, passes by an overwhelming majority. This initiative ends bilingual education in California's public schools.

2000   Massive protests against U.S. Navy bombardments of the Island of Vieques off the shore of Puerto Rico lead to arrests and harassment.

2002   Millionaire banker Antonio R. "Tony" Sánchez, Jr., runs unsuccessfully for governor of Texas.

2003   The Iraq War begins.

2004   Writer Gloria Anzaldúa dies prematurely of cancer. She authored *Borderlands/La Frontera: The New Mestiza* (1987) and other important works on gender and homophobia.

2005   Councilman Antonio Villaraigosa is elected mayor of Los Angeles, becoming the first Mexican American mayor of the city since the start of U.S. rule.

2006   Millions protest nationally on May 1 in response to proposed legislation known as H.R. 4437 that would raise penalties for illegal immigration and classify unauthorized immigrants and anyone who helps them as felons.

2007   The U.S. Census Bureau says that Latinos were the largest minority group in the nation at 42.7 million—an increase of 1.3 million, 800,000 from natural increase (births minus deaths) and 500,000 from immigration. Latinos were 3.3 times more likely to be in prison than whites; 4.2 times more likely to be in prison for murder, and 5.8 times more likely to be in prison for felony drug crimes.

PART I
Borders

When the Spaniards invaded the New World in 1494, at least 100 million people lived in the Americas. They included more than 350 major tribal groups, 15 distinct cultural centers, and more than 160 linguistic stocks. No borders existed as we know them. The present framework of the modern nation-states of Latin America and the United States came about through the conquest of the Americas and the carving up of territories into political units after the wars of independence of the early nineteenth century. The Spanish, Portuguese, and English controlled most of these units. These three colonial powers were divided along more than physical borders—there were also linguistic, religious, and racial borders. Proximity to the British colonies in North America played a role in the development of the identities of the former Spanish colonies, and the growth of the North American colonies was spurred on by what included the richest farmland in the world. Once it became its own country in North America, the United States sought to expand at the expense of British Canada to the north and New Spain, which became modern-day Mexico, to the south.

1. Excerpts from J. Eric S. Thompson, ed., *Thomas Gage's Travels in the New World, 1648*

Central America is an isthmus located at the southernmost end of North America abutting South America. It is the shortest landmass between the Atlantic and Pacific Oceans. Since the eighteenth century, the United States has seen strategically located Central America as important to its political, military, and economic interests. During the Spanish colonial period, the early 1500s to 1821, Panama served as a center of commerce for Spain's colonies in America, because Spain shipped trade items and slaves from Panama to Peru. On September 15, 1821, the colonies that made up the Captaincy General of Guatemala declared their independence from Spain. For two years, Central America was under the rule of Emperor Agustín de Iturbide, but on July 1, 1823, El Salvador, Guatemala, Honduras, Nicaragua, and Costa Rica formed the United Provinces of Central America. The following description was written by Thomas Gage, a British subject and a Spanish Dominican who spent two or three years in Guatemala City, where he began to have religious doubts. Gage published a book in 1648 describing his travels in Latin America.

The isthmus of Panama, which runneth between the north and south seas, besides gold in it, is admirably stored with silver, spices, pearls, and medicinal herbs ... Guatemala, seated in the midst of a Paradise on one side and a hell on the other [a volcano], yet never hath this hell broke so loose as to consume that flourishing city. True it is that many years ago it opened a wide mouth on the top, and breathed out such fiery ashes as filled the houses of Guatemala and the country about … The trading of the city [Guatemala] is great, for by mules it partakes of the best commodities of Mexico, Oaxaca, and Chiapa, and, southward, of Nicaragua and Costa Rica. By sea, it hath commerce with Peru, by two sea ports and havens … The Government of all the country about, and of all Honduras, Socomusco, Comayagua, Nicaragua, Costa Rica, Vera Paz, Suchitepéquez, and Chiapas is subordinate unto the Chancery [*Audencia*] of Guatemala; for although every governor over these several provinces is appointed by the King and Council of Spain, yet when they come to those parts to the enjoyment of their charge and execution office, their actions, if unjust, are weighed and judged, censured, and condemned by the Court residing in the city [of Panama] … It is held to be one of the richest places in all America, having by land and, by the river Chagres, commerce with the North Sea, and by the south, trading with all Peru, East Indies, Mexico, and Honduras.

Source: J. Eric S. Thompson, ed., *Thomas Gage's Travels in the New World* (Norman: University of Oklahoma Press, © 1958), pp. 95, 183, 186, 187, 327.

2. The Secret Treaty of San Ildefonso, October 1, 1800

The secret San Ildefonso Treaty was entered into between the French Republic and the King of Spain. Through this treaty, which was negotiated under duress when Emperor Napoleon Bonaparte of France pressured Spain to cede back the territory, Spain returned the Louisiana Territory to France. In its haste, the treaty did not clearly indicate the boundaries of the territory that was returned. This lack of specifity would open the door for the United States to make claims far in excess of the original boundaries of the Louisiana territory. The San Ildefonso Treaty became a topic of controversy for Spain and the United States after France transferred the Louisiana Territory to the United States in 1803.

His Catholic Majesty having always manifested an earnest desire to procure for His Royal Highness the Duke of Parma an aggrandizement which would place his domains on a footing more consonant with his dignity; and the French Republic on its part having long since made known to His Majesty the King of Spain its desire to be again placed in possession of the colony of Louisiana; and the two Governments having exchanged their views on these two subjects of common interest, and circumstances permitting them to assume obligations in this regard which, so far as depends on them, win assure mutual satisfaction, they have authorized for this purpose the following: the French Republic, the Citizen Alexandre Berthier General in Chief, and His Catholic Majesty, Don Mariano Luis de Urquijo, knight of the Order of Charles III, and of that of St. John of Jerusalem, a Counselor of State, his Ambassador Extraordinary and Plenipotentiary appointed near the Batavian Republic, and his First Secretary of State ad interim, who, having exchanged their powers, have agreed upon the following articles, subject to ratification.

ARTICLE 1

The French Republic undertakes to procure for His Royal Highness the Infant Duke of Parma an aggrandizement of territory which shad increase the population of his domains to one minion inhabitants, with the title of King and with all the rights which attach to the royal dignity; and the French Republic undertakes to obtain in this regard the assent of His Majesty the Emperor and King and that of the other interested states' BO that His Highness the Infant Duke of Parma may be put into possession of the said territories without opposition upon the conclusion of the peace to be made between the French Republic and His Imperial Majesty.

ARTICLE 2

The aggrandizement to be given to His Royal Highness the Duke of Parma may consist of Tuscany, in case the present negotiations of the French Government with His Imperial Majesty shall permit that Government to dispose thereof; or it may consist of the three Roman legations or of any other continental provinces of Italy which form a rounded state.

ARTICLE 3

His Catholic Majesty promises and undertakes on his part to retrocede to the French Republic, six months after the full and entire execution of the above conditions and provisions regarding His Royal Highness the Duke of Parma, the colony or province of Louisiana, with the same extent that it now has in the hands of Spain and that it had when France possessed it, and such as it ought to be according to the treaties subsequently concluded between Spain and other states.

ARTICLE 4

His Catholic Majesty will give the necessary orders for the occupation of Louisiana by France as soon as the territories which are to form the arrandizement [sic] of the Duke of Parma shall be placed in the hands of His Royal Highness. The French Republic may, according to its convenience, postpone the taking of possession; when that is to be executed, the states directly or indirectly interested will agree upon such further conditions as their common interests and the interest of the respective inhabitants require.

ARTICLE 5

His Catholic Majesty undertakes to deliver to the French Republic in Spanish ports in Europe, one month after the execution of the provision with regard to the Duke of Parma, six ships of war in good condition built for seventy-four guns, armed and equipped and ready to receive French crews and supplies.

ARTICLE 6

As the provisions of the present treaty have no prejudicial object and leave intact the rights of an, it is not to be supposed that they win give offense to any power. However, if the contrary shall happen and if the two states, because of the execution thereof, shall be attacked or threatened, the two powers agree to make common cause not only to repel the aggression but also to take conciliatory measures prosper for the maintenance of peace with all their neighbors.

ARTICLE 7

The obligations contained in the present treaty derogate in no respect from those which are expressed in the Treaty of Alliance signed at San Ildefonso on the 2d Fructidor, year 4 (August 19, 1796); on the contrary they unite anew the interests of the two powers and assure the guaranties stipulated in the Treaty of Alliance for all cases in which they should be applied.

ARTICLE 8

The ratifications of these preliminary articles shall be effected and exchanged within the period of one month, or sooner if possible, counting from the day of the signature of the present treaty.

In faith whereof we, the undersigned Ministers Plenipotentiary of the French Republic and of His Catholic Majesty, in virtue of our respective powers, have signed these preliminary articles and have affixed thereto our seals.

Done at San Ildefonso the 9th Vendemiaire, 9th year of the French Republic (October 1, 1800).

Alexandre Birthier and Mariano Luis De Urquijo

Source: Courtesy of the Avalon Project, Yale University, http://www.yale.edu/lawweb/avalon/ildefens.htm.

3. Excerpts from the Louisiana Purchase, April 30, 1803

On April 30, 1803, Napoleon Bonaparte of France sold the Louisiana Territory, more than 800,000 square miles (2 million square kilometers) of land extending from the Mississippi River to the Rocky Mountains, to the United States for about $15 million. This put the United States at the Texas border, on the rim of New Spain (Mexico). Euro-Americans viewed Texas as being controlled by a corrupt and intrusive European power. From the beginning, the United States was aggressive in its claims to Texas: U.S. President Thomas Jefferson insisted that the Rio Grande River was the western boundary of the Louisiana Territory. The U.S. claimed that it owned all of the land to and including half of New Mexico. The U.S. minister to Spain was instructed by Jefferson to insist upon the Rio Bravo (Rio Grande) but to yield in case of the probability of armed conflict. With the Louisiana Purchase, the United States doubled its size, and, more importantly, was free to navigate the Mississippi River. Although many considered the taking of more territory a violation of the U.S. Constitution since there was no specific power to purchase the land, the Senate ratified the treaty on October 20, 1803. The following articles deal with the cession of the territory and accentuate the lack of specification of clear boundaries. However, with regard to boundaries, the United States promised to honor the San Ildefonso Treaty.

ARTICLE I

Whereas by the Article the third of the Treaty concluded at St Ildefonso the 9th Vendémiaire on 1st October 1800 between the First Consul of the French Republic and his Catholic Majesty it was agreed as follows.

His Catholic Majesty promises and engages on his part to cede to the French Republic six months after the full and entire execution of the conditions and Stipulations herein relative to his Royal Highness the Duke of Parma, the Colony or Province of Louisiana with the Same extent that it now has in the hand of Spain, & that it had when France possessed it; and Such as it Should be after the Treaties subsequently entered into between Spain and other States.

And whereas in pursuance of the Treaty and particularly of the third article the French Republic has an incontestible [sic] title to the domain and to the possession of the said Territory—The First Consul of the French Republic desiring to give to the United States a strong proof of his friendship doth hereby cede to the United States in the name of the French Republic for ever and in full Sovereignty the said territory with all its rights and appurtenances as fully and in the Same manner as they have been acquired by the French Republic in virtue of the above mentioned Treaty concluded with his Catholic Majesty.

ARTICLE II

In the cession made by the preceeding [sic] article are included the adjacent Islands belonging to Louisiana, all public lots and Squares, vacant lands and all public buildings, fortifications, barracks and other edifices which are not private property. The Archives, papers & documents relative to the domain and Sovereignty of Louisiana and its dependances [sic] will be left in the possession of the Commissaries of the United States, and copies will be afterwards given in due form to the Magistrates and Municipal officers of such of the said papers and documents as may be necessary to them.

ARTICLE III

The inhabitants of the ceded territory shall be incorporated in the Union of the United States and admitted as soon as possible according to the principles of the federal Constitution to the enjoyment of all these rights, advantages and immunities of citizens of the United States, and in the mean time they shall be maintained and protected in the free enjoyment of their liberty, property and the Religion which they profess....

ARTICLE VI

The United States promise to execute Such treaties and articles as may have been agreed between Spain and the tribes and nations of Indians until by mutual consent of the United States and the said tribes or nations other Suitable articles Shall have been agreed upon....

ARTICLE X

The present treaty Shall be ratified in good and due form and the ratifications Shall be exchanged in the Space of Six months after the date of the Signature by the Ministers Plenipotentiary or Sooner if possible.

In faith whereof the respective Plenipotentiaries have Signed these articles in the French and English languages; declaring nevertheless that the present Treaty was originally agreed to in the French language; and have thereunto affixed their Seals.

Done at Paris the tenth day of Floreal in the eleventh year of the French Republic; and the 30th of April 1803.

Robt R Livingston, Jas. Monroe and Barbé Marbois

Source: The People's Vote, http://www.ourdocuments.gov/doc.php?flash=true&doc=18.

4. Excerpts from the Proclamation of Haiti's Independence by the General in Chief, Jean Jacques Dessalines, to the Haitian People in Gonaives, January 1, 1804

By the late eighteenth century, a bond was forming among Latin Americans. They had a common colonial history, and African slavery plagued many of the colonies. There was an African consciousness that formed among many of the colonies as 10 million Africans were imported to the Americas. African music and culture linked the Caribbean with Colombia, Venezuela, and Brazil. In 1791, an African slave rebellion established Haiti as a free, black republic— the first of its kind—plunging the country into civil war. It both spread fear and inspired many colonists. After initially opposing the revolt of 1791, Toussaint Louverture (1743–1803) led the rebels. His army defeated a British expeditionary force in 1798. He then led an invasion of Santo Domingo, and freed the slaves there. By 1803, Napoleon and Toussaint agreed to terms of peace. However, the French betrayed Toussaint, placing him under arrest and assassinated him. In the following document of 1804, Jean Jacques Dessalines (1758–1806) declared the independence of Haiti, sending ripples throughout the Americas. Dessalines was a Haitian nationalist and the first ruler of a free Haiti. In the late nineteenth century, the United States would claim a common American heritage with Latin America. However, unlike Haiti, which Latin Americans considered a Latin American nation, the United States' Latin American neighbors to the south considered them to be a European nation.

Citizens,

It is not enough to have expelled from your country the barbarians who have bloodied it for two centuries; it is not enough to have put a brake to these ever reviving factions which take turns to play-act this liberty, like ghost[s] that France had exposed before your eyes; it is necessary, by a last act of national authority, assure forever an empire of liberty in this country our birth place; we must take away from this inhumane government, which held for so long our spirits in the most humiliating torpor, all hope to resubjugate us; we must at last live independent or die.

Independence or death … May these sacred words bring us together, and may they be the signal of our struggles and of our gathering.

Citizens, my compatriots, I have gathered in this solemn day these courageous servicemen, who on the eve of harvesting the last crotchets rest of liberty, have given their blood to save it; these generals who led your efforts against tyranny, have not yet done enough for your well being.… The French name still glooms our countryside.

All is there to remind us of the atrocities of this barbarian people: our laws, our customs, our cities, all bear the French imprint; what do I say? There are French in our island, and you believe yourself to be free and independent of that republic which fought all nations, it is true, but who has never been victorious over those who wished to be free.

Well what! victims for over fourteen years of our own credulity and our own indulgence; defeated, not by the French armies, but by the shamefaced eloquence of the proclamation of their agents; when will we get tired of breathing the same air than them? Its cruelty compared to our moderated patience; its color to our[s]; the vast seas that keep us apart, our avenging climate, tell us enough that they are not our brothers, and that they will never become and that, if they find asylum amongst us, they will be once more the schemers of our troubles and our divisions.

Indigenous citizens, men, women, girls and children, bear your regards on all the parts of this island; look for, yourself, your spouses, your husbands, yourself, your brothers, you, your sisters; what do I say? Look for your children, your children, those that are being breast fed! What have they become? ... I tremble to say it ... the prey of these vultures. Instead of these interesting victims, your eye dismayed can only perceive their assassins; may the tigers that are still dripping their blood, and whose horrible presence reproach your insensibility and your slowness to avenge them. What are you waiting for to appease their souls? Remember that you have wished that your remains be buried near the remains of your fathers, when you had chased away tyranny; would you go down to your tomb without avenging them? No, their skeleton would push away yours.

And you, precious men, intrepid generals, whose lack of insensibility to your own misfortunes, have resurrected liberty by giving it all your blood; you should know that you have done nothing if you do not give to the nations a terrible example, but just, of the avenge that must exercise a proud people who have recovered their liberty, and jealous to maintain it; let us instill fear in all those whom would dare try to take it away from us again; let us begin with the French.... May they tremble when they approach our coasts, if not by the memory of the cruelty that they have inflicted, at least by the terrible resolution that we are about to take to devote to death, anyone born French, who would dirty of his sacrilegious foot the territory of liberty.

We dared to be free, let us dare to be so by ourselves and for ourselves, let us emulate the growing child: his own weight breaks the edge that has become useless and hamper its walk. What nation has fought for us? What nation would like to harvest the fruits of our labors? And what dishonorable absurdity than to vanquish and be slaves. Slaves! Leave it to the French this qualifying epithet: they have vanquished to cease to be free.

Let us walk on other footprints; let us imitate these nations whom, carrying their solicitude until they arrive on a prospect, and dreading to leave to posterity the example of cowardliness, have preferred to be exterminated rather than to be crossed out from the number of free peoples.

Let us be on guard however so that the spirit of proselytism does not destroy our work; let our neighbors breath[e] in peace, may they live in peace under the empire of the laws that they have legislated themselves, and let us not go, like spark fire revolutionaries, erecting ourselves as legislators of the Caribbean, to make good of our glory by troubling the peace of neighboring islands: they have never, like the one that we live in, been soaked of the innocent blood of their inhabitants; they have no vengeance to exercise against the authority that protects them.

Fortunate to have never known the plagues which have destroyed us, they can only make good wishes for our prosperity. Peace to our neighbors! but anathema to the French name! Eternal hate to France! That is our cry.

Indigenous of Haiti, my fortunate destiny reserved me to be one day the sentinel who had to watch guard the idol to which you are making your sacrifice, I have watched, fought, sometimes alone, and, If I have been fortunate to deliver in your hands the sacred trust that you had under my care, remember that it is up to you now to conserve it. Before you consolidate it by laws which assure your individual liberty, your leaders, which I assemble here, and myself, we owe you the last proof of our devotion.

Generals, and you, leaders, reunited here near me for the well being of our country, the day has come, this day which must make eternal our glory, our independence.

If there could exist amongst you a half-hearted, may he distance himself and tremble to pronounce the oath that must unite us.

Let us swear to the entire universe, to posterity, to ourselves, to renounce forever to France, and to die rather than to live under its domination.

To fight until the last crotchet rest for the independence of our country!

And you, people for too long misfortuned, witness to the oath that we are pronouncing, remind yourself that it is on your perseverance and your courage that I depended on when I threw myself in this career for liberty in order to fight against despotism and tyranny against which you struggled since fourteen years. Remind yourself that I sacrificed myself to jump to your defense, parents, children, fortune, and that now I am only rich of your liberty; that my name has become in horror to all nations who wish for slavery, and that the despots and tyrants do not pronounce it only while cursing the day that saw me born; and if for whatever reason you refused or received while murmuring the laws that the genius which watch over your destiny will dictate me for your good fortune, you would deserve the fate of ungrateful peoples.

But away from me this horrible idea. You will be the support of the liberty that you cherish, the support to the chief which command you.

Take then in your hands this oath to live free and independent, and to prefer death to all those who would love to put you back under the yoke.

Swear at last to pursue forever the traitors and the enemies of your independence.

Done at the general headquarter of Gonaives, this January 1st 1804, the first year of Independence.

Jean Jacques Dessalines

Source: "Live free or die!" Proclamation of Haiti's Independence. Haitian Arawak Movement, http://www.haitianarawak.com/documents/historical/proclamation.php.

5. Letter from John Sibley to General Henry Dearborn, October 12, 1808

Euro-American merchants played an active role in expanding borders of the United States. They were often spies or filibusterers. One of the most notorious American adventurers was John Sibley (1757–1837), a Massachusetts medical doctor who moved to Natchitoches, Texas, after the United States received the Louisiana Territory from France. Sibley became acquainted with the Red

River Valley and, in 1804, President Thomas Jefferson named Sibley an Indian Agent in the border country. Sibley later received several thousand dollars from Congress to use to bribe the Indian tribes to support Americans. The physician participated in early filibustering expeditions to take Texas from Spain and was considered a menace by Spain. Sibley's correspondence to various personages in the United States helped to shape the image of Texas. Sibley also contributed articles on Spanish Texas that were published in various U.S. newspapers. The following letter from Sibley to General Henry Dearborn concerns the Mexican War for Independence from Spain and records Euro-American reactions to this movement. It expresses the notion that Texas was part of the United States.

Natchitoches, October 12th 1808
Sir
Mr. Erwin has lately informed me that he shall leave this place On the first of April next & return Again to Philada[delphia]: I have a Son in Wilmington, N. Carolina, by the name of Samuel Hopkins Sibley, about two years younger than his brother George C. Sibley (who you know), who I take the Liberty of Recommending as the Successor of Mr. Erwin & Shall feel much obliged & gratified should you think proper to give him the appointment.

I think him as Capable as his brother & will be responsible for his good Conduct in every respect. His appointment will be perfectly Agreeable to Mr. Linnard, who wishes Mr. Erwin's place may be Supplied by the time he will leave this. I very much regret the loss of Mr. Erwin from our Small Society, for I never knew a young man of a Purer Mind, or of more Chaste morality. I shall always esteem his Virtues as well as admire his Understanding all good Men who know him cant help but wish him well.

Everything in this quarter is quiet. The season is healthy & very great Crops of everything, no Occurrence Amongst the Indians worthy of notice, everybody wishes the embargo raised; but not untill [sic] the Object for which it was laid is affected: or it is found insufficient to affect it. The late events in Spain Seems to me very much to Change our prospects in this quarter. If the Govt of Spain in Europe is destroyed by France, Mexico & its dependencies are prepared to declare themselves independent, & will place the Present Vice King of Mexico at their head, Untill [sic] some Branch of the Bourbon family shall Arrive in America, they will cultivate the friendship of the United States by all means in their power. A very friendly Intercourse on their part has already Commenced, the heart of the New Governor Salcedo is entirely with us.

About Thirty Negroes from two or three plantations on Red River about 40 Miles below this Town deserted Yesterday morning together they stole Arms, Ammunition & Horses, their persuers [sic] have not Returned. They went towards the River Sabine. Governor Salcedo Said repeatedly when here, that he would have all Such Sent Back that might Come into his Province after his Arrival, Unless he received from the King an express order to the contrary. His Sincerity will in a few days be put to proof
I am
With great Esteem
Your Obt Servant
John Sibley.

Genl. Henry Dearborn

Source: Julia Kathryn Garrett, "Dr. John Sibley and the Louisiana-Texas Frontier, 1803–1814," *Southwestern Historical Quarterly Online*, vol. 47, no. 1, http://www.tsha.utexas.edu/publications/journals/ shq/online/v047/n1/contrib_DIVL1027.html.

6. Letter from Ignacio de Allende to Fr. Miguel Hidalgo, August 31, 1810

Captain Ignacio de Allende (1779–1811) served in the Spanish Army in Colonial Mexico during the first part of the nineteenth century. He became a supporter of the Mexican independence movement in 1810. Along with Doña Josefa Ortíz de Domínguez, Juan de Aldama, and Mariano Abasolo, he was among the core conspirators. The following letter was written to Fr. Miguel Hidalgo (1753–1811), who is considered the Father of Mexico, a month before the revolt. It discusses what was being said at the meetings in preparation for the declaration of independence. The letter, dated 31/810 for the 31st of August 1810, is a window into the secret activities before the Grito de Dolores (Document 7). It also reveals some of the conspirators' prejudices toward the Indians.

Sn. Cura Dn. Migl. Hidalgo y Costilla. Sn. Mign. el Gre. Ago. 31/810. Esteemed Señor Cura: I arrived from Queretaro and have not been able to write to you because I found no messenger in whom I had confidence. On the 13th instant the anniversary of the conquest of Mejico it was arranged that there would be public celebrations [in Queretaro] which lasted three days and we [Allende and Juan de Aldama], without paying any attention to them, went to the home of the Gonzalez family, where many important matters were discussed. It was decided to work with our intentions carefully concealed, since if the movement was openly revolutionary it would not be seconded by the general mass of the people, and Second Lieutenant Dn. Pedro Se[p]tien strengthened his stand saying that if the revolution was inevitable, as the Indians were indifferent to the word liberty, it was necessary to make them believe the insurrection was being accomplished only in order to help King Ferdinand. In the next meeting I am going to propose that we start the uprising at San Juan [de los Lagos] during the days of the fair, where without being at all unprepared we will pretend to be peaceful elements; but before the meeting I want to go to see you as soon as possible so that we may always work in agreement in this cause. I wish you good health and beg God to protect you and repeat myself your appreciative, affectionate and dependable servant who attentively kisses your hand.
(Signed)

Igno. de Allende

Source: Archivo General de la Nación, Mexico City. Courtesy of Sons of DeWitt Colony Texas, Archives: Father Miguel Hidalgo, http://www.tamu.edu/ccbn/dewitt/hidalgoarchive.htm.

7. El Grito de Dolores, September 16, 1810

At midnight on September 16, 1810, Fr. Miguel Hidalgo rang his parish bell in the city of Dolores, Guanajuato, and declared Mexico's independence. The declaration of independence was called *El Grito de Dolores* (the Shout for

Independence). Hidalgo called for Mexican independence, the exile or arrest of all Spaniards in Mexico, and ended by calling out, *"Mexicanos, ¡Viva México!"* (Mexicans, long live Mexico!). The exact words that Fr. Hidalgo used have not been found, and the two quotations below are two renditions of what Fr. Hidalgo might have said.

EL GRITO DE DOLORES FR. MIGUEL HIDALGO SEP 15, 1810

"My children: a new dispensation comes to us today. Will you receive it? Will you free yourselves? Will you recover the lands stolen three hundred years ago from your forefathers by the hated Spaniards? We must act at once ... Will you not defend your religion and your rights as true patriots? Long live our Lady of Guadalupe! Death to the gachupines!"

Source: Michael C. Meyer and William L. Sherman, "Mexican Independence," in *The Course of Mexican History*, 2nd ed. (New York: Oxford University Press, 1983), pp. 287–288.

"My friends and countrymen: neither the king nor tributes exist for us any longer. We have borne this shameful tax, which only suits slaves, for three centuries as a sign of tyranny and servitude; [a] terrible stain which we shall know how to wash away with our efforts. The moment of our freedom has arrived, the hour of our liberty has struck; and if you recognized its great value, you will help me defend it from the ambitious grasp of the tyrants. Only a few hours remain before you see me at the head of the men who take pride in being free. I invite you to fulfill this obligation. And so without a patria nor liberty we shall always be at a great distance from true happiness. It has been imperative to take this step as now you know, and to begin this has been necessary. The cause is holy and God will protect it. The arrangements are hastily being made and for that reason I will not have the satisfaction of talking to you any longer. Long live, then, the Virgin of Guadalupe! Long live America for which we are going to fight!"

—Sons of the Dewitt Colony

Source: "Father Hidalgo's Grito de Dolores." Courtesy of Sons of DeWitt Colony Texas, http://www.tamu.edu/ccbn/dewitt/mexicanrev.htm.

8. José María Morelos Decree, October 13, 1811

Fr. Miguel Hidalgo's 1810 War of Mexican Independence deepened racial divisions among the various castes in Mexico. His cry, *Death to the Spaniards*, alienated many *criollos* (creoles, American-born Spaniards) and even *mestizos* (those of mixed Indian/European ancestry) who were afraid of Indian nationalism. After Fr. Hidalgo's execution in 1811 for treason, the war shifted to guerrilla warfare. José María Morelos (1765–1815), of Spanish, Indian, and African ancestry, became the principal leader of the revolution after the death of Fr. Hidalgo. In 1815, Spanish forces captured Morelos. He was put on trial by the viceroy's military court and the Spanish Inquisition. In the following document, Morelos sought to smooth out the racial rifts in order to unify the disparate castes behind the war.

Don José María Morelos, Lt. Gen. of the Army, and General of the South hereby decrees:

Albeit that a grave error has been incurred, and what we have suffered on this coast could bring upon all of us the inhabitants the worst of anarchy, or better stated a lamentable desolation. This came in part from the damage done because officials have gone beyond their boundaries and faculties. Now the inferior has proceeded with charges against the superior, their revolution has experienced difficulty in great part with little progress. Our weapons are to cut off at the root, uprisings and disorders which have come about and I am come to declare by degree this day the following points.

For in as much our system only shall be able to proceed once that the political government and military falls into the hands of "the criollos" who would be better keepers of the rights of our lord Don Fernando the Seventh [King of Spain]. And as a consequence, from hereon no distinction shall be made in categories of qualities, being that generally all of us call ourselves Americans, and looking each to the other as brothers, we ought to live in the Holy Peace that our Redeemer, Jesus Christ has left us when he made a triumphant ascension into the heavens, and it follows that all should know him, that there be no motive for those groupings that are called castes, which only want to destroy each one the other, the whites against the blacks, and these against the native Americans. For it would be the worst crime of all that man would commit, which deed would not have any equal example in all of the centuries and nations, much less we ought not to permit this [anarchy] in our time, because it would be the cause of our total destruction, both spiritual and moral.

Since the whites were the first representatives in the kingdom, and they were the first ones to take up arms in defense of the native peoples, and the other castes with them, we then owe to the whites the object of our merit and gratitude and not our hate, which easily could be formed against them.

That the officials of the troops, judges and commissioned officers ought not to show excess in their duly rights, but that they concede in their tasks, unless charged by an inferior against the superior, and then only with special allowance of the Suprema Junta [Congress], in written form, not verbally, manifesting the grievance against the person they wish to charge.

That no official acting as judge or commissioned officer, neither deputized agents without authority bring charges, the inferior against the superior until receiving special orders from me, or His Majesty the Suprema Junta, and that be done by bona fide persons.

That no individual be that who it may, take the voice of the Nation to proceed in other kinds of riots, now that we have a legitimate superior entity should bring to them their most difficult cases of betrayal of the nation and so that no one bring charges in his own authority.

Being now that it is our system, we will not bring charges against the rich, for whatever reasons, and much less against the rich *criollos*. No one dare to lay hands on their goods, no matter how rich that person may be, it will be against all rights of our neighbors to take this action, principally against the Divine Law, which prohibits us from robbing and stealing other's things against the will of their rightful owner, and even the thought of coveting things that belong to another. Even though they may be guilty as rich europeans or *criollos* none shall lay hold of their goods without express orders from a superior. This order or rules needs to be effective also against kidnapping or confiscating so that everything be done in due process.

Be it that anyone dares to commit a crime against this decree, he shall be punished with all rigor of the laws and the same punishment shall have anyone who has ideas of rioting, overthrowing the government, and in all accounts not expressly mentioned here for lack of definition, those given to evil spirits, and are against the law of God, tranquility of the inhabitants of the kingdom and progress of our arms [cause].

And so that this notice can reach everyone and no one be ignorant of the same, I order that this publication be posted in the city, on the entrance and everywhere people can read and comprehend my orders, posting it upon the pathways as is the customs. It is dated in the City of Our Lady of Guadalupe of Tecpan, Oct. 13th, 1811, José María Morelos.

Source: "War of the Castes Archives: José María Morelos." Courtesy of Sons of Dewitt Colony Texas, http://www.tamu.edu/ccbn/dewitt/morelossent.htm.

9. Excerpts from a Letter from Thomas Jefferson to Alexander von Humboldt, December 6, 1813

U.S. President Thomas Jefferson is often portrayed as an isolationist, but his correspondence to German Baron Alexander von Humboldt and others suggests otherwise. Jefferson had a expansionist view of Euro-American destiny. Jefferson had contact with world intellectuals, such as the world traveler von Humboldt, to whom he wrote the following letter on December 6, 1813. The letter suggests that Euro-Americans were making use of Humboldt's maps and information in regard to New Spain. Jefferson mentions that American explorer Zebulon Pike was a spy. In the letter, Jefferson betrays his biases toward Spain.

MY DEAR FRIEND AND BARON

I think it most fortunate that your travels in those countries were so timed as to make them known to the world in the moment they were about to become actors on its stage. That they will throw off their European dependence I have no doubt; but in what kind of government their revolution will end I am not so certain. History, I believe, furnishes no example of a priest-ridden people maintaining a free civil government. This marks the lowest grade of ignorance, of which their civil as well as religious leaders will always avail themselves for their own purposes. The vicinity of New Spain to the United States, and their consequent intercourse, may furnish schools for the higher, and example for the lower classes of their citizens. And Mexico, where we learn from you that men of science are not wanting, may revolutionize itself under better auspices than the Southern provinces. These last, I fear, must end in military despotisms. The different casts of their inhabitants, their mutual hatreds and jealousies, their profound ignorance and bigotry, will be played off by cunning leaders, and each be made the instrument of enslaving others. But of all this you can best judge, for in truth we have little knowledge of them to be depended on, but through you. But in whatever governments they end they will be American governments, no longer to be involved in the never-ceasing broils of Europe. The European nations constitute a separate division of the globe; their localities make them part of a distinct system; they have a set of interests of their own in which it is our business never to engage ourselves. America has a hemisphere to itself. It must have its separate system of interests, which must not be subordinated to those of Europe. The insulated state in which nature has placed the American continent, should so far avail it that no spark of war kindled in the other quarters of the globe should be wafted across the wide oceans which separate us from them. And it will be so. In fifty years more the United States alone will contain fifty millions of inhabitants, and fifty years are soon gone over. The peace of 1763 is within that period. I was then twenty years old, and of course remember well all the transactions of the war preceding it. And you will live to see the epoch now equally ahead of us; and the numbers which will then be spread over the other parts of the American hemisphere, catching long before that the principles of our portion of it, and concurring with us in the maintenance of the same system. You see how readily we run into ages beyond the grave; and even those of us to whom that grave is already opening its quiet bosom. I am anticipating events of which you will be the bearer to me in the Elysian fields fifty years hence....

That their Arrowsmith should have stolen your Map of Mexico, was in the piratical spirit of his country. But I should be sincerely sorry if our [Zebulon] Pike has made an ungenerous use of your candid communications here; and the more so as he died in the arms of victory gained over the enemies of his country. Whatever he did was on a principle of enlarging knowledge, and not for filthy shillings and pence of which he made none from that work. If what he has borrowed has any effect it will be to excite an appeal in his readers from his defective information to the copious volumes of it with which you have enriched the world. I am sorry he omitted even to acknowledge the source of his information. It has been an oversight, and not at all in the spirit of his generous nature. Let me solicit your forgiveness then of a deceased hero, of an honest and zealous patriot, who lived and died for his country.

You will find it inconceivable that Lewis's journey to the Pacific should not yet have appeared; nor is it in my power to tell you the reason. The measures taken by his surviving companion, Clarke, for the publication, have not answered our wishes in point of despatch. I think, however, from what I have heard, that the mere journal will be out within a few weeks in two volumes. These I will take care to send you with the tobacco seed you desired, if it be possible for them to escape the thousand ships of our enemies spread over the ocean. The botanical and zoological discoveries of Lewis will probably experience greater delay, and become known to the world through other channels before that volume will be ready. The Atlas, I believe, waits on the leisure of the engraver.

Although I do not know whether you are now at Paris or ranging the regions of Asia to acquire more knowledge for the use of men, I cannot deny myself the gratification of an endeavor to recall myself to your recollection, and of assuring you of my constant attachment, and of renewing to you the just tribute of my affectionate esteem and high respect and consideration.

Thomas Jefferson

Source: "A Hemisphere to Itself," *The Letters of Thomas Jefferson: 1743–1826*, Oxford Archives, Oxford, England.

10. Excerpts from the Adams-Onís Treaty of 1819

The Adams-Onís Treaty is also known as the Transcontinental Treaty of 1819 or the Florida Purchase Treaty. Since before the United States of America achieved independence in 1783, Americans had designs on Florida, which they considered part of U.S. territory. There were frequent border raids and Americans regarded the Seminoles as a menace. These tensions increased in December

1817, when President James Monroe ordered General Andrew Jackson to lead an expedition against Florida's Seminole Indians. Many scholars say the underlying reason for this expedition was to empower Monroe to put pressure on Spain—already having problems with independence movements throughout the Americas—to sell. Another pretext was that Spain was harboring runaway African slaves in Florida. In 1818, Jackson invaded Florida, took control of Spanish forts, and executed British nationals. Jackson's raid led to an international incident with England and put pressure on Spain to enter into negotiations regarding Spanish Florida. The Adams-Onís Treaty of 1819, signed by Spanish Foreign Minister Luis de Onís and U.S. Secretary of State John Quincy Adams, ceded Florida to the United States and settled a dispute regarding borders along the Sabine River in Texas. Among other reasons, the following treaty articles are important because they specified the new borders.

ARTICLE 2. His Catholic Majesty cedes to the United States, in full property and sovereignty, all the territories which belong to him, situated to the Eastward of the Mississippi, known by the name of East and West Florida. The adjacent Islands dependent on said Provinces, all public lots and squares, vacant Lands, public Edifices, Fortifications, Barracks and other Buildings, which are not private property, Archives and Documents, which relate directly to the property and sovereignty of said Provinces, are included in this Article. The said Archives and Documents shall be left in possession of the Commissaries, or Officers of the United States, duly authorized to receive them.

ARTICLE 3. The Boundary Line between the two Countries, West of the Mississippi, shall begin on the Gulf of Mexico, at the mouth of the River Sabine in the Sea, continuing North, along the Western Bank of that River, to the 32d degree of Latitude; thence by a Line due North to the degree of Latitude, where it strikes the Rio Roxo of Nachitoches, or Red-River, then following the course of the Rio-Roxo Westward to the degree of Longitude, 100 West from London and 23 from Washington, then crossing the said Red-River, and running thence by a Line due North to the River Arkansas, thence, following the Course of the Southern bank of the Arkansas to its source in Latitude, 42. North and thence by that parallel of Latitude to the South-Sea. The whole being as laid down in Melishe's Map of the United States, published at Philadelphia, improved to the first of January 1818. But if the Source of the Arkansas River shall be found to fall North or South of Latitude 42, then the Line shall run from the said Source due South or North, as the case may be, till it meets the said Parallel of Latitude 42, and thence along the said Parallel to the South Sea: all the Islands in the Sabine and the Said Red and Arkansas Rivers, throughout the Course thus described, to belong to the United States; but the use of the Waters and the navigation of the Sabine to the Sea, and of the said Rivers, Roxo and Arkansas, throughout the extent of the said Boundary, on their respective Banks, shall be common to the respective inhabitants of both Nations. The Two High Contracting Parties agree to cede and renounce all their rights, claims and pretensions to the Territories described by the said Line: that is to say—The United States hereby cede to His Catholic Majesty, and renounce forever, all their rights, claims, and pretensions to the Territories lying West and South of the above described Line; and, in like manner, His Catholic Majesty cedes to the said United States, all his rights, claims, and pretensions to any Territories, East and North of the said Line, and, for himself, his heirs and successors, renounces all claim to the said Territories forever.

ARTICLE 4. To fix this Line with more precision, and to place the Landmarks which shall designate exactly the limits of both Nations, each of the Contracting Parties shall appoint a Commissioner, and a Surveyor, who shall meet before the termination of one year from the date of the Ratification of this Treaty, at Nachitoches on the Red River, and proceed to run and mark the said Line from the mouth of the Sabine to the Red River, and from the Red River to the River Arkansas, and to ascertain the Latitude of the Source of the said River Arkansas, in conformity to what is above agreed upon and stipulated, and the Line of Latitude 42 to the South Sea: they shall make out plans and keep Journals of their proceedings, and the result agreed upon by them shall be considered as part of this Treaty, and shall have the same force as if it were inserted therein. The two Governments will amicably agree respecting the necessary Articles to be furnished to those persons, and also as to their respective escorts, should such be deemed necessary.

ARTICLE 5. The Inhabitants of the ceded Territories shall be secured in the free exercise of their Religion, without any restriction, and all those who may desire to remove to the Spanish Dominions shall be permitted to sell, or export their Effects at any time whatever, without being subject, in either case, to duties.

ARTICLE 6. The Inhabitants of the Territories which His Catholic Majesty cedes to the United States by this Treaty, shall be incorporated in the Union of the United States, as soon as may be consistent with the principle of the Federal Constitution, and admitted to the enjoyment of all the privileges, rights and immunities of the Citizens of the United States....

ARTICLE 8. All the grants of land made before the 24th of January 1818 by His Catholic Majesty or by his lawful authorities in the said Territories ceded by His Majesty to the United States, shall be ratified and confirmed to the persons in possession of the lands, to the same extent that the same grants would be valid if the Territories had remained under the Dominion of His Catholic Majesty. But the owners in possession of such lands, who by reason of the recent circumstances of the Spanish Nation and the Revolutions in Europe, have been prevented from fulfilling all the conditions of their grants, shall complete them within the terms limited in the same respectively, from the date of this Treaty; in default of which the said grants shall be null and void—all grants made since the said 24th of January 1818 when the first proposal on the part of His Catholic Majesty, for the cession of the Floridas was made, are hereby declared and agreed to be null and void....

John Quincy Adams and Luis De Onís

Source: Modern History Sourcebook: United States—Spain: Treaty of 1819, http://www.fordham.edu/halsall/mod/1819florida.html.

11. Plan of Iguala, February 24, 1821

The Mexican war for independence lasted just over 10 years, 1810–1821, encouraging the rise of local *caudillos* (strongmen). It also created national heroes, such as Vicente Guerrero (1782–1831), a mule driver of African, Indian, and Spanish ancestry who became commander-in-chief of the Mexican Army. Eight years later, Guerrero became president of Mexico, and he abolished slavery.

The war encouraged unity among many of the racial groups in Mexico. Along with Agustín de Iturbide (1783–1824), a former Spanish army officer, Guerrero agreed on the Plan de Iguala, known as the Plan of Three Guarantees, which called for independence, union with equality of races, and the Catholic religion. When Mexico was under Spain, it was called New Spain. The new nation of Mexico would be independent of Spain, but ruled by a constitution. Guerrero joined with the former royalist officer Iturbide to successfully overthrow Spain.

Plan or indications to the government that must be provisionally installed with the objective of ensuring our sacred religion and establishing the independence of the Mexican Empire: and it will have the title of the North American Government Junta [Assembly], proposed by Colonel D. Agustin de Iturbide to his Excellency The Viceroy of New Spain, Count del Venadito.

1st. The Religion of New Spain is and shall be catholic, apostolic and Roman, without toleration of any other.

2nd. New Spain is independent of the old and of any other power, even of our Continent.

3rd. Its Government shall be a Monarchy moderated with arrangement to the Constitution peculiar and adaptable to the kingdom.

4th. Its Emperor will be D. Fernando VII, and if he does not present himself personally for swearing in México within the term prescribed by the Courts, his Most Serene Highness the Infante [Crown Prince] Carlos, D. Francisco de Paulo, Archduke Carlos or other individual of the reining house that the Congress considers suitable will be called upon in his place.

5th. While the courts convene, there will be a Junta that will have that meeting and the assurance of compliance with the plan in all its extent as its objective.

6th. Said Junta, that will be denominated as Governing, must be composed of voters [speakers] of whom the official letter from his Excellency The Viceroy speaks.

7th. While D. Fernando VII presents himself in México to render a swearing, the Junta will govern in the name of His Majesty by virtue of the swearing of loyalty that it made to the nation; however the orders that he may have imparted will be suspended while he has not been sworn.

8th. If D. Fernando VII does not consider it worthwhile coming to México, while the Emperor to be crowned is resolved, the Junta or the Regency shall rule in the name of the nation.

9th. This government shall be supported by the army of the three warranties that will be discussed later.

10th. The courts shall resolve the continuation of the Junta, or of a Regency if one should substitute for it while a person arrives to be crowned.

11th. The courts shall immediately establish the Constitution of the Mexican Empire.

12th. All the inhabitants of New Spain, without any distinction among Europeans, Africans or Indians, are citizens of this Monarchy, with options to all employment according to their merits and virtues.

13th. The person of every citizen and his properties, shall be respected and protected by the government.

14th. The secular and regular cleric will be preserved in all its rights and pre-eminences.

15th. The Junta shall take care that all the branches of the state, and all the political, ecclesiastic, civil and military personnel remain without any alteration in the same state as they exist today. Only those that indicate to be in disagreement with the plan shall be removed, replaced by those more distinguished by virtue and merit.

16th. A protective army will be formed that shall be denominated of the three warranties, and under its protection it will take first the conservation of the Catholic, apostolic and Roman Religion cooperating by all means that are within its reach so that there will be no mixing of with any other sect and will attack opportunely the enemies that could damage it; second the independence under the manifested system; third the intimate union of American and Europeans therefore guaranteeing the bases so fundamental to the happiness of New Spain, sacrificing the life of the first to the last of its individuals before consenting to their infringement.

17th. The troops of the army will observe the most exacting discipline to the letter of the ordinances, and the chiefs and officers will continue afoot as they are today: that is in their respective classes with options to vacant employment and those to be vacated by those who would not wish to follow its flags or by any other cause, and with option to those that are considered of necessity or convenience.

18th. The troops of said army shall be considered of the line [regular army troops].

19th. The same will take place with those that follow this plan. Those that do not differ, those of the system prior to the independence that join said army immediately, and the countrymen who intend to enlist, shall be considered national militia troops, and the Courts shall dictate the form of all of them for the domestic and foreign security of the kingdom.

20th. Employment will be granted according to the true merit by virtue of reports from the respective chiefs and provisionally in the name of the Nation.

21st. While the Courts are established delinquencies will be processed in total arrangement with the Spanish Constitution.

22nd. Conspiring against independence shall be processed by imprisonment without progressing to any other action until the Courts decide the penalty for the gravest of the delinquencies after that of Divine Majesty.

23rd. Those who encourage disunion shall be watched and shall be considered conspirators against independence.

24th. Since the Courts to be installed shall be constituent, it will be necessary that the representatives [deputies] receive sufficient powers to that effect; and furthermore as it is of great importance that the voters know that their representatives will be to the Mexican Congress, and not to Madrid, the Junta shall prescribe the just rules for the elections and shall indicate the time necessary for those and for the opining of Congress. Since the elections may not be verified in March, its completion shall occur as soon as possible.

Source: Courtesy of Sons of DeWitt Colony Texas, http://www.tamu.edu/ccbn/dewitt/iguala.htm.

12. Treaty of Córdova, August 24, 1821

The agreement on the independent kingdom of Mexico was concluded in Córdova, Spain, on August 24, 1821. The treaty was signed by Don Juan O'Donnoju, Lieutenant-General of the Armies of Spain, and Don Agustín de Iturbide (1763–1823). The Treaty of Córdova adopted existing Spanish law for the Mexican nation and recognized the independence of Mexico. Because of this the Treaty of Córdova would become relevant in later land grant suits during the Euro-American occupation of the Southwest.

1st. This kingdom of America shall be recognised as a sovereign and independent nation; and shall, in future, be called the Mexican Empire.

2d. The government of the empire shall be monarchical, limited by a constitution.

3d. Ferdinand VII, catholic king of Spain, shall, in the first place, be called to the throne of the Mexican Empire, (on taking the oath prescribed in the 10th Article of the plan,) and on his refusal and denial, his brother, the most serene infante Don Carlos; on his refusal and denial, the most serene infante Don Francisco de Paula; on his refusal and denial, the most serene Don Carlos Luis, infante of Spain, formerly heir of Tuscany, now of Lucca; and upon his renunciation and denial, the person whom the cortes of the empire shall designate.

4th. The emperor shall fix his court in Mexico, which shall be the capital of the empire.

5th. Two commissioners shall be named by his excellency Senor O'Donnoju, and these shall proceed to the court of Spain, and place in the hands of his Majesty King Ferdinand VII, a copy of this treaty, and a memorial which shall accompany it, for the purpose of affording information to his Majesty with respect to antecedent circumstances, whilst the cortes of the empire offer him the crown with all the formalities and guarantees which a matter of so much importance requires; and they supplicate his Majesty, that on the occurrence of the case provided for in Article 3, he would be pleased to communicate it to the most serene infantes called to the crown in the same article, in the order in which they are so named; and that his Majesty would be pleased to interpose his influence and prevail on one of the members of his august family to proceed to this empire, inasmuch as the prosperity of both nations would be thereby promoted, and as the Mexicans would feel satisfaction in thus strengthening the bands of friendship, with which they may be, and wish to see themselves, united to the Spaniards.

6th. Conformably to the spirit of the "Plan of Iguala," an assembly shall be immediately named, composed of men the most eminent in the empire for their virtues, their station, rank, fortune, and influence; men marked out by the general opinion, whose number may be sufficiently considerable to insure by their collective knowledge the safety of the resolutions which they may take in pursuance of the powers and authority granted them by the following articles.

7th. The assembly mentioned in the preceding article shall be called the "Provisional Junta of Government."

8th. Lieutenant-General Don Juan O'Donnoju shall be a member of the Provisional Junta of Government, in consideration of its being expedient that a person of his rank should take an active and immediate part in the government, and of the indispensable necessity of excluding some of the individuals mentioned in the above Plan of Iguala, conformably to its own spirit.

9th. The Provisional Junta of Government shall have a president elected by itself from its own body, or from without it, to be determined by the absolute plurality of votes; and if on the first scrutiny the votes be found equal, a second scrutiny shall take place, which shall embrace those two who shall have received the greatest number of votes.

10th. The first act of the Provisional Junta shall be the drawing up of a manifesto of its installation, and the motives of its assemblage, together with whatever explanations it may deem convenient and proper for the information of the country, with respect to the public interests, and the mode to be adopted in the election of deputies for the cortes, of which more shall be said hereafter.

11th. The Provisional Junta of Government after the election of its president, shall name a regency composed of three persons selected from its own body, or from without it, in whom shall be vested the executive power, and who shall govern in the name and on behalf of the monarch till the vacant throne be filled.

12th. The Provisional Junta as soon as it is installed, shall govern ad interim according to the existing laws, so far as they may not be contrary to the "Plan of Iguala," and until the cortes shall have framed the constitution of the state.

13th. The regency immediately on its nomination, shall proceed to the convocation of the cortes in the manner which shall be prescribed by the Provisional Junta of Government, conformably to the spirit of Article No. 7 in the aforesaid "Plan."

14th. The executive power is vested in the regency, and the legislative in the cortes; but as some time must elapse before the latter can assemble, and in order that the executive and legislative powers should not remain in the hands of one body, the junta shall be empowered to legislate; in the first place, where cases occur which are too pressing to wait till the assemblage of the cortes, and then the junta shall proceed in concert with the regency; and, in the second place, to assist the regency in its determinations in the character of an auxiliary and consultative body.

15th. Every individual who is domiciled amongst any community, shall, on an alteration taking place in the system of government, or on the country passing under the dominion of another prince, be at full liberty to remove himself, together with his effects, to whatever country he chooses, without any person having the right to deprive him of such liberty, unless he have contracted some obligation with the community to which lie had belonged, by the commission of a crime, or by any other of those modes which publicists have laid down; this applies to the Europeans residing in New Spain, and to the Americans residing in the Peninsula. Consequently it will be at their option to remain, adopting either country, or to demand their passports, (which cannot be denied them,) for permission to leave the kingdom at such time as may be appointed before-hand, carrying with them their families and property; but paying on the latter the regular export duties now in force, or which may hereafter be established by the competent authority.

16th. The option granted in the foregoing article shall not extend to persons in public situations, whether civil or military, known to be disaffected to Mexican independence; such persons shall necessarily quits the empire within the time which shall be allotted by the regency, taking with them their effects after having paid the duties, as stated in the preceding article.

17th. The occupation of the capital by the Peninsular troops being an obstacle to the execution of this treaty, it is indispensable to have it removed. But as the Commander-in-Chief of the imperial army fully participating in the sentiments of the Mexican nation, does not wish to attain this object by force, for which, however, he has more than ample means at his command, notwithstanding the known valour and constancy of the Peninsular troops, who are not in a situation to maintain themselves against the system adopted by the nation at large. Don Juan O'Donnoju agrees to exercise his authority for the evacuation of the capital by the said troops without loss of blood, and upon the terms of an honourable capitulation. AGUSTÍN DE ITURBIDE, JUAN O'DONNOJU. (A true copy.) JOSE DOMINGUEZ. Dated in the Town of Cordova, 24th August, 1821.

Source: Courtesy of Sons of DeWitt Colony Texas, http://www.tamu.edu/ccbn/dewitt/iguala.htm.

13. Excerpts from Simón Bolívar Letter, Kingston, Jamaica, September 6, 1815

No Latin American hero is as revered as Simón Bolívar (1783–1830), the "Great Liberator" of Latin America. To this day, he has kept alive the hope of a united Latin America. Bolívar believed a united hemisphere would strengthen the hemisphere against foreign threats. On September 6, 1815, the Carta de Jamaica was written in Kingston, Jamaica. Bolívar reviewed the historical successes in the struggle for Latin American independence. The document discusses the causes and justifications for independence and calls upon Europe to help free the Latin American nations in their common struggle against Spain. Bolívar also reflects on the future of Mexico, Central America, and South America. The following excerpt discusses the centrality and importance of Central America to Latin American unity.

It is a grandiose idea to think of consolidating the New World into a single nation, united by pacts into a single bond. It is reasoned that, as these parts have a common origin, language, customs, and religion, they ought to have a single government to permit the newly formed states to unite in a confederation. But this is not possible. Actually, America is separated by climatic differences, geographic diversity, conflicting interests, and dissimilar characteristics. How beautiful it would be if the Isthmus of Panamá could be for us what the Isthmus of Corinth was for the Greeks! Would to God that some day we may have the good fortune to convene there an august assembly of representatives of republics, kingdoms, and empires to deliberate upon the high interests of peace and war with the nations of the other three-quarters of the globe ... The states of the Isthmus of Panamá, as far as Guatemala, will perhaps form a confederation. Because of their magnificent position between two mighty oceans, they may in time become the emporium of the world. Their canals will shorten distances throughout the world, strengthen commercial ties between Europe, America, and Asia, and bring to that happy area tribute from the four quarters of the globe. There some day, perhaps, the capital of the world may be located—reminiscent of the Emperor Constantine's claim that Byzantium was the capital of the ancient world ... I am, Sir, etc. etc. Simón Bolívar

Source: Simón Bolívar, Reply of a South American to a Gentleman of this Island [Jamaica], pp. 118–119. In Harold Bierck, Jr., ed., *Selected Writings of Bolivar*, vol. I (New York: Colonial Press, 1951), pp. 103–122.

14. Excerpt from Simón Bolívar's Speech before the Congress of Angostura, February 15, 1819

General Simón Bolívar advocated a centralized Spanish American government that would evolve into a democracy. At the Congress of Angostura, Bolívar laid out his vision for the foundation for the formation of the Republic of Colombia (1819–1830). It included what are now the separate countries of Colombia, Panama, Venezuela, and Ecuador. As with Mexico and Central America, divisions within the region thwarted Bolívar's plan to unite the former Spanish colonies as a new nation or confederation. The following excerpt reviews the history of the Americas and discusses the similarities with the fallout of the decline of the Spanish Empire, with the dismemberment of the Roman Empire.

We are not Europeans; we are not Indians; we are but a mixed species of aborigines and Spaniards. Americans by birth and Europeans by law, we find ourselves engaged in a dual conflict: we are disputing with the natives for titles of ownership, and at the same time we are struggling to maintain ourselves in the country that gave us birth against the opposition of the invaders. Thus our position is most extraordinary and complicated. But there is more. As our role has always been strictly passive and political existence nil, we find that our quest for liberty is now even more difficult of accomplishment; for we, having been placed in a state lower than slavery, had been robbed not only of our freedom but also of the right to exercise an active domestic tyranny.... We have been ruled more by deceit than by force, and we have been degraded more by vice than by superstition. Slavery is the daughter of darkness: an ignorant people is a blind instrument of its own destruction. Ambition and intrigue abuses the credulity and experience of men lacking all political, economic, and civic knowledge; they adopt pure illusion as reality; they take license for liberty, treachery for patriotism, and vengeance for justice. If a people, perverted by their training, succeed in achieving their liberty, they will soon lose it, for it would be of no avail to endeavor to explain to them that happiness consists in the practice of virtue; that the rule of law is more powerful than the rule of tyrants, because, as the laws are more inflexible, every one should submit to their beneficent austerity; that proper morals, and not force, are the bases of law; and that to practice justice is to practice liberty.

Although those people [North Americans], so lacking in many respects, are unique in the history of mankind, it is a marvel, I repeat, that so weak and complicated a government as the federal system has managed to govern them in the difficult and trying circumstances of their past. But, regardless of the effectiveness of this form of government with respect to North America, I must say that it has never for a moment entered my mind to compare the position and character of two states as dissimilar as the English-American and the Spanish-American. Would it not be most difficult to apply to Spain the English system of political, civil, and religious liberty: Hence, it would be even more difficult to adapt to Venezuela the laws of North America.

Nothing in our fundamental laws would have to be altered were we to adopt a legislative power similar to that held by the British Parliament. Like the North Americans, we have divided national representation into two chambers: that of Representatives and the Senate. The first is very wisely constituted. It enjoys all its proper functions, and it requires no essential revision, because the Constitution, in creating it, gave it the form and powers which the people deemed necessary in order that they might be legally and properly represented. If the Senate were hereditary rather than elective, it would, in my opinion, be the basis, the tie, the very soul of our republic. In political storms this body would arrest the thunderbolts of the government and would repel any violent popular reaction. Devoted to the government because of a natural interest in its own preservation, a hereditary senate would always oppose any attempt on the part of the people to infringe upon the jurisdiction and authority of their magistrates … The creation of a hereditary senate would in no way be a violation of political equality. I do not solicit the establishment of a nobility, for as a celebrated republican has said, that would simultaneously destroy equality and liberty. What I propose is an office for which the candidates must prepare themselves, an office that demands great knowledge and the ability to acquire such knowledge. All should not be left to chance and the outcome of elections. The people are more easily deceived than is Nature perfected by art; and although these senators, it is true, would not be bred in an environment that is all virtue, it is equally true that they would be raised in an atmosphere of enlightened education. The hereditary senate will also serve as a counterweight to both government and people; and as a neutral power it will weaken the mutual attacks of these two eternally rival powers.

The British executive power possesses all the authority properly appertaining to a sovereign, but he is surrounded by a triple line of dams, barriers, and stockades. He is the head of government, but his ministers and subordinates rely more upon law than upon his authority, as they are personally responsible; and not even decrees of royal authority can exempt them from this responsibility. The executive is commander in chief of the army and navy; he makes peace and declares war; but Parliament annually determines what sums are to be paid to these military forces. While the courts and judges are dependent on the executive power, the laws originate in and are made by Parliament. Give Venezuela such an executive power in the person of a president chosen by the people or their representatives, and you will have taken a great step toward national happiness. No matter what citizen occupies this office, he will be aided by the Constitution, and therein being authorized to do good, he can do no harm, because his ministers will cooperate with him only insofar as he abides by the law. If he attempts to infringe upon the law, his own ministers will desert him, thereby isolating him from the Republic, and they will even bring charges against him in the Senate. The ministers, being responsible for any transgressions committed, will actually govern, since they must account for their actions.

A republican magistrate is an individual set apart from society, charged with checking the impulse of the people toward license and the propensity of judges and administrators toward abuse of the laws. He is directly subject to the legislative body, the senate, and the people: he is the one man who resists the combined pressure of the opinions, interests, and passions of the social state and who, as Carnot states, does little more than struggle constantly with the urge to dominate and the desire to escape domination. This weakness can only be corrected by a strongly rooted force. It should be strongly proportioned to meet the resistance which the executive must expect from the legislature, from the judiciary, and from the people of a republic. Unless the executive has easy access to all the administrative resources, fixed by a just distribution of powers, he inevitably becomes a nonentity or abuses his authority. By this I mean that the result will be the death of the government, whose heirs are anarchy, usurpation, and tyranny…. Therefore, let the entire system of government be strengthened, and let the balance of power be drawn up in such a manner that it will be permanent and incapable of decay because of its own tenuity. Precisely because no form of government is so weak as the democratic, its framework must be firmer, and its institutions must be studied to determine their degree of stability ... unless this is done, we will have to reckon with an ungovernable, tumultuous, and anarchic society, not with a social order where happiness, peace, and justice prevail.

Source: Simón Bolívar, *An Address of Bolívar at the Congress of Angostura (February 15, 1819),* reprint ed. (Washington, D.C.: Press of B. S. Adams, 1919), *passim.* Scanned by: J. S. Arkenberg, Dept. of History, Cal. State Fullerton. Prof. Arkenberg has modernized the text. Courtesy of Paul Halsall, ed., Internet History Sourcebooks Project, Fordham University, http://www.fordham.edu/halsall/mod/1819bolivar.html.

PART II
Going West, 1820–1840s

During the first two decades of the nineteenth century, the United States through a series of purchases and aggressions expanded dramatically. The Louisiana territory in 1803, which encompassed today's Arkansas, Missouri, Iowa, Oklahoma, Kansas, Nebraska, parts of Missouri, much of North Dakota, and almost all of South Dakota, as well as portions of other states, added 820,000 square miles to the new nation. In 1819, U.S. aggressions in Florida added another 58, 664 square miles. This crossing of borders took a dramatic turn in 1821 as Mexico gained its independence from Spain. And the new nation was bordered by the United States in Texas, New Mexico, among other northern Mexican lands. The rapid expansion of the Euro-Americans had acquired a sense of uniqueness and entitlement, believing that Texas once belonged to them and that moving the U.S. Border south was not aggression but reannexing of what was already theirs. The first wave of permanent Euro-American settlers was cotton growers who wanted land and the right to own other human beings. They were followed by speculators, filibusterers, and merchants. Soon Mexican officials reacted to the belligerency of newcomers who wanted to do it their own way. Not all Mexicans resisted the encroachments—it was a class thing with many of the landed gentry profiting greatly from a change of flags. Some Mexicans admired Euro-American Republican ideas and modernizing society. In the end the border moved further south and the stage was set for the United States to "reannex" another 261,797 square miles as the borders crossed river valleys.

15. Excerpts from the Letter from Stephen Austin to Edward Lovelace or Josiah Bell, November 22, 1822

The Euro-American aggression into Texas in the 1820s was about slavery, not the desire for freedom or democracy. It was about more land and more slaves. In 1819, Moses Austin (1761–1821)—the father of Stephen Austin—received permission from the Spanish Crown to settle in Texas and bring other colonists. The settlers received vast land tracts that they did not, in most cases, have to pay for. In return for free and low-cost land, they promised to obey the laws, become Spanish subjects, and become Catholics. However, before Moses could comply with the terms of the contract, he died, and New Spain became Mexico. His son Stephen met with Mexican officials and made much the same agreement. From the beginning, the younger Austin considered slavery critical to the prosperity of the Euro-American colonists. Texas after 1821 was part of the Mexican Republic that had won its freedom in that year. Although slavery had been legal under Spain, Mexican revolutionary leaders promised to abolish slavery. Thus, Austin went to Mexico City to protect the interests of slaveholders who were part of his colony.

It is believed that this letter, which discusses political affairs in Mexico City, was written to Edward Lovelace, a planter from Louisiana who had accompanied Stephen Austin to Texas. There is some question that the letter may have been written to Josiah Bell (1791–1839) because it was found in the possession of Bell's wife. Bell was one of Austin's original 300 planters, so it is probable that the letter was to him. Regardless of the recipient, the letter makes clear that Austin was of the opinion that the only thing that could save Mexico was a monarchy.

Dear Sir:

When I arrived here Congress were sitting but progressing very slowly, the discord and jealousy manifested from the first day of the session of Congress against the Generalissimo Iturbide (now Emperor) was increasing daily and everything was at a stand[still]. There were three distinct parties in Congress, one for a Bourbon King, one for an Emperor from this country, and the other for a Republic, in this state of things the government was approximating towards Anarchy, when on the night of the 18 of May the army stationed in this city proclaimed Iturbide Emperor, the next day Congress elected him in due form and on the 21 he took the oath, these things put a stop to all business for some time—Agreeably to the Emperors Oath he could do nothing without the consent of Congress and this body moved most astonishingly slow and were more occupied in watching the Emperor than in attending to the interest of the country—On the 21 July the Emperor was crowned, and very soon after serious collisions began to arise between him and Congress, the latter wished to keep all power in their hands and things were getting worse every day all was at a dead stand, for Congress would do nothing for fear of granting a little power to the executive, and the Emperor could do nothing so long as Congress existed without its sanction—In this state of things it was in vain for an individual to urge his business ... Matters progressed in this manner from bad to worse and were again verging towards Anarchy; one dangerous conspiracy was discovered and quelled by the imprisonment of about 70, amongst whom were 20 members of Congress and at length finding that nothing but an extraordinary and desicive [sic] step could save the nation from the confusion and the established government from ruin, the Emperor desolved [sic] congress by a decree of his own on the 31 of October last and created a national Junta of his own choosing from amongst the members of Congress—since then things have gone on better and with more harmony. My business relative to the settlement is now, acting on and in less than 10 days I shall be dispatched with everything freely arranged. The principal difficulty is slavery, this they will not admit—as the law is all slaves are to be free in ten years, but I am trying to have it amended so as to make them slaves for life and their children free at 21 years—but do not think I shall succeed in this point, and that the law will pass as it now is, that is, that the slaves introduced by the settlers shall be free after 10 years—As regards all other matters there will be no difficulty, I will write you again from here after I get through and let you know the particulars. I am doubtful nothing can be done about getting land at or near Galveston, the government seems opposed to any settlement being formed so near the borders of the United States, when I return to Texas I will write you very fully—you must not be frightened at the name of an Imperial government, you like myself have lived under a Monarchy, when Louisiana belonged to Spain and I think we lived as happy then as under the government of the United States—The Emperor has his enemies and in the United States the Democrats will abuse him no doubt, but he is doing the best for his country. These people will not do for a Republic nothing but a Monarchy can save them from Anarchy.

Stephen F. Austin This is a true copy of the letter, recd from S. F. Austin. Received from Mrs. Bell and I presume was addressed to her husband Josiah H Bell.

Guy M. Bryan

Source: Courtesy of Sons of DeWitt Colony Texas, http://www.tamu.edu/ccbn/dewitt/slavery letters.htm.

16. The Monroe Doctrine, December 2, 1823

U.S. President James Monroe (1758–1831) delivered this speech to a joint session of Congress on December 2, 1823. In it, Monroe outlined the foreign policy objectives of the United States, and proclaimed that European powers should no longer colonize or interfere with the affairs of the nations of the "Americas." The United States planned to stay neutral in wars between European powers and those between Spain and its colonies. But if the latter's wars spilled over to the Americas, the United States would not permit it. America was for Americans and no longer open to European colonization. Generally, Latin Americans have interpreted the Monroe Doctrine as an expression of the United States' imperial designs toward Latin America. In contrast, the United States saw the doctrine as anti-colonialism and, in the following document, President Monroe sets out his reasons for the proclamation.

Fellow-Citizens of the Senate and House of Representatives:

At the proposal of the Russian Imperial Government, made through the minister of the Emperor residing here, a full power and instructions have been transmitted to the Minister of the United States at St. Petersburgh [*sic*] to arrange, by amicable negotiation, the respective rights and interests of the two nations on the northwest coast of this continent. A similar proposal has been made by His Imperial Majesty to the Government of Great Britain, which has likewise been acceded to. The Government of the United States has been desirous, by this friendly proceeding, of manifesting the great value which they have invariably attached to the friendship of the Emperor, and their solicitude to cultivate the best understanding with his Government. In the discussions to which this interest has given rise, and in the arrangements by which they may terminate the occasion has been judged proper for asserting, as a principle in which the rights and interests of the United States are involved, that the American continents, by the free and independent condition which they have assumed and maintain, are henceforth not to be considered as subjects for future colonization by any European powers....

It was stated at the commencement of the last session that a great effort was then making in Spain and Portugal, to improve the condition of the people of those countries, and that it appeared to be conducted with extraordinary moderation. It need scarcely be remarked, that the result has been, so far, very different from what was then anticipated. Of events in that quarter of the globe, with which we have so much intercourse, and from which we derive our origin, we have always been anxious and interested spectators. The citizens of the United States cherish sentiments the most friendly, in favor of the liberty and happiness of their fellow men on that side of the Atlantic. In the wars of the European powers, in matters relating to themselves, we have never taken any part, nor does it comport with our policy to do so. It is only when our rights are invaded, or seriously menaced, that we resent injuries, or make preparation for our defence. With the movements in this hemisphere, we are, of necessity, more immediately connected, and by causes which must be obvious to all enlightened and impartial observers. The political system of the allied powers is essentially different, in this respect, from that of America. This difference proceeds from that which exists in their respective governments. And to the defence of our own, which has been achieved by the loss of so much blood and treasure, and matured by the wisdom of their most enlightened citizens, and under which we have enjoyed unexampled felicity, this whole nation is devoted. We owe it, therefore, to candor, and to the amicable relations existing between the United States and those powers, to declare, that we should consider any attempt on their part to extend their system to any portion of this hemisphere, as dangerous to our peace and safety. With the existing colonies or dependencies of any European power we have not interfered, and shall not interfere. But with the governments who have declared their independence, and maintained it, and whose independence we have, on great consideration, and on just principles, acknowledged, we could not view any interposition for the purpose of oppressing them, or controlling, in any other manner, their destiny, by any European power in any other light than as the manifestation of an unfriendly disposition towards the United States. In the war between those new governments and Spain we declared our neutrality at the time of their recognition, and to this we have adhered, and shall continue to adhere, provided no change shall occur, which, in the judgement [*sic*] of the competent authorities of this government, shall make a corresponding change, on the part of the United States, indispensable to their security.

The late events in Spain and Portugal, show that Europe is still unsettled. Of this important fact, no stronger proof can be adduced than that the allied powers should have thought it proper, on any principle satisfactory to themselves, to have interposed, by force, in the internal concerns of Spain. To what extent such interposition may be carried, on the same principle, is a question, to which all independent powers, whose governments differ from theirs, are interested; even those most remote, and surely none more so than the United States. Our policy, in regard to Europe, which was adopted at an early stage of the wars which have so long agitated that quarter of the globe, nevertheless remains the same, which is, not to interfere in the internal concerns of any of its powers; to consider the government de facto as the legitimate government for us; to cultivate friendly relations with it, and to preserve those relations by a frank, firm, and manly policy; meeting, in all instances, the just claims of every power; submitting to injuries from none. But, in regard to these continents, circumstances are eminently and conspicuously different. It is impossible that the allied powers should extend their political system to any portion of either continent, without endangering our peace and happiness: nor can any one believe that our Southern Brethren, if left to themselves, would adopt it of their own accord. It is equally impossible, therefore, that we should behold such interposition, in any form, with indifference. If we look to the comparative strength and resources of Spain and those new governments, and their distance from each other, it must be obvious that she can never subdue them. It is still the true policy of the United States to leave the parties to themselves, in the hope that other powers will pursue the same course.

James Monroe
Washington, December 2, 1823
Source: Basic Readings in U.S. Democracy, http://usinfo.state.gov/usa/infousa/facts/democrac/50.htm.

17. Petition Concerning Slavery, June 10, 1824

An 1824 petition from the colonists at the Austin (Texas) Colony called upon the Mexican Congress to allow emigrants to bring slaves into Texas. According to the petitioners, the slaves were not for the purpose of trade or speculation. They were family servants who had been raised by them since infancy. These slaves, according to American leader Stephen Austin (1793–1836) and other Americans in Texas, were essential to make the colony prosperous since it was they who would clear the land and develop the farms.

These inhabitants respectfully represent to your sovereignty that the Slaves introduced into this establishment by the emigrants were not brought here for the purpose of Trade or speculation neither are they Africans but are the family servants of the emigrants and raised by them as such from their infancy and were intended to aid in clearing the Land and establishing their farms which these Colonists could not have effected without them for this Province is entirely uninhabited and great Labor required in Opening farms and as the Law sanctioned the introduction of slaves into the Country the emigrants felt entirely safe in bringing them. These Inhabitants therefore respectfully solicit that your sovereignty will take into Consideration the right of property they have to their slaves that they brought them here As a necessary part of the Capital required by the desert State of the Country to establish their farms and Ranches and if freed the loss of their value added to the very heavy expences [sic] of removing such a distance and settling in an entire wilderness and suffering all the miseries of Hunger, exposed to the attack of Hostile Indians will complete their total ruin—Also these Inhabitants respectfully represent that some of their friends and Relations visited this Country last spring and winter and selected their Lands as a part of the Above named 300 families After building Cabins they returned to move out their families this summer and fall and are now on the Road bringing their Slaves with them relying on the faith of the Colonization Law under which Austin's establishment is formed—Article [30] of which Law Authorises [sic] the introduction of Slaves by the Colonists those emigrants therefore who are on the Road and are detained by the excessive heat and destructive drought that now pervades this whole Country will be totally and forever ruined if on their arrival here after so much fatigue labor and expense in removing they are to loose their Slaves and besides that be liable to heavy punishment for bringing them. These Inhabitants therefore respectfully pray that your sovereignty may take their Case into Consideration and declare that the slaves and their descendents of the 300 families who emigrate to the Establishment formed by the Emprasario Stephen F. Austin in this province shall be slaves for Life … San Felipe do Austin June 10, 1824.

Signed Estevan F. Austin, Jared E. Groce, Santiago Cummins, Juan P. Coles [To Federal Congress or Executive.]

Source: Courtesy of Sons of DeWitt Colony Texas, http://www.tamu.edu/ccbn/dewitt/slaveryletters. htm#petitioncongress.

18. Decree Abolishing the Slave Trade in Mexico, July 13, 1824

Indian and African slavery existed in Mexico during the era of Spanish colonialism. Forms of de facto slavery persisted even after Mexican independence in 1821. But the nation's leaders were committed to ending this institution. On December 6, 1810, Fr. Miguel Hidalgo, a parish priest in Guanajuato, declared that slavery was abolished in Mexico. Hidalgo was executed in 1811, and Fr. José María Morelos, a priest and insurgent, reiterated the pronouncement against slavery. Once Mexico achieved independence from Spain in 1821, the question of slavery emerged again as proslavery groups attempted to exploit the fact that there were no constitutional guarantees. The Decree of July 13, 1824, prohibited slave trade, but it was not fully enforced because of the instability of the new Mexican government.

PROHIBITION OF THE COMMERCE AND TRAFFIC IN SLAVES

The Sovereign General Constituent Congress of the United Mexican States has held it right to decree the following:

1. The Commerce and Traffic in Slaves, proceeding from whatever power, and under whatever flag, is for ever prohibited, within the territories of the United Mexican States.

2. The Slaves, who may be introduced contrary to the tenor of the preceding article, shall remain free in consequence of treading the Mexican soil.

3. Every vessel, whether National or Foreign, in which Slaves may be transported and introduced into the Mexican territories, shall be confiscated with the rest of its cargo and the Owner, Purchaser, Captain, Master, and Pilot, shall suffer the punishment of ten years confinement.

4. This law will take effect from the date of its publication; however, as to the punishments prescribed in the preceding article, they shall not take effect till [*sic*] six months after, towards the Planters who, in virtue of the law of the 14th October last, relating to the Colonization of the Isthmus of Guazacoulco, and may disembark Slaves for the purpose of introducing them into the Mexican territory. (See the 21st Article of the Decree of October 11, 1823.)

Source: "Abolition of the Slave Trade: Decree of July 13, 1824." Courtesy of Sons of DeWitt Colony Texas, http://www.tamu.edu/ccbn/dewitt/slaverybugbee.htm#slavedecree1824.

19. Decree No. 16: The Colonization of the State of Coahuila and Texas, 1825

In 1825, Texas was not an independent entity—it was part of the Mexican state of Coahuila and, as such, was governed by the laws of Mexico and the state of Coahuila. The following are the laws of colonization, which Euro-Americans and other colonists had agreed to uphold. However, almost immediately upon arrival after 1822, Euro-American colonists pressured the Mexican government to change these laws and grant them more autonomy. The Mexican state, on the other hand, sought to make the new settlers comply and obey the laws.

The Governor provisionally appointed by the Sovereign Congress of this State. To all who shall see these presents; Know that the said Congress have decreed as follows.

Decree No. 16. The Constituent Congress of the Free, Independent and Sovereign State of Coahuila and Texas, desiring by every possible means, to augment the population of its territory; promote the cultivation of its fertile lands; the raising and multiplication of stock; and the progress of the arts and commerce; and being governed by the Constitutional act, the Federal Constitution, and the basis established by the National Decree of the General Congress, No. 72, have thought proper to decree the following LAW OF COLONIZATION:

Art. 1. All Foreigners, who in virtue of the general law, of the 18th August, 1824, which guarantees the security of their persons and property, in the territory of the Mexican Nation, wish to remove to any of the settlements of the state of Coahuila and Texas, are at liberty to do so; and the said State invites and calls them.

Art. 2. Those who do so, instead of being incommoded, shall be admitted by the local authorities of said settlements, who shall freely permit them to pursue any branch, of industry that they may think proper, provided they respect the general laws of the nation, and those of the state.

Art. 3. Any foreigner, already in the limits of the state of Coahuila and Texas who wishes to settle himself in it, shall make a declaration to that effect, before the Ayuntamiento [town council] of the place, which he selects as his residence; the Ayuntamiento in such case, shall administer to him the oath which he must take to obey the federal and state constitutions, and to observe the religion which the former prescribes; the name of the person, and his family if he has any, shall then be registered in a book kept for that purpose, with a statement of where he was born, and whence from, his age, whether married, occupation, and that he has taken the oath prescribed, and considering him from that time and not before, as domiciled.

Art. 4. From the day in which any foreigner has been enrolled, as an inhabitant, in conformity with the foregoing article, he is at liberty to designate any vacant land, and the respective political authority will grant it to him in the same manner, as to a native of the country, in conformity with the existing laws of the nation, under the condition that the proceedings, shall be passed to the government for its approbation.

Art. 5. Foreigners of any nation, or a native of any of the Mexican states, can project the formation of any towns on any lands entirely vacant, or even on those of an individual, in the case mentioned in 35th article; but the now settlers who present themselves for admission, must prove their Christianity, morality and good habits, by a certificate from the authorities where they formerly resided.

Art. 6. Foreigners who emigrate at the time in which the general sovereign congress may have prohibited their entrance, for the purpose of colonizing, as they have the power to do, after the year 1840, or previous to that time, as respects those of any particular nation, shall not then be admitted; and those who apply in proper time, shall always subject themselves to such precautionary measures (if national security, which the supreme government, without prejudicing the object of this law, may think proper to adopt relative to them).

Art. 7. The government shall take care, that within the twenty leagues bordering on the limits of the United States of the North, and ten leagues in a straight line from the coast of the Gulf of Mexico, within the limits of this state, there shall be no other settlements, except such as merit the approbation of the supreme government of the Union, for which object, all petitions on the subject, whether made by Mexicans or foreigners, shall be passed to the superior government, accompanied by a corresponding responding report.

Art. 8. The projects for new settlements in which one or more persons offer to bring at their expertise, one hundred or more families, shall be presented to the government, and if found conformable with this law, they will be admitted; and the government will immediately designate to the contractors, the land where they are to establish themselves, and the term of six years, within which, they must present the number of families they contracted for, under the penalty of losing the rights and privileges offered in their favor, in proportion to the number of families which they fail to introduce, and the contract totally annulled if they do not bring at least one hundred families.

Art. 9. Contracts made by the contractors or undertakers, *Empresarios* [land contractors], with the families brought at their expense, are guaranteed by this law, so far as they are conformable with its provisions.

Art. 10. In the distribution of lands, a preference shall be given to the Military entitled to them, by the diplomas issued by the supreme executive power, and to Mexican citizens who are not Military, among whom there shall be no other distinction, than that founded on their individual merit, or services performed for the country, or in equal circumstances, a residence in the place where the land may be situated; the quantity of land which may be granted, is designated in the following articles.

Art. 11. A square of land, which on each side has one league or five thousand *varas*, or what is the same thing, a superficies of twenty-five million varas, shall be called a *sitio*, and this shall be the unity for counting one, two, or more sitios; and also the unity for counting one, two or more labors, shall be one million square varas, or one thousand varas on each side, which shall compose a labor. The vara for this measurement shall be three geometrical feet.

Art. 12. Taking the above unity as a basis, and observing the distinction which must be made, between grazing land, or that which is proper for raising of stock, and farming land, with or without the facility of irrigation, this law grants to the contractor or contractors, for the establishment or a new settlement, for each hundred families which he may introduce and establish in the state, five sitios of grazing land and five labors, at least the one half of which, shall be without the facility of irrigation; but they can only receive this premium for eight hundred families, although a greater number should be introduced, and no fraction whatever, less than one hundred shall entitle them to any premium, not even proportionally.

Art. 13. Should any contractor or contractors in virtue of the number of families which he may have introduced, acquire in conformity with the last article, more than eleven square leagues of land, it shall nevertheless be granted, but subject to the condition of alienating the excess, within twelve years, and if it is not done, the respective political authority shall do it by selling it at public sale, delivering the proceeds to the owners, after deducting the costs of sale.

Art. 14. To each family comprehended in a contract, whose sole occupation is cultivation of land, one labor shall be given; should he also be a stock raiser, grazing land shall be added to complete a sitio, and should his only occupation be raising of stock, he shall only receive a superficies of grazing land, equal to twenty-four million square bars.

Art. 15. Unmarried men shall receive the same quantity when they enter the matrimonial state, and for foreigners who marry native Mexicans, shall receive one fourth more; those that are entirely single, or who do not form a part of some family whether foreigners or natives, shall content themselves with the fourth part of the above mentioned quantity, which is all that can be given them until they marry.

Art. 16. Families or unmarried men who, entirely of their own accord, have emigrated and may wish to unite themselves to any new towns, can at all times do so, and the same quantity of land shall be assigned them, which is mentioned in the two last articles; but if they do so within the first six years from the establishment of the settlement, one labor more shall be given to families, and single men in place of the quarter designated in the 15th article shall have the third part.

Art. 17. It appertains to the government to augment the quantity indicated in the 14, 15, and 16th Articles, in proportion to the family industry, and activity of the colonists, agreeably to the information given on these subjects by the Ayuntamientos [town councils] and Commissioners; the said government always observing the provisions of the 12th article, of the decree of the general congress on the subject.

Art. 18. The families who emigrate in conformity with the 16th article shall immediately present themselves to the political authority of the place which they may have chosen for their residence, who, finding in them the requisites, prescribed by this law for new settlers, shall admit them, and put them in possession of the corresponding lands, and shall immediately give an account thereof to the government; who of themselves, or by means of a person commissioned to that effect, will issue them a title.

Art. 19. The Indians of all nations, bordering on the state, as well as wandering tribes that may be within its limits, shall be received in the markets, without paying any duties whatever for commerce, in the products of the country; and if attracted by the moderation and confidence, with which they shall be treated, any of them, after having first declared themselves in favor of our Religion and Institutions, wish to establish themselves in any settlements that are forming, they shall be admitted, and the same quantity of land given them, as to the settlers spoken of in the 14th and 15th articles, always preferring native Indians to strangers.

Art. 20. In order that there may be no vacancies between tracts, of which, great care shall be taken in the distribution of lands, it shall be laid off in squares, or other forms although irregular, if the local situation requires it; and in said distribution, as well as the assignation of lands for new towns, previous notice shall be given to the adjoining proprietors, if any, in order to prevent dissentions and law suits.

Art. 21. If by error in the concession, any land shall be granted, belonging to another, on proof being made of that fact, an equal quantity shall be granted elsewhere, to the person who may have thus obtained it through error, and he shall be indemnified by the owner of such land, for any improvements he may have made; the just value of which improvements, shall be ascertained by appraisers.

Art. 22. The new settlers as an acknowledgment, shall pay to the state, for each sitio of pasture land, thirty dollars; two dollars and a half for each labor without the facility of irrigation, and three dollars and a half, for each one that can be irrigated, and so on proportionally according to the quantity and quality of the land distributed; but the said payments need not be made, until six years after the settlement and by thirds; the first within four years, the second within five years, and the last within six years, under the penalty of losing the land for a failure, in any of said payments; there are excepted from this payment, the contractors, and Military, spoken of in the 10th article; the former with respect to lands given them, as a premium, and the latter, for those which they obtained, in conformity with their diplomas.

Art. 23. The Ayuntamiento of each municipality (*Comarca*) shall collect the above mentioned funds, gratis, by means of a committee appointed either within or without their body; and shall remit them as they are collected, to the treasurer of their Funds, who will give the corresponding receipt, and without any other compensation than two and a half per cent, all that shall be allowed him; he shall hold them at the disposition of the government, rendering an account every month of the ingress and egress, and of any remissness or fraud, which he may observe in their collection of all which, the person employed, and the committee, and the individuals of the Ayuntamientos who appoint them, shall be individually responsible and that this responsibility may be at all effectual, the said appointments shall he made viva voce, and information shall be given thereof immediately to the government.

Art. 24. The government shall sell to Mexicans and to them only, such lands as they may wish to purchase, taking care that there shall not be accumulated in the same hands, more than eleven sitios, and under the condition, that the purchaser must cultivate what he acquires by this title within six years, from its acquisition, under the penalty of losing them; the price of each sitio, subject to the foregoing condition, shall be one hundred dollars, if it be pasture land; one hundred and fifty dollars, if it be farming land without the facility of irrigation; and two hundred and fifty dollars if it can be irrigated.

Art. 25. Until six years after the publication of this law, the legislature of this state, cannot alter it as regards the acknowledgement, and price to be paid or land, or as regards the quantity and quality, to be distributed to the new settlers, or sold to Mexicans.

Art. 26. The new settlers, who within six years from the date of the possession, have not cultivated or occupied the lands granted them, according to its quality, shall be considered to have renounced them, and the respective political authority, shall immediately proceed to take possession of them, and recall the titles.

Art. 27. The contractors and Military, heretofore spoken of, and those who by purchase have acquired lands, can alienate them at any time, but the successor is obliged to cultivate them in the same time, that the original proprietor was bound to do; the other settlers can alienate theirs when they have totally cultivated them, and not before.

Art. 28. By testamentary will, made in conformity with the existing laws, or those which may govern in future, any new colonist, from the day of his settlement, may dispose of his land, although he may not have cultivated it, and if he dies intestate, his property shall be inherited by the person or persons entitled by the laws to it; the heirs being subject to the same obligation and condition imposed on the original grantee.

Art. 29. Lands acquired by virtue of this law, shall not by any title whatever, pass into mortmain.

Art. 30. The new settler, who wishing to establish himself in a foreign country, resolves to leave the territory of the state, can do so freely, with all his property; but after leaving the state, he shall not any longer hold his land, and if he had not previously sold it, or the sale should not be in conformity with the 27th article, it shall become entirely vacant.

Art. 31. Foreigners who in conformity with this law, have obtained lands, and established themselves in any new settlement, shall be considered from that moment, naturalized in the country; and by marrying a Mexican, they acquire a particular merit to obtain letters of citizenship of the state, subject however to the provisions which may be made relative to both particulars, in the constitution of the state.

Art. 32. During the first ten years, counting from the day on which the new settlements may have been established, they shall be free from all contributions, of whatever denomination, with the exception of those which, in case of invasion by an enemy, or to prevent it, are generally imposed, and the produce of agriculture or industry of the new settlers, shall be free from excise duty, Alcabala, or other duties, throughout every part of the state, with the exception of the duties referred to in the next article; after the termination of that time, the new settlements shall be on the same footing as to taxes with the old ones, and the colonists shall also in this particular, be on the same footing with the other inhabitants of the state.

Art. 33. From the day of their settlement, the new colonists shall be at liberty to follow any branch of industry, and can also work mines of every description, communicating with the supreme government of the confederation, relative to the general revenue appertaining to it, and subjecting themselves in all other particulars, to the ordinances or taxes, established or which may be established on this branch.

Art. 34. Towns shall be founded on the sites deemed most suitable by the government, or the person commissioned for this effect, and for each one, there shall be designated four square leagues, whose area may be in a regular or irregular form, agreeably to the situation.

Art. 35. If any of the said sites should be the property of an individual, and the establishment of new towns on them, should notoriously be of general utility, they can, notwithstanding, be appropriated to this object, previously indemnifying the owner for its just value, to be determined by appraisers.

Art. 36. Building lots in the new towns shall be given gratis, to the contractors of them and also to artists of every class, as many as are for the establishment of their trade; and to the other settlers they shall be sold at public auction, after having been previously valued, under the obligation to pay the purchase money by installments of one third each, the first in six months, the second in twelve months and the third in eighteen months; but all owners or lots, including contractors and artists, shall annually pay one dollar for each lot, which, together with the produce of the sales, shall be collected by the Ayuntamientos, and applied to the building of churches in said towns.

Art. 37. So far as is practicable, the towns shall be composed of natives and foreigners, and in their delineation, great care shall be taken to lay off the streets straight, giving them a direction from north to south, and from east to west, when the site will permit it.

Art. 38. For the better location of the said new town, their regular formation and exact partition of their land and lots, the government on account of having admitted any project, and agreed with the contractor or contractors, who may have presented it, shall commission a person of intelligence and confidence, giving him such particular instructions as may be deemed necessary and expedient and authorizing him under his own responsibility, to appoint one or more surveyors, to lay off the town scientifically, and do whatever else that be required.

Art. 39. The Governor in conformity with the last fee bill, *Arancel*, of notary public's of the ancient audience of Mexico, shall designate the fees of the commissioner, who in conjunction with the colonists shall fix the surveyor's fees; but both shall be paid by the colonists and in the manner which all parties among themselves may agree upon.

Art. 40. As soon as at least forty families are united in one place, they shall proceed to the formal establishment of the new towns, and all of them shall take an oath, to support the general and state constitutions; which oath will be administered by the commissioner; they shall then, in his presence, proceed for the first time, to the election of their municipal authority.

Art. 41. A new town, whose inhabitants shall not be less than two hundred, shall elect an Ayuntamiento, provided there is not another one established within eight leagues, in which case, it shall be added to it. The number of individuals which are to compose the Ayuntamiento, shall be regulated by the existing laws.

Art. 42. Foreigners are eligible, subject to the provisions which the constitution of the state may prescribe, to elect the members of their municipal authorities, and to be elected to the same.

Art. 43. The municipal expenses, and all others which may be considered necessary, or of common utility to the new towns, shall be proposed to the Governor, by the Ayuntamientos through the political chief, accompanied with a plan of the taxes, *arbitrios*, which in their opinion may be just and best calculated to raise them, and should the proposed plan, be approved of by the Governor, he shall order it to be executed, subject however to the resolutions of the legislature, to whom it shall be immediately passed with his report and that of the political chief, who will say whatever occurs to him on the subject.

Art. 44. For the opening and improving of roads, and other public works in Texas, the government will transmit to the chief of that department, the individuals, who in other parts of the state, may have been sentenced to public works as vagrants, or for other crimes; these same persons may be employed by individuals for competent wages, and as soon as the time of their condemnation is expired, they can unite themselves as colonists, to any new settlement, and obtain the corresponding lands, if their reformation shall have made them worthy of such favor in the opinion of the chief of the department, without whose certificate, they shall not be admitted.

Art. 45. The government in accord with the respective ordinary ecclesiastics, will take care to provide the new settlements with the competent number of pastors, and in accord with the same authority, shall propose to the legislature for its approbation, the salary which the said pastors are to receive, which shall be paid by the new settlers.

Art. 46. The new settlers as regards the introduction of slaves shall subject themselves to the existing laws, and those which may hereafter be established on the subject.

Art. 47. The petitions now pending relative to the subject of the law, shall be dispatched in conformity with it, and for this purpose they shall be passed to the Governor, and the families who may be established within the limits of the state, without having any land assigned them, shall submit themselves to this law, and to the orders of the supreme government of the Union, with respect to those who are within twenty leagues of the limits of the United States of America, and in a straight line of the coast of the Gulf of Mexico.

Art. 48. This law shall be published in all the villages of the state; and that it arrives at the notice of all others, throughout the Mexican confederation, it shall be communicated to their respective legislatures, by the secretary of this state; and the Governor will take particular care, to send a certified copy of it, in compliance with the 16th article of the federal constitution, to the two houses of Congress, and the supreme executive power of the nation, with a request to the latter, to give it general circulation through foreign states, by means of our ambassadors. The Governor pro tem of the state will cause it to be published and circulated.

Saltillo, 24 March, 1825

Signed, RAFAEL RAMOS Y VÁLDEZ, President

JUAN VICENTE CAMOS, Member & Secretary

JOSÉ JOAQUÍN ROSALES, Member & Secretary

Therefore I command all Authorities, as well Civil as Military and Ecclesiastical, to obey and cause to be obeyed, the present decree in all its parts.

Rafael Gonzales, Governor

Source: Courtesy of Sons of DeWitt Colony Texas, http://www.tamu.edu/ccbn/dewitt/ cololaws.htm.

20. Decree of Mexican President Vicente Guerrero Abolishing Slavery, September 15, 1829

Between 1821 and 1829, the Mexican government attempted to regulate slave traffic in Texas and also make Euro-American colonists comply with Mexican laws. By 1829, Texas had a population of about 20,000, not counting slaves who numbered just over a thousand. By this time, many Mexicans feared the steady migration of Euro-Americans into Texas was undermining its sovereignty and moved to secure its borders. One of the ways suggested to stem American migration was to emancipate the slaves; the prosperity of the white colonists depended on slave labor. The abolitionists convinced Mexican President Vicente Guerrero, who was of Indian, African, and Spanish heritage, to sign the law abolishing slavery. The law is as follows.

Abolition of Slavery. The President of the United Mexican States, to the inhabitants of the Republic. Be it known; That in the year 1829, being desirous of signalizing the anniversary of our Independence by an Act of national Justice and Beneficence, which may contribute to the strength and support of such inestimable welfare, as to secure more and more the public tranquility, and reinstate an unfortunate portion of our inhabitants in the sacred rights granted them by Nature, and may be protected by the Nation under wise and just Laws, according to the

Provision in Article 30 of the Constitutive Act; availing myself of the extraordinary faculties granted me, I have thought proper to Decree:

1. That slavery be exterminated in the Republic.

2. Consequently those are free, who, up to this day, have been looked upon as slaves.

3. Whenever the circumstances of the Public Treasury will allow it, the owners of slaves shall be indemnified, in the manner which the Laws shall provide.

Mexico 15 Sept. 1829, A. D. JOSÉ MARÍA de BOCANEGRA.

Source: Courtesy of Sons of DeWitt Colony Texas, http://www.tamu.edu/ccbn/dewitt/chieftains.htm#guerroedict.

21. Excerpts from Gen. Manuel de Mier y Terán's Diaries, 1789–1832

In his diaries, Mexican Gen. Manuel de Mier y Terán (1789–1832), head of a boundary commission in 1828–1829, reports on the seditious atmosphere in Texas eight years before the revolution. The general served in the Mexican War for Independence and was active in the political life of the new nation. His mission was primarily a scientific one, taking data and critiquing the agricultural and commercial potential of the natural resources of the land. He also evaluated the political chaos and the spirit of rebellion among the Euro-American colonists.

As one covers the distance from Béxar to this town [Nacogdoches], he will note that Mexican influence is proportionately diminished until on arriving in this place he will see that it is almost nothing. And indeed, whence could such influence come? Hardly from superior numbers in population, since the ratio of Mexicans to foreigners is one to ten; certainly not from the superior character of the Mexican population, for exactly the opposite is true, the Mexicans of this town comprising what in all countries is called the lowest class—the very poor and very ignorant. The naturalized North Americans in the town maintain an English school, and send their children north for further education; the poor Mexicans not only do not have sufficient means to establish schools, but they are not of the type that take any thought for the improvement of its public institutions or the betterment of its degraded condition. Neither are there civil authorities or magistrates; one insignificant little man—not to say more—who is called an *alcalde*, and an Ayuntamiento [town council] that does not convene once in a lifetime is the most that we have here at this important point on our frontier; yet, wherever I have looked, in the short time that I have been here, I have witnessed grave occurrences, both political and judicial. It would cause you the same chagrin that it has caused me to see the opinion that is held of our nation by these foreign colonists, since, with the exception of some few who have journeyed to our capital, they know no other Mexicans than the inhabitants about here, and excepting the authorities necessary to any form of society, the said inhabitants are the most ignorant of Negroes and Indians, among whom I pass for a man of culture. Thus, I tell myself that it could not be otherwise than that from such a state of affairs should arise an antagonism between the Mexicans and foreigners, which is not the least of the smoldering fires which I have discovered. Therefore, I am warning you to take timely measures. Texas could throw the whole nation into revolution.

The colonists murmur against the political disorganization of the frontier, and the Mexicans complain of the superiority and better education of the colonists; the colonists find it unendurable that they must go three hundred leagues to lodge a complaint against the petty pickpocketing that they suffer from a venal and igno-rant alcalde, and the Mexicans with no knowledge of the laws of their own coun-try nor those regulating colonization, set themselves against the foreigners, deliberately setting nets to deprive them of the right of franchise and to exclude them from the Ayuntamiento. Meanwhile, the incoming stream of new settlers is unceasing; the first news of these comes by discovering them on land already under cultivation, where they have been located for many months; the old inhabitants set up a claim to the property, basing their titles of doubtful priority, and for which there are no records, on a law of the Spanish government; and thus arises a lawsuit in which the alcalde has a chance to come out with some money. In this state of affairs, the town where there are no magistrates is the one in which lawsuits abound, and it is at once evident that in Nacogdoches and its vicinity, being most distant from the seat of the general government, the primitive order of things should take its course, which is to say that this section is being settled up without the consent of anybody....

In spite of the enmity that usually exists between the Mexicans and the foreign-ers, there is a most evident uniformity of opinion on one point, namely the separa-tion of Texas from Coahuila and its organization into a territory of the federal government. This idea, which was conceived by some of the colonists who are above the average, has become general among the people and does not fail to cause consid-erable discussion. In explaining the reasons assigned by them for this demand, I shall do no more than relate what I have heard with no addition of my own conclusions, and I frankly state that I have been commissioned by some of the colonists to explain to you their motives, notwithstanding the fact that I should have done so anyway in the fulfillment of my duty.

They claim that Texas in its present condition of a colony is an expense, since it is not a sufficiently prosperous section to contribute to the revenues of the state administration; and since it is such a charge it ought not to be imposed upon a state as poor as Coahuila, which has not the means of defraying the expenses of the corps of political and judicial officers necessary for the maintenance of peace and order. Furthermore, it is impracticable that recourse in all matters should be had to a state capital so distant and separated from this section by deserts infected by hostile sav-ages. Again, their interests are very different from those of the other sections, and because of this they should be governed by a separate territorial government, having learned by experience that the mixing of their affairs with those of Coahuila brings about friction. The native inhabitants of Texas add to the above other reasons which indicate an aversion for the inhabitants of Coahuila; also the authority of the comandante and the collection of taxes is disputed....

The whole population here is a mixture of strange and incoherent parts without parallel in our federation: numerous tribes of Indians, now at peace, but armed and at any moment ready for war, whose steps toward civilization should be taken under the close supervision of a strong and intelligent government; colonists of another people, more progressive and better informed than the Mexican inhabitants, but also more shrewd and unruly; among these foreigners are fugitives from justice, honest laborers, vagabonds and criminals, but honorable and dishonorable alike travel with their political constitution in their pockets, demanding the privileges, authority and officers which such a constitution guarantees.

Source: Alleine Howren, "Causes and Origin of the Decree of April 6, 1830," *Southwestern Historical Quarterly*, XVI (1913), 395–398.

22. Letter from Gen. Manuel de Mier y Terán to Lucás Alamán, "¿En qué parará Texas? En lo que Dios quiera." ("What is to become of Texas? Whatever God wills."), July 2, 1832

Mexican Gen. Manuel de Mier y Terán (1789–1832) led a boundary commission tour of Texas in 1828–29. In his last letter a day before his death he wrote Lucás Alamán, the intellectual leader of the Mexican conservatives. Mier y Terán was a seasoned and respected officer and after the 1828–29 tour was made commandant general of the Eastern Interior Provinces. In this capacity, he visited Galveston Bay in November 1831. His 1828 report had a sense of urgency and he recommended strong measures to stop U.S. expansion into Texas. As a first step, he recommended more presidios or garrisons placed close to major settlements. Concerned with the growing trade with the United States, he urged closer trade ties between Mexico proper and Texas. Then he urged more Mexican and European settlers be recruited to settle in Texas. These measures were not effectively implemented. And in this letter Mier y Terán anticipated the Texas revolt of 1836 and the loss of Texas.

A great and respectable Mexican nation, a nation of which we have dreamed and for which we have labored so long, can never emerge from the many disasters which have overtaken it. We have allowed ourselves to be deceived by the ambitions of selfish groups; and now we are about to lose the northern provinces. How could we expect to hold Texas when we do not even agree among ourselves? It is a gloomy state of affairs. If we could work together, we would advance. As it is, we are lost. I believed, and with reason, that the withdrawal of the ministry would end the revolution. It only gave courage to those factions of discord who now hope to occupy all the country. There is commotion from Tampico to Mexico. The present state of affairs in Texas does not permit me to leave. The revolution absorbs the energies of men who should be working together.

From the twenty-fourth of last May I held a position in order to protect the states of San Luis and Tamaulipas from the military forces of the revolutionists, and to a certain extent overcome their influence in closing the principal means of communication; but it was impossible to stay their activities in Huasteca and other towns in Tamaulipas, from which places they were able completely to surround my camp. Particularly in Victoria did they make headway. The authorities and powers there were in a. most critical position, since the legal existence of their government depended upon my success in this fracas. As individuals, they were about equally divided in their allegiance-some favored the government and some supported the revolution. Was ever a general faced with a more insuperable obstacle? I could expect no direct aid from the state government in pursuing a rigorous plan of war. Even when I received orders from Victoria, I realized under the circumstances that they were not constitutional. The effect has been to leave me. isolated in Tamaulipas with my depleted forces. If I leave, the, state is lost. If I remain, all is lost. Martial law would be a precarious remedy, and one justified by the revolution; but our constitution makes no provision for such a law, and if it were changed so as to provide for such measures today, in Tamaulipas and everywhere in the federation it would produce such lamentable results, that it is best not to consider it. In the first place, it is an impossibility, and secondly, if it were not, I as commander would have to ask for my relief.

Moctezuma would not listen to reason. His forces now are larger than mine. His successes are due to numbers rather than to his generalship ... When I came through this country in 1829, on my way to Tampico, I noticed many places connected with the return of Iturbide to Mexico. I have seen the house where he spent his last night. The wall in front of which he was shot is still standing. This morning dawned diaphanous, radiant, beautiful. The sky was blue; the trees green, the birds were bursting with joy; the river crystalline, the flowers yellow, making drops of dew shine in their calyces. Everything pulsed with life, everything gave evident signs that the breath of God had reached nature. In contrast to these things the village of Padilla is alone and apathetic, with its houses in ruin and its thick ashen adobe walls; and my soul is burdened with weariness. I am an unhappy man, and unhappy people should not live on earth. I have studied this situation for five years and today, I know nothing, nothing, for man is very despicable and small; and—let us put an end to these reflections, for they almost drive me mad. The revolution is about to break forth and Texas is lost.

Immortality! God! The Soul! What does all this mean? Well, then, I believe in it all, but why does man not have the right to put aside his misery and his pains? Why should he be eternally chained to an existence which is unpleasant to him? And this spirit which inspires, which fills my mind with ideas-where will it go? Let us see, now; the spirit is uncomfortable, it commands me to set it free, and it is necessary to obey. Here is the end of human glory and the termination of ambition.

¿En qué parará Texas? En lo que Dios quiera. ["What is to become of Texas? Whatever God wills."]

Source: Courtesy of Wallace L. McKeehan, Sons of DeWitt Colony Texas. http://www.tamu. edu/ccbn/dewitt/teranmanuel.htm.

23. José Antonio Navarro's Letter to the Editor of the San Antonio *Ledger*, October 30, 1853

Many Tejano Mexican (those of Mexican heritage living in Texas) notables were sympathetic to Euro-American migration because of the benefits they received from an increase in trade and land values spurred by Euro-American settlement. One of the leaders of the Tejano elite was José Antonio Navarro, a conservative. He was the leader of a faction loyal to Euro-American colonists. Navarro, a second-generation Tejano born at San Antonio de Béxar in Texas on February 27, 1795, was a *criollo*, a full-blooded Spaniard born in the New World. He flaunted that his father was a native of Corsica, and claimed that his mother was from a noble Spanish family. A strong advocate of states' rights during the U.S. Civil War (1861–1865), he supported the Confederacy. He wrote the following letter in Spanish to the editor of the San Antonio, Texas, *Ledger*. In it Navarro bitterly criticizes the Mexican government and speaks of the War of Independence from Mexico in Texas.

Dear Sir:

In the issue of September 17th last, I read some historical memoirs concerning the foundation and ancient history of San Antonio de Bexar. Since I was an eye-witness of all the events described in that work, I cannot resist the temptation to correct certain substantial errors contained in that narrative. Undoubtedly, they are the result of inaccurate reports which were perhaps taken from mutilated and incomplete documents from which it is difficult to maintain chronological sequence. I have always wanted to obtain the most exact report of those events so that the customs, character, abilities and moral traits of the men and events of that epoch might be presented to posterity.

In 1813, the author of this letter was eighteen years old; he was then in San Antonio and he still retains fresh memories of that time. This act and his concern for everything pertaining to San Antonio, beloved for thousands of reasons, are the result of the present emanation and should be narrated with due respect to the truth.

You will not discover in this writing flowers of speech nor the persistence of excellence of its style but an unreserved narrative of bloody and revolutionary times. The Mexican priest named Miguel Hidalgo y Costilla, illustrious by a thousand titles, actually was the first to utter the cry of Independence in the Pueblo of Dolores. The priest José María Morelos was famous from that time to this for his military talents. He was also another one of the heroes of Mexican Independence and who later after the execution of the priest Hidalgo, convoked the first Mexican Congress of Apacigen. General Felix María Calleja, later Viceroy of Mexico, was particularly distinguished of his bloody persecutions and iniquities against the patriots Hidalgo, Guerrero, Morelos, Bravo, and others. Calleja was the most dangerous enemy of the Mexicans.

Morelos was captured, treated with ignominy and was finally shot in the old castle of San Christobal one-fourth league distance from the capital of Mexico.

José Bernardo Gutíerrez, a native of Revilla, Tamaulipas, fled to the United States immediately after the capture and imprisonment of the patriot heroes in Acatita de Bajan near Monclova, in the year 1811. He visited Washington and other cities in the United States and finally in the state of Louisiana enlisted 450 American volunteers with whom he again invaded Texas in the month of October 1812.

Nacogdoches, a military fortification on the Trinity River, was captured by him without resistance and subsequently he took La Bahía del Espiritu Santo, known today as Goliad. Manuel Salcedo, military Governor of Texas, and Simon de Herrera of Nuevo Leon, went out with more than 2,000 men and besieged La Bahía, November 15, 1812.

Generals Gutíerrez [sic], McGee, Kemper, Perry and Ross sustained the siege for the better of three months. In desperation the besieged finally went out from the wall of Goliad with almost all their force composed of American volunteers and some Mexicans. They fought the enemy and returned to the fort leaving 200 of the enemy dead and wounded and they suffered scarcely any losses. After twenty-seven regular encounters, Salcedo and Herrera discontinued the siege and retired to San Antonio towards the end of March 1813. Gutíerrez, Kemper and the others, stimulated by the forced retreat of the enemy, followed them day by day. Salcedo had not arrived at San Antonio with his army when he was ordered by Simon de Herrera to abandon the city and march to the Salado, where, at the place called "Rosilla," he encountered the army of Gutíerrez, if a band of 900 patriots could be called an army.

The two armies fought to the end of March. It was a bloody battle. Herrera lost 400 men, dead and wounded, and Gutíerrez lost only five dead and fourteen wounded. The royal army fled in disorder in the direction of San Antonio which Salcedo and Herrera had begun to fortify for the purpose of resisting Gutíerrez.

Kemper and others, after collecting the spoils of battle and burying the dead, pursued Salcedo with their victorious army and took possession of Concepción Mission, southeast of San Antonio. The following day they marched to San Antonio. The army of patriots formed in double columns in the lower labor where at present stand the private residences of Devine, Callaghan and Gilbeau. From that memorable place, Bernardo Gutíerrez demanded the unconditional surrender of Governors Salcedo and Herrera. Surrender took place March 30, 1813. On the evening of the 31st these same persons with their entire staff and other officers of high rank left Bexar on foot and met Gutíerrez and his victorious army. It was clear that nothing was known of what had happened to the conference between the victors and the conquered except that the request that their lives be spared had been guaranteed. Gutíerrez replied evasively but gave them to understand that they were in no danger of losing their lives.

Those unfortunate Spanish officers surrendered at the discretion of the enemy and so by their cowardice sealed their own doom. They surrendered their swords and were placed between two files of soldiers. Gutíerrez and his army returned to the eastern side of the river compelling their prisoners to march in front to the sound of martial music, and they entered within the walls of the Alamo, the same Alamo which in March 1836 was to become the cradle of the liberty of Texas and the scene of the marvel of valor. There, the valiant patriot[s], Gutíerrez, Kemper, Ross and their brave companions enjoyed the first sleep since the triumph of March 31st. There, they sealed the mysterious bond of those terrible events which happened in the year of 1836.

On April 1st at nine in the morning, the republican army marched to the beating of drums from the Alamo to Main Plaza of San Antonio. They crossed the river of Commerce street. The Spanish-Mexican army had disbanded and retired the preceding night and could not be seen in any part of the city. Only a few who were overcome with terror and a few citizens of San Antonio remained. Gutíerrez took possession of all the houses of Government where the beautiful store of the Mesdames Bances now stands, and immediately called an administrative Junta [committee] of civil council of those citizens who with great ardor had opposed Spanish rule and who consequently had favored Mexican Independence. This Junta was composed of from eight to ten members, a President, and a Secretary. From the writings of Gutíerrez it seems that he signed it with the sole object of court-martialing and sentencing the Spanish prisoners.

The secretary of this Junta, Mariano Rodrigues, is still living. At that time he was a youth, active and jolly. Today he is an antiquated septuagenarian who merely exists in San Antonio with a very limited recollection of the past and an extreme indifference for the future. On the fourth day of April, or possibly on the night of the fifth, a company of sixty Mexican men under the command of Antonio Delgado led out of San Antonio fourteen Spanish prisoners, including four of Mexican birth, to the eastern bank of the Salado near the same spot on which occurred the battle of Rosilla. There they alighted from their fine horses, and with no other arms than the large, dull machetes which each of those monsters carried hanging from their belts. After having heaped offensive words and insulting epithets upon them, they beheaded them with inhuman irony, some of those assassins sharpened their machetes on the soles of their boots in the presence of their defenseless victims.

Oh, shame of the human race! What a disgrace for the descendants of a Christian nation! What blood can coolly suffer in silence an act unparalleled in the annals of the history of San Antonio de Bexar? But we owe an impartial history to posterity that such horrible deeds may be known to the future generations so that through their own good conduct of the future, they may eradicate such horrible stains from our benign soil.

One day after the slaughter, I myself saw that horde of assassins arrive with their officer, Antonio Delgado, who halted in front of the houses of Government to inform Bernardo Gutíerrez that the fourteen victims had been disposed of. On that morning of ominous glory, a large number of other young spectators and I stood at the door of the Palace of the Governor and watched Captain Delgado's entrance into the hall. He doffed his hat in the presence of General Gutíerrez and stuttering, he proffered some words mingled with shame. He handed Gutíerrez a paper which, I believe, contained a list of the beheaded ones, and whose names I give below:

SPANIARDS:
Manuel Salcedo, Governor
Simon de Herrera, Colonel
Geronimo Herrera, Colonel
Juan Echevarria, Captain
José Mateos, Lieutenant
José Goescochea, Lieutenant
Juan Ignacio Arrambide, Lieutenant
Gregorio Amador, Lieutenant
Antonio López, Lieutenant
Francisco Perciva, Captain
MEXICANS:
Miguel de Arcos, Lieutenant
Luis Hijo y Francisco, Lieutenant
Juan Caso, Lieutenant

I myself saw the clothing and the blood-stained jewels which those tigers carried hanging from their saddle horns, making public festival of their crime and of having divided the spoils among themselves pro rata.

As I have said, it is certain that Gutíerrez received in the Palace of the Governor an account of that cruel affair although later he disavowed taking part in the execution of the prisoners. Gutíerrez says in a manuscript which he wrote and printed in Monterey May 6, 1827, that he had never given the order to execute those unfortunate fourteen prisoners, but that a great number of citizens who were greatly excited provoked against the Spanish Governors, induced a majority of the Junta to pass a formal order so that the guard who had custody of the prisoners should hand them over could avoid such a scandal, much less relinquish his command on seeing his cause blackened by the most infamous action that could be authorized by a leader of vandals. Consequently, Gutíerrez shared in the atrocity. He was a hypocrite; he pronounced sentence and like Pilate, washed his hands. It was not a court martial which passed sentence as has been erroneously stated.

Kemper and his American auxiliaries were horrified by so barbarous a deed and they prepared to leave the country, demanding of Gutíerrez that they be justified in the name of the Mexican Republic but due to the pleadings in chorus of Miguel Menchaca and other Mexican leaders, they consented to remain in San Antonio to help the cause of Mexican Independence.

Some days after these events, it became known with certainty that Colonel Ignacio Elizondo was marching from the Rio Grande to San Antonio with an army of more than 2,000 men. Elizondo was furious on receiving the news of the murder of the governors and by forced marches arrived at the place known as Alazan about two miles west of San Antonio. Gutíerrez and Peery met him there June 3, 1813, and from the towers of the Catholic Parish Church, a number of curious youths, including myself, watched the conflict of shining weapons through our field glasses and listened to the deep thunder of the cannons.

Elizondo, after a combat of four hours was defeated and he abandoned the field of battle, leaving 400 men dead, wounded and prisoners. Gutíerrez lost 22 men and 42 wounded. Among the dead was the aide-de-camp Maricos, a French youth, skillful, learned, with a personal valor and such bravery that not even the marshals of Napoleon could rival. Scarcely had the victors, Gutíerrez and Perry, returned to San Antonio when it was learned that the Commander in Chief of the province, Joaquín de Arredondo, was in Laredo on his way to San Antonio with more than 3,000 of the best troops of Mexico, united with the fugitives of the battles of Alazan who with the defeated Colonel Elizondo had joined them on the road. At this time, Gutíerrez, despite his victories, began to lose the confidence of his officers and soldiers. Either the barbarous and abnormal conduct of Gutíerrez towards the murdered Spaniards or the political tricks of José Alvarez de Toledo, a Spaniard who had been sent by the Cortes of Cadiz to the island of San Domingo, a liberal opposed to the rule of the King of Spain, who came from the state of Louisiana to dismiss Gutíerrez from office, all effected the feeling of the Republican officers and the army. But what is absolutely certain is that Gutíerrez' influence diminished with the same rapidity as that with which he had triumphed in a thousand battles.

Discouraged on seeing himself abandoned, Gutíerrez left Be[x]ar with some of his intimate friends for the United States. And a few days later, General Toledo took command of the army. Gutíerrez, in his proclamation of May 25, 1827, said that General Alvares de Toledo was only a hypocritical patriot of Mexican independence and that when he came to Texas to take command of the Republican troops, he was in secret correspondence with the King of Spain in an attempt to hinder the progress and the success of the patriots.

As proof of his assertion it is said that some time after the year 1813, Alvares de Toledo had returned to Spain and he was not only received by Fernando VII, but he was even rewarded with the appointment of Ambassador to one of the European Courts. Whether this is true of not is the mystery hidden in the misty twilight of time long passed. There is further proof of Toledo's having been a sincere patriot in 1813, after which he suffered the weakness of taking refuge in the amnesty and favor of the King. But if we may judge by reputation and appearances, we must confess that the assertions of Gutíerrez are confirmed by the epithets that his own countrymen have hurled in his face, "He was a politician without principles, an unlettered judge, an undisciplined soldier and cruel to the marrow."

On the other hand, Toledo was apparently a young man of 32 years, of liberal principles, affluent in speech, pleasing personality, skillful, of gentle manly demeanor and very obsequious. With this multitude of fascinating qualities, he immediately captured the hearts and goodwill of the army and the inhabitants of San Antonio, and later, he became the commanding officer.

Finally, General Arredondo became furious and impatient to pacify the minds of the people and to avenge the death of his countrymen, the Governors. On the 18th of August and not on the 13th, as it has been stated, Toledo opened battle at Medina. This general had 1,500 men including 600 American volunteers. Arredondo had 4,000 men. The battle was fought with great military skill on both sides. The American volunteers formed the regiment of infantry and the company of artillery was composed of nine cannon[s] from four to eight inches in caliber. The cavalry consisted of inhabitants of San Antonio and vicinity and of certain individuals from Tamaulipas and the Rio Grande.

By a strategic movement Arredondo caused his army to raise a unanimous cry of Long live the King! Victory is ours! At the same time the band played their notes of victory, causing the cavalry of terrorized patriots to flee from the field. However, the phlegmatic America Infantry, and its artilleries sustained the deadly fire from the eighteen heavy-calibered cannon[s] of Arredondo for more than four hours.

No one can overcome impossibilities, nor is it natural for one to combat a disproportionately large force. The America Infantry finally abandoned the artillery and hurriedly fled from the field of battle, breaking their files against the oak and mesquite trees, rather than leave them as trophies for the enemy and resolutely they gave themselves up to fate. Arredondo's cavalry pursued them with saber in hand and lance prepared, inflicting terrible slaughter upon them for six long miles, and so perished the better part of those brave compatriots. On the following day, Arredondo entered the city triumphantly, with his carts laden with wounded and dying.

At this point my hand trembles in recording the scenes of horror with which they spurred one of the bitterest enemies of Gutíerrez in requital for the previous atrocities of Gutíerrez. Arredondo avenged himself in the most infamous manner and without distinction, and he ordered the imprisonment of 700 of the most peaceful inhabitants of San Antonio.

At the same time, he imprisoned 300 unfortunate people in the cells of the Catholic priests on the night of the 20th of August. They were crowded in like sheep in the fold in the hottest months of summer. On the morning of the following day, 18 of them had perished from suffocation. The remainder were placed before the firing squad from day to day for no more response than that they had been accused of being in favor of Independence.

By a unexplicable [*sic*] coincidence, it appears that in San Antonio, in those same places where so many cruelties were committed, reserved for providence so that in happier times they might serve as lessons in devotion, justice, education and recreation, there today stands the courthouse, and facing Main Plaza is the balustrade of the hotel; the former is the sanctuary of the law, and the latter a lodging place that affords the most delicious food the gastronomist can possibly procure.

In those times, daily executions took place and often the laments of the dying were heard where now stands the Post Office through which the inner thoughts are communicated in writing, and through which knowledge and policies are diffused through the community.

Arredondo erected a large prison for women known as La Quinta. There, they suffered agony. More than 500 married and single women whose husbands and fathers were known as insurgents! For four months, an insolent guard compelled them to convert twenty-four bushels of corn into tortillas daily to feed the officers and soldiers of Arredondo.

There, the modest and gentle wives and daughters were exposed to the insults of those depraved undisciplined troops and frequently they suffered the defiled and lewd gazes and endearing remarks of officers and soldiers who enjoyed that detestable and repugnant pastime. Juana Leal de Tarín and Concepción Leal de Garza, who then lived on their farms on the banks of the San Antonio River, were among those innocent and unfortunate prisoners of La Quinta. They endured their defaming captivity with a spirited courage before submitting to the shameful proposals of their jailers.

After the battle of Medina, Col. Elizondo left San Antonio with 500 men in pursuit of the fugitives, who were on the road to the United States. At the Trinity River on the old road from San Antonio he overtook a body of men and families, and at that point 105 persons were shot.

Perhaps I shall be excused of exaggerating in giving details of the manner in which those captives were condemned and executed on the Trinity. Elizondo had for a chaplain a despicable priest known as Padre Camacho and when some of the fugitive insurgents were captured, Elizondo brought them to the confessional and ordered the said clergyman to confess them according to the rites of the Catholic Church. Belief in Christianity and hope of eternity compelled those unfortunate men to confess without reserve the part they had taken in the revolution. Padre Camacho, in the conviction of these confessions, gave a prearranged signal to the officers of the guard so that they might lead the victims immediately to the place of execution.

One other aggravating circumstance may fill the readers with horror. Padre Camacho by chance had been wounded by a spent bullet which broke the muscles of his leg at the battle of Alazan. More than once on the Trinity River, where some unfortunate condemned to death pleaded aloud for mercy, the priest, raising his clerical garments said to him, "Move on my son, and suffer the penalty in the name of God, because perhaps the bullet which wounded me may have come from your gun."

After these executions on the Trinity River, Elizondo took as prisoners all the broken families, many ladies, black eyed and beautiful. They were handcuffed and were compelled to cross the San Antonio River on foot at the very place which now is the pleasant bathing place of Mr. Hall, and Elizondo himself invited the weaker sex to bathe their delicate forms.

Who could have foretold that the heads of the famous spies of Gen. Gutíerrez, Gulas, Botas Negras and Ayamontes, whom Arredondo had had executed in San Antonio, would be crated and placed on the sharp end of a pike at the very spot where now the American flag proudly waves on Military Plaza.

Who could have foretold that thirty-three years later an emblem of terror feared by the tyrants, a flag respected by the world, would mark the place where their lifeless heads had been exhibited.

After the independence of Mexico was gained, Gov. Trespalacios crossed the Medina River towards San Antonio and upon viewing the prairies sprinkled with human skeletons, he had them collected and buried with full military honors.

I distinctly remember the following Inscription written on a square of wood which was on the trunk of an oak tree:

Here lie the Mexican heroes who followed the example of Leonides
Who sacrificed their wealth and lives
Ceaselessly fighting against tyrants.

This is an imperfect but truthful history of the events of that period.

San Antonio remained quiet and subjected to the dominion of the King of Spain after the arrival of Arredondo. He confiscated and sold the property of the patriots known as rebels who never recovered their goods, not even after the consummation of Mexico['s] Independence in the year of 1821.

The noble citizens of Bexar sacrificed their lives and property, performing prodigies of valor in the year 1813. They left to their descendants no other inheritance than the indifference and ingratitude of the Mexican Republic.

They never received my recompense of indemnity, not even the due respect and gratitude of their fellow citizens of Mexico. Our courage and heroism were cast into complete oblivion by the government of an ancient and respected country. For that reason, I do not believe that anyone will be surprised that the germ of discontent which the people of Texas nurtured and for which reason they adhere to the new order of things that is offered to us by the institutions of a great, powerful, and growing Republic. Such is the source an opportunity for the Independence of Texas which State is separated from that Government forever. Maybe this condition will continue indefinitely.

Source: The Memoirs of José Antonio Navarro: Historical Sketches about San Antonio de Bexar by an Eye-Witness, October 30, 1853. www.tamu.edu/ccbn/dewitt.htm.

24. Excerpts from Lorenzo de Zavala, *Journey to the United States of North America*, Early 1830s

Lorenzo de Zavala (1788–1836), a native of Mérida, Yucatán, was one of Mexico's most active political leaders of the 1820s. He held a number of political and diplomatic posts. But he went into exile in the early 1830s after a fallout with the conservative ruling junta. Zavala traveled throughout the United States. He later deserted the Mexican side in Texas and served as vice-president of the Lone Star State (the Republic of Texas) These excerpts telling of his travels through the United States give a glimpse into the mentality of the nineteenth-century Mexican Liberal who wanted to privatize Mexico. He was enamored with the Euro-American experiment, and his writings show the biases and racism typical of his class. Zavala, at the time his book was written, was close to many Euro-American politicos, including the former disruptive U.S. Minister to Mexico from 1825–1829, Joel Poinsett (1779–1851), who became embroiled in the domestic affairs of Mexico offending officials by trying to purchase parts of the Mexican state in 1827.

The Mexican is easy going, lazy, intolerant, generous almost to prodigality, vain, belligerent, superstitious, ignorant and an enemy of all restraint. The North

American works, the Mexican has a good time; the first spends less than he has, the second even that which he does not have; the former carries out the most arduous enterprises to their conclusion, the latter abandons them in the early stages; the one lives in his house, decorates it, furnishes it, preserves it against the inclement weather; the other spends his time in the street, flees from his home, and in a land where there are no seasons he worries little about a place to rest. In the United States all men are property owners and tend to increase their fortune; in Mexico the few who have anything are careless with it and fritter it away.

As I say these things it must be understood that there are honorable exceptions, and that especially among educated people are to be found very commendable social and domestic virtues. There are also in the United States people who are prodigal, lazy, and despicable. But that is not the general rule.

I seem to hear some of my fellow countrymen yelling: "How awful! See how that unworthy Mexican belittles and exposes us to the view of civilized peoples." Just calm down, gentlemen, for others have already said that and much more about us and about our forefathers, the Spaniards. Do you not want it said? Then mend your ways. Get rid of those eighty-seven holidays during the year that you dedicate to play, drunkenness and pleasure. Save up capital for the decent support of yourselves and your families in order to give guarantees of your concern for the preservation of the social order. Tolerate the opinions of other people; be indulgent with those who do not think as you do; allow the people of your country to exercise freely their trade, whatever it may be, and to worship the supreme Author of the Universe in accordance with their own consciences. Repair your roads; raise up houses in order to live like rational beings; dress your children and your wives with decency, don't incite riots in order to take what belongs to somebody else. And finally, live on the fruit of your labors, and then you will be worthy of liberty and of the praises of sensible and impartial men.

The people of Mexico are my Maecenas, but I do not follow in the way of others who fill a page with the praises of those persons whose patronage they solicit. The advantage of those who write without expecting a reward is that they say what they feel, and they are believed and respected....

For a Mexican who has never left his country, or who has not done so in a long time, the first impression as he arrives at any point in the United States or England is that of seeing all classes of people dressed. They say that when the Emperor Alexander visited London in 1814, he said to those about him that he found no common people in that capital. What a pleasant spectacle to the eye of the beholder is that of a society that announces by its appearance of decorum and decency, the industry, the comforts and even the morality of a people! On the contrary, how unpleasant is the aspect of nudity and lack of cleanliness and what a sad idea a nation gives of the state of its civilization and of its morality when it is inhabited by such people! In a work on Spain that he published in Paris a certain M. Faurefour years ago put on the title page of the book an engraving of a student wearing a to[rn] cloak and other rags, with a staff in his hand, begging alms for the love of God. This alone gave an idea of the object which most attracted the attention of the French traveler in the Pyrenean Peninsula....

In my *Historical Essay* on the revolutions of Mexico I have set forth my opinions concerning that beautiful and rich portion of land known formerly as the province of Texas and today as an integral part of the State of Coahuila and Texas. Once the way was opened to colonization, as it should have been, under a system of free government, it was necessary that a new generation should appear within a few years and populate a part of the Mexican Republic, and consequently that this new population should be entirely heterogeneous with respect to the other provinces or states of the country. Fifteen or twenty thousand foreigners distributed over the vast areas of Mexico, Oaxaca, Veracruz, etc., scattered among the former inhabitants cannot cause any sudden change in their ways, manners and customs. Rather they adopt the tendencies, manners, language, religion, politics and even the vices of the multitude that surrounds them. An Englishman will be a Mexican in Mexico City, and a Mexican an Englishman in London.

The same thing will not happen with colonies. Completely empty woods and lands, uninhabited a dozen years ago, converted into villages and towns suddenly by Germans, Irish, and North Americans, must of necessity form an entirely different nation, and it would be absurd to try to get them to renounce their religion, their customs and their deepest convictions. What will be the result?

I have stated it many times. They will not be able to subject themselves to a military regime and an ecclesiastical government such as unfortunately have continued in Mexican territory in spite of the republican-democratic constitutions. They will point out the institutions that should govern the country, and they will want it not to be a deceit, an illusion, but a reality. When a military leader tries to intervene in civil transactions, they will resist, and they will triumph. They will organize popular assemblies to deal with political matters as is done in the United States and in England. They will build chapels for different faiths to worship the Creator according to their beliefs. Religious practices are a social necessity, one of the great consolations for the ills of humanity. Will the government of Mexico send a legion of soldiers to Texas to enforce Article 3 of the Mexican constitution which prohibits the exercise of any other faith than the Catholic?...

In the city of New York there are a considerable number of blacks and colored people, although as in the other states to the north of Maryland slavery is not permitted. But in spite of this emancipation of the African class and its descendants, it is excluded from all political rights, and even from the common trade with the others, living to a certain degree as though excommunicated. This situation is not very natural in a country where they profess the principles of the widest liberty. Nothing, however, can overcome the concern that exists with respect to this particular subject.

The colored people have their separate homes, hotels, and churches; they are the Jews of North America. This rejection by society degrades them and takes from them the incentive to work; they resign themselves to idleness and do not try to improve a hopeless situation, circumscribed within limits so narrow that there is scarcely room to calculate self-interest. Hence the vices and laziness which with very few exceptions holds this whole class down to the lowest ranks of society. This is the great argument against the emancipation of the slaves, an argument that discourages its most ardent supporters and that would make their efforts useless if the abolition of slavery were not demanded by a necessity that within a short time will admit no further delay....

In 1830 I visited the widow of Senor Don Agustín de Iturbide in Georgetown near Washington, where she was living and looking after the education of her children. In 1834 I had the pleasure of seeing this respectable Mexican family for a second time in Philadelphia, after the president of the Mexican republic, General

Santa Anna, had lifted the banishment which condemned her to live outside her own country, although with a good pension. Senora Iturbide had achieved in good part the fruits of her endeavors; her older daughters, receiving an education according to the culture of the country, have followed the wishes of their teachers and have augmented the charms of their sex with the advantages of the mind and with the physical perfection of a material education.

Source: Lorenzo de Zavala, *Journey to the United States of North America*. Houston: Arte Publico Press, University of Houston © 2005, pp. 2–3, 50, 79, 90, 107. Wallace Woolsey, trans. John-Michael Rivera, ed. Reprinted with permission of the publisher. (Originally published as *Merida de Yucatan: Imprenta de Castillo y Compañía*, 1846.)

25. Texas Declaration of Independence, March 2, 1836

The political climate in Texas deteriorated and, by 1831, Euro-Americans from the United States flooded into Texas ready to "free" it from Mexico. There were hostilities after this point and by the mid-1830s uprising was in the making. Meanwhile, Antonio López de Santa Anna (1794–1876) marched troops to Texas in order to secure Mexico's north Texas borders. Santa Anna arrived in February and by March 1, 1836, Euro-Americans supported by a minority of Mexican elites held a convention appointing a committee of five delegates to draft a Declaration of Independence that was voted on and passed by the delegates. Like the 1776 U.S. Declaration of Independence it stated the function and responsibility of government encased by a list of grievances. Thus, Texas was declared a free and independent republic.

The Unanimous Declaration of Independence made by the Delegates of the People of Texas in General Convention at the town of Washington on the 2nd day of March 1836.

When a government has ceased to protect the lives, liberty and property of the people, from whom its legitimate powers are derived, and for the advancement of whose happiness it was instituted, and so far from being a guarantee for the enjoyment of those inestimable and inalienable rights, becomes an instrument in the hands of evil rulers for their oppression.

When the Federal Republican Constitution of their country, which they have sworn to support, no longer has a substantial existence, and the whole nature of their government has been forcibly changed, without their consent, from a restricted federative republic, composed of sovereign states, to a consolidated central military despotism, in which every interest is disregarded but that of the army and the priesthood, both the eternal enemies of civil liberty, the everready minions of power, and the usual instruments of tyrants.

When, long after the spirit of the constitution has departed, moderation is at length so far lost by those in power, that even the semblance of freedom is removed, and the forms themselves of the constitution discontinued, and so far from their petitions and remonstrances being regarded, the agents who bear them are thrown into dungeons, and mercenary armies sent forth to force a new government upon them at the point of the bayonet.

When, in consequence of such acts of malfeasance and abdication on the part of the government, anarchy prevails, and civil society is dissolved into its original elements. In such a crisis, the first law of nature, the right of self-preservation, the inherent and inalienable rights of the people to appeal to first principles, and take their political affairs into their own hands in extreme cases, enjoins it as a right towards themselves, and a sacred obligation to their posterity, to abolish such government, and create another in its stead, calculated to rescue them from impending dangers, and to secure their future welfare and happiness.

Nations, as well as individuals, are amenable for their acts to the public opinion of mankind. A statement of a part of our grievances is therefore submitted to an impartial world, in justification of the hazardous but unavoidable step now taken, of severing our political connection with the Mexican people, and assuming an independent attitude among the nations of the earth.

The Mexican government, by its colonization laws, invited and induced the Anglo-American population of Texas to colonize its wilderness under the pledged faith of a written constitution, that they should continue to enjoy that constitutional liberty and republican government to which they had been habituated in the land of their birth, the United States of America.

In this expectation they have been cruelly disappointed, inasmuch as the Mexican nation has acquiesced in the late changes made in the government by General Antonio Lopez de Santa Anna, who having overturned the constitution of his country, now offers us the cruel alternative, either to abandon our homes, acquired by so many privations, or submit to the most intolerable of all tyranny, the combined despotism of the sword and the priesthood.

It has sacrificed our welfare to the state of Coahuila, by which our interests have been continually depressed through a jealous and partial course of legislation, carried on at a far distant seat of government, by a hostile majority, in an unknown tongue, and this too, notwithstanding we have petitioned in the humblest terms for the establishment of a separate state government, and have, in accordance with the provisions of the national constitution, presented to the general Congress a republican constitution, which was, without just cause, contemptuously rejected.

It incarcerated in a dungeon, for a long time, one of our citizens, for no other cause but a zealous endeavor to procure the acceptance of our constitution, and the establishment of a state government.

It has failed and refused to secure, on a firm basis, the right of trial by jury, that palladium of civil liberty, and only safe guarantee for the life, liberty, and property of the citizen.

It has failed to establish any public system of education, although possessed of almost boundless resources, (the public domain) and although it is an axiom in political science, that unless a people are educated and enlightened, it is idle to expect the continuance of civil liberty, or the capacity for self government.

It has suffered the military commandants, stationed among us, to exercise arbitrary acts of oppression and tyrrany [sic], thus trampling upon the most sacred rights of the citizens, and rendering the military superior to the civil power.

It has dissolved, by force of arms, the state Congress of Coahuila and Texas, and obliged our representatives to fly for their lives from the seat of government, thus depriving us of the fundamental political right of representation.

It has demanded the surrender of a number of our citizens, and ordered military detachments to seize and carry them into the Interior for trial, in contempt of the civil authorities, and in defiance of the laws and the constitution.

It has made piratical attacks upon our commerce, by commissioning foreign desperadoes, and authorizing them to seize our vessels, and convey the property of our citizens to far distant ports for confiscation.

It denies us the right of worshipping the Almighty according to the dictates of our own conscience, by the support of a national religion, calculated to promote the temporal interest of its human functionaries, rather than the glory of the true and living God.

It has demanded us to deliver up our arms, which are essential to our defence, the rightful property of freemen, and formidable only to tyrannical governments.

It has invaded our country both by sea and by land, with intent to lay waste our territory, and drive us from our homes; and has now a large mercenary army advancing, to carry on against us a war of extermination.

It has, through its emissaries, incited the merciless savage, with the tomahawk and scalping knife, to massacre the inhabitants of our defenseless frontiers.

It hath been, during the whole time of our connection with it, the contemptible sport and victim of successive military revolutions, and hath continually exhibited every characteristic of a weak, corrupt, and tyrranical [*sic*] government.

These, and other grievances, were patiently borne by the people of Texas, untill [*sic*] they reached that point at which forbearance ceases to be a virtue. We then took up arms in defence of the national constitution. We appealed to our Mexican brethren for assistance. Our appeal has been made in vain. Though months have elapsed, no sympathetic response has yet been heard from the Interior. We are, therefore, forced to the melancholy conclusion, that the Mexican people have acquiesced in the destruction of their liberty, and the substitution therefor of a military government; that they are unfit to be free, and incapable of self government.

The necessity of self-preservation, therefore, now decrees our eternal political separation.

We, therefore, the delegates with plenary powers of the people of Texas, in solemn convention assembled, appealing to a candid world for the necessities of our condition, do hereby resolve and declare, that our political connection with the Mexican nation has forever ended, and that the people of Texas do now constitute a free, Sovereign, and independent republic, and are fully invested with all the rights and attributes which properly belong to independent nations; and, conscious of the rectitude of our intentions, we fearlessly and confidently commit the issue to the decision of the Supreme arbiter of the destinies of nations.

Richard Ellis, President of the Convention and Delegate from Red River, et al.

Source: Courtesy of the Avalon Project at Yale Law School, http://www.yale.edu/lawweb/avalon/texdec.htm.

26. Excerpts from the Address of the Honorable S. F. Austin, Louisville, Kentucky, March 7, 1836

Stephen Austin (1793–1836) led Euro-Americans in Texas from 1821 to 1836. He actively sought money and military support from Euro-Americans in the United States for the uprising. In this speech to supporters in Louisville, Kentucky, Austin paints Texas as an uncivilized place until the coming of Euro-Americans, who, according to him, were invited into Texas. Outside support of volunteers and arms was vital to the success of the insurrection, and many of the early volunteers came from Kentucky and neighboring southern states.

It is with the most unfeigned and heartfelt gratitude that I appear before this enlightened audience, to thank the citizens of Louisville, as I do in the name of the people of Texas, for the kind and generous sympathy they have manifested in favor of the cause of that struggling country; and to make a plain statement of facts explanatory of the contest in which Texas is engaged with the Mexican Government.

But a few years back Texas was a wilderness, the home of the uncivilized and wandering Comanche and other tribes of Indians, who waged a constant warfare against the Spanish settlements. These settlements at that time were limited to the small towns of Bexar (commonly called San Antonio) and Goliad, situated on the western limits. The incursions of the Indians also extended beyond the Rio Bravo del Norte, and desolated that part of the country.

In order to restrain these savages and bring them into subjection, the government opened Texas for settlement. Foreign emigrants were invited and called to that country. American enterprise accepted the invitation and promptly responded to the call. The first colony of Americans or foreigners ever settled in Texas was by myself. It was commenced in 1821, under a permission to my father, Moses Austin, from the Spanish government previous to the Independence of Mexico, and has succeeded by surmounting those difficulties and dangers incident to all new and wilderness countries infested with hostile Indians. These difficulties were many and at times appalling, and can only be appreciated by the hardy pioneers of this western country, who have passed through similar scenes....

The fact is, we had such guaranteed; for, in the first place the government bound itself to protect us by the mere act of admitting us as citizens, on the general and long established principle, even in the dark ages, that protection and allegiance are reciprocal—a principle which in this enlightened age has been extended much further; for its received interpretation now is, that the object of government is the well being, security, and happiness of the governed, and that allegiance ceases whenever it is clear, evident, and palpable, that this object is in no respect effected....

In 1833, the people of Texas, after a full examination of their population and resources, and of the law and constitution, decided, in general convention elected for that purpose, that the period had arrived contemplated by said law and compact of 7th May, 1824, and that the country possessed the necessary elements to form a state separate from Coahuila. A respectful and humble petition was accordingly drawn up by this convention, addressed to the general congress of Mexico, praying for the admission of Texas into the Mexican confederation as a state. I had the honor of being appointed by the convention the commissioner or agent of Texas to take this petition to the city of Mexico, and present it to the government. I discharged this duty to the best of my feeble abilities, and, as I believed, in a respectful manner. Many months passed and nothing was done with the petition, except to refer it to a committee of congress, where it slept and was likely to sleep. I finally urged the just and constitutional claims of Texas to become a state in the most pressing manner, as I believed it to be my duty to do; representing also the necessity and good policy of this measure, owning to the almost total want of local government of any kind, the absolute want of a judiciary, the evident impossibility of being governed any longer by Coahuila (for three fourths of the legislature were from there) and the consequent anarchy and discontent that existed in Texas. It was my misfortune to offend the high authorities of the nation—my frank and honest exposition of the truth was construed into threats.

At this time (September and October, 1833) a revolution was raging in many parts of the nation, and especially in the vicinity of the city of Mexico. I despaired of obtaining anything, and wrote to Texas, recommending to the people there to organize as a state de facto without waiting any longer. This letter may have been imprudent, as respects the injury it might do me personally, but how far it was criminal or treasonable, considering the revolutionary state of the whole nation, and the peculiar claims and necessities of Texas, impartial men must decide. It merely expressed an opinion. This letter found its way from San Antonio de Bexar (where it was directed) to the government. I was arrested at Saltillo, two hundred leagues from Mexico, on my way home, taken back to that city and imprisoned one year, three months of the time in solitary confinement, without books or writing materials, in a dark dungeon of the former inquisition prison. At the close of the year I was released from confinement, but detained six months in the city on heavy ball [surveillance]. It was nine months after my arrest before I was officially informed of the charges against me, or furnished with a copy of them. The constitutional requisites were not observed, my constitutional rights as a citizen were violated, the people of Texas were outraged by this treatment of their commissioner, and their respectful, humble and just petition was disregarded.

These acts of the Mexican government, taken in connexion [sic] with many others and with the general revolutionary situation of the interior of the republic, and the absolute want of local government in Texas, would have justified the people of Texas in organizing themselves as a State of the Mexican confederation, and if attacked for so doing in separating from Mexico. They would have been justifiable in doing this, because such acts were unjust, ruinous and oppressive, and because self-preservation required a local government in Texas suited to the situation and necessities of the country, and the character of its inhabitants. Our forefathers in '76 flew to arms for much less. They resisted a principle, "the theory of oppression," but in our case it was the reality—it was a denial of justice and of our guarantied [sic] rights—it was oppression itself....

In 1834, the President of the Republic, Gen. Santa Anna, who heretofore was the leader and champion of the republican party and system, became the head and leader of his former antagonists—the aristocratic and church party. With this accession of strength, this party triumphed. The constitutional general Congress of 1834, which was decidedly republican and federal, was dissolved in May of that year by a military order of the President before its constitutional term had expired. The council of government composed of half the Senate which, agreeably to the constitution, ought to have been installed the day after closing the session of Congress, was also dissolved; and a new, revolutionary, and unconstitutional Congress was convened by another military order of the President. This Congress met on the 1st of January, 1835. It was decidedly aristocratic, ecclesiastical and central in its politics. A number of petitions were presented to it from several towns and villages, praying that it would change the federal form of government and establish a central form. These petitions were all of a revolutionary character, and were called "pronunciamientos," or prenouncements for centralism. They were formed by partial and revolutionary meetings gotten up by the military and priests. Petitions in favour of the federal system and constitution, and protests against such revolutionary measures, were also sent in by the people and by some of the State Legislatures, who still retained firmness to express their opinions....

The emancipation of Texas will extend the principles of self-government, over a rich and neighbouring country, and open a vast field there for enterprise, wealth, and happiness, and for those who wish to escape from the frozen blasts of a northern climate, by removing to a more congenial one. It will promote and accelerate the march of the present age, for it will open a door through which a bright and constant stream of light and intelligence will flow from this great northern fountain over the benighted regions of Mexico.

Source: Courtesy of The Avalon Project, http://www.yale.edu/lawweb/avalon/texind01.htm.

27. Excerpt from José María Salomé Rodríguez, *The Memoirs of Early Texas*, 1913

José María Salomé Rodríguez, a member of the Mexican elite, wrote his memoirs shortly before his death on February 22, 1913. Born in San Antonio on October 29, 1829, his father, Ambrosio Rodriguez, fought on the filibusters' side. J. M. Rodríguez was judge of Webb County for 35 years. His family supported Texas breaking away from Mexico, and belonged to the landed elite that considered themselves natives. Mexicans sided with or opposed the Euro-Americans along class lines, with those with land seeing the benefits of becoming part of the United States. In this excerpt, Rodríguez recalls what had been told to him about the Alamo and the Texas War and its immediate aftermath.

BATTLE OF BEXAR AND THE ALAMO

My earliest recollection is when I was a boy about six years old. One evening I was coming with my father and mother up Soledad Street, where the Kampmann Building is now, and as we got a little further [*sic*] up the street, we were stopped by a sentry and there were other soldiers there and we saw some breastworks there. General Cos, the Mexican general, my father told me, was in possession of the town. We went a little further down where the present corner of Travis and Soledad Street is. We crossed a ditch on a plank and went up Soledad Street to see my uncle, Jose Olivarri. I heard a great deal of shooting towards the Plaza and my father said that General Burleson of the Texas Army was trying to capture the city. The next day General Cos capitulated and was allowed to take his arms and leave the city.

Ben Milam was killed at the Veramendi House. The arms the Mexicans had were old English muskets that did not reach much over fifty yards. The Texas army used long range flint rifles. Shortly after that, Colonel [William Barrett] Travis was put in command with a small garrison and he stayed at the Alamo. Colonel Travis was a fine looking man of more than ordinary height. I recollect him distinctly from the very fact that he used to come up to our house from the Alamo and talk to my father and mother a great deal, Our house was the first one after you crossed the river coming from the Alamo and Colonel Travis generally stopped at our home going and coming. He was a very popular man and was well liked by everyone. My father was always in sympathy with the Texas cause, but had so far not taken up arms on either side.

Soon after this, a report came to my father from a reliable source that Santa Ana [*sic*] was starting for San Antonio with 7,000 men, composed of cavalry, infantry and artillery, in fact a well organized army. My father sent for Colonel Travis and he came to our house and my father told him about this coming of Santa Ana and advised him to retire into the interior of Texas and abandon the Alamo. He told him he could not resist Santa Ana's army with such a small force. Colonel Travis told my father that he could not believe it, because General Cos had only been defeated less than three months, and it did not seem possible to him that General Santa Ana could organize in so short a time as large an army as that. Colonel Travis, therefore, remained at the Alamo, and at the last, Travis told my father, "Well we have made up our minds to die at the Alamo fighting for Texas." My father asked him again to retire as General Sam Houston was then in the interior of Texas organizing an army.

The Mexicans in San Antonio who were in sympathy with the war of Independence organized a company under Colonel Juan Seguin. There were twenty-four in the company including my father and they joined the command of General Sam Houston. My mother and all of us remained in the city. One morning early a man named Rivas called at our house and told us that he had seen Santa Ana in disguise the night before looking in on a fandango on Soledad Street. My father being away with General Houston's army, my mother undertook to act for us, and decided it was best for us to go into the country to avoid being here when General Santa Ana's army should come in. We went to the ranch of Dona Santos Ximenes. We left in ox carts, the wheels of which were made of solid wood. We buried our money in the house, about $800.00; it took us nearly two days to get to the ranch.

A few days after that, one morning about daybreak, I heard some firing, and Pablo Olivarri, who was with us woke me up. He said, "You had better get up on the house; they are fighting at the Alamo." We got up on the house and could see the flash of the guns and hear the booming of the cannon. The firing lasted about two hours. The next day we heard that all the Texans had been killed and the Alamo taken. A few days after that, an army consisting of about 1,200 men under General Urrea came by from San Antonio on their way to Goliad to attack Fannin. I saw these troops as they passed the ranch.

There has been a great deal of discussion with reference to what had been done with the bodies of the Texans who were slain in the Alamo. It is claimed that Colonel Seguin wrote a letter in which he stated that he got together the ashes in the following February and put them in an iron urn and buried them in San Fernando Cathedral. This does not seem possible to me; because nothing of that kind could have happened without us knowing that and we never heard of any occurrence of that kind. Seguin did not return from Houston's army until my father did, both of them being in the same command, my father a first Lieutenant and he a Colonel. It is true that the bones were brought together somewhere in the neighborhood or a little east of where the Menger Hotel is now and were buried by Colonel Seguin, but that any of them were ever buried in the Cathedral, I have never heard nor do I believe that to be true. The only person I know of being buried in the Cathedral was Don Eugenio Navarro, who was buried near the south wall of the Cathedral near the chancel.

Some days after the Urrea army passed, we heard of the massacre of Fannin's army at Goliad. My mother, along with other loyal families, determined then to move to East Texas, and we started with all our goods and chattels in ox-carts. The Flores and Seguin families were among those who went with us. Most of us traveled in the carts. Horses were very scarce, the army taking nearly all they could find. We had gotten as far as the Trinity River on the road to Nacogdoches where we heard of Santa Ana being defeated and all returned to San Antonio, except our family, who went on to Washington, which was the Texas capital, as my father was still in the field with Houston's troops.

THE BATTLE OF SAN JACINTO

The company which my father [Ambrosio Rodríquez] joined belonged to General Sam Houston's forces and were attached to General Houston's staff. My father and General Houston became very warm friends, which friendship lasted until my father's death, and continued with our family until Houston died. My father often told us the story of the Battle of San Jacinto.

He told us that General Santa Ana picked out 1,200 of his best men from his army and crossed the Brazos in pursuit of Houston under the impression that Houston was retreating toward Louisiana, and his main army of about 5,000 men or more remained on this side of the river under General Filisola. Houston discovered all these movements of Santa Ana, and he told his men that he was preparing to fight Santa Ana's advance army. Santa Ana came up within only a few miles of Houston's camp.

One evening Houston sent out a scouting party consisting of my father and others, to reconnoiter. They ran into Santa Ana's scouts and had a little brush. Santa Ana's men had a small cannon, and a cannon ball passed so close to my father's eyes that he was blinded for three or four hours. The next day about two o'clock, General Houston went around and talked to all of his men in camp and he told them, that now was the best time to fight Santa Ana and asked them would they do so, and they all agreed to it enthusiastically. Houston had about 600 men, all cavalry. The next day he prepared for the attack, and my father's company was placed on the left hand of Houston, and he told them that when they got in certain distance to lay down and drag themselves on the ground until they got in rifle shot of Santa Ana's men, who were taking a siesta. As soon as they got in range they let loose a volley into Santa Ana's men. After they had fired, they were afraid to stand up again and load. One of the company, a man named Manuel Flores, got up to load his gun and said, "Get up you cowards, Santa Ana's men are running." Then they got up, loaded their guns and commenced firing again. Santa Ana's men kept on running from the first volley and General Lamar coming up stopped the shooting, and took about six hundred prisoners. Santa Ana's horse was shot about six times. The horse was brought to General Houston and died. General Houston was slightly wounded in the leg.

A day or two after the battle, two of Houston's men went out from the camp to kill some game, and when a few miles from camp, they found a man sitting in an old log house, and they took him prisoner. As soon as they arrested him, one of the men said to him, "Look here, you are Santa Ana." The man denied this and made signs with his hands that he was a clerk; he was a scribe. The men said that as he wore a fine shirt, he could not be a common soldier because the common soldiers did not wear such shirts. They started with him for Houston's camp, but he only walked a few steps and then complained that he could not walk, so one of the men gave him his horse and kept asking him if he were not Santa Ana. One of the men thought he was Santa Ana and the others did not. Soldiers did not wear shirts trimmed with lace, so that surely must be Santa Ana.

He put the man on the horse and led him. When they got near the camp with their prisoner, the Mexican prisoners in the Texas camp began to cry, "Santa Arina [*sic*], Santa Ana." They took him into camp and as soon as they came to General Houston, Santa Ana said, "General Houston, I am General Santa Ana, your prisoner of war." General Houston said "What can I do for you?" He answered "Give me something to eat, for I am hungry." Then General Houston said to my father, "Rodríquez, you and Menchaca cook a fine Mexican dinner for General Santa Ana." There was not much to cook, but they made tortillas of flour and gave him the best they had in camp.

As soon as he had eaten dinner, General Houston asked him, "Why did you put to the sword every man in the Alamo," to which Santa Ana replied, that according to the rules of war when a superior force demanded unconditional surrender of inferior forces, if not obeyed, they forfeited their lives. General Houston told him that such was a barbarous custom and should not be practiced in these days. Then General Houston asked Santa Ana why all of Fannin's men were massacred. Santa Ana said that he had nothing to do with that; that he was not responsible. General [José María] Urrea was in full command at Goliad. General Houston asked Santa Ana then to issue an order commanding General Filisola to retire across the Rio Grande. To this, Santa Ana replied that he was not in command of the Mexican army then, he was a prisoner of war and that General Filisola was the commander and was not bound to obey his orders. General Houston told him to issue the order anyway, and if not obeyed that he, Santa Ana, would not be to blame. He gave the order and General Filisola obeyed and retired. This greatly helped the Texas cause.

General Santa Ana said he wanted to make arrangements for his liberty. General Houston replied, "I have no authority to make such arrangements. We have a Congress and a Provisional Government. We will have to submit that question to them." I omitted to state that Santa Ana, after he had come into the camp and had eaten, inquired if his aid General Almonte was alive and was told that he was alive and he sent for Almonte, who was a good English scholar and who thereafter acted as interpreter. Santa Ana asked for his baggage and it was brought to him. He took out a gold watch and offered it to the soldier who loaned him his horse. General Houston said, "My men cannot take presents." Then they had a long conversation about his liberty, and this conversation between General Houston and General Santa Ana was in my father's presence.

My father said that while Santa Ana was in the camp with Houston, some of the men of his army attempted to create a mutiny and demanded that Santa Ana be executed because of the massacre of Fannin's men and the Alamo. General Houston, being wounded, was lying down at the time and he rose up and made a speech to the men. "If we keep Santa Ana alive," said he, "We have the liberty of Texas in our hands; if we kill him, we will have the contempt and the odium of the entire world and will lose our war. If you kill him, you might as well kill me." They talked it over and finally agreed to drop the matter. My father was a witness to all of this.

A peculiar circumstance of the battle of San Jacinto is that my father's kinsman, Mariano Rodríquez also took part in that battle, but he was on Santa Ana's staff as

Captain and paymaster, and he retired to Mexico with the Mexican army and did not return until after the Mexican War was over in 1849.

The Mexican troops, having departed from Texas altogether, the Texans then organized their government, but a great portion of the army remained in the field, expecting the return of the troops from Mexico. About eight months after the battle of San Jacinto, the company in which my father served was mustered out and he was honorably discharged. While he was still in the army, a brother of my mother's came to Washington and brought us back to San Antonio, and my father after leaving the army returned to San Antonio and went to merchandising.

Two or three days after we got to San Antonio, I went to the Alamo and saw the blood on the walls.

AFTER THE WAR

Colonel [Seguin] was then appointed mayor of San Antonio and had charge of the town as to both military and civil affairs. A great many of the Mexicans who were in sympathy with the Mexican Government had fled to Mexico, and others who had been loyal to the Texas cause, returned and helped to establish the civil government. J. D. McLeod was the first Chief Justice and Jose Antonio Navarro represented Bexar County in the first Congress. My father opened a store next to our residence on Commerce Street.

Then came the Vasquez raid at which time I was at the ranch with my father, near Seguin. General Vasquez made his raid in 1841 but only remained here a short time. There was no fighting and he finally left. I am not familiar with the details of that raid.

GENERAL WOLL'S INVASION

In 1842, a report came into San Antonio that a band of robbers from Mexico was coming to rob San Antonio. The people then got together and organized two companies of citizens. My father belonged to the company with Capt. Menchaca and they had their quarters in the old court house on the corner of Market and Main Plaza. On the corner of Soledad and Main Plaza, an American named Chauncy Johnson had a company of forty men, all Americans, and they composed the divisions to fight against these robbers. As soon as they organized, they sent three Mexicans with an escort to meet this band. They met them and it turned out to be the regular army of Mexico, instead of robbers, and they kept them prisoners.

One morning, just before daybreak, I heard a gun fired, and woke up and I heard a band of music, playing an old air called La Cachucha. It was the dancing tune in those days. It was very fine music. It was a band of fifty musicians. The firing of the gun was the warning to the citizens that the army was here. As this was the regular army of Mexico, Menchaca's company agreed that they could not stand up against a whole army and withdrew to a safe distance. Chauncy Johnson, however, said his company should not disband, but would fight it out. The army then marched into town. The band was in the lead coming into Main Plaza between the Cathedral and what is now Frost's Bank. Then Johnson's men turned loose a volley on the band and killed and wounded fifteen or twenty musicians. This angered General Woll, and he placed a small cannon where the Southern Hotel now stands and fired on

Johnson's men. Johnson then raised a white flag and the Mexicans took them all prisoners and they finally were sent back to Mexico. General Woll had a fine ball given in his honor by the citizens. After the ball, a report came in that Colonel Hays was camped on the Salado preparing to attack Woll. General Woll sent a portion of his men out to the Salado to attack Col. Hays; They fought one day and night but could not dislodge Hays and the next day they retreated towards the Rio Grande. Antonio Perez, the father of the present Antonio Perez now living at San Antonio, who was with General Woll, came at night to our house and told us the army was going to retire into Mexico. While the battle was going on at the Salado, Woll sent a company of cavalry and attacked and killed Dawson's men, who were coming from Seguin to reinforce Hays. They killed and butchered nearly all of them.

After Woll's raid, General Somerville organized a force, and disobeying the orders of General Sam Houston went into Mexico and was defeated at Mier, and all were taken prisoners. Those prisoners were taken into the interior of Mexico, and one of them related to me the whole circumstance. His name was Glascock. He said that they had orders to kill one out of every ten. They filled a pitcher with black and white beans, then the men were formed into line and each man would run his hand into the pitcher and take a bean. Glascock said that when he went up to the pitcher to take his bean out that he was shivering. He ran his hand into the pitcher and got a white bean and was saved. Glascock afterwards started the first English newspaper in San Antonio.

TEXAS AS A STATE

In 1845, the Republic of Texas was annexed to the United States as a state and thus passed away the Republic of Texas.

I was sent to New Orleans in 1842, where I attended the French schools for two years. While there, I heard that Henry Clay was a candidate for President. He was opposed to the Annexation of Texas to the Union, but he was a weak candidate and was defeated and Polk was elected on the democratic platform, which favored annexation. After Polk's election, followed the annexation of Texas as a state. Then came the war with Mexico. The United States troops came, a regiment of cavalry and camped on the Salado. They were here for a time and afterwards went into Mexico. After I returned from New Orleans, I went to work in my father's store. The Mexican War, of course settled the status of this government and it then became the same as any other state of the Union and the people became interested in the politics of the United States, of which the leading issue was slavery. In this particular section of the state, there were not many slaves, because Mexican people as a rule do not believe in slavery.

My family owned some slaves, but we worked them as other servants and treated them kindly. I became interested in local politics in 1854 and was elected alderman. My father had been an alderman also, during the term Colonel Seguin was Mayor of San Antonio. Afterwards I was elected assessor and tax collector and served in these offices for two years. The secession question then came to be a burning issue. General Houston was a candidate for Governor on the Union issue and Runnels was his opponent. General Houston made an eloquent speech at San Pedro Park on the Union issue against secession; he was speaking from a small platform erected by the democrats. In his speech, he alluded to the democratic platform and said that he did not believe in platforms. He was a very fine orator, and during his speech he ridiculed the democratic platform and called out, "Platforms will not stand." Just at that moment the platform upon which he was standing fell, and General Houston went through. He continued his speech, although the people could only see his head and shoulders above the fallen stand, and said, "Ladies and Gentlemen, you see the democratic platform will not stand." He carried Bexar County by a great majority and was elected Governor by 10,000 or more votes. I saw him inaugurated and carried my sister Carolina with me to attend the inaugural ball, and General Sam Houston did us the honor to invite my sister to lead the grand march at the Inaugural ball. He was a steadfast friend of our family and had a great affection for my father.

Shortly after that, the secession convention was called and I attended it as interpreter for Colonel Basilio Benavides, representative from Webb County. Sam Smith and Jose Angel Navarro represented Bexar County. After the secession was declared and established, Houston refused to accept it by taking an oath and he was removed from office. His place was taken by Lieutenant Governor Clark. After Houston was relieved from office he went out on the capitol grounds, and before a large crowd, among whom was about 500 of McCullough's men, delivered a most magnificent address. Among other things he said, "You Southern people stand to-day as traitors to your country and your flag and you will regret the day that you made such a move because the United States is a powerful nation and they will get reinforcement from Europe. You will not be recognized as a nation by the world, and have no standing whatever, and it will not be long before you will be paying five dollars a pound for your coffee." This later came true. "You will put up a good fight and then have to surrender. You have no more right to secede than a county has from a state, you are revolutionists, and as I stand here to-day, although I am ready to risk my life for Texas, I hate to see the Texans lose their lives and property."

In the meantime there were shouts from those who opposed him, and some people would no longer listen to his speech. He retired to his home, but the war went on, and everything he predicted came to pass....

Source: Courtesy of Sons of DeWitt Colony Texas, http://www.tamu.edu/ccbn/dewitt/rodmemoirs.htm.

28. Excerpt from the Memoirs of Antonio Menchaca

Antonio Menchaca (1800–1879), a former Mexican army officer, fought on the Euro-American side in the Texas War of Independence (1836). Menchaca was close to Juan Seguín (1806–1890) and fought in the battle of San Jacinto (1836). His memoirs were published by the Yanaguana Society of San Antonio, Texas, which attempted to preserve the history of San Antonio and South Texas. This excerpt is about the events leading up to the Texas Declaration of Independence. It is important because it gives a glimpse of key players such as James Bowie (1796–1836) from Kentucky, the ambitious slave trader and land speculator who had been active in filibustering since 1819. Bowie permanently entered Texas in 1830 where he was befriended by José Martin de Varamendí (1778–1833), whose daughter Bowie married. Varamendí later became governor of Texas and Coahuila; he was pro-Euro-American. Tensions reached a boiling point with the beginning of the decade when Mexico decreed that Euro-Americans could no longer immigrate to Texas. Recently arrived adventurers like Bowie fanned the flames. In 1832, the Battle of Velasco resulted in deaths; conventions were held in 1832 and 1833. Hostilities did not occur spontaneously.

I was born in 1800. Was baptized in the church of San Fernando de Austria [San Fernando de Bexar] on the 12 Jan. same year; was raised in San F. de A. up to the year 1807....

In 1830, in March, James P. Bowie, of Kentucky, came to San Antonio, in company with Gov. [William H.] Wharton. From here, Bowie went to Saltillo. In the same year, J. M. [Juan Martín] Veramendi was appointed Lt. Gov., and started for Mexico to qualify. There, Bowie and him met and became friends. Veramendi came back with his family and Bowie accompanied him. Bowie and Ursula Veramendi became engaged ... and Bowie, not having what he considered enough to justify him in marrying, asked Veramendi to give him time to go to Kentucky and get funds, and he would then marry his daughter. Veramendi granted the request. Bowie went and returned in the month of March 1831, and married; remained three months here, then left for the interior of Texas to recruit forces for the war [with Mexico]. Returned in 1832, went to look for the S. Saba mines; returned remained here four months; again went to look for mines. While Bowie was on this second trip, news reached here that [José María de] Letona, the Governor of Mexico, had died. Veramendi had to go to Mexico to take charge of government. While Bowie was on the Colorado, he received a command from San Felipe, directed by [Stephen] Austin, that he should repair immediately to S. F. that his services were greatly needed. Upon receipt of this news, Bowie wrote a letter to his wife, telling her where he was going and on what business and that it was hard to tell when they would meet again. Veramendi, having heard of Letonia's [*sic*] death, made ready for his trip to Saltillo, started and arrived there on the 11th of November 1832. As soon as he arrived, he received his com. [commission] as Gov., which he exercised until the 7th of February 1833, when Bowie with seven other Americans arrived there also. On the following day he had an interview with Veramendi, and was introduced to the members of Congress. As soon as his acquaintance with the leading members became such as to warrant it, he told them what his object was. He received the assurances of Marcial Borrego and Jose Maria Uranga that they would aid him his enterprise. He tried, and succeeded in making them change the Congress from Saltillo to Monclova [Coahllila]. Congress having been established at Mexico, he returned to Texas. In the same year, in the month of July, Veramendi sent $10,000 to Musquiz to be sent to N. O. In the month of September, Veramendi's family, as well as Bowie's wife, with $25,000 worth of goods, were taken to Monclova, where they arrived on the 27th of September. On that day the cholera commenced there. The first who died of it being Madame Veramendi; then Madame Bowie, the balance of the family remained there until the 1st of November, when they were brought to San Antonio by A[ntonio] M[enchaca], when they arrived.

The year 1834 passed; also 1835, in which year in July, Col. Nicholas Condelle, with 500 Infantry and 100 Cavalry, arrived here; for it was reported that the Americans were gathered at S. Felipe. With these last troops there were here 1,100 soldiers, 1,000 Cavalry, and 100 Infantry. On the 23 of October, A[ntonio] M[enchaca] received a letter from Bowie in which was enclosed a note addressed to Marcial Borrego and G.M. Uranga. The letter told A[ntonio] M[enchaca] to deliver the note in person, to trust it to no one; and to be as quick about it as possible. He went, while the report here was that the Americans were at Gonzales, delivered the note, and on his return got as far as San Fernando de Rosas, where he was detained and would not be allowed to pass; though his liberty was given him upon his giving bond. Six days after the capitulation of San Antonio, a friend of his, Pedro Rodriguez, furnished him with two men and horses to bring him to San Antonio. He crossed at night at Eagle Crossing, and arrived here on the 20th of December. The companies who had assisted in the siege were still here. As soon as he arrived here, he sought Bowie who, as soon as he saw him, put his arms around his neck, and commenced to cry to think that he had not seen his wife die. He said, "My father, my brother, my companion and all my protection has come. Are you still my companion in arms?" he asked. Antonio answered, "I shall be your companion, Jim Bowie, until I die." "Then come this evening", said Bowie, "to take you to introduce you to [William Barrett] Travis, at the Alamo." That evening he was introduced to Travis, and to Col. Niel. Was well received.

On the 26th December 1835, Dn. Diego Grant left San Antonio, towards Matamoros, with about 500 men ... They here kept up guards and patrols of night. 250 men went from here to keep a lookout on Cos who had gone to Mexico, and returning here on the 5th January, 1836. On the 13 January, 1836, David Crockett presented himself at the old Mexican graveyard, on the west side of the San Pedro Creek, had in company with him fourteen young men who had accompanied him from Tennessee, here as soon as he got there he sent word to Bowie to go and receive him, and conduct him into the City. Bowie ... lodged at Erasmo Seguin's house. Crockett, Bowie, Travis, Niell and all the officers joined together, to establish guards for the safety of the City ... fearing that the Mexicans would return. On the 10 February 1836, A. was invited by officers to a ball given in honor of Crockett ... [A]t the ball, at about 1 o'clock A.M. of the 11th, a courier, sent by Placido Benavides, arrived, from Camargo, with the intelligence that Santa Ana, [*sic*] was starting from the Presidio Rio Grande, with 13,000 troops, 10,000 Infantry and 3,000 Cavalry, with the view of taking San Antonio. The courier arrived at the ball room door inquired for Col. Seguin, and was told that Col. Seguin was not there. Asked if Menchaca was there, and was told that he was. He spoke to him and told him that he had a letter of great importance, which he had brought from P.B. from Camargo, asked partner and came to see letter. Opened letter and read the following: "At this moment I have received a very certain notice, that the commander in chief, Antonio Lopez de Santa Anna, marches for the city of San Antonio to take possession thereof, with 13,000 men." As he was reading letter, Bowie came opposite him ... Travis came up, and Bowie called him to read that letter; but Travis said that at that moment he could not stay to read letters, for he was dancing with the most beautiful lady in San Antonio. Bowie told him that the letter was one of grave importance, and for him to leave his partner. Travis came and brought Crockett with him. Travis and Bowie understood Spanish, Crockett did not. Travis then said, it will take 13,000 men from the Presidio de Rio Grande to this place thirteen or fourteen days to get here; this is the 4th day. Let us dance to-night and to-morrow we will make provisions for our defense. The ball continued until 7 o'clock, A.M. ... Travis invited officers to hold a meeting with a view of consulting as to the best means they should adopt for the security of the place. The council gathered; many resolutions were offered and adopted, after which Bowie and Seguin made a motion to have A[ntonio] M[enchaca] and his family sent away from here, knowing that should Santa Anna come, A[ntonio] and his family would receive no good at his hands. A[ntonio] left here and went to Seguin's ranch, where he stayed six days, preparing for a trip. Started from there and went as far as Marcelino to sleep; then three miles the east side of Cibolo, at an old pond at sun up next morning. Nat Lewis, passed with a wallet on his back, a-foot from San Antonio, and A[ntonio] asked him why he went a-foot and he was answered that he could not find a horse; that Santa Anna had arrived at San Antonio, the day previous with 13,000 men. A[ntonio] asked what the Americans had done. He said they were in the Alamo inside the fortifications. A[ntonio] asked why N[at] did not remain there and he answered that he was not a fighting man, that he was a business man. A[ntonio] then told him to go then about his business. A[ntonio] continued his journey, got to Gonzales, at the house of G. Dewitt, and there met up with Gen. Ed Burleson, with seventy-three men, who had just got there, then, slept. And on the following day, attempted to pass to the other side with families, but was prevented by Burleson, who told him that the families might cross, but not him; that the men were needed in the army. There met up with fourteen Mexicans of San Antonio, and they united and remained there until a company could be formed ... Six days after being there, Col. Seguin, who was sent as courier by Travis, arrived there and presented himself to Gen. Burleson, who, upon receipt of the message, forwarded it to the Convention assembled at Washington, Texas. On the following day, the M. Co. was organized with twenty-two men ... [that included] Capt. Seguin; 1st. Lt. Manuel Flores, and A.M. 2nd. Lieut. On the 4th of March, the news reached that Texas had declared her Independence....

Source: Yanaguana Society, San Antonio, 1937. Courtesy of Wallace L. McKeehan, Sons of DeWitt Colony Texas, http://www.tamu.edu/ccbn/dewitt/menchacamem.htm.

29. Excerpts from José Juan Sánchez Navarro, *A Mexican View of the War in Texas*, 1830s

From a prominent northern Mexican family, José Juan Sánchez-Navarro was an adjutant inspector of the departments of Nuevo León and Tamaulipas during the 1830s. In the *Ayudantía de Inspección de Nuevo León y Tamaulipas*, his almanac, dated April 1831 to November 1839, he included notations in the form of a diary, presented here. Sánchez Navarro chronicled the tensions and major encounters between the Mexican and Texan forces in San Antonio de Béxar. Sánchez Navarro gave an eyewitness account that is among the best primary sources of the Battle of the Alamo. His feeling toward the American colonists is bitter. Much as he despised the "norteamericanos," however, Sánchez could take little comfort in the quality of Mexican leadership, as is shown in his account of his encounter with Antonio López de Santa Anna in Leona Vicario in February 1836. At the same time, in Monclova as the Mexican reinforcements were on their way to San Antonio, Sánchez described the soldiers' wretched conditions. He is consistently critical of many of the superior officers, particularly of Santa Anna, the president and commander-in-chief of the army. With reference to the recapture of the Alamo by the Mexican forces, Sánchez makes extensive comments, as shown at the end of this section. His diary is prefaced by the first passage below and other excerpts follow.

"All has been lost save honor!" I do not remember, nor am I in the mood to remember, what French king said this, perhaps under better circumstances than those in which we are today, the eleventh of December 1835. Béxar, and perhaps Texas has been lost, although the majority of the faithful subjects the Supreme Government had here for its defense cannot be blamed for such a loss. This is my humble opinion; and to prove it, I shall relate the event in so far as it is within my power to do so … [*Ayudantia de Inspección de Nuevo León y Tamaulipas, 1831–1839*, 2 vol-418ff., I:253.]

We were surrounded by some gross, proud, and victorious men. Anyone who knows the character of the North Americans can judge what our situation must have been! [*Ayudantia de Inspección de Nuevo León y Tamaulipas, 1831–1839*, 2 vol-418ff. I:245v.]

The Most Excellent President, to whom I introduced myself and who recognized me—we were classmates in officers' training … has granted the request I made him [to permit me] to return to the Texas campaign … There is much activity by way of preparation for this purpose. There are many troops and [there is] much noise; but I see no indications of good political, military, and administrative systems.

His Excellency himself attends to all matters whether important or most trivial. I am astonished to see that he has personally assumed the authority of major general … of quartermaster, of commissary, of brigadier generals, of colonels, of captains, and even of corporals, purveyors, arrieros, and carreteros.

Would it not be better for His Excellency to rid himself of such troublesome work which will occupy his time, which is more needed for the execution of the high duties of his office, by keeping each individual member of the army in complete exercise of his authority according to the provisions of the general ordinances.…

What will become of the army and of the nation if the Most Excellent President should die? Confusion and more confusion because only His Excellency knows the springs by means of which these masses of men called the army are moved. The members of the army in general have no idea of the significance of the Texas war, and all of them believe that they are merely on a military excursion. If, when questioned, one tells the truth about what one has seen there, one is considered a poor soul. As if the enemy could be conquered merely by despising him.…

Today the Most Excellent President left with his General Staff. He was accompanied by General Cos as far as Santa María. It is said that His Excellency is very economical, even miserly. Those close to him assert that whoever wants to, can make him uncomfortable by asking him for a peso; and they add that he would rather give a colonel's commission than ten pesos. Can all this be true? Even if it is, would it not be better not to mention it? I believe so. But the facts speak for themselves. When we took leave of each other, His Excellency shook my hand and expressed surprise that I was not wearing the insignia of lieutenant colonel, and he told me so. [*Ayudantia de Inspección de Nuevo León y Tamaulipas, 1831–1839*, 2 vol-418ff. II:3-3v.]

It is pitiful and despairing to go looking for provisions and beasts of burden, money in hand when there is plenty of everything in the commissaries, the almacenes, and depots, and to have everyone from the quartermaster general, who is General Woll, and the jefe político to the humblest clerk reply—as if I were a Turk and the supplies I order and for which I offer to pay cash were for the Russians—'We cannot sell that, we cannot let you have it because it is for the army.' Consequently, we are perishing from hunger and misery in the midst of plenty. [*Ayudantia de Inspección de Nuevo León y Tamaulipas, 1831–1839*, 2 vol-418ff. II:4]

When we arrived in this city [Monclova], His Excellency the President had left for Río Grande the day before. He is going to Béxar with inconceivable, rather, astonishing haste. Why is His Excellency going in such haste? Why is he leaving the entire army behind? Does he think that his name alone is sufficient to overthrow the colonists? [II:4-4v.]

On the 21st [of March 1836], Fannin and four hundred twenty one prisoners were shot at la Bahía between six and eight in the morning. Sad day! God grant that there may not be another like it! Would it not be well to save the prisoners for the purpose of using them if we should some day suffer reverses? [II:78v.]

The Most Excellent President and many of those close to him assert that the campaign is ended; but Generals Filisola, Arago—who is dying—Amador, Andrade, and Cos say that it has hardly started. I am of the opinion of the latter gentlemen. It is reported as a fact that we set fire to all the residences that are not burned by the colonists. I have made many efforts to see what there is by way of a plan for the campaign. I believe there is none; or that if there is one, it is in the mind of His Excellency the President. [II:79.]

If it is true, as is asserted, that an army of four thousand men is coming from Mexico to carry on the Texas campaign, why was the Texas army dissolved and withdrawn? Who or what circumstances can give to the generals, the jefes, the officers, and the troops that are coming now for the first time the experience and the practical knowledge of those who have been in Texas previously? Is it possible that we Mexicans must always learn by trial and error? It is indeed dangerous to expose the fate of a nation a second time. [II:93v.]

Long live our country, the Alamo is ours! Today at five in the morning, the assault was made by four columns under the command of General Cos and Colonels Duque, Romero, and Morales. His Excellency the President commanded the reserves. The firing lasted half an hour. Our jefes, officers, and troops, at the same time as if by magic, reached the top of the wall, jumped within, and continued fighting with side arms. By six thirty there was not an enemy left. I saw actions of heroic valor I envied. I was horrified by some cruelties, among others, the death of an old man named Cochran and of a boy about fourteen. The women and children were saved. Travis, the commandant of the Alamo died like a hero; Buy [Bowie], the braggart son-in-law of Beramendi died like a coward. The troops were permitted to pillage. The enemy have suffered a heavy loss: twenty-one field pieces of different caliber, many arms and munitions. Two hundred fifty-seven of their men were killed: I have seen and counted their bodies. But I cannot be glad because we lost eleven officers with nineteen wounded, including the valiant Duque and González; and two hundred forty-seven of our troops were wounded and one hundred ten killed. It can truly be said that with another such victory as this we'll go to the devil.... [II:6v.]

Source: A Mexican View of the War in Texas: Memoirs of a Veteran of the Two Battles of the Alamo, transcribed for the Second Flying Company of Alamo de Parras by Robert Durham, *The Library Chronicle,* vol. IV, no. 2. Courtesy of Sons of DeWitt Colony Texas, http://www.tamu.edu/ccbn/ dewitt/adp/archives/maps/sanchezdoc.html.

30. Excerpt from the Diary Entry of José Enrique de la Peña, 1836

Lt. Col. José Enrique de la Peña (1805–1844), an officer on Gen. Antonio López de Santa Anna's (1794–1876) staff in 1836, gives a first-person eyewitness account of the Battle of the Alamo. He reported the capture and execution of the legendary outdoorsman Davy Crockett. His account debunks the traditional story that Crockett, the former congressman from Tennessee, fought to the end, wielding his long-rifle, "Betsy."

Shortly before Santa Anna's speech, an unpleasant episode had taken place, which, since it occurred after the end of the skirmish, was looked upon as base murder and which contributed greatly to the coolness that was noted. Some seven men had survived the general carnage and, under the protection of General Castrillón, they were brought before Santa Anna. Among them was one of great stature, well proportioned, with regular features, in whose face there was the imprint of adversity, but in whom one also noticed a degree of resignation and nobility that did him honor. He was the naturalist David Crockett, well known in North America for his unusual adventures, who had undertaken to explore the country and who, finding himself in Béxar at the very moment of surprise, had taken refuge in the Alamo, fearing that his status as a foreigner might not be respected. Santa Anna answered Castrillón's intervention on Crockett's behalf with a gesture of indignation and, addressing himself to the sappers, the troops closest to him, ordered his execution. The commanders and officers were outraged at this action and did not support the order, hoping that once the fury of the moment had blown over these men would be spared, but several officers who were around the president and who, perhaps, had not been present during the moment of danger, became noteworthy by an infamous deed, surpassing the soldiers in cruelty. They thrust themselves forward, in order to flatter the commander, and with swords in hand, fell upon these unfortunate, defenseless men just as a tiger leaps upon his prey. Though tortured before they were killed, these unfortunates died without complaining and without humiliating themselves before their torturers.

Source: José Enrique de la Peña, *With Santa Anna in Texas: A Personal Narrative of the Revolution.* Carmen Perry, trans. (College Station: Texas A & M University, 1997), p. 53.

31. Excerpt from the Treaty of Velasco, May 14, 1836

The Treaty of Velasco was negotiated between officials of the interim government of the Republic of Texas and General Antonio López de Santa Anna (1794–1876) about three weeks after his capture on April 22, 1836. Santa Anna did not have the authority to negotiate the treaty that gave Texas to the United States, since all treaties have to be ratified by Congress. Hence, the status of Texas was tenuous since legally it was still part of Mexico. Tensions between slave and free states in the United States stood in the way of U.S. annexation, although the latter kept troops poised at the border. This excerpt includes a discussion of the prisoners of war taken during the Texas Revolt (1836) and relations between the Mexican and Euro-American Texas armies.

Articles of an agreement entered into, between His Excellency David G. Burnet, President of the Republic of Texas, of the one part, and His Excellency General Antonio Lopez de Santa Anna, President General in Chief of the Mexican Army, of the other part.

ARTICLE 1ST

General Antonio Lopez de Santa Anna agrees that he will not take up arms, nor will he exercise his influence to cause them to be taken up against the people of Texas, during the present War of Independence.

ARTICLE 2ND

All hostilities between the Mexican and Texian troops will cease immediately both on land and water.

ARTICLE 3RD

The Mexican troops will evacuate the Territory of Texas, passing to the other side of the Rio Grande del Norte.

ARTICLE 6TH

The troops of both armies will refrain from coming into contact with each other, and to this end the Commander of the Army of Texas will be careful not to approach within a shorter distance of the Mexican Army than five leagues.

ARTICLE 7TH

The Mexican Army shall not make any other delay on its march, than that which is necessary to take up their hospitals, baggage—and to cross the rivers—any delay not necessary to these purposes to be considered an infraction of this agreement.

ARTICLE 8TH

By express to be immediately dispatched, this agreement shall be sent to General Filisola and to General T. J. Rusk, commander of the Texian Army, in order that they may be apprised of its stipulations, and to this and they will exchange engagements to comply with the same.

ARTICLE 9TH

That all Texian prisoners now in possession of the Mexican Army or its authorities be forthwith released and furnished with free passports to return to their homes, in consideration of which a corresponding number of Mexican prisoners, rank and file, now in possession of the Government of Texas shall be immediately released. The remainder of the Mexican prisoners that continue in possession of the Government of Texas to be treated with due humanity—any extraordinary comforts that may be furnished them to be at the charge of the Government of Mexico.

ARTICLE 10TH

General Antonio Lopez de Santa Anna will be sent to Veracruz as soon as it shall be deemed proper.

The contracting parties sign this Instrument for the above mentioned purposes, by duplicate, at the Port of Velasco this fourteenth day of May 1836.

David G Burnet
Ant. Lopez de Santa Anna
Jas Collinsworth, Sec of State
Bailey Hardeman, Secy of Treasury
T W Grayson, Atty General
Ant. Lopez de Santa Anna
David G Burnet
Jas Collinsworth, Secretary of State
Bailey Hardeman, Secy of Treasury
T W Grayson, Atty General

Source: Courtesy of the Yale University Law School Library. The Avalon Project, http://www.yale.edu/lawweb/avalon/velasco.htm.

32. Letter from Vicente Córdova to Manuel Flores, July 19, 1838

In 1838, a plot was discovered against the Republic of Texas. Mexicans had been the largest portion of the population in northeast Texas before 1836. However, after the Treaty of Velasco (1836) the Euro-American population grew, and these settlers brought with them their notions of race. Aside from the Mexicans, the Indians resented the intrusion, and it was rumored that the Cherokees had made a treaty with Mexico to war on Texas. Enter Vicente Córdova (1798–1842), a prominent Mexican leader from the Nacogdoches region in Texas who had not joined the Texas Revolt. He was the reputed leader of the conspiracy. In 1838, hysteria mounted among the Euro-Americans as Córdova, with more than 100 men, revolted. In response, Lone Star Gov. Sam Houston issued a proclamation prohibiting unlawful assemblies and the carrying of arms. He further ordered all assembled without authorization to dissolve. The Córdova Revolt was put down, but Córdova escaped and made his way into Mexico. Meanwhile, the Nacogdoches District Court indicted 33 Mexicans for treason. José Antonio Menchaca (1995–?), who was second in command to Córdova, was found guilty of treason and sentenced to hang. Then Governor of Texas Mirabeau Buonaparte (1798–1859) pardoned José Antonio Menchaca (1795–?) only four days before his scheduled execution. Authorities used this incident as a pretext for the removal of the Cherokees from Texas. The document speaks to the fact that Córdova had a commission from the Mexican Army to recruit among the Indians for a revolt.

To Manuel Flores
July 19, 1838
Sir:

I hold a commission from General Vicente Filisola to raise the Indians as auxiliaries to the National Army and I have already entered upon my duties by inviting a meeting of the neighboring tribes, and being informed that you are appointed for the same purpose I would be glad to know what preliminary arrangements you have made towards the accomplishment of the objects contemplated; and I hope you will make every effort to approach with such force as you may have at your command as far as you may judge proper, and that you will make all effort to hold with me a verbal communication in order that we may have in our respective stations an understanding, and that you will bring the pipe which I understand you are in possession in order that the Indian Chiefs may smoke it of the Cherokee and other tribes, who have promised me to unite as soon as possible for action, and who have also agreed that in case our plans should be discovered. In the mean time, they then will commence operations with the force we may have at command, and it is highly desirable that you should approach to give us in such case a helping hand. We have heard here that the troops have commenced operations in La Bahia but do not know whither [*sic*] it is true. I desire we should treat with each other in full confidence which is necessary to the success of our commission. I will say no more at present than that you may act in full confidence of your friend that S.M.B. Vicente Córdova.

Source: Vicente Córdova to Manuel Flores, July 19, 1838, Texas Indian Papers, vol. 1, no. 2. Archives and Manuscripts, Texas State Library and Archives Commission, www.tsl.state.tx.us/exhibits/indian/early/cordova-1838.html.

33. Excerpts from John L. O'Sullivan's Column on "Manifest Destiny," 1839

All wars of aggression have an ideology to justify them. This is especially true of the United States, which is a Christian nation, and does not intentionally steal without rationalizing its behavior. The rationale for the Mexican-American War in 1846 was "Manifest Destiny," a religious doctrine with roots in Calvinist and Puritan ideas. It is important because it influences U.S. foreign policy to this day. According to the doctrine, God determines salvation, and He predestined the European race for salvation. The United States was the chosen land and Americans God's chosen people. Many Euro-Americans believed that God chose the United States to be the custodian of democracy and hence the nation had a mission—that is, that God had predestined Western Europeans to spread His principles. Mexico, on the other hand, was a Catholic country. John L. O'Sullivan (1813–1885), a columnist and editor for the influential *United States Magazine and Democratic Review,* coined the term "Manifest Destiny." He said that it was the destiny of the United States to annex Texas and the Oregon territory. The excerpt lays out this ideology in passionate detail.

The American people having derived their origin from many other nations, and the Declaration of National Independence being entirely based on the great principle of human equality, these facts demonstrate at once our disconnected position as regards any other nation; that we have, in reality, but little connection with the past history of any of them, and still less with all antiquity, its glories, or its crimes. On the contrary, our national birth was the beginning of a new history, the formation and progress of an untried political system, which separates us from the past and connects us with the future only; and so far as regards the entire development of the natural rights of man, in moral, political, and national life, we may confidently assume that our country is destined to be the great nation of futurity.

It is so destined, because the principle upon which a nation is organized fixes its destiny, and that of equality is perfect, is universal. It presides in all the operations of the physical world, and it is also the conscious law of the soul—the self-evident dictates of morality, which accurately defines the duty of man to man, and consequently man's rights as man. Besides, the truthful annals of any nation furnish abundant evidence, that its happiness, its greatness, its duration, were always proportionate to the democratic equality in its system of government....

What friend of human liberty, civilization, and refinement, can cast his view over the past history of the monarchies and aristocracies of antiquity, and not deplore that they ever existed? What philanthropist can contemplate the oppressions, the cruelties, and injustice inflicted by them on the masses of mankind, and not turn with moral horror from the retrospect?

America is destined for better deeds. It is our unparalleled glory that we have no reminiscences of battlefields, but in defence of humanity, of the oppressed of all nations, of the rights of conscience, the rights of personal enfranchisement. Our annals describe no scenes of horrid carnage, where men were led on by hundreds of thousands to slay one another, dupes and victims to emperors, kings, nobles, demons in the human form called heroes. We have had patriots to defend our homes, our liberties, but no aspirants to crowns or thrones; nor have the American people ever suffered themselves to be led on by wicked ambition to depopulate the land, to spread desolation far and wide, that a human being might be placed on a seat of supremacy.

We have no interest in the scenes of antiquity, only as lessons of avoidance of nearly all their examples. The expansive future is our arena, and for our history. We are entering on its untrodden space, with the truths of God in our minds, beneficent objects in our hearts, and with a clear conscience unsullied by the past. We are the nation of human progress, and who will, what can, set limits to our onward march? Providence is with us, and no earthly power can. We point to the everlasting truth on the first page of our national declaration, and we proclaim to the millions of other lands that "the gates of hell"—the powers of aristocracy and monarchy— "shall not prevail against it."

The far-reaching, the boundless future will be the era of American greatness. In its magnificent domain of space and time, the nation of many nations is destined to manifest to mankind the excellence of divine principles; to establish on earth the noblest temple ever dedicated to the worship of the Most High—the Sacred and the True. Its floor shall be a hemisphere—its roof the firmament of the star-studded heavens, and its congregation [a] Union of many Republics, comprising hundreds of happy millions, calling, owning no man master, but governed by God's natural and moral law of equality, the law of brotherhood—of "peace and good will amongst men."...

Yes, we are the nation of progress, of individual freedom, of universal enfranchisement. Equality of rights is the cynosure of our union of States, the grand exemplar of the correlative equality of individuals; and while truth sheds its effulgence, we cannot retrograde, without dissolving the one and subverting the other. We must onward to the fulfilment of our mission—to the entire development of the principle of our organization—freedom of conscience, freedom of person, freedom of trade and business pursuits, universality of freedom and equality. This is our high destiny, and in nature's eternal, inevitable decree of cause and effect we must accomplish it. All this will be our future history, to establish on earth the moral dignity and salvation of man—the immutable truth and beneficence of God. For this blessed mission to the nations of the world, which are shut out from the life-giving light of truth, has America been chosen; and her high example shall smite unto death the tyranny of kings, hierarchs, and oligarchs, and carry the glad tidings of peace and good will where myriads now endure an existence scarcely more enviable than that of beasts of the field. Who, then, can doubt that our country is destined to be *the great nation of futurity?*

Source: "The Great Nation of Futurity," *The United States Democratic Review*, vol. 6, no. 23, (Nov. 1839): 426–430. Courtesy of Cornell University Library, http://cdl.library.cornell.edu/cgi-bin/moa/sgml/moa-idx?notisid=AGD1642-0006-46.

34. Excerpt from Juan Seguín's Address to the Texas Senate, February 1840

Soon after so-called Texas independence in 1836, disillusionment set in among Mexicans in Texas, such as Juan Seguín (1806–1880), a leader of the Mexican faction and close friend of Stephen Austin (1793–1836), the deceased leader of the Euro-American colonists. Seguín, and many Mexican elites, believed that they would be treated as equals. However, many Euro-American newcomers considered all Mexicans *greasers*, a pejorative term for Mexicans. Some were driven off their land and threatened physically. Seguín was well respected among the Texas Mexican population, also known as Tejanos. Because of the growing antagonism toward Mexicans, Seguín left Texas and fought on the Mexican side during the Mexican-American War (1846–1848). After the war, he returned to Texas. The following address to the Texas Senate was written in 1840 before he left Texas, and it advocates the printing of laws in Spanish.

I wish, sir, to know upon what data the Second Auditor founded his estimate of the cost of translating and printing the Laws to be enacted by the present Congress, to the amount of $15,000. I wish to know, Mr. President, what the cost of translating the laws, enacted by the former Legislative bodies of Texas is, laws which in virtue of the existing laws upon that subject, ought to have been translated, and printed; also, what laws have been translated, and where do they exist? My constituents have, as yet, not seen a single law translated and printed; neither do we know when we shall receive them: Mr. President, the dearest rights of my constituents as Mexico-Texians are guaranteed by the Constitution and the Laws of the Republic of Texas; and at the formation of the social compact between the Mexicans and the Texians, they had rights guaranteed to them; they also contracted certain legal obligations—of all of which they are ignorant, and in consequence of their ignorance of the language in which the Laws and the Constitution of the land are written. The Mexico-Texians were among the first who sacrificed their all in our glorious Revolution, and the disasters of war weighed heavy upon them, to achieve those blessings which, it appears, are destined to be the last to enjoy, and as a representative from Bexar, I never shall cease to raise my voice in effecting the object. But, in order not to detain this honorable body, at this time any longer, I will conclude these cursory remarks, leaving my detailed observations upon the subject to a more proper occasion.

Texas State Senator, Bexar County: Honorable Juan N. Seguin

Source: The Seguin Family Historical Society, "The Original and Official Seguin Family Organization and Web Site," http://www.seguinfamilyhistory.com/index.html#address.

35. Letter from Texas President Mirabeau B. Lamar to the People of Santa Fé, April 14, 1840

After the 1836 Treaty of Velasco, the status of Texas was uncertain, and although most Euro-Americans and Mexicans knew it was a matter of time before Texas would be annexed by the United States, there was some sentiment in favor of maintaining an independent Lone Star Republic. Within Texas there was an interest in extending the border north and west to the Rio Grande. Meanwhile, there were frequent border clashes. Texas President Mirabeau B. Lamar wanted Texas to acquire control of the Santa Fé trade. On June 19, 1841, a party called the Santa Fé Pioneers set out to "liberate" New Mexico. New Mexico's Gov. Manuel Armijo misrepresented their numbers and fooled the Texans into surrendering without the firing of a single shot. Among those involved was José Antonio (1795–1871), a signer of the Texas Declaration of Independence (1836) who was captured. The prisoners were marched to Mexico City and later given clemency, all except Navarro, who spent 14 months in San Juan de Ulúa prison. This letter from President Lamar to the people of Santa Fé attempted to persuade New Mexico's residents to join Texas.

Republic of Texas Executive Department
Austin April 14, 1840
To the Citizens of Santa Fé, Friends, and Compatriots,
You have doubtless heard of the glorious Revolution by which the late Province of Texas has been emancipated from the thralldom of Mexican domination. That revolution was forced upon us by circumstances too imperative to be resisted. The Anglo American population of Texas had left the comforts and the enlightened liberty of their own country, and had immigrated to this wilderness, under the most solemn guarantees of the Constitution of 1824. We had witnessed many disastrous civil commotions in the Government of Mexico, and greatly deplored the want of harmony and the frequent convulsions which distracted our adopted country. But we still entertained an illusive hope that a dear-bought experience—the lessons of many calamities—would exert harmonizing influence, and teach the authorities of Mexico that frequent political chances and domestic discords were destructive of the prosperity and character of a people, that Union and Stability were necessary to strength; and peace and harmony to happiness.

These hopes, so long and patiently cherished, were finally dissolved forever when the Federal Constitution under which we had migrated to the Country and identified our destiny with hers, was forcibly abrogated, and a military despotism reared in its stead. Texas then resolved to be free—to endure no longer the vicissitudes of a fickle and corrupt influence which controlled the powers of Mexico, subverting, all hopes of her greatness, and all our native aspirations for tranquility at home and national respectability abroad. Impelled by these high considerations which a benignant Providence has sanctioned by conferring in unexampled prosperity upon us, we have asserted and achieved our Independence, and have entered the great family of nations as a free and sovereign people. As such we have been formally recognized by the illustrious Governments of the United States, and by the ancient Monarchy of France, and other powers of Europe are ready to extend the right hand of Fellowship. Our national resources are in a rapid progress of development; our population increasing by numerous accessions from Europe and the United States, and our commerce extending with a power and celerity seldom equalled in the history of nations.

Under these auspicious circumstances we tender to you a full participation in all our blessings. The great River of the North, which you inhabit, is the natural and convenient boundary of our territory, and we shall take great pleasure in hailing you as fellow citizens, members of our young Republic, and co-aspirants with us for all the glory of establishing, a new happy and free nation. Our Constitution is liberal as a rational and enlightened regard to human infirmities will safely permit. It confers equal politic privileges on all; tolerates all religions without distinction, and guarantees an even and impartial administration of the laws. This communication, I trust, will be received by you and by your public authorities, in the same spirit of kindness and sincerity in which it is dictated. And if nothing shall intervene to vary my present intention, I shall despatch in time for them to arrive in your section of the Country about the month of September proximo, one, or more Commissioners, gentlemen of worth and confidence, to explain more minutely the condition of our country; of the sea-board and the cor[r]elative interests which so emphatically recommend and ought perpetually to cement the perfect union and identity of Santa Fé and Texas. The Commissioners will be accompanied by a military escort for the purpose of repelling any hostile Indians that may infest the passage, and with the further view of ascertaining and opening a safe and convenient route of communication between the two sections of Country which being strongly assimilated in interests, we hope to see united in friendships and consolidated under a common Government. Until the arrival of these Commissioners, I have empowered some of your own citizens, Capt W. G. Dryden, Mr. W. H. Workman, and Mr. Rowland (to who[m] the views and feelings of this Government have been communicated) [to] confer with you upon the subject matter of this communication.

Mirabeau B Lamar

Source: Courtesy of Sons of DeWitt Colony Texas, http://www.tamu.edu/ccbn/dewitt/santafeexped.htm.

36. Excerpts from Juan Nepomuceno Seguín, *Personal Memoirs of Juan N. Seguín*

In this document, Juan Seguín, a leader of the Mexicans within the faction that supported the Euro-Americans, explains why he left Texas in the 1840s. Following independence, a flood of southerners came into the state, many of whom brought with them biases toward Catholics and people with darker skin. They resented landowners such as Seguín, who felt entitled because of their social status and contributions to the success of the war with Mexico. The tensions and threats to his life forced Seguín into exile. This explains his contributions to Texans and the reasons for his exile.

The tokens of esteem, arid evidences of trust and confidence, repeatedly bestowed upon me by the Supreme Magistrate, General Rusk, and other dignitaries of the

Republic, could not fail to arouse against me much invidious and malignant feeling. The jealousy evinced against me by several officers of the companies recently arrived at San Antonio from the United States, soon spread amongst the American straggling adventurers, who were already beginning to work their dark intrigues against the native families, whose only crime was that they owned large tracts of land and desirable property.

John W. Smith, a bitter enemy of several of the richest families of San Antonio, by whom he had been covered with favors, joined the conspiracy which was organized to ruin me.

I will also point out the origin of another enmity which on several occasions, endangered my life. In those evil days, San Antonio was swarming with adventurers from every quarter of the globe. Many a noble heart grasped the sword in the defence of the liberty of Texas, cheerfully pouring out their blood for our cause, and to them everlasting public gratitude is due; but there were also many bad men, fugitives from their country, who found in this land an open field for their criminal designs.

San Antonio claimed then, as it claims now, to be the first city of Texas; it was also the receptacle of the scum of society. My political and social situation brought me into continual contact with that class of people. At every hour of the day and night, my countrymen ran to me for protection against the assaults or exactions of those adventurers. Sometimes, by persuasion, I prevailed on them to desist; some times, also, force had to be resorted to. How could I have done other wise? Were, not the victims my own countrymen, friends and associates? Could I leave them defenceless, exposed to the assaults of foreigners, who, on the pretext that they were Mexicans, treated them worse than brutes[?] Sound reason and the dictates of humanity would have precluded a different conduct on my part....

1842. After the retreat of the Mexican army under Santa Anna, until [the] Vasquez invasion in 1842, the war between Texas and Mexico ceased to be carried on actively. Although open commercial intercourse did not exist, it was carried on by smuggling, at which the Mexican authorities used to wink, provided it was not carried on too openly, so as to oblige them to notice it, or so extensively as to arouse their avarice.

In the beginning of this year, I was elected Mayor of San Antonio. Two years previously, a gunsmith named Goodman had taken possession of certain houses situated on the Military Plaza, which were the property of the city. He used to shoe the horses of the volunteers who passed through San Antonio, and thus accumulated a debt against the Republic, for the payment of which he applied to the President to give him possession of the buildings referred to, which had always been known as city property.

The board of Aldermen passed a resolution to the effect that Goodman should be compelled to leave the premises; Goodman resisted, alleging that the houses had been given to him by the President, in payment for public services. The Board could not, of course, acknowledge in the President any power to dispose of the city property, and consequently directed me to carry the resolution into effect. My compliance with the instructions of the Board caused Goodman to become my most bitter and inveterate enemy in the city.

The term for the mortgage that Messrs. Ogden and Howard held on my property had run out. In order to raise money and comply with my engagements, I determined to go to Mexico for a drove of sheep. But fearful that this new trip would prove as fatal as the one already alluded to, I wrote to General Vasquez, who was then in command of the Mexican frontier, requesting him to give me a pass. The tenor of Vasquez' answer caused me to apprehend that an expedition was preparing against Texas, for the following month of March.

I called a session of the Board of Aldermen, (of which the Hon. S. A. Maverick was a member,) and laid before them the communication of General Vasquez, stating that according to my construction of the letter we might soon [see] the approach of the Mexicans.

A few days afterwards, Don Jose Maria Garcia of Laredo came to San Antonio; his report was so circumstantial as to preclude all possible doubts as to the near approach of Vasquez to San Antonio. Notice was immediately sent to the Government of the impending danger. In the various meetings held to devise means of defence, I expressed my candid opinion as to the impossibility of defending San Antonio. I observed that for myself; I was going to the town of Seguin, and advised every one to do the same.

On leaving the city, I passed through a street where some men were making breastworks; I stated to them that I was going to my ranch, and thence to Seguin, in case the Mexican forces should take possession of San Antonio.

From the Nueces river, Vasquez forwarded a proclamation by Arista to the inhabitants of Texas. I received at my ranch, a bundle of those proclamations, which I transmitted at once to the Corporation of San Antonio.

As soon as Vasquez entered the city, those who had determined upon defending the place, withdrew to Seguin. Amongst them were Dunn and Chevallie, who had succeeded in escaping from the hands of the Mexicans, into which they had fallen while on a reconnoitering expedition on the Medina. The latter told me that Vasquez and his officers stated that I was in favor of the Mexicans; and Chevallie further added that, one day as he was talking with Vasquez, a man named Sanchez, came within sight, whereupon the General observed: "You see that man! Well, Colonel Seguin sent him to me, when he was at Rio Grande. Seguin is with us." He then drew a letter from his pocket, stating that it was from me. Chevallie asked to be allowed to see it, as he knew my handwriting, but the General refused and cut short the interview.

On my return to San Antonio, several persons told me that the Mexican officers had declared that I was in their favor. This rumor, and some threats uttered against me by Goodman, left me but little doubt that my enemies would try to ruin me.

Some of the citizens of San Antonio had taken up arms in favor of the enemy. Judge Hemphill advised me to have them arrested and tried, but as I started out with the party who went in pursuit of the Mexicans, I could not follow his advice.

Having observed that Vasquez gained ground on us, we fell back on the Nueces River. When we came back to San Antonio, reports were widely spreading about my pretended treason. Captain Manuel Flores, Lieutenant Ambrosio Rodriguez, Matias Curbier, and five or six other Mexicans, dismounted with me to find out the origin of the imposture. I went out with several friends leaving Curbier in my house. I had reached the Main Plaza, when several persons came running to inform me that some Americans were murdering Curbier. We ran back to the house, where we found poor Curbier covered with blood. On being asked who assaulted him, he answered that the gunsmith, Goodman, in company with several Americans, had struck him with a rifle. A few minutes afterwards, Goodman returned to my house, with about thirty volunteers, but, observing that we were prepared to meet them, they did not attempt to attack us. We went out of the house and then to Mr. Guilbeau's, who offered me his protection. He went out into the street, pistol in hand, and succeeded in dispersing the mob, which had formed in front of my house. Mr. John Twohig offered me a shelter for that night; on the next morning, I went under disguise to Mr. Van Ness' house; Twohig, who recognised me in the street, warned me to "open my eyes." I remained one day at Mr. Van Ness'; next day General Burleson arrived at San Antonio, commanding a respectable force of volunteers. I presented myself to him, asking for a Court of Inquiry; he answered that there were no grounds for such proceedings. In the evening I went to the camp, and jointly with Colonel Patton, received a commission to forage for provisions in the lower ranchos. I complied with this trust.

I remained, hiding from rancho to rancho, for over fifteen days. Every party of volunteers en route to San Antonio declared, "they wanted to kill Seguin." I could no longer go from farm to farm, and determined to go to my own farm and raise fortifications, &c.

Several of my relatives and friends joined me. Hardly a day elapsed without receiving notice that a party was preparing to attack me; we were constantly kept under arms. Several parties came in sight, but, probably seeing that we were prepared to receive them, refrained from attacking. On the 30th of April, a friend from San Antonio sent me word that Captain Scott, and his company, were coming down by the river, burning the ranchos on their way. The inhabitants of the lower ranchos called on us for aid against Scott. With those in my house, and others to the number of about 100, I started to lend them aid. I proceeded, observing the movements of Scott, from the function of the Medina to Pajaritos. At that place we dispersed and I returned to my wretched life. In those days I could not go to San Antonio without peril of my life.

Matters being in this state, I saw that it was necessary to take some step which would place me in security, and save my family from constant wretchedness. I had to leave Texas, abandon all, for which I had fought and spent my fortune, to become a wanderer. The ingratitude of those who had assumed to themselves the right of convicting me; their credulity in declaring me a traitor on mere rumors when I had to plead in my favor the loyal patriotism with which I had always served Texas, wounded me deeply.

But, before leaving my country, perhaps forever, I determined to consult with all those interested in my welfare. I held a family council. All were in favor of my removing for some time to the interior of Texas. But, to accomplish this, there were some unavoidable obstacles. I could not take one step from my ranch towards the Brazos without being exposed to the rifle of the first person who might meet me, for, through the whole country, credit had been given to the rumors against me. To emigrate with my family was impossible, as I was a ruined man from the time of the invasion of Santa Anna and our flight to Nacogdoches, furthermore, the country of the Brazos was unhealthier than that of Nacogdoches, and what might we not expect to suffer from disease in a new country and without friends or means[?]

Seeing that all these plans were impracticable, I resolved to seek a refuge amongst my enemies, braving all dangers. But before taking this step, I sent in my resignation to the Corporation of San Antonio, as Mayor of the city, stating to them that, unable any longer to suffer the persecutions of some ungrateful Americans who strove to murder me, I had determined to free my family and friends from their continual misery on my account, and go and live peaceably in Mexico. That for these reasons I resigned my office, with all my privileges and honors as a Texan.

I left Bexar without any engagements towards Texas, my services paid by persecutions, exiled and deprived of my privileges as a Texan citizen, I was in this country a being out of the pale of society, and when she could not protect the rights of her citizens, they seek protection elsewhere. I had been tried by a rabble, condemned without a hearing, and consequently was at liberty to provide for my own safety....

REMARKS

After the expeditions of General Woll, I did not return to Texas till the treaty of Guadalupe Hidalgo. During my absence nothing appeared that could stamp me as a traitor. My enemies had accomplished their object; they had killed me politically in Texas, and the less they spoke of me, the less risk they incurred of being exposed in the infamous means they had used to accomplish my ruin.... The rumor that I was a traitor was seized with avidity by my enemies in San Antonio. Some envied my position, as held by a *Mexican*; others found in me an obstacle to the accomplishment of their villainous plans. The number of land suits which still encumbers the docket of Bexar County would indicate the nature of plans, and anyone, who has listened to the evidence elicited in cases of this description will readily discover the base means adopted to deprive rightful owners of their property....

I have finished my memoirs; I neither have the capacity nor the desire to adorn my acts with literary phrases. I have attempted a short and clear narrative of my public life, in relation to Texas. I give it publicity, without omit[t]ing or suppressing anything that I thought of the least interest, and confidently I submit to the public verdict.

Several of those who witnessed the facts which I have related are still alive and amongst us; they can state whether I have in any way falsified the record.

Source: Juan Nepomuceno Seguín, *Personal Memoirs of Juan N. Seguín* (San Antonio, TX: Ledger Bok and Job Office, 1858), pp. 18–27, 29–32.

PART III
The Mexican-American War

The war with Mexico pushed the borders further south crossing people, rivers, and other resources. The admission of Texas on March 1, 1845, was a provocation that made war inevitable. Even if Mexico would have accepted the loss of Texas, there was the question of the border. Mexico claimed the Nueces River (Rio Grande) that was 150 miles north of the Rio Bravo as the Mexican. The United States claimed the Rio Grande as the boundary using the Treaty of Velasco of 1836 as its authority. The only problem was that Mexico had never signed nor approved the boundary. On the basis of this fiction, the United States pushed for the war that cost Mexico more than 500,000 square miles of territory, over 25,000 dead, and valuable rivers and resources. A strong "all Mexico" movement energized a feeling of American exceptionalism and entitlement over all of Latin America. The Treaty of Guadalupe Hidalgo of 1848 ended the war but not the fallout of the crossing of borders.

37. Excerpts from the Treaty of Annexation between the United States and the Republic of Texas, April 12, 1844

The Treaty of the Annexation of Texas, negotiated in 1844, was not approved by Congress until February 28, 1845. Most Euro-Americans in Texas favored annexation to the United States, although a substantial number wanted to remain independent. Yet a majority of Texans were Southerners by birth and they wanted unification with the United States. They also felt threatened by British insistence that they emancipate their slaves. These excerpts are from the Treaty of Annexation in which the United States recognized Mexican and Texan land grants and agreed to pay its debts.

... ARTICLE II

The citizens of Texas shall be incorporated into the Union of the United States, maintained and protected in the free enjoyment of their liberty and property and admitted, as soon as may be consistent with the principles of the federal constitution, to the enjoyment of all the rights, privileges and immunities of citizens of the United States.

ARTICLE III

All titles and claims to real estate, which are valid under the laws of Texas, shall be held to be so by the United States; and measures shall be adopted for the speedy adjudication of all unsettled claims to land, and patents shall be granted to those found to be valid.

ARTICLE IV

The public lands hereby ceded shall be subject to the laws regulating the public lands in the other Territories of the United States, as far as they may be applicable; subject, however, to such alterations and changes as Congress may from time to time think proper to make. It is understood between the parties that if, in consequence of the mode in which lands have been surveyed in Texas, or from previous grants or locations, the sixteenth section cannot be applied to the purpose of education, Congress shall make equal provision by grant of land elsewhere. And it is also further understood, that, hereafter, the books, papers and documents of the General Land Office of Texas shall be deposited and kept at such place in Texas as the Congress of the United States shall direct.

ARTICLE V

The United States assume and agree to pay the public debts and liabilities of Texas, however created, for which the faith or credit of her government may be bound at the time of the exchange of the ratifications of this treaty; which debts and liabilities are estimated not to exceed, in the whole, ten millions of dollars, to be ascertained and paid in the manner hereinafter stated.

Done at Washington, the twelfth day of April, eighteen hundred and forty-four.

J. C. Calhoun, Isaac Van Zandt and J. Pinckney Henderson

Source: "The Treaty of Annexation—Texas." Courtesy of The Avalon Project, Yale University Law School, http://www.yale.edu/lawweb/avalon/texan05.htm.

38. José Joaquín de Herrera, "A Proclamation Denouncing the United States' Intention to Annex Texas," June 4, 1845

José Joaquín de Herrera (1792–1854) was president of Mexico three times (1844, 1844–1845, 1848–1851). A general in the Mexican Army, de Herrera served during the Mexican-American War (1846–1848). After the war, de Herrera reluctantly assumed the presidency after a congressional commission implored him to accept. Mexico City was still in the hands of the United States, and he was in office from 1848 until January 1851. The following proclamation was in response to U.S. hostilities toward Mexico over the annexation of Texas.

PROCLAMATION

The minister of foreign affairs has communicated to me the following decree: José Joaquin de Herrera, general of division and president and interim of the Mexican Republic, to the citizens thereof.

Be it known: That the general congress has decreed, and the executive sanctioned, the following:

The national congress of the Mexican Republic, considering:

That the congress of the United States of the North has, by a decree, which its executive sanctioned, resolved to incorporate the territory of Texas with the American union;

That this manner of appropriating to itself territories upon which other nations have rights, introduces a monstrous novelty, endangering the peace of the world, and violating the sovereignty of nations;

That this usurpation, now consummated to the prejudice of Mexico, has been in insidious preparation for a long time; at the same time that the most cordial friendship was proclaimed, and that on the part of this republic, the existing treaties between it and those states were respected scrupulously and legally;

That the said annexation of Texas to the U[nited] States tramples on the conservative principles of society, attacks all the rights that Mexico has to that territory, is an insult to her dignity as a sovereign nation, and threatens her independence and political existence;

That the law of the United States, in reference to the annexation of Texas to the United States, does in nowise destroy the rights that Mexico has, and will enforce, upon that department;

That the United States, having trampled on the principles which served as a basis to the treaties of friendship, commerce and navigation, and more especially to those of boundaries fixed with precision, even previous to 1832, they are considered as inviolate by that nation.

And, finally, that the unjust spoliation of which they wish to make the Mexican nation the victim, gives her the clear right to use all her resources and power to resist, to the last moment, said annexation;

IT IS DECREED

1st. The Mexican nation calls upon all her children to the defense of her national independence, threatened by the usurpation of Texas, which is intended to be realized by the decree of annexation passed by the congress, and sanctioned by the president, of the United States of the north.

2d. In consequence, the government will call to arms all the forces of the army, according to the authority granted it by the existing laws; and for the preservation of public order, for the support of her institutions, and in case of necessity, to serve as the reserve to the army, the government, according to the powers given to it on the 9th December 1844, will raise the corps specified by said decree, under the name of "Defenders of the Independence and of the Laws."

José Joaquín de Herrera.
Palace of the National Government,
City of Mexico, June 4, 1845.

Source: Steven R. Butler, ed., *A Documentary History of the Mexican War* (Richardson, TX: Descendants of Mexican War Veterans, 1995), p. 5, http://www.dmwv.org/mexwar/documents/herrera.htm.

39. Letter from Abraham Lincoln to Williamson Durley, October 3, 1845

The conflict between Mexico and Euro-American colonists in Texas in 1836 had brought slavery to the national stage. In the United States it heightened the debate between pro- and anti-slavery factions. The U.S. Congress approved the annexation of Texas in late February 1845, and it was only a matter of time before Texas would become part of the United States. A debate formed around the annexation and the inevitability of a war with Mexico. Opposition was led by the abolitionists, or Liberty Party. In Illinois. Abraham Lincoln (1809–1865), then a Congressman, found himself obliged to answer Democratic Party arguments for annexation. The following letter is to his friend Williamson Durley of Hennepin, Illinois, who, along with his brother Madison, advocated forming a third party. They were abolitionists who operated an underground railroad that conducted runaway African slaves to freedom. Lincoln courted the Durleys, and in the letter he argued the immorality of annexation and discussed the Texas question.

Springfield
Friend Durley:
When I saw you at home, it was agreed that I should write to you and your brother Madison. Until I then saw you, I was not aware of your being what is generally called an abolitionist, or, as you call yourself, a Liberty man; though I well knew there were many such in your county. I was glad to hear you say that you intend to attempt to bring about, at the next election in Putnam, a union of the whigs proper, and such of the liberty men, as are whigs in principle on all questions save only that of slavery. So far as I can perceive, by such union, neither party need yield any thing on the point in difference between them. If the whig abolitionists of New York had voted with us last fall, Mr. Clay would now be president, whig principles in the ascendant, and Texas not annexed; whereas by the division, all that either had at stake in the contest, was lost. An, indeed, it was extremely probably, beforehand, that such would be the result. As I always understood, the Liberty—men deprecated the annexation of Texas extremely; and, this being so, why they should refuse to so cast their votes as to prevent it, even to me seemed wonderful. What was their process of reasoning, I can only judge from what a single one of them told me. It was this:

"We are not to do evil that good may come." This general proposition is doubtless correct; but did it apply? If by your votes you could have prevented the extension, &c., of slavery, would it not have been good and not evil so to have used your votes, even though it involved the casting of them for a slaveholder? By the fruit the tree is to be known. An evil tree can not bring forth good fruit. If the fruit of electing Mr. Clay would have been to prevent the extension of slavery, could the act of electing have been evil?

But I will argue f[u]rther. I perhaps ought to say that individually I never was much interested in the Texas question. I never could see much good to come of annexation; inasmuch, as they were already a free republican people on our own model; on the other hand, I never could very clearly see how the annexation would augment the evil of slavery. It always seemed to me that slaves would be taken there in about equal numbers, with or without annexation. And if more were taken because of annexation, still there would be just so many the fewer left, where they were taken from. It is possibly true, to some extent, that with annexation, some slaves may be sent to Texas and continued in slavery, that otherwise might have been liberated. To whatever extent this may be true, I think annexation an evil. I hold it to be a paramount duty of us in the free states, due to the Union of the

States, and perhaps to liberty itself (paradox though it may seem) to let the slavery of the other states alone; while, on the other hand, I hold it to be equally clear, that we should never knowingly lend ourselves directly or indirectly, to prevent that slavery from dying a natural death—to find new places for it to live in, when it can no longer exist in the old. Of course I am not now considering what would be our duty, in cases of insurrection among the slaves.

To recur to the Texas question, I understand the Liberty men to have viewed annexation as a much greater evil than I ever did; and I would like to convince you if I could, that they could have prevented it, without violation of principle if they had chosen.

I intend this letter for you and Madison together; and if you and he or either shall think fit to drop me a line, I shall be pleased.

Yours with respect

A. Lincoln

Source: Abraham Lincoln, *Collected Works of Abraham Lincoln*, vol. 1. Roy P. Basler et al., eds. (Ann Arbor: University of Michigan Digital Library Production Services, 2001), pp. 347–48.

40. Excerpts from President James Polk's State of the Union Address, December 2, 1845

James Knox Polk (1795–1849), the eleventh president of the United States, ran on the platform of expanding the United States at the expense of Mexico and Canada. Because of the war fever he was able to override Whig opposition to the war with Mexico. In addition to securing 1.2 million square miles from Mexico, he secured the Oregon Territory (including Washington, Oregon, and Idaho) and opened the debate regarding slavery in the new territories. The following are excerpts of his State of the Union Address in which he blames Mexico for tensions between the two countries. Although Polk manipulated events to make war inevitable, he stated that he had done everything in his power to avert a confrontation.

Fellow Citizens of the Senate and of the House of Representatives:

I regret to inform you that our relations with Mexico since your last session have not been of the amicable character which it is our desire to cultivate with all foreign nations. On the 6th day of March last the Mexican envoy extraordinary and minister plenipotentiary to the United States made a formal protest in the name of his Government against the joint resolution passed by Congress "for the annexation of Texas to the United States," which he chose to regard as a violation of the rights of Mexico, and in consequence of it he demanded his passports. He was informed that the Government of the United States did not consider this joint resolution as a violation of any of the rights of Mexico, or that it afforded any just cause of offense to his Government; that the Republic of Texas was an independent power, owing no allegiance to Mexico and constituting no part of her territory or rightful sovereignty and jurisdiction. He was also assured that it was the sincere desire of this Government to maintain with that of Mexico relations of peace and good understanding. That functionary, however, notwithstanding these representations and assurances, abruptly terminated his mission and shortly afterwards left the country. Our envoy extraordinary and minister plenipotentiary to Mexico was refused all official intercourse with that Government, and, after remaining several months, by the permission of his own Government he returned to the United States. Thus, by the acts of Mexico, all diplomatic intercourse between the two countries was suspended.

Since that time, Mexico has until recently occupied an attitude of hostility toward the United States has been marshaling and organizing armies, issuing proclamations, and avowing the intention to make war on the United States, either by an open declaration or by invading Texas. Both the Congress and convention of the people of Texas invited this Government to send an army into that territory to protect and defend them against the menaced attack. The moment the terms of annexation offered by the United States were accepted by Texas the latter became so far a part of our own country as to make it our duty to afford such protection and defense. I therefore deemed it proper, as a precautionary measure, to order a strong squadron to the coasts of Mexico and to concentrate an efficient military force on the western frontier of Texas. Our Army was ordered to take position in the country between the Nueces and the Del Norte, and to repel any invasion of the Texan territory which might be attempted by the Mexican forces. Our squadron in the Gulf was ordered to cooperate with the Army. But though our Army and Navy were placed in a position to defend our own and the rights of Texas, they were ordered to commit no act of hostility against Mexico unless she declared war or was herself the aggressor by striking the first blow. The result has been that Mexico has made no aggressive movement, and our military and naval commanders have executed their orders with such discretion that the peace of the two Republics has not been disturbed. Texas had declared her independence and maintained it by her arms for more than nine years. She has had an organized government in successful operation during that period. Her separate existence as an independent state had been recognized by the United States and the principal powers of Europe. Treaties of commerce and navigation had been concluded with her by different nations, and it had become manifest to the whole world that any further attempt on the part of Mexico to conquer her or overthrow her Government would be [in] vain. Even Mexico herself had become satisfied of this fact, and whilst the question of annexation was pending before the people of Texas during the past summer, the Government of Mexico, by a formal act, agreed to recognize the independence of Texas on condition that she would not annex herself to any other power. The agreement to acknowledge the independence of Texas, whether with or without this condition, is conclusive against Mexico. The independence of Texas is a fact conceded by Mexico herself, and she had no right or authority to prescribe restrictions as to the form of government which Texas might afterwards choose to assume. But though Mexico can not complain of the United States on account of the annexation of Texas, it is to be regretted that serious causes of misunderstanding between the two countries continue to exist, growing out of unredressed injuries inflicted by the Mexican authorities and people on the persons and property of citizens of the United States through a long series of years. Mexico has admitted these injuries, but has neglected and refused to repair them. Such was the character of the wrongs and such the insults repeatedly offered to American citizens and the American flag by Mexico, in palpable violation of the laws of nations and the treaty between the two countries of the 5th of April 1831, that they have been repeatedly brought to the notice of Congress by my predecessors. As early as the 6th of February 1837, the President of the United States declared in a message to Congress that ... our Army and Navy had remained on the frontier and coasts of Mexico for many weeks without any hostile movement on her part, though her menaces were continued, I deemed it important to put an end, if possible, to this state of things. With this view I caused steps to be taken in the month of September last to ascertain distinctly and in an authentic form what the designs of the Mexican Government were whether it was their intention to declare war, or invade Texas, or whether they were disposed to adjust and settle in an amicable manner the pending differences between the two countries. On the 9th of November an official answer was received that the Mexican Government consented to renew the diplomatic relations which had been suspended in March last, and for that purpose were willing to accredit a minister from the United States. With a sincere desire to preserve peace and restore relations of good understanding between the two Republics, I waived all ceremony as to the manner of renewing diplomatic intercourse between them, and, assuming the initiative, on the 10th of November, a distinguished citizen of Louisiana was appointed envoy extraordinary and minister plenipotentiary to Mexico, clothed with full powers to adjust and definitively settle all pending differences between the two countries, including those of boundary between Mexico and the State of Texas. The minister appointed has set out on his mission and is probably by this time near the Mexican capital. He has been instructed to bring the negotiation with which he is charged to a conclusion at the earliest practicable period, which it is expected will be in time to enable me to communicate the result to Congress during the present session. Until that result is known I forbear to recommend to Congress such ulterior measures of redress for the wrongs and injuries we have so long borne as it would have been proper to make had no such negotiation been instituted.

When orders were given during the past summer for concentrating a military force on the western frontier of Texas, our troops were widely dispersed and in small detachments, occupying posts remote from each other. The prompt and expeditious manner in which an army embracing more than half our peace establishment was drawn together on an emergency so sudden reflects great credit on the officers who were intrusted with the execution of these orders, as well as upon the discipline of the Army itself. To be in strength to protect and defend the people and territory of Texas in the event Mexico should commence hostilities or invade her territories with a large army, which she threatened, I authorized the general assigned to the command of the army of occupation to make requisitions for additional forces from several of the States nearest the Texan territory, and which could most expeditiously furnish them, if in his opinion a larger force than that under his command and the auxiliary aid which under like circumstances he was authorized to receive from Texas should be required. The contingency upon which the exercise of this authority depended has not occurred. The circumstances under which two companies of State artillery from the city of New Orleans were sent into Texas and mustered into the service of the United States are fully stated in the report of the Secretary of War. I recommend to Congress that provision be made for the payment of these troops, as well as a small number of Texan volunteers whom the commanding general thought it necessary to receive or muster into our service....

James K. Polk

Source: Joint Session of Congress, State of the Union Address, 29th Congress, First Session, December 2, 1845, http://www.presidentialrhetoric.com/historicspeeches/polk/stateoftheunion 1845.html.

41. Letter from Ulysses S. Grant to Fiancée Julia Dent, July 25, 1846

In the following letter from Lt. Ulysses S. Grant (1822–1885) to his fiancée, Julia Dent, he expressed horror over the Mexican-American War, saying that it was unjust. However, it was his duty to fight in the war against Mexico—the United States was his country, whether right or wrong. In this case, Grant considered the war unjust. Throughout his memoirs, Grant was critical of the war against Mexico because he considered it a U.S. war of aggression.

Since we have been in Matamoros, a great many murders have been committed, and what is strange there seems to be very week [weak] means made use of to prevent frequent repetitions. Some of the volunteers and about all the Texans seem to think it perfectly right to impose on the people of a conquered City to any extent, and even to murder them where the act can be covered by dark. And how much they seem to enjoy acts of violence too! I would not pretend to guess the number of murders that have been committed upon the persons of poor Mexicans and our soldiers, since we have been here, but the number would startle you.

Source: John Y. Simon, *The Papers of Ulysses S. Grant*, vol. 1 (London: Feffer & Simons, 1967), p. 102.

42. Abraham Lincoln's "Spot Resolutions," December 22, 1847

President James K. Polk (1795–1849) ordered Gen. Zachary Taylor (1784–1850) into the disputed land between the Nueces and Rio Grande Rivers to provoke the Mexican Army, which fired on Taylor's troops on April 24, 1846. Polk labeled this an act of war and called for hostilities with Mexico. Abraham Lincoln (1809–1865), who was a freshman Whig congressman from Illinois at the time, questioned the "spot" where blood had first been shed in the Mexican-American War. Was it on U.S. soil? Was the president lying about the provocation? Lincoln was one of several congressmen opposing the war. On December 22, 1847, he introduced the "Spot Resolutions," in which he demanded to know the spot where American blood was spilled. This was important because Polk claimed that the Mexicans attacked U.S. troops on American soil. Lincoln's legislation was never acted upon by the full Congress. However, it earned him the nickname "Spotty Lincoln."

And whereas this House is desirous to obtain a full knowledge of all the facts which go to establish whether the particular spot on which the blood of our citizens was so shed was or was not at that time *our own soil*: Therefore, *Resolved by the House of Representatives*, That the President of the United States be respectfully requested to inform this House—

1st. Whether the spot on which the blood of our citizens was shed, as in his messages declared, was or was not within the territory of Spain, at least after the treaty of 1819 until the Mexican revolution.

2d. Whether that spot is or is not within the territory which was wrested from Spain by the revolutionary Government of Mexico.

3d. Whether that spot is or is not within a settlement of people, which settlement has existed ever since long before the Texas revolution, and until its inhabitants fled before the approach of the United States army.

4th. Whether that settlement is or is not isolated from any and all other settlements by the Gulf and the Rio Grande on the south and west, and by wide uninhabited regions on the north and east.

5th. Whether the people of that settlement, or a majority of them, or any of them, have ever submitted themselves to the government or laws of Texas or of the United States, by consent or by compulsion, either by accepting office, or voting at elections, or paying tax, or serving on juries, or having process served upon them, or in any other way.

6th. Whether the people of that settlement did or did not flee from the approach of the United States army, leaving unprotected their homes and their growing crops, *before* the blood was shed, as in the messages stated; and whether the first blood, so shed, was or was not shed within the enclosure of one of the people who had thus fled from it.

7th. Whether our *citizens*, whose blood was shed, as in his messages declared, were or were not, at that time, armed officers and soldiers, sent into that settlement by the military orders of the President, through the Secretary of War.

8th. Whether the military force of the United States was or was not so sent into that settlement after Gen. Taylor had more than once intimated to the War

Department that, in his opinion, no such movement was necessary to the defence or protection of Texas.

Source: Printed Resolution and Preamble on Mexican War: "Spot Resolutions," The Abraham Lincoln Papers at the Library of Congress, http://memory.loc.gov/cgi-bin/query/r?ammem/mal:@field(DOCID+@lit(d0007000)).

43. John C. Calhoun, "The Conquest of Mexico," 1848

U.S. Sen. John C. Calhoun (D–South Carolina) (1782–1850) had advocated the annexation of Texas, after it had broken away from Mexico and declared its independence in 1836. The status of the Lone Star State, as it was called, was tenuous, and Mexico did not recognize Texas as a separate country. Mexico let it be known that any attempt on the part of the United States to annex Texas would be a declaration of war. Calhoun had been secretary of state in the cabinet of President John Tyler in 1844–1845. However, as a U.S. senator from South Carolina, Calhoun grew suspicious of President James K. Polk's intrigues and fearful that the president's intentions of acquiring significant territory below the Rio Grande would hurt the slave states since it would be incorporating a non-white people. Hence, Calhoun abstained from the initial vote for the war and supported unilaterally withdrawing to the Rio Grande and keeping everything north of the river. Calhoun took a leading role in the senate debate over the question of incorporating Mexico. "To incorporate Mexico, would be the very first instance of the kind of incorporating an Indian race," Calhoun said, "for more than half of the Mexicans are Indians, and the other is composed chiefly of mixed tribes. I protest against such a union as that! Ours, sir, is the Government of a white race."

RESOLVED, That to conquer Mexico and to hold it, either as a province or to incorporate it into the Union, would be inconsistent with the avowed object for which the war has been prosecuted; a departure from the settled policy of the Government; in conflict with its character and genius; and in the end subversive of our free and popular institutions.

RESOLVED, That no line of policy in the further prosecution of the war should be adopted which may lead to consequences so disastrous.

In offering, Senators, these resolutions for your consideration, I have been governed by the reasons which induced me to oppose the war, and by the same considerations I have been ever since guided. In alluding to my opposition to the war, I do not intend to notice the reasons which governed me on that occasion, further than is necessary to explain my motives upon the present. I opposed the war then, not only because I considered it unnecessary, and that it might have been easily avoided; not only because I thought the President had no authority to order a portion of the territory in dispute and in possession of the Mexicans, to be occupied by our troops; not only because I believed the allegations upon which it was sanctioned by Congress, were unfounded in truth; but from high considerations of reason and policy, because I believed it would lead to great and serious evils to the country, and greatly endanger its free institutions.

But after the war was declared, and had received the sanction of the Government, I acquiesced in what I could not prevent, and which it was impossible for me to arrest; and I then felt it to be my duty to limit my course so as to give that direction to the conduct of the war as would, as far as possible, prevent the evil and danger with which, in my opinion, it threatened the country and its institutions. For this purpose, at the last session, I suggested to the Senate a defensive line, and for that purpose, I now offer these resolutions. This, and this only, is the motive which governs me. I am moved by no personal nor party considerations. My object is neither to sustain the Executive, nor to strengthen the Opposition, but simply to discharge an important duty to the country. But I shall express my opinion upon all points with boldness and independence, such as become a Senator who has nothing to ask, either from the Government or from the people, and whose only aim is to diminish, to the smallest possible amount, the evils incident to this war. But when I come to notice those points in which I differ from the President, I shall do it with all the decorum which is due to the Chief Magistrate of the Union.

When I suggested a defensive line, at the last session, this country had in its possession, through the means of its arms, ample territory, and stood in a condition to force indemnity. Before then, the successes of our arms had gained all the contiguous portions of Mexico, and our army has ever since held all that it is desirable to hold—that portion whose population is sparse, and on that account the more desirable to be held. For I hold it in reference to this war a fundamental principle, that when we receive territorial indemnity, it shall be unoccupied territory.

In offering a defensive line, I did it because I believed that, in the first place, it was the only certain mode of terminating the war successfully; I did it, also, because I believed that it would be a vast saving of the sacrifice of human life; but above all, I did so because I saw that any other line of policy would expose us to tremendous evil, which these resolutions were intended to guard against. The President took a different view. He recommended a vigorous prosecution of the war—not for conquest: that was disavowed—but for the purpose of conquering peace; that is, to compel Mexico to sign a treaty making a sufficient cession of territory to indemnify this Government both for the claims of its citizens and for the expenses of the war. Sir, I opposed this policy. I opposed it, among other reasons, because I believed that if the war should be ever so successful, there was great hazard to us, at least, that the object intended to be effected by it would not be accomplished. Congress thought differently. Ample provisions, in men and money, were granted for carrying on the war. The campaign has terminated. It has been as successful as the Executive of the country could possibly have calculated. Victory after victory has followed in succession, without a single reverse. Santa Anna was repelled and defeated, with all his forces. Vera Cruz was carried, and the Castle with it. Jalapa, Perote, and Puebla fell; and, after two great triumphs of our army, the gates of Mexico opened to us. Well, sir, what has been accomplished? What has been done? Has the avowed object of the war been attained? Have we conquered peace? Have we obtained a treaty? Have we obtained any indemnity? No, sir: not a single object contemplated has been effected; and, what is worse, our difficulties are greater now than they were then, and the objects, forsooth, more difficult to reach than they were before the campaign commenced.

So much for the past; we now come to the commencement of another campaign; and the question is, What shall be done? The same measures are proposed. It is still "a vigorous prosecution of the war." The measures are identically the same. It is not for conquest—that is now as emphatically disowned as it was in the first instance. The object is not to blot Mexico out of the list of nations, for the President is emphatic in the expression of his desire to maintain the nationality of Mexico. He desires to see her an independent and flourishing community, and assigns strong and cogent reasons for all that. Well, sir, the question is now, What ought to be done? We are now coming to the practical question, Shall we aim at carrying on another vigorous campaign under present circumstances?

Mr. President, I have examined this question with care, and I repeat, that I cannot support the recommendations of the President. There are many and powerful reasons, stronger than those which existed at the commencement of the last campaign, to justify my opposition now. The cost in money will be vastly greater. There is a bill for ten additional regiments now before the Senate, and another bill providing for twenty regiments of volunteers has been reported, making in all, not less, I suppose, than twenty-five thousand troops; raising the number of troops in the service—as, I presume, the chairman of the Committee on Military Affairs can inform you—to not much less than seventy thousand in the whole. Well, sir, the expense will be much more than that of the last campaign. It will cost not much short of sixty millions of dollars.

Sir, we have heard how much glory our country has acquired in this war. I acknowledge it to the full amount, Mr. President, chivalrously; they have conferred honor on the country, for which I sincerely thank them.

Mr. President, I believe all our thanks will be confined to our army. So far as I know, in the civilized world there is no approbation of the conduct of the civil portion of our power. On the contrary, everywhere the declaration is made that we are an ambitious, unjust, hard people, more given to war than any people of modern times. Whether this be true or not, it is not for me to inquire. I am speaking now merely of the reputation which we heard abroad—everywhere, I believe; for as much as we have gained in military reputation abroad, I regret to perceive, we have lost in our political and civil reputation. Now, sir, much as I regard military glory; much as I rejoice to behold our people in possession of the indomitable energy and courage which surmount all difficulties, and which class them amongst the first military people of the age, I would be very sorry indeed that our Government should lose any reputation for wisdom, moderation, discretion, justice, and those other high qualities which have distinguished us in the early stages of our history.

The next reason which my resolutions assign, is, that it is without example or precedent, wither [*sic*] to hold Mexico as a province, or to incorporate her into our Union. No example of such a line of policy can be found. We have conquered many of the neighboring tribes of Indians, but we have never thought of holding them in subjection—never of incorporating them into our Union. They have either been left as an independent people amongst us, or been driven into the forests.

I know further, sir, that we have never dreamt of incorporating into our Union any but the Caucasian race—the free white race. To incorporate Mexico, would be the very first instance of the kind of incorporating an Indian race; for more than half of the Mexicans are Indians, and the other is composed chiefly of mixed tribes. I protest against such a union as that! Ours, sir, is the Government of a white race. The greatest misfortunes of Spanish America are to be traced to the fatal error of placing these colored races on an equality with the white race. That error destroyed the social arrangement which formed the basis of society. The Portuguese and ourselves have escaped—the Portuguese at least to some extent—and we are the only people on this continent which have made revolutions without being followed by anarchy. And yet it is professed and talked about to erect these Mexicans into a Territorial Government, and place them on an equality with the people of the United States. I protest utterly against such a project.

Sir, it is a remarkable fact, that in the whole history of man, as far as my knowledge extends, there is no instance whatever of any civilized colored races being found equal to the establishment of free popular government, although by far the largest portion of the human family is composed of these races. And even in the savage state we scarcely find them anywhere with such government, except it be our noble savages—for noble I will call them. They, for the most part, had free institutions, but they are easily sustained among a savage people. Are we to overlook this fact? Are we to associate with ourselves as equals, companions, and fellow-citizens, the Indians and mixed race of Mexico? Sir, I should consider such a thing as fatal to our institutions.

The next two reasons which I assigned, were, that it would be in conflict with the genius and character of our institutions, and subversive of our free government. I take these two together, as intimately connected; and now of the first—to hold Mexico in subjection.

Mr. President, there are some propositions too clear for argument; and before such a body as the Senate, I should consider it a loss of time to undertake to prove that to hold Mexico as a subjected province would be hostile, and in conflict with our free popular institutions, and in the end subversive of them. Sir, he who knows the American Constitution well—he who has duly studied its character—he who has looked at history, and knows what has been the effect of conquests of free States invariably, will require no proof at my hands to show that it would be entirely hostile to the institutions of the country to hold Mexico as a province. There is not an example on record of any free State even having attempted the conquest of any territory approaching the extent of Mexico without disastrous consequences. The nations conquered have in time conquered the conquerers by destroying their liberty. That will be our case, sir. The conquest of Mexico would add so vast an amount to the patronage of this Government, that it would absorb the whole power of the States in the Union. This Union would become imperial, and the States mere subordinate corporations. But the evil will not end there. The process will go on.

The same process by which the power would be transferred from the States to the Union, will transfer the whole from this department of the Government (I speak of the Legislature) to the Executive. All the added power and added patronage which conquest will create, will pass to the Executive. In the end, you put in the hands of the Executive the power of conquering you. You give to it, sir, such splendor, such ample means, that, with the principle of proscription which unfortunately prevails in our country, the struggle will be greater at every Presidential election than our institutions can possibly endure. The end of it will be, that that branch of Government will become all-powerful, and the result is inevitable—anarchy and despotism. It is as certain as that I am this day addressing the Senate.

But, Mr. President, suppose all these difficulties removed; suppose these people attached to our Union, and desirous of incorporating with us, ought we to bring them in? Are they fit to be connected with us? Are they fit for self-government and for governing you? Are you, any of you, willing that your States should be governed by these twenty-odd Mexican States, with a population of about only one million of your blood, and two or three millions of mixed blood, better informed, all the rest pure Indians, a mixed blood equally ignorant and unfit for liberty, impure races, not as good as Cherokees or Choctaws?

We make a great mistake, sir, when we suppose that all people are capable of self-government. We are anxious to force free government on all; and I see that it has been urged in a very respectable quarter, that it is the mission of this country to spread civil and religious liberty over all the world, and especially over this continent. It is a great mistake. None but people advanced to a very high state of moral and intellectual improvement are capable, in a civilized state, of maintaining free government; and amongst those who are so purified, very few, indeed, have had the good fortune of forming a constitution capable of endurance. It is a remarkable fact in the history of man, that scarcely ever have free popular institutions been formed by wisdom alone that have endured.

It has been the work of fortunate circumstances, or a combination of circumstances—a succession of fortunate incidents of some kind—which give to any people a free government. It is a very difficult task to make a constitution to last, though it may be supposed by some that they can be made to order, and furnished at the shortest notice. Sir, this admirable Constitution of our own was the result of a fortunate combination of circumstances. It was superior to the wisdom of the men who made it. It was the force of circumstances which induced them to adopt most of its wise provisions. Well, sir, of the few nations who have the good fortune to adopt self-government, few have had the good fortune long to preserve that government; for it is harder to preserve than to form it. Few people, after years of prosperity, remember the tenure by which their liberty is held; and I fear, Senators, that is our own condition. I fear that we shall continue to involve ourselves until our own system becomes a ruin. Sir, there is no solicitude now for liberty. Who talks of liberty when any great question comes up? Here is a question of the first magnitude as to the conduct of this war; do you hear anybody talk about its effect upon our liberties and our free institutions? No, sir. That was not the case formerly. In the early stages of our Government, the great anxiety was how to preserve liberty; the great anxiety now is for the attainment of mere military glory. In the one, we are forgetting the other. The maxim of former times was, that power is always stealing from the many to the few; the price of liberty was perpetual vigilance. They were constantly looking out and watching for danger. Then, when any great question came up, the first inquiry was, how it could affect our free institutions—how it could affect our liberty. Not so now. Is it because there has been any decay of the spirit of liberty among the people? Not at all. I believe the love of liberty was never more ardent, but they have forgotten the tenure of liberty by which alone it is preserved.

We think we may now indulge in everything with impunity, as if we held our charter of liberty by "right divine"—from Heaven itself. Under these impressions, we plunge into war, we contract heavy debts, we increase the patronage of the Executive, and we even talk of a crusade to force our institutions, our liberty, upon all people. There is no species of extravagance which our people imagine will endanger their liberty in any degree. But it is a great and fatal mistake. The day of retribution will come. It will come as certainly as I am now addressing the Senate; and when it does come, awful will be the reckoning—heavy the responsibility somewhere!

Source: http://teachingamericanhistory.org/library/index.asp?documentprint=478.

44. Excerpts from Walt Whitman, *Leaves of Grass*, 1855

Poet Walt Whitman (1819–1892) was a paradox—a walking contradiction. He was a staunch abolitionist so much so that he was fired from his job as editor of the *Brooklyn Eagle*. But unlike his fellow abolitionists, he supported the war with Mexico. A romantic, Whitman had no doubt in the alleged greatness and superiority of the American nation. His poetry offered assurances of the legitimacy of the war, and his expressions communicated certainty and self-evident truth. In the following document Whitman spoke of his belief in the uniqueness of the Euro-American people; his poem "Song of Myself" heralded Euro-American exceptionalism. He saw *America* as the prime mover of human history—a belief that most Euro-Americans shared at this time.

America does not repel the past or what it has produced under its forms or amid other politics or the idea of castes or the old religions ... accepts the lesson with calmness ... is not so impatient as has been supposed that the slough still sticks to opinions and manners and literature while the life which served its requirements has passed into the new life of the new forms ... perceives that the corpse is slowly borne from the eating and sleeping rooms of the house ... perceives that it waits a little while in the door ... that it was fittest for its days ... that its action has descended to the stalwart and well shaped heir who approaches ... and that he shall be fittest for his days....

The American poets are to enclose old and new for America is the race of races. Of them a bard is to be commensurate with a people. To him the other continents arrive as contributions ... he gives them reception for their sake and his own sake. His spirit responds to his country's spirit ... he incarnates its geography and natural life and rivers and lakes. Mississippi with annual freshets and changing chutes, Missouri and Columbia and Ohio and Saint Lawrence with the falls and beautiful masculine Hudson, do not embouchure where they spend themselves more than they embouchure into him. The blue breadth over the inland sea of Virginia and Maryland and the sea off Massachusetts and Maine and over Manhattan bay and over Champlain and Erie and over Ontario and Huron and Michigan and Superior, and over the Texan and Mexican and Floridian and Cuban seas and over the seas off California and Oregon, is not tallied by the blue breadth of the waters below more than the breadth of above and below is tallied by him. When the long Atlantic coast stretches longer and the Pacific coast stretches longer he easily stretches with them north or south. He spans between them also from east to west and reflects what is between them....

The English language befriends the grand American expression ... it is brawny enough and limber and full enough. On the tough stock of a race who through all change of circumstance was never with-out the idea of political liberty, which is the animus of all liberty, it has attracted the terms of daintier and gayer and subtler and more elegant tongues. It is the powerful language of resistance ... it is the dialect of common sense. It is the speech of the proud and melancholy races and of all who aspire. It is the chosen tongue to express growth faith self-esteem freedom justice equality friendliness amplitude prudence decision and courage. It is the medium that shall well nigh express the inexpressible.

Source: Walt Whitman, *Leaves of Grass* (Brooklyn, NY: Gabriel Harrison daguerreotype, 1855), pp. iii, iv, xi. I.

45. Abraham Lincoln's Speech to Congress against Seizing Mexican Territory, January 12, 1848

Illinois Congressman Abraham Lincoln (1809–1865) continued to question the U.S. role in the Mexican-American War and claimed that its purpose was to seize Texas, California, and other Southwest land areas. According to Lincoln, James K. Polk (1795–1849), the president of the United States, had lied and taken the nation into a war of aggression against Mexico to support the South's expansionist goals. Clear and simple, it was to support the ambitions of the slave states. The document denied the claims of Texas that the Rio Grande was the boundary between the two countries.

Some, if not all the gentlemen on the other side of the House, who have addressed the committee within the last two days, have spoken rather complainingly, if I have rightly understood them, of the vote given a week or ten days ago, declaring that the war with Mexico was unnecessarily and unconstitutionally commenced by the President [James K. Polk]....

I now proceed to examine the President's evidence, as applicable to such an issue. When that evidence is analized [sic], it is all included in the following propositions:

1. That the Rio Grande was the Western boundary of Louisiana as we purchased it of France in 1803.
2. That the Republic of Texas always claimed the Rio Grande, as her Western boundary.
3. That by various acts, she had claimed it on paper.
4. That Santa Anna, in his treaty with Texas, recognised [sic] the Rio Grande, as her boundary.
5. That Texas before, and the U.S. after, annexation had exercised jurisdiction beyond the Nueces—between the two rivers.
6. That our Congress, understood the boundary of Texas to extend beyond the Nueces.

Now for each of these in its turn.

His first item is, that the Rio Grande was the Western boundary of Louisiana, as we purchased it of France in 1803; and seeming to expect this to be disputed, he argues over the amount of nearly a page, to prove it true; at the end of which he lets us know, that by the treaty of 1819, we sold to Spain the whole country from the Rio Grande eastward, to the Sabine. Now, admitting for the present, that the Rio Grande, was the boundary of Louisiana, what, under heaven, had that to do with the present boundary between us and Mexico? How, Mr. Chairman, the line, that once divided your land from mine, can still be the boundary between us, after I have sold my land to you, is, to me, beyond all comprehension. And how any man, with an honest purpose only, of proving the truth, could ever have thought of introducing such a fact to prove such an issue, is equally incomprehensible. His next piece of evidence is that "The Republic of Texas always claimed this river (Rio Grande) as her western boundary[.]" That is not true, in fact. Texas has claimed it, but she has not always claimed it. There is, at least, one distinguished exception. Her state constitution—the republic's most solemn, and well considered act—that which may, without impropriety, be called her last will and testament revoking all others— makes no such claim. But suppose she had always claimed it. Has not Mexico always claimed the contrary? So that there is but claim against claim, leaving nothing proved, until we get back of the claims, and find which has the better foundation. Though not in the order in which the President presents his evidence, I now consider that class of his statements, which are, in substance, nothing more than that Texas has, by various acts of her convention and congress, claimed the Rio Grande as her boundary, on paper. I mean here what he says about the fixing of the Rio Grande as her boundary in her old constitution (not her state constitution) about forming congressional districts, counties &c &c. Now all of this is but naked claim; and what I have already said about claims is strictly applicable to this. If I should claim your land, by word of mouth, that certainly would not make it mine; and if I were to claim it by a deed which I had made myself, and with which you had had nothing to do, the claim would be quite the same, in substance—or rather, in utter nothingness. I next consider the President's statement that Santa Anna in his treaty with Texas, recognised [*sic*] the Rio Grande, as the western boundary of Texas. Besides the position, so often taken that Santa Anna, while a prisoner of war—a captive—could not bind Mexico by a treaty, which I deem conclusive—besides this, I wish to say something in relation to this treaty, so called by the President, with Santa Anna. If any man would like to be amused by a sight of that little thing, which the President calls by that big name, he can have it, by turning to Niles' Register volume 50, page 336. [See Santa Anna Treaty.] And if any one should suppose that Niles' Register is a curious repository of so mighty a document as a solemn treaty between nations, I can only say that I learned, to a tolerable degree [of] certainty, by enquiry at the State Department, that the President himself never saw it any where else. By the way, I believe I should not err if I were to declare, that during the first ten years of the existence of that document, it was never, by any body, called a treaty—that it was never so called, till the President, in his extremity, attempted, by so calling it, to wring something from it in justification of himself in connection with the Mexican war. It has none of the distinguishing features of a treaty. It does not call itself a treaty. Santa Anna does not therein, assume to bind Mexico; he assumes only to act as the President-Commander-in-chief of the Mexican Army and Navy; stipulates that the then present hostilities should cease, and that he would not himself take up arms, nor influence the Mexican people to take up arms, against Texas during the existence of the war of independence[.] He did not recognize [*sic*] the independence of Texas; he did not assume to put an end to the war; but clearly indicated his expectation of its continuance; he did not say one word about boundary, and, most probably, never thought of it. It is stipulated therein that the Mexican forces should evacuate the territory of Texas, passing to the other side of the Rio Grande; and in another article, it is stipulated that, to prevent collisions between the armies, the Texan army should not approach nearer than within five leagues—of what is not said—but clearly, from the object stated it is—of the Rio Grande. Now, if this is a treaty, recognising [*sic*] the Rio Grande as the boundary of Texas, it contains the singular feature of stipulating that Texas shall not go within five leagues of her own boundary.

Next comes the evidence of Texas before annexation, and the United States afterwards, exercising jurisdiction beyond the Nueces, and between the two rivers. This actual exercise of jurisdiction is the very class or quality of evidence we want. It is excellent so far as it goes; but does it go far enough? He tells us it went beyond the Nueces; but he does not tell us it went to the Rio Grande. He tells us, jurisdiction was exercised between the two rivers, but he does not tell us it was exercised over all the territory between them. Some simple minded people, think it is possible, to cross one river and go beyond it without going all the way to the next—that jurisdiction may be exercised between two rivers without covering all the country between them. I know a man, not very unlike myself, who exercises jurisdiction over a piece of land between the Wabash and the Mississippi; and yet so far is this from being all there is between those rivers that it is just one hundred and fifty two feet long by fifty wide, and no part of it much within a hundred miles of either. He has a neighbour between him and the Mississippi—that is, just across the street, in that direction—whom, I am sure, he could neither persuade nor force to give up his habitation; but which nevertheless, he could certainly annex, if it were to be done, by merely standing on his own side of the street and claiming it, or even sitting down and writing a deed for it.

But next the President tells us, the Congress of the United States understood the state of Texas they admitted into the union, to extend beyond the Nueces. Well, I suppose they did. I certainly so understood it. But how far beyond? That Congress did not understand it to extend clear to the Rio Grande, is quite certain by the fact of their joint resolutions for admission expressly leaving all questions of boundary to future adjustment. And it may be added that Texas herself is proved to have had the same understanding of it that our Congress had, by the fact of the exact conformity of her new constitution to those resolutions.

I am now through the whole of the President's evidence; and it is a singular fact, that if any one should declare the President sent the army into the midst of a settlement of Mexican people, who had never submitted, by consent or by force, to the authority of Texas or of the United States, and that there, and thereby, the first blood of the war was shed, there is not one word in all the President has said which would either admit or deny the declaration. This strange omission, it does seem to me, could not have occurred but by design. My way of living leads me to be about the courts of justice; and there, I have sometimes seen a good lawyer, struggling for his client's neck, in a desperate case, employing every artifice to work round, befog, and cover up, with many words, some point arising in the case, which he dared not admit, and yet could not deny. Party bias may help to make it appear so; but with all the allowance I can make for such bias, it still does appear to me, that just such, and from just such necessity, is the President's struggle in this case.

Some time after my colleague (Mr. Richardson) introduced the resolutions I have mentioned, I introduced a preamble, resolution, and interrogatories intended to draw the President out, if possible, on this hitherto untrodden ground. To show their relevancy, I propose to state my understanding of the true rule for ascertaining the boundary between Texas and Mexico. It is, that wherever Texas was exercising jurisdiction was hers; and wherever Mexico was exercising jurisdiction was hers; and that whatever separated the actual exercise of jurisdiction of the one, from that of the other, was the true boundary between them. If, as is probably true, Texas was exercising jurisdiction along the western bank of the Nueces, and Mexico was exercising it along the eastern bank of the Rio Grande, then neither river was the boundary; but the uninhabited country between the two was. The extent of our territory in that region depended, not on any treaty-fixed boundary (for no treaty had attempted it), but on revolution Any people anywhere, being inclined and having the power, have the right to rise up, and shake off the existing government, and form a new one that suits them better. This is a most valuable—most sacred right—a right, which we hope and believe, is to liberate the world. Nor is this right confined to cases in which the whole people of an existing government may choose to exercise it. Any portion of such people that can, may revolutionize, and make their own, of so much of the territory as they inhabit. More than this, a majority of any portion of such people may revolutionize, putting down a minority, intermingled with, or near about them, who may oppose their movement. Such minority was precisely the case of the tories of our own revolution. It is a quality of revolutions not to go by old lines, or old laws; but to break up both, and make new ones. As to the country now in question, we bought it of France in 1803, and sold it to Spain in 1819, according to the President's statements. After this, all Mexico, including Texas, revolutionized against Spain; and still later, Texas revolutionized against Mexico. In my view, just so far as she carried her revolution by obtaining the actual, willing or unwilling, submission of the people, so far, the country was hers, and no farther. Now sir, for the purpose of obtaining the very best evidence, as to whether Texas had actually carried her revolution to the place where the hostilities of the present war commenced, let the President answer the interrogatories I proposed, as before mentioned, or some other similar ones. Let him answer, fully, fairly, and candidly. Let him answer with facts, and not with arguments. Let him remember he sits where Washington sat, and so remembering, let him answer as Washington would answer. As a nation should not, and the Almighty will not, be evaded, so let him attempt no evasion—no equivocation. And if, so answering, he can show that the soil was ours where the first blood of the war was shed—that it was not within an inhabited country or, if within such, that the inhabitants had submitted themselves to the civil authority of Texas, or of the United States, and that the same is true of the site of Fort Brown, then I am with him for his justification. In that case I, shall be most happy to reverse the vote I gave the other day. I have a selfish motive for desiring that the President may do this. I expect to give some votes, in connection with the war, which, without his so doing, will be of doubtful propriety in my own judgment, but which will be free from the doubt if he does so. But if he can not, or will not do this—if on any pretence, or no pretence, he shall refuse or omit it, then I shall be fully convinced, of what I more than suspect already, that he is deeply conscious of being in the wrong, that he feels the blood of this war, like the blood of Abel, is crying to Heaven against him. That originally having some strong motive—what, I will not stop now to give my opinion concerning—to involve the two countries in a war, and trusting to escape scrutiny by fixing the public gaze upon the exceeding brightness of military glory—that attractive rainbow that rises in showers of blood— that serpent's eye that charms to destroy, he plunged into it, and has swept on and on, till, disappointed in his calculation of the ease with which Mexico might be subdued, he now finds himself, he knows not where. How like the half insane mumbling of a fever-dream, is the whole war part of his late message! At one time telling us that Mexico has nothing whatever that we can get but territory; at another, showing us how we can support the war by levying contributions on Mexico. At one time, urging the national honor, the security of the future, the prevention of foreign interference, and even the good of Mexico herself, as among the objects of the war; at another, telling us that "to reject indemnity, by refusing to accept a cession of territory, would be to abandon all our just demands, and to wage the war, bearing all its expenses, without a purpose or definite object." So then, the national honor, security of the future, and every thing but territorial indemnity, may be considered the no-purposes, and indefinite, objects of the war! But, having it now settled that territorial indemnity is the only object we are urged to seize by legislation here, all that he was content to take, a few months ago, and the whole province of lower California to boot, and to still carry on the war—to take all we are fighting for and still fight on. Again, the President is resolved, under all circumstances, to have full territorial indemnity for the expenses of the war; but he forgets to tell us how we are to get the excess, after those expenses shall have surpassed the value of the whole of the Mexican territory. So again, he insists that the separate national existence of Mexico shall be maintained; but he does not tell us how this can be done after we shall have taken all her territory. Lest the questions I here suggest be considered speculative merely, let me be indulged a moment in trying [to] show they are not. The war has gone on some twenty months; for the expenses of which, together with an inconsiderable old score, the President now claims about one half of the Mexican territory; and that, by far the better half, so far as concerns our ability to make any thing out of it. It is comparatively uninhabited; so that we could establish land offices in it, and raise some money in that way. But the other half is already inhabited, as I understand it, tolerably densely for the nature of the country; and all its lands, or all that are valuable, already appropriated as private property. How then are we to make any thing out of these lands with this encumbrance on them or how, remove the encumbrance? I suppose no one will say we should kill the people, or drive them out, or make slaves of them, or even confiscate their property. How then can we make much out of this part of the territory? If the prosecution of the war has, in expenses, already equalled the better half of the country, how long its future prosecution will be in equalling the less valuable half is not a speculative, but a practical question, pressing closely upon us. And yet it is a question which the President seems to never have thought of. As to the mode of terminating the war and securing peace, the President is equally wandering and indefinite. First, it is to be done by a more vigorous prosecution of the war in the vital parts of the enem[y']s country; and, after apparently talking himself tired on this point, the President drops down into a half despairing tone, and tells us that "with a people distracted and divided by contending factions, and a government subject to constant changes, by successive revolutions, the continued success of our arms may fail to secure a satisfactory peace." Then he suggests the propriety of wheedling the Mexican people to desert the counsels of their own leaders, and trusting in our protection, to set up a government from which we can secure a satisfactory peace; telling us that "this may become the only mode of obtaining such a peace." But soon he falls into doubt of this too; and then drops back on to the already half abandoned ground of "more vigorous prossecution." All this shows that the President is, in no wise, satisfied with his own positions. First he takes up one, and in attempting to argue us into it, he argues himself out of it; then seizes another, and goes through the same process; and then, confused at being able to think of nothing new, he snatches up the old one again, which he has some time before cast off. His mind, tasked beyond its power, is running hither and thither, like some tortured creature on a burning surface, finding no position on which it can settle down and be at ease.

Again, it is a singular omission in this message, that it no where intimates when the President expects the war to terminate. At its beginning, Genl. Scott was, by this same President, driven into disfavor, if not disgrace, for intimating that peace could not be conquered in less than three or four months. But now, at the end of about twenty months, during which time our arms have given us the most splendid successes—every department, and every part, land and water, officers and privates, regulars and volunteers, doing all that men could do, and hundreds of things which it had ever before been thought men could not do—after all this, this same President gives us a long message, without showing us that, as to the end, he himself has, even an imaginary conception. As I have before said, he knows not where he is. He is a bewildered, confounded, and miserably perplexed man. God grant he may be able to show there is not something about his conscience more painful than all his mental perplexity!

Source: United States House of Representatives. The Abraham Lincoln Papers at the Library of Congress. Series 1. General Correspondence. 1833–1916. Library of Congress, http://memory.loc.gov/cgi-bin/query/r?ammem/mal:@field(DOCID+@lit(d0007400)).

46. Excerpts from the Memoirs of Ulysses S. Grant, 1885

As a lieutenant, West Point graduate Ulysses S. Grant (1822–1885) fought under the command of Gen. Zachary Taylor (1784–1850) during the Mexican-American War. Grant later became the leading Union general of the Civil War and, after the war, became president. In his memoirs, Grant gave blunt evaluations of the politics of slavery and U.S. expansionist aggression.

Generally the officers of the army were indifferent whether the annexation [of Texas] was consummated or not; but not so all of them. For myself, I was bitterly opposed to the measure, and to this day regard the war [with Mexico] which resulted as one of the most unjust ever waged by a stronger against a weaker nation. It was an instance of a republic following the bad example of European monarchies, in not considering justice in their desire to acquire additional territory.

Texas was originally a state belonging to the republic of Mexico. It extended from the Sabine River on the east to the Rio Grande on the west, and from the Gulf of Mexico on the south and east to the territory of the United States and New Mexico—another Mexican state at that time—on the north and west. An empire in territory, it had but a very sparse population, until settled by Americans who had received authority from Mexico to colonize. These colonists paid very little attention to the supreme government, and introduced slavery into the state almost from the start, [al]though the constitution of Mexico did not, nor does it now, sanction that institution. Soon they set up an independent government of their own, and war existed, between Texas and Mexico, in name from that time until 1836, when active hostilities very nearly ceased upon the capture of Santa Anna, the Mexican President. Before long, however, the same people—who with permission of Mexico had colonized Texas, and afterwards set up slavery there, and then seceded as soon as they felt strong enough to do so—offered themselves and the State to the United States, and in 1845 their offer was accepted. The occupation, separation and annexation were, from the inception of the movement to its final consummation, a conspiracy to acquire territory out of which slave states might be formed for the American Union.

Even if the annexation itself could be justified, the manner in which the subsequent war was forced upon Mexico cannot. The fact is, annexationists wanted more territory than they could possibly lay any claim to, as part of the new acquisition. Texas, as an independent State, never exercised jurisdiction over the territory between the Nueces River and the Rio Grande. Mexico never recognized the independence of Texas, and maintained that, even if independent, the State had no claim south of the Nueces. I am aware that a treaty, made by the Texans with Santa Anna while he was under duress, ceded all the territory between the Nueces and the Rio Grande; but he was a prisoner of war when the treaty was made, and his life was in jeopardy. He knew, too, that he deserved execution at the hands of the Texans, if they should ever capture him. The Texans, if they had taken his life, would have only followed the example set by Santa Anna himself a few years before, when he executed the entire garrison of the Alamo and the villagers of Goliad.

In taking military possession of Texas after annexation, the army of occupation, under General [Zachary] Taylor, was directed to occupy the disputed territory. The army did not stop at the Nueces and offer to negotiate for a settlement of the boundary question, but went beyond, apparently in order to force Mexico to initiate war. It is to the credit of the American nation, however, that after conquering Mexico, and while practically holding the country in our possession so that we could have retained the whole of it, or made any terms we chose, we paid a round sum for the additional territory taken; more than it was worth, or was likely to be, to Mexico. To us it was an empire and of incalculable value; but it might have been obtained by other means. The Southern rebellion was largely the outgrowth of the Mexican war. Nations, like individuals, are punished for their transgressions. We got our punishment in the most sanguinary and expensive war of modern times.

Source: U.S. Grant, *Personal Memoirs of U.S. Grant* (New York: Charles L. Webster & Co., 1885), pp. 22–24, http://www.bartleby.com/1011/.

47. Excerpt from Abiel Abbott Livermore, *The War with Mexico Reviewed*, 1850

Abiel Abbott Livermore (1811–1892), a minister of the Congregational Church in New England, opposed the Mexican-American War because he considered it unjust and a plot by slave states to secure more land. In 1850, he won the American Peace Prize for a graphic book, *The War with Mexico Reviewed*, which covered extensively the atrocities of the war. Not much is known about Livermore, who continued to be involved in progressive causes such as the abolitionist movement that sought to end slavery. In this excerpt, Livermore quotes an eyewitness to the atrocities committed against Mexicans during the war. Livermore represents the progressive strain within American society that has worked for peace and questioned the motives for war.

Again, the pride of race has swollen to still greater insolence the pride of country, always quite active enough for the due observance of the claims of universal brotherhood. The Anglo-Saxons have been apparently persuaded to think themselves the chosen people, anointed race of the Lord, commissioned to drive out the heathen, and plant their religion and institutions in every Canaan they could subjugate.… Our treatment both of the red man and the black man has habituated us to feel our power and forget right … The god Terminus is an unknown deity in America. Like the hunger of the pauper boy of fiction, the cry had been, 'more, more, give us more.…

[He quotes one account:]

Among the hundreds of the dead whom I saw there [at the Battle of Buena Vista], I was much touched by the appearance of the corpse of a Mexican boy, whose age, I should think, could not have exceeded fifteen years … [a bullet had struck him through the breast].

Source: Abiel Abbott Livermore, *The War with Mexico Reviewed* (Boston: American Peace Society, 1850), pp. 8, 11, 12, 139.

48. Excerpts from *The Other Side: Or Notes for the History of the War between Mexico and the United States Written in Mexico, 1846–1847*

The original articles were written from September 1848, and May 1849, under the general title of *Apuntes para la Historia de la Guerra entre México y los Estados-Unidos*. They were attributed to 15 Mexican officers. One of the principal contributors was Ramón Alcaraz, an officer in the Mexican Army during the Mexican-American War (1846–1848). He wrote many books about the topic. *Apuntes para la Historia* was translated in 1850 by Albert C. Ramsey as *The Other Side: Or Notes for the History of the War between Mexico and the United States*. It was published in Mexico, England, and the United States. The book gave the Mexican side of the Mexican-American War. The following excerpts have been attributed to Alcaraz's eyewitness accounts from the various battles in which he participated.

Matamoros is situated on the west bank of the Rio Bravo, in a vast plain, composed of wooden and brick houses, fourteen leagues distant from the coast. The proximity of the enemy indicated that they would little hesitate to attack a place presenting such important difficulties to its defenders. Open on all sides, except that where the river flowed, little resistance could be made towards the interior, and what increased the danger was that the fortifications which had existed were reduced now to a small redoubt. This had been constructed to the west of the city, and at some 600 yards distant from it, upon the bank of the river at the ford called the Anacuitas …

To sustain the attack, they could not count on a sufficient force. The garrison was composed in the beginning of the battalion of Sappers, the 2d light, the 1st and 10th infantry regiments of the line, and the 7th of cavalry, the auxiliaries of the towns of the North, several companies of Presidiales, and a battalion of the National Guard of the city of Matamoros. The artillery consisted of 20 field pieces, served by one company. Two or three days after the coming of the Americans, the marines of Tampico arrived, the 6th infantry, and a battalion of the Guarda Costa of that place. These two sections being united, they formed a total of about 3,000 men.

The munitions were not scarce, if they were not abundant. But it was not so fortunate with provisions, because the necessary supply had not been obtained in time, and before the blockade of the port. From the interior of the country it was impossible to bring them, and much less now was there an opportunity.

On the 8th it was positively ascertained from the spies, that the enemy, in number about 3,000 men with an abundance of artillery and numerous wagons, were directing their march from the Fort of Isabel to the entrenched camp in front of Matamoros. The General-in-Chief at once determined to give battle; an opportunity which he had sought for so many days. At ten o'clock in the morning our cavalry went forth upon the spacious plain of Palo Alto: the infantry followed at two in the day, and there came in sight of the enemy.

The artillery of the Americans, much superior to ours, made horrid ravages in the ranks of the Mexican [A]rmy. The soldiers yielded, not overwhelmed in a combat in which they might deal out the death which they received—not in the midst of the excitement and gallantry which the ardor of a battle brings forth, but in a fatal situation in which they were killed with impunity, and decimated in cold blood. The action was prolonged for whole hours under such unfortunate auspices, and the slain increased every minute. The troops at last, tired of being slaughtered for no use, demanded with a shout to be led on to the enemy with the bayonet, for they wished to fight hand to hand, and to die like brave men.

The fire began to spread. Its sinister splendor illuminated the camp, in which a short time before resounded the roar of artillery, and in which now were heard heart-rending groans of our wounded. As most of these were from cannon-shot, they were horribly mutilated. The sight deeply saddened, and the misfortune was complete, when nothing could be done to alleviate their sufferings, for the surgeon who carried the medicine-chests had disappeared at the first fire, without breathing where he had deposited them. There was no other choice than to send some of them to Matamoros in the carts that had brought provisions. The rest were left abandoned on the 9th in the field.

—The Battles of Palo Alto and La Resaca, Ramón Alcaraz (Mexican Army Officer), 1846

A little further on, they came up with the enemy on the field of battle known by the name of the Angostura. The ground which had to be passed over was formed of extensive and broad plains, in which it would not have been possible to resist the vigorous shock of our troops, especially of our beautiful cavalry. But where the enemy had halted to give battle, two successive series of hills and barrancas began, which formed a position truly formidable. Each hill was fortified with a battery and ready to deal its murderous fire upon any attempting to take it. The position presenting serious obstacles to an attack, manifested very plainly, that for the Mexicans to gain a victory they would have to sustain a heavy loss in men.

At the second charge of our troops, a lieutenant, D. José Maria Montoya, who was in the front rank, became mixed up with the Americans. Seeing himself alone, and not desiring to be killed nor taken prisoner, he availed himself of a stratagem to feign a parley, whereby he was carried into the presence of General Taylor. This was followed by his returning to our camp accompanied by two officers of their army, to have an interview with General Santa Anna. But Montoya, who had his reasons for not presenting himself, separated from the commissioners, who fulfilled their instructions.

General Santa Anna has not been embraced in this accusation. Friends and enemies have recognised [*sic*] the valor with which he constantly braved the fire. It is to be regretted his combinations did not correspond with his gallantry, that his errors dim the splendor of his merits, and that while it is painful to blame his conduct as a general, it is also pleasing to praise his courage as a soldier.

—The Battle of Buena Vista, Ramón Alcaraz, February 1846

At dawn on the 18th, the roar of the enemy's artillery resounded through the camps, as a solemn announcement of a battle.

Some of our soldiers now began to leave their ranks, and to descend the opposite side, attempting to mingle with the wounded who were retiring, but General Santa Anna, observing it, ordered some of his adjutants to prevent this disorder and they, either on compulsion or by the stimulus of enthusiasm, succeeded in persuading the fugitives to return.

In the meantime, General Baneneli appealed to the last resource, and ordered his men to charge bayonets. They, eager to join in an action which they had only heard, immediately hastened this movement in full force to come up to where they were directed; but, surprised at finding themselves hand to hand with an enemy so superior in numbers and surrounded on all sides, were panic-struck in an instant, fell into disorder, and their commander in vain endeavored to keep them in their ranks. Being himself involved in the crowd with the chiefs of engineers and other officers who endeavored, sword in hand, to keep back the men, they were actually rolled together down the opposite declivity, borne along by the multitude, which poured onward like a torrent from the height.

Among the fire and smoke, and above the mass of blue formed by the Americans behind the summit of the Telégrafo, still floated our deserted flag. But the banner of the stars was soon raised by the enemy upon the same staff, and for an instant both became entangled and confounded together, our own at length falling to the ground, amidst the shouts and roar of the victors' guns, and the mournful cries and confused voices of the vanquished.

When the Telégrafo was lost, the 6th infantry had retreated to the positions on the right, where they capitulated with the other corps. The grenadier battalion, which had been drawn out from the battery of the centre to the foot of the hill, chiefly dispersed, in spite of the exertions made to collect it.

An enthusiastic officer harangued the troops at the pitch of his voice, assuring them that they had yet lost nothing, wishing to reanimate the spirit now dead in all that unfortunate crowd. General Baneneli, rushing in with his horse and full of wrath, poured forth a thousand horrible imprecations upon his soldiers, and with the butt of his pistol threatened particularly one of his captains. The General-in-Chief vented his rage upon the officers who had lost their positions; and the agitation of the multitude, and the difficulties of the ground, with the general dangers and desperation, rendered the scene indescribable.

Horrible, indeed, was the descent by that narrow and rocky path, where thousands rushed, disputing the passage with desperation, and leaving a track of blood upon the road. All classes being confounded, all military distinction and respect were lost, the badges of rank became marks for sarcasms, that were only meted out according to their grade and humiliation. The enemy, now masters of our camp, turned their guns upon the fugitives. This augmented more and more the terror of the multitude crowded through the defile, and pressed forward every instant by a new impulse, which increased the confusion and disgrace of the ill-fated day.

Cerro-Gordo was lost! Mexico was open to the iniquity of the invader.

—The Battle of Cerro Gordo, Ramón Alcaraz, Mexican Army, April 1847

We will speak in the first place of Chapultepec, the key of Mexico, as then was commonly said, and whose reminiscences and traditions made it doubly important for the enemy, and moreover for the military projects they had conceived.

On the exterior it had the following fortifications. A horn-work in the road which leads to Tacubaya. A parapet in the gate at the entrance. Within the [e]nclosure which surrounds the woods to the south side, a breast-work was constructed, and a ditch eight yards wide and three in depth.

The artillery defending this fortification were 2 pieces of twenty-fours, 1 of eight, 3 field of fours, and 1 howitzer of 68, in all, 7 pieces.

The chief of the castle was General D. Nicolas Bravo and the second General, D. Mariano Monterde.

At dawn on the 12th, the enemy's battery, situated in the hermitage, opened its fire on the garita of the Niño Perdido, without any other object, as we can learn from the documents published by the American chiefs, than to call attention, and to properly be able to plant the ordnance which should batter Chapultepec in the places which we have mentioned.

In effect, in a few minutes, these batteries began to fire upon Chapultepec. At first, they caused no destruction. But rectifying their aim, the walls of the building commenced to be pierced by balls in all directions, experiencing great ravages also in the roofs, caused by the bombs which the mortar threw that, as we have said, was concealed in the court of the Molino. The artillery of Chapultepec answered with much precision and accuracy. The engineers worked incessantly to repair the damage done by the enemy's projectiles, and the troops quite behind the parapets suffered from this storm of balls. The most intelligent in the military art judge that the troops could have been placed at the foot of the hill to avoid the useless loss, leaving in the building only the artillerymen and the requisite engineers. This was not done, and the carcasses of the bombs and hollow balls killed and wounded many soldiers, who had not even the pleasure of discharging their muskets.

—The Battle of Chapultepec, Ramón Alcaraz

Source: Ramón Alcaraz et al., eds., *The Other Side: Or Notes for the History of the War between Mexico and the United States Written in Mexico*, Albert C. Ramsey, trans. (New York: John Wiley, 1850), pp. 33–38, 45–50, 122–129, 208–214, 353–365.

49. Excerpts from George B. McClellan, "On Volunteers in the Mexican War"

As in the case of many other generals who participated in the U.S. Civil War (1861–1865), George B. McClellan (1826–1885) served as a lieutenant during the Mexican-American War. Like many junior officers, he had doubts about the war and the conduct of U.S. volunteers who committed atrocities. The following excerpts are from his *Mexican War Diary* in which he criticizes the behavior of many Euro-American volunteers.

December 1846

I was perfectly disgusted coming down the river. I found that every confounded Voluntario in the "Continental Army" ranked me, to be ranked and put aside for a soldier of yesterday, a miserable thing with buttons on it, that knows nothing whatever, is indeed too hard a case. I have pretty much made up my mind that if I cannot increase my rank in this war, I shall resign shortly after the close of it. I cannot stand the idea of being a Second Lieutenant all my life. I have learned some valuable lessons in this war. I am (I hope and believe) pretty well cured of castle building. I came down here with high hopes, with pleasing anticipations of distinction, of being in hard fought battles and acquiring a name and reputation as a stepping stone to a still greater eminence in some future and greater war. I felt that if I could have a chance I could do something; but what has been the result—the real state of the case? The first thing that greeted my ears upon arriving off Brazos was the news of the battle of Monterey—the place of all others where this Company and its officers would have had an ample field for distinction. There was a grand miss but, thank heaven, it could not possibly have been avoided by us. Well, since then we have been dodging about—waiting a week here, two weeks there for the pontoon train, a month in the dirt somewhere else, doing nothing, half the company sick, have been sick myself for more than a month and a half—and here we are going to Tampico. What will be the next thing it is impossible to guess at. We may go to San Luis, we may go to Vera Cruz, we may go home from Tampico, we may see a fight, or a dozen of them, or we may not see a shot fired. I have made up my mind to act the philosopher—to take things as they come and not worry my head about the future, to try to get perfectly well, and above all things to see as much fun as I can "scare up" in the country.

I have seen more suffering since I came out here than I could have imagined to exist. It is really awful. I allude to the sufferings of the Volunteers. They literally die like dogs. Were it all known in the States, there would be no more hue and cry against the Army, all would be willing to have so large a regular army that we could dispense entirely with the volunteer system. The suffering among the Regulars is comparatively trifling, for their officers know their duty and take good care of the men.

Source: William Starr Myers, ed., *The Mexican War Diary of George B. McClellan* (Princeton: Princeton University Press, 1917), pp. 16–21.

50. Excerpts from Samuel E. Chamberlain, *My Confessions*

Samuel E. Chamberlain (1829–1908) was a soldier, artist, and author who traveled throughout the Southwest and Mexico. At the age of 15 he left home and joined the Second Illinois Volunteer Regiment that was headed to Texas. Once in Texas, he joined the regular army. He participated in border fights and rode with the Glanton gang who took Mexican scalps. *My Confessions* documents Euro-American racism and destruction during the Mexican-American War. The book was apparently based on Samuel Chamberlain's scrapbook, MC092, at the San Jacinto Museum of History, Houston, Texas. The book was published long after Chamberlain's death. The following excerpts are a report from the Mexican city of Parras (Coahuila, Mexico).

We found the patrol had been guilty of many outrages.... They had ridden into the church of San José during Mass, the place crowded with kneeling women and children, and with oaths and ribald jest had arrested soldiers who had permission to be present.

[He described a massacre by volunteers, mostly from Yell's Cavalry, at a cave:] On reaching the place we found a "greaser" shot and *scalped*, but still breathing; the poor fellow held in his hands a Rosary and a medal of the "Virgin of Guadalupe," only his feeble motions kept the fierce harpies from falling on him while yet alive. A Sabre thrust was given him in mercy, and on we went at a run. Soon shouts and curses, cries of women and children reached our ears, coming apparently from a cave at the end of the ravine. Climbing over the rocks we reached the entrance, and as soon as we could see in the comparative darkness, a horrid sight was before us. The cave was full of our volunteers yelling like fiends, while on the rocky floor lay over twenty Mexicans, dead and dying in pools of blood. Women and children were clinging to the knees of the murderers shrieking for mercy ... Most of the butchered Mexicans had been scalped; only three men were found unharmed. A rough crucifix was fastened to a rock, and some irreverent wretch had crowned the image with a bloody scalp. A sickening smell filled the place. The surviving women and children sent up loud screams on seeing us, thinking we had returned to finish the work!... No one was punished for this outrage.

Source: Samuel E. Chamberlain, *My Confessions* (New York: Harper & Row, 1956), pp. 75, 87–88.

51. Excerpts from the Treaty of Guadalupe Hidalgo, 1848

With the Treaty of Guadalupe Hidalgo, Mexico ceded Arizona, New Mexico, California, and parts of Utah, Nevada, and Colorado to the United States. Mexico was forced to relinquish claims to Texas—recognizing the Rio Grande as the boundary (Article V) between the two countries. The United States paid Mexico for taking half its territory. The United States paid Mexico $15,000,000 in compensation for war-related damage to Mexican property and agreed to compensate American citizens for debts owed to them by the Mexican government. These debts were mostly related to the loss of runaway slaves who found refuge in Mexico. The Treaty called for the property and civil rights of Mexican nationals on what was to become the U.S. side of the border. Finally, the United States promised to police its boundaries. The Senate ratified the treaty by a vote of 34–14 on March 10, 1848. It only passed by a one-vote margin since a two-thirds majority was required for passage. Article X, which guaranteed the protection of Mexican land grants, was deleted. The following are key articles of the Treaty.

... ARTICLE V

The boundary line between the two Republics shall commence in the Gulf of Mexico, three leagues from land, opposite the mouth of the Rio Grande, otherwise called Rio Bravo del Norte, or opposite the mouth of its deepest branch, if it should have more than one branch emptying directly into the sea; from thence up the middle of that river, following the deepest channel, where it has more than one, to the point where it strikes the southern boundary of New Mexico; thence, westwardly, along the whole southern boundary of New Mexico (which runs north of the town called Paso) to its western termination; thence, northward, along the western line of New Mexico, until it intersects the first branch of the River Gila; (or if it should not intersect any branch of that river, then to the point on the said line nearest to such branch, and thence in a direct line to the same); thence down the middle of the said branch and of the said river, until it empties into the Rio Colorado; thence across the Rio Colorado, following the division line between Upper and Lower California, to the Pacific Ocean.

The southern and western limits of New Mexico, mentioned in the article, are those laid down in the map entitled "Map of the United Mexican States,["] as organized and defined by various acts of the Congress of said republic, and constructed according to the best authorities. Revised edition. Published at New York, in 1847, by J. Disturnell, of which map a copy is added to this treaty, bearing the signatures and seals of the undersigned Plenipotentiaries. And, in order to preclude all difficulty in tracing upon the ground the limit separating Upper from Lower California, it is agreed that the said limit shall consist of a straight line drawn from the middle of the Rio Gila, where it unites with the Colorado, to a point on the coast of the Pacific Ocean, distant one marine league due south of the southernmost point of the port of San Diego, according to the plan of said port made in the year 1782 by Don Juan Pantoja, second sailing-master of the Spanish fleet, and published at Madrid in the year 1802, in the atlas to the voyage of the schooners Sutil and Mexicana; of which plan a copy is hereunto added, signed and sealed by the respective Plenipotentiaries.

In order to designate the boundary line with due precision, upon authoritative maps, and to establish upon the ground land-marks which shall show the limits of both republics, as described in the present article, the two Governments shall each appoint a commissioner and a surveyor, who, before the expiration of one year from the date of the exchange of ratifications of this treaty, shall meet at the port of San Diego, and proceed to run and mark the said boundary in its whole course to the mouth of the Rio Bravo del Norte. They shall keep journals and make out plans of their operations; and the result agreed upon by them shall be deemed a part of this treaty, and shall have the same force as if it were inserted therein. The two Governments will amicably agree regarding what may be necessary to these persons, and also as to their respective escorts, should such be necessary.

The boundary line established by this article shall be religiously respected by each of the two republics, and no change shall ever be made therein, except by the express and free consent of both nations, lawfully given by the General Government of each, in conformity with its own constitution.

    …

ARTICLE VII

The River Gila, and the part of the Rio Bravo del Norte lying below the southern boundary of New Mexico, being, agreeably to the fifth article, divided in the middle between the two republics, the navigation of the Gila and of the Bravo below said boundary shall be free and common to the vessels and citizens of both countries; and neither shall, without the consent of the other, construct any work that may impede or interrupt, in whole or in part, the exercise of this right; not even for the purpose of favoring new methods of navigation. Nor shall any tax or contribution, under any denomination or title, be levied upon vessels or persons navigating the same or upon merchandise or effects transported thereon, except in the case of landing upon one of their shores. If, for the purpose of making the said rivers navigable, or for maintaining them in such state, it should be necessary or advantageous to establish any tax or contribution, this shall not be done without the consent of both Governments. The stipulations contained in the present article shall not impair the territorial rights of either republic within its established limits.

ARTICLE VIII

Mexicans now established in territories previously belonging to Mexico, and which remain for the future within the limits of the United States, as defined by the present treaty, shall be free to continue where they now reside, or to remove at any time to the Mexican Republic, retaining the property which they possess in the said territories, or disposing thereof, and removing the proceeds wherever they please, without their being subjected, on this account, to any contribution, tax, or charge whatever.

Those who shall prefer to remain in the said territories may either retain the title and rights of Mexican citizens, or acquire those of citizens of the United States. But they shall be under the obligation to make their election within one year from the date of the exchange of ratifications of this treaty; and those who shall remain in the said territories after the expiration of that year, without having declared their intention to retain the character of Mexicans, shall be considered to have elected to become citizens of the United States.

In the said territories, property of every kind, now belonging to Mexicans not established there, shall be inviolably respected. The present owners, the heirs of these, and all Mexicans who may hereafter acquire said property by contract, shall enjoy with respect to it guarantees equally ample as if the same belonged to citizens of the United States.

ARTICLE IX

The Mexicans who, in the territories aforesaid, shall not preserve the character of citizens of the Mexican Republic, conformably with what is stipulated in the preceding article, shall be incorporated into the Union of the United States and be admitted at the proper time (to be judged of by the Congress of the United States) to the enjoyment of all the rights of citizens of the United States, according to the principles of the Constitution; and in the mean time, shall be maintained and protected in the free enjoyment of their liberty and property, and secured in the free exercise of their religion without restriction.

ARTICLE X [STRICKEN BY U.S. AMENDMENTS]

ARTICLE XI

Considering that a great part of the territories, which, by the present treaty, are to be comprehended for the future within the limits of the United States, is now occupied by savage tribes, who will hereafter be under the exclusive control of the Government of the United States, and whose incursions within the territory of Mexico would be prejudicial in the extreme, it is solemnly agreed that all such incursions shall be forcibly restrained by the Government of the United States whensoever this may be necessary; and that when they cannot be prevented, they shall be punished by the said Government, and satisfaction for the same shall be exacted all in the same way, and with equal diligence and energy, as if the same incursions were meditated or committed within its own territory, against its own citizens.

It shall not be lawful, under any pretext whatever, for any inhabitant of the United States to purchase or acquire any Mexican, or any foreigner residing in Mexico, who may have been captured by Indians inhabiting the territory of either of the two republics; nor to purchase or acquire horses, mules, cattle, or property of any kind, stolen within Mexican territory by such Indians.

And in the event of any person or persons, captured within Mexican territory by Indians, being carried into the territory of the United States, the Government of the latter engages and binds itself, in the most solemn manner, so soon as it shall know of such captives being within its territory, and shall be able so to do, through the faithful exercise of its influence and power, to rescue them and return them to their country or deliver them to the agent or representative of the Mexican Government. The Mexican authorities will, as far as practicable, give to the Government of the United States notice of such captures; and its agents shall pay the expenses incurred in the maintenance and transmission of the rescued captives; who, in the mean time, shall be treated with the utmost hospitality by the American authorities at the place where they may be. But if the Government of the United States, before receiving such notice from Mexico, should obtain intelligence, through any other channel, of the existence of Mexican captives within its territory, it will proceed forthwith to effect their release and delivery to the Mexican agent, as above stipulated.

For the purpose of giving to these stipulations the fullest possible efficacy, thereby affording the security and redress demanded by their true spirit and intent, the Government of the United States will now and hereafter pass, without unnecessary delay, and always vigilantly enforce, such laws as the nature of the subject may require. And, finally, the sacredness of this obligation shall never be lost sight of by the said Government, when providing for the removal of the Indians from any portion of the said territories, or for its being settled by citizens of the United States; but, on the contrary, special care shall then be taken not to place its Indian occupants under the necessity of seeking new homes, by committing those invasions which the United States have solemnly obliged themselves to restrain.

...

ARTICLE XV

The United States, exonerating Mexico from all demands on account of the claims of their citizens mentioned in the preceding article, and considering them entirely and forever canceled, whatever their amount may be, undertake to make satisfaction for the same, to an amount not exceeding three and one-quarter millions of dollars. To ascertain the validity and amount of those claims, a board of commissioners shall be established by the Government of the United States, whose awards shall be final and conclusive; provided that, in deciding upon the validity of each claim, the boa[rd] shall be guided and governed by the principles and rules of decision prescribed by the first and fifth articles of the unratified convention, concluded at the city of Mexico on the twentieth day of November, one thousand eight hundred and forty-three; and in no case shall an award be made in favour of any claim not embraced by these principles and rules.

If, in the opinion of the said board of commissioners or of the claimants, any books, records, or documents, in the possession or power of the Government of the Mexican Republic, shall be deemed necessary to the just decision of any claim, the commissioners, or the claimants through them, shall, within such period as Congress may designate, make an application in writing for the same, addressed to the Mexican Minister of Foreign Affairs, to be transmitted by the Secretary of State of the United States; and the Mexican Government engages, at the earliest possible moment after the receipt of such demand, to cause any of the books, records, or documents so specified, which shall be in their possession or power (or authenticated copies or extracts of the same), to be transmitted to the said Secretary of State, who shall immediately deliver them over to the said board of commissioners; provided that no such application shall be made by or at the instance of any claimant, until the facts which it is expected to prove by such books, records, or documents, shall have been stated under oath or affirmation.

Source: Treaty of Guadalupe Hidalgo, February 2, 1848, The Avalon Project at Yale Law School, http://www.yale.edu/lawweb/avalon/diplomacy/mexico/guadhida.htm.

52. Deleted Article X from the Treaty of Guadalupe Hidalgo, 1848

Article X of the Treaty of Guadalupe Hidalgo used strong terms to guarantee the property rights of Mexicans and Indians who remained in the ceded territory. However, there was some question whether the article applied to Texas. There was also sentiment against leaving large amounts of lands in Mexican hands. The debate was heated and many U.S. senators did not want to make any concessions to the vanquished nation. The Senate finally approved the Treaty of Guadalupe Hidalgo without Article X, which guaranteed the protection of Mexican land grants, and with changes made to Article IX that obligated the United States to police its boundaries, on March 10, 1848. U.S. Secretary of State James Buchanan sent a letter to the Mexican Congress giving reasons for the elimination of Article X and the revision of Article IX. He wrote that the U.S. Constitution already promised to protect private property. Article IX was changed because it violated precedents in treaties negotiated with France and Spain. The Querétaro Protocol was given to the Mexican Congress prior to the U.S. ratification of the treaty giving the reasons why the United States had changed the original. In short, it said "Trust us." The U.S. Constitution would protect Mexican Americans. The protocol's interpretation of the treaty, however, had no legal force.

ARTICLE X

All the land grants made by the Mexican government or by the competent authorities which pertained to Mexico in the past and which will remain in the future within the boundaries of the United States will be respected as valid, with the same force as if those territories still remained within the limits of Mexico. But the grantees of lands in Texas who had taken possession of them and who because of the conditions of the state since discord began between the Mexican Government and Texas, may have been impeded from complying with all the conditions of the grants, have the obligation of fulfilling the same conditions under the stated terms of the respective grants, but now counted from the date of the exchange of the ratifications of this Treaty; for failing to do this the same grants are not obligatory upon the State of Texas, in virtue of stipulations contained in this article.

Source: Article X, Treaty of Guadalupe Hidalgo, http://www.digitalhistory.uh.edu/mexican_voices/voices_display.cfm?id=62.

53. President James K. Polk (1795–1849) on Article X of the Treaty of Guadalupe Hidalgo, February 22, 1848

President James K. Polk sent U.S. Minister Nicholas Trist (1800–1874), a seasoned diplomat, to Mexico in the spring of 1847 to negotiate a treaty of peace for ending the Mexican-American War. By August 1847, negotiations were well underway. However, President Polk was not pleased with the outcome of the negotiations and wanted more of Mexico's land. The Treaty of Guadalupe Hidalgo ceded 55 percent of Mexico's territory to the United States in exchange for $15 million in compensation for war-related damage to Mexican property. Polk actively campaigned against the inclusion of Article X guaranteeing the protection of Mexican land grants. He did not want strong guarantees to protect Mexican property—opining that the U.S. Constitution already protected Mexicans in the United States. Polk pressured senators to vote against the inclusion of Article X. The following document raises what he called serious flaws in Article X, saying there was no need for the article since U.S. law would protect property rights.

IN EXECUTIVE SESSION, SENATE OF THE U. STATES.
WEDNESDAY, FEBRUARY 23, 1848.

The following message was received from the President of the United States, by Mr. Walker, his secretary:

To the Senate of the United States:

I lay before the Senate, for their consideration and advice as to its ratification, a treaty of peace, friendship, limits, and settlement, signed at the city of Guadalupe Hidalgo, on the second day of February 1848, by N. P. Trist on the part of the United States, and by plenipotentiaries appointed for that purpose on the part of the Mexican government.

I deem it to be my duty to state that the recall of Mr. Trist as commissioner of the United States, of which Congress was informed in my annual message, was dictated by a belief that his continued presence with the army could be productive of no good, but might do much harm by encouraging the delusive hopes and false impressions of the Mexicans; and that his recall would satisfy Mexico that the United States had no terms of peace more favorable to offer. Directions were given that any propositions for peace, which Mexico might make, should be received and transmitted by the commanding general of our forces, to the United States.

It was not expected that *Mr. Trist* would remain in Mexico, or continue in the exercise of the functions of the office of commissioner, after he received his letter of recall. He has, however, done so, and the plenipotentiaries of the government of Mexico, with a knowledge of the fact, have concluded with him this treaty. I have examined it with a full sense of the extraneous circumstances attending its conclusion and signature, which might be objected to; but, conforming, as it does substantially on the main questions of boundary and indemnity, to the terms which our commissioner, when he left the United States in April last, was authorized to offer, and animated, as I am, by the spirit which has governed all my official conduct towards Mexico, I have felt it to be my duty to submit it to the Senate for their consideration, with a view to its ratification.

To the tenth article of the treaty there are serious objections, and no instructions given to Mr. Trist contemplated or authorized its insertion. The public lands within the limits of Texas belong to that State, and this government has no power to dispose of them, or to change the conditions of grants already made. All valid titles to land within the other territories ceded to the United States will remain unaffected by the change of sovereignty; and I therefore submit that this article should not be ratified as a part of the treaty.

There may be reason to apprehend that the ratification of the "additional and secret article" might unreasonably delay and embarrass the final action on the treaty by Mexico. I therefore submit whether that article should not be rejected by the Senate.

If the treaty shall be ratified as proposed to be amended, the cessions of territory made by it to the United States, as indemnity, the provision for the satisfaction of the claims of our injured citizens, and the permanent establishment of the boundary of one of the States of the Union, are objects gained of great national importance; while the magnanimous forbearance exhibited towards Mexico, it is hoped may insure a lasting peace and good neighborhood between the two countries.

I communicate herewith a copy of the instructions given to *Mr. Slidell* in November 1845, as enjoy extraordinary and minister plenipotentiary to Mexico; a copy of the instructions given to *Mr. Trist* in April last, and such of the correspondence of the latter with the Department of State, not heretofore communicated to Congress, as will enable the Senate to understand the action which has been had with a view to the adjustment of our difficulties with Mexico.

James K. Polk
Washington, February 22, 1848.

Source: U.S. Senate, 30th Cong., 1st Sess., Executive Order 68. *Congressional Record*.

54. The Querétaro Protocol, May 26, 1848

The Mexican Congress reluctantly ratified the Treaty of Guadalupe Hidalgo by the U.S. Senate on March 10, 1848. One vote against the treaty would have lacked the two-thirds majority required. Article 10 was absent from the ratified version of the treaty and changes to Article 11 had lessened the obligation of the United States to protect Mexican property. The treaty passed the Mexican Congress by a one-vote margin and was ratified on May 19, 1848. Some Mexican legislators relied on a letter of protocol by American negotiators, known as the Querétaro Protocol, that assured Mexicans that their rights would be protected by the U.S. Constitution and that the deletion of Article X and parts of the other articles was in their interest. Many Mexican legislators did not trust the United States and wanted a guarantee of property rights as well as the inclusion of parts of Article IX that guaranteed Mexicans left behind full citizenship, guaranteeing immediate statehood to the Mexican Southwest, and obligated the United States to police its borders.

1st. The American Government by suppressing the IXth article of the Treaty of Guadalupe Hidalgo and substituting the IIId article of the Treaty of Louisiana, did not intend to diminish in any way what was agreed upon by the aforesaid article IXth in favor of the inhabitants of the territories ceded by Mexico. Its understanding is that all of the agreement is contained in the 3d article of the Treaty of Louisiana. Inconsequence of all the privileges and guarantees civil, political, and religious, which would have been possessed by the inhabitants of the ceded territories, if the IXth article of the treaty had been retained, will be enjoyed by them, without any difference, under the article which has been substituted.

2nd. The American Government by suppressing the Xth article of the Treaty of Guadalupe Hidalgo did not in any way intend to annul the grants of lands made by Mexico in the ceded territories. These grants notwithstanding the suppression of the article of the treaty, preserve the legal value which they may possess, and the grantees may cause their legitimate (titles) to be acknowledged before American tribunals. (Titles: those which were legitimate titles up to the 13th of May, 1846, and in Texas up to the 2nd March, 1836.)

Source: Protocol of Quéretaro, http://www.digitalhistory.uh.edu/mexican_voices/voices_display. cfm?id=65.

55. Excerpt from Manuel Crescion Rejón on the Treaty of Guadalupe Hidalgo, 1848

Many Mexican intellectuals expressed doubt as to the good faith of the United States in 1848. For them, the United States had unjustly invaded Mexico. In 1848, at the time the treaty was signed, Mexican diplomat Manuel Crescion Rejón predicted that Mexicans in the United States would be at the mercy of the Euro-Americans and, because of their race, would be treated as second-class citizens in the United States.

Our race, our unfortunate people, will have to wander in search of hospitality in a strange land, only to be ejected later. Descendants of the Indians that we are, the North Americans hate us, their spokesmen depreciate us, even if they recognize the justice of our cause, and they consider us unworthy to form with them one nation and one society, they clearly manifest that their future expansion begins with the territory that they take from us, and pushing aside our citizens who inhabit the land.

Source: Antonio de la Peña y Reyes, *Algunos Documentos Sobre el Tratado de Guadalupe-Hidalgo* (México, D.F.: Sec de Rel. Ext., 1930), p. 159, quoted in Richard Gonzales, "Commentary on the Treaty of Guadalupe Hidalgo." In Feliciano Rivera, *A Mexican American Source Book* (Menlo Park, CA: Educational Consulting Associates, 1970), p. 185.

PART IV
The Border and Reannexation

The existing Mexican and United States border is the result of the Texas and Mexican-American Wars. After these wars, establishing a line was not easy. Both nations sent out survey teams; often where the border was had to be negotiated. Meanwhile, politicos lobbied for extending the line to favor their interests. Texas claimed the Rio Grande to and including half of New Mexico, and expansionists talked about the reannexation of land that was supposedly their land. The documents in this section address "The Mexican Border." We use the term *reannex* because Euro-Americans thought of it in those terms.

The lines on the maps were meant to designate the limits of Mexico—not the limits of the United States. Drawing lines was highly political. The boundary that was drawn at the time of the signing of the Treaty of Guadalupe Hidalgo was based on J. Disturnell's 1847 Map. It was a faulty map that made the drawing of the line almost impossible. The task of Boundary Commissioner James Bartlett was complicated by members of the U.S. Congress and the territorial governor of New Mexico who questioned his decisions and even accused him of selling out the United States.

56. Henry Clay's Resolutions on the Compromise of 1850, January 29, 1850

The annexation of Texas to the United States and the acquisition of a huge portion of Mexican territory did not decrease tensions between the North and the South. The Treaty of Guadalupe Hidalgo ended the Mexican-American War (1848) but almost immediately the north and the south sought to further their interests—the South wanted slavery legalized in the newly acquired land and the North wanted to exclude slavery. Before going to war, Congress had passed the Wilmot Proviso (1846) as an amendment to a House of Representatives bill that prohibited slavery in any land acquired from Mexico. However, once the war was over, slave interests were not satisfied and a crisis similar to that of the Missouri Compromise of 1820 ensued. In the case of the latter, Missouri in 1818 had sufficient population to be admitted as a state. An amendment was proposed that prohibited slavery from entering Missouri. The amendment passed the House but not the Senate. In 1820, a compromise was reached in which Maine was admitted as a free state, and Missouri was not required to prohibit slavery. Slavery was prohibited in the Louisiana Territory (obtained through the Louisiana Purchase [1803]) above 36° 30′ (latitude/longitude)—except for Missouri. In 1849, there was a similar stalemate and five laws were passed that became known as the Compromise of 1850. As with the Missouri Compromise, the purpose of the Compromise of 1850 was to balance the interests of the slaveholding states and the free states and to avert a split. In sum, California was designated as a free state; Texas received money to give up its claims to the Rio Grande to the east that included New Mexico, Arizona, and parts of Utah; the slave trade was prohibited, but slavery was not outlawed except in the District of Columbia; and fugitive slave laws were passed, requiring the return of runaway slaves. Henry Clay, U.S. senator from Kentucky, offered the following resolution that encapsulated the compromise.

It being desirable, for the peace, concord, and harmony of the Union of these States, to settle and adjust amicably all existing questions of controversy between them arising out of the institution of slavery upon a fair, equitable and just basis: therefore,

1. Resolved, That California, with suitable boundaries, ought, upon her application to be admitted as one of the States of this Union, without the imposition by Congress of any restriction in respect to the exclusion or introduction of slavery within those boundaries.

2. Resolved, That as slavery does not exist by law, and is not likely to be introduced into any of the territory acquired by the United States from the republic of Mexico, it is inexpedient for Congress to provide by law either for its introduction into, or exclusion from, any part of the said territory; and that appropriate territorial governments ought to be established by Congress in all of the said territory, not assigned as the boundaries of the proposed State of California, without the adoption of any restriction or condition on the subject of slavery.

3. Resolved, That the western boundary of the State of Texas ought to be fixed on the Rio del Norte, commencing one marine league from its mouth, and running up that river to the southern line of New Mexico; thence with that line eastwardly, and so continuing in the same direction to the line as established between the United States and Spain, excluding any portion of New Mexico, whether lying on the east or west of that river.

4. Resolved, That it be proposed to the State of Texas, that the United States will provide for the payment of all that portion of the legitimate and bona fide public debt of that State contracted prior to its annexation to the United States, and for which the duties on foreign imports were pledged by the said State to its creditors, not exceeding the sum of dollars, in consideration of the said duties so pledged having been no longer applicable to that object after the said annexation, but having thenceforward become payable to the United States; and upon the condition, also, that the said State of Texas shall, by some solemn and authentic act of her legislature or of a convention, relinquish to the United States any claim which it has to any part of New Mexico.

5. Resolved, That it is inexpedient to abolish slavery in the District of Columbia whilst that institution continues to exist in the State of Maryland, without the consent of that State, without the consent of the people of the District, and without just compensation to the owners of slaves within the District.

6. But, resolved, That it is expedient to prohibit, within the District, the slave trade in slaves brought into it from States or places beyond the limits of the District, either to be sold therein as merchandise, or to be transported to other markets without the District of Columbia.

7. Resolved, That more effectual provision ought to be made by law, according to the requirement of the constitution, for the restitution and delivery of persons bound to service or labor in any State, who may escape into any other State or Territory in the Union. And,

8. Resolved, That Congress has no power to promote or obstruct the trade in slaves between the slaveholding States; but that the admission or exclusion of slaves brought from one into another of them, depends exclusively upon their own particular laws.

Source: Compromise of 1850, U.S. Congress, http://www.ourdocuments.gov/doc.php?flash=true&doc=27&page=transcript.

57. Excerpt from Governor William Carr Lane's Manifesto Regarding the Drawing of the Boundary between Mexico and the United States, 1853

The Treaty of Guadalupe Hidalgo (1848) mandated a joint boundary commission to determine the boundary between the United States and Mexico. In December 1848, President James K. Polk (term of office 1845–1849) named Ambrose Sevier as U.S. Commissioner but he died before he could be confirmed to head the U.S. commission. John B. Weller (1812–1875), a former Congressman from Ohio, replaced Sevier and on July 6, 1849, met with Mexican Commissioner Gen. Pedro García Conde. The joint commission ran a line from the Pacific Ocean to the Gila and Colorado Rivers. They planned to meet in El Paso. Weller was forced to leave the commission because of political intrigue and infighting. He was replaced by John Russell Bartlett (1805–1886) and the commission resumed its work in the El Paso, Texas, area. Immediately, an impasse developed over the location of the southern boundary of New Mexico. Controversy developed when several serious discrepancies were found in the official Disturnell Treaty map used by the framers of the Treaty of Guadalupe Hidalgo (1848) to set the boundaries. Bartlett and García Conde reached a compromise in the spring of 1851. This agreement resulted in a crisis that was not resolved until the Gadsden Purchase was negotiated in 1853. Federal, state, and local representatives from New Mexico and the rest of the country claimed that Bartlett had sold them out by giving "their" land to Mexico. The following document is an excerpt from a manifesto issued by New Mexico Territorial Governor Willam Carr Lane (1789–1863), a Whig who had served as mayor of St. Louis from 1837 to 1840. President Millard Fillmore (1800–1874) appointed him in 1852 to be the new governor of the New Mexican Territory. The statement inflamed Mexican authorities in neighboring Chihuahua who charged that the United States was attempting to goad Mexico into another war in order to seize more land.

The mere fact, without any other reason, that the President and Congress of the United States have disapproved and repudiated the provisional boundary line which has been run from the Rio Grande to the Gila, is of itself an ample justification of the act of the Government of New-Mexico in promulgating the proclamation of the 19th inst., and the want of special instructions from Mexico does not in the slightest degree invalidate this official act. Whatever your Excellencies may have heard to the contrary from persons as ignorant as presumptuous, it is none the less true that my authority is to be found in the laws and constitution of the United States, in the law of nations, in the treaty with Mexico, and in the duties of my office as Governor of this Territory.

Your Excellencies have affirmed that the southern boundary line of New-Mexico terminated at New-Mexico, twenty-two miles north of the provisional line of Mr. Bartlett, while a degree of the Mexican Congress fixes the line at El Paso; this decree has never, to my knowledge, been revoked.

In your communication your Excellencies frankly admit that Chihuahua never exercised its jurisdiction over the territory in dispute, before the running of Mr. Bartlett's line, notwithstanding it was entreated by the inhabitants so to do. And why did it not exercise its jurisdiction? I will answer for your Excellencies—it was because it was well known that the territory belonged to New-Mexico, and not to Chihuahua.

The error committed by Mr. Bartlett, when he determined the said line, induced Chihuahua into error, and it is now incumbent upon Chihuahua to correct it.

"If we should have to suspend for a time the work on one portion of the line, by reason of a difference of opinion, or any other cause, we may go on and determine some other part, so that, in case we should not agree as to the southern boundary line, and should therefore have to refer to our respective Governments, the work on the Gila may progress, should it be deemed expedient." To these reasonable propositions, Mr. Bartlett turned a deaf ear, and obstinately insisted upon his established line, without the concurrence of his colleagues, even though the latter had shown the said line to be wrong....

(Signed)

WM. CARR LANE,
Governor of the Territory of New-Mexico.

Source: New York Daily Times, June 20, 1853, p. 3.

58. Excerpt from Commissioner James Bartlett's Reply to William Carr Lane, 1853

John Russell Bartlett (1805–1886), the head of the U.S. Boundary Commission, kept a journal of the United States–Mexican Boundary Survey Commission's work. In 1854, he published the two-volume *Personal Narrative of Explorations and Incidents in Texas, New Mexico, California, Sonora, and Chihuahua, 1850–1853* (1856). While commissioner, he was under constant criticism from expansionists like the New Mexican Territorial Governor, William Carr Lane (1789–1863), who wanted a more liberal interpretation of the mandate of the Guadalupe Treaty and accused Bartlett of giving away American soil. The expansionists wanted the entire Mesilla Valley. In the following passage, Bartlett explains why the boundaries were drawn as they were and he answers New Mexico Territorial Gov. Lane's claim that Bartlett had sold out U.S. interests and given away the Mesilla Valley to Mexico.

Mesilla is the diminutive of the Spanish word *mesa*, table, i.e., table land, or plateau; and is applied to a lesser plateau in the valley of the Rio Grande, beneath that of the great *mesa*, plateau, or table land which extends for several hundred miles in all directions from the Rio Grande. It means, therefore, little plateau, or little table land.

It is situated on the western side of the Rio Grande, about fifty miles above El Paso, in latitude about 32° 18' North; and until the year 1850, it was without an inhabitant.

Immediately preceding, and after the war with Mexico, the Mexican population occupying the eastern bank of the Rio Grande in Texas and New Mexico, were greatly annoyed by the encroachments of the Americans, and by their determined efforts to despoil them of their landed property. This was done by the latter, either settling among them, or, in some instances, forcibly occupying their dwellings and cultivated spots. In most cases, however, it was done by putting *"Texas head-rights"* on their property. These head-rights, were grants issued by the State of Texas, generally for 640 acres, or a mile square, though they sometimes covered very large tracts. They were issued to persons who had served in her wars, and resembled our military land warrants; or to original settlers. These certificates or "head-rights" are still bought and sold in that State. The owner of them may locate his land where he pleases, unless previously occupied, or in lawful possession of another.

With these land certificates or "head-rights," many Americans flocked to the valley of the Rio Grande, and located them in many instances on property which, for a century, had been in the quiet possession of the descendants of the old Spanish colonists. The latter, to avoid litigation, and sometimes standing in fear of their lives, abandoned their homes, and sought a refuge on the Mexican side of the river. Dona Ana, a modern town on the eastern bank of the Rio Grande, 55 miles above El Paso, and near the "initial point;" being a well located and desirable place, and moreover, selected by the United States for one of its military posts, became an attractive point among speculators, and was, in consequence, pounced upon by them and covered by the "Texas head-rights" or land-warrants. Whether the Mexican occupants of the town and lands adjacent were the lawful owners or not, it is needless to state; it is sufficient to say that they had long been in undisturbed possession. They now became alarmed. Litigations commenced. Some applied to the authorities of NewMexico, Texas or the United States for protection. Failing to obtain it, in despair, several hundred abandoned their property and homes, determined to seek an asylum within the territory of Mexico, preferring the very uncertain protection they could obtain there, to remaining as citizens of the United States.

With this resolution, a spot was selected on the opposite or western side of the river, eight or ten miles below Dona Ana, which, it was believed, would be within the limits of Mexico. In the month of May 1850, this persecuted people established themselves there, and named the place "La Mesilla," i.e., the little table. To increase the colony, the Government of Mexico offered to give lands to other actual settlers, which offer induced large numbers of dissatisfied Mexicans living in New-Mexico and in the small settlements along the Rio Grande, in Texas, to remove there. More than half the population of Dona Ana removed to Mesilla within a year.

When the boundary line was agreed upon, in December 1850, and it became certain that La Mesilla was south of it, according to the treaty map, a day was set apart for public rejoicing, for the astronomers had been observing near them, and led them to doubt on which side of the line their valley would fall. The day came, and the event was celebrated by firing of cannon and a grand ball, which many from El Paso attended. After this, the population increased much on account of the inducements offered, and in October 1852, the Prefect of El Paso stated that the population numbered 1,900 souls. Very few Americans ever settled there; in fact, none but traders, and it is probable that there neve[r] were twenty altogether.

Last Summer, some Mexican speculators attempted to practice the same impositions upon them as were practiced when they were citizens of New-Mexico, by claiming their lands. This created great dissatisfaction, and then they threatened to abandon their lands and again become citizens of the United States. At this time, some mischievous persons put an idea into their heads to deny the jurisdiction of Mexico, and thus save their property; and this is, doubtless, the foundation of Gov. LANE's assertion, that they desire to be *reannexed* to New-Mexico.

B.

Source: "The Mesilla Valley," *New York Daily Times*, May 5, 1853, p. 6.

59. A Letter from John Disturnell to the *New York Daily Times* on the Drawing of the New-Mexican Boundary, May 6, 1853

John Disturnell (1801–1877) was the most influential and well-known U.S. mapmaker of the nineteenth century. When the United States turned to an authority to establish the U.S.-Mexican border, they based their assumptions on Disturnell's map since it was the most authoritative. But, his 1847 map was flawed and caused a dispute over the placing of the U.S.-Mexico boundary around the El Paso area. An error in the coordinates of the map raised the issue as to whether the lines in that area should be disputed. El Paso was incorrectly located on the official map 34 miles too far north and 100 miles too far east. The dispute was resolved by a compromise between U.S. Boundary Commissioner James Bartlett and Mexican Commissioner Pedro García Conde (1806–1851). This compromise caused uproar with U.S. politicos claiming that Bartlett had given away U.S. territory. In the following letter, Disturnell defended the Boundary Commission's compromise and called the Mesilla dispute of imaginary value and an attempt to take advantage of Mexico. The letter is fundamental to understanding the dispute and the Euro-American maneuver of reannexation.

THE NEW-MEXICAN BOUNDARY

To the Editor of the New York Daily Times:

The article in your paper of the 5th inst., on the subject of "*The Mexican Boundary,*" signed "W.H.S." is one-sided, and partly erroneous in regard to the matter in dispute. For a correct view of the subject, the public should read the article in the *National Intelligencer* of the 5th of April, signed "P.F.," which quotes from the instructions given to N.P. Trist, Esq., the Commissioner on the part of the United States, and who signed the Treaty of Peace and Limits, Feb. 2, 1848. Also refer to the Constitution of Chihuahua, as revised in 1847, which defines the northern boundary between New-Mexico, at 32° 57' 43" north latitude. Then examine a map of the Republic of Mexico, certified to by Don Garcio Conde in 1845, which valuable and authentic map is in the possession of the late Commissioner to settle the boundary between the two countries; and in conclusion, refer to the "*Treaty Map,*" revised edition, 1847, which indicates, on careful examination, the line in dispute to run parallel to 32° 22' north latitude—being no doubt the fair and equitable *boundary line*, according to the letter of said Treaty.

As to the imaginary value of the Mesilla Valley, or tract in dispute, it has no force other than a greater inducement for a stronger party to despoil a weaker foe.

As regards the *Treaty Map* of the Republic of Mexico, which has of late so often been referred to, it was first published in the City of New-York, in 1828, being then considered the most correct map of Mexico, and certified to as such by competent authority. Since then, in many respects, the map has been improved and corrected from time to time, as new information has been received from the Departments at Washington and otherwise.

In December 1847, it was discovered that a geographical error existed in regard to the true position of El Paso, a frontier town of Chihuahua, which error was corrected from official documents, derived in Washington by the publisher of said map. In changing the boundary between New-Mexico and Chihuahua, the compiler was guided by new and supposed reliable American authority, which, however, seems to have been an error in regard to said boundary, according to the import of the able article in the *National Intelligencer*, and from an official map of Chihuahua, which has recently been shown to me by J. R. Bartlett, Esq., the late Commissioner on the part of the United States, to settle the boundary between the two countries, as called for by the Treaty of 1848.

Yours, &c.,

John Disturnell
New York, May 6, 1853

Source: New York Daily Times, May 7, 1853, p. 3.

60. Excerpts from the Gadsden Purchase Treaty, December 30, 1853

The U.S. minister to Mexico, James Gadsden (1788–1858), attempted to purchase Sonora and northern Mexico from Mexico. When Mexico was unwilling to sell this area, Gadsden used heavy-handed methods in the negotiations, threatening Mexican ministers that, if they did not sell southern Arizona and parts of New Mexico, "we shall take it." Under pressure, Mexico ceded over 45,000 square miles, of which some 35,000 were in southern Arizona, for $10 million. The Gadsden, or Mesilla, Treaty settled the controversy surrounding where the boundary between the countries should be placed. The following documents are excerpts of the treaty that deal with the Mesilla Valley's transfer to the United States and the relieving of the United States of responsibility for Indian raids emanating from U.S. territory.

ARTICLE I

The Mexican Republic agrees to designate the following as her true limits with the United States for the future: retaining the same dividing line between the two Californias as already defined and established, according to the 5th article of the Treaty of Guadalupe Hidalgo limits between the two republics shall be as follows: Beginning in the Gulf of Mexico, three leagues from land, opposite the mouth of the Rio Grande, as provided in the 5th article of the Treaty of Guadalupe Hidalgo;

thence, as defined in the said article, up the middle of that river to the point where the parallel of 31° 47' north latitude crosses the same; thence due west one hundred miles; thence south to the parallel of 31° 20' north latitude; thence along the said parallel of 31° 20' to the 111th meridian of longitude west of Greenwich; thence in a straight line to a point on the Colorado River twenty English miles below the junction of the Gila and Colorado Rivers; thence up the middle of the said River Colorado until it intersects the present line between the United States and Mexico.

For the performance of this portion of the treaty, each of the two governments shall nominate one commissioner, to the end that, by common consent the two thus nominated, having met in the city of Paso del Norte, three months after the exchange of the ratifications of this treaty, may proceed to survey and mark out upon the land the dividing line stipulated by this article, where it shall not have already been surveyed and established by the mixed commission, according to the treaty of Guadalupe Hidalgo, keeping a journal and making proper plans of their operations. For this purpose, if they should judge it necessary, the contracting parties shall be at liberty each to unite to its respective commissioner, scientific or other assistants, such as astronomers and surveyors, whose concurrence shall not be considered necessary for the settlement and of a true line of division between the two Republics; that line shall be alone established upon which the commissioners may fix, their consent in this particular being considered decisive and an integral part of this treaty, without necessity of ulterior ratification or approval, and without room for interpretation of any kind by either of the parties contracting.

The dividing line thus established shall, in all time, be faithfully respected by the two governments, without any variation therein, unless of the express and free consent of the two, given in conformity to the principles of the law of nations, and in accordance with the constitution of each country respectively.

In consequence, the stipulation in the 5th article of the treaty of Guadalupe Hidalgo upon the boundary line therein described is no longer of any force, wherein it may conflict with that here established, the said line being considered annulled and abolished wherever it may not coincide with the present, and in the same manner remaining in full force where in accordance with the same.

ARTICLE II

The government of Mexico hereby releases the United States from all liability on account of the obligations contained in the 11th article of the treaty of Guadalupe Hidalgo and the said article and the thirty-third article of the treaty of amity, commerce, and navigation between the United States of America and the United Mexican States concluded at Mexico, on the fifth day of April 1831, are hereby abrogated.

BY THE PRESIDENT: FRANKLIN PIERCE

W. L. Marcy,
Secretary of State.

Source: The Avalon Project, Yale University Law School, http://www.yale.edu/lawweb/avalon/diplomacy/mexico/mx1853.htm.

61. Excerpt from a letter of Joaquín Corella, Head of Arizpe's *Ayuntamiento* (Town Council) to Sonoran Gov. Manuel Gándara, January 25, 1856

This document is from Joaquín Corella, head of Arizpe's (Sonora, Mexico) town council. He was critical of the 1853 Gadsden Treaty that ceded the Mesilla Valley to the United States. Much of the Mesilla belonged to Sonora. Apache raids had decimated Sonora. Mexicans blamed the Euro-Americans for the raids. Corella saw the Gadsden Treaty as absolving U.S. authorities from a guarantee of the Treaty of Guadalupe Hidalgo (1848) to prevent Indian raids into Mexico and predicted this would have disastrous consequences.

The Gadsden Treaty [1853], we repeat, has again brought misfortune to Sonora; it has deprived the state of its most valuable land, as well as resulting in the protection of the Apache who launch their raids from these lands [Arizona] and to North Americans [bandits] who live among them, because in less than twenty-four hours they can cross the boundary; there the robbers and assassins remain beyond punishment; in our opinion it is vital as well as indispensable to garrison the border with sufficient troops that are always alert, since only in this way can their operation be successful and [only in this way] can they defend the integrity of a state threatened by filibusters....

Source: Fernando Pesqueira, "Documentos Para la Historia de Sonora," 2nd series, vol. 3 (Manuscript in the University of Sonora Library, Hermosillo, Sonora), Rodolfo Acuna and Guadalupe Compean, trans.

62. Excerpt from "From the Rio Grande," March 7, 1855

The total length of the U.S.–Mexico border is 1,951 miles; from its mouth on the Gulf of Mexico to El Paso, Texas, the border is about 1,254 miles. The Rio Grande dips into the heartland of Mexico, placing U.S. cities like Brownsville, Texas, less than 1,000 miles from Mexico City and close to major Mexican populations. After Texas became part of the United States, U.S. merchants sought to establish a hegemony over trade along the Mexican side of the border. In the early 1850s, a so-called Merchants War broke out due to the uncertainty of the Rio Grande boundary and Mexico's tariff laws that sought to end Euro-American economic encroachments. U.S. merchants claimed that these privileges had been granted by the treaty of Guadalupe Hidalgo. Article XXII specified that if war ever broke out that merchants of either republic residing in the other country could remain for twelve months and settle their affairs. They would be protected and respected. The merchant claimed Favored Nation Status.

Intrigue bristled along the border as filibusters sought their fortune. Often they were joined by Mexian Americans. Take José María Jesús Carbajal (?–1874), born in San Fernando de Béxar (San Antonio), an ardent Protestant, whose family supported the Texas Revolt. Carbajal was a leader of expeditions financed by Texas merchants. He led four expeditions into Mexico between 1850 and 1853, attempting to set up the Republic of the Rio Grande, consisting of the Mexican states of Tamaulipas, Nuevo León, and Coahuila. The expeditions became known as the Merchants War. The following is an excerpt describing filibustering activities emanating from Brownsville, Texas. It mentions Carbajal.

The Brownsville *Flag* of the 21st inst., says: A grand ball came off in Brownsville on the evening of the 19th, in honor of Mr. Castillo late Mexican Consul at that place. The *Flag* describes it as a brilliant affair.

The *Flag* has the following:

Fillibusters on the Rio Grande—It is stated that $60,000 have been subscribed by the merchants at Brownsville, Texas, and the Mexicans residing there to fit out a filibustering expedition against Mexico, to be commanded by Gen. Carvajal, and that the citizens of Monterey have pledged themselves to raise $100,000 for the same purpose. Gen. [Adrián] Woll [1795–1875], the Mexican commander, had stopped all communication with the American side of the Rio Grande. He has 1,000 men at Matamoras [sic], 100 at Reynosa, 400 at Camargo, 400 at Mier and 100 at Guerro [sic].

We find the above paragraph in several of our exchanges, without credit. Like other counterfeits, its fabricator is ashamed of the production. Instead of $60,000, the merchants of Brownsville have not subscribed 60 cents to aid any fillibuster organization nor do we believe that the Mexicans residing here have. Our towns on the Rio Grande, as yet, are chiefly commercial, and for this commerce we are dependent, almost wholly, upon our neighbors of Mexico. To secure this trade, quiet on the frontier is absolutely necessary, and our merchants have had time to be taught by experience the futility of border revolutions—revolutions instigated, in most instances, by visionary aspirants for fame and place, rather than from motives of patriotism and the welfare of their countrymen. The citizens of Brownsville have hospitably received political exiles from Mexico—those who have fled from persecution under the present rulers of that country—and would be as ready to extend the same hospitality and afford the same refuge to the persecutors, should, as it is by no means improbable, the continual changes of fortune render such a refuge necessary. The spirit and genius of our institutions guarantee this to all alike, without partiality.

The above paragraph is wholly untrue. There is no organization forming here. Aside from a harmless paper warfare occasionally waged, the whole of the northern frontier of Mexico is quiet. The new commandant, Gen. Vega, seems to give general satisfaction. Many of those engaged in the late revolution have been pardoned and returned to their homes, where their valorous swords and stout lance poles have been exchanged for pruning knives and plowshares, for the peaceful cultivation of the soil. Carvajal is still on this side; but, in the retirement of the shades of private life, is, so far as we know, complying with the laws of the country whose protection he has sought.

Source: New York Daily Times, March 7, 1855, p. 3.

63. Excerpt from "The French in Sonora and Dominica—The Monroe Declaration," December 16, 1852

The Treaty of Guadalupe Hidalgo (1848) and the Gadsden Purchase (1853) crossed Mexican land. Some Euro-Americans believed that all of northern Mexico belonged to them, and pressed their economic and territorial interests. Often Euro-Americans were paranoid of European designs on what they believed belonged to them. They were especially covetous of Sonora, which was renowned for its vast mineral resources, and kept an eye on the colony of Count Gaston Raousset Boulbon in that Mexican state. Raousset (1817–1854) was a French nobleman who had gone to California to seek his fortune. He and other Frenchmen encountered prejudice in California and sought to colonize Sonora, Mexico. The following excerpt from an article in the *Washington Union* was balanced and minimized efforts of the French to plant a colony in Sonora, but noted increased French presence in the Caribbean and raised the Monroe Doctrine as a justification for the U.S. action against France. The United States, according to the article, could not let France gain a foothold on the continent.

THE FRENCH IN SONORA AND DOMINICA—THE MONROE DECLARATION

From the Washington Union

The recent extraordinary intelligence of the revolt of a French colony in the Mexican province of Sonora, of the defeat of the Federal troops by the insurgent forces under command of Count Raousset Boulbon, and the annexation of the Department to the Empire of France, by the proclamation of the victorious adventurer, excited throughout the country a mingled sensation or doubt and astonishment. Viewing the announcement in connection with the speculations of a portion of the French press, respecting the propriety of encouraging European colonization in Mexico, to prevent its absorption by the United States, some of our journals were disposed to credit the singular story, and to anticipate an attempt on the part of the French Government to accept and make good the conquest. By a subtle and ingenious method of reasoning, other circumstances were adduced in support of this position.

In our opinion the importance of this affair is very much exaggerated, and its aim and tendency altogether misapprehended. We have no idea that the French Government is in the least implicated in the movement, or that it originates in any concerted plot; nor do we apprehend that it will receive the sanction of the Emperor of France. We take it to be one of a class of adventurous and indefinite outbreaks of ambition or cupidity by which the supremacy of law and social order in the republic of Mexico is prostrated and the fields of industry made desolate. It is agreed that the immediate provocation of the conflict between Count Boulbon's followers and the Mexican authorities grew out of some misunderstanding in relation to the title to the mine of Arizona; and that the origin of the French colony in Sonora was accidental and for commercial ends, rather than formed by design and for political effect. Moreover, by one, and in our judgment the more probable, account, Boulbon has simply proclaimed the independence of Sonora, without reference to its annexation to France. The same account intimates that the probable result of the affair will be the annexation of Sonora to—the United States.

The view here presented of the insurrection in Mexican Sonora strikes us as the correct view of the matter. However ambitious Napoleon III may be of colonial conquest, he is hardly so stupid as to believe that this Government will suffer him to plant his foot on the confines of California. He would not expend his energies in so foolish and futile an effort as this Sonora plot. If he covets a foothold on this hemisphere, he will, doubtless seek to compass his purpose by some surer, safer, and wiser scheme.

That the French Government does entertain the purpose of extending its power on the American continent is scarcely a matter of doubt; in fact, at this very moment, this purpose is in process of accomplishment. Some time since, it was announced that a French squadron had taken possession of the Peninsula of Samana, in the Republic of Dominica, with the avowed intention of fortifying it and converting it into a naval station. This is a most significant and important event.

By incredible effort the force of the French navy has been increased, until it is scarcely inferior to that of the British war marine. As a basis for the operation of this immense navy in the waters of the American Continent, the Peninsula and Bay of Samana are appropriated by the French Government, under the plausible pretext of protecting the Spanish population of Hayti [sic] from the ravages of the negro neighbor, the savage Soulouque. It is said that the President of the Dominican Republic is entirely in the interests of France, and that he has surrendered the independence of his country to French domination. The effect of the cession of Samana to France, and the establishment of a French naval station in its bay, will undoubtedly give that Government a supreme control over the Dominican Republic. By some it is contended that France has in prospect the ulterior object of subjugating the Empire of Hayti, and reducing the entire island to its dominion: but we do not believe this to be the policy of the French Government. Its object is the *establishment of a naval depot in the Bay of Samana, whence it may securely exert its influence on the affairs of the American Continent.*

The Bay of Samana affords the finest harbors in the world, and by the fortification of the Peninsula can be made inaccessible to any hostile assault by water. It commands absolutely the Mona passage between Hayti and Puerto Rico, and would enable any naval power possessing it to harrass [sic], if not destroy our commerce around Cape Horn, and with the West Indies and Central America. With a naval force securely stationed in the Bay of Samana, France might exert a powerful influence on the political condition of the West India isles, and in the event of war with this country might easily ravage our commerce and desolate our coasts.

Will the Government of the United States suffer France to effect a foothold on this continent, or establish a position in its waters whence it may operate so imperiously on American affairs? *Will not this Government remove the pretext under which France acts, by itself assuming the protectorate of Dominica?* Shall the Monroe doctrine be maintained or shall we surrender the principle that the "American Continents are not to be considered as subjects for Colonization by any European power?" The aggressions of France in Dominica have imposed upon our Government the imperative duty of deciding this question at once. If it be an open question—if the submission of this Government to the usurpations of Great Britain in Central America be not deemed a surrender of the Monroe principle—then it is time to revive it, to reassert and to stand by it, when a chief power of Europe plants itself right in the pathway of our commerce, and frowns menacingly on our flag. The Government of the United States has formally disclaimed any design of interfering in the affairs of Europe; the time has come when it should enforce the observance of the principle of non-intervention in the affairs of this Continent, on the ambitious powers of Europe.

Source: Washington Union, no date, reprinted in *New York Daily Times*, December 16, 1852, p. 5.

64. Letter from John Forsyth to Hon. Lewis Cass on the Execution of Colonel Henry Crabb and Associates, Message from the President of the United States of America, February 16, 1858

California was a hotbed of filibustering activity. Many expeditions were launched from there with the objective of annexing Mexican land. They wanted to recreate another Texas (1836). Sonora, Mexico, was attractive because of its renowned mineral wealth, especially silver. This attracted Euro-American and European filibusterers. Sonora also had fertile farmlands, watered by rivers such as the Yaqui and Mayo—two of the most productive rivers in Mexico. Another factor that made Sonora attractive was that it had one of the best natural harbors on the Gulf of California that connected to the Pacific Ocean. One of the most notorious filibustering expeditions to Sonora was led by Henry Crabb, a former California state senator and Whig, in 1857. He was ordered out of the state, and when he refused he was attacked by Sonoran troops who captured him and cut off his head. President James Buchanan (1791–1868) tried to use the incident as a pretext to invade and occupy Sonora, calling the beheading of Crabb barbaric. Buchanan's true intention was to unify the United States in a foreign war so as to take attention away from the sectional conflict. On December 19, 1859, Buchanan requested that the U.S. Congress approve occupation of Sonora as well as Chihuahua. The following document from the U.S. Minister to Mexico discusses the filibusters and how far the U.S. consular agents should go to protect the encroachers. Its tone is moderate and a departure from Buchanan's bellicose rhetoric.

Mr. Forsyth to Mr. Cass
No. 32.
LEGATION OF THE UNITED STATES,
City of Mexico, April 24,1857
SIR: The Mexican papers have been filled for two months past, with rumors of a filibustering expedition from California, under one General Crabb, against Sonora. As we have no commercial or consular agents in that part of the republic, I am without other information on the subject than I can gather from the California and Mexican journals. The minister of relations has, upon several occasions, inquired of me what advices I had on a subject which gives the government a good deal of concern. While I have not been able to add to his stock of information, I have taken occasion to assure him that expeditions of this character against the sovereign rights of Mexico, were viewed by my government with displeasure, and would be prevented, so far as it was in its power to do it. I think there is little doubt that a body of armed men from California—some three hundred in number, and the advance guard of a larger force—are on their march to, if not already arrived in, Sonora. If so, we have the beginning of a series of personal tragedies which will impose a serious and delicate duty on this legation. In the natural course of the conflict between the invaders and the Mexican troops, some of our misguided countrymen will fall into the hands of the latter, and will, doubtless, be summarily dealt with. In such a contingency I should be glad to have the instructions of my government how far to interfere in their behalf. In the absence of instructions, I should hold it to be my duty to demand for them a fair and regular trial, and if condemned, to use my influence, official and personal, to save their lives, not as a demand of right, but as a matter of grace and policy. The expeditionists

have certainly chosen an unfortunate time for their movements as regards the interests of the United States in their relations with Mexico. The invasion is calculated to produce an unhappy influence, adverse to the efforts which I have constantly and perseveringly made to eradicate from the Mexican mind the deeply-seated distrust of Americans, and to establish in its stead a confidence in the friendly and honorable sentiments of our government and people towards them. My observation has taught me to believe that nothing but this distrust and fear of our people has prevented the States bordering on the United States—especially those like Chihuahua and Sonora, overrun by savages and receiving no protection from the Mexican government—from breaking their feeble ties with the central government, and seeking, in annexation with us, that security for life and property of which they are now wholly destitute. The people of Mexico have been taught to believe, from the examples cited to them in California and Texas, that their proper titles, especially to land, would not be respected by their new rulers. I have the opinions of the most intelligent men I meet here, that this circumstance alone has saved to the republic of Mexico the fidelity of Tamaulipas, New Leon, Chihuahua, and Sonora.

I am, very respectfully, your obedient servant,

John Forsyth

Hon. LEWIS CASS, &c., &c., &c.

Source: John Forsyth to Hon. Lewis Cass, Execution of Colonel Crabb and Associates, Message from the President of the United States of America, February 16, 1858, pp. 2–3.

65. Excerpt from a Special Correspondent, "A Tour in the Southwest," 1854

Racial attitudes of Euro-Americans toward Mexicans were formed by popular articles published by travelers along the almost 2,000-mile U.S.–Mexican border. The following excerpt is an account of a traveler along the Rio Grande that was printed in the *New York Daily Times*. It speaks of Mexicans in racial terms and perpetuates stereotypes that were rampant at the time.

It must be remembered that the Mexican population within the territory is large and increasing, and that it is a dark-colored, mixed race, including often no small proportion of African blood, so much so, that it requires the eye of an expert to distinguish many of those held as slaves, on account of their color, from others among the Mexicans who are constitutionally eligible to the highest offices. The Mexicans have no repugnance, but rather the contrary, to equality and the closest intimacy with negroes. But the intelligence, the enterprise, and the peculiar habits of mind which are the effects of early industrial training, that exist as most important elements in the Germans, as well as the rational regard for liberty, as a right of man, which they generally have, is wanting in the degraded Mexicans.

Source: New York Daily Times, June 3, 1854, p. 2.

66. Excerpts from the *New York Daily Times*, "New Mexico—Its Social Condition," 1852 (author unknown)

Along with Euro-American merchants and U.S. soldiers who moved into the occupied territory along the Rio Grande, Protestant missionaries descended on the newly occupied territory that once belonged to Mexico. Much like the

Spanish missionaries, they entered Mexico with their cultural and racial biases. They believed that the Mexicans were pagans and that through their conversion to Christianity, not only would their souls be saved, but they would become civilized. The following document from a Protestant minister comments on Mexicans in New Mexico and their "depraved" state.

He found there some 6,000 Mexicans who had never heard a gospel sermon. There were numbers of American traders there, and a host of gamblers. The state of society was most deplorable and alarming. It does not materially differ from the society of some of the other heathen territories. Ignorance, superstition and idolatry were prevalent in such a degree as I had never before heard of in any uncivilized country. There never had been a school-house or institution of learning of any kind for the instruction of the youth, neither were there any school books of any description.

The Mexicans are a depraved, lawless set of desperadoes. Gambling is a universal habit. I believe there is not a single Mexican, man or woman, boy or girl, of the age of eight years, but knows how to gamble. Mothers teach their children from infancy the art of gambling. They are trained up in the school of deception by their parents until able to deceive, cheat and gamble on their own hook. The most depraved and wicked are the greatest to be respected. Licentiousness in all its deplorable malignity—in the worst conceivable forms—stalks abroad at mid-day. Until this vice is checked, little can be done for the elevation of the people, and unless missionaries are sent there to teach them, their reformation is hopeless. It is a lamentable fact that since the conquest by the Americans, their vices have increased. The Americans have been instrumental in carrying among them.

Their christenings, their weddings, and their funerals are celebrated in the most debasing and humiliating debauchery.

Source: *New York Daily Times*, September 21, 1852, p. 6.

67. Excerpt from O. Henry, "Tamales," 1912

O. Henry is the pen name of Euro-American writer William Sydney Porter (1862–1910). He wrote more than 400 short stories. The following excerpt of his poem, "Tamales," expresses the racism toward Mexicans that was prevalent during the time it was written.

This is the Mexican
Don José Calderón
One of God's countrymen.
Land of the buzzard.
Cheap silver dollar, and
Cacti and murderers.
Why has he left his land
Land of the lazy man,
Land of the pulque
Land of the bull fight,
Fleas and revolution.

This is the reason,
Hark to the wherefore;
Listen and tremble.

One of his ancestors,
Ancient and garlicky,
Probably grandfather,
Died with his boots on.
Killed by the Texans,
Texans with big guns,
At San Jacinto.
Died without benefit
Of Priest or clergy;
Died full of minie balls,
Mescal and pepper.

Don José Calderon
Heard of the tragedy.
Heard of it, thought of it,
Vowed a deep vengeance;
Vowed retribution
On the Americans,
Murderous gringos,
Especially Texans.
"Valga me Dios! Que
Ladrones, diablos,
Matadores, mentidores,
Caraccos y perros,
Voy a matarles,
Con solos mis manos,
Toditas sin falta."
Thus swore the Hidalgo
Don José Calderon.

He hied him to Austin.
Bought him a basket,
A barrel of pepper,
And another of garlic;
Also a rope he bought.
That was his stock in trade;
Nothing else had he.
Nor was he rated in
Dun or in Bradstreet,
Thought he meant business,
Don José Calderon.
Seeker of vengeance.

With his stout lariat,
Then he caught swiftly
Tomcats and puppy dogs,
Caught them and cooked them,
Don José Calderon.
Vower of vengeance.
Now on the sidewalk

Sits the avenger
Selling Tamales to Innocent purchasers.
Dire is thy vengeance,
Oh, José Calderon,
Ritiless Nemesis
Fearful Redresser
Of the wrongs done to thy
Sainted grandfather.

Now the doomed Texans,
Rashly hilarious,
Buy of the deadly wares,
Buy and devour.
Rounders at midnight,
Citizens solid,
Bankers and newsboys,
Bootblacks and preachers,
Rashly importunate,
Courting destruction.
Buy and devour.
Beautiful maidens
Buy and devour,
Gentle society youths
Buy and devour.

Buy and devour
Thins thing called Tamale;
Made of rat terrier,m
Spitz dog and poodle.
Maltese cat, boarding house
Steak and red pepper.
Garlic and tallow,
Clorn meal and shucks.
Buy without shame
Sit on store steps and eat,
Stand on the street and eat,
Ride on the cars and eat,
Strewing the shucks around
Over creation.

Dire is thy vengeance,
Don José Calderon.
For the slight thing we did
Killing thy grandfather.
What boots it if we killed
Only one greaser,
Don José Calderon.
This is your deep revenge,
You have greased all of us,
Grease a whole nation

With your Tamales,
Don José Calderon
Santos Espiriton,
Vicente Camillo,
Quitana de Rios,
De Rosa y Ribera.

Source: O. Henry. *Rolling Stones* (New York, Collier & Sons, 1912), pp. 257–258.

68. Excerpt from William D. Carrigan and Clive Webb, "The Lynching of Persons of Mexican Origin or Descent in the United States, 1848 to 1928"

The Euro-American people had made war on the Native American for two centuries. They also considered the Mexican an Indian. Phrases such as *the only good Indian is a dead Indian* were part of their vernacular. Euro-Americans transferred these racial and cultural attitudes to Mexicans upon moving into what was formerly Mexican land. This racism created barriers that reinforced inequality and led to a lack of protection from the law for Mexicans that is prevalent up to this day. The brutality was not confined to groups such as the Texas Rangers (formed in 1823), who were infamous for their brutal treatment of Mexicans, but also from ordinary people who saw the Mexican as an intruder and menace to the American way of life. Hence, in the name of justice, many white Americans executed hundreds of Mexican migrants and residents without any repercussions. This gave rise to vigilante groups, often called *Minute Men*, who perpetuated atrocities. Lynchings were the worst of these atrocities. Studies, such as that from which the following excerpt is taken, suggest that 473 out of every 100,000 Mexican migrant workers during this time period died as lynching victims. The following excerpt describes the extent of the lynching of Mexicans in the Southwest.

Although no comprehensive work on the lynching of Mexicans was ever produced, several historians have addressed the subject of mob violence against Mexicans in more general terms. Despite the extensive documentation of anti-Mexican mob violence provided by these scholars, historians of lynching continue to ignore the brutal repression of Spanish-speakers in the United States. One reason is that no scholar has attempted to provide an actual count of Mexican lynching victims. Discussions of African American lynching victims in the South have rested upon an actual count of individual cases since the turn of the twentieth century. The treatment of Mexican lynching victims, by contrast, often rests upon impressionistic estimates. In 1949, Carey McWilliams wrote in *North from Mexico* that "vast research would be required to arrive at an estimate of the number of Mexican lynchings"....

Between 1848 and 1928, mobs lynched at least 597 Mexicans. Historian Christopher Waldrep has asserted that the definition of lynching has altered so much over the course of time as to render impossible the accurate collection of data on mob violence. It is therefore essential to familiarize the reader from the outset with the interpretation of lynching used to compile the statistics in this essay. The authors regard lynching as a retributive act of murder for which those responsible claim to be serving the interests of justice, tradition, or community good. Although our notion as to what constitutes a lynching is clear, it is still impossible to provide a precise count of the number of Mexican victims. We have excluded a significant number of reported lynchings when the sources do not allow for verification of specific data such as the date, location, or identity of the victim. The statistics included in this essay should therefore be considered a conservative estimate of the actual number of Mexicans lynched in the United States.

Frontier conditions undoubtedly fostered the growth of vigilantism in general. Nonetheless, the conventional interpretation of western violence cannot be applied to the lynching of Mexicans. The most serious criticism of the "socially constructive" model of vigilantism espoused by Richard Maxwell Brown is that it legitimates the actions of lawbreakers. There is an implicit presumption in the civic virtue of the vigilantes and the criminal guilt of their victims. In truth, the popular tribunals that put Mexicans to death can seldom be said to have acted in the spirit of the law. According to Joseph Caughey, vigilante committees persisted in their activities "long after the arrival" of the law courts. However, Anglos refused to recognize the legitimacy of these courts when they were controlled or influenced by Mexicans. Determined to redress the balance of racial and political power, they constructed their own parallel mechanisms of justice. This is precisely what occurred in Socorro, New Mexico, during the 1880s when an Anglo vigilance committee arose in opposition to the predominantly Mexican legal authorities. These committees showed little respect for the legal rights of Mexicans, executing them in disproportionately large numbers. Their actions therefore amounted to institutionalized discrimination....

The lynching of Mexicans not only occurred in areas where there was a fully operating legal system but often involved the active collusion of law officers themselves. In February 1857, a Justice of the Peace assembled an unwilling audience of Mexicans outside the San Gabriel mission to watch as he decapitated Miguel Soto and then stabbed repeatedly at the corpse. The most systematic abuse of legal authority was by the Texas Rangers. Their brutal repression of the Mexican population was tantamount to state-sanctioned terrorism. Although the exact number of those murdered by the Rangers is unknown, historians estimate that it ran into the hundreds and even thousands. In March 1881, Rangers crossed the border into Mexico and illegally arrested Onofrio Baca on a charge of murder. Baca was returned without extradition orders to the United States where he was handed over to a mob "and strung up to the cross beams of the gate in the court house yard until he was dead." The terrorizing of Mexicans continued well into the twentieth century. On October 18, 1915, Mexican outlaws derailed a train traveling toward Brownsville, killing several passengers. Some who survived the crash were robbed and murdered by the bandits. The Rangers exacted brutal revenge. Two Mexican passengers aboard the train were shot for their supposed assistance of the raid. The Rangers then executed eight suspected Mexican criminals along the banks of the Rio Grande....

Source: William D. Carrigan and Clive Webb, "The Lynching of Persons of Mexican Origin or Descent in the United States, 1848 to 1928." *Journal of Social History* 37.2 (2003), pp. 412–417.

69. José María Loaiza's Claim for the Lynching of His Wife Josefa and His Banishment by a Mob in Downieville, California, July 4, 1852

In 1851, a Downieville, California, kangaroo court sentenced a 26-year-old Mexican woman called Juanita (her real name was Josefa) to hanging. She was the first woman hanged in California. Early accounts minimized the gravity of the lynching, claiming that Juanita Loaiza was a prostitute who lived with a gambler, José María Loaiza. On July 4, 1851, during a drunken rage, Fred Cannon, one of the miners in Downieville, in northern California, intentionally broke down Josefa's door and tried to force sexual favors from her. She ran him off. When Josefa and her husband approached Cannon the next day and asked him to pay for the door, he called her a whore. Josefa went to the door of her home and said, "This is no place to call me bad names, come into my house and call me that." Josefa stabbed Cannon with a knife. Although the miners wanted to lynch Josefa and José on the spot, they held a kangaroo trial. Cannon's body was displayed in a tent, dressed in a red flannel shirt, unbuttoned to show the wound. A pregnant Josefa was convicted. She was hanged from a bridge, while over 2,000 men lined the river to watch. For years, the lynching of Josefa was excused because, according to the defenders of the vigilantes, she was a whore.

The following document from the Rodolfo F. Acuña Archives at California State University Northridge presents an electronic mail message from Sacramento, California historian Roberto Carrillo Gantz in which he summarizes his research on the Josefa Loaiza lynching and exposes the lie that she was a prostitute. Gantz, who is a vocational instructor for Sacramento County, historian, and screenwriter, was moved by a Public Broadcasting television program about the California Gold Rush and the lynching of Josefa. He did quite a bit of research on the subject at the California State Library in Sacramento while researching the injustice for a screenplay. While browsing microfiche on the U.S. Mexican Claims Commission, he came across a claim made by Josefa's husband.

A claim made by José María Loaiza, filed against the U.S. government for "the lynching of his wife and the banishment of himself by a mob ... July 4, 1852 ... Downieville, California." The date was inaccurate but further research verified that it was Josefa's husband. Josefa and José María Loaiza were from Sonora. "Schedule of Mexican Claims against the United States," Senate Executive Document 31, 44th Congress 2nd Session. Docket Number 904. José María Loaiza made a claim for the lynching of his wife Josefa and his banishment by a mob on July 4, 1852 in Downieville, California. The claim was made on June 11, 1875. The claim was dismissed by the commissioner.

Source: Rodolfo F. Acuña Archives, Special Collections, California State University Northridge.

70. Letter from "Dame Shirley" Concerning San Francisco Vigilante Committee Activities against Chileans, 1852

Mexicans were not the only victims of vigilantism from 1848–1928. Chinese, blacks, and other Latinos also were targeted. Not all Latinos went to the mine fields and a sizeable colony grew in San Francisco, California. The following document is a letter from Louise Amelia Knapp Smith Clappe (1819–1906), who used the pseudonym Dame Shirley, to her sister Molly in Massachusetts. It is about the San Francisco Vigilante Committee and its activities in San Francisco and views the committees as an improvement from more spontaneous lynchings and an attempt to purge civic sins.

This frightful accident recalled the people to their senses, and they began to act a little less like madmen, than they had previously done. They elected a vigilance committee, and authorized persons to go to The Junction and arrest the suspected Spaniards.

The first act of the Committee was to try a Mexicana, who had been foremost in the fray. She has always worn male attire, and on this occasion, armed with a pair of pistols, she fought like a very fury. Luckily, inexperienced in the use of fire-arms, she wounded no one. She was sentenced to leave the Bar by day-light, a perfectly just decision, for there is no doubt she is a regular little demon. Some went so far as to say she ought to be hanged, for she was the indirect cause of the fight. You see always, it is the old, cowardly excuse of Adam in Paradise—the woman tempted me, and I did eat—as if the poor frail head, once so pure and beautiful, had not sin enough of its own, dragging it forever downward, without being made to answer for the wrong-doing of a whole community of men.

The next day, the Committee tried five or six Spaniards, who were proven to have been the ringleaders in the sabbath-day riot. Two of them were sentenced to be whipped, the remainder to leave the Bar that evening, the property of all to be confiscated to the use of the wounded persons. Oh Mary! imagine my anguish when I heard the first blow fall upon those wretched men.

Source: Indian Bar, August 4, 1852. Louise Amelia Knapp Smith Clappe, *The Shirley Letters from California Mines in 1851–1852: Being a Series of Twenty-Three Letters from Dame Shirley ... to Her Sister in Massachusetts ... Reprinted from the Pioneer Magazine of 1854–55,* Thomas C. Russell, ed. (San Francisco: Thomas C. Russell, 1922), pp. 263–264. Quoted in Leonard Pitt, *California Controversies: Major Issues in the History* (New York: Scott, Foresman and Company, 1968), p 72.

71. Excerpts from Jay Monaghan, *Chile, Peru, and the California Gold Rush of 1849,* 1973

Chileans arrived in San Francisco soon after the discovery of gold in 1848. Since Chile was on the Pacific side of the Western Hemisphere, Chileans were closer to California than the first wave of 49ers who came from the East overland. The Chileans arrived before this group of Euro-Americans. Like Mexicans they were young, single, and did not speak English. The first wave went to the gold fields, often staking out the best claims. They suffered from the history of racism toward Mexicans. They were darker than Euro-Americans, spoke Spanish, and were Catholics. They used the gold fields as a base. Some started businesses in San Francisco, Sacramento, and Monterey where small communities formed. Those that prospered had some capital and they engaged in the importation of flour and mining equipment from Chile. Euro-Americans grew jealous of the Chileans' prosperity, believing that all of the wealth belonged to them. An anti-Chilean hysteria developed and, on July 15, 1849, angry mobs in San Francisco attacked the peaceful Chileans. The following excerpt is from Jay Monaghan's book on the California Gold Rush, a classic in the field.

Many of the Chileans in town were men of property who had come to San Francisco with goods to sell, and one of them who established a shop in his tent had trouble on June 21, 1849. That day, while the shopkeeper was serving a customer, two entered and quarreled about an alleged payment. In apparent fright, the shopkeeper drew a pistol. One of the gangsters pled with him and the other one fled. As he ran out the door the handgun fired. Who pulled the trigger was never known, the bullet hit the running man and he died the next day. His name was Benjamin B. Bailey, a private in the recently banded New York regiment. The sound of the shot attracted a crowd, and by the time the sheriff arrived with a warrant the Chilean shopkeeper had disappeared. His tent and goods auctioned off to the crowd, and the self-righteous Hounds, several of whom had served in the regiment with Bailey, maintain; that his death justified them in organizing themselves as the city's Regulators. The editor of *Alta California* protested, holding the Chilean shopkeeper's right to protect his property with a gun. Obviously two points of view were beginning [to] polarize in San Francisco, and at this time businessmen who happened to be Chileans were respected by the best citizens.

The sudden influx of displaced Chileans from the placers [mining areas] during the last weeks of June gave the city a real problem. The refugees came in an ugly mood and rotos [broken-derogatory word referring to a person in poverty and of vulgar habits] were known dangerous characters. Policemen were needed, but the city had no money to pay them. Perhaps the self-styled Regulators might serve in this capacity. They claimed to be upholders of law and order. Some persons welcomed them and lauded the grotesque costumes they wore while marching, two by two, through the streets. Tradesmen smiled indulgently when the Regulators (or Hounds) ended their march at a saloon, where the drinks were "charged to the dust so the rain could settle it."

These young men crossed the bay to Contra Costa on Sunday, July 15, to parade there, and Sam Roberts, who would be convicted for leading the Hounds in the notorious riot, entered upon the scene. He was an odd ruffian from Valparaiso. Unable to read or write, he had served on a Chilean man-of-war and had probably deserted to come to California with a United States regiment. He may have been a member of the New York volunteers to which Ben Bailey belonged. Certainly, he marched with the Hounds wearing a lieutenant's uniform. Between parades he had operated a boat for landing incoming passengers, and no doubt he resented the necessity of competing in this occupation with newly arrived Chileans who supported themselves temporarily as boatmen the way Pérez Rosales' companions had done.

Nevertheless, Sam did have friendly relations with some Chileans, and, knowing Spanish, he was naturally attracted to Washington Hall on the plaza. This Chilean house of prostitution later became famous when the beautiful spitfire, Mariquita, stabbed the equally fair Camille La Reine. Her crime was considered totally inexcusable because the death of her victim....

Sam, knowing Spanish, led a group of some twenty men to the saloon tent of Dominguez Cruz at Clark's Point. Inside, along the bar, he saw the backs of twenty Chileans. Sam marched his party in and, with drawn pistol, ordered the drinkers to disperse. Dominguez recognized Sam, the ex-sailor from Valparaiso, and served his men a round or two of drinks. They proclaimed his saloon their headquarters, then marched out. Thus, if a full-scale riot ensued, one Chilean saloonkeeper would be on the rioter's side....

The extent of the depredations committed by Sam and his gang cannot be determined. Certainly he tried to recruit followers from other gangs by attracting attention with fife, drum, and shouts of encouragement through his megaphone. Before dawn, however, he returned to Dominguez' saloon, bringing loot to be stored there.

The next morning many outraged citizens appealed to alcalde [mayor], who claimed that he could do nothing without an armed constabulary, or what the Chileans called *vigilantes,* an ominous word in California history. He did, however, call a meeting in the plaza for three o'clock that afternoon. So Chileans believed, erroneously, that the alcalde had resigned, a natural assumption when they saw distinguished citizens assemble to take the government into their own hands. At meeting, Sam Brannan, always eager to address any audience, spoke out in his best auctioneer voice, insisting on justice for Chileans, the good people from a neighboring republic. California, Brannan boomed, depended on Chile for flour, on skilled artisans for laying bricks, on her bakers for bread. He did not mention that Chileans under Pérez Rosales had paid him well for poor accommodations on his decrepit craft to Sacramento, but he insisted that a collection be taken to reimburse those who had been robbed. The Hounds, he thundered must be suppressed....

Somewhat different indictments were rendered against nineteen other Hounds, and seventeen of these men were arrested immediately. Since there was no jail in San Francisco, they were confined on the United States war sloop *Warren* in the bay. Three Hounds, including Sam Roberts, could not be found in town, but before arraignment two days later they had all been apprehended. Roberts was on a schooner headed for Stockton.

The trial commenced on July 18. Prompt justice surely! Pioneers did not believe in legal procrastination. Many witnesses were called, including Sam's woman, Felice, and the badly wounded Rinaldo Alegria, whose mother and sister helped him into court. The poor fellow died soon afterward from the bullet in his abdomen.

According to the evidence, thirty-eight Chileans had been either assaulted or intimidated. Rioters had stolen $6,300 in coin, gold dust worth $1,500, and clothes, jewelry, and firearms valued at $1,400. In addition, the looters had carried off many casks of wine and brandy.

The defense attorney cross-examined all witnesses with care, and in his concluding argument, begged for leniency, basing his plea on General Smith's proclamation against foreigners and a lack of identification of the looters. He proved effectively that there were no organized Hounds, although an unfinished constitution had been written to form the Regulators into an association for mutual benefit in case of illness.

Several witnesses testified that the leader of the rioters wore a military uniform. Some described it to be more like a major general's than a lieutenant's uniform, and the jury decided that the resplendent man must be Sam Roberts. Consequently they adjudged him guilty on all counts in the indictment. He was sentenced to hard labor for ten years in whatever penitentiary the governor of California might select. The other prisoners who were found guilty received lesser sentences according to their crimes, but for one reason or another none of the terms were served.

The prompt decision from the jury and the severity of the sentences might have been consoling to some Chileans in San Francisco, but hundreds of their fellow countrymen had already returned to Valparaiso with bitter memories of their treatment in California. By the time they reached home, dozens of ships carrying Argonauts from the eastern United States would be stopping at Valparaiso. What a chance to give those yanquis some of their own medicine when they came ashore! Trouble between the two peoples seemed sure to erupt next in South America....

Source: Jay Monaghan, *Chile, Peru, and the California Gold Rush of 1849* (Berkeley, CA: University of California Press, © 1973), pp. 164–170.

72. Excerpts from Jill L. Cossley-Batt, "The Capture of Joaquín Murieta," 1928

The legend of the so-called Mexican bandit Joaquín Murieta (whose spelling varies according to source) has fascinated Hollywood. The legendary Zorro was fashioned on his times. The story is simple. Murieta was attacked by Euro-Americans who raped his wife and killed his family members. Unable to obtain justice, he turned to creating his own justice. The story is a mixture of fact and fantasy. Even the great Chilean poet, Pablo Neruda (1904–1973), claimed Joaquín as a Chilean. However, through the tireless work of Alfredo Figueroa, a composer and Chicano activist from Blythe, California, we know that the California Rangers got the wrong man, and the real Joaquín Murieta died of old age in Sonora, Mexico. The following is an excerpt from Jill L. Cossley-Batt's book describing the death of Murrieta.

On May 17 of this year the State Assembly, then in session at Benicia, passed a joint resolution empowering Governor John Bigler to organize a joint company of determined men to be known as "The California Rangers," and to offer three thousand dollars reward for the capture of Joaquín Murrieta....

"There's Joaquín!"

Captain Love detailed John White to follow Murieta, while a general battle took place between the remaining bandits and Rangers. Three-Fingered-Jack put up a game fight; two of his wounds were mortal, and it is known that he fired his last shot after his heart had been pierced with a bullet from the rifle of George Chase.

The bandits were armed exclusively with six-shooters, whereas the Rangers, being fitted out with rifles, revolvers, and shot-guns, had the advantage, and soon made short work of the swarthy desperadoes. Twelve were killed outright and two were taken prisoners. The Rangers were uninjured, but Captain Love had experienced a "close shave."

While all this fighting was going on, John White, mounted on a fresh steed which he had been leading for any possible emergency, experienced little difficulty in overtaking the fleeing bandit chieftain. Joaquín was riding "Injun fashion" with one hand clutching the mane of his mount, and only his feet exposed to view, his body being shielded by that of the horse he was riding.

As the two men came into close quarters, White discharged his revolver at Murrieta. The first shot missed him, as he moved quickly to one side; a second shattered the hand that clutched the animal's mane, causing the rider to fall on the ground. Quickly rising to his feet and holding the bleeding hand aloft in [a] token of submission, the wounded man addressed his captor in Spanish, saying:

"Mira mi mano, amigo!" ("Look at my hand, friend!")

White, who had formerly been the trusted lieutenant of Jack Hayes, a renowned Indian fighter, was exceptionally courageous, but too chivalrous to take advantage of a wounded man. He said to Joaquin, "I arrest you," and the young Mexican surrendered. At this moment, however, the other Rangers arrived upon the scene, and some of them, seeing Joaquín's arm lowered, and thinking the two were still in combat, shot the bandit to pieces.

This impulsive action upset many of the Rangers, for they were anxious to take Joaquín alive in order to present substantial proof, when claiming the reward which had been offered for his capture.

The whole affair happened about eighty miles from Fresno, and a question arose concerning the proper disposition of the dead bandit's body. After considerable discussion they decided to cut off Murieta's head, sever the hand of Three-Fingered-Jack, and take these trophies along for the purpose of satisfying public anxiety and giving tangible proof that the bloodthirsty bandits were out of the way.

One of the prisoners, when fording the river, committed suicide by plunging under the water and holding on to the growth beneath, thus defying the efforts of the Rangers to save him. The other was placed in jail, but the jail was mobbed at night, and the next day he was found hanging near the spring of a prominent citizen.

The head and hand were taken to Fresno and preserved in alcohol, then placed in the office of Doctor Leach for safety's sake. Here they were identified by Mr. Dorsey and several others from Mariposa, where Joaquín Murieta was well known. Later they were moved to Hornitos, where Edward Connor and Captain Howard helped to prepare the affidavits establishing the capture and identity of the dead bandit. After a while Black and Henderson placed them on exhibition in San Francisco, where an admission of twenty-five cents was charged. They attracted so much attention that the same men exhibited them in New York, where they netted a large amount of money. Then the Rangers raised so much objection that the relics were brought back to San Francisco, where they were destroyed in the great earthquake and fire of 1906, which wiped out almost every landmark and relic of the gold-rush days.

Some of the old Spanish families appear thoroughly convinced that Joaquín Murieta was not killed—that it was one of the other Joaquíns. However, the head was inspected by Governor Bigler, and the bill granting the reward passed the Senate, May 13, 1854. Captain Howard states that there was no doubt as to its being Joaquín Murieta; also that the terrible murders and robberies ceased from that time forth, and that Californians lived in a reasonable degree of peace until 1872, when there was a revival of banditry under the leadership of Vasquez. This later criminal was eventually captured by the Sheriff's posse and executed in the Santa Clara jail, San José, March 19, 1875.

According to the following letter written to Howard by Edward Connor (later Gen. Connor), there was some doubt as to whether Harry Love would divide the three thousand dollars reward that had been offered for the capture of Joaquín Murieta. It appears that Connor went to Sacramento in order that he might be on hand should anything unjust occur.

Source: Jill L. Cossley-Batt, *The Last of the California Rangers* (New York: Funk & Wagnalls, 1928), http://www.yosemite.ca.us/library/california_rangers/joaquin_murieta.html.

73. Excerpts from David Bacon, "Interview with Antonio Rivera Murrieta" [descendant of Joaquín Murrieta], December 15, 2001

The following is an interview by journalist David Bacon with Antonio Rivera Murrieta, a descendant of Joaquín Murrieta—the most famous Mexican bandit of the 1850s. The story goes that he and his family were robbed by white Americans who raped and killed his wife. Unable to get justice from the Euro-American system, he turned to the highway avenging his wife's death. Many experts claim that Joaquín was not killed by California Ranger Harry Love who cut off Joaquín's head and the hand of his accomplice, Three Finger Jack. There was a reward for the capture of Murrieta. Recent studies say that there were as many as five dozen Joaquíns and, in fact, the real Joaquín Murrieta died of old age in Sonora, Mexico. David Bacon (DB) is a well-known author and photographer of the border and Mexico. The interview recounts recollections of the family of Joaquín and confirms that he died in Sonora, Mexico.

DB: *Where are you from?*

My name is Antonio Rivera Murrieta. I was born on February 19th at a very beautiful place in the state of Sonora—in Trincheras, on the land of Joaquín Murrieta. I called it Joaquín Murrieta's land because that's what my great grandfather told me and he was Murrieta's cousin.

DB: *What did they say to you in your youth about Joaquín Murrieta?*

They spoke about him as the one who went to California at the time to guide the others from Sonora, to mine gold there. There used to be 10,300 people living in California who were from Sonora back then. After they returned to Mexico, they were afraid because of the persecution against Murrieta, and they didn't speak much about him. That was very true of my grandfather, although not my great grandfather.

They feared that the people who persecuted Murrieta would follow them all the way to Trincheras. In addition, people from our family, the Murrietas, couldn't come to the United States—it was taboo. Many would be denied entry, many were denied a passport, and others were denied entrance. One of them was Juan Murrieta— brother of the president of the association of Murrieta's descendants in Trincheras. It took the U.S. government more than 3 years to give me a visa because they'd ask me if I was in the Communist Party, or if I was an activist against the Mexican government. They made a lot of excuses, but I knew what the problem was. It was that I had the last name of Murrieta. The name bothered them. So it took 3 years. I had an appointment every 6 months and finally after 3 years they gave me my passport in Sonoita, Sonora.

DB: *What happened with Juan Murrieta?*

Juan Murrieta was passing through Nogales and they said they asked him, "are you related to Joaquín Murrieta?" When he answered that he was, they told him that he no longer had a passport, and they ripped it up. This happened in 1946–47.

DB: *So almost 100 years after Joaquín Murrieta died, they still feared him?*

They still had that fear because the textbooks in the primary schools in Arizona and California said he was a "gringo eater," that he killed one for breakfast, one for lunch and another for dinner. They said he killed people in knife fights, and called him a bandit, an assailant. But we all know that Joaquín Murrieta was a social fighter. He wanted to retrieve the part of Mexico that was lost at that time in the Treaty of Guadalupe Hidalgo.

DB: *When I was a child I read the kinds of things you're talking about in the schools I attended in California. What was the real story of Joaquín Murrieta? Where was he from and what did he do?*

The true story is that the people from Sonora living in California, Arizona, New Mexico, Texas—the Mexicans here—were the last ones to realize that the land wasn't part of Mexico any more, and that they were no longer Mexicans. There wasn't mail in those days, or anything that could have told them that this happened. They started to realize it when Anglos came and wanted to take away their mines, their farms, their cattle, their way of living and the little they had. In addition, they were assaulted in Yuma.

There were many Joaquín Murrietas. Many Mexicans were angry during that time and fought, but Joaquín Murrieta lasted the longest because he had more luck and was more organized.

He wanted to recover that part of Mexico that was ours. There is talk that he had contact with the Mexican federal government back then, but the federal government didn't support his effort to recover that lost part of Mexico. So the only thing left for him was to defend himself and the rights of the Mexicans—the people from Sonora who were still living there.

DB: Who were these people?

They were country people. They were the ones who showed the Anglos how to mine the gold, to extract the gold from the earth. Up until then, in the United States there weren't many gold mines, only one in North Carolina. So the Anglos who arrived in California didn't know how to mine the gold. It was the people from Sonora who showed them. That's what we want to explain, so that North Americans understand the fundamental value that Mexicans made to the development of California and what it is today. That's the point. The gold fever was the foundation that made California, and people from Sonora had the principal role in teaching the Anglos how to mine the gold. Joaquín Murrieta was not a bandit. He was not a killer of North Americans. He was a social fighter, and that's why Mexicans called him a patriot.

DB: And now, 150 years later, why is Joaquín Murrieta's life still something important or relevant?

I would like North Americans to better understand us, the Mexicans—the fundamental value that we have—because we still come to work here. We come to develop this country. They, of course, pay us, thank God, but we are a very important part of this country. Chicanos and Mexicans still come to work in industry, the restaurants, the cleaning, in the warehouses, and the fields. Without Mexicans, the crops wouldn't be harvested, because, let's be honest, the majority of the North Americans don't want to work as farmworkers because it's hard work. We do. Why? Possibly because we're already used to hard work. That's what we want them to learn. And we need to learn more about North Americans as well.

DB: When did you get interested in social movements, and when did it become part of your own life?

I began to participate in forming the social movement of the International Association of the Descendents of Joaquín Murrieta in 1987. Before that, we had conversations with Alfredo Figueroa in Blythe, California, who is the president of the association. But in 1988, we started to openly fight to clear Joaquín Murrieta's name, and for these ideas of social justice. We fight for our people here that can't get a drivers license, and whose car insurance costs them triple that of a resident or a North American. Just because someone is an illegal, it doesn't mean that he doesn't know how to drive.

DB: So the Association of the Descendents of Joaquín Murrieta is part of a broader movement for the civil rights of the undocumented here?

We want mutual understanding between the North Americans and the Mexicans of who Murrieta was, to dissipate from the minds of children and adults of that Murrieta was a "gringo killer"—that he was [a] bandit, a pistolero, that he stole and murdered. We want people to understand that he fought to recover part of his fatherland and that he defended the Mexicans of that time.

To us, that's part of a better understanding between North Americans and Mexicans that since we're here, we have to fight for the undocumented as well, against the abuse they suffer. We have more than 3 million undocumented right now in the United States and we have no way to document them. We want an agreement that these people have rights, that they get paid better, that they can get a green card, a driver's license, car insurance, and a house to live in.

Since we started, we've helped the clinic in Trincheras, where Joaquín Murrieta lived. We have taken them medication and medical instruments, and an ambulance. We are in the process of getting them a school bus and a few other things: clothes, typewriters. We have two complete computers with printers for the high school in Trincheras. We still don't have the 23 kilometers that are needed of asphalt, to pave the primary road to the state highway.

DB: Hector Moroyoqui, the high school teacher in Trincheras, says cultural activities are needed to encourage more respect toward the indigenous heritage of the people that live there, from the Mayos, the Yaquis, the Papagos, and other indigenous groups. Is the Murrieta Association also supporting this effort?

Yes, we have always been in contact with the indigenous groups. The governor of the Papagos, Rafael Garcia-Valencia, is a consultant to us. He is an assistant to the mayor of Caborca, and is a teacher in Quitovac, near Sonoita, an indigenous Papago community. Because of the current change in the political party of the president of the republic, we feel that indigenous people have more support. So we're going to take advantage of that opportunity for us to ask more from the government.

The municipal president of Trincheras is of Mayo origin, from Navojoa. He helped us get into contact with the Mayo, and for the first time, three and a half years ago, we were able to bring a strong group of the Mayo to dance at our fiesta. A Yaqui group also came from Ciudad Obregon.

DB: So the association has two areas of emphasis, one to establish this dialog between the Mexicans and North Americans to have more respect towards the Mexicans and also to have more recognition of the indigenous heritage of the people in Sonora in the area of Trincheras and Caborca?

Yes, that's it. We are doing both things—supporting the indigenous people, the Mexican Indians: the Otum, the Guarillios, the Papago, the Mayo, the Yaqui, the Cucapaz, the Mujavi, the Chimahuevo, because those are the people of Murrieta. Back then, Joaquín Murrieta was guided by them. He wasn't born familiar with the trails where they walked from Trincheras to California. That was a 6-month trip. He was guided by the Papagos, in the Trincheras region of Caborca. The Papagos and the Pimas and the Opotas, were the ones who guided Murrieta all the way to California. The authentic paths are still there—the "Devil's Path," where Murrieta passed.

Thirty years ago, on a mountain near Caborca, I saw a rock with Joaquín Murrieta's name on it, that says 1850 with a[n] arrow next to it, next to the Devil's Path. But we have not been able to find that rock again. It disappeared as though through an act of magic. We are still looking for it.

I think Murrieta himself also had indigenous blood because his last name was Orozco from his mother's side, and that name is associated with the Otum and Pima. Even more, he could have Mayo blood, because the original Murrietas, Joaquín's parents and uncles, came from Alamo, Sonora. Alamo was the Mayos' fundamental area then. So I think that the principal blood that we, the Murrietas have, is Mayo blood.

DB: Many things remaining from that era are disappearing. I saw and photographed some of the iron crosses on the graves in the cemetery in La Cienega, that were made in the time of Murrieta, but many of them have now disappeared.

Yes. La Cienega is the place where Joaquín Murrieta had his ranch, where he kept almost 2,000 horses. It was called La Verruga. That's where he stored the horses, weapons, and ammunition he planned to use to take the part of Mexico back that was taken from us, supposedly sold by Antonio Lopez Santana after the war in Texas....

Source: Interview with Antonio Rivera Murrieta, Phoenix AZ (12/15/01). From *Communities Without Borders* (Cornell/ILR Press, 2006), © David Bacon, http://dbacon.igc.org.

74. Excerpts from Horace Bell, *Reminiscences of a Ranger; or, Early Times in Southern California*, 1881

Horace Bell (1830–1918), an attorney, wrote his autobiography in a gossip-like fashion about the lawless days of Los Angeles in the 1850s. Although he chased the Mexican bandit Joaquín Murrieta and contemporary gangs of Mexican bandits, in the following excerpt he was very critical of fellow Euro-Americans in California, conceding that Murrieta and other Mexican rebels were justified in rebelling against white American racism and mistreatment.

On the morning following my arrival in the city of the Angels I walked around to take notes in my mind as to matters of general interest. First I went immediately across the street to a very small adobe house with two rooms, in which sat in solemn conclave, a sub-committee of the great constituted criminal court of the city. On inquiry I found that the said sub-committee had been in session for about a week, endeavoring to extract confessions from the miserable culprits by a very refined process of questioning and cross-questioning, first by one of the committee, then by another, until the whole committee would exhaust their ingenuity on the victim, when all of their separate results would be solemnly compared, and all of the discrepancies in the prisoner's statements would be brought back to him and he be required to explain and reconcile them to suit the examining committee; and the poor devil, who doubtless was frightened so badly that he would hardly know one moment what he had said the moment previous, was held strictly accountable for any and all contradictions, and if not satisfactorily explained, was invariably taken by the wise heads of the said committee to be conclusive evidence of guilt. Six men were being tried, all Sonoranians, except one, Felipe Read, a half-breed Indian, whose father was a Scotchman; all claimed, of course, to be innocent; finally one Reyes Feliz made a confession, probably under the hypothesis that hanging would be preferable to such inquisitorial torture as was being practiced on him by the seven wise men of the Angels. Reyes said in his confession that he and his brother-in-law, Joaquín Murietta, with a few followers, had, about a year previous, ran off the horses of Jim Thompson from the Brea ranch, and succeeded in getting them as far as the Tejon, then exclusively inhabited by Indians; that old Zapatero, the Tejon chief, on recognizing Jim Thompson's brand, arrested the whole party, some dozen in all, men and women, and stripped them all stark naked, tied them up, and had them whipped half to death, and turned loose to shift for themselves in the best way they could. Fortunately for the poor outcasts, they fell in with an American of kindred sympathies, who did what he could to relieve the distress of the forlorn thieves, who continued their way-as best they could toward the "Southern Mines" on the Stanislaus and Tuolumne, no mining being done south of those points at that time. In the meantime, brave old Zapatero, who was every inch a chief, sent Thompson's herd back to him—an act for which I hope Jim is to this day duly grateful.

At the time this confession was made, Joaquín was walking around, as unconcerned as any other gentleman; but when the minions of the mob went to lay heavy hand upon him he was gone, and from that day until the day of his death, Joaquín Murietta was an outlaw and the terror of the southern counties. Until that confession he stood in this community with as good a character as any other Mexican of his class.

Reyes Feliz denied all knowledge of the murder of General Bean. One of the prisoners, Cipriano Sandoval, the village cobbler of San Gabriel, also, after having for several days maintained his innocence, and denied any and all knowledge of the murder, came out and made a full confession. He said he was on his way home from the maromas (rope-dancers) at about 11 o'clock one night, it being quite dark. He heard a shot, and then the footsteps of a man running toward him; that a moment after he came in violent contact with a man whom he at once recognized as Felipe Read. They mutually recognized each other, when Felipe said: "Cipriano, I have just shot Bean. Here is five dollars; take it, say nothing about it, and when you want money come to me and get it." That was the sum total of his confession. All the others remained obdurate, and what I have related was the sum of the information elicited by the seven days [of] inquisition. The committee had certainly found the murderer of General Bean.

The fact was, I believe, that Bean, who kept a bar at the Mission, had seduced Felipe's mistress, and Indian woman, away from him, and hence the assassination. Three days after my arrival the "inquisitors" announced themselves as ready to report. In the meantime I went around taking notes in my mind. Los Angeles, at the time of my arrival, was certainly a nice looking place—the houses generally looked neat and clean, and were well whitewashed. There were three two-story adobe houses in the city, the most important of which is the present residence of Mrs. Bell, widow of the late Capt. Alex. Bell; then the Temple building, a substantial two-story, at the junction of Main and Spring Streets; and the old Casa Sanchez, on what is now Sanchez Street. The lower walls of the latter are still there, the house having been razed. The business of the place was very considerable; the most of the merchants were Jews, and all seemed to be doing a paying business. The fact was, they were all getting rich. The streets were thronged throughout the entire day with splendidly mounted and richly dressed caballeros, most of whom wore suits of clothes that cost all the way from $500 to $1,000, with saddle and horse trappings that cost even more than the above named sums. Of one of the Lugos, I remember, it was said his horse equipments cost over $2,000. Everybody in Los Angeles seemed rich, everybody was rich, and money was more plentiful, at that time, than in any other place of like size, I venture to say, in the world.

The question will at once suggest itself to the reader: Why was it that money was so plentiful in Los Angeles at the time referred to? I will inform him. The great rush to the gold mines had created a demand for beef cattle, and the years '48, '49, and

'50 had exhausted the supply in the counties north of San Luis Obispo, and purchasers came to Los Angeles, then the greatest cow county of the State. The southern counties had enjoyed a succession of good seasons of rain and bountiful supply of grass. The cattle and horses had increased to an unprecedented number, and the prices ranged from $20 to $35 per head, and a man was poor indeed who could not sell at the time one or two hundred head of cattle, and many of our first class rancheros, for instance the Sepulvedas, Abilas, Lugos, Yorbas, Picos, Stearns, Rowlands, and Williams, could sell a thousand head of cattle at any time and put the money in their pockets as small change, and as such they spent it.

On the second evening after my arrival, in company with a gentleman, now of high standing in California, I went around to see the sights. We first went to the "El Dorado" and smiled at the bar. The "El Dorado" was a small frame building, a duplicate of the "Imprenta," wherein the Star was published; the room below being used as a bar and billiard room, while the upper room was used as a dormitory. The place was kept by an elegant Irishman, John H. Hughes, said to have been a near Kinsman of the late great church dignitary, Archbishop Hughes. John was a scholar, and without doubt, so far as manners and accomplishments went, was a splendid gentleman, and the whole community accorded to him the honor of being a good judge of whisky. The "El Dorado" was situated at about the southeast corner of the Merced theater.

Along toward the spring of 1853, the Rev. Adam Bland, without the fear of the virtuous community before his eyes, purchased the "El Dorado," pulled down its sacred sign, and profanely converted it into a Methodist church! Alas, poor Hughes! I believe it broke his heart. He never recovered from the blow. It broke his noble spirit, and a few years later, when a fair Señorita withheld her smiles from the brilliant Hughes, it was the feather that broke the camel's back, and the disconsolate Hughes joined the Crabbe filibustering expedition to Sonora and was killed.

From the "El Dorado" we betook ourselves to Aleck Gibson's gambling house on the plaza, where a well kept bar was in full blast, and some half dozen "monte banks" in successful operation, each table with its green baize cover, being literally heaped with piles of $50 ingots, commonly called "slugs." Betting was high. You would frequently see a ranchero with an immense pile of gold in front of him, quietly and unconcernedly smoking his cigarrito and betting twenty slugs on the turn, the losing of which produced no perceptible discomposure of his grave countenance. For grave self-possession under difficult and trying circumstances, the Spaniard is in advance of all nationalities that I know of.

From the great gambling house on the plaza we hied us to the classic precincts of the "Calle de los Negros," which was the most perfect and full grown pandemonium that this writer, who had seen the "elephant" before, and has been more than familiar with him under many phases since, has ever beheld. There were four or five gambling places, and the crowd from the old Coronel building on the Los Angeles street corner to the plaza was so dense that we could scarcely squeeze through. Americans, Spaniards, Indians, and foreigners, rushing and crowding along from one gambling house to another, from table to table, all chinking the everlasting eight square $50 pieces up and down in their palms. There were several bands of music of the primitive Mexican-Indian kind, that sent forth most discordant sound, by no means in harmony with the eternal jingle of gold—while at the upper end of the street, in the rear of one of the gambling houses was a Mexican "Maroma" in uproarious confusion. They positively made night hideous with their howlings. Every few minutes a rush would be made, and may be a pistol shot would be heard, and when the confusion incident to the rush would have somewhat subsided, and inquiry made, you would learn that it was only a knife fight between two Mexicans, or a gambler had caught somebody cheating and had perforated him with a bullet. Such things were a matter of course, and no complaint or arrests were ever made. An officer would not have had the temerity to attempt an arrest in "Negro Alley," at that time.

I have no hesitation in saying that in the years of 1851, '52, and '53, there were more desperadoes in Los Angeles than in any place on the Pacific Coast, San Francisco with its great population not excepted. It was a fact, that all of the bad characters who had been driven from the mines had taken refuge in Los Angeles, for the reason that if forced to move further on, it was only a short ride to Mexican soil, while on the other hand all of the outlaws of the Mexican frontier made for the California gold mines, and the cut-throats of California and Mexico naturally met at Los Angeles, and at Los Angeles they fought. Knives and revolvers settled all differences, either real or imaginary. The slightest misunderstandings were settled on the spot with knife or bullet, the Mexican preferring the former at close quarters and the American the latter....

As stated in the beginning of this history, on the arrest and confession of Reyes Feliz, Joaquín Murietta [another spelling], his brother-in-law, who had for one or two years been domiciled among the angels, decamped, and was not heard of until the spring of 1853, when he commenced a succession of bold and successful operations in the southern mines, beginning at San Andres, in Calaveras County. His acts were so bold and daring, and attended with such remarkable success, that he drew to him all the Mexican outlaws, cut-throats and thieves that infested the country extending from San Diego to Stockton. No one will deny the assertion that Joaquín in his organizations, and the successful ramifications of his various bands, his eluding capture, the secret intelligence conveyed from points remote from each other, manifested a degree of executive ability and genius that well fitted him for a more honorable position than that of chief of a band of robbers. In any country in America except the United States, the bold defiance of the power of the government, a half year's successful resistance, a continuous conflict with the military and civil authorities and the armed populace—the writer repeats that in any other country in America other than the United States—the operations of Joaquín Murietta would have been dignified by the title....

there is little doubt in the writer's mind that Joaquin's aims were higher than that of mere revenge and pillage. Educated in the school of revolution in his own country, where the line of demarcation between rebel and robber, pillager and patriot, was dimly defined, it is easy to perceive that Joaquín felt himself to be more the champion of his countrymen than an outlaw and an enemy to the human race....

Source: Major Horace Bell, *Reminiscences of a Ranger; or, Early Times in Southern California* (Los Angeles: Yarnell, Caystile & Mathes, Printers, 1881), pp. 23–29, 72, 108, http://memory.loc. gov/cgi-bin/query/r?ammem/calbk:@field(DOCID+@lit(calbk103)).

75. Excerpt from a Statement by Tiburcio Vásquez, 1874

Tiburcio Vásquez (1839–1875), from the San Jose, California area, was perhaps the best-known Mexican bandit of his time after Joaquín Murrieta, exemplifying what British historian E. J. Hobsbawm called a "primitive rebel" or "social bandit." He was not a revolutionary because his intent was not independence but instead a revolt against injustice. In his case, injustice was fueled by the racism of the times. His career spanned 15 years and, like Jesse James and even Bonnie and Clyde, he was supported by his people. In the following excerpt he talks about his early life and why he became an outlaw.

I was born in Monterey County, California, at the town of Monterey, August 11, 1835.... I can read and write, having attended school in Monterey. My parents were people in ordinarily good circumstances; owned a small tract of land and always had enough for their wants.

My career grew out of the circumstances by which I was surrounded as I grew to manhood. I was in the habit of attending balls and parties given by the native Californians, into which the Americans, then beginning to become numerous, would force themselves and shove the native-born men aside, monopolizing the dances and the women. This was about 1852.

A spirit of hatred and revenge took possession of me. I had numerous fights in defense of what I believed to be my rights and those of my countrymen. The officers were continually in pursuit of me. I believed that we were unjustly and wrongfully deprived of the social rights which belonged to us. So perpetually was I involved in these difficulties that I at length determined to leave the thickly settled portion of the country, and did so.

I gathered together a small band of cattle and went into Mendocino County, back of Ukiah and beyond Fallis Valley. Even here I was not permitted to remain in peace. The officers of the law sought me out in that remote region, and strove to drag me before the courts. I always resisted arrest.

I went to my mother and told her I intended to commence a different life. I asked for and obtained her blessing, and at once commenced the career of a robber. My first exploit consisted in robbing some peddlers of money and clothes in Monterey County. My next was the capture and robbery of a stagecoach in the same county. I had confederates with me from the first, and was always recognized as leader. Robbery after robbery followed each other as rapidly as circumstances allowed, until in 1857 or '58 I was arrested in Los Angeles for horse-stealing, convicted of grand larceny, sent to the penitentiary and was taken to San Quentin and remained there until my term of imprisonment expired in 1863.

Up to the time of my conviction and imprisonment, I had robbed stagecoaches, houses, wagons, etc., indiscriminately, carrying on my operations for the most part in daylight, sometimes, however, visiting houses after dark.

After my discharge from San Quentin I returned to the house of my parents and endeavored to lead a peaceful and honest life. I was, however, soon accused of being a confederate of Procopio and one Sato, both noted bandits, the latter of whom was afterward killed by Sheriff Harry Morse of Alameda County. I was again forced to become a fugitive from the law-officers, and, driven to desperation, I left home and family and commenced robbing whenever opportunity offered. I made but little money by my exploits, I always managed to avoid arrest. I believe I owe my frequent escapes solely to my courage. I was always ready to fight whenever opportunity offered, but always tried to avoid bloodshed.

Source: Los Angeles Star, May 16, 1874.

76. Excerpts from Robert Greenwood,
The California Outlaw: Tiburcio Vásquez, 1960

Author Robert Greenwood's account is the best known biography of Tiburcio Vásquez, who for some 15 years robbed mostly white merchants and establishments throughout California (1859–1875). He was supported and shielded by the Mexican community. In the following excerpts, Greenwood quotes Vásquez on his motives for becoming an outlaw, and quotes George A. Beers, a special correspondent for the *San Francisco Chronicle,* on why Vásquez became a bandit and how he captured the imagination of the Mexican populace.

Vásquez turned to the life of a bandido because of the bitter animosity then existing, and which still exists, between the white settlers and the native or Mexican portion of the population. The native Californians, especially the lower classes, never took kindly to the stars and stripes. Their youth were taught from the very cradle to look upon the American government as that of a foreign nation. This feeling was greatly intensified by the rough, brutal conduct of the worst class of American settlers, who never missed an opportunity to openly exhibit their contempt for the native Californian or Mexican population—designating them as "d——d Greasers."

Source: Robert Greenwood, *The California Outlaw: Tiburcio Vásquez* (Los Gatos, CA: Talisman Press, 1960), pp. 12, 75.

PART V
Texas

The border between Matamoros, Texas, and Tijuana, Mexico, stretches 1,969 miles; the outcome of the United States' crossing borders. The distance from the mouth on the Gulf of Mexico to El Paso/Cuidad Juarez is 1,254 miles. Just under two-thirds of the U.S. side of the border falls in Texas. The loss of the Rio Grande was a major one for Mexico since the river sustained considerable agriculture and Mexican towns sprang up along the river. This concentration of population on the border distinguished it from the rest of the international border. It was where the two peoples clashed and the Mexican population in South Texas was caught in the middle. The racism of most white Americans who felt entitled to the little that the Mexican had prevented the assimilation of the Mexican in South Texas and led to what British historian E. J. Hobsbawn has called social banditry—bandit-rebel—robbers and outlaws who were seen by many Mexican Americans as champions of the people rather than criminals. Driven too far, the border people sporadically rose up to defend their way of life and dignity. Because of the intensity of the contact Texas deserves special note during the 1860s and 1870s.

77. Judge José Tomás Canales on Juan Cortina, 1949

Mexicans had lived on what would be the Mexican-American border well before the Euro-American takeover of 1836. While many more affluent Mexicans sided with the Euro-Americans, others resented the colonization. Many of those who were initially pro–Euro-American grew disillusioned. Most of the descendants, whatever side they belonged to, preserved memories of the past. On his mother's side, Judge José Tomás Canales (1877–1976), a prominent politico, was related to the Cavazos and the Garza families who were prominent border landowners on both the U.S. and Mexican sides of the border. Canales was active politically and was a player in the political machines during the first decades of the twentieth century. Canales became a judge and legislator. By the late 1910s, Canales was locked in a fight with the Texas Rangers who, from 1915–1950, brutalized the Mexican population. He held hearings showing flagrant abuses that led to the disbandment of the rangers.

Canales was related to Juan Cortina (1824–1892), born in Camargo, Tamaulipas, a member of the Cavazos family. Cortina was branded an outlaw after he shot a marshal after he made a racial slur in 1859. Cortina raised an army and challenged U.S. authorities. He operated out of Tamaulipas where he became the governor until the mid 1870s. Canales endorsed the work of

Charles W. Goldfinch, saying that he did not believe that the Mexican side of Cortina's story would ever be told.

When Charles W. Goldfinch informed me in 1947 that he had decided to write his Master's Thesis on the life and character of Juan N. Cortina, I tried to dissuade him from doing so. Cortina's life is quite an enigma and practically all that has been written about him is most derogatory in effect; and since Mr. Goldfinch had married into my family, I was afraid he would only echo what had been written about Cortina, which would have earned him a dislike and disapproval of the family; as, traditionally, Cortina has been considered a patriot and hero, who sacrificed himself fighting against racial hatred and discrimination. But Mr. Goldfinch argued that Cortina had not had anyone who was fair enough to interpret the facts from his (Cortina's) point of view; that all who had written about him were either his enemies, like Adolphus Glavecke, or persons who were prejudiced against him on account of his race, and those who resented his taking the side of the recently conquered Mexicans. He insisted that Cortina was entitled to have an unbiased presentation of the facts from his viewpoint as even a common felon would be entitled to that much if he were on trial. When I saw that Mr. Goldfinch had already made up his mind to make Cortina the subject of his Master's Thesis, I then turned over to him all the data that I had. For many years, I had intended to write the life of Juan N. Cortina for I had felt that no one had done justice to him nor had truly understood, or interpreted Cortina's actions. I admit that I possess neither the aptitude nor the ability to write a biography such as this and, also, that Mr. Goldfinch has done an excellent work.

Those who have never experienced the humiliating feeling of being pointed out as a member of an inferior race cannot truly interpret Cortina's life. That is why neither Professor J. Frank Dobie, nor Professor J. Fred Rippy, nor Dr. Walter Prescott Webb (although all are excellent gentlemen and true Texans) have interpreted the actions of Cortina in any other light, except that of a bandit and a thief. Perhaps a personal experience would explain this point:

Some years ago, I was trying a case in the City of Alice, Texas, County Seat of Jim Wells County. One morning, on my way to the Court House, I passed in front of what appeared to be a very nice looking barber shop, whose owner I knew personally. I needed a haircut and a shave and decided to enter the place. The owner, somewhat embarrassed, told me: "Mr. Canales, I am sorry that I cannot serve you, because you do not belong to the right race." I retorted: "I thought that only registered stock were required to show a pedigree"; and left the place.

My feeling[s] must have been very similar to those of Cortina when the Anglo-Americans of his time not only refused to recognize him us an American citizen, but scornfully referred to him as "a damned 'Mexican Greaser.'" Had I been Cortina at the time of the incident above related, perhaps I would have shot the barber, even at the risk of getting shot myself; but I do not believe in using force in vindication of my own rights; much less to take human life. This incident strongly reminded me, at the time, of what Juan N. Cortina must have felt and what he had to endure, and, I believe, what undoubtedly caused him to resort to violence.

On the other hand, Mr. Carey McWilliams, in his excellent book *North from Mexico*, although not a Texan, but one who, as a reporter, had actually seen the great injustices done to people of the Mexican race in California in the Zoot-Suit Riots comes nearer to understanding Cortina's true character, when he says of him: "there was unquestionably something of the Robin Hood about Cortina."

There has been some controversy as to the personal appearance of Cortina. J. Frank Dobie says: "the expression of his face sinister, sensual and cruel." Col. J. S. (Rip) Ford, who knew him personally, in his unpublished memoirs (page 705) says: "He is of medium size, with regular features, and a rather pleasing countenance. He is rather fairer than most men of his nationality. He is fearless, self-possessed, and cunning. In some cases he has acted towards personal and political enemies with a clemency worthy of imitation." And this from Cortina's mortal enemy, the one who fought him most and did his best to kill him! Again, on page 1111, Col. Ford further says: "In regard to the manner in which Cortina treated citizens of the United States, and of Texas, while he was in power in the State of Tamaulipas (1864) was worthy of remembrance. There were Americans in Matamoros known to have been personally unfriendly to Cortina, and he treated them kindly and honorably."

These incidents are related solely to explain why, at the beginning of this Foreword, I refer to Cortina as an enigma. It requires a complete familiarity with the facts and an intimate acquaintance with the life-habits and customs of Cortina and of his family and people, in order to arrive at a true estimate of his real character.

Unquestionably, Cortina's frank and open sympathy towards the Union Forces during the Civil War and the fact that he was a friend of Governor Edmund J. Davis, whom he had befriended in Matamoros (while the latter was a refugee from the Confederate State of Texas), contributed largely to his being branded "a cattle thief" in addition to the epithet of "bandit" when the attempt was made during the Reconstruction Period (1871) to have him pardoned. So long as Cortina remained in Mexico and would decide to stay there, his enemies were, apparently, well satisfied; but when they heard that a Petition had been presented to the Legislature to have him pardoned that he might return to Texas, his enemies would not permit this for they would have to meet him on equal terms and perhaps, face him on equal ground. A fair and impartial examination of the facts surrounding the application for a pardon and the sudden activity taken by his enemies, at that time, show this to be a fact.

While at first I did not approve of Mr. Goldfinch's choice of theme for his thesis; yet, after he had written it and I had read it, I must confess that it has given me a great personal satisfaction; I also feel that it should be made public for many of the facts stated and commented therein have not been fully revealed or made clear by any writer on Texas History. By the reading of this thesis we may not only learn new and important facts in Texas History, but we may, also, find a new and better way of interpreting historical events which may enable us to solve many of our present problems fraught with biases and racial prejudice. The labor and great research required in the preparation of this thesis fully justifies its printing and publication.

BROWNSVILLE, TEXAS, OCTOBER 1949

J. T. Canales

Source: Preface to Charles W. Goldfinch, "Juan Cortina 1824–1892: A Re-Appraisal," MA dissertation, University of Chicago, 1949, 1–3.

78. Excerpts from Report of Major Samuel P. Heintzelman to Colonel Robert E. Lee, March 1, 1860

Col. Robert E. Lee (1807–1870) was sent to the Rio Grande to pursue Juan Cortina (1824–1894), who was called the scourge of the Río Grande by Euro-Americans. Cortina (misspelled by many sources) became a fugitive in 1859, when he shot a marshal who was pistol-whipping one of his mother's former servants and called him what amounted to "a dirty Mexican." When the white townspeople lynched an old man who was a friend of Cortina's, he raised an army and attacked Euro-American towns. For the next 15 years he was hunted by U.S. rangers, state militia, and the U.S. Army. Lee, much as General John Pershing was sent years later to pursue Pancho Villa (1878–1923) in 1916, was unable to find the elusive Cortina. The following letter is from Maj. Samuel P. Heintzelman (1805–1880) to Lee, reporting extensively on the status of the chase and hostilities on the border near Brownsville, Texas.

MAJOR HEINTZELMAN TO COLONEL LEE

Headquarters Brownsville Expedition
Fort Brown, Texas, March 1, 1860
In compliance with Special Order No. 103, headquarters department of Texas, San Antonio, November 12, 1859, I repaired to San Antonio and reported to the commanding general for instructions.

I was directed to proceed towards Brownsville and disperse any hostile parties I might meet, &c. From accounts received soon after, the reports were believed to be greatly exaggerated and the expedition was broken up. But I was directed to proceed to Brownsville and make full inquiries there and on the frontier above.

I reached Brownsville on the night of the 5th of December.

Juan Nepomosina Cortinas, (or Cortina,) the leader of the banditti who have for the last five months been in arms on the Lower Rio Grande, murdering, robbing, and burning, is a ranchero, at one time claiming to be an American, and at another a Mexican, citizen. At the time General Taylor arrived on the banks of the Rio Grande, he was a soldier in General Arista's army. He has been for years noted as a lawless, desperate man.

Ten years ago he was indicted for murder, and the sheriff attempted to arrest him, which made him, for a long period, keep out of the way until the witnesses were gone. In 1854, he again began to be seen about; but no effort was made to arrest him until in the spring of 1859, when he was indicted for horse stealing, and he has since been a fugitive from justice. When he came to town he was always well armed, or had some of his friends around him, making it dangerous to interfere with him. His principal business has been dealing in stock, purchasing or stealing, as was the most convenient. He had great influence with his class of the Mexican population, and thus, as he controlled so many votes, was courted at elections by politicians.

He has a ranch called San José, a few miles from town, and whenever there was any danger of arrest he would retire to this place and keep himself surrounded by a band of outlaws, as desperate as himself. Leading this lawless life, he and those around him made numerous enemies. On the 13th of July last he was in Brownsville with some of his ranchero friends, when a man who was formerly a servant of his was arrested by the city marshal for abusing a coffee-house keeper. Cortinas attempted to rescue the man; he fired twice on the marshal, the second shot wounding him in the shoulder, and rescued the prisoner. He mounted his horse, took the prisoner up behind him, and with his friends around him, rode off defying the authorities to arrest him. He escaped to Matamoras, and there was treated with consideration and lauded as the defender of Mexican rights.

For this, an effort was made by the sheriff to arrest him. A party was got up, but they did not succeed in getting what they considered a sufficient force and the posse never started. Several of the men who were active on this occasion were known to Cortinas, and they were marked.

It has been reported that he held a captain's commission in the Mexican Army. He at one time was a lieutenant under General Garcia, but was detected selling the horses given to him for a remount, and was dismissed. Since these troubles commenced he has offered his services with fifty men to General Garcia, but they were declined.

He probably held some commission in the custom-house or maritime guards. Under this pretext he recruited men and purchased arms. Don Miguel Tigerino, his first cousin, on the 28th of September, said in Brownsville to some of his friends that he "was a desperate, contrary, fellow. When every one thought that he had started for the interior he turned up suddenly in Brownsville." He no doubt, when he came over here, intended to kill all his enemies that he could catch, and then go into the interior.

Before daylight on the morning of the 28th of September, Cortinas entered the city of Brownsville with a body of mounted men, variously estimated at from forty to eighty, leaving two small parties [on] foot outside—one near the cemetery, the other near the suburb of Framireno. The citizens were awakened by firing and cries of "Viva cheno Cortinas!" "Mueran los Gringos!" "Viva Mexico!" ["Long live Cheno Cortinas!" "Death to the Gringos!" Long live Mexico!"] The city was already in his possession, with sentinels at the corners of the principal streets and armed men riding about. He avowed his determination to kill the Americans, but assured Mexicans and foreigners that they should not be molested. Thus was a city of from two thousand to three thousand inhabitants occupied by a band of armed bandits, a thing till now unheard of in these United States.

He made his headquarters in the deserted garrison of Fort Brown, and sent mounted men through the streets hunting up their enemies. He broke open the jail, liberated the prisoners, knocked off their irons, and had them join him. He killed the jailer, Johnson, a constable named George Morris, young Neale in his bed, and two Mexicans; was after Glaseche, the wounded city marshal, and others. One of his men was killed by the jailer, in the attack on the jail.

Cortinas himself rode up to a store on the levee and called for spirits of turpentine. A few minutes after this, General Caravajal made his appearance on the levee, and said that he would try and put a stop to all this, and seeing Don Miguel Tiguino [*sic*] on the opposite bank of the river, called to him to cross over to this side instantly. This he did, on horseback, accompanied by Don Agassito Longosia. General Caravajal then sent for Cortinas, and, after a talk with him, he with his men, mounted and on foot, numbering about sixty, marched along the levee out towards his mother's rancho, about nine miles above the town.

Matamoras [*sic*] came over at 11 o'clock P.M., at the request of those Mexican gentlemen, to persuade the people of Brownsville to comply with his demand, whilst an express awaited, on the other side, their answer, to carry it to Cortinas. His demand was refused, but he was informed that the man was in the hands of the sheriff, to be dealt with by the laws of the country.

The night after the arrival of Captain Tobin's company, Cabrera was found hung.

Cortinas, with forty men, crossed the river the same night. He received their answer, and took up his old quarters, at his mother's rancho. Here he collected men and arms, and prepared to carry out his threats, occasionally sending threatening communications to the authorities. His men would make their appearance on the outskirts of the town in open daylight; but the citizens had now organized and armed, and kept a guard day and night.

Some Mexican troops, who had been called over about the 30th of September, and who had returned home when Cortinas recrossed to the Mexican side, were now invited over again. About seventy-five men came over, with a piece of artillery, to join an expedition which the citizens were preparing for the purpose of attacking Cortinas. They were of the National Guards, of Matamoras [sic], under the command of Colonel Loranco and Don Miguel Tigerino, who accompanied the expedition as a volunteer.

There were about twenty Americans, under Captain Thompson, and forty Mexicans, from the town and ranches below, under a Mexican called Portillo, all mounted. They took along a four-pounder howitzer.

The expedition started on the 22d of October, met the enemy nine miles from town on the 24th, routed him from his first position, and followed him up as he retreated into the chaparral, from which, without being seen, he kept up a constant fire. Here, the Mexican gun stuck in the mud, and on the second discharge it was dismounted, and was then abandoned. The advance fell back. The other gun, with its ammunition, was also abandoned, but, it is said, not until it was thrown into the river. However, both the guns were in Cortinas's camp that night. The flight now became general, all being anxious to be the first to reach Brownsville. The Mexican troops had four men wounded, and brought up the rear. One Mexican with Portillo was also badly wounded. Two men of Cortinas's—all that he lost—were killed by the Mexican troops.

The Mexican troops had but from eight to twelve rounds of ammunition, and they did not retreat until it gave out. They are accused, but I think most unjustly, of having fired blank cartridges, and that the cap squares were loosened to dismount the gun.

Cortinas now had two pieces of artillery, and was much emboldened by his success. Large reinforcements joined him, some voluntarily, others he compelled from the neighboring ranches. He commenced levying contributions of arms, horses, beef cattle, corn, everything that he wanted for his men, sometimes giving receipts for what he took.

He intercepted all the mails to and from this place, except the Point Isabel, by capturing the mail riders, cut open the mail bags, and had the letters read to him; he cannot read or write. Once he sent in the letters opened, with a note apologizing to the postmaster, "as it was a matter of necessity for him to know what steps were taken against him." By this means he knew more of what was going on outside of Brownsville than its citizens.

He knew when the rangers with Captain Tobin were expected, and made arrangements to intercept them. Glaseche, however, went and guided them in about midnight, without their meeting any one. The same night, Cortinas was known to be hovering about town, and Tobin's men were received with a shower of grape, fired at them before they were recognized. This was the 10th of November.

About eight days after, thirty men were sent under Lieutenant Littleton, towards the Arroyo Colorado, to meet Captain Donaldson's company. He missed Donaldson, but on the Palo Alto prairie fell into an ambuscade prepared by Cortinas, and lost three men killed and one wounded and a prisoner. The next day, when a party went out to bring the dead they found this man murdered and all the dead mutilated. They went to Santa Rita, seven miles from here, to attack Cortinas, but knowing that he had artillery, and thinking he was too strong, they only made a demonstration and returned to the city. All this only served to give Cortinas and his followers confidence. He now believed that he could stand his ground against the whole State of Texas.

In the meantime more volunteers arrived. On the 22d of November the rangers under Captain Tobin, numbering about two hundred and fifty men, including in this Captain Kenedy's company of citizens from Brownsville, the Indianola company, and a 24-pounder howitzer in charge of Lieutenant Langdon, United States artillery, who volunteered, again started out to exterminate Cortinas. On the 24th, Captain Tobin had his whole force collected at Santa Rita, seven miles above town. Here he left the 24-pounder and about sixty men, and advanced with the main body of his force to make a reconnoissance [sic]. The advance, when near the intrenchment, two miles above Santa Rita, was fired upon by both cannon and small arms. The fire was returned. Captain Tobin now gave the order to fall back and wait for the artillery, but the whole force fell back to Santa Rita. Here there was another council and a misunderstanding, and the next morning sixty men started back to town. The next day (25th) Captain Tobin again advanced, but when near the barricades there was another consultation, and it was decided to be imprudent to risk an attack, and the whole force marched back to Brownsville.

It was a wise decision. In their disorganized condition an attack would have brought certain defeat. About a month before, this the streets of Brownsville were barricaded.

Cortinas was now a great man; he had defeated the "Gringos," and his position was impregnable; he had the Mexican flag flying in his camp, and numbers were flocking to his standard. When he visited Matamoras [sic] he was received as the champion of his race—as the man who would right the wrongs the Mexicans had received; that he would drive back the hated Americans to the Nueces, and some even spoke of the Sabine as the future boundary. The lower order of Mexicans hate Americans, and the educated classes are not always exempt from this feeling. This is well shown from the difficulty we had in obtaining information. When his force and all his movements were well known in Matamoras [sic], with daily intercourse with his camp, we were answered with vague and exaggerated accounts. Men who have lived here for years, and are united to Mexican women, could learn nothing reliable.

A party of forty men, under Santo Cadena, joined him from Agua Leguas, in Nueva [sic] Leon, remained until they were loaded with plunder and then returned to their homes. Another party of sixty convicts escaped from prison at Victoria, in Tamuulipas [sic], armed themselves, and, after a fight with the authorities, marched through the country to the Rio Grande, and joined him. Affairs remained in this state until we arrived here on the night of the 5th of December.

I entered the town that night with Captain Stoneman's company "E," 2d cavalry, forty-six men, and "L" and "M" companies, 1st artillery, sixty-six men, and five men of the 1st infantry—in all, five officers and one hundred and seventeen men. In Fort Brown, were Captain Rickett's company, 1st artillery, of forty-eight men.

On our march from the Nueces to the Arroyo Colorado we only met two Americans and a Mexican cart; all travel had ceased for some time. At the arroyo we first learned to a certainty that Captain Tobin was in Brownsville, but that he had not dislodged Cortinas, and got the most exaggerated accounts of the latter's forces.

The morning after our arrival I endeavored to get information as to the number, position, and objects of Cortinas; every one appeared to be as ignorant of these matters as I was; accounts ranged as high as fifteen hundred men. I finally satisfied myself that he could not have over three hundred and fifty men, and that he occupied a fortified position across the river road, about nine miles above town, and that his works were armed with two pieces of artillery. As to his objects no one knew.

Captain Tobin informed me that he had about one hundred and fifty rangers, and placed himself under my command; I wished him to send out parties to reconnoitre [*sic*] their position; several went, but none of them ever got near enough to give me any information. At 1 o'clock A.M., the 14th of December, we marched out of Brownsville with one hundered and sixty-five officers and men of the regular army, and one hundred and twenty rangers; half an hour before day I halted a mile and a half from the point where I was told his intrenchment was.

I was desirous of having a reconnoisance [*sic*] made before proceeding further; the rangers were so thoroughly stampeded by their previous expedition that it was only after much difficulty and delay that I could get any one to go, and then only by Judge Davis, who had been out with them before, volunteering to go with them; we advanced and found that the intrenchment had been abandoned apparently for a week; it consisted of a heavy breastwork of ebony logs and earth mixed with brush across the road, with two embrasures and a ditch in front; about one hundred yards beyond another had been commenced to face the other way; the first was badly located and could easily have been turned.

After a short delay in clearing a road around these obstructions, the march was resumed. About three miles f[a]rther, where the road is straight and passing through a very dense chaparral with ebony trees, our attention was attracted by the waving of a flag six or seven hundred yards in advance, with a few men about it. In a moment more, a burst of smoke and a round shot down the road informed me that the enemy was before us. Until this event, the general impression was that Cortinas would not dare fire upon the United States troops.

I immediately ordered the guns unlimbered and the fire returned. The rangers seeing with how much coolness the regular troops stood the fire of the enemy regained confidence, and were finally induced to advance to the attack. With the aid of "L" and "M" companies, 1st artillery, they took the enemies' camp, at Vicente Guenais, a few hundred yards beyond, capturing some provisions and arms. The pursuit was continued about two miles further. Some horsemen made their escape across the river into Mexico. Where the enemy was posted, the chaparral was so dense that but a small portion of the force was engaged. This was one of Cortinas's principal camps, and had been long occupied, but he was not in it. The infantry were commanded by Pancho Balli, and the artillery by Antonio Juarez, or Jantes, and in all about sixty men. The resistance they made was quite trifling. We had two men of the artillery slightly wounded, and a ranger mortally. The enemy lost eight.

Here, whilst we halted to refresh the men and animals, Major Ford came up with fifty-five men. He heard the firing in the morning, and rode forty miles, *via* Brownsville, to join us.

A rain set in, and continuing, the next morning we returned to town. I had learned that Cortinas was behind us, back in the country, and would probably come in on the river. We reached town without meeting any of the enemy.

I was, on my return to town, informed that Cortinas was on his way to attack Point Isabel and burn the custom-house, full of valuable goods, and that he had also large parties towards the Arroyo Colorado. I sent out three strong parties, but in a few days they returned with out meeting any one. I was now satisfied that he had concentrated his whole force, and was retiring up the river to lay waste the country.

I started on the 21st of December with all the force I could collect, amounting to one hundred and fifty regulars and one hundred and ninety-eight rangers. I had information that was deemed reliable that Cortinas had fortified himself at the Baston, thirty-five miles from town, in Mr. Neale's brick house, loop-holed and surrounded by corrals. We came in sight of the Baston at twelve o'clock [P.]M. on the 23d, found the fences, corrals, and jacales [thatch-roofed huts] burned, the house sacked, and the enemy gone.

The next place I was told that we should certainly meet him was in a bend of the river a mile beyond—Edinburg. We reached Edinburg on Sunday, the 25th of December. Although we met several Mexicans from Reynosa, Mexico, not one could tell us anything about him, except that he had left after plundering the cus-tom-house, post office, &c., which we could see ourselves. His next position was a canebrake, a few miles beyond Edinburg; but when we arrived he had left.

The next day I learned that Cortinas was occupying Ringgold barracks and Rio Grande City, with his troops encamped on the plaza. Major Ford, who was in advance here, sent Colonel Lockridge with the information. I determined to surprise him by a night march. As our march was most of the way in full view from the Mex-ican side of the river, we went into camp at the usual time and in the usual manner. At midnight we resumed our march in silence, and an hour before daylight were three miles from Rio Grande City. Here, our spies met us with the assurance that he was still encamped in Rio Grande City.

I now made the arrangement for Ford's and Henon's companies, eighty-five men, to make a detour, and get on the road to Koma, above the city, and Captain Tobin, with Tomlinson's and Hampton's companies, one hundred and thirteen men, to move in advance of our right flank, whilst the regulars, giving the rangers half an hour's start, would advance with the artillery along the road, and attack him in front.

We advanced in this order, but when we reached the barracks some ranger rode up and reported that Major Ford could not get beyond on the road, and had com-menced the attack in front. On entering the town, I learned that most of his men had encamped about half a mile beyond. Here, he had been attacked by Ford, who was supported by Captain Tobin, with his, Tomlinson's, and Hampton's companies. The enemy made a vigorous resistance, but as soon as he saw the regular troops, with the "white-topped wagons" rise the ridge back of the town, he gave way. He here abandoned his provisions, half-cooked breakfast, and a baggage cart, but carried off his artillery.

I ordered up more troops, but the men, fatigued by a march of forty miles since the morning before, could not overtake the advance, and were sent after those who had escaped into the chapparal. At this time a dense fog set in, enabling many of the enemy to escape into the thick chapparal which lined the whole road. I rode forward, and found the ranger companies all broken up, and strewed along the road, with most of the officers in advance. I soon overtook Major Ford, and gave direc-tions to press the pursuit, as our victory would not be complete if they succeeded in carrying off their guns. After a pursuit of more than nine miles, we captured both his guns, loaded. There was no more attempt made at resistance, and here the last dispersed.

Within a few minutes after the capture of the second gun, the men on foot and guns and all our wagons were up. They had made a march of nearly fifty miles in twenty-five hours, thirty of them without stopping for water. There was not a straggler from the regular troops.

The defeat was complete. We captured his guns, ammunition and baggage carts, provisions, everything he could throw away to lighten his flight, and entirely dispersed his force.

We had sixteen rangers wounded, mostly very slight cases. Cortinas had between five and six hundred men, and his loss was about sixty killed and drowned in the river. Most of them who escaped got across the river into Mexico, and without arms. He fled to Grunoro, where he made his appearance next day. He afterwards was seen at Mier Camargo, Keynosa, and so continued down the river collecting able stragglers. Many small parties were seen on the Mexican side of the river, but generally unarmed. I sent Captain Stoneman's company the same evening to Koma for its protection. Captain Dawson, with "L" and "M" companies, first artillery, left on the 29th of December to garrison Fort Brown. I went to Koma, and remained until the 15th of January, 1860, then returned to this place to collect, in compliance with instructions, the names of the killed and amount of damage done by Cortinas.

A difficulty about the organization and command of the rangers created much embarrassment and delay. An election was held, and Tobin was elected major. I endeavored to have the rangers distributed along the river in small parties to prevent the reorganization of the enemy's forces but my orders were never fully carried out.

Two commissioners of the State of Texas, Messrs. Navarro and Taylor, now arrived in Brownsville, to inquire into the causes of this disturbance, and authorized to reorganize the rangers. They mustered all out of service, and then mustered in Ford's and Littleton's companies.

I was called upon by the commissioners to say what force of rangers would be sufficient for the protection of the frontier. With but one company of cavalry I was of the opinion that the two then in service would be sufficient. They were placed under my command.

I placed Captain Stoneman's cavalry and Ford's and Littleton's companies of rangers on the river between here and Rio Grande City with orders to keep out small parties. Cortinas's men were very active at this time crossing over and driving stock into Mexico.

Cortinas, soon after his defeat at Rio Grande City, established a camp at La Bolza, thirty-five miles above here, with the avowed object of attacking the steamboat Ranchero, on her return from the towns above. This being her first trip since last September, it was well known that she would have a valuable freight. Her whole cargo was valued by the officer of the boat at $200,000.

During his stay at La Bolza, Cortinas recruited men, procured arms, ammunition, and supplies. He crossed at Las Rusias to the American side of the river, intercepted the United States mail carrier, cut open the mail bags, and rifled them of their contents. He threatened the carrier with death for serving the Americans, and only spared him because the contractor is a Mexican. He was taken to La Bolsa and there kept until he made his escape in the confusion of the fight of the 4th of February. At La Bolsa, a frequent subject of conversation was the intercepting and robbing of the steamboat. During the time, Cortinas was in constant communication with the inhabitants of Matamoros [*sic*] and other towns on the river.

On the 31st of January I called, with one of the Texas commissioners and the American consul, on General Garcia, the Mexican commander of the line of the Brazos. He showed us the instructions he had to cooperate with the United States forces in arresting Cortinas and dispersing his bands. He told as that he had sent out but could not learn where Cortinas was to be found. We had known for near a month past that he was at La Bolsa.

On the 4th of February, near La Bolsa, Cortinas's men fired from the Mexican side of the river on a party of Captain Ford's men, mortally wounding one, and also a few minutes after, on the steam boat; to repel this attack, and to protect the lives and property on board the boat it was advisable to cross into Mexico; Captain Ford, with Major Tobin and Captain Tomlinson, crossed with forty-nine men, attacked Cortinas in his camp, and after a sharp skirmish, drove him out of it. Cortinas is said to have had about two hundred men, and that his loss was twenty-nine killed and forty wounded. We had but two men slightly wounded. Captain Stoneman, who was a few miles below, hastened up with his company, and before daylight the next morning we had over two hundred men on the ground.

At 10 1/2 o'clock P.M., an express reached me with a report of what had occurred. The town was wild with excitement; people declared that war had commenced. A party got together with the object of crossing at this ferry and seizing the ferryboats, which are kept at night on the Mexican side in charge of a guard. As there has been for some time past considerable alarm of an invasion of filibusters and rangers, a strong Mexican guard has been kept at the ferry.

Some gentlemen who met them came and told me as I was returning to the garrison. I found the party armed on the bank of the river; I had but little difficulty in convincing them of the folly of such an act; that it would only complicate affairs; that the boats were now in our power, but that we were not prepared nor authorized to occupy Matamoras.

The next morning I addressed a note to General Garcia, informing him of what had occurred, and calling upon him now to co-operate with me in arresting Cortinas. I knew that he had received an express an hour or two earlier than we, and that from eighty to a hundred men had left the same night, but it was believed more to aid Cortinas than to arrest him. The object of my note was more to learn the feelings of the Mexican authorities than from any expectation of any action on their part towards arresting Cortinas. He had too many friends in Matamoras, and I doubt whether they had the power, if they had the inclination, to arrest him.

A few hours brought me a reply, in which General Garcia informed me that he had sent out a portion of the rural police, and would send more as soon as they could be organized, and asking me to withdraw our troops. Don Miguel G. Cabezas, the second alcalde, and Don Manuel Trevino, the Mexican consul, brought the letter, and were authorized to give me explanations.

I learned from these gentlemen that about forty men of the police force had gone, and that more would leave in the afternoon and evening. More went, as promised. In the conversation with them I impressed upon them the absolute necessity for the most prompt and energetic measures on their part to arrest this man, for if he was permitted to go on, the most grave consequences would follow. As we had accomplished our object and as I did not wish to continue this cause of irritation, I sent orders for the troops to recross which they did the next day, after an interview with the commander of the police force.

When Captain Ford came in sight of the police force there was a large number of armed men around. Some sixty of those withdrew to our side. These men the police force would not vouch for. They were evidently Cortinas's men.

The prudence of Captain Ford and the good order he had observed, together with his prompt withdrawal, have quieted down the excitement. After the fright at La Bolsa, some one along, but not of his command and contrary to Captain Ford's orders, set fire to the jacales and fences, and they were consumed. On the 7th of February Inaquin Arguilles, who succeeded General Garcia in the command, addressed me a note making reclamations for the burning of these jacales, as some compensation for the violation of their territory. In my reply I justified the act, as they had failed in their international obligations in permitting Cortinas, after having been driven from our soil, to occupy their territory, recruit, arm, and equip his men, and occupy those jacales for weeks, for the avowed object of attacking this steam-boat engaged in lawful traffic, &c. To this I have received no reply.

A few days after his defeat at La Bolsa we again heard of Cortinas, with from forty to sixty men, encamped near a rancho called "La Mesa," about six miles f[a]rther from the river and nearly opposite his old place.

Captain Ford took post on our side of the river, nearly opposite, and was getting minute information as to the localities, with the intention of surrounding his camp. A few days ago he broke up this camp and went up the river, it is supposed by some, to Camargo, and by others for the interior. Linaus and Cadruta are mentioned. He has evidently left this frontier. His brother says that he intends to join the Indians. His mother and a brother are desirous to return to this side of the river and to reoc-cupy their ranches. This has strengthened me in the belief that he has left permanently.

In reviewing the events of the past five or six months, I arrive at the following facts:

Cortinas has been an outlaw and fugitive from justice for the last ten years. Some politicians found that he could influence a large vote amongst his countrymen, and during an election he was courted. Thus there was never any great effort made to bring him to justice. His mother owns ten leagues of land in a body near town, much of it covered with a dense chapparal. A few miles back from his house, near the river, he built a rancho called San José, which is arranged for a secure retreat, where it would be difficult to surprise any one. This was an asylum for horse and cat-tle thieves, robbers, and murderers, for those whose enemies would not permit them to live on the Mexican side of the river, or who dared not show themselves in the thickly settled parts of this State.

In Brownsville there were several persons who had made themselves obnoxious to him and his associates. His first object in coming here was, no doubt, revenge to get rid of these. Then he would have gone off into the interior with some of his friends, in a government employment, until his deeds were forgotten. But the arrest of Cab-rera, as he was ready to leave, kept him back. He recrossed the river to rescue Cab-rera, and punish those who held him in custody. The idle and the dissolute flocked around him, lured by the prospect of plunder. He soon gained notoriety, and the affair grew beyond his control. The hatred of Americans on the frontier, amongst all classes of Mexicans, brought him men and means. Our side of the river furnished some horses and beef; with but few arms. Most of his arms, ammunition, and supplies to maintain his forces for so many months, came from Mexico, and principally from Matamoras. Most of his men were "pelados" from the towns and ranches along the Rio Grande. On the Mexican side he always found a market for his plunder. At Rio Grande City, in an ammunition box which we captured, were orders in which he is styled "General on Gefe" ["Chief General"], and he went about with a body guard.

The whole country from Brownsville to Rio Grande City, one hundred and twenty miles, and back to the Arroya [sic] Colorado, has been laid waste. There is not an American, or any property belonging to an American, that could be destroyed in this large tract of country. Their horses and cattle were driven across into Mexico, and there sold, a cow, with a calf by her side, for a dollar.

At Rio Grande City, in answer to the complaints of his men that he had not fulfilled his promises, he told them that they should the next day have "manos libres" ["men available"] from ten to twelve. Our unexpected arrival saved the city from being sacked and burned, and the few Americans left from murder.

Rio Grande City is almost depopulated, and there is but one Mexican family in Edinburg. On the road this side I met but two ranchos occupied, and those by Mexicans. The jacales and fences are generally burned. The actual loss in property can give but a faint idea of the amount of the damage. The cattle that were not carried off are scattered in the chapparal, and will soon be wild and lost to their owners. Business, as far up as Lerido [Laredo], two hundred and forty miles, has been interrupted or suspended for five months. It is now too late to think of preparing for a crop, and a whole season will be lost.

The amount of the claims for damages presented is three hundred and thirty-six thousand eight hundred and twenty-six dollars and twenty one cents: many of them are exaggerations, but then there are few Mexicans who have put in any.

There have been fifteen Americans and eighty friendly Mexicans killed, Cortinas has lost one hundred and fifty-one men killed; of the wounded I have no account.

The severe punishment that this people have received it is to be hoped will long deter any one from another such undertaking. A small garrison in Fort Brown would have prevented a thought of such a thing. No people care less for the civil, and are more afraid of the military power.

His idea and that of his dupes was that this was in the nature of a Mexican pronunciamento; that he would, when he became formidable, be bought off by the authorities; that his men would return unmolested to their homes, and soon all be forgotten.

The citizens of Brownsville are not entirely guiltless. Had they performed their civil duties, and brought this man to justice in the first part of his career, or had they even have had a military organization, the morning of the 28th of September Cortinas would have been shot down or arrested.

It will be a long time before the ill-feeling engendered by this outbreak can be allayed. It is dangerous for Americans to settle near their boundary. The river is narrow, and now low, and easy to cross. A robbery or murder is committed, and in a few minutes the criminal is secure from pursuit. Both banks must be under the same jurisdiction. It will at once add to the value of the lands and promote settlement. The industrious, enterprising, active race on one side cannot exist in such close proximity with the idle and vicious on the other without frequent collisions.

The class of the Mexican population (pelados) who joined Cortinas, are an idle, thriftless, thieving, vicious people, living principally on jerked beef and corn, a frijole as a luxury. The climate is such that they require but little in the way of clothing, or to shelter themselves from the weather, and the soil produces spontaneously much that they live upon. When they have enough to eat they only work on compulsion, which the system of peonage furnishes on the Mexican side of the river.

For the protection of the frontier, I think that it will be necessary to station at least one company of infantry at Fort Duncan, one at Fort McIntosh, one at Fort Ringgold barracks, and two at Fort Brown. Until there is a more stable government on the other side, I would keep two companies of cavalry in the field, between Ringgold barracks and Brownsville.

My thanks are due to the officers and men of the regular army, and to those of the rangers for their cheerful and efficient aid during the last four months. I also am much indebted for valuable information to Judge Haris, Mr. Yturia, Mr. Cummins, and Mr. Galsan.

The accompanying lists give the names of the killed and the accounts of damages with the claims. I also add a few letters which, with my previous reports, will give you a full history of what has occurred. The two field returns give the names of the officers engaged on the 14th and 27th of December 1859.

Respectfully submitted,

S. P. Heintzelman,
Major 1st Regiment Infantry, Com'dg Brownsville Expedition.
Captain John Withers,
Ass't Adj't Gen., U.S.A., San Antonio, Texas.
Source: Troubles on Texas Frontier, House of Representatives, 36th Congress, 1st Session, Ex. Doc. No. 81, Letter from the Secretary of War, pp. 2–14.

79. Excerpts from *Report of the Mexican Commission on the Northern Frontier Question*, 1875

Juan Cortina (1824–1894) had become, according to Euro-Americans, an outlaw for shooting a marshal who pistol-whipped an elderly servant of his mother and called Cortina a "greaser" when he intervened. The Texas press and many merchants demanded more troops and forts on the border. Many Mexicans charged that the hysteria was manufactured and that the threat was exaggerated. The motive, they believed, was to pressure the government to sustain military forts on the border so that the merchants could make fortunes through supply contracts necessary to maintain the forts and to insure the flow of money spent by soldiers in the nearby towns. Considerable diplomatic pressure was put on the Mexican government to arrest Cortina with many Euro-Americans demanding that the United States invade Mexico. Tired of the accusations, the Mexican government conducted its own investigation. Some of the findings follow in a Mexican Commission Report that some historians consider one of the most important documents of its time.

Desirous of hearing the complaints of the sufferers of injuries received, the Commission issued copies of the regulations of the 21st November, and invited the citizens of Mexico and Texas to present their claims before them. They then set about to collect all the facts relative to cattle stealing on the United States frontier, whether favorable or adverse to the Mexican Republic. Besides this, and in compliance with the law of Congress, their duties extended to the hearing and investigation of the complaints of American citizens, and to this end the above-named regulations were issued, as follows:

Although testimonial evidence on all these points has been most useful and important, yet circumstantial proofs culled from the archives have in all cases been more conclusive. In those examined by the Commission are a series of regulations framed by the municipal and police authorities for the suppression of horse thieves in the towns lying on the bank of the river. Very few of these measures looked to the prevention of the traffic in stolen cattle from Texas, from which it would seem that this evil did not exist to the same extent; whilst on the contrary, the laws had in view the damages resulting from horse stealing in Mexico, and the transportation of the horses into Texas, proving that this was the greater traffic, and the one that needed greater legislation. Measures for the prevention of this crime have been issued in every town along the river, from which it may be deduced that like injuries were experienced in every village on the Mexican line; and as these preventive measures were constant and frequently repeated, it would seem that the injuries were constant and frequently recurring....

The great weight of these proofs cannot be estimated from a few isolated measures of this kind, but must be judged as a whole; for whilst instituting a repressive system of horse stealing on the Mexican frontier for the Texan market, since 1848, they also indicate the robberies organized on the Texan shore of the Rio Bravo, in injury to Mexican proprietors.

They are contemporaries, at least, in the robberies committed in 1848, and which have since continued. Adolfo Glaevecke is one of those who have most actively engaged in horse stealing in Mexico, ever since the Rio Bravo has been the dividing line between the two nations.

Persons who have belonged to the police corps, accomplices of Glaevecke, and persons who have appeared in court at various times to reclaim stolen animals, have appeared before the Commission as witnesses against Glaevecke, so that with all the overwhelming testimony before them, the Commission feels confident to express an opinion as to his character. Glaevecke owns a horse pen on the Texas shore of the river, which used to bear the name of Santa Rita, but is now called Linero. On one side of this enclosure was the ford known as Tia Morales. Here the thieves in the employ of Glaevecke congregate, and to this pen, or enclosure, are the animals stolen in Mexico carried; driven for the most part across the ford Tia Morales. The evidence of title witnesses on this point is corroborated by documentary testimony. This ford was the object of the most active vigilance on the part of the authorities, and the extracts from the documents in Matamoros show that seizure was here often made of thieves and stolen animals, and that various enactments of law were made to guard the ford of Tia Morales.

Since 1848 to the present, for the space of twenty-five years, there has existed in Texas the trade in goods stolen in Mexico, without the attempt at interference on the part of the authorities to punish the offenders of law in this illicit traffic. During this same period the collection of droves of animals at certain periods of each year along the whole American line has been permitted, with the knowledge that these animals were stolen from Mexican territory. Finally, there had been tolerated the public organization of bands of robbers, who under the patronage of influential persons have gone to Mexico to steal for the benefit of their patrons.

We quote the following extracts from a correspondence dated at Rome, Star County, and published in a Texan newspaper:

"In Guerrero, Mexico," says the correspondent, "I was informed by the city authorities that there was an organized band of robbers, whose constant occupation was to steal horses in Mexico and carry them to Texas, where they in return stole horses and cattle to bring back to Mexico. The three principal leaders are, Atilano Alvarado, Procopio Gutierrez, and Landin, the former being the foreman of Captain R. King, on whose rancho he has lived for a number of years, and is well known to the stock-raisers of that section of the country; our informer says also, I am sure they have many accomplices and co-operators on the ranches of Texas on this side of the river and all along the coast. Procopio Gutierrez resides a part of the time in Texas, on San Bartolo rancho, Zapote county, with his adoptive father.

I crossed afterwards to the American side and investigated the matter in the most secret manner possible, and found all these things to be perfectly correct.

I asked several persons of the city whether they were doing anything to put a stop to the robbery. *What can we do?* they replied. Our sheriff lives on a ranch twenty-two miles from here: and has not come within the county.

for several months, and even he himself has aided in transporting the stolen animals through his rancho over into Mexico on the 10th or 12th of November. No one knows or can swear with any certainty that said cattle had been stolen, but it is presumed that the whole or a part of them were stolen, as the drivers kept away from the collector of customs and from the inspector of hides and cattle; and when an authority of the county connives in the robbery, instead of preventing it, there is nothing to be done against such powerful bands of robbers."—Daily *Ranchero*, Brownsville, January 12th, 1873, p. 84

The residents of Texas have complained constantly that the Mexican authorities have not taken all the necessary precautions to prevent the stealing of cattle on our borders; that the State of Texas has, to the contrary, done all in its power by way of keeping the laws. Now an investigation has become indispensable in order to ascertain what has occurred on both frontiers....

The question relative to Texas presents four aspects—her legislation, her public administration, her police, and her administration of justice.

The Texas legislation is imperfect. It contains no efficacious, energetic means to prevent the robberies which take place in the branding pens, and which contribute to maintain a state of perfect disorder, in the prolongation of which the proprietors who give themselves up to these depredations are interested. To commit these depredations they require accomplices—men destitute of conscience, who rob for others without any other consideration than the pay which they receive; and it is certain that these men, accustomed not to respect property, rob on their own account whenever it is possible.

One of the proprietors who has distinguished himself most in these depredations is Ricardo King, owner of the estate Santa Gertrudis, county of Nueces. He has had as chief, Tomas Vasquez, accomplice in robberies of Mexican horses, and in the robberies of cattle committed in Texas, and Fernando Lopez, accomplice in the last. He has kept in his rancho this Atilano Alvarado, who is thought to be chief of a party of robbers stationed in Guerrero. They appear also in the dispatches drawn up before the Commission, the dates of which are not very accurate with regard to the robberies in which the individuals have participated who have been in his service. Ricardo King had a large band who ran constantly in all directions of the country marking calves, though they did not belong to him. It is impossible to admit that the people forming that party possessed any sentiments of morality. The laws of Texas offer no energetic remedies for this evil, and are insufficient.

His revolt was brought about by the following circumstances. He saw the sheriff at Brownsville dragging a Mexican along by the collar; [Juan] Cortina remonstrated with him; the sheriff made use of insulting language in his reply; Cortina then shot at and wounded him, and carried off the prisoner. This occurred on the 13th of July, 1859. On the 28th of September of the same year, he again appeared at Brownsville with some fifty men, and took possession of the town. Several of those who, it was alleged, had been guilty of outrage toward the "Texan Mexicans," were killed, and all the prisoners who joined him were released. At the request of various persons he left the city and retired to his ranch; he was disposed to lay down his arms and leave Texas; several parties saw him for this purpose, and he agreed to it, requiring only from four to six days to transfer to the Mexican side some cattle which some of his companions had, and divide his people into small parties of three or four each, to avoid their being pursued by the Mexican authorities at the time of their crossing the river. He did so, but shortly after he was told that one of his followers bad been hung at Brownsville, upon which he went into Texas and began gathering people together, giving his movement a more definite character.

It is worthy of notice that when the revolt assumed this aspect it was highly popular among the "Texan Mexicans," that is, among all the Mexican population which had settled in Texas before or after the Treaty of Guadaloupe [sic]. The fact that Cortina was joined by a large number of these, some of whom were land owners, can be attributed to no other reason....

Richard King has in his service a large band; he makes use of it for depredating upon other people's cattle, by seizing all of the unbranded calves, which are then branded with King's brand, notwithstanding the ownership of the calves is shown by their following cows bearing other people's brands. These depredations are continuous, because King's band is almost always uninterruptedly in movement. He thus develops and maintains demoralization among a great number of people, because only men without principle could accept the position of instrument for the commission of such crimes. He has had among his herders the accomplices in robberies committed in Texas or Mexico, as, for example, Fernando Lopez and Tomas Vazquez: nevertheless, he states that his injuries amount to millions.

MONTEREY, May 15th, 1873

Emilio Velasco, Ygnacio Galindo,
Antonio Garoia Carrillo and Augustin Silacio, *Secretary*

Source: Report of the Mexican Commission on the Northern Frontier Question: Investigating Commission of the Northern Frontier (New York, Baker & Goodwin Printer, 1875), pp. 3, 13, 28, 39, 83–84, 105–106, 126–129, 176.

80. Excerpt from "A Little War on the Border," 1877

Like water, salt is essential for life in arid environments. A power struggle broke out in the late 1860s as to who would control the salt deposits located in the Guadalupe Mountains 110 miles east of El Paso. Mexicans had not made an effort to secure ownership of the beds that supplied all of western Texas, southern New Mexico, and Mexico with salt. Mexicans engaged in the salt trade during bad times and used the salt free of charge. In the 1870s bloody battles broke out when unscrupulous elements attempted to monopolize the salt, which would deprive Mexicans of a needed resource. A Salt Ring comprised of influential Euro-American politicos led the monopolists. Two factions maneuvered to control the salt beds for commercial purposes. The following excerpt from The New York Times reports on conditions around the El Paso area and the friction between whites and Mexicans.

Gen. Sheridan seems to have taken from the first a common-sense view of the latest troubles on the Texan frontier. His brief comment on the El Paso affair, which he described as "a row about some salt," was a dash of cold water on the fire which a few sensational newspapers had kindled. According to the military critics and international lawyers who infest some of the newspaper offices, a cause of war existed on the frontier. It was distinctly declared that at least 400 Mexicans had crossed the Rio Grande, had captured the civil authorities of El Paso County, and had, as in such case is made and provided, "inaugurated a reign of terror." The immediate object of this invasion was not clear. But it was evident to those who were clamorous for war that hostilities had been begun, and that nothing but armed reprisals would vindicate the honor of the United States. Within a few days, and while The Times was making fun of these "invasions," the hysterical appeals to arms which the war newspapers were uttering suffered modification. It was then asserted that the Mexican residents of El Paso County, Texas, reinforced by arrivals from the further side of the Rio Grande, had defied the local authorities, and were in a state of revolt. The "invaders" became "insurgents," and it was asserted that they openly declared that El Paso County belonged to Mexico. By a clumsy reversal of all the facts in the case, it was argued that this latest difficulty was only the legitimate result of the failure of the United States Government to demand, at the cannon's mouth, the extradition of the Mexican citizens who lately took out of Rio Grande City Jail certain of their compatriots and retreated with them to Mexican soil. The *World*, which is naturally the organ of these filibusteros, coolly said that it was of no consequence what the cause of the local disturbance might be. The general question remained the same. Anarchy and disorder on the other side of the Rio Grande perpetually threatened the peace and good-will which notoriously prevail on our side of the boundary.

It will not encourage these amateur warmakers to learn that the "invaders" or "insurgents" of El Paso are known to the military authorities as "the mob," and that the officer commanding has not only had several confabs with the leaders, but that the mob has dispersed, after the General commanding had given orders that they should be left to the authorities of the State, to deal with as was thought best. Sheridan was right when he said that the whole trouble, so wickedly and willfully exaggerated by demagogues, was only "a row about some salt." There were no invaders, no insurgents. About thirty miles from the town of El Paso is the salt spring which has been such a prolific source of trouble. It is a considerable lake, which yields salt so abundantly that it is only necessary for the people who visit it to shovel it into their wagons. For more than two hundred years this natural deposit has been considered common property, and has been the source to which people inhabiting the territory now known as Texas, New-Mexico, and Northern Mexico have resorted for supplies. Recently some land-grabbers, said to be New-Yorkers, have seized upon the lake, and have covered it with a paper title under what is known as the "Desert Lands Law"—a statute of doubtful expediency and more than doubtful paternity. These persons having seized upon the property, demanded forty cents a bushel for the salt taken from the lake, and, to enforce their claim, they made such improvements as were considered necessary to perfect their title. The people of the region, who are as largely of Mexican origin as are the voters of New-Mexico and Arizona, resisted what they considered an invasion of popular rights. Most likely their resistance was illegal; certainly it was violent and sanguinary. The mob assaulted the civil authorities, who were only doing their duty by upholding the rights of those who, at least, had the forms of law on their side. The result was a riot, in which several people were killed. It was a lamentable affair, very much such as often disgraces an older state than Texas, when a neighborhood quarrel over a line fence or right of way culminates in murder and defiance of law. But only the most distempered imagination could connect this local disturbance with the supposed dark designs of Mexican invaders. The disturbers were of all races, and the so-called "insurgents" were intent only on preserving what they considered their right to shovel salt. They had no more thought of "invading" the United States than they had of invading the planet Mars.

It is not claimed, however, that the population on the Mexican side of the Rio Grande is peaceable and orderly. From the time of Carbrajal, in 1850, until now, the country has been as frequently agitated by risings and petty revolts as any other part of the Mexican Republic. As soon as a rising takes place, the so-called insurgents harry the Americans on this side of the boundary, and, secure from the effects of any demand made by our Government upon that of Mexico, continue their work of brigandage until the "revolution" drops into pieces. On the other hand, it cannot be claimed for our own citizens that they are the lamblike non-resistants and long-suffering peace-makers which they have claimed to be. Those who are at all familiar with the border Texan will laugh at the assertion that the Mexicans have been the only aggressors in all these recent disturbances. It is the fixed belief of the Texan that the Sierra Madre, not the Rio Grande, should be the boundary line betwixt the two Republics. A long series of raids and "revolutions," in which the Americans have been the moving spirits, have harassed Mexico during the past twenty-five years. A correspondent of The Times, whose letter is printed to-day, makes mention of some of these disgraceful affairs. And our correspondent, whose statements are impartial and worthy of credence, points out some of the difficulties of the situation. Chief among these is the inadequacy of existing extradition treaties. Our convention with Mexico provides for the return of American citizens who have been indicted under the laws of the United States. But it is demanded sometimes, as in the case of the raid upon the jail at Rio Grande City, that Mexican criminals should be sent over to us to be tried under the laws of the United States. This demand, in any event, would be an unusual one; and as long as the extradition treaty would not justify it, such a request must be made with moderation. Nevertheless, some of the warlike newspapers, with more zeal than knowledge, have actually proposed that a formidable force be sent to the Rio Grande to coerce the Mexican authorities into giving up their own citizens for trial in our country. Let us imagine, if we can, the howl of rage and indignation which these belligerent editors would emit if they heard of a similar demand being made upon the United States by Mexican officials. The correspondence to which we have just referred does not encourage us to hope for speedy peace on the frontier. But it is evident that, while the Mexicans are lawless, uneasy spirits are constantly committing all manner of acts from our side of the line for the purpose of embroiling the two Republics in war.

Source: New York Times, October 22, 1877, p. 4.

81. Excerpt from W. M. Dunn's Report to War Department, Bureau of Military Justice, April 19, 1878

The Mexicans and Euro-Americans often clashed in many ways after the U.S. occupation of South Texas as newly arrived Euro-American settlers forced Mexican farmers off the land. The two peoples also clashed culturally and had different attitudes toward the use of land, water, and salt. An example of this clash of cultures took place around the small town of San Elizario, near present-day El Paso, Texas, in 1877, over salt beds in the Guadalupe Mountains 110 miles east of El Paso that supplied all of western Texas, southern New Mexico, and Mexico with salt. Two competing groups, one led by the Salt Ring and another by Father Antonio Borrajo and Louis Cardis (1825–1877), a local politician, formed as each side sought to obtain ownership of the beds. Local Mexicans supported Father Borrajo's cabal. Charles Howard (1842–1877), a Democratic politician, at first supported the Borrajo-Cardis faction but Howard and Cardis quarreled over ownership of the salt. Things got ugly when Howard took control of the salt flats in 1877, and he shot and killed Cardis. Howard, a former Texas Ranger, enlisted the support of the rangers and with a troop of 20 Texas Rangers rode into San Elizario. The Mexicans defended themselves and captured Howard and two of his men, executing them in front of a firing squad. This gave Euro-Americans the pretext for the Salt War of 1877, which led to Euro-American mob action and widespread vigilantism. The rangers and the army also indiscriminately attacked Mexicans. The following document by the Judge Advocate General W. M. Dunn relates how Howard was killed.

The outbreak was, it is believed, the result of a desire for revenge for the murder of [Louis] Cardis, a crime which had no justification, which was deliberate and brutal, and which exasperated the people beyond control. [Charles] Howard was brought before a justice of the peace for the murder, but was released at once on bail, in violation of law, and as not long before he had caused the arrest and imprisonment of two men for the mere offense of *saying* that they meant to get salt from the ponds, law or no law, the Spanish-American populace naturally thought they saw that there was no equality of justice, and felt compelled to take the law into their own hands.

Of the mob of five hundred which captured the town of Elizario and the Texas force and killed Howard, perhaps one hundred were men from the Mexican side, who had come over in defiance of the Mexican authorities. These, or the guiltier of these, the extradition against [agent?], Judge Blacker, has officially demanded. No answer has yet been received.

The amount of damage by robbing and destruction wrought by the mob is estimated at about $12,000.

The evidence is abundant that a small force of United States soldiers would have prevented all the trouble. That an outbreak would sooner or later follow the withdrawal of troops the testimony shows was predicted months before.

It seems apparent from the opinions of the leading citizens, embodied in the testimony, that another emeute of the same sort may occur at any moment under provocation, the first one having met with so much success and such impunity from punishment. Many outrages were committed on innocent people in the neighborhood during the excitement, but of these not a few were perpetrated by members of the State force, raised under authority of the governor of Texas by Sheriff Kerber, who recruited his men from Silver City, N.M. These last seem especially to be responsible for the rapes, homicides, and other crimes of which the people justly complained.

The evidence makes it manifest that the Spanish population on both sides of the Rio Grande hold the American military in the highest awe, while they feel no dread of State levies, and despise the civil authorities unless protected by the military arm. Of these civil authorities not a few are Spaniards who took part in the emeute; of the others the county judge is an inveterate drunkard, disqualified by his habits to enforce order, and the rest are powerless for want of jails, a posse, or an armed force.

The members of the board selected and appointed by the governor of Texas appends a statement to the record of proceedings, in which, after expressing his full concurrence in the board's recommendations, he protests against some of its opinions and inferences, and announces his intention to forward, as soon as possible, a minority report.

W. M. Dunn,
Judge-Advocate-General
The Secretary of War
(Through the General of the Army)

Source: "El Paso Troubles in Texas," Letter from the Secretary of War, House of Representatives, 45th Cong., 2d. Sess., Ex. Doc. No. 93, May 28, 1878, pp. 3–5. Congressional Record.

82. Excerpt from "El Paso Troubles in Texas," Letter from Colonel John H. King, Secretary of War, House of Representatives, to the Bureau of Military Justice, April 19, 1878

The following is a summary of the report of the military inquiry board into the causes of the Salt War commencing in 1877. It was based on testimonies by local residents of San Elizario, a small town near El Paso, Texas, as to why Charles Howard (1842–1877) was seized and executed in a dispute over the ownership of salt beds just over a hundred miles from El Paso. A Mexican faction had formed around parish priest Antonio Borajo who, with Italian Louis Cardis (1825–1877), claimed the beds. Borajo-Cardis had been partners of Howard but broke when Howard unilaterally claimed the salt, and Howard shot and killed Cardis with a shotgun. The Mexicans fought back when a troop of 20 Texas Rangers led by Howard entered the region. They captured Howard and two of his cohorts and, on orders of Fr. Borajo, executed them. During the investigation, the Mexican population was reluctant to testify. The report pieces together the events leading to Howard's death, which touched off the so-called war. It took oral testimonies.

EL PASO, TEX., March 16, 1878.
The Board met pursuant to adjournment at 8 P.M.
Present: Col. John H. King, Ninth Infantry; Lieut. Col. William H. Lewis, Nineteenth Infantry; Maj. John B. Jones, Frontier Battalion.

The Board adopted the following as its final report, which is signed by two members, one, Maj. J. B. Jones, dissenting, and handing in a communication, which was received by the Board and agreed to, and is attached to its report, following next after.

PRELIMINARY

The Board met with noticeable reluctance on the part of many people, in the different localities where its sessions were held, to testify upon all the points which it was within its province to examine. Some, fearing that their statements might be published after leaving the hands of the Board, and finding their way, through the medium of the press, back to this neighborhood, so excite local animosities as to lead to their ruin, refused to testify at all. Hence, also, the guarded language to be found in many of the statements made by intelligent parties.

The Board in the prosecution of the duties devolving upon it, visited, on two different occasions, the towns of Ysleta, Socorro, and San Elizario, Texas, and pursuant to its instructions submit the following result of its labors:

SUMMARY

The Board finds that at San Elizario, in the latter part of September (September 29, 1877), Charles H. Howard, Gregoria N. Garcia, the county judge and a justice of the peace, were, for causing the arrest of two Mexicans, citizens of that town, named Maadonia [*sic*] Gandara and Jose Maria Juarez, for saying they intended to go and get salt from the salt lakes (as charged in affidavits), themselves arrested confined in durance, and threatened by an armed mob numbering about fifty or sixty men, of whom ten were from the Mexican side of the Rio Grande; they were led by Cisto Salcido and Leon Granido, at that time citizens of Texas. It is believed that even then Howard's life was in danger, but at the earnest and united petitions of the Rev. Pierre Bourgad, the priest of the parish, and Louis Cardis, as stated in their own words, it was spared, and both he and the two officials were released, but on condition that the first should bind himself in the sum of $12,000, with good security, to relinquish his interests in the Salinas, and then to leave the county never to return, nor yet to prosecute them for their action in the matter. As for the county judge and the justice, they were released on tendering the resignation of their respective offices. (Appendix E, No. 5; F, Nos. 8 and 9; and L, Nos. 3, 7, and 20.)

In the beginning of November following, Howard returned to the county, notwithstanding the pledge he had given to remain away, whereupon the Mexicans became incensed and gathered together again, some with arms in their hands, to the number of about two hundred, of whom about twenty were citizens of Mexico, living on this and the other side of the river, and threatened the lives of the bondsmen to enforce the payment of the bond which they declared was rendered forfeit by Howard's return. But the timely arrival of an officer of the State of Texas, Maj. John B. Jones, who came before their junta accompanied by the parish priest as interpreter, prevented their half-matured plans from culminating into any overt acts of disorder. They expressed themselves satisfied with the interview, and as a result of his visit promised to disband and disperse and await the decisions of the courts. (Appendix L, Nos. 3, 7, and 20.) But their professions and promises must have been insincere, for as found (see Appendix B, Nos. 1 to 25), the people, early in

December, that is to say, December 12, 1877, rose *en masse* and armed themselves for the mischief that ensued. Yet with imperfect organization and little discipline they were speedily joined by friends and sympathizers who came, some to fight and others to steal, from across the river in squads of a few at a time, until their numbers grew to formidable proportions. Their exact force is difficult to compute. Their leaders who know are in foreign parts, and the estimate of those who have testified differs widely, but there could not have been far from 400, of whom not less than one-third were Mexican citizens, the remainder being from El Paso County, Texas. All were under the leadership of Francisco (*alias* Chico) Barcla, with Desiderio Apodaca as second in command, and these were assisted by Ramon Sambrano, Leon Granido, Cisto Salcido, Anastasio Montez, and Acaton Porras, all residents of Texas, except Montez, who was from Mexico. (Appendix H, No. 1 to 5; F, Nos. 8 and 9.) They assembled in the town of San Elizario and made no secret of their intentions to kill Charles H. Howard (who had gone there under escort of a small company of the Texas Battalion of Rangers), but disavowing at the same time, so it is said, any purpose to become involved with the United States Government. Here the mob remained in possession from the 12th to the 17th of December. They surrounded and besieged the house and corral where the rangers were quartered, and, after some casualties on both sides, compelled their surrender and disarmament. They plundered stores and warehouses of goods and provisions, and carried the booty across the river. They killed on the 12th Mr. Charles E. Ellis, whose store and mill they afterward robbed. On the 13th they shot down in the street Sergt. C. E. Mortimer, of the Frontier Battalion of Rangers, and on the 17th, after the surrender, in broad daylight and in cold blood, they murdered Charles H. Howard, John G. Atkinson, and John E. McBride; the last-named was one of the rangers, the other two were quartered in the building for protection. The death of Mortimer was the only loss suffered by the rangers during the siege. The number and extent of the casualties on the side of the mob is not known, and probably never will be. It must have been large. (Appendix D, No. 1, and F, Nos. 8, 9, 11.)

It is impracticable as yet to fix the true value of the property destroyed and stolen, as the principal losers are dead, but it is believed that the amount is rather more than instead of less than $12,000. (Appendix F, No. 9, and L, Nos. 5 and 8, P, No. 6.)

No evidence taken substantiates the report heretofore prevalent, that the people coming from Mexico and taking part in these criminal proceedings were an organized body previously drilled and disciplined by officers of the Mexican Army. One Ferris Lermo, or, as known by the Mexicans, Teniente Lermo, who was formerly a lieutenant in the Mexican Army, but not connected with it for many years, and now an old man, did assist the mob of November by written advice and personal instruction in tactics, but finding they were disposed to adopt extreme measures, which he could not second and from which he would have dissuaded them, he incurred their dislike, and went or was driven away before the rising, and there is nothing to show that he returned. (Appendix L, Nos. 7 and 20.)

The inhabitants of the adjacent towns on both sides of the river have hitherto, for many years, lived in a state of amity, and are intimately connected by the bonds of a common faith, like sympathies and tastes, and are related in numerous instances by marriage; hence each would naturally support and defend the other, if occasions real or fancied demanded their aid, to any sacrifice. In the words of one who ought to know them well, if they have a good man to lead them, there is not a more pacific, easily governed, and loyal people on the face of the earth; if they have a bad one they will be just as bad as he would have them. (Appendix P, No. 6.) The statements of reliable citizens, showing the character of the people, in this view are important and worthy of consideration. They will be found in Appendix C. Nos. 1 to 4....

John H. King,
Colonel Ninth Infantry, President of Board
W. H. Lewis,
Lieutenant Colonel Nineteenth Infantry, Member of Board
Leonard Hay,
First Lieutenant and Adjutant Ninth Infantry, Recorder

Source: "El Paso Troubles in Texas," 45th Cong., 2d. Sess., Ex. Doc. No 93, May 28, 1878, pp. 13–18.

The section on Voices Mexianas could very well be dominated by Spanish language newspapers that were common wherever there was a concentration of Mexican people. The main regional concentrations of Spanish language newspapers were Californis, the Upper Rio Grande Valley, and South Texas. From 1848–1876, San Francisco, California, housed ten newspapers—among them *El Eco del Pacific*, a daily. In Brownsville, Texas, seven Spanish-language newspapers were published. Los Angeles, Santa Fe, and Las Cruces also circulated Spanish-language newspapers. As the Mexican population increased along the Texas-Mexico border so did the number of newspapers. New Mexico was also fertile territory with many weeklies. The daily *La Voz del Pueblo* served the people of Las Vegas, New Mexico, from 1879–1929. In Tucson, Arizona, *El Fronterizo*, a weekly, was printed from 1878. This section could very well have been all about these newspapers that tell about the everyday life of the Mexicans who the border had crossed. However, in order to diversify the voices, we have included excerpts from an oral interview taken by Hubert Howe Bancroft, selections from the first Mexican woman novelist María Amparo Ruiz de Burton, and an excerpt from the autobiography of Miguel Antonio Ortero II of New Mexico. Many of these voices are being recovered by Nicolás Kanellos' "Recovering the U.S. Literary Heritage Project," at *Arte Público Press* at the University of Houston.

83. Excerpts from the Testimony of Eulalia Pérez Regarding Her Life in Mexican California, 1877

Eulalia Pérez (1768–1878) was the "keeper of the keys" at Mission San Gabriel Arcángel and the owner of Rancho del Rincón de San Pascual in Alta, California. She was born in Baja, California. Court records show that she lived to be 140, but her descendants agree that she was only 110 years old when she died. This testimony from a Native American is one of the few to survive history. In the following passage, she described her duties as a housekeeper in a California mission in 1823. The testimony was taken by Hubert Howe Bancroft, who conducted some 100 interviews with descendants of the original Californios (Californians of Mexican extraction) to preserve the early history of the state. Of these 100, 12 testimonies were from women.

I, Eulalia Pérez, was born in the Presidio of Loreto in Baja California.

My father's name was Diego Pérez, and he was employed in the Navy Department of said presidio; my mother's name was Antonia Rosalia Cota. Both were pure white.

I do not remember the date of my birth, but I do know that I was fifteen years old when I married Miguel Antonio Guillen, a soldier of the garrison at Loreto Presidio. During the time of my stay at Loreto I had three children—two boys, who died there in infancy, one girl, Petra, who was eleven years old when we moved to San Diego, and another boy, Isidoro, who came with us to this [Alta] California.

I lived eight years in San Diego with my husband, who continued his service in the garrison of the presidio, and I attended women in childbirth.

I had relatives in the vicinity of Los Angeles, and even farther north, and asked my husband repeatedly to take me to see them. My husband did not want to come along, and the commandant of the presidio did not allow me to go either, because there was no other woman who knew midwifery.

In San Diego everyone seemed to like me very much, and in the most important homes they treated me affectionately. Although I had my own house, they arranged for me to be with those families almost all the time, even including my children.

In 1812, I was in San Juan Capistrano attending Mass in church when a big earthquake occurred, and the tower fell down. I dashed through the sacristy, and in the doorway the people knocked me down and stepped over me. I was pregnant and could not move. Soon afterwards I returned to San Diego and almost immediately gave birth to my daughter Maria Antonia, who still lives here in San Gabriel.

After being in San Diego eight years, we came to the Mission of San Gabriel, where my husband had been serving in the guard. In 1814, on the first of October, my daughter Maria del Rosario was born, the one who is the wife of Michael White and in whose home I am now living....

When I first came to San Diego the only house in the presidio was that of the commandant and the barracks where the soldiers lived.

There was no church, and Mass was said in a shelter made out of some old walls covered with branches, by the missionary who came from the Mission of San Diego.

The first sturdy house built in San Diego belonged to a certain Sanchez, the father of Don Vicente Sanchez, alcalde [administrator] of Los Angeles and deputy of the Territorial Council. The house was very small, and everyone went to look at it as though it were a palace. That house was built about a year after I arrived in San Diego.

My last trip to San Diego would have been in the year 1818, when my daughter Maria del Rosario was four years old. I seem to remember that I was there when the revolutionaries came to California. I recall that they put a stranger in irons and that afterwards they took them off.

Some three years later I came back to San Gabriel. The reason for my return was that the missionary at San Gabriel, Father Jose Sanchez, wrote to Father Fernando at San Diego—who was his cousin or uncle—asking him to speak to the commandant of the presidio at San Diego requesting him to give my son Isidoro Guillen a guard to escort me here with all my family. The commandant agreed.

When we arrived here, Father Jose Sanchez lodged me and my family temporarily in a small house until work could be found for me. There I was with my five daughters—my son Isidoro Guillen was taken into service as a soldier in the mission guard.

At that time, Father Sanchez was between sixty and seventy years of age—a white Spaniard, heavy set, of medium stature—a very good, kind, charitable man. He, as well as his companion Father Jose Maria Zalvidea, treated the Indians very well, and the two were much loved by the Spanish-speaking people and by the neophytes and other Indians.

Father Zalvidea was very tall, a little heavy, white; he was a man of advanced age. I heard it said that they summoned Zalvidea to San Juan Capistrano because there was no missionary priest there. Many years later, when Father Antonio Peyri fled from San Luis Obispo—it was rumored that they were going to kill the priests—I learned that Zalvidea was very sick, and that actually he had been out of his mind ever since they took him away from San Gabriel, for he did not want to abandon the mission. I repeat that the father was afraid, and two Indians came from San Luis Rey to San Juan Capistrano; in a rawhide cart, making him as comfortable as they could, they took him to San Luis, where he died soon after from the grueling hardships he had suffered on the way.

Father Zalvidea was very much attached to his children at the mission, as he called the Indians that he himself had converted to Christianity. He traveled personally, sometimes on horseback and at other times on foot, and crossed mountains until he came to remote Indian settlements, in order to bring them to our religion.

Father Zalvidea introduced many improvements in the Mission of San Gabriel and made it progress a very great deal in every way. Not content with providing abundantly for the neophytes, he planted [fruit] trees in the mountains, far away from the mission, in order that the untamed Indians might have food when they passed by those spots.

When I came to San Gabriel the last time, there were only two women in this part of California who knew how to cook [well]. One was Maria Luisa Cota, wife of Claudio Lopez, superintendent of the mission; the other was Maria Ignacia Amador, wife of Francisco Javier Alvarado. She knew how to cook, sew, read, and write and take care of the sick. She was a good healer. She did needlework and took care of the church vestments. She taught a few children to read and write in her home, but did not conduct a formal school.

On special holidays, such as the day of our patron saint, Easter, etc., the two women were called upon to prepare the feast and to make the meat dishes, sweets, etc.

The priests wanted to help me out because I was a widow burdened with a family. They looked for some way to give me work without offending the other women. Frs. Sanchez and Zalvidea conferred and decided that they would have first one woman, then the other and finally me, do the cooking, in order to determine who did it best, with the aim of putting the one who surpassed the others in charge of the Indian cooks so as to teach them how to cook. With that idea in mind, the gentlemen who were to decide on the merits of the three dinners were warned ahead of time.

One of these gentlemen was Don Ignacio Tenorio, whom they called the Royal Judge, and who came to live and die in the company of Father Sanchez. He was a very old man, and when he went out, wrapped up in a muffler, he walked very slowly with the aid of a cane. His walk consisted only of going from the missionary's house to the church.

The other judges who also were to give their opinions were Don Ignacio Mancisidor, merchant; Don Pedro Narvaez, naval official; Sgt. Jose Antonio Pico—who later became lieutenant, brother of Gov. Pio Pico; Don Domingo Romero, who was my assistant when I was housekeeper at the mission; Claudio Lopez, superintendent at the mission; besides the missionaries. These gentlemen, whenever they were at the mission, were accustomed to eat with the missionaries.

On the days agreed upon for the three dinners, they attended. No one told me anything regarding what it was all about, until one day Father Sanchez called me and said, "Look, Eulalia, tomorrow it is your turn to prepare dinner—because Maria Ignacia and Luisa have already done so. We shall see what kind of a dinner you will give us tomorrow."

The next day I went to prepare the food. I made several kinds of soup, a variety of meat dishes and whatever else happened to pop into my head that I knew how to prepare: The Indian cook, named Tomas, watched me attentively, as the missionary had told him to do.

At dinner time those mentioned came. When the meal was concluded, Father Sanchez asked for their opinions about it, beginning with the eldest, Don Ignacio Tenorio. This gentleman pondered awhile, saying that for many years he had not eaten the way he had eaten that day—that he doubted that they ate any better at the King's table. The others also praised the dinner highly.

Then the missionary called Tomas and asked him which of the three women he liked best—which one of them knew the most about cooking. He answered that I did.

Because of all this, employment was provided for me at the mission. At first they assigned me two Indians so that I could show them how to cook, the one named Tomas and the other called "The Gentile." I taught them so well that I had the satisfaction of seeing them turn out to be very good cooks, perhaps the best in all this part of the country.

The missionaries were very satisfied; this made them think more highly of me. I spent about a year teaching those two Indians. I did not have to do the work, only direct them, because they already had learned a few of the fundamentals.

After this, the missionaries conferred among themselves and agreed to hand over the mission keys to me. This was in 1821, if I remember correctly. I recall that my daughter Maria del Rosario was seven years old when she became seriously ill and was attended by Father Jose Sanchez, who took such excellent care of her that finally we could rejoice at not having lost her. At that time I was already the housekeeper.

The duties of the housekeeper were many. In the first place, every day she handed out the rations for the mess hut. To do this, she had to count the unmarried women, bachelors, day-laborers, vaqueros—both those with saddles and those who rode bareback. Besides that, she had to hand out daily rations to the heads of households. In short, she was responsible for the distribution of supplies to the Indian population and to the missionaries' kitchen. She was in charge of the key to the clothing storehouse where materials were given out for dresses for the unmarried and married women and children. Then she also had to take care of cutting and making clothes for the men.

Furthermore, she was in charge of cutting and making the vaqueros' outfits, from head to foot—that is, for the vaqueros who rode in saddles. Those who rode bareback received nothing more than their cotton blanket and loin-cloth, while those who rode in saddles were dressed the same way as the Spanish-speaking inhabitants; that is, they were given shirt, vest, jacket, trousers, hat, cowboy boots, shoes, and spurs; and a saddle, bridle, and lariat for the horse. Besides, each vaquero was given a big silk or cotton handkerchief, and a sash of Chinese silk or Canton crepe, or whatever there happened to be in the storehouse.

They put under my charge everything having to do with clothing. I cut and fitted, and my five daughters sewed up the pieces. When they could not handle everything, the father was told, and then women from the town of Los Angeles were employed, and the father paid them.

Besides this, I had to attend to the soap-house, which was very large, to the wine-presses, and to the olive-crushers that produced oil, which I worked in myself. Under my direction and responsibility, Domingo Romero took care of changing the liquid.

Luis the soap-maker had charge of the soap-house, but I directed everything.

I handled the distribution of leather, calf-skin, chamois, sheepskin, Morocc[an] leather, fine scarlet cloth, nails, thread, silk, etc., everything having to do with the making of saddles, shoes, and what was needed for the belt- and shoe-making shops.

Every week I delivered supplies for the troops and Spanish-speaking servants. These consisted of beans, com, garbanzos, lentils, candles, soap, and lard. To carry out this distribution, they placed at my disposal an Indian servant named Lucio, who was trusted completely by the missionaries.

When it was necessary, some of my daughters did what I could not find the time to do. Generally, the one who was always at my side was my daughter Maria del Rosario.

After all my daughters were married—the last one was Rita, about 1832 or 1833—Father Sanchez undertook to persuade me to marry First Lt. Juan Marine, a Spaniard from Catalonia, a widower with family who had served in the artillery. I did not want to get married, but the father told me that Marine was a very good man—as, in fact, he turned out to be—besides, he had some money, although he never turned his cash-box over to me. I gave in to the father's wishes because I did not have the heart to deny him anything when he had been father and mother to me and to all my family.

I served as housekeeper of the mission for twelve or fourteen years, until about two years after the death of Father Jose Sanchez, which occurred in this same mission.

A short while before Father Sanchez died, he seemed robust and in good health, in spite of his advanced age. When Capt. Barroso came and excited the Indians in all the missions to rebel, telling them that they were no longer neophytes but free men, Indians arrived from San Luis, San Juan, and the rest of the missions. They pushed their way into the college, carrying their arms, because it was raining very hard. Outside the mission, guards and patrols made up of the Indians themselves were stationed. They had been taught to shout "Sentinel on guard!" and "On guard he is!" but they said "Sentinel open! Open he is!"

On seeing the Indians demoralized, Father Sanchez was very upset. He had to go to Los Angeles to say Mass, because he was accustomed to do so every week or fort-night, I do not remember which. He said to me, "Eulalia, I am going now. You know what the situation is; keep your eyes open and take care of what you can. Do not leave here, neither you nor your daughters." (My daughter Maria Antonia's hus-band, named Leonardo Higuera, was in charge of the Rancho de los Cerritos, which belonged to the mission, and Maria del Rosario's husband, Michael White, was in San Blas.)

The father left for the pueblo, and in front of the guard some Indians surged for-ward and cut the traces of his coach. He jumped out of the coach, and then the Indians, pushing him rudely, forced him toward his room. He was sad and filled with sorrow because of what the Indians had done and remained in his room for about a week without leaving it. He became ill and never again was his previous self. Blood flowed from his ears, and his head never stopped paining him until he died. He lived perhaps a little more than a month after the affair with the Indians, dying in the month of January, I think it was, of 1833. In that month, there was a great flood. The river rose very high and for more than two weeks no one could get from one side to the other. Among our grandchildren was one that they could not bring to the mission for burial for something like two weeks, because of the flood. The same month—a few days after the father's death—Claudio Lopez, who had been superintendent of the mission for something like thirty years, also died.

In the Mission of San Gabriel there was a large number of neophytes. The married ones lived on their rancherias with their small children. There were two divisions for the unmarried ones: one for the women, called the nunnery, and another for the men. They brought girls from the ages of seven, eight, or nine years to the nunnery, and they were brought up there. They left to get married. They were under the care of a mother in the nunnery, an Indian. During the time I was at the mission, this matron was named Polonia—they called her "Mother Superior." The alcalde was in charge of the unmarried men's division. Every night, both divisions were locked up, the keys were delivered to me, and I handed them over to the missionaries.

A blind Indian named Andresillo stood at the door of the nunnery and called out each girl's name, telling her to come in. If any girl was missing at admission time, they looked for her the following day and brought her to the nunnery. Her mother, if she had one, was brought in and punished for having detained her, and the girl was locked up for having been careless in not coming in punctually.

In the morning the girls were let out. First they went to Father Zalvidea's Mass, for he spoke the Indian language; afterwards they went to the mess hut to have breakfast, which sometimes consisted of corn gruel with chocolate, and on holidays with sweets—and bread. On other days, ordinarily they had boiled barley and beans and meat. After eating breakfast each girl began the task that had been assigned to her beforehand—sometimes it was at the looms, or unloading, or sewing, or whatever there was to be done.

When they worked at unloading, at eleven o'clock they had to come up to one or two of the carts that carried refreshments out to the Indians working in the fields. This refreshment was made of water with vinegar and sugar, or sometimes with lemon and sugar. I was the one who made up that refreshment and sent it out, so the Indians would not get sick. That is what the missionaries ordered.

All work stopped at eleven, and at twelve o'clock the Indians came to the mess hut to eat barley and beans with meat and vegetables. At one o'clock they returned to their work, which ended for the day at sunset. Then all came to the mess hut to eat supper, which consisted of gruel with meat, sometimes just pure gruel. Each Indian carried his own bowl, and the mess attendant filled it up with the allotted portion....

The Indians were taught the various jobs for which they showed an aptitude. Others worked in the fields, or took care of the horses, cattle, etc. Still others were carters, oxherds, etc.

At the mission, coarse cloth, serapes, and blankets were woven, and saddles, bridles, boots, shoes, and similar things were made. There was a soap-house, and a big carpenter shop as well as a small one, where those who were just beginning to learn carpentry worked; when they had mastered enough they were transferred to the big shop.

Wine and oil, bricks, and adobe bricks were also made. Chocolate was manufactured from cocoa, brought in from the outside; and sweets were made. Many of these sweets, made by my own hands, were sent to Spain by Father Sanchez.

There was a teacher in every department, an instructed Indian.

Source: Carlos N. Hijar, Eulalia Pérez, and Agustín Escobar, *Three Memoirs of Mexican California, 1877* (University of California, Bancroft Library, 1988), pp. 73–82.

84. Francisco Ramírez, "El Dia de Muertos" ("The Day of the Dead"), 1857

El Clamor was founded by 18-year-old Francisco Ramírez, who published the newspaper in Los Angeles, California, from 1855–1859. The young publisher was well read, having been tutored by local Californios (a name given to Californians of Mexican extraction), which was the custom of the day. Spanish–language newspapers such as *El Clamor* and Tucson's *El Fronterizo* (1889–1929) were common and provided a voice for the Mexican people. *El Clamor* championed equal rights for Mexicans, condemned the lynchings of the times, and led a back-to-Mexico movement. Ramírez's writing is all the more remarkable since there were no schools in colonial California and Ramírez was self-taught. In the following article, the author describes the Day of the Dead in Los Angeles, California, which is, to this day, celebrated by people of Mexican extraction.

The Day of the Dead is near. On this day, fighting in the city stops: the day is the day that memories of those who are no longer with us excite our heart. Tearful faces show their pain. They have expressions of mourning. The raspy sounds of the bells affect the heart, and each sound arouses a sad and melancholy memory. A cemetery is a deplorable sight of images of death ... an old man wipes his tears, tears for a wife whom death seized; farther away there is a beautiful and innocent young girl accompanied by her brother, who prays for the soul of their mother, whose death abandoned them to the miseries of the orphanhood; they cry, they moan, and they ask their mother to protect them, requesting that upon their death to reunite with her ... All moan this day, the father, the son, the husband, the lover, the friend, releasing expressions of their pain; the fisherman, the day laborer, the domestic servant, the poor man ... Human misery! The moment man is born until he dies, he suffers pain in this world ... condemned to support the loss of loved ones; although it is horrible to see a dead friend who sweetened our lives ... it is preferable to lose a friend through death than through infidelity: the man who we believed true and is unfaithful ... this is a misfortune worse than death ... the ingratitude. Because of this, the saintly God, floods man with many sufferings? Sinks him into misery? Drowns him in misfortune?... Without hope what would man be in this world? This hope makes us wish death without horror, it sustains us in virtue, and it alleviates and it mitigates our evils.

Source: El Clamor Publico (Los Angeles), October 31, 1857; Trans. Guadalupe Compean.

85. Francisco Ramírez, "Let There Be Justice," 1856

Francisco Ramírez, the 18-year-old publisher of Los Angeles' *El Clamor Público*, published from 1855 to 1859, was steeped in the rational thinking of many Latin American intellectuals during the mid-nineteenth century. His

Spanish-language newspaper carried articles from Latin American newspapers, especially from Sonora, Mexico, and other parts of Mexico. This article analyzes the concept of justice. A parish priest had brought a complaint against defendants who had broken down a cemetery's gate. The jury found for the defendants and ordered the plaintiff to pay for the costs of the trial. The article takes this decision apart and shows there was no justice.

Let there be justice! (Even if the skies fall) a criminal lawsuit took place a few days ago in this city, before a Justice of the Peace, whose aim was very extraordinary. It was not a civil case, but criminal suit, an action taken by the State of California caused when the defendant broke down the door of the cemetery. The complaint was signed by the Rev. Párraco. It seems that the defendant was set free, and the priest who swore out the complaint was sentenced to pay the costs of the jury which was made up of young people, who had chosen with very little care and in a matter of minutes, and as it appears, without much reflection; the failures of the jury, the verdict that the criminal was not guilty, and that the case was brought with malice and without cause by the priest. The Justice of the Peace decided there was no probable cause.... Civilized countries generally have good laws; but the injustice arises from bad execution in applying them. This has been borne out in this judgment.... In the first place, juries do not have right to say more than the defendant was guilty or not guilty ... the defendant was declared not guilty ... it was not a charge for the jury to determine whether the complaint was malicious or without probable cause ... hence the jury exceeded its authority ... the judge based his sentence on the jury's verdict which was illegal and thus null and void according to the law.... the question of the malice or probable cause could be considered and argued by the lawyer of the Priest, but the Justice of the Peace arbitrarily refused to listen to a single word in favor of the Priest.... the Justice of the Peace erred and should have examined the complaint and the offense, and whether the circumstances justified the arrest order; and if it was not an offense he did not have to file it. There is a very profound contradiction in the conduct of this Justice of the Peace who issued the order of arrest and hence admitted that there was probable cause to arrest the defendant; and later ruled that it was without probable cause. The whole world knows that the Rev. Father is young person that just arrived from Spain, that he is ignorant of American laws, and knows very little English ... it is evident that his declaration was made without malice or bad faith.

Source: El Clamor Público, "Let There Be Justice," Los Angeles, July 5, 1856, pp. 2–3, ed. Francisco Ramírez, trans. Guadalupe Compean.

86. Manuel Retes, "Emigration to Sonora," 1858

El Clamor Público's publisher, Francisco Ramírez, at first advocated living under the American flag. He believed that the U.S. Constitution would protect the rights of Mexicans in the United States. However, he was soon disillusioned by racism and the lynching of Mexicans, and advocated the return to Mexico as the only means of achieving justice. Manuel Retes was an agent for the return-to-Mexico movement and regularly advertised in *El Clamor* with the support of Ramírez. This circular advertises a meeting at the home of the last Mexican governor, Pio Pico (1801–1894).

EMIGRATION FOR SONORA

(Circular)

The Board responsible for promoting emigration to Sonora, informs its countrymen that registration in this county has started and so far has, amounts five hundred fifty to date. In view of the support for this movement ... that has barely begun ... the organizing board still has had no time to start in other counties; and considering that the number of those wishing to emigrate continue multiply, the Board Representative believes that it is now time this venture should be put under the protection and consideration of the Government of Sonora, and the Supreme Court of Mexico.... Accordingly, it is agreed as of 16 October a commissioner will be appointed on 1st of next January.... all Hispanic American residents currently in this county are invited to a General Board meeting, with this end in mind, in this city, to be held at twelve noon, in the house of tiles of D. Pio Pico, located in the plaza. At this time, a discussion will be submitted to the General Board according to the terms proposed, the commissioner, to the [Sonoran] government, to be considered and discussed, and approved by all emigrants.

Chamber of Sessions, Los Angeles, December 16 of 1858.

Manuel Retes and Manuel Escalante,
President

Source: El Clamor Publico, Los Angeles, December 18, 1858; trans. Guadalupe Compean.

87. Excerpts from María Amparo Ruiz de Burton, *Who Would Have Thought It?*, 1872

María Amparo Ruiz de Burton (ca. 1832–1895), one of California's first female novelists, wrote from the perspective of the Mexican elite of her time. Born in Baja, California, she moved to U.S. soil after marrying a Euro-American captain. The following are excerpts from her first novel about a young Mexican girl as she is delivered from Indian captivity in the Southwest and comes to live in the household of a New England family. The author gives her insight into culture and perspectives on national history and identity clash. The passages criticize the dominant society's opportunism and hypocrisy, and showcase northern racism. The novel is set in Massachusetts and New England. The main character is Dr. James Norval, a geologist, who returns home with dark skinned María Dolores Medina, a.k.a. Lola. Norval had been captured by Indians along the Colorado River and encountered Lola and her mother who were also captives. Lola's mother dies and Norval escapes with Lola, returning home. Lola's presence causes friction with Norval's racist wife Jemina. Through the tension Ruiz de Burton critiques the hypocrisy of New England's Puritan society as well as northern righteousness. The first passage contrasts Norval's humanity with his wife's snobbery. The last passage discusses the French occupation of Mexico during this same period of the 1860s.

"What would the good and proper people of this world do if there were no rogues in it—no social delinquents? The good and proper, I fear, would perish of sheer inanity—of hypochondriac lassitude—or, to say the least, would grow very dull for want of convenient whetstones to sharpen their wits. Rogues are useful."

So saying, the Rev. Mr. [John] Hackwell scrambled up the steep side of a crazy buggy, which was tilting ominously under the pressure of the Rev. Mr. Hammerhard's weight, and sat by him. Then the Rev. Hackwell spread over the long legs of his friend Hammerhard a well-worn buffalo-robe, and tucked the other end carefully under his own graceful limbs, as if his wise aphorism upon rogues had suggested to him the great necessity of taking good care of himself and friend, all for the sake of the good and dull of this world....

But Mrs. [Jeminia] Norval was so shocked at this that the doctor, tired as he was in body by his journey, and in mind by all the harassing little incidents and disputes which had occurred since his arrival, left the matter for that night to his wife's discretion. The child, then, was sent with Hannah to share her room for the night.

The doctor kissed Lola several times and embraced her to bid her good night, and she, sobbing as if her heart would break, and looking back several times as she left the room, went away to sleep the sleep of the orphan under that inhospitable roof....

"Don't you know, doctor, that you kissed that Indian child more affectionately than you kissed your own daughters?" Mrs. Norval said fiercely to her husband when they had closed their bedroom door to the outer world.

"Maybe I did, for I pity the poor orphan. My daughters, thank God, have yet their parents to take care of them, but this poor little waif has no one in the world, perhaps, to protect her and care for her but myself."

"As for that, she'll get along well enough. She is not so timid as to need anybody's particular protection. Her eyes are bold enough. She will learn to work—I'll see to that—and a good worker is sure of a home in New England. Mrs. Hammerhard will want just such a girl as this, I hope, to mind the baby, and she will give her some of her castoff clothes and her victuals."

"Cast-off clothes and victuals!" the doctor repeated, as if he could not believe that his ears had heard rightly.

"Why, yes. We certainly couldn't expect Mrs. Hammerhard would give more to a girl ten years old to mind a little baby in the cradle."

"And how is she to go to school, if she is to mind Mrs. Hammerhard's baby for old clothes and cold victuals?"...

[Issac in the land of the Aztecs] Don Felipe and Don Luis, therefore, had been among the firm and most prompt supporters of the republican government up to winter of 1863. In December of this year, however, and just about time of Isaac's arrival in Mexico, these letters which the two gentlemen perused so eagerly as Isaac was riding towards them had come. These letters said that there was a very strong probability—almost a certainty—that the Archduke Maximilian would accept the proposed throne of Mexico; that he still hesitated, but that, as a great field for a noble and lofty ambition was thus opened to him, and he was known to be of generous impulses, the friends of monarchism anticipated [he] would accept in the hope of effecting a great good by giving the Mexican people a stable government, which would bring to them peace and prosperity and raise them to a high rank among the civilized nations of the world.

Source: María Amparo Ruiz de Burton, *Who Would Have Thought It?* Edited and introduced by Rosaura Sanchez and Beatrice Pita. Houston: Arte Publico Press—University of Houston © 1997, pp. 9, 21–22, 196. Reprinted with permission of the publisher.

88. Excerpts from María Amparo Ruiz de Burton, *The Squatter and the Don*, 1885

María Amparo Ruiz de Burton (ca. 1832–1895) wrote two novels in English. Born in Loreto, Baja California, Mexico, she belonged to an elite land holding family. She lived through the 1846 U.S. invasion of La Paz, Baja California. Ruiz married a captain of the invading army, Henry S. Burton. She attended President Abraham Lincoln's 1861 inauguration. However, she acquired pro-Confederate sympathies. Aside from her novels, she left a treasure trove of letters and a play. She criticized Euro-American materialism and also lamented the decline of the Californios (Californians of Mexican extraction) who were exploited by Euro-Americans. *The Squatter and the Don* is about a Californio rancher, Don Mariano Alamar. Published in 1885, it was from the perspective of the conquered. As the editors of the reprint point out, *"The Squatter and the Don* avoids addressing the dispossession of the Indians, seen here only as ranch hands and servants; neither does it essentialize ethnicity in and of itself, nor limit the characters to one spatial dimension.'' The following passages are excerpts from this novel describing the Californios and the loss of their patrimony. William Darrell was a formed squatter—one of many Euro-Americans who moved on California and challenged the legal titles of the owners in the courts using them to steal the Califonios' land.

THE SQUATTER AND THE DON

But [William] Darrell [of Alameda County] was no longer the active squatter that he had been. He controlled many votes yet, but in his heart he felt the weight which his wife's sad eyes invariably put there when the talk was of litigating against a Mexican land title.

This time, however, Darrell honestly meant to take no land but what belonged to the United States. His promise to his wife was sincere, yet his coming to Southern California had already brought trouble to the Alamar rancho.

Don Mariano Alamar [of San Diego] was silently walking up and down the front piazza of his house at the rancho; his hands listlessly clasped behind and his head slightly bent forward in deep thought. He had pushed away to one side the many armchairs and wicker rockers with which the piazza was furnished. He wanted a long space to walk. That his meditations were far from agreeable could easily be seen by the compressed lips, slight frown, and sad gaze of his mild and beautiful blue eyes. Sounds of laughter, music, and dancing came from the parlor, the young people were entertaining friends from town with their usual gay hospitality, and enjoying themselves heartily. Don Mariano, though already in his fiftieth year, was as fond of dancing as his sons and daughters, and not to see him come in and join the quadrille was so singular that his wife thought she must come out and inquire what could detain him. He was so absorbed in his thoughts that he did not hear her voice calling him, "What keeps you away? Lizzie has been looking for you; she wants you for a partner...."

"But, as George is to marry my [Don Alamar's] daughter, he would be the last man from whom I would ask a favor" [to use his influence on the Attorney General on Don Alamar's behalf].

"What is that I hear about not asking a favor from me?" said George Mechlin, coming out on the piazza with Elvira on his arm, having just finished a waltz. "I am interested to know why you would not ask it."

"You know why, my dear boy. It isn't exactly the thing to bother you with my disagreeable business."

"And why not? And who has a better right? And why should it be a bother to me to help you in any way I can? My father spoke to me about a dismissal of an appeal, and I made a note of it. Let me see, I think I have it in my pocket now," said George, feeling in his breast pocket for his memorandum book, "yes, here it is—'For uncle to write to the attorney general about dismissing the appeal taken by the squatters in the Alamar grant, against Don Mariano's title, which was approved.' Is that the correct idea? I only made this note to ask you for further particulars."

"You have it exactly. When I give you the number of the case, it is all that you need say to your uncle. What I want is to have the appeal dismissed, of course, but if the attorney general does not see fit to do so, he can, at least, remand back the case for a new trial. Anything rather than this killing suspense. Killing literally, for while we are waiting to have my title settled, the *settlers* (I don't mean to make puns) are killing my cattle by the hundred head, and I cannot stop them."

"But are there no laws to protect property in California?" George asked.

"Yes, some sort of laws, which in my case seem more intended to help the law-breakers than to protect the law-abiding," Don Mariano replied.

"How so? Is there no law to punish the thieves who kill your cattle?"

"There are some enactments so obviously intended to favor one class of citizens against another class that to call them laws is an insult to law, but such as they are, we must submit to them. By those laws any man can come to my land, for instance, plant ten acres of grain, without any fence, and then catch my cattle which, seeing the green grass without a fence, will go to eat it. Then he puts them in a '*corral*' and makes me pay damages and so much per head for keeping them, and costs of legal proceedings and many other trumped up expenses, until for such little fields of grain I may be obliged to pay thousands of dollars. Or, if the grain fields are large enough to bring more money by keeping the cattle away, then the settler shoots the cattle at any time without the least hesitation, only taking care that no one sees him in the act of firing upon the cattle. He might stand behind a bush or tree and fire, but then he is n[ot] seen. No one can swear that they saw him actually kill the cattle, and jury can convict him, for although the dead animals may be there, lying on the ground shot, still no one saw the settler kill them. And so it is at the time. I must pay damages and expenses of litigation, or my cattle [get] killed almost every day.

"It could be done, perhaps, if our positions were reversed, and the Spanish people— '*the natives*'—were the planters of the grain fields, and the Americans were the owners of the cattle. But as we, the Spaniards, are the owners of the Spanish Mexican-land grants and also the owners of the cattle ranchos, our State legislators will not make any law to protect cattle. They make laws '*to protect agriculture*' (they say proudly), which means to drive to the wall all owners of cattle ranchos. I am told that at this session of the legislature a law more strict yet will be passed, which will be ostensibly '*to protect agriculture*' but in reality to destroy cattle and ruin the native Californians. The agriculture of this State does not require legislative protection. Such pretext is absurd."

"I thought that the rights of the Spanish people were protected by our treaty with Mexico," George said.

"Mexico did not pay much attention to the future welfare of the children she left to their fate in the hands of a nation which had no sympathies for us," said Dona Josefa, feelingly.

"I remember," calmly said Don Mariano, "that when I first read the text of the treaty of Guadalupe Hidalgo, I felt a bitter resentment against my people; against Mexico, the mother country, who abandoned us—her children—with so slight a provision of obligatory stipulations for protection. But afterwards, upon mature reflection, I saw that Mexico did as much as could have been reasonably expected at the time. In the very preamble of the treaty the spirit of peace and friendship, which animated both nations, was carefully made manifest. That spirit was to be *the foundation* of the relations between the conqueror and conquered.

How could Mexico have foreseen then that when scarcely half a dozen years should have elapsed the trusted conquerors would, *In Congress Assembled*, pass laws which were to be retroactive upon the defenseless, helpless, conquered people, in order to despoil them? The treaty said that our rights would be the same as those enjoyed by all other American citizens. But, you see, Congress takes very good care not to enact retroactive laws for Americans, laws to take away from American citizens the property which they hold now, already, with a recognized legal title. No, indeed. But they do so quickly enough with us—with us, the Spano-Americans, who were to enjoy equal rights, mind you, according to the treaty of peace. This is what seems to me a breach of faith, which Mexico could neither presuppose nor prevent."

"It is nothing else, I am sorry and ashamed to say," George said. "I never knew much about the treaty with Mexico, but I never imagined we had acted so badly."

"I think but few Americans know or believe to what extent we have been wronged by Congressional action. And truly, I believe that Congress itself did not anticipate the effect of its laws upon us and how we would be despoiled," said Don Mariono sadly....

[conclusion: reviews the fraud committed by Cols. P. Huntington and the Central Pacific Railroad Co.] This, surely, is an *"aggravation of excess!"*

The House Committee on Public Lands in their report on the *"forfeiture of the Texas Pacific land grant,"* reviewed Mr. Huntington's acts with merited severity. Amongst many other truths the report says: "The Southern Pacific claims to 'stand in *the shoes*' of the Texas Pacific. Your committee agrees that 'standing in the shoes' would do if the Southern Pacific *filled the shoes.*" But it does not. It never had authority or recognition by Congress east of Yuma. For its own purpose, by *methods which honest men have denounced,* greedy to embrace all land within its network of rails, to secure monopoly of transportation, surmounting opposition, and beating down all obstacles in its way, and in doing so, crushing the agent Congress has selected as instrument to build a road there, *doing nothing, by governmental authority or assent even, and having succeeded in defeating a necessary work and rendering absolutely abortive the attempt to have one competing transportation route to the Pacific built, it coolly asks to bestow upon it fifteen millions of acres of lands; to give it the ownership of an area sufficient for perhaps one hundred thousand homes, as a reward for that result."*

And the committee (with one dissenting voice only) reported their opinion that the Southern Pacific Railroad Company had *neither legal nor equitable* claim to the lands of the Texas Pacific which Mr. Huntington wished to appropriate.

But is it not a painful admission that these few men should have thwarted and defeated the purpose and intent of the Government of the United States of having a competing railway in the Texas Pacific? Not only Col. Scott, and Hon. John C. Brown, and Mr. Frank T. Bond, the President and Vice President of this road, but also Sen. Lamar, Mr. J. W. Throckmorton, Mr. House, Mr. Chandler of Mississippi, and many, many other able speakers, honorable, upright men, all endeavored faithfully to aid the construction of the Texas Pacific. All failed. The falsehoods disseminated by ex-Sen. Gwin, which Sen. Gordon and others believed, and thus in good faith reproduced, had more effect when backed by the monopoly's money.

But Tom Scott is laid low, and so is the Texas Pacific; now the fight for greedy accumulation is transferred to California. The monopoly is confident of getting the land subsidy of the Texas Pacific—after killing it; of getting every scrap that might be clutched under pretext of having belonged to the decapitated road. Thus, the lands that the City of San Diego donated to Tom Scott *on condition* that the Texas Pacific should be built, even these, the monopoly has by some means seized upon. No Texas Pacific was built, but nevertheless, though clearly specified stipulations be violated, San Diego's lands must go into the voracious jaws of the monster. Poor San Diego! After being ruined by the greed of the heartless monopolists, she is made to contribute her widow's mite to swell the volume of their riches! This is cruel irony indeed.

Source: María Amparo Ruiz de Burton, *The Squatter and the Don*. Edited and introduced by Rosaura Sanchez and Beatrice Pita. Houston: Arte Público Press—University of Houston © 1997, pp. 62–66, 340. Reprinted with permission of the publisher.

89. Excerpts from Sostenes Betancourt, "The Wife of Joaquín Murieta and el Ferrocarril del Sur," 1885

Spanish-language newspapers were abundant in the United States during the nineteenth century. Almost every established Latino community had a newspaper. They carried news of other Spanish-speaking communities in the United States and Mexico. The following article is from *El Cronista* of San Francisco and tells of the travels of Sostenes Betancourt through the San Jose area. He describes the vivid life of Latinos in the mid-1880s. Aside from describing people of distinction, he relates an account of a scam perpetrated by a woman claiming to be the widow of the legendary Mexican bandit or freedom fighter Joaquín Murieta (1829–1853), who was allegedly killed by Capt. Harry Love and his rangers—even thirty years after his alleged death Murieta was remembered by the Mexican community.

Commissioned by the Southern Pacific Railroad, I made an inspection tour of the beautiful lands traveled by the railroad ... I chose the northern route, which extends 143 miles, from the Pacific's Metropolis all the way to La Soledad's limit where the splendid mountain range almost dissolves, it is an exuberant and florid picture of the opulent valleys of Santa Clara, Salinas, Hollister, Tres Pinos, and others.

But before I begin my narrative, which is an exact replica of my travel notes, I would like to make it clear that I have neither the desire for honor or benefit, nor do I fear antagonizing powerful companies, to compromise my telling the truth....

If deserved praises of North American railroads, principally, Southern Pacific Railroads, are not welcomed by some readers, I will be sorry, because as I said at the beginning, I am obliged to honor the company which granted me the honor, honor that even the North American writers themselves rarely receive.

On April 2nd, a day of great remembrances for all Mexicans, I began the trip. Barely leaving the city, you see the beauty of this privileged land, rich in gold and soft to the touch of the sowing hand of the working men.

From San Bruno to La Soledad, one valley follows another; tight as a billiards table, the greenery of an ocean, delineated by two funny ranges that protect it from the sea and the lack of elevation, an eternal emerald cloth.

A curious fact: the range on the right, going from here, is covered in luxurious vegetation. There are no palm trees, but one can guess the immensity beyond; there are no huge tamarind trees, but the leaves of those trees have a dreamy whispering as those found on the Mexican coast.... And to the left, covered in vegetation, exuberant mint, which seduces you even more with its attractive and immense wheat granaries of different shades, depending on the sautéing they reach and its silvery threads of innumerable formed creeks. To the right, the reflection of the sun attracts birds of colored feathers, yellow and red.... confused with flowers of identical color, birds' blue wings as active as the golondrina [swallow]. To the left ... the land forms creeks, in a swamp and soft bed.... Everywhere, on mountain tops, slopes, and valleys, huge sheep herds, cow herds, which [one beast] because of his size reminds me of the cow seen in the dreams of the Egyptians' Pharaoh, life and its multiple manifestations of wealth, the agribusiness is felt and admired as we get some distance from the city....

To the working men, the honest family man, the loving husband who wishes to give his companion a peaceful home, I would happily advise him to establish himself on any of the land plots which crosses the Southern Railroad that are easily acquired. The mundane life in San Francisco is very difficult and very expensive. The poor, with some job and thrift ... can become a property owner in a few years, and then, work for himself and not for a salary. Even more, in the countryside there is no fragmentation of the city, nor need for religious bread for the soul, nor the intelligence bread of instruction. There are schools, churches for different cults that the human race adopts, and the child, the men, the women, can attend without the worries that exist in the cities. In the countryside, the greatest preoccupation consists in the cleanliness of the body which reflects the cleanliness of the soul....

San Bruno, Milbrae, Oak Grove, San Mateo, Belmont, Redwood City, Fair Oaks, Menlo Park, Mayfield, Mountain View, Murphy's Lawrence's Santa Clara, are within 47 miles, 13 stations perfectly attended line the path. In each one there are excellent hotels, telegraph, telephone, and express available to the guests. In order to avoid mistakes, the conductor is obliged to speak in a loud voice, the name of each station as well as the next one. There are no changing cars till Gilroy; therefore a child can travel without the fear of getting lost. There is a waiting room, warm in the winter and cooled in the summer. Vanity Room for the ladies and gentlemen. Books to read while waiting, which is never prolonged, since the train works exactly as the [rider expects, keeping to] its scheduled time.

The admirable beauty of certain points, such as the poetry of our own memories, are powerful motives so that we at least mention them in these notes, at least the way one greets an old acquaintance. One can hear the Castilian language here.... during siesta time it is common to see those honest working men resting while reading a newspaper of their absent land.

With such noble workers, forced out countrymen, I have seen you cry as children when reading the paper of our Minister of Foreign Relations refuting the revolution started by barrios de Guatemala, and your tears and loneliness in the fields, are the most convenient proof that the Mexican government knew how to interpret the sentiment of Mexicans. Belmont, the name says it, is a beautiful and splendid mountain, well known because every year there are delicious picnics in the countryside. Menlo Park is a very nice area of recreation; it protects from the wind lovely little orchards, so well known that only with an expert guide one can get close to them. It is said that Santa Clara is like the Athens of California ... at all hours of the day, young people of both sexes walk through the spacious avenues studying voluminous books and abstracts yanking from science its secrets. Santa Clara is known for its Jesuit College established there, where young people honor their generation by getting an education. San Jose, head of Santa Clara's county, is a well-known city. In a small scale, they have all the comforts of that great metropolis. Well populated, in its downtown, all business transactions from many southern towns transpire. Its all-seasons' benign climate is famous. Only Monterey has better climate, but is chosen by those unfortunate ill, for kindness of its climate and the fact that it possesses miraculous thermal waters which instantly cure rheumatism and painful ailments. There is a great number of Mexicans, Chileans, and Argentines, and among them are very distinguished people because of their education and the positions they hold.

On the first and second of each month the movement is extraordinary. On those days, the government pays teachers of both sexes, and the county schools, which are many, those days are not close[d] but deserted, because habit becomes law, and it is complete rigor that all students accompany the teachers to the government offices to collect their pay.... A bit more than 30 miles to the south of San Jose is Gilroy, passing by readied stations of Eden Vale, Coyote, Perris, Madrone, and tenants. A new town of 1,600 inhabitants is dedicated to farming. On the northeast sierras, [there are] huge vineyards, and sarsaparilla is grown. The Fahrenheit thermometer, in the shade, at the meridian hour marks 60°. There are several Mexicans that get together at night, after work, in a saloon of a Chilean named Fernando Devia. Gilroy's business is paralyzing. With the exception of the bank's appearance, which does not allow comparison with stores of fifth or sixth level in the city, gold or silver coins are nowhere to be found. There are three well-furnished hotels, protestant temples, one catholic, and one mason, fire department, and a billiard saloon. The property is well depreciated, since an acre of good land for growing vineyards can be purchased for $15 dollars. We were assured that in time of harvest this, an essentially agricultural town, presents a non-use mercantile movement. We sadly noticed that there some of our compatriots live badly and look worse. During 30 hours, we visited D. Fernando Devia several times, and from the first to the last, we noticed players persevering at billiard, Panguingui, and other similar games. Moreover, the saloon does not speak very well in favor of the parishioners' culture. It is true that they are workers, but the traveler's comparison won't cease to clash when compared between this and other recreation places. Regarding the weather, it is the undeniable kindness of Gilroy, where spring continues ... good weather, the abundance of medicinal plants, the tranquility one enjoys there, the easiness to get nutritious and healthy meals at a low cost, Gilroy is not only convenient for the ill but also for the industrialists to settle somewhere else when in need of abundant resources. To the gentlemen, courtesy of Don Estolano N. Larios, merchant, we owe those 18 agreeable hours in Los Tres Pinos. Not only did he offer us his honest hospitality, such are the customs of our ancestors, he accompanied us to the most notable places of the area and gave us facts which helped us [in] writing the story of our trip. Tres

Pinos is a town of only one street, a population of 250, of which 50 are Mexican. Since this is the end of the South Pacific and due to land deals, the company is in litigation and it is feared that the railroads will not continue, most businessmen or industrialists have refused to improve the town the railroad is going through. However, there are some establishments that give certain representation. Two hotels, wood-processing plant, public school where Mass is given on Sundays, meat-shop, shoe store, bars, mixed stores, dancing halls, postal office, express, telegraph, two extensive granaries.... The principal sources of public wealth consist of agriculture and cattle raising. There are large vineyards and fruit tree farms, so much that the idea of starting a factory for fruit preserves seems to be growing.

Tres Pinos is surrounded by distinguished ranches, among them are "Santa Anita," "Quien Sabe," "Los Muertos," where all the extensive labor, although seasonal, give each year abundant harvests. The rich personalities of Spanish origin, among them Don Joaquin Bolado, Don E. Anzar, Dona Dolores de Laveaga, are justly esteemed for their excellent qualities. So that the great Hoax which took place two years ago, 70 miles south of the Tres Pinos, be understood, we need to refresh the memory with few paragraphs of history. Father Magin, a Franciscan, was the first missionary of Santa Clara. Famous for his virtues, dies as a saint and, according to tradition, God Almighty interceded for him.

In all those valleys, they talk about extraordinary adventures, as if they had occurred yesterday, of the legendary Joaquín Murieta. They talk of his wife Mariana, without anyone truly knowing how she disappeared. Twenty years ago the "crazy one," that is what they called her, associated with a French man, set up a tent near San Luis Obispo; and in a close-by creek sowed gold sputters. Soon word got out.... Adventurous men and women came in mass, they formed a town, and during the night they lost the game at the tent of Mariana and the French man, the fraudful who took all the gold and more that had been collected during the day. Finally, their fraudulent deception was exposed and the fleeced victims were able to leave town considering themselves lucky with their lives ... Almost three years ago Mariana reappeared, still accompanied by the French man, and also Carperio Ramadas, Guadalupe Olivas, and two assistants. This time, she appeared where the Santa Cruz valley narrows on the side of Nueva Indria, very close to the abrupt boulder Gavilán, where Joaquín Murieta held meetings with his subordinates. They preached the end of the world, claimed they were authorized by Father Magin who appeared to thousands of people ... through his interpreter, to supposedly preached the destruction of the world.

Mariana made running water flow from the boulders, she would say where on the earth to dig and surprised spectators with the innumerable treasures in diamonds and other rocks, silver, and gold.

Close to the day when Mariana and her two assistants disappeared, there were up to six thousand penitents. Even today there are people who are very respectable, but can not explain the miracles they believed. There are many who believe that in their desire to have the heavenly kingdom, they lost all their earthly possessions. Now they vegetate in the cursed land they once called holy. Mariana ran away with some capital, which according to the people, was no less than eight thousand dollars. In the Salinas Valley, 118 miles south of this city, a town is growing which is taking the same name as the valley. The population is 3,500 people; close to one thousand are of Spanish origin. Generally, they are in Monterey County which at one point was the best of California, the happiest Mexican people with their original customs and their generous talent. The principal source of wealth in Salinas consists of agriculture, cattle ranching, industrial factories and mercantile businesses. In a small scale, all the negotiations are handled here, even though generally these are implemented in the large mercantile nucleus.

An excellent friend of ours, businessman *sic*, son of the country, Don W. A. Richardson, showed us the best places in the city and even had the kindness of introducing us to people in high places. The city is surrounded by swamps, however, the low lands of the valley look good. However, it needs a well organized police and a cleaning crew or a public works inspection. The two proud institutions would benefit since it is a public health issue. The effects of humidity and squalor are diphtheria, paralysis, and rheumatism, which are the prevalent diseases of today. With respect to public buildings, there are some well-known buildings. The Justice Department ... cost the county 60,000 dollars. There are four churches or temples, but the highest valued at $20,000 is a Catholic one.... Focused and hard-working men carry out all types of banking transactions. Director Don W. S. Johnson is a well respected and loved gentleman ... his wife was a native.

There is a business plaza, six or seven hotels, workers from all industries, railroad, telephone, telegraph, casinos, saloons, recreational places, and many more [establishments that] clearly indicate a profile of a civilized population. Let's not doubt even for a second that Salinas has an excellent future. An acre of land, depending on the location, can be bought from twenty to one thousand pesos, so persons of means will find it easy to get established, and the poor who has nothing but the patrimony of his work will find permanent work in the Salinas Valley. That the Spanish language is as easily spoken as English will attract those of our nationality who live sadly in San Francisco. In Salinas, they would find a social niche: there are beautiful young marrying women, and there are permanent jobs. At the end of the south of the state, a mission was called San Vicente the Great during colonial times. In its memory, La Soledad was founded, its northern borders [meet] with the Southern Pacific Railroad. From 250 inhabitants, which the provisional small town has, almost all the thirty workers would be Mexican. There is a great element of wealth, outside of the one railroad line, [that] consists of sowing the land and raising sheep. The valley still extends beyond La Soledad.... The Salinas River crosses through the middle of the Rancho San Vicente and ... gets lost in the hills or stubborn brooks. It is truly a shame to see that those rivers' water is not used to water the fields. In that area, innumerable patriots are descendants of wealthy Mexican families, among them Don Gregorio Soberanes, owner of the most comfortable hotel in La Soledad, owner of the San Vicente Convent; and he has hanging from a gold nail, the key of the hall where the priests celebrated their rituals.

Source: El Cronista, San Francisco, year 11, no. 62, Saturday, April 18, 1885. Trans. Guadalupe Compean.

90. Excerpts from Miguel Antonio Otero II, *My Life on the Frontier 1864–1882*

Miguel Antonio Otero II (1859–1944) was from a prominent New Mexico family. Like the elites of other territories and states taken from Mexico, he intermarried and had business dealings with prominent Euro-Americans immigrating to the territory. Otero became governor of New Mexico Territory from

1897 to 1906. He was the son of Miguel Antonio Otero, a prominent businessman and New Mexico politician. The following passages are from his
autobiography, a trilogy, which tells of life in New Mexico, largely from the
viewpoint of an elite "New Mexican."

My father, Don Miguel Antonio Otero I, had declined a renomination as New
Mexico delegate to the United States Congress because of a determination to retire
from politics. He had also refused the appointment as Minister to Spain which President Lincoln....

It was my father's strong conviction that he devote his time and energies entirely
to the business he had previously formed with David Whiting. Whiting & Otero was
engaged in the multiform profitable activities of banking, outfitting, wholesaling....

During our stay at Don Juan's home [upon returning to New Mexico,] we saw
some of the lawlessness that prevailed in that part of the Territory. A band of Tex-
a[n]s had debouched into northern New Mexico ... and were rustling all the cattle
and horses in the country. In their raids they had killed several herders who had
opposed them. I saw the large herd of cattle these Texans had stolen near Las Vegas.
The rustlers all wore chaps and were armed to the teeth with rifles and pistols.

The presence of this outfit was naturally a great source of excitement to Las
Vegas people, and, as my father had arrived the day before, a delegation of the most
prominent citizens of northern New Mexico appealed to him to do something to
relieve the section from this scourge, their notion being that a man of my father's
prominence might have some influence with the rustlers. My father undertook the
mission, without much hope of success, and to our great delight he allowed my
brother and me to accompany him.

We all rode out to their camp, located where East Las Vegas now stands. When
my father asked for the leader of the band, a large, red-headed man with chin
whiskers, weighing fully two hundred and twenty-five pounds, presented himself. My
father urged him to have greater regard for the property of the citizens of New Mexico. When my father had finished, the leader of the Texans answered thus:

"These God damn greasers have been stealing our horses and cattle for the past
fifty years, and we got together and thought we would come up this way and have a
grand roundup, and that is why we are here. What is more, we intend to take all the
horses and cattle we come across and drive them back to their old ranges in Texas,
where they belong. My advice to you fellows is: Don't attempt to interfere with what
we are doing unless you are looking for trouble."

My father did not attempt to argue the matter further, knowing that it was useless. I have never forgotten the episode, for it revealed that hostile and vengeful
feeling displayed by the Texans which produced acts of lawlessness calculated to
make the name "Tejano" a hated word among the New Mexicans. It is said that
mothers were in the habit of censuring their children with the dire threat: "If you
are not good, I'll give you to the Tejanos, who are coming back."

In this instance, as in many others, the New Mexicans were long suffering. The
people of the northern part of the Territory had suffered heavily from these pillagers
and reasoned that it would cost them their lives to interfere in any way with the
northern ruffians. So they stood the losses and allowed the Texans to proceed on
their way. Two days after my father made his plea, the whole herd and the Tejanos
had disappeared in a southeasterly direction. It was afterwards learned that the

leader of this band of marauders took the proceeds of the raid and invested it in Denver, erecting one of that city's largest office buildings.

After a pleasant renewal of friendship with their many acquaintances in Las Vegas, my parents started for Santa Fe on the Barlow & Sanderson Stage, taking all of us children with them. On our arrival, we took rooms in a building which stood just across the street from the old Exchange Hotel, called the "La Fonda," celebrated as being the end of the Santa Fe Trail (on the site where H. H. Dorman now has his real estate office), and here we remained until conveyances arrived to take us to my uncle's home at La Constancia.

My uncle's home was a typical hacienda, or country estate, located in the richest and most desirable part of the Territory—the valley of the Rio Grande, extending from Penña Blanca to El Paso, Texas. At such haciendas, the life was lavish and luxurious to a degree hard to imagine nowadays; in many respects it resembled the principality of some foreign prince. The owners of these haciendas were fittingly called "Don" and "Dona," titles of respect and honor.

Uncle Manuel and Aunt Doloritas were very fond of entertaining, and while we were there, they gave several dances. The dances usually lasted until sunrise, refreshments and wines being served from midnight on. A good hot breakfast was furnished [to] all the guests before they started for their homes.

Source: Miguel Antonio Otero, My *Life on the Frontier 1864–1882* (New York: Arno Press, 1974), pp. 1, 61–63.

Land has always been important to Mexicans. Many Mexican old-timers would symbolically put dirt to their mouths and taste the land. It meant the place where they were raised, lived and passed on memories to their children. Land has been associated with liberty. Different people had different interpretations of land. For the Native American, it meant life—not ownership—and land was not tied to profit. Under Spanish and Mexican frontier law, their laws provided for the communal use of lands and private and public space was often shared. The latter was a semi-feudal society and communal lands were given to villages to settle frontier areas; even in the case of large grants the community was, in theory, protected. The United States concept of land differed, and it was tied to the free market. The Euro-American approach to land was tied to the notion of race and entitlement. They conjured up myths such as that they paid for the land with their blood. During the first three decades after the Treaty of Guadalupe Hidalgo (1848) there was a massive transference of land in which Mexicans lost most of their land grants and all of their communal lands. This huge transference of land was abetted by government and the courts. This transference ignored the provisions of the Treaty of Guadalupe Hidalgo (1848) that guaranteed a respect for Mexican land titles. In theory, a treaty is the law of the land—in practice the Treaty of Guadalupe Hidalgo was given separate status and allowed local courts jurisdiction over the adjudication of land titles. The confusion encouraged squatters' rights or the moving onto other people's land and claiming it. The latter had the burden to prove title which was a lengthy and costly proposition. In the case of communal lands the commons were taken from them and often given to capitalist farmers.

91. Excerpt from "The Concept of Common Lands Defines Community Land Grants," 2007

Land policy differs from country to country and is often based on the environment and tradition. For example, water laws in arid countries like Mexico and Spain differ from those in wet places like England. After the U.S. conquest of 1848, the United States was forced to use Mexican water use laws to avoid conflicts. In the Mexican tradition, water belonged to the public—or at least this was how it was supposed to work. The Spanish and Mexican governments followed a similar logic; to settle their northern frontier, the Spanish Crown, and later the Mexican government in the eighteenth and early nineteenth centuries, the governors of California, New Mexico, and Coahuila y Tejas granted or sold land to individuals and communities. The Spanish crown distributed grants to groups of people to form towns or villages. The Treaty of Guadalupe Hidalgo (1848) explicitly protected the rights of holders of private and communal lands. The original Article IX of the treaty also included language that required the immediate admission of former Mexican territories as states so the Mexican settlers would have a say in their governance. The U.S. government violated the treaty and rather than simply accepting titles to Spanish or Mexican land grants, Congress required claimants to confirm the legality of their land grants through a lengthy and expensive legal process before courts or commissions. Meanwhile, the communal lands were privatized and villagers lost their use of common lands and forests. Grantees had the burden of proof, which was often at an expense that was beyond their means. Judges and commissioners unfamiliar with Spanish and Mexican land law (let alone the Spanish language) weighed the evidence.

From the end of the seventeenth century to the middle of the nineteenth century, Spain and México issued grants of land to individuals, groups, towns, pueblos, and other settlements in order to populate present-day New Mexico. Academic treatises and popular literature typically divide these grants into two types: "individual grants" and "community land grants." Grants to towns and other settlements were modeled on similar communities created in Spain, where the king granted lands adjacent to small towns for common use by all town residents. Under Spanish and Mexican law in the territory of New Mexico, officials made grants to towns and other communities. Such grants were in keeping with Spanish laws, including the 1680 Recopilación de las Leyes de los Reynos de las Indias. However, local laws, practices, and customs often dictated how grants were made and confirmed.

After achieving independence from Spain in 1821, México continued to adhere to Spanish law by extending additional land grants to individuals to encourage settlements in unoccupied areas and to stave off U.S. encroachment on Mexican territory. The Mexican-American War began in 1846 and formally ended with the signing of the Treaty of Guadalupe Hidalgo in 1848. Under the treaty, México ceded most of what is presently the American Southwest, including the present day states of New Mexico and California, to the United States for $15 million....

Land grant documents contain no direct reference to "community land grants" nor do Spanish and Mexican laws define or use this term. Scholars, land grant literature, and popular terminology use the phrase "community land grants" to denote land grants that set aside common lands for the use of the entire community. We adopted this broad definition for the purposes of this report.

To determine the meaning of the term "community land grants," we first reviewed land grant documents, and found that grant documents do not describe grants as community land grants. We also did not find applicable Spanish and Mexican laws that defined or used the term. However, as a result of our review of land grant literature, court decisions, and interviews with scholars, legal experts, and grantee heirs, we found that the term is frequently used to refer to grants that set aside some land for general communal use (*ejidos*) or for specific purposes, including hunting (*caza*), pasture (*pastos*), wood gathering (*leña*) or watering (*abrevederos*). Our definition coincides with the way in which scholars, the land-grant literature, and grant heirs use the term.

Under Spanish and Mexican law, common lands set aside as part of an original grant belonged to the entire community and could not be sold. Typically, in addition to use of common lands, settlers on a community land grant would receive individual parcels of land designated for dwelling (*solar de casa*) and growing food (*suerte*). Unlike the common lands, these individual parcels could be sold or otherwise disposed of by a settler who fulfilled the requirements of the grant, such as occupying the individual parcel for a continuous period. For example, the documentation for the Antón Chico grant, issued by México in 1822, contains evidence that common lands were part of the original grant. The granting document provided for individual private allotments and common lands. Congress confirmed the Antón Chico grant in 1860 and the grant was patented in 1883.

APPROXIMATELY FIFTY-TWO PERCENT OF ALL NEW MEXICO LAND GRANTS MAY BE CLASSIFIED AS COMMUNITY LAND GRANTS

[there were] three types of community land grants, totaling 152 grants, or approximately 52 percent of the 295 land grants in New Mexico. In 79 of the community land grants, the common lands formed part of the grant according to the grant documentation. Scholars, grant heirs, and others have found an additional 51 grants that they believe to contain communal lands; and we located 22 grants of communal lands to the indigenous pueblo cultures in New Mexico....

The third type of community land grants ... encompasses grants extended by Spain to the indigenous pueblo cultures in New Mexico to protect communal lands that had existed for centuries before the Spanish settlers arrived. For the most part, the pueblo settlements these colonists encountered in the sixteenth century were permanent, communally owned villages, where inhabitants engaged in agricultural pursuits. Spain declared itself guardian of these communities, respected their rights to land adjacent to the pueblos, and protected pueblo lands from encroachment by Spanish colonists. Spain made grants to these communities in recognition of their communal ownership of village lands. México continued to recognize pueblo ownership of land and considered pueblo residents to be Mexican citizens.

After the Treaty of Guadalupe Hidalgo, the Congress required the Surveyor General to investigate and report on pueblo claims. The Congress subsequently confirmed Spanish grants to 22 pueblos on the recommendation of the Surveyor General....

Source: U.S. Government Accounting Office, http://www.gao.gov/guadalupe/commland.htm.

92. Excerpts from Herbert O. Brayer, *William Blackmore: The Spanish Mexican Land Grants of New Mexico and Colorado, 1863–1878*

New Mexico was the most heavily populated Mexican province at the time of the signing of the Treaty of Guadalupe Hidalgo (1848). Because so many people were dispossessed there as a result of land grabs, the Land Question—or the question of from whom the land was stolen—continues to be important to this day. Under Mexican law, two types of grants existed: private grants to individuals and communal grants, made to villages in frontier regions. These types of communal land grants were made to frontier settlers and to the pueblos for tribal use. The Mexican signers of the Treaty of Guadalupe Hidalgo (1848) wanted to protect property rights, but they believed the promises of U.S. negotiators that their property would be respected.

Further, Article 8 of the treaty provided that "property of every kind now belonging to Mexicans not established there shall be inviolably respected." However, in 1854, the office of the Surveyor General of New Mexico was set up to review titles. It was supposed to respect Spanish and Mexican laws, usages, and customs in reviewing the claims. In all, this office reviewed approximately 180 claims (not including grants to pueblo villages) and confirmed 46 of these non-pueblo grants. In 1891, the Court of Private Land Claims was established to judge land grant claims in New Mexico and the Southwest. In the next 13 years, the Court reviewed 282 claims to land grants in New Mexico and confirmed 82. The following passages are by Herbert O'Brayer, the state archivist of Colorado, in his biography of William Blackmore, an infamous British entrepreneur and spectator in Spanish and Mexican land grants in Colorado and New Mexico who represented English mining interests in New Mexico after the Civil War. Here Brayer reviews Anglo-Saxon law and attitude and their applicability to New Mexico and gives a brutal assessment.

Anglo-Saxon principles of law, taxation and land holding, as well as the new-found trade and commerce, also made definite, though for a time unnoticeable, inroads on the traditional economy of the territory. The terms of the [T]reaty of Guadalupe Hidalgo had pledged the United States to respect and protect the private property rights of the former Mexican citizens within the ceded territory. Unfortunately for the owners of New Mexico land grants, the methods devised by Congress for confirming their holdings became so involved, prolonged, and expensive, that many owners ultimately lost their lands instead of obtaining confirmation of them. The legal process established by the government was, in theory, relatively simple. A grant claimant was called upon to present his evidence of title to the newly created Surveyor General of New Mexico who examined the documents, held hearings, and, after determining the validity of the title to each grant, reported his findings to Congress with the recommendation that final confirmation be made by that body. In practice, however, the system failed to function so easily. Many of the grantees, unable to understand the English language, and naturally suspicious of the "gringo," flatly refused to submit their documents to the surveyor general, believing that they were well protected by the provisions of the treaty with Mexico.

To further complicate matters, a group of shrewd, and not too scrupulous Yankee lawyers, many of them ex-soldiers who had entered with the army of occupation or had settled in the territory after the Civil War, took advantage of the situation and within a few years had not only succeeded in obtaining control of many of the more important grants, but had actually obtained ownership of them. Since the native was dependent upon large tracts of land for the successful grazing of his flocks, this practice contributed largely to the breakup of the traditional economy by forcing the New Mexican to contract his operations or to seek other, less desirable lands. Impoverishment, dispossession, and the dislocation of population was the inevitable result. The method practiced by these representatives of "Yankee" law was to approach the native land grant residents and, after grossly exaggerating the intricacies of the confirmation process and their influence with officials both in Santa Fe and in Washington, to offer their services as attorneys for the claimants. The gullible land owners, desiring to avoid all personal contact with the new and frequently misunderstood government, readily consented. As only a few of the grantees could afford monetary remuneration, the astute lawyers generously agreed to accept payment in land. It took a good many acres at twenty-five to thirty-five cents an acre to pay the well-padded expense accounts and retainer fees charged by the counselors. Land became the usual media for payment of legal services by the natives. In one acknowledged instance, a noted Santa Fe attorney received title to more than 50,000 acres of one of the most valuable grants in the territory as payment for his efforts in defending a native charged with murder. The success of a small group of politically powerful attorneys in literally "cornering the land grant market," led to much controversy. This famous clique controlled territorial politics for more than half a century, exercising undue influence over the territorial courts, and obtaining powerful support both in Congress and in the executive branch of the federal government....

Slowly, the process whereby over eighty percent of the grants were to be lost to their hispanic settlers and owners set in and destroyed the economic equilibrium of New Mexico. The changes wrought by the imposition of the Anglo-American culture were very real, but in 1870 were not readily discernible to the casual observer. The native New Mexican remained essentially a subsistence farmer, utilizing centuries' old agricultural methods and implements....

Source: Herbert O. Brayer, *William Blackmore: The Spanish Mexican Land Grants of New Mexico and Colorado, 1863–1878*. Volume 1. Denver: Bradford Robinson, © 1949, pp. 16–19.

93. Petition of Antonio María Pico et al. to the Senate and House of Representatives of the United States, 1859

After California became part of the United States in 1848, land ownership became the major cause of hostility between the conquered and the conquerors. With the heavy immigration of Euro-Americans, the question of the validity of Mexican land titles was raised. The discovery of gold brought hoards of new settlers who contested Mexican ownership of land. California had been an isolated Spanish colony and then a Mexican province. The governors had liberally handed out land. As in other former Mexican states and territories, the U.S. government, under the pretext of validating titles, encouraged squatters to compete for land titles distributed before 1848. Mexican law provided that any Californian wanting a land grant applied to the governor. The applicant listed his or her name, age, country, vocation, and the quantity and description of the desired land. Surveying was very expensive so the applicant made a hand-drawn map, or diseño, laying out the boundaries of the grant. The U.S. system evolved at a different time in history and required a more involved process. The American process required that the land was surveyed and plotted on a grid system. In 1851, in order to clear up the confusion over land ownership in California, Congress established the California Land Commission, which placed the burden of proof of land ownership on the claimant. This was an expensive burden that included appeals of the Commission's decisions to the federal courts. Land owners were required to hire attorneys, who often took their land as collateral. Litigation over land grants lasted years. The following is a petition by Antonio María Pico and other Californios to the U.S. Congress presenting their grievances.

We, the undersigned, residents of the state of California, and some of us citizens of the United States, previously citizens of the Republic of Mexico, respectfully say:

That during the war between the United States and Mexico the officers of the United States, as commandants of the land and sea forces, on several occasions offered and promised in the most solemn manner to the inhabitants of California, protection and security of their persons and their property and the annexation of the said state of California to the American Union, impressing upon them the great advantages to be derived from their being citizens of the United States, as was promised them.

That, in consequence of such promises and representations, very few of the inhabitants of California opposed the invasion; some of them welcomed the invaders with open arms; a great number of them acclaimed the new order with joy, giving a warm reception to their guests, for those inhabitants had maintained very feeble relations with the government of Mexico and had looked with envy upon the development, greatness, prosperity, and glory of the great northern republic, to which they were bound for reasons of commercial and personal interests, and also because its principles of freedom had won their friendliness.

When peace was established between the two nations by the Treaty of Guadalupe Hidalgo, they joined in the general rejoicing with their new American fellow countrymen, even though some—a very few indeed—decided to remain in California as Mexican citizens, in conformity with the literal interpretation of that solemn instrument; they immediately assumed the position of American citizens that was offered them, and since then have conducted themselves with zeal and faithfulness and with no less loyalty than those whose great fortune it was to be born under the flag of the North American republic—believing, thus, that all their rights were insured in the treaty, which declares that their property shall be inviolably protected and insured; seeing the realization of the promises made to them by United States officials; trusting and hoping to participate in the prosperity and happiness of the great nation of which they now had come to be an integral part, and in which, if it was true that they now found the value of their possessions increased, that was also to be considered compensation for their sufferings and privations....

They heard with dismay of the appointment, by Act of Congress, of a Commission with the right to examine all titles and confirm or disapprove them, as their judgment considered equitable. Though this honorable body has doubtless had the best interests of the state at heart, still it has brought about the most disastrous effects upon those who have the honor to subscribe their names to this petition, for, even though all landholders possessing titles under the Spanish or Mexican governments were not forced by the letter of the law to present them before the Commission for confirmation, nevertheless all those titles were at once considered doubtful, their origin questionable, and, as a result, worthless for confirmation by the Commission; all landholders were thus compelled de facto to submit their titles to the Commission for confirmation, under the alternative that, if they were not submitted, the lands would be considered public property.

The undersigned, ignorant then, of the forms and proceedings of an American court of justice, were obliged to engage the services of American lawyers to present their claims, paying them enormous fees. Not having other means with which to meet those expenses but their lands, they were compelled to give up part of their property, in many cases as much as a fourth of it, and in other cases even more.

The discovery of gold attracted an immense number of immigrants to this country, and, when they perceived that the titles of the old inhabitants were considered doubtful and their validity questionable, they spread themselves over the land as though it were public property, taking possession of the improvements made by the inhabitants, many times seizing even their houses (where they had lived for many years with their families), taking and killing the cattle and destroying their crops; so that those who before had owned great numbers of cattle that could have been counted by the thousands, now found themselves without any, and the men who were the owners of many leagues of land now were deprived of the peaceful possession of even one acre.

The expenses of the new state government were great, and the money to pay for these was only to be derived from the tax on property, and there was little property in this new state but the above-mentioned lands. Onerous taxes were levied by new laws, and if these were not paid, the property was put up for sale. Deprived as they were of the use of their lands, from which they had now no lucrative returns, the owners were compelled to mortgage them in order to assume the payment of taxes already due and constantly increasing. With such mortgages upon property greatly depreciated (because of its uncertain status), without crops or rents, the owners of those lands were not able to borrow money except at usurious rates of interest. The usual interest rate at that time was high, but with such securities it was exorbitant; and so they were forced either to sell or lose their lands; in fact, they were forced to borrow money even for the purchase of the bare necessities of life. Hoping that the Land Commission would take quick action in the revision of titles and thus relieve them from the state of penury in which they found themselves, they mortgaged their lands, paying compound interest at the rate of from three to ten percent a month. The long-awaited relief would not arrive; action from the Commission was greatly delayed; and, even after the Commission would pronounce judgment on the titles, it was still necessary to pass through a rigorous ordeal in the District Court; and some cases are, even now, pending before the Supreme Court of the nation. And in spite of the final confirmation, too long a delay was experienced (in many cases it is still being experienced), awaiting the surveys to be made by the United States Surveyor-General ... Congress overlooked making the necessary appropriations to that end, and the people were then obliged to face new taxes to pay for the surveys, or else wait even longer while undergoing the continued and exhausting demands of high and usurious taxes. Many persons assumed the payment of the surveyors and this act was cause for objection from Washington, the work of those surveyors rejected, and the patents refused, for the very reason that they themselves had paid for the surveys. More than 800 petitions were presented to the Land Commission, and already 10 years of delays have elapsed and only some 50 patents have been granted.

The petitioners, finding themselves unable to face such payments because of the rates of interest, taxes, and litigation expenses, as well as having to maintain their families, were compelled to sell, little by little, the greater part of their old possessions. Some, who at one time had been the richest landholders, today find themselves without a foot of ground, living as objects of charity—and even in sight of the many leagues of land which, with many a thousand head of cattle, they once had called their own; and those of us who, by means of strict economy and immense sacrifices, have been able to preserve a small portion of our property, have heard to our great dismay that new legal projects are being planned to keep us still longer in suspense, consuming, to the last iota, the property left us by our ancestors. Moreover, we see with deep pain that efforts are being made to induce those honorable bodies to pass laws authorizing bills of review, and other illegal proceedings, with a view to prolonging still further the litigation of our claims.

Source: Manuscript HM 514, Huntington Library, San Marino, California.

94. Excerpts from *de Arguello v. United States*, 1855

The de Arguello family appealed to the U.S. Supreme Court on the ruling of a California Court on the disposition of their land grant. As early as 1795, José de Arguello, the commandant of the Presidio of San Francisco, occupied the ranch known as "Las Pulgas." Rancho de las Pulgas, at that time, encompassed an area of 35,260 acres. Upon José's death (ca. 1820), the rancho passed to his son, Luis Arguello. Apparently the original proof of title was lost, which was common at the time. In 1820 or 1821, Gov. Pablo Vincente de Sola gave a new title to Luis. In 1830, after the death of Luis, his family remained in possession of the rancho. Over the years, challenges were made to the title of the grant, but the Arguellos prevailed. In 1855, *de Arguello v. United States* was one of a series of cases ignoring the Treaty of Guadalupe (1848) and the Querétaro Protocol (1848), which guaranteed former Mexican citizens equal protection of their property rights. Under the California Land Act of 1851, each grantee had to present his or her claim to protect her or his interests. The commissioners and the court confirmed the Arguellos' legal title of the Las Pulgas grant, but not to the valley. The court said the Arguellos did not prove their title, although there was considerable evidence to the contrary. The U.S. Supreme Court upheld the lower court and found that there was no trace of evidence of a grant from the Mexican governor. The Court held the Arguellos' occupancy of the land was not evidence of ownership. The Court discounted oral evidence and insisted on archival proof, which, considering the circumstances and the times, was a very strict standard. The following excerpts of the case give the Court's rationale for their decision.

The following is a U.S. Supreme Court case on a California Land Grant case:

In a Mexican claim, where the archives of government show no trace or evidence of a grant from the Governor, and its existence is not proved by any one who had seen it, its existence and loss being assumed because none can be found, the grant is not proved by pasturing or cutting timber on the land, nor are such acts ground of an adverse claim. Nor does the refusal of the Governor to grant the land to another, because it belonged to or was claimed by claimant, operate to give title by estoppel.

When the equity of claimant has been adjudicated and the boundary and quantity ascertained, it is conclusive. Distinction between "empresario" contracts for colonization, and grants to Mexican citizens. Construction of Act in relation thereto Restraint by the Mexican Act of 1724 of grants of land within the littoral leagues had no application except to colonies of foreigners; not to Mexican citizens.

On the 26th of November 1835, the governor of California gave an order that the petitioner should have a tract of land without specifying the boundaries, which was done by an order, having the formalities of a definitive title on the 27th. This latter document must govern the case. No good title is shown which can include the valley on the west....

The appellants represent the heirs of Don Luis Arguello, who died about the year 1830.

1. They allege that Don Jose Dario Arguello, father of Don Luis, being one of the founders of the country, and in its military service as commandant of the Presideo [*sic*] at San Francisco, was the owner of a tract called "Las Pulgas," by virtue of some title or license derived from Don Diego Borica, then governor of the province, who was in possession of it as early as 1795; that this early title has been lost, and remains only in tradition.

2. That, in 1820 or 1821, Don Pablo Vincente de Sola made a new title to Don Luis Arguello, who had succeeded his father, Don Jose, in the possession.

3. That after the death of Don Luis, in 1830, his family remained in possession; that in August, [**479] 1835, one Alvisu petitioned the governor for a grant of the "Canada de Raymundo," and, it being found that the heirs of Arguello claimed that valley to be within the bounds of their rancho Pulgas, notice was ordered to be given to the widow and heirs, of Alvisu's petition. That they appeared by their attorney, Estrada, before the governor, and protested against the grant to Alvisu; and that the governor on inquiry, acknowledged the justice of the claim of the Arguello, and refused to grant the valley to Alvisu.

4. That in October 1835, Estrada, the executor of Luis Arguello, and acting as agent for the family, made application to the governor, setting forth their long possession and praying a corresponding title to be issued in their names; and that the governor, after examining into the justice of their claim, issued a decree of concession dated 26th of November 1835, which was approved by the territorial assembly on the 10th of December following. This last-mentioned decree or grant thus approved is the only documentary evidence of title exhibited by the claimants. If it includes within its boundaries the "Canada de Raymundo," as part of "Las Pulgas," it will follow that the claimants have shown a complete title thereto; and our inquiry would end here. Therefore, though last in order in the claimants' deraignment of their title, we shall consider it first.

On the 27th of October, 1835, Don Jose Estrada, executor of Don Luis Arguello, presented his petition on behalf of the widow and heirs, to Don Jose Castro, the governor, praying for a grant of the "rancho of Las Pulgas," and describing its boundaries as "from the Creek of San Matteo to the Creek of San Francisquito, and from the Estheros, (the estuary or bay) to the Sierra, or mountains." The petition alleged also that the Arguellos had "been in possession of the same since 1800, as is publicly and notoriously known, but the papers of possession had been mislaid."

The alcalde made a report, accompanied by the testimony of three witnesses, who proved an occupancy of the rancho of Las Pulgas by the Arguellos for many years as a cattle range. One describes it as extending from east to west (evidently a mistake for north to south) four leagues, and from the estuary to the hills (lomas) situate[d] at the west of Monte Redondo and Canada "Raymundo." This would include the valley now claimed ... order, dated 26th November 1835:

Monterey, November 26, 1835.

In view of the petition with which this expedient begins, and the information of three competent witnesses, and in conformity with the laws and regulations of the subject, the minor orphans of the deceased citizen, Don Louis Arguello, at the petition of Jose Estrada, citizen, are declared the owners in property of the tract known under the name of "Las Pulgas"; reserving the approval of the M.E. territorial deputation, to which this expedient shall be sent, the corresponding patent to be signed, and recorded in the corresponding book, delivering it to the interested parties for its suitable uses. Senor Don Jose Castro, senior member (vocal) of the M.E. territorial deputation, and political chief, ad interim, of Upper California, thus ordered, decreed, and signed; to which I certify.

[The U.S. Supreme Court] The document of the 26th has none of the characteristics of a definitive grant. It shows only that the governor assents that the petitioner shall have a grant of a tract of land called "Las Pulgas." It describes no boundary, and ascertains no quantity. It contemplates a "corresponding patent," and does not purport itself to be such document. On the contrary, the document of the 27th that has all the formalities of a definitive title, and purports on its face to be made for that purpose. It gives the boundaries of the tract known as "Las Pulgas," namely: "On the south the creek San Francisquito, on the north the San Matteo, on the east the estuary, on the west the Canada de Raymundo, four leagues in length and one in breadth." [The court is attempting to limit the Arguello grant of "Las Pulgas"— they are claiming more.]

The Mexican authorities have themselves given a construction to this grant in 1840, when they granted the Canada de Raymundo to Coppinger, calling for "Las Pulgas" as its eastern boundary. Moreover, jurisdical possession was given to the Arguellos, establishing the western boundary of the Las Pulgas, one league west of the estuary or bay of San Francisco. The commissioners and the court below having confirmed the claim of the appellants to the extent of this legal title, the question on their appeal is, whether they have shown any title to the valley of Raymundo, or for any land west of the boundary adjudged to Las Pulgas by the Mexican authorities, so many years ago. In support of their claim the appellants rely upon a supposed grant from Governor Borrica to Don Jose Arguello, at an early day, and a regrant or new title to Don Luis Arguello in 1820 or 1821, by De Sola.

Much parol testimony, and some historical documents, have been introduced on this subject. The value and effect of this evidence has been very fully discussed by the commissioners and the court below. We fully concur in their conclusions on this subject, but do not think it necessary to indicate our opinion by a special and particular examination of it. It will be sufficient to state the results at which we arrived after a careful consideration.

1. There is no sufficient evidence to satisfy our minds that any grant was ever made by Governor Borrica, or by De Sola. The archives of government show no trace of evidence of such a grant from either of them. They have not proved the existence of it by the testimony of any one who had seen it; they assume the existence and loss of the documents, from the fact that none can now be found. Without stopping to inquire, whether, by the Spanish law, a subject could claim against the king by prescription, we will assume, for the purposes of this case, that as a presumption of fact, the court would be justified in presuming a grant on proof of fifty years' continuous, notorious, adverse possession of a tract of land having certain admitted and well-defined boundaries; and inquire whether we have such evidence as regards this

valley of Raymundo, and the eight additional leagues of land now claimed to belong to the ranches of Las Pulgas. Don Jose Arguello was, for many years, commandant of the Presidio of San Francisco; after his death he was succeeded in the command by his son Don Luis. As early as 1797, the king's horses were pastured and herded on this rancho. As early as 1804, soldiers, under the command of Don Jose, resided in huts on the land included in the grant made to appellants in 1835, and had charge of cattle said to belong to the commandant Don Jose. The sheep of the neighboring mission of Santa Clara were sometimes pastured on it. The king's cattle, as well as those of the commandant, were pastured on it as late as 1821. After the death of Don Jose, his son and successor in office, Don Luis, continued the occupation of it, by his herds and herdsmen. The cattle on this rancho, at some seasons, wandered over the valley of Raymundo, and to the foot of the western sierra. Don Luis also cut timber at one time on the hills west of said valley. About 1821, Gov. Sola had the king's cattle removed, and permitted Don Luis to remain in possession of the rancho, which he continued to claim as his own up to the time of his death; though he took no steps towards obtaining a definitive title. As to the extent of his claim; his eastern, northern, and southern boundaries by the creek and the estuary were well known and ascertained. The western, though said to be the hills, or mountains, and, in one sense, a fixed boundary, was very uncertain. It might be at one league from the bay to the first range of woody hills, or four leagues to the highest summit of the main ridge of the sierra. Not one of the witnesses who attempt to establish this title by tradition can state what number of square leagues it contained.

The fact that the governor, in 1835, refused to grant this valley to Alvisu, because it belonged or was claimed by the heirs of Arguello, cannot operate to give a title to them by way of estoppel.

2. We come now to the consideration of the appeal entered on behalf of the United States.

The authenticity of the patent or concession to the claimants for Las Pulgas, in 1835, is not disputed; but it is contended that it is void, "because, under the regulations of 1824, lands lying within the literal leagues could not be granted by territorial governors, but only by the supreme government." On the contrary, it is contended by the counsel for the claimants, "that this clause in the colonization laws is not intended as a general prohibition of grants of land within those boundaries, but refers only to foreign colonization; and is applicable to States only, and not to the Territories of the republic." It is evident from an inspection of this act of 1824, and consequent regulations of 1828, that they contemplate two distinct species of grants. 1. Grants to impresarios, or contractors, sometimes called pobladores, who engaged to introduce a body of foreign settlers. 2. The distribution of lands to Mexican citizens, "families or single persons."

On the whole, we are of [the] opinion that the judgment of the district court is correct, and it is adjudged that the said claim of the petitioners is valid as to that portion of the land described in the petition, which is bounded as follows, to wit: On the south by the Arroygo, or creek of San Francisquito, on the north by the creek San Matteo, on the east by the Esteras, or waters of the bay of San Francisco, and on the west by the eastern borders of the valley known as the "Canada de Raymundo," said land being of the extent of four leagues in length and one in breadth, be the same more or less, and it is therefore hereby decreed that the said land be, and the same is hereby confirmed to them; and it is further adjudged and decreed that the said petitioners have and hold the same under this confirmation in the following shares or proportions, to wit: Maria de la Solidad Ortega Arguello, one equal undivided half thereof; Jose Ramon Arguello, one equal undivided fourth part thereof; Luis Antonio Arguello, one equal undivided tenth part thereof; and S. M. Mezes three equal undivided twentieth parts of said premises....

*Source: Maria de la Solidad de Arguello et al., Claimants and Appellants, v. the United States. The United States, Appellants, v. Maria de la Solidad de Arguello et al. Supreme Court of the United States *59 U.S. 539;* 15 L. Ed. 478; 1855 U.S. LEXIS 730; 18 HOW 539 May 12, 1856, Decided; December 1855 Term.*

95. Excerpts from W. W. Robinson, *The Story of Mission Lands, Ranchos, Squatters, Mining Claims, Railroad Grants, Land Scrip, Homesteads*, 1948

William Wilcox Robinson (1891–1972) was a prolific writer of pamphlets, articles, and books on the history of Southern California. In *The Story of Mission Lands, Ranchos, Squatters, Mining Claims, Railroad Grants, Land Scrip, Homesteads,* Robinson described California's early Spanish land laws and institutions, then selected San Pascual (Pasadena) as their archetype, and narrated California's land history. He wrote about changes in land institutions and laws that followed the Mexican-American War, profiling San Francisco and Los Angeles. The following passage describes the phenomenon of squatterism in California.

Every American is a squatter at heart—or so it seems if we think of the tide of adventurous men that began moving west at the close of the Revolutionary War, men impatient of governmental authority and as contemptuous of the rights of Indians as of wild animals, men who believed land should be free as air. This tide finally reached the westernmost boundary of California.

Squatterism is as old as our country. George Washington, in 1784, was making entries in his diary about his experiences with squatters on lands he owned west of the Alleghenies. The squatter movement that began in the eastern states continued steadily west and farther west, greatly influencing the land policies of the government. It found its climax, but hardly its conclusion, when gold-hungry pioneers looked enviously and graspingly on the vast ranchos held by Californians under Mexican laws. Squatterism in California has never entirely died out, although shotguns gave way to lawyers. In recent years, with California rancho titles all settled, we still find mild flare-ups of the squatter spirit, for the desire to settle upon the good lands held by another person dies hard. Who does not want to get something for nothing!

Even before California became a part of the Union—September 9, 1850—the wagons of the immigrants were moving in and coming to a stop on the good valley lands of the rancheros. Squatters began early to organize into armed bands to get what they wanted. Some were interested in ranches. Some began staking out, or helping themselves to, lots on the outskirts of growing towns like San Francisco and Sacramento.

Many years were to elapse before a land commission, authorized under Act of Congress in 1851, and the courts to which its decisions could be appealed, could pass upon all of the 800 and more private land claims in California. Meanwhile, adventurous American immigrants, who believed—as in the popular song—that "Uncle Sam is rich enough to give us all a farm," found on their arrival that all the best land in California, or at least the most usable, was included in enormous grants made by the Mexican regime. To many of these "North American adventurers," as native Californians liked to refer to them, the great landowners were merely monopolists who, like the Indians, were obstructing the path or progress of civilization. After all, California had been captured, as well as bought, from Mexico.

No doubt some of these newcomers brought with them the honest notion that this territory obtained from Mexico was inevitably public land and that they, therefore, had the right to preempt and settle upon lands in California as freely as they had been doing upon any part of the public domain in other states. When they found the best areas under Mexican titles or held by speculators who had bought them up, clashes were inevitable. Hardly any part of California was free from violence. The story of squatterism in California is just one chapter in the story of mob law in America....

In May 1853, Jack Powers, who was a squatter on land of Nicholas Den near Santa Barbara, barricaded himself with fifteen of his friends behind logs and wagons and defied the sheriff's attempt to oust him. They were armed with revolvers, rifles, and shotguns and were supplied with liquor and food. In the battle that developed there were killed and wounded on both sides.

Trespassers and squatters roamed and mined at will along the creek beds of John Charles Fremont's ore-rich Mariposas grant, and when the final survey showed valuable mines included within the rancho's boundaries, Fremont's settlement became an armed camp. Miners attempted to seize the mines they had worked. Bloodshed and riots followed.

Source: W. W. Robinson, *The Story of Mission Lands, Ranchos, Squatters, Mining Claims, Railroad Grants, Land Scrip, Homesteads.* Berkeley, CA: University of California Press, © 1979, pp. 111–113, 126.

96. Excerpts from *Gonzales v. Ross*, 1887

The history of Texas land grants after 1848 is even more tortuous than that of Californian and New Mexican territory (which, up to the mid-1860s, included Arizona). Portions of Texas had been part of Coahuila, Tamaulipas and Chihuahua, Mexico—which had made land grants to encourage settlements through the colonization law of 1825. Between 1821–1836, Mexico made various grants to Mexican ranchers and Euro-American colonists in Texas. In 1836, the so-called Republic of Texas claimed disputed land that belonged to Tamaulipas that continued to issue land titles in the Trans-Nueces region until 1848. Texas had officially recognized the land grants made under Spanish and Mexican rule as valid. In 1850, the Texas legislature established a board of commissioners to manage the land grant question and issue a report. Later, the legislature passed a law that gave jurisdiction to district courts for confirming Spanish and Mexican titles. *Gonzales v. Ross* was brought by the heirs of Juan Gonzales. They sued the International and Great Northern Railroad Company and their tenant for trespass and for the recovery of eleven leagues of land situated in Kinney County, Texas, adjoining the Rio Grande. A jury was waived by the court, which found for the defendants. The court said that the plaintiffs failed to prove their title. Significantly, the court had overruled and dismissed testimony offered by the plaintiffs as evidence that their ancestor, Juan Gonzales, owned the land. The U.S. Supreme Court, in a rare instance, overruled the lower court and said that it should have accepted the testimonies of proof of title by Gonzales.

The Congress of Coahuila and Texas on the 28th April 1832, passed a law respecting the grant of public lands. One Gonzales applied for a grant under this law, and, on the 16th October 1832, the governor made the grant of the land in dispute under which the plaintiffs claim in the customary form for such grants. A commissioner was appointed to give possessory title to the tract, and on the 18th April 1834, he delivered to the grantee at Dolores formal possession of the tract, and executed and delivered a formal "testimonio" thereof. On the 26th March 1834, the Congress of Coahuila and Texas at Monclova repealed the act of April 28, 1832. The laws of the Mexican states did not then take effect in any part of the country until promulgated there. There was no evidence of the promulgation of the repealing act at Dolores, but there was presumptive evidence tending to show that on the 3d May 1834, it had not been promulgated there. Held: that under all the circumstances, and in view of the distances of Dolores from Monclova, the presumption was that the repealing act had not been promulgated when the commissioner extended the title to Gonzales.

The act of the Congress of Coahuila and Texas of March 26, 1834, creating a new system of disposing of the public lands, did not abrogate the grants and sales which had been made under the act of April 28 1832, nor abolish the office and function of commissioners necessary for extending such grants.

From the notorious public history of the colony of Beales and Grant, and from other notorious facts which are stated in the opinion of the court, it is Held, that the governor in the gran[t] to Gonzales, which is the subject matter of this suit, intended to designate and did designate the commissioner of the neighboring enterprise as the officer to locate the grant and deliver possession to the grantee, and that his official acts therein, having been accepted and acquiesced in by the government, must be considered as valid, even if done by him only as commissioner de facto.

The public officer who extended the lands in dispute must be presumed to have extended them in the proper department, and this presumptive conclusion of law is made certain in fact by examining the laws referred to in the opinion of the court.

In 1834, the state of Coahuila and the department of Monclova extended eastwardly at least as far as the river Nueces.

As all favorable presumptions will be made against the forfeiture of a grant, and as it will be presumed, unless the contrary be shown, that a public officer acted in accordance with law and his instructions, and as the government acquiesced in the commissioner's acts in extending the grant in dispute and no attempt had been made to revoke them or to assert a forfeiture; Held, that he had authority to extend the title, and his acts must be considered valid.

The testimonio in this case sufficiently connects itself with the original grant and subsequent steps taken under it: it is not necessary that it should be attached to it by a physical connection.

The grant in this case gave power and authority to the commissioner to extend it, and no further order was necessary.

The extension of the title of the grantee by the commissioner in a Mexican grant completed the title, without patent or other act of the government, and notwithstanding the imposition of conditions subsequent; and the non-performance of such conditions subsequent constituted no objection to the admission of plaintiff's evidence to show such extension.

If a forfeiture of a Mexican land grant from non-payment or condition subsequent can be availed of by a private person at all, it can only be after he has shown some right to the land in himself by virtue of a subsequent purchase or grant from the sovereignty of the soil.

Prior to the adoption of the constitution of 1876 the laws of Texas did not require that a title under a Mexican grant should be registered in the county or deposited among the archives of the land office, in order to give it vitality; and it was only void as against third persons acquiring title from the sovereignty of the soil, not having notice of it.

Defences [sic] against Spanish and Mexican titles in Texas under Art. XIII of the constitution of Texas of 1876 constitute no objection to the admission of evidence in support of such titles. Quoere, as to the effect of the provisions in that article prohibiting the future registration of titles, or the depositing of them in the land office....

OPINION: ... MR. JUSTICE BRADLEY delivered the opinion of the court.

This is an action of trespass to try title, brought by the heirs of Juan Gonzales against The International and Great Northern Railroad Company and their tenant in possession (Ross), to recover eleven leagues of land situate[d] in Kinney County, Texas, adjoining the Rio Grande. The defendants pleaded not guilty, and title from the sovereignty of the soil. At the trial a jury was waived, and the court ... rendered judgment for the defendants. The judgment is based upon the failure of the plaintiffs to make out their title; and their failure to make title arose from the court's overruling and rejecting the testimony offered by the plaintiffs as evidence of the extension of title to their ancestor, Juan Gonzales.

The court found and decided that the plaintiff had shown an application for, and concession of, eleven leagues of land in the name of Juan Gonzales, in the state of Coahuila and Texas, and gave the purport of the documents showing the same, being an exemplification of the original in the archives of the government of Coahuila, at Saltillo. These documents were in Spanish, accompanied by a verified translation. They were exemplified under date of August 20, 1874, and had been duly recorded in the clerk's office in the records of Kinney County on the 8th of February, 1878, as appeared by the clerk's certificate thereon.

The application of Gonzales, as translated, was as follows, to wit:

"To his Excellency: The citizen Juan Gonzales, before your Excellency, with greatest respect, states:

"That in accordance with the provisions of the law of colonization of the state your Excellency will please grant me the sale of eleven sitios of land of those vacant lands of the department of Monclova and places by me designated, promising to introduce in them the number of stock required by the same law and paying the value, delivering at once the fourth part of the same and binding myself to fulfil [sic] all requirements of the same law. Praying your Excellency will grant this petition as requested, will receive grace and justice.

"JUAN GONZALES."

The grant, bearing date, Leona Vicario, October 16, 1832, was attached to the application, and was in the name of the Governor in the usual form, and, as translated, was as follows:

"In accordance to Article 13 of the new law of colonization enacted by the honorable Congress of the state, April 28, 1832, I grant the sale to petitioner of the eleven sitios of land prayed for at the place designated by him, provided that they shall be all in one tract and not under any title belonging to any corporation or person whatsoever.

"The commissioner for the division of lands in the enterprise to which corresponds the one which petitioner solicits, and in his default, or in case there is none, or not being engaged in any other enterprise, the alcalde 1st, or the only one acting of the respective municipality or the nearest one, complying with [the] order given in the matter, will place him in possession of the said sitios, and will extend the corresponding title to the same, first classifying the quality of said lands, so as to be able to state the amount to be paid the state, which payment must first be paid by the interested party in the manner and terms specified in the last part of said Article 13, making the payment at once as provided by this article, in the treasury of the state, receipt of which he will present to the secretary, so that the secretary, upon sight of it, will proceed to give [the] interested party [a] copy of his petition, with which he will go to the commissioner and have its requirements complied with.

"ECA Y MUSQUIZ. (One rubric.)

"SANTIAGO DEL VALLE, Secretary. (One rubric.)"

The court next found as follows:

"Second. That Fortunato Soto was duly appointed by the proper authority of the state of Coahuila and Texas, as commissioner to extend titles in the colony contracted for by Juan Carlos Beales and Diego Grant. That his commission of authority was dated March 13th, 1834, and was signed by Francisco Vidann y Vallastenor, the then governor of the state of Coahuila and Texas and by J. Mijuel [*sic*] Falcon, the then secretary of [the] state of Coahuila and Texas.

"Third. The plaintiffs are the legal heirs of Juan Gonzales, the beneficiary and grantee of the concession referred to in decision number one, above set forth.

"Fourth. That defendants are in possession of the land described in plaintiff's petition.

"Fifth. That the boundaries of the colony contracted for by Juan Carlos Beales and Diego Grant are shown by the following ... contract of colonization entered into with the citizen Diego Grant and Don Juan Carlos Beales as empresarios to introduce 800 families in the vacant lands of the state."

The contract referred to, between the government of Coahuila and Texas and Juan Carlos Beales and Diego Grant, is then set out in full, the application bearing [the] date October 5, 1832, and the concession October 9, 1832. It included, first, a grant for the whole territory lying between the Rio Grande and Nueces Rivers, and bounded south by the state of Tamaulipas, and north by the 29th parallel of latitude; secondly, a grant of a tract formerly granted to Woodbury and Vehlein, and subject to their right to colonize 200 families, embracing a territory over 200 miles in length, bounded north by the 32d parallel of latitude, south by the old road leading from Rio Grande to Bexar, west by the 100th degree of west longitude, and east by other grants in the interior of Texas. The first tract adjoins the southwest corner of the second; and Kinney County, in which the lands in question are situated, lies in the angle between the two tracts, but outside of both.

The 9th Article of the concession to Beales and Grant has the following provision: "This colony shall be regulated and their lands divided by a commissioner of the government, who in proper time will be appointed, and will discharge his duties in accordance with the laws and instructions that for said officials have been approved by the honorable Congress."

The bill of exceptions then exhibits two maps given in evidence by the plaintiffs, certified by the Secretary of State of the United States, one being a copy taken from Disturnell's map of the united Mexican states, published in 1847, and deposited with the Treaty of Guadalupe Hidalgo, 1848; the other showing the boundary line between the United States and Mexico, as laid down in Melish's map, published in 1818, and agreed to in the treaty of January 12, 1828. These maps show that the province of Texas did not then embrace any territory west of the river Nueces.

In view of this evidence and the findings of the court thereon, the plaintiffs then offered in evidence a paper purporting to be a testimonio, with formal and sufficient proof of its execution, by which testimonio it appeared that in April, 1834, the possessory title of the land in controversy was extended to Juan Gonzales, the ancestor of the plaintiffs, by Fortunato Soto, commissioner for the state in the colony of Rio Grande. This paper was in the Spanish language, and together with the authentications and translation thereof, had been recorded in the clerk's office of Kinney County on the 21st of June 1878, as appears by the clerk's certificate thereon. The following is a copy of the said document as translated, to wit:

"In the village of Dolores, state of Coahuila, Texas, on the 18th day of the month of April, 1834, I, the citizen Fortuato Soto, as commissioner for the supr. government of the state in the colony of the Rio Grande, and in compliance with the contract celebrated (entered into) between said government and the citizen Juan Gonzales, and in accordance with the requirements and stipulations which the law provides in this matter, I extend the present title, in the name of the government and in accordance with the provision in its superior decree of the 16th of October 1832, contained in the aforesaid contract, to the citizen Juan Carlo Bealers, as attorney of the said citizen Juan Gonzales, which power of attorney he presented, of the eleven sitios of land to which said contract has reference, which said lands in their actual state I have classed as pasture lands, and which said boundaries are: Commencing from the place where the boundary line of the property of Dona Dolores Soto do Beales forms an angle between south and west, a line will be drawn to the south, prolonging in the same direction, which will there terminate the said section at a distance of thirteen thousand seven hundred and fifty varas; from whence another line will be drawn in a right angle, which, crossing the arroyo (creek) of Piedra Pinta, will have the length of twenty thousand varas; and from this point another line will be drawn towards the north parallel with the first, and of the same length, and ends with another line to the east that, crossing the same arroyo (creek), will extend up to the place of beginning; so that in all form and right he, the said citizen Juan Gonzales, may at all times prove his rights to the said eleven sitios of land, I went with his attorney, citizen Juan Carlos Beales, which, after being surveyed by the surveyor, C. Guillo Egerton, I put him in possession, and taking him by the right hand, and in the name of the supreme government of the state, walked him over the said eleven sitios of land and caused him to perform all the

other ceremonies, as provided by the laws in this case of real possession, being witnesses the citizens Eduardo Little, Enrique Brown, and George Colwell, beside those
of my assistance [*sic*], all residents of the village, who for the validity of it signed
with me, and the interested party said day, month and year, pledging himself to
replace the proper paper with the seal that is required, not having at present any of
the seal in this village nor its surroundings.
    "FORTUNATO SOTO.
    "THOS. H. F. O'S. ADDICKS, De Assistencia.
    "THOMAS PLUNCKETT, De Assistencia.
    "JUAN CARLOS BEALES.
    "ENRIQUE BROWN.
    "EDUARDO LITTLE.
    "GEORGE COLWELL."
    "I, the citizen, Fortunato Soto, commissioner for the Supreme Government of
the state of Coahuila and Texas in this colony, certify that the preceding testimonio
is a literal copy legally taken from its original, which is of record in the proper book
of these archives, and in compliance with Article 8 of the instructions of the 25th
of April 1830, I give the present to the interested party as title, which is given on
common paper, not having any of the proper seal, and for the validity of the same I
signed it with the assisting witnesses in said village the 18th of April 1834.
    "FORTUNATO SOTO.
    "THOS. H. F. O'S. ADDICKS, De Assistencia.
    "THOS. SAM. PLUNCKETT, De Assistencia."
    To the introduction of this paper the defendants objected for the following
reason:
    1st. It has not been proved and recorded according to law, and its registration was
not authorized by law when it pretends to have been recorded. No protocol or matrix of
it has been shown ever to have been filed in the archives of the General Land Office,
and no such is or ever was an archive of such office; no possession of the land claimed
by any one holding under it has been shown; no payment of taxes thereon by plaintiffs,
or any one for them, has been shown; no compliance with or fulfillment of the conditions of the law under which it purports to have been issued has been or attempted to
be proved; and if it ever had any validity, it appears from the face thereof that it is such
a claim as was never perfected, but wholly abandoned, and the land remitted to the
public domain, and that it is a stale demand and void.
    2d. It does not contain and is not based upon any executive grant, concession, or
primitive title, nor does it contain any petition or application of the pretended
grantee for a concession or for a survey of the land or the execution of final title of
possession, nor any order referring it to the empresario order of survey, surveyor's field
notes, or other constituent element of an expediente of final title, nor apt words to
express a grant of land from the state by way of sale as required by law at its date; but
it purports to be a kind of grant unknown to and not authorized by such law, and it
appears therefrom that the same issued without authority of and against law.
    3d. It purports to have been issued by one unknown to the law, claiming to exer-
cise the powers and perform the functions of an office not then existing, but the existence, powers, and jurisdiction whereof had already been repealed, styling himself
commissioner of a colony not shown to have existed, and which, it is well known,
never did exist; and it is claimed to be title embracing and relating to land situated

in Kinney County, as averred in the petition, which is well known to have been embraced within the Woodbury colony district at the date it bears, for which colony the person purporting to have issued it was not, and does not by the terms of the instrument pretend to have been, a commissioner or officer.

4th. It appears there from that its matrix or protocol, if it is in fact a testimonio of such, contained no executive concession or petition for such; no petition or application for a survey of the land, nor for the execution of final title; no reference to the empresario order of survey nor surveyor's field notes, and no one of the requisite antecedent steps, papers, documents, or acts entering into and forming the expediente of a valid final title or grant under the law in force when and where it purports to have been issued; none of which can be established by parol.

5th. It does not express any consideration paid, or to be paid, or conditions to be performed or required by law.

6th. It purports to have been executed pursuant to a contract stated to have been ratified with the executive, while the only one so to be ratified was that of an empresario.

7th. It pretends to be an absolute grant in fee, which was not authorized or contemplated by the law.

8th. If the contract it refers to was an executive concession by way of sale, this instrument shows it to have been forfeited under the law, and constituting no authority for the execution of this paper on the 18th of April 1834.

9th. It has vices before the law, and is defective in manner and form, using bad grammar, awkward construction, and a form and style diverse from the usual general practice, and contains unaccustomed clauses without any reason therefor.

10th. It is not written upon sealed or stamped paper, as required by law, nor upon paper validated by the proper officers of the municipality or any other; and its execution has not been proved, and no attempt has been made to show that the persons purporting to have signed it did so when and where it bears date or in the capacity therein stated.

11th. It was never registered, as required by law, under the former government of Coahuila and Texas, nor under the republic or state of Texas; it was never presented nor any payment on it made to the collector of the former government, nor to any officer of the republic or state of Texas; it was never presented to either of the commissions established by law to investigate titles to land in the section of the state where the demanded premises are situate, nor was it ever brought forward or set up as a claim to land till more than forty years after its date, and now only with the greatest want of verisimilitude in the matters it contains and expresses.

12th. It attempts to conceal the fact that the land, if it relates to the demanded premises, was, at its date, embraced within a colony for which the one purporting to have executed it did not by its terms pretend to be a commissioner or officer, and falsely claims to have been issued in and by the commissioner of a colony which never existed.

13th. It has no receipt for any instalment [*sic*] of the purchase money written out at the bottom of it, as required by law, nor has any attempt been made to prove such payment.

14th. It is incompetent and irrelevant, and shows upon its face that it is not a subject of judicial cognizance, and it does not describe or identify the demanded premises, but is void for want of certainty.

15th. It is prohibited from being used in evidence by the thirteenth article of the constitution of Texas, and if it ever had any validity, it is stale and forfeited, and the land to which it relates was reunited to the public domain by legislative equivalent for reunion by office found.

The bill of exceptions states that the court sustained the said objections, and refused to admit the said document in evidence, mainly on the ground that the same was issued without authority of law, the law and instructions under which the commissioner pretended to act having been repealed prior to the execution thereof; to which ruling rejecting said documents plaintiffs, by counsel, excepted.

The court thereupon rendered judgment for the defendants.

We will first consider the main reason assigned by the court below for rejecting the evidence offered, namely, that the law and instructions under which the commissioner pretended to act had been repealed prior to the execution thereof. The law under which the grant was made to Juan Gonzales, and under which the commissioner acted in extending the title, was that passed by the Congress of Coahuila and Texas, April 28, 1832. This law, it is true, was repealed and supplied by an act of the Congress passed at the city of Monclova, March 26, 1834, and the testimonio offered in evidence is dated at the village of Dolores, April 18, 1834, some three weeks afterwards. But the laws of the Mexican states did not take effect in any part of the country until they were promulgated there; and as Dolores was situated in the present county of Kinney, about 200 miles from Monclova, and probably much more than that as the roads there ran, and as the means of communication in that region at that time were difficult and dilatory, it is not probable that the act of March 26 was promulgated at Dolores prior to the 18th of April. Besides, the commissioner was a public officer, having a public duty to perform, and in the absence of evidence to the contrary, the presumption would be that he acted in accordance with the law as known at the time. This presumption is strengthened by the language of another act passed in the same session of the Congress, on the 3d day of May 1834, which declared that certain favorable terms as to the price of lands, proffered by a law of 1830, should "be understood only in respect to the price of lands acquired until (hasta) the publication of the decree of 26th of March of this year," implying, it would seem, that the law of the 26th of March had not yet been published. Looking at the matter in every point of view, we think the presumption is, that this act, which was the repealing act referred to, had not been promulgated at Dolores, or in that vicinity, when the commissioner extended the title of possession to Gonzales....

although the act of 26th March 1834, created a new system of disposing of the public lands, and repealed the act of 1832, it did not abrogate the grants and sales which had been made under it; nor did it abolish the office and functions of commissioner, necessary for extending such grants....

On the whole we think it clear that Fortunato Soto had authority to extend the title in question, or, at least, that his official acts were acquiesced in by the government, and are to be considered as valid.

We are, therefore, of opinion that the court below should have admitted the testimonio in evidence, unless it was incompetent by reason of some matter or thing occurring after its execution and delivery to Gonzales.

Analyzing the various and somewhat confused and multifarious objections of the defendants, we find three such matters assigned as grounds for rejecting the evidence: First, the non-fulfilment of the conditions of the grant; secondly, that no protocol, or matrix of the concession or testimonio, was amongst the archives of the land office, nor on record in the proper county in proper time; thirdly, that, not being amongst the archives, and not being recorded in proper time, and never being followed by actual possession, the testimonio was an absolute nullity by force of the XIIIth Article of the Constitution of 1876.

These matters may constitute very good and substantial grounds of defence, and we are not disposed to intimate anything to the contrary in this opinion. But we think they can only be effectual by way of defence....

As to the matter of registration, the laws of Texas prior to the adoption of the constitution of 1876, so far as we can discover, did not require that a title should be registered in the county, or deposited amongst the archives of the land office, in order to give it validity. It was only void as against third persons acquiring title from the sovereignty of the soil, not having notice of it. In this respect the laws of Texas were not dissimilar to those of most of the states of the Union. Indeed, the original titles could not be deposited in the land office when, as was often the case, they belonged to the archives of the foreign government at Saltillo, or other place where they were originally deposited. Copies of them, amounting to second originals, or testimonies of the final title, might be so deposited, or might be registered in the proper county; but even that was not necessary to their validity, although it might be necessary to protect the owners against titles subsequently acquired without notice of their existence. It is manifest, however, that titles thus subsequently acquired, if relied on by a defendant, must be proved as matter of defence, and cannot be urged against the competency of the plaintiff's evidence of his title....

The judgment of the Circuit Court is reversed, and the case is remanded, with directions to award a new trial.

Source: Gonzales v. Ross. Supreme Court of the United States. 120 U.S. 605; 7 S. Ct. 705; 30 L. Ed. 801; 1887 U.S. LEXIS 2007. Submitted November 2, 1886. March 14, 1887, Decided.

97. Excerpt from Las Gorras Blancas (The White Caps) Manifesto, 1890

Las Gorras Blancas (The White Caps) was a group of New Mexicans, mostly around the Las Vegas, New Mexico, area, who fought to retain community control of the common lands in the 1880s and 1890s. They conducted raids on white farmers who threatened native-owned land near Las Vegas. They cut fences and destroyed property. On August 12, 1890, Le Baron Bradford Prince, Governor of the New Mexico territory, begged officials in Washington to send federal troops to patrol the area around Las Vegas. Many of the white ranchers had built fences to separate cattle from flocks of sheep belonging to the native inhabitants. The enclosure movement accelerated after 1870 with the introduction of cheap barbed-wire fencing. The following excerpt summarizes the grievances of the native farmers.

Not wishing to be misunderstood, we hereby make this our declaration.

Our purpose is to protect the rights and interests of the people in general; especially those of the helpless classes.

We want the Las Vegas Grant settled to the benefit of all concerned, and this we hold is the entire community within the grant.

We want no "land grabbers" or obstructionists of any sort to interfere. We will watch them.

We are not down on lawyers as a class, but the usual knavery and unfair treatment of the people must be stopped.

Our judiciary hereafter must understand that we will sustain it only when "Justice" is its watchword.

The practice of "double-dealing" must cease.

There is a wide difference between New Mexico's "law" and "justice." And justice is God's law, and that we must have at all hazards.

We are down on race issues, and will watch race agitators. We are all human brethren, under the same glorious flag.

We favor irrigation enterprises, but will fight any scheme that tends to monopolize the supply of water courses to the detriment of residents living on lands watered by the same streams.

We favor all enterprises, but object to corrupt methods to further the same.

We do not care how much you get so long as you do it fairly and honestly.

The People are suffering from the effects of partisan "bossism" and these bosses had better quietly hold their peace. The people have been persecuted and hacked about in every which way to satisfy their caprice. If they persist in their usual methods, retribution will be their reward.

We are watching "political informers."

We have no grudge against any person in particular, but we are the enemies of bulldozers and tyrants.

We must have a free ballot and a fair count, and the will of the majority shall be respected.

Intimidation and the "indictment" plan have no further fears for us. If the old system should continue, death would be a relief to our sufferings. And for our rights our lives are the least we can pledge.

If the fact that we are law-abiding citizens is questioned, come out to our homes and see the hunger and desolation we are suffering; and "this" is the result of the deceitful and corrupt methods of "bossism."

Be fair and just and we are with you, do otherwise and take the consequences.

The White Caps, 1,500 Strong and Growing Daily

Source: Las Vegas Daily Optic, March 12, 1890.

PART VIII
Latinos South of the Border

The Mexican border marks where the first world ended and the third, according to many Americans, began. In reality, Euro-American interests in the other America did not end with the acquisition of Florida and the Mexican cession as Euro-Americans sought to incorporate much of the Caribbean and secure its interests in Central America—both of which were keys to the projected construction of a "U.S." inter-ocean canal. The Gem of the Antilles was Cuba whose trade was vital to U.S. commercial interests and its land was also coveted by Euro-American slave owners. This gave rise to the Cuban Question that discussed American interests within the island—90 miles off the shore of Florida. Sectional interests within the United States made its forcible acquisition much more complicated than the invasion of Mexico (1846). Nevertheless, the 1850s were a period of filibustering expeditions—often financed by private Euro-American capital. Tensions were also heightened by crude U.S. diplomatic efforts to purchase Cuba. As the canal fever grew hotter, and U.S. merchant and sea power increased—so did interest in the rest of the Caribbean. Puerto Rico was a thousand miles away but it was strategically located in routes to Panama. Cuba and Puerto Rico were the last two islands in Spain's possession. And in the 1860s, independence movements emerged in these two locations. The United States before 1865 was divided over the question of the acquisition of Cuba due to the slave issue. After this it continued to deny belligerency status to rebels because of U.S. economic interests on the island, and its desire to maintain the status quo. There were those who argued that the United States did not want Cuban independence but favored the status quo until such time as Spain sold the island to it.

98. Author Unknown, Excerpts from "Cuba," 1849

Once Florida became part of the United States in 1819, U.S. commercial and political interest turned their attention to Cuba that was only 90 miles off the southern tip of Florida. Cuba was the largest of the Caribbean Islands and had vast acres of land available for plantation-type crops such as sugar and tobacco. By the mid-nineteenth century, the United States had additional reason to covet Cuba and the Caribbean. Its strategic location made it vital to U.S. sea power, which needed fueling ports. These ports were essential to the defense of U.S. business interests in Central American and to the future of a canal through the isthmus. Moreover, the political competition between the North and the South over representation heated up during the 1850s. More states meant more votes in Congress and Cuba, because of its plantation-like economy and climate, would be in the slave column. Hence, slaveholders saw it as part of the south; U.S. merchants saw Cuba as vital to U.S. hegemony in the isthmus; and the U.S. Navy and military saw the Caribbean as militarily essential. Spain owned these lands. At first, the United States tolerated Spanish rule since it feared that Great Britain would step into the vacuum if Cuba won its independence and the British would gain a foothold in the region. The following article, published in 1849, introduces a discussion of the Cuban Question and addresses the activities of Cuban independistas in the United States. It includes a letter of a Cuban in the United States asking for U.S. aid in securing Cuban independence. The writer advocates for the Cuban independistas. During the 1850s, Cuban exiles routinely used the United States as a staging area. Euro-Americans often supported these ventures economically purchasing arms for favored rebels. According to the article, it would not take much to take over Cuba.

The island of Cuba possessed of soil of unsurpassed fertility, and the most salubrious climate ... The slave population does not naturally increase, but is sustained by a constant arrival of large importations from Africa ... The creole population are the occupiers of the land, and owners of the slaves producing the wealth of the island ... sugar, coffee and tobacco ... affairs [in Cuba] have now reached [the point] that the Cuban is taxed beyond the exactions imposed on the citizens of any other known community.... The Cubans, in their natural aspirations for liberty, have been checked by the fact, that being deprived of arms by the government, they are placed on one hand in danger of the insurrection of slaves forced upon them, and on the other at the mercy of a foreign mercenary and licentious soldiery quartered among them. Under these circumstances they perceive that their only chance of freedom is foreign aid, in some force, around which they can rally, give expression to their opinions, and assert their rights in the government. They now pay $20,000,000 per annum to their oppressors.... Accordingly an extensive organization was formed in Cuba and out of it. In New York was established an able periodical, La Verdad, to advocate the cause of Cuban freedom ... Several persons accused of writing those articles [in La Verdad] were arrested in Cuba [among them Cirilo Villaverde] ... a scholar, full of the generous enthusiasm and patriotism natural to a cultivated mind.

[His letter follows]

SAVANNAH, APRIL 19, 1849.

My Dear T,

At last I am resting under the wings of the American Eagle.

It may be that you are already apprised of my miraculous escape from the prison of Havana, where, as a man guilty of high treason, and accused of a capital crime by the District Attorney (Fiscal). I was lately watched with the greatest diligence. First, be it known to you that the District Attorney (Fiscal) had accused M, and me of a capital crime and that the Council decreed ten years' transportation against you, (three of the members being of opinion that you should be condemned to death), and against M and me six years' transportation. I succeeded in escaping two days after the Council of War had met, that is to say, the 31st of March, in the night. Since then I have received no intelligence from Havana and I do not know yet whether the Captain General has approved or disapproved the sentences. However, I believe he will approve it and then the unfortunate M, who remained in chains in the Castle ... to bear the torments of the iron hand that condemns him. Unfortunate youth!

CIRILO VILLAVERDE.

That our treaty obligations forbid any armed expedition to be fitted out within our borders against nations with which we are at peace, is undoubtedly the case; but the assumption that armed citizens are going to march against some particular state with which we are at peace, is a most absurd stretch of power. That American citizens have the full and undoubted right to enter into the service of any foreign nation, has frequently been asserted, and acted upon. Our gallant officers entered freely into the service of the Texans, when struggling for independence, and the Texans loaned money, bought arms, and procured aid among us, as did also Don Carlos, in London, when he attempted to seize the crown of Spain. Hundreds of similar instances present themselves, affording precedents that justify the entering into the service of the Cubans, against their ruthless oppressors. The practicability of the enterprise is unquestionable. A force of 3[000] to 4,000 Americans, landed in Cuba, in the winter months, would have to contend with perhaps 14,000 Spaniards, divided in small garrisons, throughout the island, each at the mercy of the people, if those people have a sufficient rallying point. Sixty days probably would suffice to place a provisional government at the head of affairs, declare the independence of the island, organize its revenues, and bid defiance to the utmost power of Spain.

Under the influence of annexation, the property of the Cubans would immediately equalise with that of similar property in the United States, and the sugar plantations of Louisiana would find, in the hitherto untouched soil of Cuba, the means of underselling the world in sugar; while the capacity of Cuba, to purchase and consume the beef, ham, flour, and other supplies of the Western states, would develope [sic] itself in an almost limitless degree. The $20,000,000 now drawn from the island, annually, for remittances to Madrid, accumulating in the island as a capital in the employment of its free industry, would draw desirable settles from all nations to avail themselves of its limitless advantages.

Source: The United States Magazine, and Democratic Review, Vol. 25, No. cxxxv, September 1849, pp. 197, 198, 200, 203, 205, http://cdl.library.cornell.edu/cgi-bin/moa/moa-cgi?notisid=AGD 1642-0025&byte=226352056.

99. Excerpts from a Letter from U.S. Secretary of State James Buchanan to R. M. Saunders, June 17, 1848

This excerpt is part of a set of a dozen letters exchanged between Secretary of State James Buchanan and R. M. Saunders of the American legation in Madrid, Spain. In this particular letter, Buchanan calls attention to conditions in Cuba and explains how much more productive the island would be as a part of the United States. It expresses the thinking of the time that as long as the island was under Spanish rule, the United States could tolerate it but it did not want Cuba to fall into another country's hands. The letters talk about rumors of Great Britain's interest in Cuba and the American fear of a British presence so close to the U.S. coastline.

Mr. Buchanan to Mr. Saunders—[Extract.]
[No. 21.] Department of State,
Washington, June 17, 1848.

Sir: By direction of the President, I now call your attention to the present condition and future prospects of Cuba. The fate of this island must ever be deeply interesting to the people of the United States. We are content that it shall continue to be a colony of Spain. Whilst in her possession, we have nothing to apprehend. Besides, we are bound to her by the ties of ancient friendship, and we sincerely desire to render these perpetual.

But we can never consent that this island shall become a colony of any other European Power. In the possession of Great Britain, or any strong naval power, it might prove ruinous both to the domestic and foreign commerce, and even endanger the Union of States. The highest and first duty of every independent nation is to provide for its own safety; and, acting upon this principle, we should be compelled to resist the acquisition of Cuba by any powerful maritime State, will all the means which Providence has placed at our command.

Cuba is almost within sight of the coast of Florida, situated between that State and the peninsula of Yucatan, and possessing the deep, capacious, and impregnably fortified harbor of Havana. If this island were under the dominion of Great Britain, she could command both the inlets to the Gulf of Mexico. She would thus be enabled, in time of war, effectively to blockade the mouth of the Mississippi, and to deprive all the Western States of this Union, as well as those within the Gulf, teeming as they are with an industrious and enterprising population, of a foreign market for their immense productions. But this is not the worst: she could also destroy the commerce by sea between our ports on the Gulf and our Atlantic ports, a commerce of nearly as great a value as the whole of our foreign trade. Is there any reason to believe that Great Britain desires to acquire the island of Cuba? We know that it has been her uniform policy, throughout her past history, to seize upon every valuable commercial point throughout the world, whenever circumstances have placed this in her power. And what point so valuable as the Island of Cuba? ... Were Cuba a portion of the United States, it would be difficult to estimate the amount of breadstuffs, rice, cotton, and other agricultural as well as manufacturing and mechanical productions; of lumber, of the produce of our fisheries and of other articles which would find a market if that island, in exchange for their coffee, sugar, tobacco, and other productions.

Yours, very respectfully,
James Buchanan

Source: Important Documents. Attempted Purchase of Cuba. *New York Daily Times,* November 24, 1852; front page.

100. Excerpts from the Clayton-Bulwer Treaty, 1850

The chief rival of the United States in the Caribbean and Central America was Great Britain. Great Britain had the mightiest navy in the world and maintained a global empire. Spain was on the decline; most of its American colonies had won their independence; its last major colonies in the New World were Cuba and Puerto Rico. The U.S. and Great Britain competed over who would build and control an Atlantic-Pacific inter-ocean canal throughout the 1850s. However, despite its bluster that the Americas were for Americans, and the waving of the Monroe Doctrine (1823), the United States could ill afford a war with Great Britain. In Central America, Great Britain claimed

Belize, the Mosquito Coast, and the Bay Islands. The United States had treaties with Nicaragua and Honduras. In order to ease tensions, the United States and Great Britain signed the Clayton-Bulwer Treaty in 1850. The chief negotiators were U.S. Secretary of State John M. Clayton and Great Britain's Sir Henry Lytton Bulwer. The Treaty stipulated that neither the United States nor Great Britain would ask for exclusive control of an inter-ocean canal. The treaty said that neither the United States nor Great Britain would "occupy, or fortify, or colonize, or assume or exercise any dominion over Nicaragua, Costa Rica, the Mosquito Coast, or any part of Central America."

ARTICLE I

The governments of the United States and Great Britain hereby declare, that neither the one nor the other will ever obtain or maintain for itself any exclusive control over the said ship canal; agreeing that neither will ever erect or maintain any fortifications commanding the same or in the vicinity thereof, or occupy, or fortify, or colonize, or assume or exercise any dominion over Nicaragua, Costa Rica, the Mosquito coast, or any part of Central America; nor will either make use of any protection which either affords or may afford, or any alliance which either has or may have, to or with any State or people, for the purpose of erecting or maintaining any such fortifications, or of occupying, fortifying, or colonizing Nicaragua, Costa Rica, the Mosquito coast, or any part of Central America, or of assuming or exercising dominion over the same; nor will the United States or Great Britain take advantage of any intimacy, or use any alliance, connection, or influence that either may possess, with any State or government through whose territory the said canal may pass, for the purpose of acquiring or holding, directly or indirectly, for the citizens or subjects of the one, any rights or advantages in regard to commerce or navigation through the said canal which shall not be offered on the same terms to the citizens or subjects of the other.

...

ARTICLE VIII

The governments of the United States and Great Britain having not only desired, in entering into this convention, to accomplish a particular object, but also to establish a general principle, they hereby agree to extend their protection, by treaty stipulations, to any other practicable communications, whether by canal or railway, across the isthmus which connects North and South America, and especially to the inter oceanic communications, should the same prove to be practicable, whether by canal or railway, which are now proposed to be established by the way of Tehuantepec or Panama. In granting, however, their joint protection to any such canals or railways as are by this article specified, it is always understood by the United States and Great Britain that the parties constructing or owning the same shall impose no other charges or conditions of traffic thereupon than the aforesaid govern[ments] shall approve of as just and equitable; and that the same canals or railways, being open to the citizens and subjects of the United States and Great Britain on equal terms, shall also be open on like terms to the citizens and subjects of every other State which is willing to grant thereto such protection as the United States and Great Britain engage to afford.

Source: Convention between the United States of America and Her Britannic Majesty; April 19, 1850. Courtesy of The Avalon Project at Yale Law School, http://www.yale.edu/lawweb/avalon/diplomacy/britain/br1850.htm.

101. Excerpts from President Millard Fillmore's State of the Union Address, December 2, 1851

Millard Fillmore (1800–1874), the 13th president of the United States, served from 1850 to 1853. He became president when Zachary Taylor (1784–1850) died in office. As president, Fillmore focused on strengthening U.S. hegemony in the hemisphere and limiting the nation's commitments elsewhere in the world. The Clayton-Bulwer Treaty of 1850 did not end the competition between United States and Great Britain over control of the Caribbean and Central America nor who would control the construction of a canal joining the Atlantic and Pacific Oceans. During his tenure Fillmore acted aggressively, dispatching warships to protect U.S. merchant ships from British interference. Fillmore also supported filibustering expeditions bound for Cuba from American soil. The most notorious was that of Venezuelan Narciso López (1797–1851), who was captured and executed by Spanish troops in 1851. In the following excerpt, President Fillmore describes American attitude toward Spain and Cuba and the expedition of Narciso López as well as events in the Isthmus of Panama.

Fellow-Citizens of the Senate and of the House of Representatives:

Since the close of the last Congress certain Cubans and other foreigners resident in the United States, who were more or less concerned in the previous invasion of Cuba, instead of being discouraged by its failure have again abused the hospitality of this country by making it the scene of the equipment of another military expedition against that possession of Her Catholic Majesty, in which they were countenanced, aided, and joined by citizens of the United States. On receiving intelligence that such designs were entertained, I lost no time in issuing such instructions to the proper officers of the United States as seemed to be called for by the occasion. By the proclamation a copy of which is herewith submitted I also warned those who might be in danger of being inveigled into this scheme of its unlawful character and of the penalties which they would incur. For some time there was reason to hope that these measures had sufficed to prevent any such attempt. This hope, however, proved to be delusive. Very early in the morning of the 3rd of August, a steamer called the *Pampero* departed from New Orleans for Cuba, having on board upward of 400 armed men with evident intentions to make war upon the authorities of the island. This expedition was set on foot in palpable violation of the laws of the United States. Its leader was a Spaniard, and several of the chief officers and some others engaged in it were foreigners. The persons composing it, however, were mostly citizens of the United States.

Before the expedition set out, and probably before it was organized, a slight insurrectionary movement, which appears to have been soon suppressed, had taken place in the eastern quarter of Cuba. The importance of this movement was, unfortunately, so much exaggerated in the accounts of it published in this country that these adventurers seem to have been led to believe that the Creole population of the island not only desired to throw off the authority of the mother country, but had resolved upon that step and had begun a well-concerted enterprise for effecting it. The persons engaged in the expedition were generally young and ill informed. The steamer in which they embarked left New Orleans stealthily and without a clearance. After touching at Key West, she proceeded to the coast of Cuba, and on the night between the 11th and 12th of August, landed the persons on board at Playtas, within about 20 leagues of Havana.

The main body of them proceeded to and took possession of an inland village 6 leagues distant, leaving others to follow in charge of the baggage as soon as the means of transportation could be obtained. The latter, having taken up their line of march to connect themselves with the main body, and having proceeded about 4 leagues into the country, were attacked on the morning of the 13th by a body of Spanish troops, and a bloody conflict ensued, after which they retreated to the place of disembarkation, where about 50 of them obtained boats and reembarked therein. They were, however, intercepted among the keys near the shore by a Spanish steamer cruising on the coast, captured, and carried to Havana, and after being examined before a military court were sentenced to be publicly executed, and the sentence was carried into effect on the 16th of August.

On receiving information of what had occurred, Commodore Foxhall A. Parker was instructed to proceed in the steam frigate *Saranac* to Havana and inquire into the charges against the persons executed, the circumstances under which they were taken, and whatsoever referred to their trial and sentence. Copies of the instructions from the Department of State to him and of his letters to that Department are herewith submitted.

According to the record of the examination, the prisoners all admitted the offenses charged against them, of being hostile invaders of the island. At the time of their trial and execution, the main body of the invaders was still in the field making war upon the Spanish authorities and Spanish subjects. After the lapse of some days, being overcome by the Spanish troops, they dispersed on the 24th of August. [Narciso] López, their leader, was captured some days after, and executed on the 1st of September. Many of his remaining followers were killed or died of hunger and fatigue, and the rest were made prisoners. Of these, none appear to have been tried or executed. Several of them were pardoned upon application of their friends and others, and the rest, about 160 in number, were sent to Spain. Of the final disposition made of these, we have no official information.

Such is the melancholy result of this illegal and ill-fated expedition. Thus, thoughtless young men have been induced by false and fraudulent representations to violate the law of their country through rash and unfounded expectations of assisting to accomplish political revolutions in other states, and have lost their lives in the undertaking. Too severe a judgment can hardly be passed by the indignant sense of the community upon those who, being better informed themselves, have yet led away the ardor of youth and an ill-directed love of political liberty. The correspondence between this Government and that of Spain relating to this transaction is herewith communicated.

Although these offenders against the laws have forfeited the protection of their country, yet the Government may, so far as consistent with its obligations to other countries and its fixed purpose to maintain and enforce the laws, entertain sympathy for their unoffending families and friends, as well as a feeling of compassion for themselves. Accordingly, no proper effort has been spared and none will be spared to procure the release of such citizens of the United States engaged in this unlawful enterprise as are now in confinement in Spain; but it is to be hoped that such interposition with the Government of that country may not be considered as affording any ground of expectation that the Government of the United States will hereafter feel itself under any obligation of duty to intercede for the liberation or pardon of such persons as are flagrant offenders against the law of nations and the laws of the United States. These laws must be executed. If we desire to maintain our respectability among the nations of the earth, it behooves us to enforce steadily and sternly the neutrality acts passed by Congress and to follow as far as may be the violation of those acts with condign punishment.

But what gives a peculiar criminality to this invasion of Cuba is that, under the lead of Spanish subjects and with the aid of citizens of the United States, it had its origin with many in motives of cupidity. Money was advanced by individuals, probably in considerable amounts, to purchase Cuban bonds, as they have been called, issued by López, sold, doubtless, at a very large discount, and for the payment of which the public lands and public property of Cuba, of whatever kind, and the fiscal resources of the people and government of that island, from whatever source to be derived, were pledged, as well as the good faith of the government expected to be established. All these means of payment, it is evident, were only to be obtained by a process of bloodshed, war, and revolution. None will deny that those who set on foot military expeditions against foreign states by means like these are far more culpable than the ignorant and the necessitous whom they induce to go forth as the ostensible parties in the proceeding. These originators of the invasion of Cuba seem to have determined with coolness and system upon an undertaking which should disgrace their country, violate its laws, and put to hazard the lives of ill-informed and deluded men. You will consider whether further legislation be necessary to prevent the perpetration of such offenses in future.

No individuals have a right to hazard the peace of the country or to violate its laws upon vague notions of altering or reforming governments in other states. This principle is not only reasonable in itself and in accordance with public law, but is Engrafted into the codes of other nations as well as our own. But while such are the sentiments of this Government, it may be added that every independent nation must be presumed to be able to defend its possessions against unauthorized individuals banded together to attack them. The Government of the United States at all times since its establishment has abstained and has sought to restrain the citizens of the country from entering into controversies between other powers, and to observe all the duties of neutrality. At an early period of the Government, in the Administration of Washington, several laws were passed for this purpose. The main provisions of these laws were reenacted by the act of April 1818, by which, amongst other things, it was declared that—

If any person shall, within the territory or jurisdiction of the United States, begin, or set on foot, or provide or prepare the means for, any military expedition or enterprise to be carried on from thence against the territory or dominions of any foreign prince or state, or of any colony, district, or people, with whom the United States are at peace, every person so offending shall be deemed guilty of a high misdemeanor, and shall be fined not exceeding $3,000 and imprisoned not more than three years.

And this law has been executed and enforced to the full extent of the power of the Government from that day to this.

In proclaiming and adhering to the doctrine of neutrality and nonintervention, the United States have not followed the lead of other civilized nations; they have taken the lead themselves and have been followed by others. This was admitted by one of the most eminent of modern British statesmen, who said in Parliament, while a minister of the Crown, "that if he wished for a guide in a system of neutrality he should take that laid down by America in the days of Washington and the secretaryship of Jefferson"; and we see, in fact, that the act of Congress of 1818 was followed the succeeding year by an act of the Parliament of England substantially the same in its general provisions. Up to that time there had been no similar law in England, except certain highly penal statutes passed in the reign of George II, prohibiting English subjects from enlisting in foreign service, the avowed object of which statutes was that foreign armies, raised for the purpose of restoring the House of Stuart to the throne, should not be strengthened by recruits from England herself.

All must see that difficulties may arise in carrying the laws referred to into execution in a country now having 3,000 or 4,000 miles of seacoast, with an infinite number of ports and harbors and small inlets, from some of which unlawful expeditions may suddenly set forth, without the knowledge of Government, against the possessions of foreign states.

"Friendly relations with all, but entangling alliances with none," has long been a maxim with us. Our true mission is not to propagate our opinions or impose upon other countries our form of government by artifice or force, but to teach by example and show by our success, moderation, and justice, the blessings of self-government and the advantages of free institutions. Let every people choose for itself and make and alter its political institutions to suit its own condition and convenience. But while we avow and maintain this neutral policy ourselves, we are anxious to see the same forbearance on the part of other nations whose forms of government are different from our own. The deep interest which we feel in the spread of liberal principles and the establishment of free governments and the sympathy with which we witness every struggle against oppression forbid that we should be indifferent to a case in which the strong arm of a foreign power is invoked to stifle public sentiment and repress the spirit of freedom in any country.

The Governments of Great Britain and France have issued orders to their naval commanders on the West India station to prevent, by force if necessary, the landing of adventurers from any nation on the island of Cuba with hostile intent. The copy of a memorandum of a conversation on this subject between the charge' d'affaires of Her Britannic Majesty and the Acting Secretary of State and of a subsequent note of the former to the Department of State are herewith submitted, together with a copy of a note of the Acting Secretary of State to the minister of the French Republic and of the reply of the latter on the same subject. These papers will acquaint you with the grounds of this interposition of two leading commercial powers of Europe, and with the apprehensions, which this Government could not fail to entertain, that such interposition, if carried into effect, might lead to abuses in derogation of the maritime rights of the United States. The maritime rights of the United States are founded on a firm, secure, and well-defined basis; they stand upon the ground of national independence and public law, and will be maintained in all their full and just extent. The principle which this Government has heretofore solemnly announced, it still adheres to, and will maintain under all circumstances and at all hazards. That principle is that in every regularly documented merchant vessel the crew who navigate it and those on board of it will find their protection in the flag which is over them. No American ship can be allowed to be visited or searched for the purpose of ascertaining the character of individuals on board, nor can there be allowed any watch by the vessels of any foreign nation over American vessels on the coast of the United States or the seas adjacent thereto. It will be seen by the last communication from the British charge' d'affaires to the Department of State that he is authorized to assure the Secretary of State that every care will be taken that in executing the preventive measures against the expeditions which the United States Government itself has denounced as not being entitled to the protection of any government, no interference shall take place with the lawful commerce of any nation.

In addition to the correspondence on this subject herewith submitted, official information has been received at the Department of State of assurances by the French Government that in the orders given to the French naval forces they were expressly instructed, in any operations they might engage in, to respect the flag of the United States wherever it might appear, and to commit no act of hostility upon any vessel or armament under its protection.

Ministers and consuls of foreign nations are the means and agents of communication between us and those nations, and it is of the utmost importance that while residing in the country they should feel a perfect security so long as they faithfully discharge their respective duties and are guilty of no violation of our laws. This is the admitted law of nations and no country has a deeper interest in maintaining it than the United States. Our commerce spreads over every sea and visits every clime, and our ministers and consuls are appointed to protect the interests of that commerce as well as to guard the peace of the country and maintain the honor of its flag. But how can they discharge these duties unless they be themselves protected? And if protected, it must be by the laws of the country in which they reside. And what is due to our own public functionaries residing in foreign nations is exactly the measure of what is due to the functionaries of other governments residing here. As in war the bearers of flags of truce are sacred, or else wars would be interminable, so in peace ambassadors, public ministers, and consuls, charged with friendly national intercourse, are objects of especial respect and protection, each according to the rights belonging to his rank and station. In view of these important principles, it is with deep mortification and regret I announce to you that during the excitement growing out of the executions at Havana, the office of Her Catholic Majesty's consul at New Orleans was assailed by a mob, his property destroyed, the Spanish flag found in the office carried off and torn in pieces, and he himself induced to flee for his personal safety, which he supposed to be in danger. On receiving intelligence of these events I forthwith directed the attorney of the United States residing at New Orleans to inquire into the facts and the extent of the pecuniary loss sustained by the consul, with the intention of laying them before you, that you might make provision for such indemnity to him as a just regard for the honor of the nation and the respect which is due to a friendly power might, in your judgment, seem to require. The correspondence upon this subject between the Secretary of State and Her Catholic Majesty's minister plenipotentiary is herewith transmitted.

I am happy to announce that an interoceanic communication from the mouth of the St. John to the Pacific has been so far accomplished as that passengers have actually traversed it and merchandise has been transported over it, and when the canal shall have been completed according to the original plan, the means of communication will be further improved. It is understood that a considerable part of the railroad across the Isthmus of Panama has been completed, and that the mail and passengers will in future be conveyed thereon. Whichever of the several routes between the two oceans may ultimately prove most eligible for travelers to and from the different States on the Atlantic and Gulf of Mexico and our coast on the Pacific, there is little reason to doubt that all of them will be useful to the public, and will liberally reward that individual enterprise by which alone they have been or are expected to be carried into effect. Peace has been concluded between the contending parties in the island of St. Domingo, and, it is hoped, upon a durable basis. Such is the extent of our commercial relations with that island that the United States can not fail to feel a strong interest in its tranquility.

Source: PresidentialRhetoric.com, http://www.presidentialrhetoric.com/historicspeeches/fillmore/stateoftheunion1851.html.

102. Excerpts from Martin R. Delany, "A Glance at Ourselves, Conclusion," 1852

Over 10 million African slaves were imported to the Americas. In the United States, there was interest among the descendants of the original slaves to learn about their presence in the disparate parts of the Western Hemisphere. This interest was heightened by the abolitionist movement. By the 1840s, there were a number of free African Americans in the United States who were writing books and articles and speaking for their own cause of freedom. In 1852, Martin R. Delany (1812–1885) wrote *The Condition, Elevation, Emigration, and Destiny of the Colored People in the United States.* Delany had been taught to read by his mother and, when his father purchased the family's freedom in 1823, Delany went to the North. Delany wrote articles that were published in William Lloyd Garrison's anti-slavery newspaper, the *Liberator.* Along with Frederick Douglass, he founded the *North Star,* an African American freedom newspaper. Delany was admitted to Harvard Medical School in 1850 but was dismissed because of the racist backlask from fellow students. He practiced medicine in Pittsburgh. Delaney evolved into a Black nationalist and advocated African American immigration to Africa. In his search for a Black Israel, Delany called for the immigration of African Americans to Central America and other parts of the Americas because he believed that these places would be conducive to African American settlement and he recognized the presence of large African populations already there.

We have advised an emigration to Central and South America, and even to Mexico and the West Indies to those who prefer to go to either of the last named places, all of which are free countries, Brazil being the only real slave holding State in South America, there being nominal slavery in Dutch Guiana, Peru, Buenos Ayres, Paraguay, and Uruguay, in all of which places colored people have equality in social, civil, political, and religious privileges; Brazil making it punishable with death to import slaves into the empire.

Our oppressors, when urging us to go to Africa, tell us that we are better adapted to the climate than they, that the physical condition of the constitution of colored people better endures the heat of warm climates than that of the whites; this we are willing to admit, without argument, without adducing the physiological reason why, that colored people can and do stand warm climates better than whites; and find an answer fully to the point in the fact that they also stand modified that white people can stand; therefore, according to our oppressors's own showing, we are a superior race, being endowed with properties fitting us for all parts of the earth, while they are only adapted to certain parts. Of course, this proves our right and duty to live wherever we may choose; while the white race may only live where they can. We are content with the fact, and have ever claimed it. Upon this rock, they and we shall ever agree. Of the West India Islands, Santa Cruz, belonging to Denmark; Porto Rico and Cuba with its little adjuncts, belonging to Spain, are the only slaveholding Islands among them, three fifths of the whole population of Cuba being colored people who cannot and will not much longer endure the burden and the yoke. They only want intelligent leaders of their own color, when they are ready at any moment to charge to the conflict to liberty or death. The remembrance of the noble mulat[t]o, Placido, the gentleman, scholar, poet, and intended Chief Engineer of the Army of Liberty and Freedom in Cuba; and the equally noble black, Charles Blair, who was to have been Commander in Chief, who were shamefully put to death in 1844, by that living monster, Capt. Gen. O'Donnell, is still fresh and indelible to the mind of every bondsman of Cuba. In our own country, the United States, there are three million five hundred thousand slaves; and we, the nominally free colored people, are six hundred thousand in number; estimating one sixth to be men, we have one hundred thousand able bodied freeman, which will make a powerful auxiliary in any country to which we may become adopted, an ally not to be despised by any power on earth. We love our country, dearly love her, but she don't love us, she despises us and bids us begone, driving us from her embraces; but we do go, whatever love we have for her, we shall love the country none the less that receives us as her adopted children.... Doomed by the Creator, to servility and degradation; The SERVANT of the white man, And despised of every nation!

Source: Martin R. Delany, *The Condition, Elevation, Emigration, and Destiny of the Colored People of the United States*, and *Official Report of the Niger Valley Exploring Party*. Philadelphia: The Author, 1852. In Chapter XXIII. Courtesy of the West Virginia Humanities Council and the George Washington Carver Institute, http://www.libraries.wvu.edu/delany/conclude.htm.

103. Excerpts from Pierre Soulé, "The Cuban Question: Defence of the López Expedition," January 25, 1853

U.S. senator from Louisiana, Pierre Soulé (1801–1870), was born in Paris, France, and migrated to New Orleans, Louisiana, via Haiti. Soulé became a lawyer and prospered in this largely French-speaking part of Louisiana. Elected to the Louisiana State Senate in 1845, he was appointed to the United States Senate in 1847, Soulé was a rogue, charming and multi-lingual. In 1853, President Franklin Pierce offered Soulé the mission to Spain with the hope of acquiring Cuba from Spain. News of Soulé's mission leaked out and when he arrived in Spain he was told he was a persona non grata. This is a passage from a speech by Soulé in the U.S. Senate where he speaks against a resolution by Sen. Lewis Cass (1782–1866) of Michigan to respect Spain's sovereignty over Cuba. Relations between the United States and Spain had worsened since Spain's execution of the Venezuelan filibuster Narciso López and many of his soldiers—some of whom were Americans. The Senate split along sectional grounds. The following documents includes Cass's resolution and Soulé's vigorous arguments against it. He takes this occasion to defend the López expedition and U.S. pretensions to Cuba.

Resolved by the Senate and House of Representatives of the United States of America in Congress assembled, That the United States do hereby declare that "the American Continents, by the free and independent position which they have assumed and maintain, are henceforth not to be considered as subjects for future colonization by any European power;" and while "existing rights should be respected," and will be by the United States, they owe it to their own "safety and interests" to announce, as they now do, "that no future European colony or dominion shall, with their consent, be planted or established on any part of the North American continent;" and should the attempt be made, they thus deliberately declare that it will be viewed as an act originating in motives regardless of their "interests and their safety," and which will leave them free to adopt such measures as an independent nation may justly adopt in defense of its rights and its honor.

And be it further resolved, That while the United States disclaim any designs upon the Island of Cuba inconsistent with the laws of nations and with their duties to Spain, they consider it due to the vast importance of the subject to make known, in this solemn manner, that they should view all efforts on the part of any other power to procure possession, whether peaceably or forcibly, of that island, which, as a naval or military position, might under circumstances easy to be foreseen, become dangerous to their southern coast, to the Gulf of Mexico, and to the mouth of the Mississippi, as unfriendly acts directed against them, to be resisted by all the means in their power.

Mr. Soule: The sole object I had in view, Mr. President, when, on a former occasion I moved the postponement of this question or debate, was to protect myself against the danger of a too hasty expression of sentiment with reference to so great and momentous a subject, as that in the discussion of which we are now engaged. I felt much unwillingness to give my judgment crudely upon any scheme of speculative or abstract policy, concerning matters which in the significant language of my honorable friend from Michigan, (Mr. Lewis Cass,) were so liable to present themselves from hour to hour for practical consideration.

[The] occasion was taken to censure the President for ... disclosing all the Cuban correspondence. Why so? Was it because by so doing, he disclosed the fact that we were willing to purchase that island, and then in the same breath we state to the world, that we ourselves are ready now and ever to purchase it, if it should ever be for sale? Was it because it disclosed the price which one of our Presidents was willing to give for it? Yet honorable Senators stated from their seats here, that they are now ready to purchase it at any price. I cannot see why we should pass censure upon the President, for doing the very thing that we are doing in our places in this Hall. But while we censured him for matters which in themselves do not perhaps strictly justify the censure, I had wished that some voice here might have been heard denouncing the fact of placing before the public eye a correspondence which the present administration must have found in a private place under seal, and considered by those who preceded them as a secret of State. But while we thus unsparingly denounce him for having abused the discretion left to him in the choice of the papers which he was to send to the other House, we praise him for the course which he pursued with reference to our late difficulties with the Cuban authorities.

I cannot give my assent to the course which the present Administration pursued towards Spain in whatever difficulties have arisen between that Power and our own citizens. And God knows I am unwilling to do any wrong to Spain, as I shall presently show. But I cannot yield my commendation to this Administration for the course which they have thought proper to pursue.

Now, in the first occurrences which took place upon the occasion of the unfortunate expedition of [Narciso] Lopez, what do we find! We find that though our own citizens had been left without protection, had been awarded none of those securities which under the treaty, they were entitled to claim at the hands of the Spanish authorities, when Com. Parker approaches the Captain General and asks for information as to the motives which could have impelled him to follow such a course, his answer was—"Your own President has denounced these men as pirates, and as pirates I have treated them." And when our Consul, Mr. Owen, approaches him, pleading for mercy, says [General José de la] Concha—"You know well that what you do here is against the will and wishes of the President of the United States." Against his wishes! And is his Administration to receive Democratic commendation for having thus used their power in the contest between our own citizens and the Spanish authorities of Havana? Are we ready to endorse Mr. Fillmore's [Millard] (1800–1874) proclamation, the edict of Concha [General José de la Concha—a field marshal of Spain] which I have just read, and the slaughter of the gallant [Col. W. S.] Crittenden [a member of the López expedition who was executed] and his fifty associates who were immolated at Havana! Are we ready to endorse all this in the face of facts which I have thus cursorily laid before the Senate! I cannot do so.

But these young men are branded again and again with those ugly names which are to be found in almost every column of those newspaper which seem to be devoted exclusively to denouncing whoever may show the least sympathy for the suffering Cubans. They are called "Marauders." Ah! were they Marauders, these youthful enthusiasts who congregated in one of our southern cities, at the call, as they thought, of their suffering brethren who went to a foreign country, landed there, knowing that they were to meet a million of inhabitants and 25,000 soldiers in arms to protect them? What kind of marauders were they who chose to go to such a country with the hope of plunder, and who, upon setting their feet upon the island, sent off, with their last adieus to their mothers and sisters, the very vessel that had brought them there? Why, Sir, they were young men against whom to this very day Spain herself has not been able to bring successfully the charge of the least delinquency. And yet we brand them with names declined to hand them down to posterity as common robbers.

Mr. Seward—Will the honorable gentlemen from La. [Louisiana], (Mr. Soule) allow me to ask, by way of information and explanation, as I known he wishes to be perfectly fair and just, whether in any official document issued by this Government, these persons were stigmatized as or termed pirates? Does he affirm such to be the fact?

Mr. Soule—[Gen.] Concha did not care much about the terms used, but he took care of the meaning. And if you place a man beyond the law, if you denounce him as being no longer under its protection, call him robber, or pirate, or outcast— names signify nothing; he is doomed.

I was going on to ask whether he was a common robber, a common robber, that young Crittenden, who so nobly met his fate? Were his last words the words of a robber, when, summoned to kneel, he proudly answered, "I never kneel but to my God!" Was he a common robber whose last words could be these: "You may kill me, but you cannot kill that hope which bounds within my heart, and denounces your cruelty at the bar of the future?" No, he was not a common robber.

But the honorable Senators disagree with the President in other respects. They are for purchasing Cuba now and ever: the President is against purchasing at present. It must be somewhat interesting to know what his reasons are for objecting to the acquisition of the Island of Cuba at present ... the present administration feels unwilling, at the present time, to have Cuba incorporated into the Union. The condition of the present population of that island is one ground, the other is predicated upon domestic considerations ... what are the domestic considerations which constitute an impediment at the present time in the way of the acquisition of Cuba, which may not constitute an impediment hereafter? I will put the question to Southern Senators particularly. What are those circumstances, what is the condition of the present population of Cuba, and what are the domestic considerations which constitute our impediment now to this Administration accepting the transfer of the Island of Cuba to us, which could not be an obstacle hereafter?

It is known that upon all hands, in every Administration, from the lips of every statesman who has addressed himself to the subject, we have the admission that Cuba is bound to be ours—so say they; and still, though bound to become ours, the time has not yet arrived. My honorable friend, with feelings I am sure congenial with my own, says: Let the fruit become ripe, it is sure to fall, and falling, to fall in our lap. Not so with the President. My friend is ready to purchase at any time and at any price. The President is unwilling to do so. Why? Because of the present condition of its population; because of domestic reasons ... Viscount Palmerston to Lord Howden, dated, "Foreign Office, Oct. 20, 1851" ... "the slaves of Cuba form a large portion, and by no means an unimportant one, of the population of Cuba, and that any steps taken to provide for their emancipation would, therefore, as far as the black population is concerned, be quite in unison with the recommendation made by Her Majesty's Government, that measures should be adopted for contenting the people of Cuba, with a view to secure the connection between that island and the Spanish crown; and it must be evident that, if the negro population of Cuba were rendered free, that fact would create a most powerful element of resistance to any scheme for annexing Cuba to the United States, where slavery still exists."

[Soulé]—If England has any power, any influence with Spain, you may now see in what condition you will find the Island. Tear up the veil that conceals the proximate future, and ask yourselves this question: If we do wait, in what condition will Cuba be? I am against purchasing Cuba—I shall come to that presently. I am now arguing upon the premises which are furnished me by those who have spoken upon this subject, and by the President himself; and I ask you, in what condition do you expect to find the Island of Cuba, if you wait much longer? I will tell you.

Here is a Madrid paper referring to the same subject and showing what impression had already been produced by the communication of Viscount Palmerston.

"It is well for all to know, whether native or foreign that the Island of Cuba can only be Spanish or African. When the day comes when the Spaniards will be found to abandon it, they will do so by bequeathing their sway to the blacks."

Here stands, in bold relief before you, the destiny which, under British influence, awaits your relations with that Island. Let Southern senators, particularly ponder this.

You deny the policy of the past. Statesmen who have preceded you have asserted, in their communications, that the idea of purchasing Cuba would only be taken into consideration if there should be an impossibility of maintaining Spain in the possession of that island. We have asserted, heretofore—and an English writer very pointedly refers to these repeated assertions—that our object was not to get possession of the island, but to maintain Spain in the dominion. And therefore, as far as that goes, our present disposition to purchase, alters the policy of the past. Sir, I am against purchasing Cuba. Whoever knows anything of Castilian pride, must be aware that Spaniards can never be brought to sell Cuba to us.

No, sir, I have still another objection against purchasing Cuba. There is something there that speaks aloud for those suffering Cubanos who call upon us for assistance. They are proud, and would not consent to this purchase. I am unwilling to move their susceptibilities; and thus, as far as a wish of mine can have any bearing upon any policy which might now or hereafter be pursued, the idea of purchasing Cuba has become an obsolete one and must be abandoned.... Spain is unwilling to sell, and from the surrounding political atmosphere, I do not know that we would run less danger in purchasing than in conquering the Island. I am against purchasing it. But, sir, I cannot dissemble the fact that in the present condition of the popular mind in these United States, a question is broken out which actually threatens us with peril. It may be upon us tomorrow, and it may not come to present its exigencies before a quarter of a century. But it may be upon us tomorrow, and it is for us to face the danger.

I want now to test the question whether England has always been as scrupulous herself with reference to that very possession, as she seems to be now-a-days, when we are ourselves interested.

It may seem strange, yet it is not the less true, that as early as 1739, England had attempted and had considered a *projet* of buccaneering, for the purpose of getting hold of that Island. I have it in my hands. I want to put the Senate in possession of one of the most curious facts of history in the last century.

A Proposal *to take the Island of Cuba with very little expense to England, by a Force raised in the American Colonies.*

If the Crown of England could become possessed of the Island of Cuba, that key of all America, no man of knowledge can denye [sic] but that Great Britain, in that case, must become possessed of the whole trade of the Spanish Empire there; and if the simple privilege of trading with those people, upon very high terms, is now become one of the greatest prizes contended for by all the Powers in Europe, surely England will not neglect any opportunity which is offered of acquiring such a possession as must infallibly secure that whole invaluable trade to its subjects alone, especially since Great Britain is now in a fair way of losing all the trade she has hitherto had with those ports. It is proposed, therefore, to take Cuba without putting England to any material expense or trouble, in ye following manner, viz:

For a person of conduct and experience to be commissioned from hence for the chief command in this expedition, to take Cuba, &c. That the number of men thus raised and armed shall consist of 10,000 ... it will be necessary to send instructions of the same import to the several Governors in America, to issue orders, and give their best assistance to fit out, with all expedition, such transports, &c., and men so equipped.

That when each Province has furnished their quota of transports and men, according to their ability, these shall immediately repair to one place appointed, which may be at South Carolina, and from thence proceed, under the command and direction of the person to be commissioned, from hence. They may, (if it shall appear advisable) in their passage, make a feint to take St. Augustine—and having managed that stratagem properly, they are to proceed to the Island of Cuba, and land in the Bay of Matanzas—that being a good harbor, and not guarded, yet lying the nearest of any other proper one to ye Havana. Here they shall land 700 or 800 men, more or less, as necessity shall require, and with that force to march down and pitch at a proper distance, to surround the Havana and cut off all manner of provisions going thereto by land; at the same time that some ships shall lye [*sic*] before the town, to prevent any provisions or relief coming to it by sea; in which situation that important place must surrender in a very short time. In order to render this conquest both sure and expeditious, it will be necessary to send six or eight sixty-gun ships, and two bomb ketches, with about 2,000 troops on board them.

If the conquest of Cuba is effected, a small part of the forces when does that, may, with very little trouble, take Porto Rico and St. Augustine, if it will appear advisable so to do. The British colonies in America, lying so near the object now in view, before ye knowledge of ye proposed attempt, can reach to Europe ye whole designe will be executed.

It may be asked, were Cuba taken, how it would be garrisoned without forces from England? for it is to be understood that ye American people who are proposed to be raised must not be compelled to stay in ye garrison against their own inclination. In answer to ye, it is enough to say, that ye proposer has also conceived a pretty certain method to garrison not only that, but all ye places mentioned, if they are taken, without much expense to England, but which he beggs leave to reserve to himself, it being too long to insert it here, till he sees how this proposal will be approved of Y. H.

Endorsed. "Proposals for taking Cuba, in America." In Mr. Hamilton's, of May ye 14th, 1739.

The Senate will see that these American filibusters and buccaneers who have, of late seemed to have attracted the attention of the whole world, had some precidents to follow; and it behooves not England to show herself very scrupulous with reference to anything which may take place here, when we find in her own archives such strange indications of similar *projets* of undertakings having been entertained by herself.

The communication of the British Minister, and that of the French Minister to our Government [protesting attempts to seize Cuba], contain nothing less than a threat, a positive and unequivocal threat, that if any attempt of the kind made by Lopez should be renewed, the United States would be made answerable for it. That threat remains still unanswered and unexplained, either by the Secretary of State or by any Senator upon this floor. Here is the precise language used: "The attacks which have been lately made upon the Island of Cuba, by lawless bands of adventurers from the United States, with the avowed design of taking possession of that island, have engaged the serious attention of Her Majesty's Government, the more especially as they are most anxious that the friendly relations now existing between

Great Britain and the United States should not be endangered, as they must be by a repetition of attacks such." Thus the United States are made answerable by France and England, for the attacks of "lawless bands of adventurers from the United States, with the avowed design of taking possession of that island." The correspondence acknowledges that the United States have in no way been engaged in those undertakings, yet we are here threatened, upon a renewal of the same undertaking, by another band of disorderly citizens, to be made answerable for it—and why? Because, I suppose they felt encouraged to hold that language to the United States, from the manner in which their interposition last year, their appearance in the waters of the Gulf of Mexico, had been received and treated by us. In vain did Mr. Crittenden insist upon an explanation from the British Minister. The only answer he could get from him, was a renewal of the assertion, for which the explanation had been demanded. And now we are told by those two proud powers, that if a new attempt be made upon the Island of Cuba, and made as described here, "by a lawless band of adventurers with the avowed design of taking possession of that island," peace between those two powers and the United States will be endangered.

One may well ask what interest do these two powers feel in the matter that should prompt them to take the subject in hand and to press it upon us in the threatening form which they have chosen to adopt!? In the instructions from the Ministers of France to M. Sartiges—I wish to remark here that the whole correspondence throughout bears the impress of such a perfect understanding existing between the two powers of France and Great Britain that the letters written by their respective representatives here are identical, word for word, the only difference being that the one is written in English and the other in French; but they are to all intents and purposes identical so are the instructions with that single difference ... I translate from the French as I read. "We have, therefore, sent to the commanders of our naval forces, in the Gulf of Mexico, instructions prescribing, that if the occasion should arise, to take the necessary measures in order to cooperate with the Spanish authorities for the purpose of defending the island (of Cuba) and maintaining its sovereignty in Spain. The Government of Her Britannic Majesty, prompted by the same feeling of respect for the rights of the Crown of Spain, and actuated by the same principles, has taken analogous steps in order to maintain Spain in the possession of Cuba, a possession which imports no loss to the relations between the great maritime powers than to Spain herself. Here we have the assertion upon the part of England and France, that their interests in Cuba arising out of the relations which now exist, is as great as that of Spain herself. That also has not been noted by the able Secretary of State who took in hand to answer that communication. Here, then, two powers come forth and tell you in the very teeth of your declaration, that you had no concern at all in the expedition of Lopez—they tell you that should that expedition be renewed you shall be made answerable for it. And why so? I suppose because they abrogate to themselves the right of instructing America as to what course she should pursue in reference to anything which passes within its borders; and it is because the interest which they feel in the occupancy of Cuba by Spain, arising out of those relations which have been lately created between France and England, is as deep as that of Spain herself. And yet we are told here, it will not do for us to take any steps in this matter; we are to remain still; we must not disturb the calm waters of the political sea. We may remain still, Mr. President, but we may yet find that the quiet we preserve is to be paid for dearly. But I shall come to this matter again.

And why should we speak of bucanneering [*sic*] now? ... I can hardly account for the forbearance we have exhibited whenever that question from any quarter has been pressed upon the consideration of this country. It is one thing certain, that the United States cannot be willing to disparage themselves in the eyes of the world by any interposition in the affairs of other nations that would not be justified by the strictest rules of propriety. That, no one can doubt. And while we are ready to let the world know that we shall respect the rights of others, it is proper that the world should also know, that, above all other rights, is the right of protecting ourselves. The right of self-defence is above every other right. What that right may be under peculiar exigencies, is not for me to say. Enough for those who may have the control of the destinies of this nation to decide for themselves as circumstances may demand. But in the mean time, I cannot bear the idea that we should divorce ourselves with respect to any attempt that may be made by European powers upon this continent, from the policy of the past.

[Soulé invokes the Monroe Doctrine (1823)] Why, sir, in the same message, on the occasion of the interept which we felt in the destinies of the Southern Republics of this continent, we find the following declaration:

"The United States consider any attempt on the part of the European powers to extend their system to any portion of this hemisphere, as dangerous to their peace and safety."

Here, again, whatever movement on the part of the European powers might be construed as having a tendency, in any way, to extend to this continent their own system, was considered as a flagrant *casus belli*. And will the Senate allow me to ask, what was the occasion which prompted President Monroe to lay down this principle? Was it, as it would seem from assertions which I have heard, that we were here being threatened by the European Powers? Not in the least. There had been no movement on the part of any European Power that could be constued by us as a threat. They had not sent their ambassadors here to teach us how we should deal with a neighboring island.

But this is not all; the doctrine of proximity—for this Monroe doctrine is not in the dark—the doctrine which, upon considerations of proximity, has been deemed by all writers on public laws as authorizing a government, in self protection, to do at times what, in the absence of that necessity, might be considered as wrong—that doctrine did not originate with Mr. Monroe; and it may be a matter of surprise for some Senators to learn—for it may have escaped many of them, as it has escaped me—that [Sen.] Rufus King (1755–1827) was originator, as far as American statesmen are concerned with it, of that doctrine. In 1801, being then at the Court of London, he hears that France is about to obtain possession of Louisiana by means of a retrocession on the part of Spain, of that country. He at once interposes, and interposes upon what ground? Upon the ground that the proximity, in which that possession is with the other possessions of the United States, made it a matter of paramount interest to us. And it is curious to see what he says in that respect. He was exceedingly guarded in his relations with the British Minister, and he contented himself with a very witty allusion, by which he meant to say, that though at present we could not be willing to endanger our situation in order to take possession of Louisiana, still we might insist upon Louisiana remaining in the possession of Spain. In speaking of the rumored cession of Louisiana by Spain to France, he supports the opinion that our policy should be to take care that it remains with Spain, and he quotes Montesquieu in the following words:

"It is happy for trading powers that God has permitted Turks and Spaniards to be in the world, since, of all nations, they are most proper to possess a great Empire with insignificance."

It was injustice to Spain on the part of Montesquieu no doubt; but it is important in the presentation of the present view, in order to show where originated the first idea that our interest required that this possession, which was in the hands of Spain, should go to no other power but the United States.

My object, Mr. President, has been merely to present the danger with which this delicate question is surrounded. I have sedulously abstained to express any opinion as to what course it might suit the policy of our Government, present or future, to pursue. It is not a matter of mine; it belongs to other hands. But, at the same time, I have deemed it my duty to show that the policy of the past teaches us, that wherever there is danger, it is our duty to provide for it. We have been reminded of the time when a mere invasion into Spain was considered a proper occasion for signifying to the world that we should not suffer European Powers to transfer to these shores anything of their own system of Government. We are told that the doctrine of 1824 was not intended to be carried beyond the circumstances in which it originated. What were they? I have already shown that not an act of the European powers could have been considered on the part of our Government as a threat. None of their vessels made their appearance here. Is it so now? See the fleet of England in the waters of Havana, French vessels in the Bay of Samana, the Bay Islands colonized, and lately, Belize transformed into a British Colony. And, if I am well instructed—and I think I am—while we are here debating these questions, in the presence of the correspondence that came to us yesterday, where repeated declarations are to be found on the part of England, as late as 1849 and 1850, that she does not mean, that she never meant to colonise—in the face of all these declarations, we have the fact staring us in the face that she has colonized the Bay Islands, and is now colonizing Belize. And something more; she has taken it for granted that Queen Isabel Secunda [sic] possesses all the rights in her real authority which her predecessors possessed over this continent. And she takes for granted, though the recognition of the independence of most of the South American Republics may have divested Spain of her title in so far as the limits of those Republics extend, that in so far as Belize is concerned, the title remains still in Spain. So says England, and she is at this very day suing for an actual transfer on the part of Spain of the absolute title to the whole strip of territory between the Atlantic and Pacific oceans.

Such is the situation, and while she is thus daring—while she shows us this unmistakable indication of her boldness, we are told, sir—politely told, as far as diplomatic communication can go, that two must enter into a treaty with England and France, not to lay hands on Cuba. Clearly, sir, should no circumstance justify on the part of the United States, any such attempt, and should nothing arise which could bring us forcibly to the necessity of placing our hands over that possession, Spain has nothing to apprehend from us. Our dispositions are and will be most friendly; but she would commit a great blunder if she could remain blind to the intimations of proximity to us. Let her take counsel of the experience of the past. Let her realise, under the promptings of that generosity so becoming to her race.... If she does it, why she may secure to herself all the advantages which she now enjoys from Cuba, by entering into treaties with that newly-created power. And, sir, I have no doubt, if Spain could be induced to view the question in that light, Cuba, proud as she is, herself, would not hesitate to tender her hand to the mother country, and probably to assume a part of the heavy burdens which weigh upon her. And, perhaps, I may be permitted to say, that, if in that struggle of generosity between the regenerated island and the mother country, a sponsor were necessary, the United States would easily tender themselves to become such for the island. But beyond that I repudiate all idea of possessing ourselves of that island in any other manner than those which the strict law of nations will authorize. If there is no danger for us in leaving that Island in the condition it now is, our duty is to maintain Spain in her possession; but if circumstances not within our control—circumstances over which two great maritime powers of Europe have assumed a controlling influence—if any such circumstances should arise, and if we should be placed in that situation where delay might be loss of our position for the future—then, of course, let us expect that our Government will take counsel from the exigency of the moment, and act as behooves a great nation....

Source: New York Daily Times, January 28, 1853, p. 1.

104. Ostend Manifesto, October 18, 1854

In a letter to President James Monroe on October 24, 1823, Thomas Jefferson (1743–1826) wrote, "I candidly confess that I have ever looked on Cuba as the most interesting addition which could ever be made to our system of States. The control which, with Florida, this island would give us over the Gulf of Mexico, and the countries and isthmus bordering on it, as well as all those whose waters flow into it, would fill up the measure of our political well-being." Jefferson was not alone in this sentiment and many Americans considered Cuba as appendage of this country that was politically and commercially vital to its prosperity. Given this mindset, and the experiences of the Texas War (1836) and the Mexican American War (1846–1848), both of which brought huge amounts of land and riches to the United States, many Americans looked for a pretext to seize Cuba. In March 1854, an incident occurred that encouraged American invention: the American steamer *Black Warrior* anchored in Havana, Cuba. Spanish authorities apprehended the ship, its cargo, and its crew. Only sectional struggle between northern and southern states averted a confrontation with Spain. About then, the Ostend Manifesto (1854) came to light. The manifesto was a secret document written by U.S. diplomats at Ostend, Belgium. Its purpose was to grab Cuba from Spain. The plan was for the United States to pay Spain $120 million for Cuba, a considerable sum considering that the entire Mexican Cession (1848) cost $15,000. When the contents of the document were made public, they outraged abolitionists, Spaniards, and Cubans alike. The cabal was composed of James Buchanan (1791–1868) who was later president, Virginia Senator James Mason (1798–1871) and Louisiana Senator Pierre Soulé (1801–1870). The Ostend Manifesto argued that U.S. occupation of Cuba was vital to national security of the United States and, hence, taking Cuba off Spain's hands was in the best interest of that country. The Ostend Manifesto sparked a debate not only along the lines of free versus slave states but also as to whether the United States should become an imperial power.

SIR:—The undersigned, in compliance with the wish expressed by the President in the several confidential despatches you have addressed to us, respectively, to that effect, have met in conference, first at Ostend, in Belgium, on the 8th, 10th, and 11th instance, and then at Aix la Chapelle in Prussia, on the days next following, up to the date hereof.

There has been a full and unresolved interchange of views and sentiments between us, which we are most happy to inform you has resulted in a cordial coincidence of opinion on the grave and important subjects submitted to our consideration.

We have arrived at the conclusion, and are thoroughly convinced, that an immediate and earnest effort ought to be made by the government of the United States to purchase Cuba from Spain at any price for which it can be obtained, not exceeding the sum of.

The proposal should, in our opinion, be made in such a manner as to be presented through the necessary diplomatic forms to the Supreme Constituent Cortes about to assemble. On this momentous question, in which the people both of Spain and the United States are so deeply interested, all our proceedings ought to be open, frank, and public. They should be of such a character as to challenge the approbation of the world.

We firmly believe that, in the progress of human events, the time has arrived when the vital interests of Spain are as seriously involved in the sale, as those of the United States in the purchase, of the island and that the transaction will prove equally honorable to both nations.

Under these circumstances we cannot anticipate a failure, unless possibly through the malign influence of foreign powers who possess no right whatever to interfere in the matter.

We proceed to state some of the reasons which have brought us to this conclusion, and, for the sake of clearness, we shall specify them under two distinct heads:

1. The United States ought, if practicable, to purchase Cuba with as little delay as possible.

2. The probability is great that the government and Cortes of Spain will prove willing to sell it, because this would essentially promote the highest and best interests of the Spanish people.

Then, 1. It must be clear to every reflecting mind that, from the peculiarity of its geographical position, and the considerations attendant on it, Cuba is as necessary to the North American republic as any of its present members, and that it belongs naturally to that great family of States of which the Union is the providential nursery.

From its locality it commands the mouth of the Mississippi and the immense and annually increasing trade which must seek this avenue to the ocean.

On the numerous navigable streams, measuring an aggregate course of some thirty thousand miles, which disembogue themselves through this magnificent river into the Gulf of Mexico, the increase of the population within the last ten years amounts to more than that of the entire Union at the time Louisiana was annexed to it.

The natural and main outlet to the products of this entire population, the highway of their direct intercourse with the Atlantic and the Pacific States, can never be secure, but must ever be endangered whilst Cuba is a dependency of a distant power in whose possession it has proved to be a source of constant annoyance and embarrassment to their interests.

Indeed, the Union can never enjoy repose, nor possess reliable security, as long as Cuba is not embraced within its boundaries.

Its immediate acquisition by our government is of paramount importance, and we cannot doubt but that it is a consummation devoutly wished for by its inhabitants.

The intercourse which its proximity to our coasts begets and encourages between them and the citizens of the United States, has, in the progress of time, so united their interests and blended their fortunes that they now look upon each other as if they were one people and had but one destiny.

Considerations exist which render delay in the acquisition of this island exceedingly dangerous to the United States.

The system of immigration and labor lately organized within its limits, and the tyranny and oppression which characterize its immediate rulers, threaten an insurrection at every moment which may result in direful consequences to the American people.

Cuba has thus become to us an unceasing danger, and a permanent cause of anxiety and alarm.

But we need not enlarge on these topics. It can scarcely be apprehended that foreign powers, in violation of international law, would interpose their influence with Spain to prevent our acquisition of the island. Its inhabitants are now suffering under the worst of all possible governments, that of absolute despotism, delegated by a distant power to irresponsible agents, who are changed at short intervals, and who are tempted to improve the brief opportunity thus afforded to accumulate fortunes by the basest means.

As long as this system shall endure, humanity may in vain demand the suppression of the African slave trade in the island. This is rendered impossible whilst that infamous traffic remains an irresistible temptation and a source of immense profit to needy and avaricious officials, who, to attain their ends, scruple not to trample the most sacred principles under foot. The Spanish government at home may be well disposed, but experience has proved that it cannot control these remote depositaries of its power.

Besides, the commercial nations of the world cannot fail to perceive and appreciate the great advantages which would result to their people from a dissolution of the forced and unnatural connexion [sic] between Spain and Cuba, and the annexation of the latter to the United States. The trade of England and France with Cuba would, in that event, assume at once an important and profitable character, and rapidly extend with the increasing population and prosperity of the island.

2. But if the United States and every commercial nation would be benefited by this transfer, the interests of Spain would also be greatly and essentially promoted.

She cannot but see what such a sum of money as we are willing to pay for the island would effect in the development of her vast natural resources.

Two-thirds of this sum, if employed in the construction of a system of railroads, would ultimately prove a source of greater wealth to the Spanish people than that opened to their vision by Cortez. Their prosperity would date from the ratification of that treaty of cession.

France has already constructed continuous lines of railways from Havre, Marseilles, Valenciennes, and Strasbourg, via Paris, to the Spanish frontier, and anxiously awaits the day when Spain shall find herself in a condition to extend these roads through her northern provinces to Madrid, Seville, Cadiz, Malaga, and the frontiers of Portugal.

This object once accomplished, Spain would become a centre of attraction for the traveling world, and secure a permanent and profitable market for her various productions. Her fields, under the stimulus given to industry by remunerating prices, would teem with cereal grain, and her vineyards would bring forth a vastly increased quantity of choice wines. Spain would speedily become, what a bountiful Providence intended she should be, one of the first nations of Continental Europe—rich, powerful, and contented.

Whilst two-thirds of the price of the island would be ample for the completion of her most important public improvements, she might, with the remaining forty millions, satisfy the demands now pressing so heavily upon her credit, and create a sinking fund which would gradually relieve her from the overwhelming debt now paralyzing her energies.

Such is her present wretched financial condition, that her best bonds are sold upon her own Bourse at about one-third of their par value; whilst another class, on which she pays no interest, have but a nominal value, and are quoted at about one-sixth of the amount for which they were issued.

Besides, these latter are held principally by British creditors who may, from day to day, obtain the effective interposition of their own government for the purpose of coercing payment. Intimations to that effect have been already thrown out from high quarters, and unless some new source of revenue shall enable Spain to provide for such exigencies, it is not improbable that they may be realized.

Should Spain reject the present golden opportunity for developing her resources, and removing her financial embarrassments, it may never again return.

Cuba, in its palmiest days, never yielded her exchequer after deducting the expenses of its government, a clear annual income of more than a million and a half dollars. These expenses have increased to such a degree as to leave a deficit chargeable on the treasury of Spain to the amount of six hundred thousand dollars.

In a pecuniary point of view, therefore, the island is an incumbrance [*sic*], instead of a source of profit, to the mother country.

Under no probable circumstances can Cuba ever yield to Spain one per cent on the large amount which the United States are willing to pay for its acquisition. But Spain is in imminent danger of losing Cuba, without remuneration.

Extreme oppression, it is now universally admitted, justifies any people in endeavoring to relieve themselves from the yoke of their oppressors. The sufferings which the corrupt, arbitrary, and unrelenting local administration necessarily entails upon the inhabitants of Cuba, cannot fail to stimulate and keep alive that spirit of resistance and revolution against Spain, which has, of late years, been so often manifested. In this condition of affairs it is vain to expect that the sympathies of the people of the United States will not be warmly enlisted in favor of their oppressed neighbors.

We know that the President is justly inflexible in his determination to execute the neutrality laws; but should the Cubans themselves rise in revolt against the oppression which they suffer, no human power could prevent citizens of the United States and liberal minded men of other countries from rushing to their assistance. Besides, the present is an age of adventure, in which restless and daring spirits abound in every portion of the world.

It is not improbable, therefore, that Cuba may be wrested from Spain by a successful revolution; and in that event she will lose both the island and the price which we are now willing to pay for it—a price far beyond what was ever paid by one people to another for any province.

It may also be remarked that the settlement of this vexed question, by the cession of Cuba to the United States, would forever prevent the dangerous complications between nations to which it may otherwise give birth.

It is certain that, should the Cubans themselves organize an insurrection against the Spanish government, and should other independent nations come to the aid of Spain in the contest, no human power could, in our opinion, prevent the people and government of the United States from taking part in such a civil war in support of their neighbors and friends.

But if Spain, dead to the voice of her own interest, and actuated by stubborn pride and a false sense of honor, should refuse to sell Cuba to the United States, then the question will arise, What ought to be the course of the American government under such circumstances? Self-preservation is the first law of nature, with States as well as with individuals. All nations have, at different periods, acted upon this maxim. Although it has been made the pretext for committing flagrant injustice, as in the partition of Poland and other similar cases which history records, yet the principle itself, though often abused, has always been recognized.

The United States have never acquired a foot of territory except by fair purchase, or, as in the case of Texas, upon the free and voluntary application of the people of that independent State, who desired to blend their destinies with our own.

Even our acquisitions from Mexico are no exception to this rule, because, although we might have claimed them by the right of conquest in a just war, yet we purchased them for what was then considered by both parties a full and ample equivalent.

Our past history forbids that we should acquire the island of Cuba without the consent of Spain, unless justified by the great law of self-preservation. We must, in any event, preserve our own conscious rectitude and our own self-respect.

Whilst pursuing this course we can afford to disregard the censures of the world, to which we have been so often and so unjustly exposed.

After we shall have offered Spain a price for Cuba far beyond its present value, and this shall have been refused, it will then be time to consider the question, does Cuba, in the possession of Spain, seriously endanger our internal peace and the existence of our cherished Union?

Should this question be answered in the affirmative, then, by every law, human and divine, we shall be justified in wresting it from Spain if we possess the power, and this upon the very same principle that would justify an individual in tearing down the burning house of his neighbor if there were no other means of preventing the flames from destroying his own home.

Under such circumstances we ought neither to count the cost nor regard the odds which Spain might enlist against us. We forbear to enter into the question, whether the present condition of the island would justify such a measure? We should, however, be recreant to our duty, be unworthy of our gallant forefathers, and commit base treason against our posterity, should we permit Cuba to be Africanized and become a second St. Domingo, with all its attendant horrors to the white race, and suffer the flames to extend to our own neighboring shores, seriously to endanger or actually to consume the fair fabric of our Union.

We fear that the course and current of events are rapidly tending towards such a catastrophe. We, however, hope for the best, though we ought certainly to be prepared for the worst.

We also forbear to investigate the present condition of the questions at issue between the United States and Spain. A long series of injuries to our people have been committed in Cuba by Spanish officials and are under dressed. But recently a most flagrant outrage on the rights of American citizens and on the flag of the United States was perpetrated in the harbor of Havana under circumstances which, without immediate redress, would have justified a resort to measures of war in vindication of national honor. That outrage is not only unatoned, but the Spanish government has deliberately sanctioned the acts of its subordinates and assumed the responsibility attaching to them.

Nothing could more impressively teach us the danger to which those peaceful relations it has ever been the policy of the United States to cherish with foreign nations are constantly exposed than the circumstances of that case. Situated as Spain and the United States are, the latter have forborne to resort to extreme measures.

But this course cannot, with due regard to their own dignity as an independent nation, continue; and our recommendations, now submitted, are dictated by the firm belief that the cession of Cuba to the United States, with stipulations as beneficial to Spain as those suggested, is the only effective mode of settling all past differences and of securing the two countries against future collisions.

We have already witnessed the happy results for both countries which followed a similar arrangement in regard to Florida.

Yours, very respectfully,

James Buchanan, J. Y. Mason, Pierre Soulé

Source: Hon. Wm. L. Marcy, Secretary of State, *House Executive Documents*, 33rd Cong., 2nd Sess., Vol. X, pp. 127–136.

105. "Designs upon Cuba," 1856

William Walker (1824–1860), a 5-foot, 2-inch Tennessean, led filibustering expeditions into Baja California and Nicaragua. Called a visionary by southerners, he wanted to add more slave states to the Union. Walker's plan included annexing Central America, the Caribbean, and Cuba to the United States. Pro-slave interests supported his military ventures with arms, money, and volunteers.

The following article alleges that the success of annexing Cuba depended on the success of Walker's filibustering expeditions. Walker had invaded Nicaragua and controlled its government. He was heralded as a patriot and compared to the heroes of the Alamo (1836) who seized Texas from Mexico. The 1850s were the heyday of Euro-American filibusterers; pirates who led military expeditions into Latin American nations hoping to repeat the theft of Texas. The authority for the United States to annex Cuba and Central America was Manifest Destiny—the doctrine that held Americans were God's chosen people and that the United States was not violating the rights of other nations but that it was only reannexing land that already belonged to them.

DESIGNS UPON CUBA

We have satisfactory evidence that the ultimate object of the Walker expedition to Nicaragua is, not so much to conquer that country as *to obtain a foothold for a renewed invasion of Cuba.* The neutrality laws of the United States were found to interfere seriously and fatally with the project while it was prosecuted in this country. At the outset of the Administration of Gen. Pierce, while it was hoped that he would be found favorable to such attempts, and that the Federal authorities would wink at the outfit of a new invading force, the leading filibusters directed their efforts to the recruitment of men and the raising of money for a renewal of the invasion which came to so fatal an end under Gen. [Narciso] Lopez. But it was soon found that nothing could be hoped from this quarter. The Administration was not ready for such a movement. Europe was then at peace—and it was only when the Russian war broke out that Mr. Buchanan and other American Ministers abroad united in proclaiming that the United States should purchase Cuba, if possible, and seize her, if not. But our Government was not even then prepared for open action upon such a policy. Mr. Marcy's conservation and good sense prevailed over the rash councils of his Cabinet associates. And even after Walker had obtained a foothold in Nicaragua, and when his position there appeared to be much stronger than ever, before or since, his Minister was rejected, and the President refused to recognize his Government.

But this policy was suddenly changed. Those who had been the leading men in the crusade against Cuba espoused the Walker movement in Nicaragua. Gen. Goicuria—a native Cuban, a man of wealth, ability, and character, who since his exile had been the life and soul of the Cuban movement, left New York, which had been his head-quarters, joined Walker in Nicaragua, took command under him and was engaged in some of the late skirmishes with the Costa Rican troops. At the same time, the Administration reversed its policy, without the slightest apparent cause, ignored the cogent reasons it had previously assigned for not recognizing Walker's Government, received his Minister and proclaimed its purpose to regard his rule as an established fact. This was speedily followed by the nomination at Cincinnati of the author of the Ostend Manifesto—through the active exertions of Messrs. Soule, Sickles, Saunders, and other prominent filibusters, and the declaration, by the Democratic Party in the Cincinnati platform, of a purpose to insist—not upon equality and neutrality in the affairs of the Isthmus, but upon *our absolute preponderance* in everything relating to Central America, and our *naval ascendency* in the Gulf of Mexico. And close upon the heels of this come Mr. James Buchanan's declarations to Hon. A. G. Brown—made officially in reply to the announcement of his nomination—that he believed the possession of Cuba would speedily become a "national necessity"—and that he regarded its acquisition as one of the great objects of his Administration. Upon this point, as well as upon all others relating to Southern interests, Mr. Brown declares that Mr. Buchanan is "as much entitled to *Southern* confidence and *Southern* votes, as Mr. [John C.] Calhoun himself."

The plan is to avoid the appearance of direct invasion from the United States—as this would subject us to complaints and probable hostility from England and France as well as Spain. But [William] Walker's rule is to be recognized and consolidated in Nicaragua. When this is effected, Nicaragua will be made the headquarters of the Cuban invaders. They will then have ground where they can organize their forces outside the jurisdiction of the United States—and our Government will thus be able entirely to evade the responsibility of the movement. But if England or France should then interfere—it "will be for our Government to consider," in the words of the Ostend Manifesto," whether the possession of Cuba is a national necessity"—and whether our "preponderance" and "supremacy" in the affairs of Central America do not require us to resist such interference, by force of arms.

That this is the programme of operations, to which the Cuban filibusters, Walker's Government and Mr. Buchanan and his political friends are parties, we have no doubt. There are several contingencies in the way of its execution. The first grows out of the difficulty which Walker is likely to experience, in maintaining his position—and the second springs from the doubt of Buchanan's election. The success of both Walker and Buchanan is essential to the scheme; and yet just now the chances of both seem clouded and desperate.

Source: New York Daily Times, August 16, 1856, p. 4.

106. Excerpt from Speech Given by William Walker in New Orleans, May 30, 1857

Gen. William Walker (1824–1860), the epitome of the ugly American in Latin America, was a 5-foot, 2-inch Tennessean. He wanted to repeat the taking of Texas from Mexico in 1836. The base of Walker's support in the United States was the American South where he recruited volunteers and raised money for arms. The following speech was given in New Orleans, Louisiana, in 1857, to 20,000 wildly applauding admirers. He laid out his plan of incorporating Central America into the United States. According to Walker, Nicaragua was the first step in the liberation of the region; according to him, Nicaraguans implored him on bended knees to be their president. Walker said Central America was in bad shape because of the mongrelization of its people and needed the United States to save it.

Fellow Citizens: I stand before you, not to vindicate a cause, for it needs none; what is just needs no vindication. This concourse of citizens and the sympathy here manifested, attest the interest you fele [feel]. But I stand to vindicate Americans, and the acts by which the American cause has been upheld by American citizens.

In examining the motives of these acts, I ask you to discard all prejudices; to stand here as if you were posterity, to judge of history—to judge without fear and without favor. Many and unscrupulous have been the means resorted to for the purpose of placing me in a false light before my countrymen. These reports it is necessary to explain: and I challenge my enemies to stand and point to a single act of mine which has been in violation of either civil, national, or international rights [cheers]; I challenge any one present to name any act of mine in Nicaragua which has not been stamped with the seal of justice.

There are those who have charged upon me such motives as to attempt to vindicate would be a sheer mockery. There are those who have charged upon me avarice and mere personal gain; from such I scorn to exonerate myself. The men who were with me in Nicaragua—my fellow-countrymen in arms will exculpate me from the charge of ever having entertained such motives. But there are other insinuations not so degrading at the first blush—that I was a mere soldier of fortune, attempting to carry out an ambitious scheme, and endeavoring to make for myself a name and a fame. This imputation I reject as equally unfounded, and I hope to convince you that such were not my motives—that I was not a mere soldier of fortune and adventure—risking the lives of my countrymen for selfish purposes—the actions of my hand prove a more noble purpose. If I have exerted myself for any thing and for and purpose, *it has been to extend American influence and Americanize Nicaragua.*

For thirty five years, a struggle for liberty had been going on among the Central American Republics. Civil wars showed that that people were incapable of self government. Nicaragua was in a State of anarchy when I received the offer of Castillon; but, after my arrival there, I refused to act in open violation of the laws of the United States; but I replied to the Cabinet that there would be no violation of the laws of our country in their asking me to fight in behalf of the Democratic Party. I sent an agent to Castillon to inform him that the contract between us must be made accordingly; that I had an invitation to assist the Hondurians [*sic*] from Gen. Cambaras, and would go there if Castillon apprehended any danger from the presence of Americans in Nicaragua. *On bended knees, and in the most suppliant terms, the Provisional President of the Republic insisted that I should remain*—he wished the Americans to be on his side, for he knew they were loyal, brave and true. [Applause.]

After my success on the Transit route, I made a treaty, by which the presence of Americans was approved by Corral and his party. I did this to secure the good will of all, and there was not a Nicaraguan who, in the face of this treaty, could say he did not approve the presence of Americans of their soil. Seven days after, in the awful presence of the priests, before whom Gen. Corral and myself had sworn to the treaty, and ere the ink was scarcely dry upon the paper, he penned encouraging letters to the people of Honduras against the Americans; these fell into my hands, and I felt that I might have brought him to the block, and by the provisions of the treaty could not evade his execution. This traitor proved to be guilty, and proved nothing in his extenuation, but begged for mercy: but I felt then as I do now, that *a Court of Justice was a thing of wisdom, and mercy the part of folly.* [Applause.]

I felt that justice and mercy would still be meted out, and that in six months after Corral's death, his party would be vanquished. After the execution of Corral, the Rivas party went over to the Democratic side, and Gen. Cabanas assisted the Hondurans. I went, by invitation, to the assistance of the Nicaraguans. Gen. Hebez joined in the application that was made to me. Every exertion was made to influence me to take the Americans to Honduras. I replied that the Americans were there as friends to all parties. By my suggestions, Commissioners were sent to Honduras and all the States, stating that we desired peace, and that our policy was pacific, and that, under the circumstances, to take sides was illiberal. Hebez acknowledged the truth of my suggestion. He was not a Democrat, and was not in favor of aiding Cabanas.

Deputies were sent by my advice, stating that the Nicaraguans desired peace. We shall see how far it was granted. In the meantime, an important event transpired— at the suggestion of Don Patricio Rivas, an American was sent to represent the republic at Washington. *I opposed this as bad policy,* but I was not in authority, and my opposition was unavailable. They wanted an American to speak the American language. You all know, fellow-citizens, how he was received, and now can paint the surprise of the Nicaraguans, because, on the plea of Pierce and Marcy, he was rejected on account of his being born in the United States. I well knew the result, and told them of the relations that existed between this country and Nicaragua, but I assured them that my countrymen knew a power higher than that of Cabinets and Presidents, and that I had infinite confidence in that higher power, which the people held in their own hands—the true American sovereignty. [Applause.]

The alliance which followed, between the four States of Central America—the combination against American citizens in Nicaragua, due to Pierce and Marcy, under their rejection of the Nicaraguan Minister—brought the matter to maturity, for immediately the Costa Ricans—the supposed weakest party of the combination—commenced hostilities by an open declaration of war. Then followed the almost anomalous decree, by which the Costa Ricans made war, not against a State, but the Americans in Nicaragua. Thus commenced the war of the races—the great battle of the mongrels and the white men.

This war, then, *was not started by Americans in Nicaragua*, and I challenge the mention of a single act in which they did anything but uphold the pledges made by the whole people of Nicaragua. After this it appears that Don Patricio Rivas plotted with the Northern States for effecting the desertion of such Americans as he could not expel by force. American rights were ignored in Nicaragua; bribes of money, and even lands, were freely offered, in the face of our having braved war in its worst forms, and suffered the loss of life by the rage of famine and pestilence.

They pretended to be convinced as to my assurances, and were willing that the merits of an election should go before the people. This I desired, for I well knew that the mass of the people detested, with an implacable hatred, the forced military services of the Costa Ricans.

The election was decreed, but only think! the result was scarcely declared before Rivas was found plotting a revolution, under the pretence that the people were overawed by my presence. But "the wicked flee when no man pursueth"; I was not there—they were running from their own consciences. Notwithstanding this conduct of Rivas, an election was had, and I was declared President of the Republic. [Great applause.]

By this election I stood forth as the only protector and lawful representative of the Nicaraguans. Rivas was previously but the provisional President. I was commander-in chief of one portion of the army, and it was through me that Rivas was named for the provisional. I was joint sponsor of his choice and after the *death of Corral* was the sole cause of his elevation. I was bound by oath to put Rivas out when I was sworn in, but I was justified by the unmistakable voice of the Nicaraguans, who knew the facts under which I had been elected.

I need not recount the events that followed: but to vindicate the Americans in Nicaragua, you all know how long and successfully I strived with, and I forced back the enemy—braved that worst of foes, the lurking pestilence, then raging with violence in Granada. But for a new influence—an influence which, I regret to say, comes little less from my own than a foreign country—we might still be in arms in Nicaragua. It is probable we had no right to expect sympathy of the British, even if determined at the sacrifice of the honor and rights of British officers. But I need not tell you that officers of the British service encouraged desertion from our army, themselves forgetting their swords, and pretending to have honor in their hearts, they were but bound to obey the dictum from a superior authority. But, whatever the position of these officers, I could not but think that, unless governed by some strange collusion, they would not thus have interfered with American citizens. It is impossible to explain it but supposing that Americans were on the British side.

Our worst enemies were Americans. Oh! That they had been born in some other country. It is to our shame that they should have drawn the same breath with honest Americans. It was not until the last exigency—that of reverse and danger—an American, bearing the name and arms of an American officer, consummated what

British ingenuity had begun. It is a duty to myself to explain why we are no longer in arms—and that however insignificant might be the representative of our Government, I would respect the American flag as much in him as in the highest officer, and that on surrendering I reserved the right of appeal, not to the Government, but to the people themselves.

Capt. Davis made representations which I could hardly believe were true, an American as he was, permitted an act which was really an act of war in Nicaragua. But consider, fellow-citizens, that little vessel, the *Granada*, was covered with glory, at American hands, she was manned by Americans; had met the vessel of the enemy; come off victorious in an engagement unequaled in the annals of warfare, ever since the days of J. Paul Jones. Yes, fellow-citizens, that event, in which the little Nicaragua schooner was successful, will be recurred [referred] to with pride by the historian, and the eleventh of April will long be remembered by the American people. Who of you cannot feel proud of the spirit of manhood manifested by an American, one born within your midst? Yes, gentlemen, you can but feel that that little vessel was a fact in the history of American enterprise, surrounded with glorious memories that cannot be erased; yet, despite the glories which she attached to our fame, there was not wanting an American to commit an act of which every lover of his country will be ashamed. Yes, it was reserved for Capt. Davis to make himself a party to an alliance between the British and the mongrels of Central America, in order to drive his own race from the Isthmus.

He expressed his determination to seize the *Granada* and we were bound to yield to him; yes, fellow-citizens, we were forced to make terms, to surrender to an officer of the American Navy. Great was our indignation when we learned that the Americans had thus interfered with the American cause in Nicaragua. Why this action of Davis? Because he had received instructions from Washington: *but, why were these instructions given! It was because, here was presented the real issue between the Marcy Treaty as it was, and the Americans in Nicaragua. Here was the starting source. The American Minister in Great Britain, and the Abolitionists at the North determined, that Slavery should be excluded from a place over which Americans had no control.* I care not what may be the ideas of those present, or what they may say in justification, it was but a combination to exclude an action of a sovereignty of Honduras from the Bay Islands. Between the States of New Granada and Costa Rica, there existed a question of boundary, originated mainly through men at New York, the agents of the Steamship Company. There was also a question of territory between New Granada and Costa Rica, and Costa Rica and Nicaragua, in relation to Buenacosta and the Mosquito country.

The idea of this question was to have New-Granada to enter into an agreement with Nicaragua that Slavery should be excluded. He commenced British intrigue, in the desire to confound the relation of this Government with our domestic institutions. Here let me say that I do not wish to excite political feeling on this subject. It is perhaps fortunate that I was born on Southern soil; it may be unfortunate *that I cannot consider Slavery a moral or political wrong.* My teachings may not have been altogether of Wilberforce I may have touched a too sensitive point, but I feel that I have but struck upon the pivot of British interference.

Look back to the origin of Slavery in American history; who introduced it into this country? Was he a man without honor? Certainly few have stood higher in moral worth than La Casas, the Spanish priest, who was the head and front of this offending. He introduced it in the Sixteenth Century for the relief of the Indians from the Spanish subjection. It were better that he had fixed it permanently not only in Cuba, but other regions than Central America. Certainly, *he was wise and far more liberal for his day than the present followers of Clarkson and Wilberforce.*

Central America was in a worse condition than under the Spanish rule. The government was going to ruin. Mongrelism was the secret of its waning fortune. What was to be done? It was left for us to Americanize Central America; on whom rests the right of regenerating the amalgamated race, and no other than the people of the United States, and especially of the Southern States. *I call upon you therefore, to execute this mission.* You cannot, in justice to yourselves shrink from your duty. You cannot but continue your energies in carrying out the great principle of American influence. As for myself, forced here as I am, I can but appeal to you to assist in retaining the American ascendancy. My duty has been paid, and I would turn back on the path I have traversed. No, gentlemen, *forced here against my will, I feel that my duty calls upon me to return.* [Applause.]

All who are nearest and dearest to me are there. There sleep the men, soldiers, and officers, whose rights I cannot fail to see respected; here, too, the heirs of those who have perished claim that I should return; *nor, while I draw one breath, shall I leave a single stone unturned in securing them in their inheritance.* I call upon you, then, fellow-citizens, male and female, whose friends and relatives have perished, to lend your aid—upon the men to assist with their fortunes and purses; upon the mothers, to belt the swords about their sons; upon the maiden, as she listens to the lover at her feet, until he shall vow to go forth on the mission of his duty. Aye, fellow-citizens, I call upon you all, by the glorious recollections of the past, and the bright anticipations for the future, *to assist in carrying out and perfecting the Americanization of Central America.* [Tremendous applause.]

The General closed, and the band struck up "Yankee Doodle," and the loud plaudits of an admiring audience, who accompanied him *en masse* to the St. Charles Hotel, his present place of abode. Such a gathering has seldom been seen in New Orleans; and never, upon any previous occasion, have we witnessed so much enthusiasm among the people.

Source: "Filibusterism," *New York Daily Times*, June 8, 1857, p. 2.

107. "Gen. Walker's Letter," September 21, 1857

In this letter to the *New York Daily Times* the correspondent, Aqviday, takes issue with filibusterer William Walker (1824–1860), who declared himself president of Nicaragua (1856–1857) and his statement that he had not gone to Nicaragua to extend slavery. The correspondent questions Walker's statement and says that Walker planned to spread slavery into Central America and South America. As proof, he cites the fact that Walker targeted the South for support. The correspondent alleges that the South had a mission to extend slavery throughout Mexico, Central, and South America.

GEN. WALKER'S LETTER

The Extension of Slavery into the Central and South American States.
Correspondence of the New York Times.
Washington, Monday, Sept. 21, 1857.

Whatever serves to develop the intentions of the South on the subject of Slavery deserves public attention. As an indication of Southern policy, I cannot but regard the last published letter of William Walker in support of his scheme for reestablishing the institution in Nicaragua with profound interest. Disposed to deny him the possession of abilities requisite for the conduct of great affairs. I am yet forced to concede that this letter is a most skillfully [sic] framed appeal to the South, and that it is marked by great power of thought and correctness of argument. No publication has lately appeared presenting in so clear a manner the general idea of Southern expansion as a means of securing the permanent domination of the great Southern institution. It is worth as much for what it unwittingly suggests to the conservatism of the South for its incitements to unlawful aggressions upon the territories and rights of the neighbors and friends of that section. Let us analyze Mr. Walker's statements and reasoning.

Walker admits that though he did not go to Central America to establish Slavery, that measure was the guiding star of his policy after he got there. He admits, too, that the decree issued with this object in view was his individual act, and that it was opposed by the whole body of native inhabitants. He asserts also that the measure was resorted to by him as part of a system for promoting "the increase of negro Slavery on this Continent," which system he calls upon the South to support as the corner-stone of its safety. What he says about the benevolence of Las Casas in suggesting the situation of Negro for Indian Slavery, is only true in part. Las Casas was a Dominican monk, celebrated as an Abolitionist. He opposed the Slavery imposed upon the Indians upon grounds hostile to any kind of Slavery. He was supported by his sect, but was bitterly reviled and threatened by the Franciscans, who were conservatives, and the Spanish settlers, who were owners of Indian slaves. In a public debate before Charles V., Las Casas contended against the Bishop of Darien that it was inhuman and irreligious to hold that any race had been designed by God for servitude. Why he consented to Negro Slavery does not clearly appear, but it seems that he regarded it as a temporary expedient necessary for the liberation of his Indians, of whom he had been appointed by Zimenes "Protector."

Walker proves by a methodical and consistent statement the existence of a combination among all the people of Spanish America from the Rio Grande to Chili, "for the purpose of excluding slavery forever from the territories now occupied by them." He then goes on to show that England has joined this combination, and that she furnished the Costa Ricans arms to aid them in the defence of their country against him and his filibusters. He notices that the new Mexican Constitution has a clause forbidding the making of any treaty for the extradition of fugitive slaves, and sums up upon the testimony thus:

"In fact, you have but to read the journals of the Spanish American Republics from Mexico to Chili to be satisfied of the enmity—active as well as passive—to the people and institutions of the Southern States."

I do not see how there can be any doubt of the correctness of this conclusion. All the people threatened by the South with invasion and subjugation have combined to defend themselves. Walker then asks the people of the South whether they intend to submit to this; whether they will be *hemmed in on the South as on the North*; whether they will surrender the right of carrying their slaves into other countries, and reducing to servitude the people who now inhabit those countries? These are momentous questions, and Walker is quite right in asking the South to pause now and consider them. They may be stated, however, in another form, as thus: Have not the people of Spanish-America a right to be free? Have they not a right to resist invasion if they suspect "the South," which is their North, of an intention to seize their several countries and enslave their free citizens, is it not their duty to combine for their defence? And if they did not so combine, would not all mankind denounce them as dolts and cowards?

No man of common sense, and especially no one who could write such a letter as this which I am commenting upon, can affect to believe that "the South" has any other or better right to move on farther south for purposes of conquest and propagandism than the North has. Now, if the South has a mission to seize Mexico, the West Indies, Central America, Venezuela, the Guianas, New-Granada, Peru, and Chili for the purpose of fixing therein African Slavery forever, which Walker avows, by implication, to be his design, who can deny to the Free States of the Union the right to move on after the South, to occupy the present Slave States, and to extirpate the "peculiar," institution of African Slavery forever? Let it be borne in mind that while the South claims the right to extend over all America an institution which she declares to be "peculiar," the institutions of the North are not peculiar, but are in harmony with those of the Christian and civilized world.

But directly after making this important disclosure, Mr. Walker proceeds to relieve his mind by this portentous admonition:

"If the South is desirous of imitating the gloomy grandeur of the Eschylian Prometheus, she has but lie supine a little while longer, and force and power will bind her to the rock, and the vulture will descent to tear the liver from her body. In her agony and grief she may console herself with the idea that she suffers a willing sacrifice."

Is this a confession, or what is it? Does Mr. Walker mean to say that Slavery is a vulture which is tearing out the liver from the body of the South? This is exactly what he means. He tells the people of the South that Slavery is a vulture that is feeding upon their hearts; but they must not kill the vulture, they must only enlarge the area of the rock, and allow the *obscenus volucres* [obscene vultures] to feed away at its leisure.

The point of a powerful combination already formed to resist the ambition and rapacity of the South, is certainly very suggestive of the necessity of caution in increasing the strength of this combination. It is the most overwhelming argument for the dependence of the South upon the Federal Union that I have ever heard. Southern conservatives will at once perceive that when the secessionists and incendiaries of the Jefferson and Toombs and Keitt school get the upper hand of them, and set up their exclusive Slave Empire, the North, above Mason and Dixon's, must form an offensive and defensive alliance with tropical America to limit and, if need be, to cripple the new aggressive power forever. And if Great Britain is now hostile to the South, and is forming combinations against her expansion, what would be her policy after the principle of territorial aggression had been inaugurated in a new government informed by no other motive?

It is said that Mr. Jenkins, to whom Mr. Walker addresses his manifesto, will repudiate the plan developed. This is very likely. Mr. Jenkins is a so-called conservative, who in 1852 was nominated for Vice President on the ticket which had Mr. Webster's name at its head. As a man of sense, who knows the real design, and the true wants of the South, he cannot assume any responsibility for the sentiments and recommendations of his correspondent.

Source: New York Times, September 23, 1857, p. 4.

108. Excerpts from *The United States Democratic Review,* "The Nicaraguan Question," 1858

Gen. William Walker (1824–1860), a 5-foot, 2-inch Tennessean, drifted into California in the 1850s and launched a series of filibustering expeditions against Mexico. He caught the imagination of Euro-Americans in 1853, when he landed a party in Sonora, Mexico, and invaded Baja California. He was kicked out. But in 1855, he enlisted some 60 men and sailed for Nicaragua where he led a successful coup. Walker was opposed by Com. Cornelius Vanderbilt, a wealthy banker, who built a route through Nicaragua and then a railroad through Panama that joined the Atlantic and Pacific Oceans. Costa Rica declared war on Walker and, in May 1857, forced him to surrender and leave Nicaragua. His departure did not end Euro-American dreams of annexing Nicaragua. Walker led an invasion of Honduras where he was captured and executed in 1860. His successes inspired debate on the Nicaraguan Question, which concerned the status of Nicaragua within the U.S. sphere of influence. While many Americans coveted its land, the thinking of most was influenced by racial doctrines that saw Nicaragua as a land of mongrels. The following excerpt deals with how Americans viewed Nicaraguans and the impediments to democracy there. The article argues that Euro-Americans had good reason to disown the "abominable bastard democracies of Central and South America." This antipathy was overcome by the potential profits that would be derived from its rich lands.

The first objection to this method is that *there are no democracies,* in the American sense, nor can be, in the Spanish American republics. A collection of negroes, mestizoes, mulattoes, and renegades of all colors, without political ideas, a sense of right, or notions of common humanity, much less of progressive civilization, must not be dignified with the name of a Democracy. We resolutely protest against it, and the good sense of the nation will go with us. The same objections that apply to the sudden emancipation of Negro slave populations, apply to these misnamed democracies of Negroes and Indians. They are mere sluggish anarchies, liable at any moment to despotism, their natural end, or to barbarism, their natural and real condition. It is unbecoming the dignity of the Federal Government, or people of the United States, to lend themselves to such contemptible fallacies. If we disown Mormonism, as [many] good reasons can be found for disowning the abominable bastard democracies of Central and South America.

It has been proposed, in a spirit of opposition, and in order to turn the scale of immigration in favor of the North, to encourage northern laborers, artisans from Massachusetts, farmers with "subsoil ploughs," and McCormick's reapers, to in large bodies to Nicaragua. Those who propose an emigration of this character to Nicaragua are either very ignorant or very cruel. When we consider that the mortality of white men in Nicaragua is as great as at Cayenne or the mouths of the Niger, and that not one person in a hundred escapes the fever, the idea of sending shiploads of emigrants with "subsoil ploughs" will be abandoned. Subsoil ploughs will never be used in Nicaragua. Agricultural labor in that climate is simple: it consists only in "keeping down the weeds and killing vermin." The wealth of the soil is generally excessive and inexhaustible. One year of neglect turns a ploughed field into an impenetrable thicket of thorns and brambles.

It is hardly necessary to develop at large, or in many words, the commercial importance of the Nicaraguan Isthmus. It is in fact the key to the Pacific. During the last two years there has been a desperate struggle among the great steamship and transit owners of California and New York to gain exclusive possession of the Nicaraguan Isthmus. These steamship owners, independently of Southern sympathy, have been the real instigators and supporters of the private war waged by adventurers against the governments of Central America for the possession of the Isthmus. The ships of these ambitions speculators have transported armies with their provisions and munitions of war to obtain by force what they had failed to secure by negotiation. Not less than five thousand lives, in all, of white men, and some fifteen thousand of Central Americans have been destroyed by lead, steel, and fever, in this contest of transit monopolists. Another five or ten thousand are waiting to be shipped away and poured into the same deadly abyss.

If our intelligent but unprincipled speculators stand ready to throw entire armies into that Nicaraguan gulf which lies midway between New York and California, to fill it up even with human bones, over which to build a solid causeway for commerce, the Federal Government needs no other apology for laying its powerful hand upon the territory.

Without violating any individual or territorial right, without sacrificing the least interest of a political nature at home; without favoring the claims of South or North, or even so much as taking these into consideration, we may purchase the Nicaraguan right of way, and as much territory as may be necessary to open it for gradual and healthy colonization.

Source: The United States Democratic Review, Vol. 41, Issue 2 (New York: J & H.G. Langley, etc. Publishers, February 1858), pp. 115–123. Courtesy of Cornell University Library, Making of America, http://cdl.library.cornell.edu/cgi-bin/moa/sgml/moa-idx?notisid=AGD1642-0041-24.

109. "The Cuban Scheme," January 10, 1859

The fervor to gain Cuba had not cooled by the end of the 1850s. The center of the southern lobby was the state of Louisiana where U.S. Sen. John Slidell (1793–1871) proposed a bill in which the United States would set aside $30 million as an installment for the $100 million purchase of Cuba. Similar proposals had been made prior to 1859, but Slidell had a large following in the Senate. During the 1840s he had served on a commission that attempted to purchase California and New Mexico from Mexico. The bill failed because, by this time, the die was cast in the struggle between the free and slave states and the South did not have sufficient votes to pass the bill. The following article calls for a more aggressive policy in acquiring Cuba and favored the Slidell bill.

THE CUBAN SCHEME

Important Movement of Resistance among the Virginia Democracy.
From the Richmond Enquirer, Jan. 10
The proposition of Sen. Slidell to place $30,000,000 "as an installment for the purchase of Cuba," in the hands of the President, is treated by the press with a superficial comment scarcely more satisfactory than the marked indifference to its

passage or rejection, which seems to possess both Houses of Congress, with regard to most of the startling propositions, Executive or Legislative in their origin, which have distinguished the present session of Congress.

Mr. Slidell's proposition will not, however, we sincerely trust, be allowed to pass through default of opposition, or by sufferance. The serious financial embarrassment in which it cannot fail to involve us, offers a very serious obstacle to a scheme which affords no perceptible promise of countervailing advantage.

When a proposition is made to raise the public debt (which, twelve months ago, stood at "0") by a single coup, to $100,000,000, we have the right to demand some substantial evidence of good to be accomplished, of benefit to be derived. What is the immediate object or necessity to be met by this appropriation of money to coax a purchase? The sum offered, however important at this time to our depleted treasury, is entirely too insignificant to tempt the cupidity of Spain. It is not even pretended that this $30,000,000 would be regarded as a sufficient equivalent for the purchase of Cuba. Indeed, it is regarded as a mere "installment" by the proposer himself.

In what manner, then, is this installment to be rendered an inducement to Spain for the sale of Cuba? In the earlier years of our Republic, when the galvanic wire of Alexander Hamilton had scarcely revived the pallid corpse of public credit, when our Government was as yet a mere experiment, when the permanency of the Union was as doubtful and more doubted than the solvency of the treasury, it was natural that foreign nations should demand some pledge in the way of prospective appropriation, before negotiating for the transfer of valuable territories. But now, will it be pretended that Spain doubts or can doubt the ability of the Federal Government, to raise and appropriate without delay or impediment the whole sum, however large, which may, and whenever it may be required for the purchase of Cuba? Equally flimsy would be the presence that this appropriation is necessary to convince Spain of the willingness of the Legislative Department of the Government, to cooperate with the Executive in the purchase of Cuba. Spain knows, England knows, France knows, everybody knows that both Legislature and Executive, as well as the people themselves, are only too desirous to secure this darling object.

Why, then, shall the appropriation be made? If it is intended as a link in the policy of practical argument by which it is attempted to force on us an increase of tariff duties—that line of vicious management which would increase expenditures, present and prospective, for the purpose of increasing the rates of taxation, only for the ultimate purpose of stimulating certain branches of industrial pursuit at the expense of all other pursuits and occupations—then we owe it to ourselves, and to the principles of the party to which we owe our honest loyalty, to crush this bantling as remorselessly as we would assail the protective system itself. Nay, the qualifying "if" is scarcely necessary, for whatever be the *intent* of Mr. Slidell's proposition, its tendency of domestic influence is obviously what we indicate.

But there is another supposition. The most probable of all, and one which will not fail to receive immediate credence in Europe, to be exclusion of all others; that this appropriation is intended, not as an installment of a round sum to be fixed by a future treaty as the amount of purchase money to be paid over to Spain, but *a bonus to be employed in secret negotiation with Spanish officials, so as to induce the accomplishment of a treaty of purchase.*

We will not pause to discuss the morality of such an arrangement, not the probability of such intent. Whether this be the intent or not, *it will at once be recognized as such by European diplomatists, and this alone will be sufficient to delay the acquisition of Cuba.* The ostentatious publicity which has unfortunately been given to diplomatic documents bearing on this question, and the loose, vague, devil-may-care tone of undetermined rashness and undefined purpose which has marked Congressional discussions on the same subject have already served to awaken and irritate the selfish apprehensions of England and France, to call into exercise all their resources of diplomatic management and powerful influence at the Court of Madrid to arouse in Spain, if not in Cuba, all the opposition of national jealousy. *We have lost much ground, both as regards time and international confidence, by inopportune movements for the acquisition of Cuba.*

At present, an abstinence from all public demonstration, if not an entire "masterly inactivity," is what is needed to ripen this fruit of territorial aggrandizement.

There are more reasons than one to justify such a conservative course, and to require its adoption. In order to succeed in any of the great objects of domestic or home policy, we must retrench not only the present rates of expenditure, but also *the extravagant list of magnificent schemes which has received the sanction of the Executive.* To accomplish anything at all we must refrain from attempting too much. The great Napoleon himself, with all the resources of an empire at his sole command, never ventured the simultaneous accomplishment of so many daring projects. The acquisition of Cuba, at a minimum expense of $100,000,000, the construction of a Pacific Railroad, at perhaps double the figure; a Mexican protectorate, international preponderance in Central America, in spite of all the powers of Europe; the submission of distant South American States; the repulse of unwarrantable demands, in which the selfish British policy of foreign encroachment is deeply interested; the enlargement of the navy; a largely increased standing army; a vital reactionary change in the mode of collecting revenue, directly opposed to the current of free-trade sentiment which is now drawing into its channel all the nations of the earth; a gigantic financial revolution, which contemplates a transfer of all the power over banking and industrial corporations from the hands of the States to those of the Federal Government. Involving a monopoly of monetary command at the centers of trade—*what Government on earth could possibly meet all the exigencies of such a flood of innovations? What Treasury could afford the drain required to supply it?*

No, this sort of thing is out of the question. This chasing after a multitude of objects will inevitably lose us everything of solid benefit, besides involving us in complicated embarrassments, which the wisdom of a subsequent century will hardly be sufficient to unravel. *We want a Napoleon in the field. We want some man who can concentrate all the energies and resources, Governmental and national, on some one great point of reform or advancement.* Abundant promises, magnificent and various, although mutually destructive, may indeed win for an Administration, an agglomeration of tolerance, *not of support,* from conflicting interests and interested contestants. But the Administration which aims to secure for itself, or for the party which it represents, the confidence and the earnest cooperation of popular support, or which aims still higher at the speedy accomplishment of great and beneficial public measures, such an Administration must be chary of promises, and must resort to a concentration of purpose, and a provident consolidation of public resources.

We must at once take hold on the first point of policy, the comparative importance and present urgency of which command the most immediate attention.

In the domain of foreign policy, a Virginia Representative, the Hon. A. G. Jenkins, seems to have recognized the clue to the disentanglement of our international complications. Before we can calculate the expediency of any other step, the abrogation of the Bulwer-Clayton Treaty must be effected.

Source: New York Times, January 21, 1859 (as obtained from the *Richmond Enquirer*, January 10, 1859), p. 2.

110. Democratic Party Platform, June 18, 1860

In 1860, two Democratic Party platforms emerged when the Democratic Convention split into North and South. The majority faction nominated Stephen Douglas (1813–1861) for president, and its platform was adopted at both the Charleston, North Carolina, and Baltimore, Maryland, conventions. Because the party nominated Douglas it was called the Douglas Platform. Along with protecting slavery, the Platform appealed to the southern dissidents by resolving to annex Cuba, which was popular among southerners. However, southern Democrats bolted from the party and held their own convention in Richmond, Virginia, where they selected Kentucky senator and U.S. Vice President John C. Breckenridge (1821–1875) as their nominee for president.

Resolved, that we, the Democracy of the Union in Convention assembled, hereby declare our affirmance of the resolutions unanimously adopted and declared as a platform of principles by the Democratic Convention at Cincinnati, in the year 1856, believing that Democratic principles are unchangeable in their nature, when applied to the same subject matters; and we recommend, as the only further resolutions, the following:

Inasmuch as difference of opinion exists in the Democratic party as to the nature and extent of the powers of a Territorial Legislature, and as to the powers and duties of Congress, under the Constitution of the United States, over the institution of slavery within the Territories,

Resolved, That the Democratic party will abide by the decision of the Supreme Court of the United States upon these questions of Constitutional Law.

Resolved, That it is the duty of the United States to afford ample and complete protection to all its citizens, whether at home or abroad, and whether native or foreign born.

Resolved, That one of the necessities of the age, in a military, commercial, and postal point of view, is speedy communications between the Atlantic and Pacific States; and the Democratic Party pledge such Constitutional Government aid as will insure the construction of a Railroad to the Pacific Coast, at the earliest practicable period.

Resolved, that the Democratic Party are in favor of the acquisition of the Island of Cuba on such terms as shall be honorable to ourselves and just to Spain.

Resolved, That the enactments of the State Legislatures to defeat the faithful execution of the Fugitive Slave Law, are hostile in character, subversive of the Constitution, and revolutionary in their effect.

Resolved, That it is in accordance with the interpretation of the Cincinnati platform, that during the existence of the Territorial Governments the measure of restriction, whatever it may be, imposed by the Federal Constitution on the power of the Territorial Legislature over the subject of the domestic relations, as the same has been, or shall hereafter be finally determined by the Supreme Court of the

United States, should be respected by all good citizens, and enforced with promptness and fidelity by every branch of the general government.

June 18, 1860.

Source: See TeachingAmericanHistory.org, *A Project of the Ashbrook Center for Public Affairs at Ashland University*, http://teachingamericanhistory.org/library/index.asp?document=79.

111. El Grito de Lares, Principles of Unity, 1867

The Puerto Rican Independence movement gained ground in the 1860s. The leader was medical doctor Ramón Betances (1827–1898) who had been exiled for sedition because he raised the issue of Puerto Rican independence. By the day's standards, Puerto Rico was heavily populated with estimates of a million people. Although it was influenced by movements in Cuba, Puerto Rico was some 900 miles from Cuba and 1,000 miles from the United States. There were several factions—on opposite sides were those calling for more autonomy within the Spanish government and those wanting independence. On September 23, 1868, the rebels called for Puerto Rican independence from Spain. The movement was influenced by successful struggles throughout Latin America. However, the revolt was premature and failed. Only a year before, Betances and his fellow revolutionaries founded the Revolutionary Committee of Puerto Rico. They issued the following principles of unity, which formed the building blocks of the independence movement. It is known today as El Grito de Lares (the Cry of Lares). After this point, Puerto Ricans formed a government in exile, operating from New York and Latin American capitals where they recruited money for arms and supporters.

THE TEN COMMANDMENTS OF FREE MEN

1. Abolition of slavery
2. The right to fix taxes
3. Freedom of worship
4. Free press
5. Free speech
6. Free trade
7. Freedom of assembly
8. Right to bear arms
9. Civil liberties of the citizens
10. Right to elect their own public officials

Source: World of Guazabara Federation, http://guazabara.com/GritodeLares.htm.

112. Excerpt from Correspondent Quasimodo, "Cuba," 1868

Spain, on the eve of the conquest of the Caribbean Islands in the 1490s, had become a major sugar producer. Plantations in the south of Spain and in the Azore and Canary Islands were expanded in the Caribbean. Cuba, under the Spanish crown, had one of the largest land masses in the Caribbean and was ideal for sugar cultivation. During the 1800s, a worldwide abolitionist movement led mostly by England limited the number of Africans imported to the island. After 1865, the United States joined in the abolition of the slave trade. The following article notes the decline of the African population in Cuba in 1868, and talks about the labor shortage on the sugar plantations. Plantation owners turned to China for laborers who were treated abysmally.

CUBA

Proposed Revival of the Slave Trade
How Plantation Hands Are Treated—A Cuban Loan—Distinguished Visitors—Movements of Gen. Lersundi

Havana, Saturday, March 18, 1868.

From Our Own Correspondent.

Summer has made its appearance somewhat too soon for the comfort of these who are compelled to remain in this hot climate. The warm weather has a peculiar influence on the population, and manifests its power in many ways. Among those most affected by it are undoubtedly the editors of the Havana journals. These gentlemen form a very peculiar class, judging from their ponderous leaders, which advocate the most absurd and even criminal measures, such as the revival of the slave-trade, a suggestion put forward by the *Diario de la Marina*. That paper had not expressed the fact in so many plain words, but has published several articles demonstrating, after a fashion, the impossibility of obtaining the field hands needed to cultivate the sugar-cane fields, and giving utterance to a firm conviction that a free white or a forced Chinese immigration can never supply the places vacated by the hundreds of Africans who are annually sacrificed to fill the pockets of the planter.

The black population is continually decreasing instead of multiplying, as was the case in the Southern States while Slavery existed there. The reason for this is obvious and well known to everybody who has been enabled to observe the treatment of the slaves on most Cuban plantations. In the first place, the negroes are poorly fed. The usual daily allowance of food on most plantations is so small that it is hardly worth while mentioning, being merely a hash of sweet potatoes, plantains, and a little jerked beef, and in many instances even the jerked beef is dispensed with. How the human frame can long sustain itself with such insufficient victuals is a wonder, and it is not therefore to be marveled at that the negroes and Chinamen die so soon. The Chinamen receive a ration of rice at every meal, as otherwise they would rise is mutiny at once. The allowance of rice to these ill-treated Asiatics can therefore not be ascribed to the liberality of the planter, but to fear. Fresh meat is an article which is known on many plantations only by name, as the article, when given, is of such a wretched quality and so limited in quantity that the blacks might as well not have any. There are some plantations, it is true, where the slaves are better cared for than on others, but the above statement holds good when applied to the generality.

The second grand cause for the annual lessening of the number of slaves is the overwork. During the grinding season the slaves of both sexes, and irrespective of age, work from nineteen to twenty-two hours per day. This appears incredible, but it is a well-known and authenticated fact, having come under the personal observation of your correspondent on several occasions. The negroes retire at midnight from the sugar-house, after working from 4 o'clock in the morning, to obtain from three to four hours' sleep before beginning the next day's labor. There is no Sunday, no day of rest; it is a continual succession of days of labor; no rest or relaxation is afforded the poor negro, for the owner of the plantation must have money enough to support his town establishment, and save enough for a Summer trip to Saratoga or to Europe; he must have his carriages and boxes at the opera, while his friends must be entertained. Is it a wonder, therefore, that the working population should be decreasing and that the planters should clamor for field hands? The white population increases fast enough; in fact they may be classed as super prolific, but its off-spring not that which is wanted or needed by the planter, who can always find drivers and overseers in abundance. Yet it must be conceded that these whites are fully as capable of performing a reasonable snare of farm labor as the blacks, unless they should also be compelled to work twenty hours a day.

Source: *New York Times*, April 26, 1868, p. 10.

113. Excerpts from the Address of Manuel de Quesada of Cuba to the United States, December 4, 1873

Manuel de Quesada (1830–1886), a Cuban patriot born in Puerto Rico, was forced to immigrate to Mexico in 1853, because of his anti-Spanish government activities. He joined the ranks of Mexican President Benito Juárez (1806–1872) and fought against the French from 1861 to 1868. Promoted to brigadier general, he became governor of Coahuila and Durango, Mexico. When the first popular Cuban insurrection began in 1868, he organized a revolutionary expedition in U.S. territory and landed at Guanaja, in the northern part of Cuba. In 1870, he left the island, to tour the United States and the South American republics while recruiting for Cuban independence. The Spaniards captured one of his steamers, *Virginius*, and the crew, including his son, was executed at Santiago de Cuba. After the insurrection failed, he moved to Costa Rica. The following address is one of his early appeals to the United States for support. In the letter to President U.S. Grant Quesada aligns the interests of Cuban independist with anti-slavery forces in the United States. Quesada makes a case for a recognition of Cuban belligerency and foreign assistance from the United States. This is a very important document because it documents early Cuban migration to the United States, and it methodically reviews United States policy toward Cuba.

THE REPRESENTATIVES OF THE CUBAN REPUBLIC IN FOREIGN LANDS, TO HIS EXCELLENCY THE PRESIDENT OF THE UNITED STATES

Your Excellency [President Ulysses S. Grant]—even at a time when, by order of the Spanish officials in the island of Cuba, the captain, crew, and a large portion of the passengers of the American steamer "*Virginius*," captured, near Jamaica by a Spanish man-of-war, have been executed, and the survivors remain subjected to ... [cruel] treatment ... [and] the American people and the whole civilized world stand amazed at the horrors of the transaction ... your Excellency's high minded ...

Message to Congress strengthened the hopes ... that the Cuban question was at last to receive the solution demanded by the interest of civilization and the spirit of American institutions....

II

As the war in Cuba broke out a short time after [the U.S. Civil War (1861–65)], the men engaged in the contest here [the U.S.], were perhaps inclined to regard the Cubans as holding the same relations to the Spanish government that the seceding States did to the government of this Union, and looked upon them as rebels to the mother country.... a great part of the American merchants resident in the island [of Cuba], or having business relations therewith ... [had] interests ... identical with those of the slave-trading Spaniards who constituted the real Spanish government of Cuba. The commerce of the United States with the Island represents more than $100,000,000 yearly, and many of the Americans engaged in it are the very energetic, though not avowed, defenders of the Spanish power in the island. And, for the reason that such power furnishes for them the slave labor which produces the sugar, coffee, and tobacco, the traffic in which makes them rich.

The men in this country who sustain this commerce necessarily exert a great influence, without appearing to mingle in any political questions, and they may have created in Washington a feeling opposed to Cuba, which will prevent the question being seen in its true light.

The Cubans constituted a colony of Spain, without political rights or rights of any kind; the South [the Confederacy] belonged to a confederation of free States, bound to submit to the decision of the greater number; the Cubans fight to abolish slavery, the South fought to preserve it; the Cubans desire to be allied to the Union, the South only wished to be separate there from. To sum up the whole matter, the South, whether wrong or otherwise, decided to establish, by an appeal to arms, the new principle of the right of a portion of a nation to separate from the main body; the Cubans have the long since admitted [the] right of independence belonging to every oppressed colony, as proclaimed in 1776 by the fathers of this country [the U.S.]. They had many times asked political rights from Spain, which had been as often denied them, and when they had lost every hope, they took to the field. Whether they are entitled to any credit for the manner they have conducted themselves, is a question not to be treated as idle words, as, it is feared, has been done heretofore.

In Cuba was formed a respectable society, augmented by emigration from Florida, St. Domingo, and all Spanish America, and influenced by the fact that a certain market for their productions could be found in the United States. The families who there acquired wealth, not finding an opportunity of educating their sons in a satisfactory manner under Spanish rule, adopted the habit of sending them to foreign lands, and in this way, after many years, there grew up in that country a population—refined and cultured—in opposition to the aims and wishes of the government of Spain. When this population decided to break the ties which bound them to the mother country, propositions were made to inaugurate the movement in April 1869, at which time it was thought all the arms and necessary supplies could be obtained and properly distributed; but the intention having been discovered by the Spaniards the outbreak was anticipated by several months, and on the 10th of October of the year previous it took place. The Cubans preferred to go to the field without arms rather than remain and be executed in cold blood by the Spaniards. From that moment the only question has been how to obtain arms from abroad. The Spanish government, being well aware that the oppressed people of the great Antille had means enough to arm their forces and to create a navy, confiscated the property of a great part of them. This property amounted to several hundreds of millions of dollars, as can be proved by the official records in Havana. This measure could not, however, prevent the patriots from buying arms, though it diminished to an immense extent the revolutionary resources. By private subscriptions of Cubans only there have been purchased fourteen steamers, sixteen sailing vessels, and 40,000 rifles. Unfortunately, as the requisite funds could not be collected rapidly, it was impossible to apply them on as large a scale as necessary to evade the Spanish blockade and not to break in any respect the neutrality laws of this country. The expeditions, sometimes owing to the scarcity of resources and at others to the want of experience—natural under the circumstances—have not always arrived at their destinations. It was essential to employ a greater amount of money at one time than could be obtained from private subscriptions. There were three methods of raising such money—sending to sea to prey upon Spanish commerce, exchanging for funds those products remaining within the extent of the insurgent lines, and to negotiate a foreign loan. To the first was presented the obstacle that the worthy representatives of the Cuban Republic at that time did not dare to assume the responsibility, as they were made aware that the American government would not view favorably the existence of Cuban privateers when it was pressing the Alabama claims. To the second existed the obstacle, that Cuban belligerency not being recognized, it was impossible to excite the spirit of gain to engage in any enterprises the object of which was to run the blockade. The third had for its obstacle that all the European and some American houses disposed to enter upon its negotiation, imposed always as a *sine qua non* condition the previous recognition of the belligerency by the United States. Consequently, the main object of all our diplomatic efforts has been, during a certain time, to bring about such recognition. The Spaniards, on their part, knowing that the immediate loss of the island would result from this recognition, stopped at no means to prevent it [*sic*] accomplishment, and without doubt they have displayed herein great diplomatic sagacity. But if on the field of intrigue they gained the result which they desired, they were not equally fortunate on the field of battle. As was natural, the greater part of the unarmed Cubans and families who were within the theatre of the war were dispersed or sent away in the midst of the military movements. At the same time, a regular army was formed, equipped by the arms and materials furnished by the successful expeditions and with those taken from the enemy, which army has during the past five years, been increasing in numbers, morale and strength.

The Spanish army in Cuba had lost, during the first four years of the war, 60,000 men, and it was supposed that the Cuban loss had been correspondingly great. As the Spaniards are naturally interested in belittling the importance of the insurrection, it may be concluded these figures are not exaggerated. Admitting that the loss, during the past year, the most bloody of all, has been in proportion equally large, it will be seen that since the beginning of the war 150,000 men have perished.

The loss resulting from the destruction of property is immense.

The value of the productions which could have been controlled by the republican government of Cuba, during the first months of the war is estimated at $10,000,000.

These productions were afterwards lost through the military operations which followed. The value of the crops in those districts which constitute the seat of war, and which have been lost, can be estimated at $15,000,000 a year ... notwithstanding all these immense losses of life and property, the non-recognition of the belligerency of the Cubans by the United States and the supreme efforts made to suppress them by Spain, they are now, as no one will deny, stronger than ever, and they have an army which renders nugatory all the efforts of their foes in the field. Their hearts have been tempered until they are injustice proof ... the delay in the recognition of their belligerency by this [U.S.] country, will compel the postponement of their [Cuban] independence until the ruin of the Antille is complete. With the slow but inevitable march of the cancer, the liberating army is encroaching upon the Spanish dominion in the island. As time moves on, this dominion is constantly growing weaker in the midst of its furious convulsions, while the revolution is constantly spreading, and the ultimate result will be to destroy in America the ignominious power of the nation of Torquemada, Alva, and Burriel.

The Cubans, notwithstanding the embargoes and confiscations from which they have suffered, are always enabled to raise funds among themselves, and every effort made by them to give assistance to the liberating army is always succeeded by another, and there is no possibility of a cessation of these efforts.... The patriots have never been wanting in fighting material, as every man capable of bearing arms has always been inclined to do so. They have done and they do everything alone, entirely alone, notwithstanding the fact that they have been opposed by an army stronger than that which Great Britain sent to this country to suppress the American Revolution, added to the number which Spain herself sent out to suppress the revolts against her power in Mexico and in her South American colonies. There were never forty thousand British soldiers on American soil; there were never forty thousand Spanish soldiers on the continent they lost. In Cuba there were during the first four years of the existing struggle, sixty thousand regular troops, and besides, some thousands of Spanish volunteers, who garrisoned the towns. With all this extraordinary force, with a formidable navy and the best American weapons, the Spanish government has year after year seen its battalions disappear, and it has no resources to-day to replace them.

Every Cuban, every progressive man, will always admire the history of this wonderful country [the United States], whose noble and intelligent people have changed materially and morally the world with the marvels of electricity, of steam, and of liberal institutions. This beloved land of America, this powerful nation, is the natural ally of Cuba. It is the market of Cuba. Its society is that which must be interlaced with the society of Cuba. Its glories reflect upon Cuba, its misfortunes are hers, and she ever prays for its success in all endeavors. The defenders of the island, however, are inclined to believe that their patriotism is not inferior to the patriotism of the fathers of the American revolution.... The lesson of the historian is, that without foreign assistance it is probable its first effort for independence would have been suppressed and George Washington died on the scaffold—treated by the British writers as a filibuster; a term applied to-day by an eminent jurist to the men of education and high position in society who have recently sacrificed their lives for the liberty of their country, and among whom the undersigned has the glory to count a son, a youth eighteen years old. [Quesada reviews the history of the American Revolution and the crucial support of France.]...

But this assistance, so secretly afforded, did not satisfy the French people, and many volunteers, depending upon their own resources, came hither to offer their lives in defense of the independence of this nation, when the news of the loss of New York and the retreat through the Jerseys made most foreigners despair of the American cause, as said Hildreth:

"The Marquis of Lafayette, a youth of nineteen, belonging to one of the most illustrious families of France, who had just arrived in America, and whom Washington now met, in Philadelphia, for the first time ... like all other French nobles of that date, he had received a military education, and held a commission in the French Army. In garrison at Metz, he had been present at an entertainment given by the Duke of Gloucester, brother of the British king, and on that occasion, from the Duke's lips he heard, first, the story of the American rebellion. His youthful fancy was fired by the idea of this trans-Atlantic struggle for liberty, and, though master of an ample fortune, and married to a wife whom he tenderly loved, he resolved at once to adventure in it. For that purpose, he opened a communication with Deane. His intention becoming known, the French Court, which still kept up the forms of neutrality, forbade him to go. But he secretly purchased a ship, which Deane loaded with military stores, and set sail at a moment when the news of the loss of New York and the retreat through the Jerseys made most foreigners despair of the American cause."

With the reception of these resources, the Americans were enabled to enter upon a new and active campaign which proved one of victories, though with occasional reverses....

The Modern Greek, too, as is well known, owes his independence, first to recognition of his belligerent rights by the leading powers of Europe, and, subsequently, to the practical assistance of the same. And lately Lombardy and Venetia owe their independence of Austria to the alliance of Italy and Prussia. It cannot be inferred from this that they were not entitled to their independence, that they did not fight bravely—the Americans, Spaniards, South Americans, Greeks, Lombards and Venetians....

no people has acquired its independence without foreign assistance, is it to be assumed that Cuba, which has had no such aid, is to be conquered by the Spanish? No; the immense misfortunes which have fallen upon that unhappy country appear to be a punishment for the horrors and abominations which have been manifested in its fields in order to coin gold from the blood of the slaves. For this great crime, both Spaniards and Cubans are responsible, as well as those who in any way foster the productions of slavery. It is true that as soon as the Cubans rose in arms against Spanish domination, they began to cleanse their skirts of the dark spot, declaring freedom to the slaves and making them their equals before the law; but it was necessary that they should expiate the abominations of the slave-trade, of the whip and the anvil block, with sufferings proportionate to them, and the ferocity of the Spaniards in Cuba has cleansed them from all the guilt of this so great crime. The spirit of evil, incarnate in these Spaniards, and extending through the island, has furnished to the Cubans an expiation for the sins of their fathers, and as they have not a single ally on earth, they have the alliance of Providence. This is not a common expression, nor without significance in the sphere of fact. In that splendid island which Columbus pronounced "the most beautiful land that human eye ever dwelt upon," under its clear skies, amid its picturesque seas, among its odorous flowers, its birds of brilliant plumage, and its proud forests, Mother Nature has placed a germ of disease, deadly to the European—the malaria.

the complete exhaustion of the Spanish treasury, as has already been said, has rendered it impossible for Spain to send to Cuba the necessary number of troops to maintain her present military position. This leads to the conclusion that if Spain, with all the moral and material assistance of this nation, has not been able to sustain herself victoriously against the Cubans, the latter would easily have conquered, had they, from the beginning, been enabled to introduce into the island the arms they needed. Your Excellency will, may be, answer this, that the high interest of this [his] country would not permit her to take any steps in this matter, and that the wiser and more prudent course was the one which has been adopted.... [Quesada complains] Meanwhile, the Spanish ambassador was an especial favorite in Washington. Nor was this all. In this country was constructed a squadron of gunboats to aid in suppressing the Cuban movement; and from this country, too, were sent the artillery and the Remington rifles used by the Spanish Army in Cuba. The record of the aid extended by this great Republic to rivet the chains upon a people struggling to be free will not be complete without referring to the order of American war vessels, cruising along the coast of the island, to receive all deserters from the Cuban forces who might make application to be taken on board—an order which constituted a true armed intervention on the part of this country in the struggle in favor of Spain. That this is so is evident from the fact that Spain, though so punctilious regarding any interference in her affairs from without, has, so far as is known, made no remonstrance—found no fault. In the meantime, the government at Madrid was sending thousands upon thousands of soldiers to the island, and, in order to prevent any change of policy on the part of the American government, a change which was demanded by the American people, it resorted to the subterfuge of proclaiming several times the entire pacification of Cuba. This was done by the Captains General, De Rodas and Valmaseda, during 1869, and in 1870, the Spanish Cortes extended a unanimous vote of thanks to the former for his action in bringing about the alleged pacification. Their object, in these deceitful declarations, has been to gain time, and to continue the American government bound to inaction, knowing that the recognition at Washington of the belligerency of the Cubans would be the death-blow to their power in America.

The slave question was also used by them to win the good graces of the American government. Striving to make it appear that they were inspired by a spirit of abolition, they issued laws with bombastic preambles, which, so far from abolishing the criminal institution in the island, only resulted in its continuance. Thus, year after year has passed away without the Cubans obtaining that recognition to which they were entitled. Unquestionably, had they been less vigorous, they would have succumbed.

Cuban authorities, becoming convinced of the enmity of the American government, withdrew their representatives accredited it, though giving to the undersigned full powers in every respect, including authority to treat with the American government, whenever it should be deemed proper to recognize the Cubans as a people struggling for independence. This action of the modest government, established on the battlefields of Cuba Libre, might perchance seem ridiculous and contemptible were the executive mansion at Washington occupied by a man less high-minded and noble than the one who shook hands with Lee on the banks of the Appomatox.... What other conviction could the Cuban government have had than that the American Administration was hostile to it? What could it do but recall its minister in this country, seeing he was always repulsed by the authority to which he was accredited? Cuba, conscious of its own inherent strength, accepted with sorrow the apparently undeniable fact of the hostility of the administration at Washington, and determined to continue its struggle for independence, relying solely upon its own resources and convinced of its ultimate triumph. This confidence was incited not alone by the justice of its cause, but by the unanimity of sentiment among the natives, and the fact that every man, no matter what his situation in life, or place of residence, was doing something to advance the interests of the cause.

As a general rule, the Spaniards, born in the Iberian Peninsula and settled in the American colonies, have been far more despotic and pitiless in their treatment of the descendants of Spaniards born therein, than has the government of Madrid.

The codes embodying the laws of the Indies and the municipal laws were, perhaps, not perfect models of liberalism, but, considering the times in which they were enacted, were calculated to bring about the prosperity of the societies affected by them, had not the Spanish residents always prevented their execution, in order to retain a monopoly of every good thing. In fact, the Creole population throughout Spanish America could well have endured the tyranny of the government at Madrid, and been resigned to remain thereunder, but they could not endure the tyranny of the Spanish residents, who condemned them to imbecility, misery, and death. And thus it is with Cuba, as is indicated in the recent message of Your Excellency. The Spaniards established in the island have always bitterly opposed any measures for the improvement of the natives, interested only in the slave trade and in accomplishing the total degradation of the Cubans. Far from composing the aristocratic portion of the people, as has been erroneously reported to Your Excellency, they constitute an uneducated population of bachelors, and careful to create no ties in the country. They are thus left free to indulge in their hatred to the people, which they never relinquish. When the war for independence broke out they formed themselves into militia organizations, called "The Volunteers," more ferocious than the Janizaries and Mamelukes. In order to overawe the native population they have grossly exaggerated their numbers, but there are, nevertheless, as many as 25,000 of them in the island, doing garrison duty in all the towns, the natives thereof being defenceless, as arms are prohibited them. Besides the volunteers and regular troops there are but few Spaniards in the island. It is not easy to estimate the entire population, as the government and the volunteers have always been interested in preventing a reliable census, and they have fixed as they liked the returns. It may be safely assumed that of the 1,500,000—the estimated population—500,000 are colored. Of the latter, more than 300,000 are slaves. There are in all 100,000 Spaniards on the island. The Volunteers being the only armed bodies in the towns, they are enabled to perpetrate their outrages with impunity. They began their murders in January 1869, in Havana; and, not satisfied with having shot without trial several thousands in Bayamo, Manzanillo, Holguin, Camaguey, Matanzas, and Santiago de Cuba, the theatre of the late massacre by Burriel, they have rebelled against every Captain-General who has not obeyed them, and in one way or another they have sent back to Spain Dulce, De Rodas, Ceballos, and Pieltain.

The secret of their power can be easily understood. They have the monopoly of the interior commerce and retail trade; they have the slave trade, which still exists, though carried on with the greatest secrecy, and they have the management of the embargoed properties of the Cubans. In fact, they are in league with the Spanish government to appropriate to themselves all the agricultural wealth of the island, resulting from the labors of the natives. Holding as they do the cities, the triumph of the Spanish cause would be the signal for exterminating the Cubans, as has already been done in many of the interior towns....

The Cubans can only expect death from these Volunteers. They realize that with the suppression of the insurrection, the work of extermination would commence, in one form or another: by immense deportations from the island, as in the case of the Fernando Po prisoners, so conducted that few, if any, would survive, without for a moment neglecting the easier task of daily shootings.... If the Cubans could for a moment doubt that this is the fate reserved for them in case of their being routed, they would easily be convinced of it by a consideration of the treatment accorded to the blacks in 1844. There existed on the island at that time a numerous and wealthy colored population. The Spaniards determined on a scheme to deprive them of their money. To this end, they affected to believe that a conspiracy existed among them, a conspiracy of which no proof has been found after thirty years, and under the lash and by the rifle, they were all exterminated. A great poet, Placido, perished among them. Considering these precedents, demonstrating as they do that the Cubans are fighting for life, it is easy to see how they have been able to neutralize the most energetic efforts of the Spaniards....

The United States long since became a resort of all the Cuban families, as could be seen at Saratoga, Newport, and, above all, in the Empire City, and, not satisfied with this yearly trip, they, soon began to purchase real estate and establish their residence in this country, making Cuba their winter resort. Meanwhile all their available means were invested in this country in national securities, railroad bonds, &c. This transfer of property from the Antille to the United States has assumed large proportions since 1865, and, had the outbreak been postponed for three years, there would have remained only a few wealthy Cuban families not established in this country. In the early part of 1869, the decree of confiscation against many of them was issued, but already large numbers naturalized as Americans had a great part of their fortunes in this [the U.S.] country.

Thus it can be easily seen from what source are drawn these very, very considerable expenditures. Moreover, the assassinations which took place, after the insurection [*sic*] of Yara, in the towns of the island, drove very many of the inhabitants to these hospitable shores. Not all of them were rich, and the poor soon began to employ themselves in a manner profitable to both the country which had received them and to the patriotic cause. They mostly dedicated themselves to the manufacture of cigars, and, according to the statistics, they have increased fivefold the wealth of the nation in this branch of industry since 1868. At least it cannot be denied that during the intervening time, large factories have been established in Key West, New Orleans, Baltimore, Philadelphia, New York, and other places. These honest men, earning from $3 to $5 a day, have contributed constantly to the patriotic fund, reducing as much as possible their personal expenses that they might contribute the more. It is worthwhile here to mention the middle class—composed of those who could not save their property before the Revolution and those who have adopted professional careers or are devoted to literary and artistic pursuits. By the first of these, this mercantile community has been enlarged in wealth and numbers, and by the latter, scientific and illustrated papers of a higher order have been established in New York, which propagate the progress and glories of the United States throughout all Spanish America, and, to an extent, in Spain itself. In medical science they have some distinguished representatives in this country, and the musical societies and the picture galleries of this enlightened city are sustained to a large degree by Cubans eminent in their respective fields. All contribute, whether rich or poor, to the patriotic fund, and will continue to do so, and while doing this they also contribute with their blood to bring about the independence of their native country. In every one of the expeditions which have been fitted out—the *Henry Burden, Salvador, Peril, Grapeshot, Catharine Whiting, Lilian Anna, Upton, Virginius, Edgar Stuart*, and many others—it has been necessary to reject applications from Cubans, as the lists were full. As many of them have gone to Cuba as could be provided with means of transportation. Notwithstanding all these well-established facts there are those who accuse the Cubans of lack of patriotism, and it is believed that there are here many thousands who do not honorably represent their cause. It is to them a sorrowful matter that, instead of receiving a due appreciation of their efforts and sacrifices, they only meet with misrepresentation and revilement. As these misrepresentations have been so often repeated without refutation, the representative of the Cuban Republic takes advantage of this occasion to make a full statement of the facts. According to the most reliable information, collected and on file in this office, the natives of Cuba resident in the United States, including old people, women, and children, do not exceed 5,000. Of those capable of bearing arms only a few remain; the balance are in the field. Of those few, many are detained here as being the only support of families. The journals who for sensational purposes make so much of the Cubans in this country ought to realize that the importance attached to them springs rather from their wealth and sacrifices than from their numbers. In order to conclude the matter, it may be added that this emigration, though so small in numbers, may have been more profitable to the country than others which have been very large. They are free from those habits of intemperance which, unfortunately, are so prevalent in some other classes of society. They do not disturb public tranquility with violent demonstrations. The assurance can be made that, with the recognition of belligerency and the consequent facilities for obtaining arms, there will be none left capable of carrying a rifle, and even many of the old men will go. It is to be hoped that, hereafter, they will be regarded in the true light. It is not so easy a matter—as has often been said—to leave home, wealth, and every enjoyment to enter upon a fearful campaign.... The United States recognized the belligerency and independence of Texas because they considered it to their own interest. The same United States treated Mexico as a republic when she was a *de facto* empire because they considered this course to their own interest. Interest, and before everything, interest, has always ruled diplomacy since this modern invention was applied by Louis XI and Ferdinand V. And there is no other conclusion than that, in the disposition of the Cuban question, interest, and only interest, will control the action of this nation.

The principle accepted, the question will, at the end, be reduced to one of dollars and cents. What has been, what is the interest of the United States in this Cuban question? Let us examine this point, placing on one side justice, humanity, and duty. First, what has been? When the Spanish American colonies accomplished their independence, Bolivar decided that Spain should be entirely expelled from the New

World, and for this purpose he organized a formidable expedition to invade Cuba to act in co-operation with the natives, it being well known that the principal families were engaged in the conspiracies of the Aguila Negra and Soles de Bolivar. This expedition, fully organized and equipped by Colombia and Mexico, with the squadron in readiness to transport it to the shores of Cuba, was on the point of embarking when the United States notified the powers engaged in it that they would not allow the proposed operations to be carried out, and that they would assist, with their military and naval forces, Spain to retain under her dominion the Island of Cuba.... The movement for independence in Spanish America being essentially abolitionist in its character, the American administration of that period could not see, with pleasure, the liberty of the blacks in Cuba brought about; not only because, as these notes indicated, the results would be detrimental to the peace and prosperity of this nation, but, as was carefully concealed, it hoped eventually to bring it within the Union as a slave State. Moreover, the independence of Cuba at that time might have resulted in a European protectorate in the Antilles, and perhaps the occupation of the island by England with the assent of the natives. Spain, a weak nation, having no navy, was preferred by the United States to hold temporarily the island, as she would preserve slavery in it, and the expectation was entertained that, at some future day, it would be ceded by her ... from 1848 to 1850 and 1854, the government of the United States, controlled by the slave interest, took some steps in favor of the annexation of the island. The Southern States saw with alarm the growing influence and increasing development of northern principles, and out of this grew this movement for annexation. The Cubans, though, they have always been inclined to substitute free labor for slave.... In 1854, another annexation scheme was presented in the slave interest. Gen. Quitman, of Mississippi, was to command a formidable expedition. The conspiracy was discovered, and Pinto and several others were executed by the Spaniards. The interest of the dominant party lay in the acquisition of the Gem of the West Indies, to be divided into three States, to add to the influence of the South; and if this scheme did not succeed it was because France and England intervened in the matter, proposing to the United States the tripartite alliance to guarantee to Spain the possession of Cuba....

What is now the interest of this nation? When the American civil war brought about as a trophy of victory to the North, the abolition of slavery, the government changed entirely its fundamental basis. It had no further reasons for desiring the preservation of the island in the power of Spain or to accomplish annexation with slave labor. Spain, instead of being a nation without a navy, as it was in 1826, had become a maritime power. Cuba, instead of being, with her slaves, a pleasant picture to the United States, became a monument of their own past ignominy that they could not tolerate at their own doors—and this, even though the island remained faithful to the crown of Spain. The Cubans, as has been so often repeated, in 1868, took to the field to gain their independence. They took possession of a large portion of the island and from the very beginning declared free all of its inhabitants. The new Republic was in accordance with the regenerated Republic of the northern continent. At this moment, this nation was compelled to look to its interest in the question, and it appears the government thought it had found it in the propositions made by Mr. Sickles to the cabinet of Madrid. If it is true that these propositions were for the Cubans to purchase the island from Spain, with the guarantee of the United States, it is to be supposed that they would be advantageous to three contracting parties. But Spain did not accept them, though she employed the diplomatic arts referred to, and such a solution should have been abandoned. Was it the interest of the United States after that to preserve the *status quo*, that the horrors of the war should be continued, the natives not being allowed to arm themselves? This was in some respects the interest of Spain, but certainly not that of the United States.

It appears that the United States—abandoning the Cuban question to itself and without reference to justice—thought it was their interest to retain their connection with the slave power in Cuba as long as possible. The recognition of Cuban belligerency would produce a declaration by Spain of the blockade of the island, and, as a consequence, the right of the Spaniards to search American vessels according to the treaty of 1795; this, of course, was a bad prospect for the commerce sustained with the slave power. May be it was considered that the continued arrival of sugar and tobacco from Cuba, paying its high duties, amounting to several millions of dollars, was preferable to any other solution for the present.

It is true that such commerce grew out of slave labor, and that the United States have made it appear that they desire the abolition of such labor in Cuba and everywhere; but the question of slavery could be treated diplomatically, and extended through an indefinite period, the United States meanwhile deriving all the advantage from such traffic and from the duties on such articles. Though the Cubans, notwithstanding the course of the United States, persisted in imitating the founders of the great nation who fought for independence, nothing could be done which would change the relation of the country to such slave power....

It is very easy to comprehend, moreover, that, with the abolition of the custom houses in Cuba, or—if, unhappily, this measure should be considered too progressive—the suspension of the export duties on these commodities, and the reduction on the import duties there imposed upon the supplies and machinery required by the planters would result in an immense saving to both these planters and the merchants in the United States. This would more than recompense the former for the losses consequent on passing from slave to free labor, while the latter would find their remuneration in the increased profits on their wares, thus relieved of the onerous duties now imposed upon them. At the same time, Cuba would become a market for a large number of exports from this country which are now shut out from the island by the high duties imposed, in order that they may not compete with the productions of the peninsula.... These undeniable facts being borne in mind, it seems the interests of the United States, at the breaking out of the revolution was to favor, at least morally, the Cubans in their efforts to become independent....

The opportunities which the government has had since the outbreak of the war to assume a position favorable to the patriots have been very numerous. In March 1869, the American brig *Mary Lowell* was captured at Ragged Island, brought to Havana and condemned as a good prize, having on board a valuable cargo.

This was an act more in contravention of international law than even the seizure of the *Virginius*. According to the treaty of 1795, the right of search and seizure of American vessels by the Spaniards extended only to the time of war. The infraction of this treaty, in the taking of the *Mary Lowell*, constituted a just cause for the American government to declare that the Spanish authorities had, by their action, virtually admitted the existence of a war in Cuba. The United States, therefore, should have recognized such war, and declared their neutrality in it. From this would have resulted a rapid termination of the struggle without these immense losses of property which have since occurred, to say nothing of the great destruction of American lives. After this remarkable event, which produced only a lengthy official correspondence, the American steamer *Florida* was overhauled and searched on two occasions by Spanish men-of-war in 1871. And so well satisfied was the administration at Washington that the action of the Spanish war vessels demonstrated the existence of a war in Cuba that on the 16th of July 1869, the honorable Secretary of State, in a protest against the edict of the Captain-General de Rodas, of the 7th of that month, stated the same in unequivocal language: "The United States cannot fail to regard any exercise on the part of Spain of the right of visit and search of American vessels, under color of the treaty of 1795, as involving the logical conclusion of the recognition by Spain of a state of war in Cuba," is the idea conveyed. Notwithstanding that the government of the United States could not "fail to regard" any exercise on the high seas, near the island of Cuba, by any vessel of war or privateer of Spain, of the right to visit or board any vessel of the United States, under color of the provisions of the treaty of 1795, as involving the logical conclusion of a recognition by Spain of a state of war in Cuba, it is unhappily true that the American government did fail, when the boarding and search of the *Florida* occurred. The whole matter can be closed with the expression of a hope that this government will not fail, now, to take the action indicated in the protest referred to. Admitting that the nationality of the *Virginius* is a matter of doubt, and that her antecedents cannot be justified, this does not affect the question, as in the case of the *Florida* no such doubt, no such antecedents exist. She had never been to the coast of Cuba, and never carried arms or expeditionists there. The American government has maintained, in an official note, that certain acts involved the logical conclusion of a recognition by Spain of a state of war in Cuba. Spain has performed such acts, and so it must be concluded such war exists. The recognition of this war by Spain should be followed by the recognition of it by the United States and a declaration of its neutrality therein. This would be sufficient, and only will free America of the ignominious presence of the never-wearying murderers who have established themselves in that wealthy and beautiful island. This would increase the glory and wealth of this great nation....

The Cubans await the decisions of the American government at this critical moment. If it is in favor of justice, humanity, and freedom, they will bow in gratitude to Providence, acting in conformity to the sacrifices already made. In favor of the maintenance of the present condition of affairs, they shall continue to the end in the struggle in which they have so long, and at the cost of so much blood and treasure, been engaged....

This question must be considered in the light of the facts so clearly stated by your Excellency in your message. In that document it is recognized that in Cuba, besides the forces of the government of Spain, there exists what is called the insurrection of Yara and the pro-slavery party, the latter being "an element," says your Excellency, "opposed to granting any relief from misrule and abuse, with no aspirations after freedom, commanding no sympathy in generous breasts, aiming to rivet still stronger the shackles of slavery and oppression." Such an element, which "has seized many of the emblems of power in Cuba, is still a power in Madrid, and recognized by the government."

The undersigned, in the name of the government which he has the honor to represent, anticipates the expression of his gratitude to the government of the United States.... It is impossible to suppose that the high-minded statesmen of the great republic have determined upon a *status quo* which will leave the Cubans unable to obtain their independence through want of the requisite arms and materials—the Spaniards at the same time unable to suppress their efforts—until both parties become so weakened that the island will fall an easy prey to the government they represent. This would be far more ferocious and cruel than the conduct of the Spanish Volunteers of Havana, which is so much deprecated by the civilized world. No Machiavellian policy ever adopted in the history of mankind could be compared with this. No; it would be unjust so to insult the high and Christian members of the American government.

Your Excellency's obedient servant,
M. QUESADA
New York, December 4, 1873.

Source: M. Quesada, *Address of Cuba to the United States* (New York: Comes, Lawrence & Co., Stationers and Printers, 1873), pp. 1–40, Library of Congress, http://memory.loc.gov/cgi-bin/query/r?ammem/murray:@field(DOCID+@lit(lcrbmrpt2502div2)).

114. Excerpt from a U.S. Senate Debate Regarding Whether the United States Should Annex Santo Domingo, 1870

Santo Domingo gained its independence from Spain in 1821. A year later, Haitians who shared the island invaded the Dominican Republic. In 1844, Dominicans ousted the Haitians but continued Haitian attacks bankrupted the republic. Conditions deteriorated to the point that, in 1870, President Buenaventura Báez (1812–1884) asked the United States to annex Santo Domingo. A congressional debate was touched off by President Ulysses S. Grant (1869–1877) annual message that proposed Congress should authorize a commission to negotiate an annexation treaty with San Domingo. Grant favored annexation. Congress passed a resolution in January 1871, authorizing the appointment of a commission. The document below reviews Báez's request; it was one of many documents representing the pro and con arguments for further U.S. expansion. This issue was debated in the forty-first U.S. Congress, third Session, 1870–1871, Senate.

The Congress of the United States is now being called upon to settle a question of the very greatest importance. This is the annexation of San Domingo, which Baez, for the last year, has been asking at the hands of the government at Washington. In every age, the people of a country have been consulted with regard to their wishes in the matter of being annexed to other countries, but such a rule has not been followed in the present case. On the 29th of November last, a treaty was signed for the annexation of San Domingo to the Union, without the people of that country being, in the slightest manner, informed thereof.

The fourth article of the treaty states that the people of San Domingo "shall in the shortest possible time, express in a manner conformable to the laws, their will concerning the cession herein provided for, and the United States shall until such expression shall he had, protect the Dominican Republic against foreign intervention (Cabral and his party), in order that the national expression shall be free."

It is clear that the people of San Domingo had not, up to the 29th of last November, expressed the slightest wish for annexation. They were first annexed by treaty, and then were provided a mode, but a very poor one, of backing out from its provisions. The United States government not only appears to have given protection, but to have actively intervened in a struggle, which has been going on in that country for a year past. It has done more; for the facts show that it has actively aided the Baez party by a money contribution of $150,000; by the presence of ships of war, and by sending down cannon and material of war. Latterly, it has gone a step further, for Admiral Poor has just noticed the Haytiens [Haitians], who are the friends of the Cabral party, that they must do nothing whatever towards aiding that party.

It would seem that Congress ought to have some respect for the laws of San Domingo, especially if it would imbue that people with a spirit of kindness. The Constitution of the Republic prohibits by Article 7th, all sale or alienation of territory, or any part of the same—and a law was passed by the Congress of the Republic in 1867, which declared that man a traitor to his country who should propose a sale or alienation of any part of the soil. Has there been anything done which manifests a change of public sentiment in that regard? The accompanying documents will show that the so-called re-incorporation of San Domingo into the Spanish Monarchy was productive of bad results. Yet the Spaniards claim that the vote of the Republic was voluntary. That vote has been repeated in the swindling management restored to but a few days ago by Baez. The Spaniards came into the country—a four years war did not make their fortunes better, and they had to retire ignominiously from the soil. Is it quite certain that, if the present annexation project be carried out, the people of that country, who according to the Spaniards at the time of abandoning the island, preferred above all times, the independence of the soil, may not exhibit signs of dissatisfaction, would they not have the sympathies of all free nations, because of the abstract justice of their cause?

We first hear of this negotiation in June 1868, when Baez addressed a confidential letter to Mr. S. Reward, in which he said that HE was willing to sell the Peninsula of Samana to the United States, upon substantially the same terms the United States had heretofore to the administration of Cabral. On the 8th of July, Mr. Seward replied (confidentially) by saying, that this communication would be held under consideration. The astute Secretary of State further said: "National transactions, however desirable and however important, sometimes depend upon *occasions* quite as much as they do upon the merit of the policy involved. On the 18th of July, Baez replied by saying, that he desired the material assistance of the United States to establish his government permanently, and for such aid will recompose [recompense] the United States with Samana," etc. It will be here seen that Baez wants to treat; "will recompense," etc., but not a word is heard from the San Domingo people in the affair. On the 18th of August, the President complains that the New York papers had spoken of one Fabeus as his Commissioner for the purpose of concluding the Samana negotiation, and informs Mr. Seward "that he had no special Commissioner or agent," etc., but at the same moment Mr. Fabens had a regular Commission as such in his pocket, duly signed by the Secretary of State of San Domingo. This letter was written to conceal from his own people what he was doing, and he went so far as to seize all letters coming from the United States, and to prohibit the circulation in San Domingo of any and all newspapers coming from the States.

On the 9th of November 1868, Baez wrote again to Mr. Seward, the purport of which was as follows:

1. He desired "the protection of the United States over the Dominican Republic. The United States to take possession of Samana, or any other position that they may deem necessary, and must *send troops and a fleet* (to the island)."

2. "In case they (the United States) cannot give protection, without the sale of Samana, it will be sold."

3. "The government is composed of men WHO DO NOT COMPROMISE THEMSELVES USELESSLY. They would like to have $200,000 paid down on the signing of the Convention! An answer was returned to this by Mr. Seward, the nature of which may be divined from the reply of Baez: "He is well aware," said the Dominican Secretary of State, "that the Congress of the United States may not be inclined to bring about the annexation of any State or country by an act of war—or what might be considered as conquest, but only by the free and general consent of the people expressed in a constitutional manner. The government of the Dominican Republic is prepared to obtain this national declaration by the common vote, or by acclamation, or in any other form that the United States government may indicate as satisfactory." "It is necessary, however, that the United States should first give the assurance, by means of a formal dispatch [*sic*], that the measure, proposed by the Dominican government, is accepted, and, at the same time, send out to this city a vessel of war with a treaty, and the sum of $300,000. One vessel of war would be sufficient at present," etc.

Baez then threatens Mr. Seward with being compelled to effect a negotiation with an English company, in case he should not be able to succeed with the United States. The next communication is forwarded to Washington, under date of 9th of January 1869. Caliral was at that time operating in the South East, and the President was seriously alarmed.

The following extraordinary question was asked in the letter forwarded to Mr. Seward: "What step would the United States take in the event that the different provinces should, at once, hoist the American flag and proclaim, by acclamation, that they placed themselves under the government of United States?" Remarking at the same time, "that such was the state of feeling existing throughout the country that the President, even if disposed, could scarcely restrain a movement which may occur at any time."

"The re-annexation of Dominica, as a province to Spain, was the personal act of President Samana, and is not a parallel case with the measures now proposed," continues the President, "where a sister Republic, by spontaneous consent of its people, desires to be admitted into the American Union."

"If the possession of Samana Bay is considered a necessity for the future operations, which the government of the United States may yet have to undertake in the Western Hemisphere, then there can be no doubt that the moment has arrived for the realization of this idea; and, if so, it is essential now to reflect about the manner by which negotiations can be effected without complications."

"The purchase of the Peninsula is a simple question, but ought not its sale to be considered as prejudicial to the interests of England, France, and Spain in this quarter of the world, and may not those powers act conjointly in offering to purchase it for a general depot?"

The same line of argument was pursued by the wily President, who added: "The Dominican government entertains no fear of being vanquished by its enemies outside, but the real danger is *that it may fail on absolute want of means to carry it on* (the war), unless speedily assisted," etc.

To this Mr. Seward replied, under the date of February 5th. He acknowledges "the receipt of the letter which has been addressed by President Baez to the

President of the United States, and which contains a favorable response to the sentiments expressed by the President of the United States in his annual message to
Congress, on the condition of the political affairs in the two Republics of San Domingo and Hayti." All these papers," he says, "have been submitted to the President of
the United States. Soon after the opening of Congress, Mr. Banks, Chairman of the
Committee on Foreign Affairs, in the House of Representatives, submitted a proposition, authorizing the President of the United States, with the consent of the
Republic of St. Domingo, to extend a naval protection to that Republic. On the first
of February, Mr. Orth, from the same committee, submitted to the House of Representatives a resolution, declaring the consent of Congress to the annexation of the
Dominican Republic to the United States, with the consent of the people and government of the Republic. This resolution was laid upon the table, by a vote of one
hundred and ten against sixty-two in favor of the resolution. I am informed that the
same resolution, or one of similar effect, will be again brought before the House of
Representatives on the 8th day of February, with the prospect of increased favor."

"There is always a necessity for the practice of much reserve on the part of the
Executive in treating of questions of a Legislative character, upon which Congress is
actually engaged. Writing under the restraint of this reserve, I think I may say two
things for the information of the Dominican Republic. First, that the strong vote of
the House of Representatives unfavorable to the resolutions, which I have mentioned, was largely due to the fact that the movers of the resolutions proceeded upon
information, which is regarded by the Executive department as confidential, and
therefore not in possession of the House of Representatives. That information, however, is regarded by the President of the United States, but with such considerations
of propriety and delicacy as may be becoming toward the government and people of
Dominica. Secondly, such proceedings, as are indicated by the resolution upon
which the House of Representatives were engaged, are regarded by a part of Congress and the American people as being inconvenient in the present juncture of our
domestic affairs; while, on the other hand, those proceedings are believed to be in
harmony with the general sentiments and expectations of the government and people of the United States."

It may be here asked, if the Dominican people were willing to dispose of the most
valuable part of the Republic, wherefore were all these propositions made in such a
confidential manner?

Mr. Fish has displayed more zeal in the matter than his predecessor. Without
demanding any basis or conditions which might tend towards preventing the United
States' Treasury from being defrauded by a set of sharpers, he signs two treaties; one
for the lease of Samana for fifty years, at an annual rent of $150,000, and makes the
first payment in advance ($147,229.91), and another for the annexation of the
Republic to the American Union.

Source: Annexation of San Domingo. New York, J. Dickson, printer, 1870, pp. 1–7. Library of
Congress, http://lcweb2.loc.gov/cgi-bin/query/r?ammem/murray:@field(DOCID+@lit(lcrbmrpt2505div1)):
@@@REF.

By the 1870s, most Latin American colonies had become independent republics. The only two remaining under the Spanish yoke were Cuba and Puerto Rico. The two islands were generously populated; Cuba was however closer to the United States and larger. Culturally and intellectually they were part of the region that can be described as south of the border. Ideas flowed freely across the borders of the disparate Latino nations—many of whose newspaper articles flowed into the United States bonding the Spanish speaking people there. Because of the proximity of Cuba to the United States, and its fertile soil, the imperial designs on it were most persistent. Meanwhile, the independista movement grew on both islands and crystalized during the post U.S. Civil War (1861–1865). This led to the Spanish government brutally repressing uprisings in Cuba which led to the exile of independista leaders and workers to the United States. Spain, during this period, granted Puerto Rico more autonomy, but by this time it was too late, and Puerto Ricans had formed their own national identity. This section draws heavily from the writings of the Apostle of Cuban Independence, José Martí (1853–1895) and other independistas during the thirty years of heavy sacrifices made by Cuban and Puerto Rican freedom fighters and their people.

115. Excerpt from María Eugenia Echenique, "The Emancipation of Women," 1876

In 1876, Argentine feminist María Eugenia Echenique (1851–1878) wrote the following critique on the role and rights of women. There was a budding feminist movement throughout Latin America at the time. Latinas were well acquainted with Harriet Beecher Stowe (1811–1896) and had read *Uncle Tom's Cabin*. Stowe's views on emancipation were applied to the emancipation of women. In her journal, Stowe wrote, "I wrote what I did because as a woman, as a mother, I was oppressed and brokenhearted, with the sorrows and injustice I saw, because as a Christian I felt the dishonor to Christianity, because as a lover of my country I trembled at the coming day of wrath." While downplaying Stowe's views on race, many Latina feminist writers emphasized gender inequality. The following excerpt is in the context of a six-month debate between María Eugenia Echenique and poet and novelist Josefina Pelliza de Sagasta (1848–1888) in the journal *La Ondina del Plata*. Echenique passionately advocates the emancipation of women.

When emancipation was given to men, it was also given to women in recognition of the equality of rights, consistent with the principles of nature on which they are founded, that proclaim the identity of soul between men and women. Thus, Argentine women have been emancipated by law for a long time. The code of law that governs us authorizes a widow to defend her rights in court, just as an educated woman can in North America, and like her, we can manage the interests of our children, these rights being the basis for emancipation. What we lack is sufficient education and instruction to make use of them, instruction that North American women have; it is not just recently that we have proclaimed our freedom. To try to question or to oppose women's emancipation is to oppose something that is almost a fact, it is to attack our laws and destroy the Republic.

So let the debate be there, on the true point where it should be: whether or not it is proper for women to make use of those granted rights, asking as a consequence the authorization to go to the university so as to practice those rights or make them effective. And this constitutes another right and duty in woman: a duty to accept the role that our own laws bestow on her when extending the circle of her jurisdiction and which makes her responsible before the members of her family.

This, assuming that the woman is a mother. But, are all women going to marry? Are all going to be relegated to a life of inaction during their youth or while they remain single? Is it so easy for all women to look for a stranger to defend their offended dignity, their belittled honor, their stolen interests? Don't we see every day how the laws are trodden underfoot, and the victim, being a woman, is forced to bow her head because she does not know how to defend herself, exposed to lies and tricks because she does not know the way to clarify the truth?

Far from causing the breakdown of the social classes, the emancipation of women would establish morality and justice in them; men would have a brake that would halt the "imperious need" that they have made of the "lies and tricks" of litigations, and the science of jurisprudence, so sacred and magnificent in itself but degenerated today because of abuses, would return to its splendor and true objective once women take part in the forum. Generous and abnegated by nature, women would teach men humanitarian principles and would condemn the frenzy and insults that make a battlefield out of the courtroom.

"Women either resolve to drown the voice of their hearts, or they listen to that voice and renounce emancipation." If emancipation is opposed to the tender sentiments, to the voice of the heart, then men who are completely emancipated and study science are not capable of love. The beautiful and tender girl who gives her heart to a doctor or to a scientist, gives it then, to a stony man, incapable of appreciating it or responding to her; women could not love emancipated men, because where women find love, men find it too; in both burns the same heart's flame. I have seen that those who do not practice science, who do not know their duties or the rights of women, who are ignorant, are the ones who abandon their wives, not the ones who, concentrated on their studies and duties, barely have time to give them a caress.

Men as much as women are victims of the indifference that ignorance, not science, produces. Men are more slaves of women who abuse the prestige of their weakness and become tyrants in their home, than of the schooled and scientific women who understand their duties and are capable of something. With the former, the husband has to play the role of man and woman, because she ignores everything: she is not capable of consoling nor helping her husband, she is not capable of giving tenderness, because, preoccupied with herself, she becomes demanding, despotic, and vain, and she does not know how to make a happy home. For her, there are no responsibilities to carry out, only whims to satisfy. This is typical, we see it happening every day.

The ignorant woman, the one who voluntarily closes her heart to the sublime principles that provoke sweet emotions in it and elevate the mind, revealing to men the deep secrets of the All-Powerful; the woman incapable of helping her husband in great enterprises for fear of losing the prestige of her weakness and ignorance; the woman who only aspires to get married and reproduce, and understands maternity as the only mission of women on earth—she can be the wife of a savage, because in him she can satisfy all her aspirations and hopes, following that law of nature that operates even on beasts and inanimate beings.

I would renounce and disown my sex if the mission of women were reduced only to procreation, yes, I would renounce it; but the mission of women in the world is much more grandiose and sublime, it is more than the beasts', it is the one of teaching humankind, and in order to teach it is necessary to know. A mother should know science in order to inspire in her children great deeds and noble sentiments, making them feel superior to the other objects in the universe, teaching them from the cradle to become familiar with great scenes of nature where they should go to look for God and love Him. And nothing more sublime and ideal than the scientific mother who, while her husband goes to cafés or to the political club to talk about state interests, she goes to spend some of the evening at the astronomical observatory, with her children by the hand to show them Jupiter, Venus, preparing in that way their tender hearts for the most legitimate and sublime aspirations that could occupy men's minds. This sacred mission in the scientific mother who understands emancipation—the fulfillment of which, far from causing the abandonment of the home, causes it to unite more closely—instead of causing displeasure to her husband, she will cause his happiness.

The abilities of men are not so miserable that the carrying out of one responsibility would make it impossible to carry out others. There is enough time and competence for cooking and mending, and a great soul such as that of women, equal to that of their mates, born to embrace all the beauty that exists in Creation of divine origin and end, should not be wasted all on seeing if the plates are clean and rocking the cradle.

Source: Courtesy of Paul Brians, Mary Gallwey, Douglas Hughes, Azfar Hussain, Richard Law, Michael Myers, Michael Neville, Roger Schlesinger, Alice Spitzer, and Susan Swan, eds. Translated by Francisco Manzo Robledo. Excerpt from *Reading About the World, Volume 2*, Harcourt Brace Custom Books, 1999. http://www.wsu.edu:8080/wldciv/world_civ_reader/world_civ_reader_2/echenique.htm.

116. Letter from José Martí to the Editor of the *New York Evening Post,* March 25, 1889

José Martí (1853–1895), perhaps the most beloved Cuban hero, spent much of his life exiled from his beloved Cuba. A renowned poet, he campaigned for Cuban independence and led several military expeditions. Martí briefly returned to Cuba in 1878, but was again exiled for conspiring against the Spanish authorities. Throughout the following years, Martí was in and out of the United States where he organized with fellow independentistas. In the United States, Martí was at first optimistic about the United States, but confronted with indifference and racism, he grew disillusioned. In the late 1880s, U.S. President Benjamin Harrison's administration renewed efforts to purchase Cuba from Spain. The United States had a budget surplus and Cuban sugar was a good investment. On Thursday, March 21, 1889, the *New York Evening Post* published a reprint of a short article entitled, "A Protectionist," which revealed racist opinions that generated a strong response from the Cuban community. Martí responded in the following letter.

To the editor of The Evening Post:

Sir: I beg to be allowed the privilege of referring in your columns to the injurious criticism of the Cubans printed in the *Manufacturer* of Philadelphia, and reproduced in your issue of yesterday.

This is not the occasion to discuss the question of the annexation of Cuba. It is probable that no self-respecting Cuban would like to see his country annexed to a nation where the leaders of opinion share towards him the prejudices excusable only to vulgar jingoism or rampant ignorance. No honest Cuban will stoop to be received as a moral pest for the sake of the usefulness of his land in a community where his ability is denied, his morality insulted, and his character despised. There are some Cubans who, from honorable motives, from an ardent admiration for progress and liberty, from a prescience of their own powers under better political conditions, from an unhappy ignorance of the history and tendency of annexation, would like to see the island annexed to the United States. But those who have fought in war and learned in exile, who have built, by the work of hands and mind, a virtuous home in the heart of an unfriendly community; who, by their successful efforts as scientists and merchants, as railroad builders and engineers, as teachers, artists, lawyers, journalists, orators, and poets, as men of alert intelligence and uncommon activity, are honored wherever their powers have been called into action and the people are just enough to understand them; those who have raised, with their less prepared elements, a town of workingmen where the United States had previously a few huts in a barren cliff; those, more numerous than the others, do not desire the annexation of Cuba to the United States. They do not need it. They admire this nation, the greatest ever built by liberty, but they dislike the evil conditions that, like worms in the heart, have begun in this mighty republic their work of destruction. They have made of the heroes of this country their own heroes, and look to the success of the American commonwealth as the crowning glory of mankind; but they cannot honestly believe that excessive individualism, reverence for wealth, and the protracted exultation of a terrible victory are preparing the United States to be the typical nation of liberty, where no opinion is to be based in greed, and no triumph or acquisition reached against charity and justice. We love the country of Lincoln as much as we fear the country of Cutting.

We are not the people of destitute vagrants or immoral pigmies that the *Manufacturer* is pleased to picture; nor the country of petty talkers, incapable of action, hostile to hard work, that, in a mass with the other countries of Spanish America, we are by arrogant travellers and writers represented to be. We have suffered impatiently under tyranny; we have fought like men, sometimes like giants, to be freemen; we are passing that period of stormy repose, full of germs of revolt, that naturally follows a period of excessive and unsuccessful action; we have to fight like conquered men against an oppressor who denies us the means of living, and fosters-in the beautiful capital visited by the tourists, in the interior of the country, where the prey escapes his grasp—a reign of such corruption as may poison in our veins the strength to secure freedom; we deserve in our misfortune the respect of those who did not help us in our need.

But because our Government has systematically allowed after the war the triumph of criminals, the occupation of the cities by the scum of the people, the ostentation of ill-gotten riches by a myriad of Spanish office-holders and their Cuban accomplices, the conversion of the capital into a gambling-den, where the hero and the philosopher walk hungry by the lordly thief of the metropolis; because the healthier farmer, ruined by a war seemingly useless, turns in silence to the plough that he knew well how to exchange for the *machete*; because thousands of exiles, profiting by a period of calm that no human power can quicken until it is naturally exhausted, are practising [*sic*] in the battle of life in the free countries the art of governing themselves and of building a nation; because our half-breeds and city-bred young men are generally of delicate physique, of suave courtesy and ready words, hiding under the glove that: polishes the poem, the hand that fells the foe—are we to be considered, as the *Manufacturer* does consider us, an "effeminate" people? These city-bred young men and poorly built half-breeds knew in one day how to rise against a cruel government, to pay their passages to the seat of war with the product of their watches and trinkets, to work their way in exile while their vessels were being kept from them by the country of the free in the interest of the foes of freedom, to obey as soldiers, sleep in the mud, eat roots, fight ten years without salary, conquer foes with the branch of a tree, die—these men of eighteen, these heirs to wealthy estates, these dusky striplings—a death not to be spoken of without uncovering the head. They died like those other men of ours who, with a stroke of the *machete*, can send a head flying, or by a turn of the hands bring a bull to their feet. These "effeminate" Cubans had once courage enough, in the face of a hostile government, to carry on their left arms for a week the mourning for Lincoln.

The Cubans have, according to the *Manufacturer*, "a distaste for exertion"; they are "helpless," "idle." These "helpless," "idle" men came here twenty years ago empty-handed, with very few exceptions; fought against the climate; mastered the language; lived by their honest labor, some in affluence, a few in wealth, rarely in misery; they bought or built homes; they raised families and fortunes; they loved luxury and worked for it; they were not frequently seen in the dark roads of life; proud and self-sustaining, they never feared competition as to intelligence or diligence. Thousands have returned to die in their homes; thousands have remained where, during the 'hardships of life, they have triumphed, unaided by any help of kindred language, sympathy of race, or community of religion. A handful of Cuban toilers built Key West. The Cubans have made their mark in Panama by their ability as mechanics of the higher trades, as clerks, physicians, and contractors. A Cuban, Cisneros, has greatly advanced the development of railways and river navigation in Colombia. Marquez, another Cuban, gained, with many of his countrymen, the respect of the Peruvians as a merchant of eminent capacity. Cubans are found everywhere, working as farmers, surveyors, engineers, mechanics, teachers, journalists. In Philadelphia, the *Manufacturer* has a daily opportunity to see a hundred Cubans, some of them of heroic history and powerful build, who live by their work in easy comfort. In New York, the Cubans are directors of prominent banks, substantial merchants, popular brokers, clerks of recognized ability, physicians with a large practice, engineers of world-wide repute, electricians, journalists, tradesmen, cigar-makers. The poet of Niagara is a Cuban, our Heredia; a Cuban, Menocal, is the projector of the canal of Nicaragua. In Philadelphia itself, as in New York, the college prizes have been more than once awarded to Cubans. The women of these "helpless," "idle" people, with "a distaste for exertion," arrived here from a life of luxury in the heart of the winter; their husbands were in the war, ruined, dead, imprisoned in Spain; the "Senora" went to work; from a slave-owner she became a slave, took a seat behind the counter, sang in the churches, worked button-holes by the hundred, sewed for a living, curled feathers, gave her soul to duty, withered in work her body. This is the people of "defective morals."

We are "unfitted by nature and experience to discharge the obligations of citizenship in a great and free country." This cannot be justly said of a people who possess, besides the energy that built the first railroad in Spanish dominions and established against the opposition of the Government all the agencies of civilization, a truly remarkable knowledge of the body politic, a tried readiness to adapt itself to its higher forms, and the power rare in tropical countries of nerving their thought and pruning their language. Their passion for liberty, the conscientious study of its best teachings, the nursing of individual character in exile and at home, the lessons of ten years of war and its manifold consequences, and the practical exercise of the duties of citizenship in the free countries of the world, have combined, in spite of all antecedents, to develop in the Cuban a capacity for free government so natural to him that he established it, even to the excess of its practices, in the midst of the war, vied with his elders in the effort to respect the laws of liberty, and snatched the sabre, without fear of consideration, from the hands of every military pretender, however glorious. There seems to be in the Cuban mind a happy faculty of uniting sense with earnestness and moderation with exuberance. Noble teachers have devoted themselves since the beginning of the century to explain by their words and exemplify by their lives the self-restraint and tolerance inseparable from liberty. Those who won the first seats ten years ago at the European universities by singular merit have been proclaimed, at their appearance in the Spanish Parliament, men of subtle thought and powerful speech. The political knowledge of the average Cuban compares well with that of the average American citizen. Absolute freedom from religious intolerance, the love of man for the work he creates by his industry, and theoretical and practical familiarity with the laws and processes of liberty, will enable the Cuban to rebuild his country from the ruins in which he will receive it from its oppressors. It is not to be expected, for the honor of mankind, that the nation that was rocked in freedom, and received for three centuries the best blood of liberty—loving men, will employ the power thus acquired in depriving a less fortunate neighbor of his liberty.

It is, finally, said that "our lack of manly force and of self-respect is demonstrated by the supineness with which we have so long submitted to Spanish oppression, and even our attempts at rebellion have been so pitifully ineffective that they have risen little above the dignity of farce." Never was ignorance of history and character more pitifully displayed than in this wanton assertion. We need to recollect, in order to answer without bitterness, that more than one American bled by our side, in a war that another American was to call a farce. A farce! the war that has been by foreign observers compared to an epic, the upheaval of a whole country, the voluntary abandonment of wealth, the abolition of slavery in our first moment of freedom, the burning of our cities by our own hands, the erection of villages and factories in the wild forests, the dressing of our ladies of rank in the textures of the woods, the keeping at bay, in ten years of such a life, a powerful enemy, with a loss to him of 200,000 men, at the hands of a small army of patriots, with no help but nature! We had no Hessians and no Frenchmen, no Lafayette or Steuben, no monarchical rivals to help us; we had but one neighbor who confessedly "stretched the limits of his power, and acted against the will of the people" to help the foes of those who were fighting for the same Chart of Liberties on which he built his independence. We fell! a victim to the very passions which could have caused the downfall of the thirteen States, had they not been cemented by success, while we were enfeebled by procrastination; a procrastination brought about, not from cowardice, but from an abhorrence of blood, which allowed the enemy in the first months of the war to acquire unconquerable advantage, and from a childlike confidence in the certain help of the United States: "They cannot see us dying for liberty at their own doors without raising a hand or saying a word to give to the world a new free country!" They "stretched the limits of their powers in deference to Spain." They did not raise the hand. They did not say the word.

The struggle has not ceased. The exiles do not want to return. The new generation is worthy of its sires. Hundreds of men have died in darkness since the war in the misery of prisons. With life only will this fight for liberty cease among us. And it is the melancholy truth that our efforts would have been, in all probability, successfully renewed, were it not, in some of us, for the unmanly hope of the annexationists of securing liberty without paying its price; and the just fears of others that our dead, our sacred memories, our ruins drenched in blood, would be but the fertilizers of the soil for the benefit of a foreign plant, or the occasion for a sneer from the *Manufacturer* of Philadelphia.

With sincere thanks for the space you have kindly allowed me, I am, sir, yours very respectfully,

José Martí

Source: From *José Martí: Selected Writings* by José Martí, introduction by Roberto Gonzalez Echevarria, edited by Esther Allen, translated by Esther Allen, copyright © 2002 by Esther Allen. Used by permission of Viking Penguin, a division of Penguin Group (USA) Inc. pp. 263–267.

117. "My Race," by José Martí, April 16, 1893

José Martí (1853–1895) was born in La Habana (also called Havana), Cuba. He became politically active at a young age, helping to found an anti-colonial newspaper, for which he was arrested and sentenced to six years of hard labor at age 15. In 1871, after serving three years, Martí moved to Spain, and in 1878, he moved to Mexico City where he joined other exiles from various Latin American countries. In 1881, Martí moved to New York where he worked as a journalist and organized Cuban and Puerto Rican dissidents. In the following article he reacts to the term *racist*. Racism was fully developed within the Cuban community since colonial times—but in the United States it took on a new meaning.

"Racist" is becoming a confusing word, and it must be clarified. No man has any special rights because he belongs to one race or another: say "man" and all rights have been stated. The black man, as a black man, is not inferior or superior to any other man; the white man who says "my race" is being redundant, and the black man who says "my race" is also redundant. Anything that divides men from each other, that separates them, singles them out, or hems them in, is a sin against humanity. What sensible white man thinks he should be proud of being white, and what do blacks think of a white man who is proud of being white and believes he has special rights because he is? What must whites think of a black man who grows conceited about his color? To insist upon the racial divisions and racial differences of a people naturally divided is to obstruct both individual and public happiness, which lies in greater closeness among the elements that must live in common. It is true that in the black man there is no original sin or virus that makes him incapable of developing his whole soul as a man, and this truth must be spoken and demonstrated, because the injustice of this world is great, as is the ignorance that passes for wisdom, and there are still those who believe in good faith that the black man is incapable of the intelligence and feelings of the white man. And what does it matter if this truth, this defense of nature, is called racism, because it is no more than natural respect, the voice that clamors from man's bosom for the life and the peace of the nation. To state that the condition of slavery does not indicate any inferiority in the enslaved race—for white Gauls with blue eyes and golden hair were sold as slaves with fetters around their necks in the markets of Rome—is good racism, because it is pure justice and helps the ignorant white shed his prejudices. But that is the limit of just racism, which is the right of the black man to maintain and demonstrate that his color does not deprive him of any of the capacities and rights of the human race.

And what right does the white racist, who believes his race has superior rights, have to complain of the black racist, who also believes that his race has special traits? What right does the black racist who sees a special character in his race have to complain of the white racist? The white man who, by reason of his race, believes himself superior to the black man acknowledges the idea of race and thus authorizes and provokes the black racist. The black man who trumpets his race when what he is perhaps trumpeting instead is only the spiritual identity of all races—authorizes and provokes the white racist. Peace demands the shared rights of nature; differing rights go against nature and are the enemies of peace. The white who isolates himself isolates the Negro. The Negro who isolates himself drives the white to isolate himself.

In Cuba there is no fear whatsoever of a race war. "Man" means more than white, more than mulatto, more than Negro. "Cuban" means more than white, more than mulatto, more than Negro. On the battlefields, the souls of whites and blacks who died for Cuba have risen together through the air. In that daily life of defense, loyalty, brotherhood, and shrewdness, there was always a black man at the side of every white. Blacks, like whites, can be grouped according to their character—timid or brave, self-abnegating or egotistical—into the diverse parties of mankind. Political parties are aggregates of concerns, aspirations, interests, and characters. An essential likeness is sought and found beyond all differences of detail, and what is fundamental in analogous characters merges in parties, even if their incidental characteristics or motives differ. In short, it is the similarity of character—a source of unity far superior to the internal relations of the varying colors of men, whose different shades are sometimes in opposition to each other—that commands and prevails in the formation of parties. An affinity of character is more powerful than an affinity of color. Blacks, distributed among the diverse or hostile specialties of the human spirit, will never want or be able to band together against whites, who are distributed among the same specialties. Blacks are too tired of slavery to enter voluntarily into the slavery of color. Men of pomp and self-interest, black and white, will be on one side, and generous and impartial men will be on the other. True men, black or white, will treat each other with loyalty and tenderness, taking pleasure in merit and pride in anyone, black or white, who honors the land where we were born. The word "racist" will be gone from the lips of the blacks who use it today in good faith, once they understand that that word is the only apparently valid argument-valid among sincere, apprehensive men—for denying the Negro the fullness of his rights as a man. The white racist and the Negro racist will be equally guilty of being racists. Many whites have already forgotten their color, and many blacks have, too. Together they work, black and white, for the cultivation of the mind, the dissemination of virtue, and the triumph of creative work and sublime charity.

There will never be a race war in Cuba. The Republic cannot retreat and the Republic, from the extraordinary day of the emancipation of blacks in Cuba and from its first independent constitution of April 10, in Guaimaro, never spoke of whites or blacks. The rights already conceded out of pure cunning by the Spanish government, and which have become habitual even before the Island's independence, can no longer be denied now, either by the Spaniard, who will maintain them as long as he draws breath in Cuba-in order to continue dividing Cuban blacks from Cuban whites—or by the independent nation, which will not, in liberty, be able to deny the rights that the Spaniard recognized in servitude.

As for the rest, each individual will be free within the sacred confines of his home. Merit, the clear and continual manifestation of culture and inexorable trade will end by uniting all men. There is much greatness in Cuba, in blacks and in whites.

—April 16, 1893

Source: From José Martí: *Selected Writings by José Martí*, introduction by Roberto Gonzalez Echevarria, edited by Esther Allen, translated by Esther Allen, copyright © 2002 by Esther Allen. Used by permission of Viking Penguin, a division of Penguin Group (USA) Inc. pp. 318–321.

118. "To Cuba!" José Martí, January 27, 1894

José Martí (1853–1895), like so many other Latin American revolutionaries, used established Latino colonies in the United States to recruit volunteers, raise money, and popularize the Cuban struggle for independence from Spain. Martí and his cohorts also identified with the struggles of Latinos in the United States and sought to give them a voice. In January 1894, the tobacco workers in Cayo Hueso (Key West), Florida, protested that the owners had replaced many of them with Spanish workers brought directly from Cuba. The Cuban dissident workers were supporters of the revolution who lived in a shanty town called Marti City. The following article discusses the tensions. While Martí identified and championed the rights of the Cuban workers, he cautioned them that they had no right to object to Spaniards because they were Spanish. He encouraged them to fight oppressive conditions.

When has the cry "To Cuba!" burst from the Cuban heart with greater reason— and greater anguish and love—than today, after the events in Key West and the loathsome spectacle of a town built by its adoptive sons that is straying from its own soil and laws to bring the enemies of those sons in from outside.

The city of Key West emerged triumphant from its early trials. In Yankee hands it was no more than sand and shacks, but now it can point proudly to factories that in their continual thought and study are like academies of learning; schools where the hand that rolls the tobacco leaf by day lifts a book and teaches by night; societies of art and recreation from which only those unfaithful to their *patria* are, for reasons of moral hygiene, excluded; homes whose great virtue makes their poverty scarcely noticeable. Key West was built by the poorest, neediest Cubans, along with a wealthy *criollo* or two, led there by his love of the sun, and later by a handful of fervent soul, both moneyed and destitute, drawn there by that loyal town's reputation for being like a single family. From his hybrid mixture—into which a corrupted Havana poured its crimes by the boatload—from this Cuban core, where all the sublimity of hope sprang from all the miseries of life; and where the humble worker's quota for Cuban honor was, year after year, the primary support of the proud, from this everyday mingling of dethroned master and emancipated slave, eating the same bread together at the workingman's productive table, arose, with no counsel or teaching but that of our island soul, a virtuous and orderly industrial city that then spilled over and gave life to the gray state, animating moribund coast with Tampa's industries, creating and sustaining railroads and steamers throughout that region of Florida, and transforming the Yankee village of small farmers and fishermen into a city of free academies and schools and generous gentlemen of industry: the principal port of the State of Florida. Those who silence this fact of deny it are paper men, with a magazine covering one eye and the other one blinded by preoccupation, for this is a fact acknowledged by men of truth, who work themselves and admire workingmen and know that the hands of masons, who assemble and construct, must be hardened by stone and stained by lime. We must cast into the fire—for its impurity and uselessness—the silken hand that, by way of greeting, licks the bloodied, debased hand of its country's corrupter, and instead beckon the rough hand that works the rifle which must drive the insolent to the sea, and the saintly hand, sometimes bony from hunger, that caresses and constructs in darkness, with the hope of the humble, the just and warm hearted *patria* that will rise from sea to sky with arms open to all mankind.

Excessive gratitude and trust were the principal and perhaps the only errors of that budding community: trust in the Washington of legend, who was more the offspring of his people than their father, and in the love of Lincoln, for whom we Cubans wore mourning, and who showed ineffable goodness in everything, except in consenting to make Cuba the dumping ground for all his nation's aggravations. Because of that blind admiration for North American liberties, which is just another form, natural in any progressive man, of the hatred of Spanish injury, blood-rule, and un-Americanism, and because of the forthright nature of the Cuban, who has been deeply marked by a long-rooted affection for the land in which he could at least think freely and work without dishonor, the Cubans of Key West came to love this harboring republic so well and to be so thoroughly taken in by the liberty if wears as a mask for the conquest it nurtures in its bosom that with their very hands they delivered to the few native settlers the government of the town that, before the Cubans arrived, had never been built. The grateful Cuban, already converted into an enthusiastic American citizen, carried this love for his adopted country into his domestic life: one quarreled with his friends for the sake of an American vote-hunter; another, though devoted to his mother island, spent his whole savings on building a house, as the monument of his affection, by the hospitable sea; another blessed every morning, from under the trees he had planted, the land where his family, persecuted and impoverished in Cuba, had brightened again into hope and prosperity; a daughter was born to another and he called her by the name of a state of the Union; many had Blaine's picture on the mantelpiece, believing that crafty manipulator of national prejudices to be the friend of Cuba; many had Cleveland's picture in their parlor, honoring him as steely foe of the republic of privileges and unjust monopolies that must everywhere be stamped out.

American industry had been living off of the future, assuming that when the domestic market was replete it would be ever so easy to empty their excess products into the torpid lands of the American continent: this and this alone was the purpose of their farcical reciprocity treaties and the shamelessness, averted in time, of the Pan-American Congress. The Hispanic republics did not lack forethought or clear-eyed sentinels and the plan failed, so the North has lived since then with its hands tugging at its purse strings, unable to pay for the production of its surplus manufactures and still less able to sell them. The sumptuary industries such as cigar-making were naturally the first to suffer from the stringency and alarm that greeted the sudden and unexpected imbalance in the nation's accounts. But the Cubans of Key West did not much mind their penury. Hadn't the city's founders lived there for twenty-five years? Hadn't the workingman, by his own sweat, bought his home there? Weren't the poor aged mother, the wife with her callused hands, and the first-born son buried there, in that white sand? Hadn't the former slave, the oppressed campesino, and the urchin of the city streets learned all the delights of liberty there and all the arrogance of men? Work was scarce or slack, there was only one meal a day, and shoes were only for Sunday; but there they remained, hundreds and thousands of them, unemployed but faithful to the family tombs and the beloved town, faithful to Key West.

Suddenly one of the city's factories, which had been closing and reopening for some time and had recently been shored up by two new Spanish partners, began negotiating with the rival city of Tampa, which offered manufacturers land and privileges that Key West unwisely refused them. The North Americans in Key West asked why Seidenberg wanted to go to Tampa, only to hear that it was because he could not bring Spanish workers to Key West. Subterranean forces, which buy and keep watch, stirred up the unbridled greed of the English-speaking population. And that city, built by Cuban effort, those merchants whose every dollar was increased a hundredfold by the Cuban Saturday, those judges placed on their benches by Cuban votes, those drunkards cured of their deliria by Cuban doctors, those sons of emancipated colonies who cannot, without denying their own history, wonder at the natural fact that the Cubans wish to rid Cuba of its masters, just as they themselves wished to be rid of the English tax on tea—those very men whom the Cubans upheld in true friendship filled the public square in anger, calling the Cubans ruffians, expressing a foul wish "to hang some Cubans," and deserting the positions they owe to the trust and prosperity of the Cuban community and the patriotism and labor of the sons of the Cuban revolution. They left the city created by the Cuban revolution to beg a foreign monarchy for soldiers known to be the rabid enemies of the American-born men who built the town for them; they began bringing new workmen, simply because those workmen were Europeans and sworn enemies of the Cuban community, to the city where hundreds of the workmen who built it had been unemployed for a year.

It was not a blow to their income; it was a blow to the heart. Those men were loved like brothers, and they had turned against their brothers. Those men were seen as the embodiment of the liberty for which the Cubans yearned, the freedom and republicanism, the justness and prestige of the law, the progress and emancipation of America—and they filled our homes with terror, took the bread from our workingmen's mouths, sent innocent men to jail, locked a messenger who was taking a note to the jail in a cell, asked for a gallows to be put up for the Cubans, and bore on their breasts as a badge of honor the colors that are in America the emblem of tyranny and that have waved, stained with blood, over the ruins of our households and the corpses of our brothers. The republicans of America were wearing the emblem of murder upon their bosoms! The men of a free people were knocking at the door of a hypocritical foreign despot to ask him for workers and soldiers with whom to impoverish and humiliate those whose only guilt is to seek, as the North Americans once sought, freedom for their country! No greater shock could have stricken the Cubans had they seen those they love most killed by a knife in their beds. Was this blue sea a sea of blood, too, like the one back in Cuba? Were they, too to be ousted, like the zorros of California or the last tejanos, from the town they had built by the product of their industry, and, more important, by their earnest and uncompromising patriotism!

One Cuban wanted to uproot his new house and throw it into the ray; another wanted to take his nine children and leave to seek justice somewhere in the world; another wanted to change his daughter's name. There is no greater and more irreparable horror than seeing that which we loved become contemptible or infamous. Is this whole universe thus? Can no merit or virtue, no persecution or misfortune, ever move a stranger's heart? Is it futile, then, to have raised, before the eyes of a nation that the world supposes to be judicious and manly, stone by stone, out of the defective remnants of a tyrannical civilization, a city where the disorder and crime of despotism have been compressed and ordered into honest industry and the frank and diverse life of liberty? Can it be, then, that the world's leading republic is a nation without love, without charity, without friendship, without gratitude, without laws? Even in the leading republic of the world there is no harbor for a people seeking refuge from ignominious slavery! What right does a man without patria have to the security of a patria? Let he who wants a safe patria conquer one. He who does not will live in exile under the lash, hunted down like a wild animal, cast from one country to another with a beggar's smile on his face to hide the death in his soul from the disdain of free men. There is no solid ground but the ground on which one was born. "To Cuba!" says our whole soul, after this deceit in Key West, this brutal wound to our love and our illusions: to the only country in the world from which we shall not be chased away like the *zorros* from California and the *tejanos* from Texas!

Had there been some provocation, some relation between a Cuban offense and the action of the North Americans, had in fact the Cubans violated the right of free transit, until recently conceded to all men with no exception by the United States Constitution, it could never have been sufficient pretext for the North Americans to go forth—in patent violation of international law and the labor laws of their own country—and ask a foreign government for workers to import into a market glutted with labor, and for enemies to provoke a conflict in the city whose peace they should be preserving. However, in stark justice, which is the only sort of justice to which a sensible and dignified man must appeal, the Key West authorities would be right to uphold the law against any abusive, untenable resistance by the Cubans. If the Cubans want a land of special privilege, where they can command, they must win their own land, as the Yankee won his from the Englishman. A Yankee who has conquered his land is not equal but superior to a Cuban who has not conquered his, just as the Yankees who fought the Englishman for their freedom are superior to the Yankees who are going to ask a foreign power for help in impoverishing and humiliating the sons of America who are fighting for their own freedom! And while the Cuban revolutionaries who populated and enriched Key West out of their love for Cuban independence believe they have a moral, though not a legal, right to keep their city free of Spanish persecution, it is also true that the history and spirit of the American nation gave them some right to hope that it would show for the sons of an American nation who are fighting for emancipation from a European monarchy the same sacred indulgence that the Irish who fight to emancipate themselves from Great Britain enjoy here. But that indulgence is up to the North Americans, and it falls to the Cubans to abide by the law of the country.

Cubans have no right whatever to forbid a Spaniard, because he is a Spaniard, to disembark on United States territory. The United States can and must punish whoever breaks this law or any other. But before a violation is punished, the law must have been violated and proof of the violation must be established in accordance with the law and the guarantees that the law furnishes to the accused. Years ago, a passion for independence may have driven a handful of fanatical Cubans, who can fight as well on a Key West pier as when they face the Spaniard's artillery, to brandish punitive clubs, and one Cuban or another might have waited on the pier, club in hand, for the Spaniards who, not content with driving the Cuban away from all of his own worktables, pursue him to a foreign country to rob him of the industry that the Spaniard learned from the Cuban. Have the Spaniards no heart, that they do not see the injustice of this? Have the North Americans no heart, that they can assist in this injustice? For on the basis of something that a handful of Cubans may have attempted in the past, when the disorderly life of Key West had not yet been gathered into the superior social order of today—and which, even in the past, because of the Cuban's natural nobility, never was nor could have been anything like the South's barbaric lynchings or the continual murders perpetrated by men in white masks in the Northeast—a law-abiding people, a people of sensible, honorable, just, and friendly men, cannot presume, against truth and all appearances, that the law has been violated in a much later case, and with rabid rage and wicked vengeance turn against an entire city of men who have done it only good, to punish in advance a crime no one has committed.

Did not a friendship of so many years' standing at least demand a proper investigation of the idiotic conspiracy that a few Spanish-speaking rogues groundlessly charged the Cubans with? Do not the moral grounds for the Cubans' unhappiness at seeing the city they have peopled and where they live today without work occupied by workers who despoil them in their own country at least deserve the respectful affection and generous courtesy of right-thinking North Americans, rather than their frenzied hatred? What mysterious hand [is] at work there? What North

American scoundrel took money from the government of Spain to incite the greed and discredit the republicanism of his compatriots? What vengeful losing candidate or base and venomous heart inflamed the unjust suspicions of those of the North against the Cubans, whose labor of twenty-five years was forgotten in an hour? Why does the city that owes us its commerce, its industry, its renown, and the intimate love we once had for it, rise up unquestioningly against us, and organize, with cries of terror, a resistance that is completely out of proportion to the vague rumor that seems to have given rise to it? Who prepared this resistance, which was so well prepared? For how long had it been planned, to have sprung up so fully formed? Who paid for it, and was so well served? Why did the good men of Key West yield, out of passion, ignorance, or a false idea of their true interests, to what was obviously a coalition of the private interests of demagogues who make their living catering to public prejudices, and pedants who are unable to understand a people they disdain and who, in one hour of revolt, vented the wrath they had suppressed for years at having lived from their favor and their votes? Or is the entire North American nation incapable of justice, and the respect that is virtues due, and the gratitude that is an obligation of friendship? Is the entire North American nation so ferocious and ungrateful? Is there in the soul of that race such a hatred of the Hispanic criollo, so false an idea of his moral and political capacities, that the most despicable men of the North dare to disdain the Cuban's most admirable virtues simply because the Cuban has maintained them amid impoverishment and slavery? Are there no honorable men there who feel ashamed of what they have helped to do, and are turning against those who, with wicked deceit, forced them to violate the laws of their nation, of all nations, and of humanity? And as for rights, did the North Americans have any right whatsoever to commit such acts, to hold the accusatory meeting in the public square, and distribute the inexcusable printed protest, to go and negotiate, without permission from their country, with a foreign and despotic monarch, to request military aid from a foreign government by which to injure and provoke their fellow citizens, to bring more workers from abroad, against the law of the country and the natural generosity of mankind, to a country where hundreds of workers are unemployed? All of this was done because it was said that nineteen Cuban conspirators had decided to oppose the landing of the Spaniards. But when the most highly respected men in the city, heroes of antique lineage in the Cuban revolution, justly venerated apostles of the rights of citizens, and former mayors of Cuban cities, asked in the name of their people for some evidence of the conspiracy, and volunteered their help in punishing it, no one presented them with any evidence, and no one could give them an answer. And when a lawyer, alone in that unfriendly and terror-stricken city, demanded the immediate release of the two Cubans unlawfully imprisoned as the heads of the conspiracy, the court released both men immediately, because no charges had been brought against them.

Why, Spanish tyranny, did we fly from you only to find all your horrors in an American republic? Why did we trust and love this inhuman and ungrateful land? There is no patria, Cubans, but the one we shall win with our own efforts. The foreign sea, too, is a sea of blood. No one loves or forgives except our own country. The only solid ground in the universe is the ground on which we were born. We will be brave, or we will wander. We will finally put our efforts to the test, or we will be outcasts, roaming the world from one country to another. The very ones we love shall bite us in the heart like rabid dogs. Cubans, there is no man without a patria, and no patria without freedom. This insult has made us all the stronger, has further united us, and has taught us, better than books and diplomas, that we are all of one soul: Spain is our only enemy, in Cuba we are trapped and corrupted, and outside of Cuba we are harassed, wherever there is a man of honor or a table with bread on it. We have no other friend or source of help than ourselves. Once more, Cubans, with our homes at our backs, abandoning our dead, we must make our way across the sea! Cubans: to Cuba!

—January 27, 1894

Source: From José Martí: *Selected Writings by José Martí*, introduction by Roberto Gonzalez Echevarria, edited by Esther Allen, translated by Esther Allen, copyright © 2002 by Esther Allen. Used by permission of Viking Penguin, a division of Penguin Group (USA) Inc. pp. 325–329.

119. Letter from José Martí to Manuel Mercado, May 18, 1895

Cuban poet and journalist José Martí (1853–1895) lived in the United States for 15 years where he grew increasingly disillusioned with white Americans. The Cuban War for Independence from Spain had been going on for 30 years, and many Cuban rebels had hoped that the United States would help them. Martí had returned to his beloved island and in the heat of the battle he warned his fellow revolutionaries to guard against possible U.S. intervention. The day before he was killed, Martí wrote an unfinished letter to Manuel Mercado (1838–1909) about his fear of U.S. imperialism in the region. Mercado was born in Michoacán, Mexico, where he met Martí. They formed a close friendship.

Dos Rios Camp, May 18, 1895

Mr. Manuel Mercado

My dearest brother: Now I can write, now I can tell you with what tenderness and gratitude and respect I love you, and your home that is my own—and with what pride and commitment. Every-day now I am in danger of giving my life for my country and duty—since I understand it and have the spirit to carry it out—in order to prevent, by the timely independence of Cuba, the United States from extending its hold across the Antilles and falling with all the greater force on the lands of our America. All I have done up to now and all I will do is for that. It has had to be concealed in order to be attained: proclaiming them for what they are would give rise to obstacles too formidable to be overcome. The nations such as your own and mine, which have the most vital interest in keeping Cuba from becoming, through an annexation accomplished by those imperialists and the Spaniards, the doorway—which must be blocked and which, with our blood, we are blocking—to the annexation of the peoples of our America by the turbulent and brutal North that holds them in contempt, are kept by secondary, public obligations from any open allegiance and manifest aid to the sacrifice being made for their immediate benefit. I lived in the monster, and I know its entrails—and my sling is the sling of David: Even now, a few days ago, in the wake of the triumph with which the Cuban people greeted our free descent from the mountains where six expenditionaries walked for fourteen days, a correspondent from the *New York Herald* took me from my hammock and hut and told me about the activities aimed at annexation—which is less fearsome because of the scant realism of those who aspire to it—by men of the legal ilk who, having no discipline or creative power of their own, and as a convenient disguise for their complacency and subjugation to Spain, request Cuba's autonomy without conviction, content that there be a master, Yankee or Spaniard, to maintain them and grant them, in reward for their services as intermediaries, positions as leaders, scornful of the vigorous masses, the skilled and inspiring mestizo mass of this country—the intelligent, creative masses of whites and blacks.

And did the *Herald* correspondent, Eugene Bryson, tell me about anything else? About a Yankee syndicate, backed by the Customs Office, in which rapacious white Spaniards have a deep hand, and that may become a toehold in Cuba for those from the North, whose complex and entrammeled political constitution fortunately leaves them unable to undertake or support this plan as the project of their government. And Bryson told me something else, though the truth of the conversation he reported to me can only be understood by one who has seen at close hand the vigor with which we have launched the revolution, and the disorder, reluctance, and poor pay of the raw Spanish army—and the inability of Spain to muster, either in or out of Cuba, the resources with which to fight this war, resources that, during the last war, it extracted from Cuba alone. Bryson told me about a conversation he had with Martinez Campos at the end of which he was given to understand that no doubt, when the time came, Spain would prefer to reach an agreement with the United States than to hand the Island over to the Cuban people. And Bryson told me still more: about an acquaintance of ours who is being groomed in the North as the United States' candidate for the presidency of Mexico, once the current President has disappeared. I am doing my duty here. The Cuban war—a reality that is superior to the vague and disparate desires of the annexationist Cubans and Spaniards whose alliance with the government of Spain would give them only relative power—has come at the right hour in America to prevent, even against the open deployment of all these forces, the annexation of Cuba to the Unites States, which would never accept the annexation of a country that is at war, and which, since the revolution will not accept annexation, cannot enter into a hateful and absurd commitment to crush, for its own benefit and with its own weapons, an American war of independence.

And Mexico? Will it not find a wise, effective, and immediate way of supplying aid, in time, to those who are defending it? Yes, it will, or I will find one on Mexico's behalf. This is life or death; there is no room for error. Discretion is the only option. I would have found and proposed a way already, but I must have more authority myself, or know who does have it, before acting or advising. I have just arrived. The constitution of a simply, practical government may take two more months, if it is to be real and stable. Our soul is one, I know that, and so is the connections', timeliness, and compromise. I represent a certain constituency, and I do not want to do anything that might appear to be a capricious expansion of it.

I arrived in a boat with General Maximo Gomez and four other men, taking the lead oar through a storm to land on an unknown, rocky stretch of one of our beaches. For fourteen days I carried my rucksack and rifle on foot across brambles and high places—rousing the people to take up arms as we passed through. I feel, in the benevolence of these souls, the root of my attachment to the pain of mankind and to the justice that will alleviate it. The countryside is undisputedly ours, to such a degree that in a month I've heard gunfire only once; at the gates of the cities we either win a victory or pass three thousand armed men in review, to an enthusiasm akin to religious fervor. We are going on now to the center of the Island where, in the presence of the revolution that have given rise to, I will lay aside the authority given me by the Cubans off the island, which has been respected on the island, and which an assembly of delegates of the visible Cuban people, the revolutionaries now in arms, must renew in accordance with their new state. The revolution desires full liberty for the army, without the nee imposed on it by a Chamber of Deputies with no real authorization, or by the suspicions of a younger generation that is its republicanism, or by jealousy and fear of the excessive future prominence of some painstaking and farsighted caudillo. However at the same time, the revolution wants concise and respectable republican representation—the same spirit of humanity and decency, full for individual dignity, in the republic's representatives as is revolutionaries on and keeping them at war. For myself, I understand that a nation cannot be made to go against the spirit that moves it, or to do without that spirit, and I know how to set hearts on fire and how to use the ardent and gratified state of those hearts for incessant agitation and attack. But where forms are concerned, there is room for many ideas, and the things of men are made by men. You own me. For myself, I will defend only that which I believe will or serve the revolution. I know how to disappear. But my ideas would not disappear, nor would my own obscurity embitter me. And as long as we have a form, we will work, whether the fulfillment of it falls to me or to others.

And now that matters of the public interest have gone first, I'll tell you about myself. Only the emotion of this duty was able to raise from coveted death the man who knows you best—now that Najera no longer lives where he can be seen—and who cherishes the friendship which you distinguish him like a treasure in his heart. I know you have been scolding me, silently, since my journey began. We give him all our soul, and he is silent! What a disappointment! How callused his soul must be if the tribute and honor of our affection has not been enough to make him write one letter more, among all the pages of letters and newspaper articles he writes each day! There are affections of such delicate honesty.

Source: From José Martí: *Selected Writings by José Martí*, introduction by Roberto Gonzalez Echevarria, edited by Esther Allen, translated by Esther Allen, copyright © 2002 by Esther Allen. Used by permission of Viking Penguin, a division of Penguin Group (USA) Inc., pp. 346–349.

120. Excerpt from "The Labor Strikes," 1875

By 1859, almost 10,000 tobacco plantations with around 1,300 cigar factories were situated near Havana, Cuba. The first large wave of Cuban cigar makers arrived in the United States in the early 1870s. Eventually some manufacturers moved to Key West. One of the first centers was Ybor City, which started out as 40 acres of swamp and scrub and northeast of Tampa. Ybor City and Tampa were separated by thick palmetto scrub. Soon cigar manufacturers from Havana, Key West, and the northern United States moved their plants to Ybor City, which became renowned for the finest Cuban cigars; it was known as the "Cigar Capital of the World," and eventually 200 cigar factories employed 12,000 tabaqueros (cigar makers), producing 700 million cigars a year. Ybor City became known as "Little Havana." With a large worker population it became a mecca for labor organization. The following news item reports on one of the first cigar-maker strikes in the United States.

THE LABOR STRIKES THE CIGAR MAKERS NOT AT WORK— THE BROWN-STONE RUBBERS' DIFFICULTIES NEARLY ENDED

The strike of the Cuban journeymen cigar-makers still continues, but like all similar strikes seems destined to a brief career. Mr. Lierena, Secretary of the Cuban Cigar Manufacturers' Association, stated yesterday that by the time the manufacturers required employees the strike would be at an end. Nearly all of the manufacturers have large stocks of cigars on hand, owing to the dull season and the small demand for high-priced cigars. Yesterday the strikers assembled in groups in the vicinity of their former places of business, and discussed the situation in their native language until the Police dispersed them. Mr. Lierena stated that the article recently published in a morning paper, placing the reduction in the rates paid at from $18 to $16 per thousand, was erroneous. The reduction made was from $20 to $18 per thousand cigars, as stated in The Times some days since. A strike is contemplated among the journeymen cigar-makers at Key West and Havana, who have been receiving about the same rate of wages as that provided in the proposed reduction. Consequently the manufacturers in this City have abandoned the proposition to import men from Cuba to fill the vacancies caused by the strike.

The strike of the brown-stone rubbers is virtually ended. The society men are now working nine hours a day in nearly all the yards. In some instances they have objected to working with non-society men, and their employers have favored them in their objection by refusing to employ non-society men. Messrs. Tate & Osborne yesterday employed six society men at $2.60 per day, for ten hours work, in addition to the number of non-society men already in their employ, thus ignoring all the rules and stipulations of the Brown-stone Rubbers' Society. James Kenney, the man who was so badly beaten by James Myers, the President of the East-side Rubbers' Society, was yesterday notified that counsel would be provided for him by the brown-stone cutters of the Mechanics' Exchange, for the purpose of prosecuting his assailant when the case comes up for trial in the Court of General Sessions.

Source: New York Times, April 7, 1875, p. 2.

121. "The Strike of the Cigar Men," 1883

Throughout the nineteenth century, cigar makers lived in immigrant ghettos and worked in sweatshops in places such as Union City, New Jersey, and in Miami and Tampa, Florida. Cigar making was a highly specialized craft. In 1857, the Society of Mutual Aids of Craftsmen and Day Laborers of Havana was formed to provide mutual aid to its members and their families. In 1866, the Union of Workers of the Branch of Tabaquerías was created. During the War of Ten Years (1868–1878) as revolutionary activity grew in Cuba, the Spanish government became more repressive toward workers' organizations and mutual aid societies became more proactive as they were transformed into labor unions. That is, they evolved from fraternal organizations into labor organizations intent on controlling production. In 1872, a union arose from the Escogedores, the wrappers, who distinguished shades of color, and took care that all of the cigars in the box were the exact same shade. In 1875, the Union of Despalilladores (strippers) was formed. These different currents evolved into the Gremio de Tabaqueros (Union of Cigar Makers) and had locals in Havana, Key West, Vera Cruz, New Orleans, and other cities. By the 1880s, these unions were ideological, with many having anarchist and socialist tendencies that were aired in their own newspapers. A milestone was Oscar Hammerstein's 1883 patenting of the first cigar rolling machine. This led to factory owners tightening work conditions and, in some cases, lowering wages in hopes of making huge profits after the lowering of an excise tax on cigars that was passed during the Civil War (1861–1865). Labor responded militantly and, in New York, a strike ensued at Lozano Pendas & Company. Lozano Pendas & Company had a factory in Ybor City, Florida. The following article also mentions the 1883 strike for a $2 per day pay increase.

The strike of the Spanish and Cuban cigar-makers for an advance of wages still continues. At the head-quarters of the strikers several employers were reported yesterday as having promised to pay the advance demanded. The Executive Committee of the Germio de Tabaqueros issued a notice stating that the strikers were willing to suffer the inconveniences arising from the suspension of work for any length of time that it might be necessary to obtain the additional $2, and resolving that in case the strike be prolonged that the strikers would go to Havana, Key West, Vera Cruz, New-Orleans, and other cities. They were, however, very hopeful that the manufacturers would in a short time accede to their demands, because they were short of stock. There were several informal conferences among the manufacturers, and a prominent manufacturer said that a conference would be held this afternoon. The cigar dealers had asked for a reduction of $3 in the price of cigars, and the manufacturers wrote informing them that the workmen had struck for an advance of $2, and that the tobacco-strippers were also clamoring for an the increase of wages, and that they could not increase the wages of their workmen and reduce the prices of stock.

Source: "The Strike of the Cigar Men," *The New York Times*, April 27, 1883.

122. "Cigarmakers Protesting," 1884

Not every cigar maker in the United States in the late nineteenth century was Cuban, Puerto Rican, or Spanish. But they were among the best. At this point, not many Puerto Ricans migrated to the United States. Puerto Rico was 1,000 miles away and workers had to travel by water. Spaniards came by way of Cuba which was only 90 miles away. There were a large number of German cigar makers who learned the craft in Europe. Samuel Gompers (1850–1924), a founder of the American Federation of Labor (AFL) in 1886, learned the craft from his father. His family emmigrated to New York where a relatively few cigar sweat shops packed as many as 75 employees into a small space. Thousands of small children worked in these sweatshops and factories, helping their parents. Gompers worked his way up through the union and, in 1881, Gompers was sent as the delegate of the cigar makers to a conference that formed the Federation of Organized Trades and Labor Councils, which evolved into the AFL. Gompers was elected as this group's first president, and held the presidency for nearly 40 years. The following article talks about a committee of workers from the AFL that was sent to Washington, D.C., to lobby the Committee on Foreign Affairs not to sign a treaty with Spain that would lower the tariff on foreign-made cigars by 50 percent and allow the tobacco leaves to be imported to the United States duty free. Cuban American cigar makers played a role in union affairs. The stream of Cubans to the United States quickened after the 1868 Cuban war of independence broke out. There were over 80 cigar factories by 1883. These factories employed almost 2,703 Cuban cigar workers. They founded the first trade unions in the U.S. South. The Cuban cigar makers were highly politicized. In 1864, cigar makers introduced lectores (readers), that workers paid to read them literary and political works as they rolled cigars. They were educated through these readings.

CIGARMAKERS PROTESTING TO USE EVERY EFFORT TO HAVE THE TREATY REJECTED

The cigarmakers held a meeting yesterday afternoon at No. 189 Bowery to discuss the best means to prevent the ratification of the Spanish treaty, by which the import tax on cigars is to be reduced 50 per cent and the duty on tobacco leaf is to be abolished altogether. This was an adjourned meeting from a previous one, at which the cigarmakers expressed their unqualified opposition to the treaty as not only derogatory to the tobacco manufacturing interests of the country, but also as prejudicial to themselves as workingmen, as such a treaty would lower their wages to the level of those of European workmen, and cause them great sufferings, if it did not drive a great portion of that industry out of the country. All were agreed as to the necessity of opposing the ratification of the treaty, and the only question was what was the best method to do it.

For the first time in a long while, the manufacturers and workingmen were in unison, and behind the cigarmakers there stand many large cigar and tobacco manufacturing firms in the country. Among these are the firms of Lesano & Pendas, manufacturers of fine Havana tobacco cigars; Lichtenstein Brothers, Wengler & Co., Brown & Earle, McCoy, Sutro & Newmark, Sanchez, Hayga & Co., C. Upman, Kaufman Brothers, George P. Lies, Powell, Wenigman & Smith, A. A. Suma & Co., C. Bartolini, M. Stachelberg & Co., and M. Hutchinson & Co. Although none of these manufacturers have taken part in the meetings of the workmen or have been known to be present at any of them, they are not any the less interested in the agitation, and are working on their own account to obtain the same result—the rejection of the treaty by the Senate. A committee of 11 was appointed at the first meeting to go to Washington to appear against the treaty before the Senate Committee on Foreign Affairs or any other committee to whom it might be referred. There were a number of workmen, however, who wanted to call a mass meeting of cigarmakers to protest against the treaty, to pass resolutions demanding its rejection, and to discuss the subject more thoroughly, and another meeting was called for yesterday afternoon, at which Samuel Gompers presided.

A motion was made to hold a mass meeting, but that did not receive as much support as its friends expected. It was argued that while a great deal of indignation would undoubtedly be expressed, the reports of the arguments that would be made at the mass meeting would hardly be presented to the Senators, while the advocates of the treaty would be on the spot with all their arguments and persuasions. Nevertheless, some of the German cigarmakers insisted on a mass meeting being held, and

Mr. Feltenberg, one of the Committee of Eleven, made an earnest appeal for one. The Senators, he declared, were the public servants of the workingmen, who had a right to demand the rejection of the treaty, and it was the duty of the Senators and of Congress to accede to the demands of the voters. All that the cigarmakers had to do would be to call a mass meeting and to make known their demands. Unless a mass meeting was called, Mr. Feltenberg threatened to resign from the committee, and, with his supporters, to withdraw from the agitation.

Another more philosophic delegate remarked that there might not be time enough to call and make preparations for a mass meeting upon a grand scale, and that meanwhile the enemy might steal a march upon them. Still another delegate who supported Feltenberg suggested that all cigarmakers and other trades unions throughout the country be requested to make demonstrations. Mr. Gompers, in reply to Mr. Feltenberg, remarked that it was true that workingmen had a right to make certain demands upon Senators and Congressmen, but when they did not have the power to enforce those demands it was unwise and a waste of time to make them. It was better to ask for what they wanted in a practical manner and to present their arguments in such a way as to obtain the desired result. The advocates of the treaty were on the spot, trying their utmost to make an impression upon the Senators and push the treaty through, while the workingmen were away in New York and other cities, far the scene of action.

Mr. Gompers had acted as a committeeman to Washington upon a former occasion, and he knew that even if the Senators were honest in their intentions they were not posted on everything that came up before them. When he was last in Washington as a member of a committee they found that the Senators were to a great extent ignorant of the wants of the workingmen. Senator Allison requested Mr. Gompers to write out the workingmen's case just as he would write it for an entirely ignorant man, and the Senator would thus be enabled to use it in his argument on the floor of the Senate.

A black-eyed and black-haired woman came into the meeting room, and after giving her name to the Chairman, was introduced as Mrs. Velasquez, of Washington. She spoke English fluently and said that she was a Cuban and had come to help the cigarmakers. She was an old worker in Congress, although she wanted it to be understood that she was not a woman's rights agitator. She had been requested by several Senators to come on to New York and confer with the cigarmakers and sugar manufacturers. One hundred and forty members of Congress and 41 Senators were decidedly opposed to the treaty. The speaker said she was very well acquainted with Messrs. Edmunds, Blair, Sherman, Randall, and numerous other Senators and Congressmen. Mr. Foster's object in drafting the treaty was to further his own individual interests and the interests of his friends, and they would do all that lay in their power to push it through the Senate.

Mrs. Velasquez was not only opposed to the treaty, but she wanted to see Cuba annexed, and there were many in Washington who wanted that, too. Mr. Hill, of Ohio, was in her office on Saturday, and she had a letter from Senator Blair asking her to see the different societies in this city. She urged the cigarmakers to send representatives to Washington, where committees would arrive from New Orleans, California, and other places, and if the workingmen only showed sufficient interest in the matter the treaty would undoubtedly be rejected.

The motion to hold a mass meeting was finally tabled.

Source: "The Cigarmakers Protesting." *The New York Times*, December 8, 1884, p. 1.

123. Letter from Maximo Gómez to U.S. President Grover Cleveland, February 9, 1897

Máximo Gómez (1836–1905) was a leader in the Cuban War for Independence. Born in Santo Domingo in 1836, he served in the Spanish Army and fought for Spain. Upon visiting Cuba in 1865, he was converted to the cause of Cuban independence and he changed sides in the war for independence. Traveling to the United States, Gómez met José Martí and other independistas who were lobbying for support and raising money. Gómez was a military man and his advice was valuable. Martí would ask Gómez to lead the rebel Cuban Army in 1895. In December 1896, U.S. President Grover Cleveland announced that the United States might reconsider its policy of nonintervention if Spain did not resolve the civil war. Gómez wrote Cleveland that although Cubans welcomed assistance, their request for help from the United States should not be considered a license to intervene in the affairs of Cuba. Many Latin Americans feared the growing U.S. interest in the region and were afraid that United States would use the war as a pretext for occupying the Caribbean islands.

Sancti Spíritus, February 9, 1897

Mr. Grover Cleveland, President of the United States

Sir: Permit a man whose soul is torn within him by the contemplation of unutterable crimes to raise his voice to the supreme chief of a people free, cultivated, and powerful.

Do not, I beg, regard this action as an inopportune act of officialism. You yourself authorized it when you conceded to me a place in your last message to Congress.

Even more, I beg you, do not regard it as a request for intervention in our affairs. We Cubans have thrown ourselves into this war, confident in our strength. The wisdom of the American people should alone decide what course of action you should take.

I will not speak of the Cubans in arms. No; I raise my voice only in the name of unarmed Americans—victims of a frightful cruelty. I raise it in the name of weakness and of innocence sacrificed, with forgetfulness of the elementary principles of humanity and the external maxims of Christian morality—sacrificed brutally in the closing days of the nineteenth century, at the very gates of the great nation which stands so high in modern culture; sacrificed there by a decaying European monarchy, which has the sad glory of setting forth the horrors of the middle ages.

Our struggle with Spain has an aspect very interesting to that humanity of which you are so noble an exemplar, and to this aspect I wish to call your illustrious attention. Look through the world and you will see how all people, with the possible exception of the Americans, contemplate with indifference, or with sentimental platonism, the war which makes red the beautiful fields of fertile Cuba as if it were a thing foreign to their interests and to those of modern culture; as if it were not a crime to forget in this manner the duties of social brotherhood.

But you know it is not Cuba alone; it is America, it is all Christianhood, it is all humanity, that sees itself outraged by Spain's horrible barbarity.

Well it is that the Spanish struggle with desperation, and that they are ashamed to explain the methods they employ in this war. But we know them, and we expected them.

We accept it all as a fresh sacrifice on the altar of Cuban independence.

It is logical that such should be the conduct of the nation that expelled the Jews and the Moors; that instituted and built up the terrible Inquisition; that established the tribunals of blood in the Netherlands; that annihilated the Indians and exterminated the first settlers of Cuba; that assassinated thousands of her subjects in the wars of South American independence, and that filled the cup of iniquity in the last war in Cuba.

It is natural that a people should proceed thus who, by hint of superstitious and fanatical education, and through the vicissitudes of its social and political life, have fallen into a sort of physiological deterioration, which has caused it to fall back whole centuries on the ladder of civilization.

It is not strange that such a people should proclaim murder as a system and as a means of putting down a war caused by its desires for money and power. To kill the suspect, to kill the criminal, to kill the defenseless prisoner, to kill the helpless wounded, to kill all who are able to impede its desolating action—all this is comprehensible as the way that the Spaniards have always understood and carried on warfare.

But not to pause at the holy and venerated hearth, personification of all most peaceful and noble; nor at women, emblem of weakness; nor at children, overwhelming symbol of inoffensive innocence. To bring upon these destruction, ruin and murder, constant and cruel; ah, sir, how horrible this is! The pen falls from my hand when I think of it, and I doubt at times human nature, in contemplating with my eyes dim with tears, so many hearts outraged, so many women sacrificed, so many children cruelly and uselessly destroyed by the Spanish columns.

The Spanish, unable to exercise acts of sovereignty over the interior of Cuba, have forced the peasants to concentrate in villages, where it is hoped misery will force them to serve in the armies of a Government which they abhor. Not only are these unhappy ones forced to abandon the only means by which they can live; not only are they forced to die of starvation, but they are branded as decided supporters of our arms, and against them, their wives and children, is directed a fearful and cruel persecution.

Ought such facts to be tolerated by a civilized people? Can human powers, forgetting the fundamental principles of Christian community, permit these things go on? Is it possible that civilized people will consent to the sacrifice of unarmed and defenseless men? Can the American people view with culpable indifference the slow but complete extermination of thousands of innocent Americans? No. You have declared that they can not; that such acts of barbarity ought not to be permitted nor tolerated. We see the brilliant initiative you have taken in protesting strongly against the killing of Europeans and Christians in Armenia and in China, denouncing them with evidence of heartfelt energy.

Knowing this, I today frankly and legally appeal to you, and declare that I can not completely prevent the acts of vandalism that I deplore.

It does not suffice that I protect the families of Cubans who join us, and that my troops, following the example of civilization, respect and put at immediate liberty prisoners of war, cure and restore the enemy's wounded, and prevent reprisals. It still appears that the Spaniard are amenable to no form of persuasion that is not backed up by force.

Ah, sir, the vicissitudes of this cruel struggle have caused much pain to the heart of an old and unfortunate father, but nothing has made me suffer so much as the horrors which I recite unless it is to see that you remain indifferent to them.

Say to the Spaniards that they may struggle with us and treat us as they please, but that they must respect the pacific population; that they must not outrage women nor butcher innocent children.

You have a high and beautiful precedent for such action. Read the sadly famous proclamation of the Spanish general, Balmaceda, of 1869, proclaiming, practically, the reproduction of this war, and remember the honorable and high-minded protest that the Secretary of State formulated against it.

The American people march legitimately at the head of the Western Continent, and they should no longer tolerate the cold and systematic assassination of defenseless Americans less history impute to them a participation in these atrocities.

Imitate the high example that I have indicated above. Your conduct, furthermore, will be based solidly on the Monroe doctrine, for this can not refer only to the usurpation of American territories and not to the defense of the people of America against European ambitions. It can not mean to protect American soil and leave its helpless dwellers exposed to the cruelties of a sanguinary and despotic European power. It must extend to the defense of the principles which animate modern civilization and form an integral part of the culture and life of the American people.

Crown your honorable history of statesmanship with a noble act of Christian charity. Say to Spain that murder must stop, that cruelty must cease, and put the stamp of your authority on what you say. Thousands of hearts will call down eternal benedictions on your memory, and God, the supremely merciful, will see in it the most meritorious work of your entire life.

I am, your humble servant,
Máximo Gómez

Source: J.A. Sierra, ed. A&E Television Networks, http://www.historyofcuba.com/history/gomez4.htm.

124. U.S. Resolution on the "Recognition of the Independence of Cuba" and the Teller Amendment, 1898

The following resolution was passed in response to a message sent to Congress by William McKinley, U.S. president from 1897 to 1901, asking for permission to intervene in Cuba and go to war with Spain. The support of the United States was important to the rebels because they did not have a navy and needed supplies and food. At this time, the United States considered Cuba and Puerto Rico vital to its interests in the Caribbean and Central America—both would become staging areas for future intervention and the building and protection of the Panama Canal.

The fourth and final resolution presented in the following document, is known as The Teller Resolution, named for its author, U.S. Sen. Henry M. Teller (1830–1914) (D-Colorado) who, like many Americans, feared that the United States had imperial designs on Cuba and that the war was a pretext for grabbing more territory. His resolution specified that the United States would not establish permanent control over Cuba and it disclaimed any intention of annexing the island. It was passed without opposition in Congress. However, after Spanish troops left the island in 1898, the United States occupied Cuba until 1902 after which Cuba, for all intents and purposes, became a U.S. protectorate.

JOINT Resolution for the recognition of the independence of the people of Cuba, demanding that the Government of Spain relinquish its authority and government in the Island of Cuba, and to withdraw its land and naval forces from Cuba and Cuban waters, and directing the President of the United States to use the land and naval forces of the United States to carry these resolutions into effect.

Whereas, the abhorrent conditions which have existed for more than three years in the Island of Cuba, so near our own borders, have shocked the moral sense of the people of the United States, have been a disgrace to Christian civilization, culminating, as they have, in the destruction of a United States battle-ship, with two hundred and sixty-six of its officers and crew, while on a friendly visit in the harbor of Havana, and can not longer be endured, as has been set forth by the President of the United States in his message to Congress of April eleventh, eighteen hundred and ninety-eight, upon which the action of Congress was invited: Therefore,

Resolved, by the Senate and House of Representatives of the United States of America in Congress assembled, First. That the people of the Island of Cuba are, and of right ought to be, free and independent.

Second. That it is the duty of the United States to demand, and the Government of the United States does hereby demand, that the Government of Spain at once relinquish its authority and government in the Island of Cuba, and withdraw its land and naval forces from Cuba and Cuban waters.

Third. That the President of the United States be, and he hereby is, directed and empowered to use the entire land and naval forces of the United States, and to call into the actual service of the United States, the militia of the several States, to such extent as may be necessary to carry these resolutions into effect.

Fourth. That the United States hereby disclaims any disposition or intention to exercise sovereignty, jurisdiction, or control over said Islands except for the pacification thereof, and asserts its determination, when that is accomplished, to leave the government and control of the Island to its people.

Approved, April 20, 1898.

Source: "Recognition of the Independence of Cuba, 1898." *American Historical Documents, 1000–1904,* The Harvard Classics, 1909–14. http://www.bartleby.com/43/45.html.

125. "Interment of José Martí," 1895

The following article describes the burial of José Martí (1853–1895), the apostle for Cuban independence. Martí was a poet, journalist, and independista. He is credited with creating sympathy for the Cuban Revolution in the United States, and in the mid-1890s took command of the armed struggle on the island. The following document describing his burial ceremonies would be the equivalent of a document describing George Washington's burial.

INTERMENT OF JOSE MARTI

Official Documents Relative to the Death of the Insurgent
Correspondence of The United Press
HAVANA, June 1—The official documents relative to the burial of Marti have been published in full. An epitome of them is as follows:

"In the General Cemetery of Santiago de Cuba, at 8 A.M., May 27, there was a meeting of a military commission named by his Excellency the Military Governor of Santiago. Among the prominent men were Col. Sandoval, who commanded the troops at the engagement of Dos Rios, May 19; Gen. Garrich, Col. Caberro, and many others. The Governor's commission was read. It empowered them to proceed to the identification and burial of the body of the so-called chief of the rebels, one José Martí.

"Several of the senior officers knew Martí in his lifetime, having known him during the 1868 to 1878 rebellion, and several having seen him during recent engagements. After a close and careful scrutiny of the remains, they were unanimously of the opinion that the body before them was that of José Martí.

"Following the identification, Col. Sandoval, acting for the Spanish Government, authorized the sepulture of the body in Compartment No. 134 of the Bovedas.

"All the legal requirements having been complied with in every detail, the certificate of death and identification of the body of José Martí was signed by the following: Manuel Tejerizo, Enrique Ubieta Maurl, Enrique Yatue, Pablo A. de Valencia, José X. de Sandoval.

"At the conclusion of the official ceremonies, Col. Sandoval addressed the vast concourse, asking if any relative or friend of Martí was present. Such friend or relative was at liberty to step forward and take part in the last offices to the dead. No one offering to do so, Col. Sandoval addressed the people, saying that in the presence of death the past was forgotten. Martí had ceased to be an enemy of Spain, and the body before them was worthy of honorable and Christian burial.

"The coffin was then placed in its niche, and the opening was closed with the usual stone tablet. When this had been done, Gen. Salcedo, in an eloquent address, said that if Spanish soldiers knew how to overcome enemies, they knew also how to respect the vanquished and how to pay honors to the dead.

"This closes the Martí incident—the one and only Martí is literally and legally dead."

Source: "Interment of José Martí" *New York Times,* June 9, 1895, p. 5.

126. "Porto Rico in Rebellion," 1895

In 1850, Cuba had a population of 1.2 million—605,560 of whom were white. That year 205,570 were free Africans and the rest were slaves. According to a royal census, in 1858, 300,430 Puerto Ricans were white, 341,015 were free Africans, and 41,736 were slaves. By 1894, the Cuban population had grown substantially with about 709,000 Spanish immigrants arriving between 1868 and 1894. Puerto Rico had a total population of about a million people. To the United States, the main difference between the two island nations was that Puerto Rico was 1,000 miles away whereas Cuba was only 90 miles away. U.S. business interests had already invaded Cuba. Like in Cuba, Puerto Rico witnessed the growth of a pro-independence movement. Spain initially responded by conceding colonial reforms such as establishing the first national political parties, the abolition of slavery, and a short-lived experiment in autonomy under the Spanish crown. In other words, Puerto Rico had representation in the Spanish courts (parliament). Like other Latin

American nations, Puerto Rico developed an identifiable culture. As with Cuba, Puerto Rico's struggle for independence came to a head in 1895. Puerto Rico had had a strong presence in the Cuban Revolutionary Party. The following article predicts that Puerto Rico would soon declare its independence and describes the activities of the Puerto Rican Separatist Party as well as its independence activities in New York City where it worked with the Cuban Revolutionary Party to raise, funds, seek volunteers, and win U.S. popular support.

PORTO RICO IN REBELLION

NEW YORK, Dec. 11—A local paper says that in her struggle for independence Cuba has found a powerful ally in the Island of Porto Rico. According to the latest intelligence, Spain has now two insurrections on her hands, or will have if the plans maturing are carried into execution. Porto Rico has gone so far, it is said, as to issue a declaration of independence and will soon join her sister island in the active struggle for liberty. An army is being formed by the Separatist party of Porto Rico, and as soon as the leaders are ready the new campaign will open.

As in the Venezuelan affair, the revolutionists are Cuban patriots residing in this city, and the same secrecy attended their movements. At a meeting held at the home of Dr. Julio Hanna, business calculated to further harass the Spanish government was transacted. It was that the initial steps were taken in the country towards a revolution in Porto Rico. If these plans and those formulated by the leaders on the island are carried out the first blow against Spain will be struck in a very short time. It may be but a few days before the people of Porto Rico, the only Spanish province in the West Indies which is not revolting against the mother country, will be in arms against Spain.

The leaders here declare that a vigorous declaration of independence has been prepared by the leaders of the Porto Rican Separatist party and that it is their intention to issue this as soon as they feel sure that they can defend themselves against any action Spain may take. One of the most prominent Porto Ricans in New York declared that this may be in less than a week. The declaration of independence was prepared on the island and at least one copy of it was sent to this city for the leaders to pass upon. They have given it their approval and have so informed the Separatist party in Porto Rico.

In starting this new revolution in Porto Rico, the leaders are fully carrying out the original plans of Gen. José Martí, the late leader of the Cuban revolution, which were to first get the Cuban insurrection well under way and then to encourage, or rather create, a similar uprising in Porto Rico. There were to be two separate revolutions, the army of each of the two provinces acting independently as far as possible, but necessarily in conjunction when a crisis was reached, but each striving for the same object, the defeat of Spain. If a victory should be won, it was arranged that the sister island should form entirely separate governments, the republic of Cuba and the republic of Porto Rico.

In formulating this plan, Gen. Martí consulted prominent Porto Ricans who are now in this city, one of whom corroborated the above statement last night. These men are among those who are arranging the present proposed coup. Cuba's cause and Porto Rico's cause, they say, are identical.

Source: Los Angeles Times, December 12, 1895, p. 3.

127. Letter from Col. Charles Gordon to the U.S. Consul to Cuba on the Death of Cuba's Gen. Antonio Maceo, January 1, 1897

The following document is an account of the death of Cuba's Gen. Antonio Maceo (1845–1896). Col. Charles Gordon sent this information to the U.S. Consul in Cuba, Fitzhugh Lee. Antonio Maceo, the son of a Venezuelan mulato and an Afro-Cuban mother, was one of the main leaders of the Cuban struggle for independence. He is credited with liberating western Cuba while leading an Afro-Cuban army. After his death in battle, Maceo was called the "Titan of Bronze." He had taken part in the Ten Years' War of 1868–1878, and the final war, which began in 1895 and would end two years after his death in 1898. When he died at age 51, Maceo was second-in-command of the Cuban Army of Independence.

Friday Jan. 1st, 1897

Dear Sir,

Some time ago, about Dec. 20th, I wrote a letter to a friend of mine, Dr. Guitierez [*sic*] at Key West, in which I described our passage of the Trocha and Maceo's death, which I requested him, after reading, to forward to the "World", for publication, but I am afraid, the Spaniards have the letter, as I intrusted it to Lieut. Col. Pacio to forward, and his fate just now is unknown. I will therefore write about it once more.

On December. 4th at 2 P.M. Gen. A. Maceo, accompanied by about 30 persons on his staff, assistants, and a few cavalrymen commanded by Comandante Varios, left San Felipe at the foot of the Gobernador (a large conspicuous hill); and as my clothes had not come, although I had dispatched two messengers, the General told me to come without them. About 6 P.M. we got to the beach, between Cabanas and Mariel, where the boat was hidden in the woods; but there was a very strong northerly wind and very heavy sea, so as to make it very dangerous, if not impossible to launch the boat.

We therefore picked the boat up on our shoulders, even the General taking hold several times, and carried it about a mile and a half across a neck of land, launching it inside the harbor of Mariel, not more than 2 miles outside the town, about 10 P.M. Gen. A. Maceo, Gen. Pedro Diaz, Panchito Gomez [son of Maj. Gen. Máximo Gómez] and I were the first 4 to cross, with one guide and two boatmen.

We landed after a passage of about 20–25 minutes at a little wharf near what I took to be some bathhouses, and all of us picking up a load, started a march of about $2\frac{1}{2}$ miles, when we stopped at a deserted house. The guide went back, and shortly returned with the 2nd group, namely Brig. Gen. Miro, Col. Nordarse, Dr. Zertoucha, Com. Justis and Ramon Umaha.

By 2 A.M. the rest, namely, Com. Piedra and Beaberes, one captain, and 5 assistants had joined us and we went about $\frac{1}{2}$ mile further, to a safer point, where we waited for daylight. About 6 A.M. on the 5th we started on the march and about 7 A.M. near La Merced, met Lt. Vazquez and some of his men, who took us to a house, where we camped all day. Next day, Dec. 6th, we left about noon, mounted on the horses of Vazquez's men, as our horses had not come yet; met Lt. Col. Baldomero Acosta with men and horses 2 P.M. and camped at Gara 4 P.M.–9 P.M. Then resumed the march and camped at Baracoa [a Havana province] at midnight. At 4 A.M. Dec. 7th resumed the march and met Brig. Silverio Sanchez, encamped with about 300 men, at 8 A.M. at San Pedro. As we had not had much sleep and there was nothing to eat, most of us (the Grl. Staff) went to sleep and the General had his hammock put up as well. We naturally had all confidence in Brig. Sanchez, but he did not have any exploradores and when suddenly about 2 P.M. without any warning, heavy firing commenced at our advance guard, all was for a moment confusion. Not enough, to be without exploration, but the advance guard was so near the camp, that when the fire opened, the bullets entered and passed beyond the camp.

Naturally we all mounted as quick as possible, and the General, Miro, Diaz, Nodarse, I, and 3–4 more were riding in a group, when immediately outside the little wood, in which was the camp, we met our retreating and, at no great distance, saw the enemy advancing and firing en guerilla. The General gave his horse the spurs and drawing his machete, shouted to the retreating men, "Atras! al machete!" The men and others who were all the time coming from the camp to the front seemed electrified, and with enthusiastic shouts wheeled their horses and charged, while the enemy precipitately retreated about 200 yards where he took position behind a strong stonewall about 4 feet high and, even dismounting his cavalry, opened a terrific fire by volleys.

The General at this moment told me to collect what men I could, and charge the enemy's right flank (on our left) while he himself charged on the left. I collected about 35–40 men, and seeing the stonewall not extended very far, also knowing it to be impossible for a small cavalry to take a wall like that from infantry by a direct charge, I went about 500 yards further to our left and then charged around the end of the wall.

I broke their first line of fire, but was losing men fast, and when I fell wounded with 3 bullets, my men put me on another horse and retreated. As I went back, I saw the General [Antonio Maceo (Daley)], with [a] small group, not more than 6–8, charging away on our right, and it seemed but a moment, when all but 2 or 3 were on the ground.

Commander Manuel Sanchez, was charging at the General's side, when a bullet entered the chin of Maceo, coming out at the back of the neck. The General fell forward on his horse's neck and Sanchez catching his arm exclaimed, "General, no soy cobarde!" Maceo could not speak, but gave him a terrible look and at this moment Sanchez received a bullet through his right leg which, after traversing his horse, also entered the stomach of the General.

Maceo fell but a short distance from the stone wall and it seems it was impossible for our people to advance and get his body. Some of the Spaniards advanced and robbed both him and Panchito Gomez, but they never got their bodies as the fire of our men drove then back. Near dark about 5 P.M. the enemy retreated and our people then got the bodies. And I here wish to protest against the horrible custom of the Spanish to kill the wounded.

They say Panchito Gomez committed suicide and I saw a picture in one of the Spanish papers, where he put the revolver to his brain. But that are all lies. First and foremost he had no revolver; on Dec. 2nd before we crossed, we have a nice little fight near San Felipe, and Panchito was wounded in the left shoulder and also lost his revolver. Second, he had no bullet wound in the head. He had besides his old wound in the shoulder, only one bullet wound in the left side of the stomach; but they found him alive with that by the side of the General and gave him a pinch (thrust) with the point of a sword in the right breast, a cut in the hollow of the left arm, and a horrible machetazo, that laid open the whole back of his head and left side of the neck.

All of us who crossed with the General were wounded except Gen. Diaz and Zertucha and Com. Justis who was killed. I received a bullet in the right knee, one through the right arm and another in the left side, but the last 2 light wounds are about well. The bullet in the knee is one of those confounded copper bullets that make a hole, size of your thumb, and besides it hurts the bone.

I believe you want to know also about some of the atrocities of the soldiers towards Pacificos, and I could write lots that I have personally witnessed, but I refer you to Mr. George Bronson Rhea, who has a host of well authenticated instances at your disposal.

Still if you wish for some more, let me know, and I will supply them. As for the talk of the papers and Gen. Weyler about his speedy pacification of the island do not believe a word of it. In Pinar del Rio are at least 6,000 armed Cubans, besides 4–6,000 more with machetes. They have a splendid general (Rius Rivera) there and at present plenty to eat. I was there sometime and never went hungry, besides had the satisfaction there to see Weyler with 25,000 men unable to force our position for 5 days, when we had not more than 80 men.

Of course everyone deplores the loss of Maceo, but I find nobody discouraged; on the contrary everybody, soldiers as well as leaders, are strong in the determination, to fight till [sic] their island is free. They all have still great hopes of American intervention, but even without that, they will fight on, trusting to tire out Spain, and especially Spaniard finances. Let me know if you wish to know more.

Yours,
El Coronel Carlos Gordon
Source: http://www.spanamwar.com/maceodeath.htm.

128. George Reno, "History of the Brilliant Career of Gen. Mario Menocal," 1899

Gen. Mario Menocal (1866–1941), president of Cuba from 1913–1921, served in the liberation war from Spain (1895–1898). Educated in the United States, he was well liked by Euro-American politicos. He became a conservative politician and initiated a "businessman" government in Cuba that was corrupt and arbitrary. The following *Los Angeles Times* article hails Menocal's selection as chief of police of Havana in the early days of his political career and portrays him as a friend of the United States who wanted to place Cuba under the protection of the United States. He secured U.S. support for his Cuban presidency by taking Cuba into World War I.

HISTORY OF THE BRILLIANT CAREER OF GEN. MARIO MENOCAL

Cuba has today for the first time in her four centuries of history, a man at the head of the police department who is a Cuban. And he is the coming man of Cuba.

The selection of Gen. Mario Menocal as Chief of Police of Havana has a significance which is understood and appreciated all over the island. His appointment by Gen. Brooke was not only a recognition of Menocal's merit and executive ability, but was to a certain extent a reward for perhaps the most striking act of personal heroism performed in the Cuban war, or for that matter in any war in any country.

It was in the spring of [18]97 that the city of Guaymaro in Camaguey was besieged by Garcia's forces and captured after a stubborn resistance on the part of the enemy. Americans now know what kind of a fight Spaniards can make when placed behind entrenchments and fortifications. At Guaymaro, after the outer defenses had been abandoned, a massive stone cathedral in the center of the place, heavily garrisoned by men who kept up a merciless fire from the long, narrow windows and protected arches, minarets and belfries, promised to be almost impregnable. The insurgents had fought their way into the city, but to approach within range of this fortified church was simply sure death. While this citadel remained in the hands of the Spaniards, the capture of Guaymaro was impossible.

In this emergency, Menocal came to the rescue. Under a heavy fire, encumbered with a torpedo of dynamite, he made his way, where possible along protecting walls, where shelter could not be found he dashed across the open from house to house, but with each step approaching nearer to the church. From which came a perfect hail storm of bullets. Had one of them but touched the explosive he carried in his arms, Menocal would have been blown into eternity. Watching his chance, little by little, slowly but surely, he neared the cathedral; one last dash and he gained the shelter of the edifice itself, placed the bomb under the edge of the great stone wall, and in an instant was away again. From a protected point fifty yards distant he seized the rifle of a companion and sent a bullet into the dynamite.

The explosion which followed tore out the entire end of the cathedral, whereupon the garrison hauled down the Spanish flag, surrendered to Gen. Garcia, and Guaymaro became henceforth the city of Cuba Libre.

The courage of the Cuban has been not only questioned, but at times absolutely denied, but I have reason to believe that even our brave Col. Roosevelt or Lt. Hobson might have hesitated a moment before offering to carry twenty-five pounds of dynamite up San Juan Hill on July 1. For this heroic deed, Col. Menocal was made a brigadier-general.

In September of the same year came the attack on Victoria de las Tunas. Slowly but surely, the Cuban lines enveloped the Spanish stronghold. On the morning of the third day, the dynamite gun, under the direction of Aristo Portuondo, was brought up to a position where it could be rendered effective. Several shots from it struck the base and sides of a stone fort which was the key to the city's defenses, and at last a shot penetrated the roof; the effect of the explosion which followed was marvelous. The walls of the fort simply bulged outward and the structure collapsed; nearly every man within or near was instantly killed. Consternation and terror momentarily overwhelmed the Spanish forces. Brig. Gen. Menocal saw his opportunity. Without waiting to consult his general, at the head of his brigade, he immediately charged and carried the enemy's trenches, and before the Spaniards could recover from their surprise, Victoria de las Tunas was in the hands of the Cuban forces, there to remain. For this gallant action, Menocal was made a general of division.

Not long before our late unpleasantness with Spain resulted in war, Gen. Menocal was sent to the West and placed in command of the insurgent forces of Havana province. It was thought at that time that we would be compelled to take Havana by storm, and Menocal was selected as one of the ablest Cuban officers in the anticipated attack.

Up to the time of his appointment as chief of Havana Police, Gen. Menocal was stationed at Marianao, where the excellent influence which he exercised over the men in his command won the admiration of Gen. Brooke and the entire staff of American officers in Havana. It is needless to say that he is loved in his native city, where his family have held a high social position for more than a century.

Mario Menocal was sent from Cuba to this country to be educated when only sixteen. He remained in New York eight years, and was graduated with high honors from Cornell University as a civil, mining, and military engineer. A little before the breaking out of the last revolution he returned to Havana, where Gen. Martinez Campos ordered him to proceed as an engineer to Porto Principe to give color to this proposed construction of a railroad from the latter city to Santa Cruz, on the south coast. This proposition was intended to pacify the people of that province and prevent them from joining the revolt. But no sooner did Gen. Máximo Gómez cross the line from Oriente into Camaguey, than Menocal dropped his quadrant, shouldered his rifle, and presented himself to the commander of the insurgent forces. Gen. Gómez immediately placed him on his staff as a lieutenant, and soon promoted him to the rank of captain, for bravery and ability displayed at the battles of Altagracia and Mulato, which took place in the summer of 1895, and afterward made him a commandante, or major.

In such high esteem were Menocal's services held that he was elected Assistant Secretary of War by the Cuban Assembly which met in the following September. The young officers, however, preferred the more active duties of the field, and in the spring of 1896, he was transferred to the forces of Gen. Calisto Garcia, who had just landed near Baracoa. Garcia made him his chief of staff, and in this capacity he assumed nearly all of the arduous detail and much of the responsibility of the fortunate campaign of the Oriente, in which Gen. Garcia became virtually master of the situation in the province of Santiago de Cuba.

It was during this campaign in May of 1896, that I first met Mario Menocal, then a colonel, near the Cauto River, "It seems good," he remarked, "to meet some one once more, who has come to the field direct from New York. It is a great old town," he sighed. After a moment which evidently recalled some pleasant recollection, he continued; "Tell me, what is now on at the Broadway theaters?" This, within hearing of rifle volleys which the Spanish forces of Jiguani were firing at a party of Cuban cavalry, suggested anything but the lawful realities of war.

I told him of the different plays then running, as well as I could recall them, while mounted couriers momentarily brought reports of the success of the insurgent force which was engaged in driving away cattle from under the enemy's guns in the fortified suburbs of the town nearby.

In the operations which were carried on in Holgain district soon after, Col. Menocal did enough work for any five men. Our hammocks were usually swung near each other, and night after night officers and practicos were reporting to him and receiving orders until long after midnight. We were always up, saddled, and on the march before dawn.

"Are you never going to take a night off and indulge in a good rest?" I once asked him.

"I shall not care to until Cuba is free," was his quiet reply.

During the summer of 1896, I saw many evidences of Menocal's coolness and unerring judgment at critical moments in different engagements with the enemy.

Although a quiet, serious man, he greatly enjoyed a joke, even at his own expense. One morning previous to my departure from Gen. Garcia's command for the head-quarters of the provisional government some two hundred miles distant, I rode alongside of Col. Menocal and noticed him eyeing my horse very carefully.

"That's s splendid animal you're riding, Reno," he remarked.

"Yes, isn't he a beauty?" I replied.

"Where did you get his mouse-colored majesty?" he asked.

"I traded a new dollar-and-a-quarter machete for him last night."

"It was a good bargain. He'll carry you from one end of the island to the other, if you take care of that little sore under the saddle."

"How did you discover that there is a sore under my saddle?"

"Oh, easily enough. That pacifico traded you my reserve horse, that's all," he replied.

I at once offered to restore the property to its rightful owner, but he would not have it so.

"He is just what you need. Don't say a word, the joke is on me, that's all."

Aside from the excellent work inaugurated in the police department by its new Chief, Menocal is serving as a valuable object lesson to that large body of ill-informed and pessimistic Americans, who, not only doubt, but with singular assur-ance, assert that all talk about the Cubans governing themselves for at least several years to come is idiotic.

When a few days ago in Havana, I referred one of these doubting individuals, a New York ex-alderman, to some of the new chief's executive work which merited approval, he exclaimed: "Why, he's no Cuban; he's got blue eyes and he speaks English."

It is true that Gen. Menocal speaks English, perfect English, and that he has blue eyes, but he is, nevertheless, a Cuban, born in Havana. The Menocals have been conspicuous as leaders in every revolution against Spanish rule in Cuba since the people of that unfortunate country commenced to send their sons to the United States to be educated. The mother, sisters, and daughters of the Menocal family are equally patriotic with the male members. I can recall but two women, Caridad Aguero and Concha Agramonte Sanchez, who sent her five sons to the field, whose enthusiasm for the cause of independence quite equals that of Gen. Menocal's mother. She sent her four sons, all she had to battle for freedom, and when at Marianao, she visited the general a few days ago, joy and pride were pictured in ev-ery lineament of her handsome face.

"As chief of police," she said. "Mario can do much good. Of course, I am proud of him; he has fought for Cuba since the first battle cry of liberty was sounded by José Martí. Were he not my son, I would exact of him a renewal of his promise never to desist in his efforts until our island republic is firmly and honorably estab-lished under the protection of the United States."

The new chief's uncle, Aniceto Menocal, is the celebrated engineering expert of Washington, who was intrusted with the report on the Nicaragua Canal route. One of his cousins is the well-known surgeon and physician of Havana, Dr. Raimundo Menocal. Another is the distinguished artist, Armando Menocal, who painted that famous masterpiece of the Fortuny School, which was exhibited at the World's Fair, Columbus in Chains.

It is needless to state that Gen. Menocal is making an efficient and satisfactory Chief of Police. Untiring energy, quickness in thought and action, perfect control of temper, and absolute fearlessness in the face of danger are his most prominent characteristics. Although under thirty, the four years in the field have given him a wonderful experience in enforcing obedience and in controlling both large and small bodies of men. Added to these qualifications, he has had the benefit of a thorough American education and possesses a practical knowledge of "the way we do things in the United States."

More than all, he has the respect, confidence, and esteem and will receive the support of the better element of Havana, Cubans and Spaniards alike. The corrupt know that they cannot buy him, and the criminal that they cannot trifle with him. From the moment that Spain's flag was lowered over Havana and Old Glory was sent up in its place, a new day dawned, a new regime commenced in the control of the city's affairs.

He has already closed those theaters which, under Spanish protection, have been a blot upon the city's reputation, and the dissolute classes have been driven into a locality where they may be confined and controlled. Against publishers and disseminators of vile literature, who have so long thrived unmolested. If not absolutely protected under the old order of things, he has inaugurated a war of extermination.

"I may not be able to make Havana a morally ideal city," he recently remarked, "but I can and will at least remove it from the category of places which disgrace the civilization of the century."

Chief McCullagh, who was sent to Havana this winter for the purpose of inspecting the police department, has reported that it is one of the most orderly cities of its size in the world.

George Reno

Source: Los Angeles Times, March 26, 1899, p. 9.

PART X
The Occupation

The Nineteenth Century was a period of adjustment and consolidation for most Latin American Republics as they formed distinct nationalities. They remained united by a colonial experience which in most part unified them through a common culture or language. This process of nationalism was greatly affected by the resources and location of the country viz-á-viz its proximity to the United States of America. Most of the republics won their independence in the early nineteenth century— Haiti from France in 1804, most from Spain or Portugal by the 1820s. The transition into modern states was tumultuous as in the case of most former colonial subjects for whom the free market is never a kind place. The invasions of Mexico in 1836 and ten years later sent ripples throughout the hemisphere forecasting the future of the Americas. Soon afterward Euro-Americans made their intentions known and moved to obtain Cuba. As the U.S. merchant and naval fleets grew, its world view of the Caribbean and Central America formed in which the isthmus was the cornerstone of U.S. commercial and national interests. The factor that deterred U.S. seizure of Cuba was the U.S.'s sectional problems that were resolved by the American Civil War (1861–1865). The end of this war was a great American milestone that saw the last two Spanish colonies launch their thirty years wars of independence. Both by this time had sizeable populations; both had large slave populations that the independistas wanted to free. In the final days of the wars for independence, the United States stepped in and unilaterally signed the Treaty of Paris (1898) with Spain that ceded it Puerto Rico and control of Cuba. The following section deals with the consequences of U.S. involvement in the area and its domination of the Caribbean and Central America. Because Puerto Rico was now a vassal of the United States, the commercialization of its institutions was accelerated, and this created an almost immediate uprooting of small farmers—many of whom had to leave the island to find work.

129. Excerpts from the Treaty of Paris between the United States and Spain, 1898

The 1898 Treaty of Paris granted Cuba independence from Spain. The following excerpts show that the treaty was solely between Spain and the United States, giving the United States the right to occupy Cuba. Spain ceded to the United States the island of Puerto Rico and other islands then under Spanish control in the West Indies, as well as the island of Guam in the Marianas or

Ladrones. This treaty also began the occupation of the Philippines by the United States. The treaty was criticized by anti-colonial forces because it did not take into account the wishes of the nations fighting for their independence. The following excerpts from the treaty deal with the granting of independence to Cuba.

The United States of America and Her Majesty the Queen Regent of Spain, in the name of her august son Don Alfonso XIII, desiring to end the state of war now existing between the two countries, have for that purpose appointed as plenipotentiaries:

The President of the United States,

William R. Day, Cushman K. Davis, William P. Frye, George Gray, and Whitelaw Reid, citizens of the United States;

And Her Majesty the Queen Regent of Spain,

Don Eugenio Montero Rios, president of the senate; Don Buenaventura de Abarzuza, senator of the Kingdom and ex-minister of the Crown; Don Jose de Garnica, deputy of the Cortes and associate justice of the supreme court; Don Wenceslao Ramirez de Villa Urrutia, envoy extraordinary and minister plenipotentiary at Brussels; and Don Rafael Cerero, general of division;

Who, having assembled in Paris, and having exchanged their full powers, which were found to be in due and proper form, have, after discussion of the matters before them, agreed upon the following articles:

ARTICLE I

Spain relinquishes all claim of sovereignty over and title to Cuba. And as the island is, upon its evacuation by Spain, to be occupied by the United States, the United States will, so long as such occupation shall last, assume and discharge the obligations that may under international law result from the fact of its occupation, for the protection of life and property.

ARTICLE II

Spain cedes to the United States the island of Porto Rico and other islands now under Spanish sovereignty in the West Indies, and the island of Guam in the Marianas or Ladrones.

ARTICLE III

Spain cedes to the United States the archipelago known as the Philippine Islands, and comprehending the islands lying within the following line.

...

ARTICLE VI

Spain will, upon the signature of the present treaty, release all prisoners of war, and all persons detained or imprisoned for political offences, in connection with the insurrections in Cuba and the Philippines and the war with the United States.

Reciprocally, the United States will release all persons made prisoners of war by the American forces, and will undertake to obtain the release of all Spanish prisoners in the hands of the insurgents in Cuba and the Philippines.

The Government of the United States will at its own cost return to Spain and the Government of Spain will at its own cost return to the United States, Cuba, Porto Rico, and the Philippines, according to the situation of their respective homes, prisoners released or caused to be released by them, respectively, under this article.

ARTICLE VII

The United States and Spain mutually relinquish all claims for indemnity, national and individual, of every kind, of either Government, or of its citizens or subjects, against the other Government, that may have arisen since the beginning of the late insurrection in Cuba and prior to the exchange of ratifications of the present treaty, including all claims for indemnity for the cost of the war.

The United States will adjudicate and settle the claims of its citizens against Spain relinquished in this article.

ARTICLE VIII

In conformity with the provisions of Articles I, II, and III of this treaty, Spain relinquishes in Cuba, and cedes in Porto Rico and other islands in the West Indies, in the island of Guam, and in the Philippine Archipelago, all the buildings, wharves, barracks, forts, structures, public highways and other immovable property which, in conformity with law, belong to the public domain, and as such belong to the Crown of Spain.

And it is hereby declared that the relinquishment or cession, as the case may be, to which the preceding paragraph refers, can not in any respect impair the property or rights which by law belong to the peaceful possession of property of all kinds, of provinces, municipalities, public or private establishments, ecclesiastical or civic bodies, or any other associations having legal capacity to acquire and possess property in the aforesaid territories renounced or ceded, or of private individuals, of whatsoever nationality such individuals may be.

The aforesaid relinquishment or cession, as the case may be, includes all documents exclusively referring to the sovereignty relinquished or ceded that may exist in the archives of the Peninsula. Where any document in such archives only in part relates to said sovereignty, a copy of such part will be furnished whenever it shall be requested. Like rules shall be reciprocally observed in favor of Spain in respect of documents in the archives of the islands above referred to.

In the aforesaid relinquishment or cession, as the case may be, are also included such rights as the Crown of Spain and its authorities possess in respect of the official archives and records, executive as well as judicial, in the islands above referred to, which relate to said islands or the rights and property of their inhabitants. Such archives and records shall be carefully preserved, and private persons shall without distinction have the right to require, in accordance with law, authenticated copies of the contracts, wills and other instruments forming part of notorial protocols or files, or which may be contained in the executive or judicial archives, be the latter in Spain or in the islands aforesaid.

ARTICLE IX

Spanish subjects, natives of the Peninsula, residing in the territory over which Spain by the present treaty relinquishes or cedes her sovereignty, may remain in such territory or may remove there from, retaining in either event all their rights of property, including the right to sell or dispose of such property or of its proceeds; and they shall also have the right to carry on their industry, commerce, and professions, being subject in respect thereof to such laws as are applicable to other foreigners. In case they remain in the territory they may preserve their allegiance to the Crown of Spain by making, before a court of record, within a year from the date of the exchange of ratifications of this treaty, a declaration of their decision to preserve such allegiance; in default of which declaration they shall be held to have renounced it and to have adopted the nationality of the territory in which they may reside.

The civil rights and political status of the native inhabitants of the territories hereby ceded to the United States shall be determined by the Congress.

...

ARTICLE X

The inhabitants of the territories over which Spain relinquishes or cedes her sovereignty shall be secured in the free exercise of their religion....

...

ARTICLE XVII

The present treaty shall be ratified by the President of the United States, by and with the advice and consent of the Senate thereof, and by Her Majesty the Queen Regent of Spain; and the ratifications shall be exchanged at Washington within six months from the date hereof, or earlier if possible.

In faith whereof, we, the respective Plenipotentiaries, have signed this treaty and have hereunto affixed our seals.

Done in duplicate at Paris, the tenth day of December, in the year of Our Lord one thousand eight hundred and ninety-eight.

[Seal] William R. Day
[Seal] Cushman K. Davis
[Seal] William P. Frye
[Seal] Geo. Gray
[Seal] Whitelaw Reid
[Seal] Eugenio Montero Rios
[Seal] B. de Abarzuza
[Seal] J. de Garnica
[Seal] W. R. de Villa Urrutia
[Seal] Rafael Cerero

Source: U.S. Congress, 55th Cong., 3d sess., Senate Doc. No. 62, Part 1 (Washington: Government Printing Office, 1899), pp. 5–11.

130. Excerpts from the Diary of General Máximo Gómez, January 8, 1899

Máximo Gómez Baez (1836–1905) was born in Santo Domingo. A member of the Spanish armed forces, he supported and fought in Cuba's Ten Years' War from 1868 to 1878, which was the first major insurgency and the beginning of the wars for independence. He traveled to the United States where he met José Martí (1853–1895), who spent his life dedicated to the cause of Cuban independence. Martí was a poet and journalist, as well as the leader of Cubans in exile. Gómez bristled at Euro-Americans' attitude of superiority toward Cubans. In the following excerpt he decries the American occupation of Cuba, saying that it was too high a price to pay for the military aid that Cubans received from the United States in the last year of the war. He concludes that the Euro-Americans turned the Cuban victory from a joyous occasion to a bitter experience. Cuban nationalists from this time forward would accuse the United States of imperialism rather than solidarity with Cubans and other Latin American nations.

The Americans' military occupation of the country is too high a price to pay for their spontaneous intervention in the war we waged against Spain for freedom and independence. The American government's attitude toward the heroic Cuban people at this history-making time is, in my opinion, one of big business. This situation is dangerous for the country, mortifying the public spirit and hindering organization in all of the branches that, from the outset, should provide solid foundations for the future republic, when everything was entirely the work of all the inhabitants of the island, without distinction of nationality.

Nothing is more rational and fair than that the owner of the house should be the one to live in it with his family and be the one who furnishes and decorates it as he likes and that he not be forced against his will and inclination to follow norms imposed by his neighbor.

All these considerations lead me to think that Cuba cannot have true moral peace—which is what the people need for their happiness and good fortune—under the transitional government. This transitional government was imposed by force by a foreign power and, therefore, is illegitimate and incompatible with the principles that the entire country has been upholding for so long and in the defense of which half of its sons have given their lives and all of its wealth has been consumed.

There is so much natural anger and grief throughout the island that the people haven't really been able to celebrate the triumph of the end of their former rulers' power.

They have left in sadness, and in sadness we have remained, because a foreign power has replaced them. I dreamed of peace with Spain; I hoped to bid farewell with respect to the brave Spanish soldiers with whom we always met, face to face, on the field of battle. The words peace and freedom should inspire only love and fraternity on the morning of concord between those who were combatants the night before; but, with their guardianship imposed by force, the Americans have turned the Cubans' victorious joy to bitterness and haven't sweetened the grief of the vanquished.

The situation that has been created for this people—one of material poverty and of grief because their sovereignty has been curbed—is ever more distressing. It is possible that, by the time this strange situation finally ends, the Americans will have snuffed out even the last spark of goodwill.

Source: J. A. Sierra and HistoryofCuba.com, http://www.historyofcuba.com/history/gomez.htm.

131. Campaign Speech Given by Albert Beveridge, September 16, 1898

Albert Beveridge (1862–1927), was a fervent advocate of Euro-American imperialism which meant U.S. control of territories outside its borders.

Beveridge and others claimed that the United States had the right and duty to control less developed nations. Cuba served as the model for forging an empire. In the following campaign speech made on September 16, 1898, during Beveridge's successful race for the U.S. Senate (from Indiana), he embraced the notion of the United States becoming an imperial power, saying the Philippines were ours forever, it was "territory belonging to the United States." This notion of entitlement and Euro-American superiority rankled Latin Americans and contributed to their distrust of the United States.

It is a noble land that God has given us; a land that can feed and clothe the world; a land whose coastlines would inclose half the countries of Europe; a land set like a sentinel between the two imperial oceans of the globe, a greater England with a nobler destiny.

It is a mighty people that He has planted on this soil; a people sprung from the most masterful blood of history; a people perpetually revitalized by the virile, man-producing workingfolk of all the earth; a people imperial by virtue of their power, by right of their institutions, by authority of their Heaven-directed purposes—the propagandists and not the misers of liberty.

It is a glorious history our God has bestowed upon His chosen people; a history heroic with faith in our mission and our future; a history of statesmen who flung the boundaries of the Republic out into unexplored lands and savage wilderness; a history of soldiers who carried the flag across blazing deserts and through the ranks of hostile mountains, even to the gates of sunset; a history of a multiplying people who overran a continent in half a century; a history of prophets who saw the consequences of evils inherited from the past and of martyrs who died to save us from them; a history divinely logical, in the process of whose tremendous reasoning we find ourselves today.

Therefore, in this campaign, the question is larger than a party question. It is an American question. It is a world question. Shall the American people continue their march toward the commercial supremacy of the world? Shall free institutions broaden their blessed reign as the children of liberty wax in strength, until the empire of our principles is established over the hearts of all mankind?

Have we no mission to perform, no duty to discharge to our fellow man? Has God endowed us with gifts beyond our deserts and marked us as the people of His peculiar favor, merely to rot in our own selfishness, as men and nations must, who take cowardice for their companion and self for their deity—as China has, as India has, as Egypt has?

Shall we be as the man who had one talent and hid it, or as he who had ten talents and used them until they grew to riches? And shall we reap the reward that waits on our discharge of our high duty; shall we occupy new markets for what our farmers raise, our factories make, our merchants sell—aye, and please God, new markets for what our ships shall carry?

Hawaii is ours; Porto Rico is to be ours; at the prayer of her people Cuba finally will be ours; in the islands of the East, even to the gates of Asia, coaling stations are to be ours at the very least; the flag of a liberal government is to float over the Philippines, and may it be the banner that Taylor unfurled in Texas and Fremont carried to the coast.

The Opposition tells us that we ought not to govern a people without their consent. I answer, The rule of liberty that all just government derives its authority from the consent of the governed, applies only to those who are capable of self-government We govern the Indians without their consent, we govern our territories without their consent, we govern our children without their consent. How do they know what our government would be without their consent? Would not the people of the Philippines prefer the just, humane, civilizing government of this Republic to the savage, bloody rule of pillage and extortion from which we have rescued them?

And, regardless of this formula of words made only for enlightened, self-governing people, do we owe no duty to the world? Shall we turn these peoples back to the reeking hands from which we have taken them? Shall we abandon them, with Germany, England, Japan, hungering for them? Shall we save them from those nations, to give them a self-rule of tragedy?

They ask us how we shall govern these new possessions. I answer: Out of local conditions and the necessities of the case methods of government will grow. If England can govern foreign lands, so can America. If Germany can govern foreign lands, so can America. If they can supervise protectorates, so can America. Why is it more difficult to administer Hawaii than Ne[w] Mexico or California? Both had a savage and an alien population: both were more remote from the seat of government when they came under our dominion than the Philippines are today.

Will you say by your vote that American ability to govern has decayed, that a century's experience in self-rule has failed of a result? Will you affirm by your vote that you are an infidel to American power and practical sense? Or will you say that ours is the blood of government; ours the heart of dominion; ours the brain and genius of administration? Will you remember that we do but what our fathers did—we but pitch the tents of liberty farther westward, farther southward—we only continue the march of the flag?

The march of the flag! In 1789, the flag of the Republic waved over 4,000,000 souls in thirteen states, and their savage territory which stretched to the Mississippi, to Canada, to the Floridas. The timid minds of that day said that no new territory was needed, and, for the hour, they were right. But Jefferson, through whose intellect the centuries marched; Jefferson, who dreamed of Cuba as an American state, Jefferson, the first Imperialist of the Republic—Jefferson acquired that imperial territory which swept from the Mississippi to the mountains, from Texas to the British possessions, and the march of the flag began!

The infidels to the gospel of liberty raved, but the flag swept on! The title to that noble land out of which Oregon, Washington, Idaho, and Montana have been carved was uncertain: Jefferson, strict constructionist of constitutional power though he was, obeyed the Anglo Saxon impulse within him, whose watchword is, "Forward": another empire was added to the Republic, and the march of the flag went on!

Those who deny the power of free institutions to expand urged every argument, and more that we hear today; but the people's judgment approved the command of their blood, and the march of the flag went on!

A screen of land from New Orleans to Florida shut us from the Gulf, and over this and the Everglade Peninsula waved the saffron flag of Spain; Andrew Jackson seized both, the American people stood at his back, and, under Monroe, the Floridas came under the dominion of the Republic, and the march of the flag went on! The Cassandras prophesied every prophecy of despair we hear today, but the march of the flag went on!

Then Texas responded to the bugle calls of liberty, and the march of the flag went on! And, at last, we waged war with Mexico, and the flag swept over the southwest, over peerless California, past the Gate of Gold to Oregon on the north, and from ocean to ocean its folds of glory blazed.

And, now, obeying the same voice that Jefferson heard and obeyed, that Jackson heard and obeyed, that Monroe heard and obeyed, that Seward heard and obeyed, that Grant heard and obeyed, that Harrison heard and obeyed, our President today plants the flag over the islands of the seas, outposts of commerce, citadels of national security, and the march of the flag goes on!

Distance and oceans are no arguments. The fact that all the territory our fathers bought and seized is contiguous, is no argument. In 1819, Florida was farther from New York than Porto Rico is from Chicago today; Texas, farther from Washington in 1845 than Hawaii is from Boston in 1898; California, more inaccessible in 1847 than the Philippines are now. Gibraltar is farther from London than Havana is from Washington; Melbourne is farther from Liverpool than Manila is from San Francisco.

The ocean does not separate us from lands of our duty and desire—the oceans join us, rivers never to be dredged, canals never to be repaired. Steam joins us; electricity joins us—the very elements are in league with our destiny. Cuba not contiguous? Porto Rico not contiguous! Hawaii and the Philippines not contiguous! The oceans make them contiguous. And our navy will make them contiguous.

But the Opposition is right—there is a difference. We did not need the western Mississippi Valley when we acquired it, nor Florida! nor Texas, nor California, nor the royal provinces of the far northwest. We had no emigrants to people this imperial wilderness, no money to develop it, even no highways to cover it. No trade awaited us in its savage vastnesses. Our productions were not greater than our trade. There was not one reason for the landlust of our statesmen from Jefferson to Grant, other than the prophet and the Saxon within them. But, today, we are raising more than we can consume, making more than we can use. Therefore we must find new markets for our produce.

And so, while we did not need the territory taken during the past century at the time it was acquired, we do need what we have taken [in] 1898, and we need it now. The resource[s] and the commerce of the immensely rich dominions will be increased as much as American energy is greater than Spanish sloth.

In Cuba, alone, there are 15,000,000 acres of forest unacquainted with the ax, exhaustless mines of iron, priceless deposits of manganese, millions of dollars' worth of which we must buy, today, from the Black Sea districts. There are millions of acres yet unexplored.

The resources of Porto Rico have only been trifled with. The riches of the Philippines have hardly been touched by the fingertips of modern methods. And they produce what we consume, and consume what we produce—the very predestination of reciprocity—a reciprocity "not made with hands, eternal in the heavens." They sell hemp, sugar, cocoanuts, fruits of the tropics, timber of price like mahogany; they buy flour, clothing, tools, implements, machinery, and all that we can raise and make. Their trade will be ours in time. Do you indorse that policy with your vote?

Cuba is as large as Pennsylvania, and is the richest spot on the globe. Hawaii is as large as New Jersey; Porto Rico half as large as Hawaii; the Philippines larger than all New England, New York, New Jersey, and Delaware combined. Together they are larger than the British Isles, larger than France, larger than Germany, larger than Japan.

If any man tells you that trade depends on cheapness and not on government influence, ask him why England does not abandon South Africa, Egypt, India. Why does France seize South China, Germany the vast region whose port is Kaouchou?

Our trade with Porto Rico, Hawaii, and the Philippines must be as free as between the states of the Union, because they are American territory, while every other nation on earth must pay our tariff before they can compete with us. Until Cuba shall ask for annexation, our trade with her will, at the very least, be like the preferential trade of Canada with England. That, and the excellence of our goods and products; that, and the convenience of traffic; that, and the kinship of interests and destiny, will give the monopoly of these markets to the American people.

The commercial supremacy of the Republic means that this Nation is to be the sovereign factor in the peace of the world. For the conflicts of the future are to be conflicts of trade—struggles for markets—commercial wars for existence. And the golden rule of peace is impregnability of position and invincibility of preparedness. So, we see England, the greatest strategist of history, plant her flag and her cannon on Gibraltar, at Quebec, in the Bermudas, at Vancouver, everywhere.

So Hawaii furnishes us a naval base in the heart of the Pacific; the Ladrones another, a voyage further on; Manila another, at the gates of Asia—Asia, to the trade of whose hundreds of millions American merchants, manufacturers, farmers, have as good right as those of Germany or France or Russia or England; Asia, whose commerce with the United Kingdom alone amounts to hundreds of millions of dollars every year; Asia, to whom Germany looks to take her surplus products; Asia, whose doors must not be shut against American trade. Within five decades the bulk of Oriental commerce will be ours.

No wonder that, in the shadows of coming events so great, free—silver is already a memory. The current of history has swept past that episode. Men understand, today, the greatest commerce of the world must be conducted with the steadiest standard of value and most convenient medium of exchange human ingenuity can devise. Time, that unerring reasoner, has settled the silver question. The American people are tired of talking about money—they want to make it.

There are so many real things to be done—canals to be dug, railways to be laid, forests to be felled, cities to be builded [sic], fields to be tilled, markets to be won, ships to be launched, peoples to be saved, civilization to be proclaimed and the [fl]ag of liberty [h]ung to the eager air of every sea. Is this an hour to waste upon triflers with nature's laws? Is this a season to give our destiny over to wordmongers and prosperity-wreckers? No! It is an hour to remember our duty to our homes. It is a moment to realize the opportunities fate has opened to us. And so is [it the] hour for us to stand by the Government.

Wonderfully has God guided us Yonder at Bunker Hill and Yorktown. His providence was above us at New Orleans and on ensanguined seas His hand sustained u[s]. Abraham Lincoln was His minister and His was the altar of freedom the Nation's soldiers set up on a hundred battlefields. His power directed Dewey in the East and delivered the Spanish fleet into our hands, as He delivered the elder Armada into the hands of our English sires two centuries ago [*Note:* actually in 1588]. The American people can not use a dishonest medium of exchange; it is ours to set the world its example of right and honor. We can not fly from our world duties; it is ours to execute the purpose of a fate that has driven us to be greater than our small intentions. We can not retreat from any soil where Providence has unfurled our banner; it is ours to save that soil for liberty and civilization.

Source: "Modern History Sourcebook: Albert Beveridge: The March of the Flag." Courtesy of Fordam University's Internet Modern History Sourcebook, http://www.fordham.edu/halsall/mod/1898beveridge.html.

132. Excerpts from "The Field Laborer," Testimony of Severo Tulier, 1899

In 1898, the United States took military possession of Puerto Rico as a result of the Treaty of Paris. The Puerto Rican people did not have a say in the treaty or in becoming part of the United States. The stated purpose of Euro-American leaders was that Puerto Rican bases were strategic for their naval operations. A majority of Puerto Ricans initially welcomed U.S. forces, believing that they would soon leave. The following excerpts are from an interview between Henry K. Carroll and Severo Tulier, the owner of a small farm in Vega Baja before the occupation. The U.S. occupation had an immediate impact on his life as he was forced to sell his farm in 1899, because he could not compete with the commercial plantation economy that came to Puerto Rico with the U.S. occupation. The commercialization of the island uprooted small farmers, some of whom—like Tulier—would continue to labor in the fields. In the following interview, he describes life in Puerto Rico.

Tulier: The usual rate [of wages] is 25 centavos and breakfast, and 37½ centavos to the better class of workmen. A few laborers who have some special skill receive as high as 50 centavos a day, but it should be borne in mind that where 50 centavos is paid, payment is made in vales, which are mere tokens … redeemable at the company's store....

The customary hours of work are from six to six; that is, for work in the field. For work in the shops and on the sugar machinery, they have to go earlier, sometimes as early as 4 o'clock in the morning....

Carroll: What do they have to eat in the evenings?

Tulier: The basis of their evening meal is a big plantain, which they sometimes make into a mess with rice and beans.... They have meat only on Sundays.... Their food improves a little during the corn season, as that forms an addition to the daily diet. Their three chief articles of food, it may be said, are sweet potatoes, plantains, and corn....

Carroll: What about their houses?

Tulier: The house is made of poles, thatched about with palm, and about 4 or 5 varas square [a vara is about 33 inches] partitioned off into a parlor, a bedroom and a kitchen.... The kitchen has no flooring, and the parlor and bedroom flooring is badly laid. Frequently the house lets in the rain.... Their wardrobe consists of two changes—one that is being worn and the other that is being washed.... The children, as a rule, have only one shirt, and while the mother is washing that one they must run about without any clothing.

The number of [infant] deaths caused from want of medical assistance is not considerable, because the women lead a free, out-of-door life, but owing to want of proper nourishing food, a great many [infants] succumb from weakness.... The poor people are absolutely in want of medical assistance in the country places, and if they go to the village to obtain medical aid they can only do so through the charity of the doctors, as they are not able to pay for such services.

Usually about five persons live in a house of the kind I have described. They all sleep together—father, mother, grown-up sons and daughters—and when they haven't sufficient beds, they sleep on piles of palm leaves.... The peasant is naturally intelligent, and his mind is as fertile as the land which he works and is only waiting the implements of education. As a proof of this I will cite an instance. When it was known that autonomy was to be granted and that suffrage was limited to men of 25 years of age who knew how to read and write, I formed a class in my district and offered to teach free all men of that age and over, to fit them to vote. I had men in the class whose ages ranged from 25 to 60 years, and some of them after a few lessons knew the letters of the alphabet at sight and could write them. This was done without the aid of any modern appliances used in teaching, a piece of rough board and chalk being the only materials at hand.... The desire of everybody to learn was manifest.

Source: Henry K. Carroll, *Report on the Island of Puerto Rico*, U.S. Treasury Department Document 2118 (Washington D.C.: Government Printing Office, 1899), pp. 724–726.

133. Excerpts from "La Miseria: A Los Negros Puertorriqueños," a Letter from Ramón Romero Rosa to Black Puerto Ricans, March 27, 1901

Ramón Romero Rosa (1863–1907), a Puerto Rican anarchist, was dedicated to organizing the working class. He was a printer, playwright, and agitator. He used the theater to teach workers to defend themselves against the power of the ruling class. Romero Rosa opposed the ideology of individualism popular in the years after the Spanish-American War and expressed a strong racial consciousness. For Romero Rosa, the recognition of African culture was essential. European traditions had been superimposed on Puerto Ricans, hiding the African essence. "A Los Negros Puertorriqueños" ("To the Black Puerto Ricans") was a pamphlet circulated in 1899 and published in 1901. In it, Romero Rosa says that "the children of Africa" were the first "brought over to settle this untamed region, constituted our first working people after the conquest." It was as if the African heritage had come out of the closet. The following excerpt is in response to a proposal from a member of the Puerto Rican elite that encouraged the exportation of Black Puerto Ricans while promoting white immigration.

TO BLACK PUERTO RICANS: MISERY

You unfortunate martyrs have doubly suffered unjust exploitation at the hands of the white slave trader of all times and of all ages.... listen to the horrible sentence just dictated against you by a miserable man, who if his skin is clear, it is because his entrails are dark. My pen refuses to write his name, because the ink, as black as ebony, is ashamed to trace it. However, it is important that you know who he is ... so you can spit on his face. His name is Don Ramón de Castro Rivera.

This miserable creature, who if he is Puerto Rican dishonors his own origin, has written to the Civil Governor, cynically telling him the importance of keeping emigration at a ratio of two thirds Blacks and mulattos and one third white, and not to permit the immigration of Blacks onto the island; that as many whites as possible be brought to the island from the United States, but not a single Black, since there are already many on the island and there should be an effort to get rid of them, since there is absolutely no need for them. Also, he advocates the fomenting of the emigration of Blacks to Ecuador since there are few and there will be no complaints of this emigration. Oh, unspeakable the shame of this miserable creature! That means, that the country's Blacks, those unfortunate workers who created the wealth of Puerto Rico, today THERE IS NO NEED FOR THEM AT ALL and you get must rid of them: How is this unfortunate race repaid for their good service. In what miserable conditions they have placed this people of virtuous and honest men who have only worked and worked to produce the gold which has been wasted by the vagabonds of this earth; the white who only have known how to handle the shameful whip of slavery and prostitution. We are not to become unraveled with insults that is not or ever will be how we behave: our minds are fresh and our hearts are honest. But we shall take our notes to the neurotic brain of this miserable being and at least remind him certain points of the history of Blacks in Puerto Rico.

Listen, Ramón de Castro Rivera, and also listen, white exploiters of the Borinquen country, the wealth that today you hold hidden, has been extracted from the blood of Blacks. Listen to those features in the history of slavery in Puerto Rico. Four centuries and eight years have gone by since the first day, in the name of Christianity, the Spain of Catholic Kings robbed the natives of their land. Maybe the immortal Colón did not imagine that his discovery would be the major cause of slavery and infamous cruelty for the Black race.

However, what happened after the discovery was a crime against humanity: the Borinquen Indians, not only were pulled from their collective way of life, they were completely exterminated by the sharp arrows and sharp blades of the scribes of the Catholic Kingdom and bourgeois aristocracy of the middle ages. All perversity is disguised with a benevolent end; and to that we repeat, in name of Christianity and European civilization the natives were expropriated of their own land and massacred. In the name of Christianity, the conquest legalized the usurpation by the expropriators of the Borinquen, and with another horrific crime substituted the fully exterminated natives. And now we get into history. It was the commercial trade of this unfortunate race from Africa, this race that today you are asking for its annulment in Puerto Rico, the ones that populated this region and were once free in their country and owned their own piece of land and who were taken by force by the cursed slave-traders, with their white faces, and a heart of darkness. European aristocracy committed this horrendous crime. Understand correctly, it was the sons of Africa, the unfortunate beings who were brought to colonize this Indian land, the first working people after the conquest. And we would fail Reason and Justice, if the richness and wealth produced in this land is denied ... to all unfortunate workers, twice slaves of the tyrannical patronage and of the state. Even today there is a scarcity of white workers arriving in Puerto Rico. The haciendas, the factories, the fields, the shops, and in all that is practical and useful the majority are black hands.

Ramón de Castro Rivera's white hands are only used to maneuver the shameful whip and to horde the wealth which was produced and continues to be produced with the sweat and blood of Blacks.

Now Ramón de Castro Rivera can see, as well as all the white bourgeoisie criminals, that with the blood and sweat of Blacks who they no longer need, made and fomented the making of all the wealth of the bourgeoisie expropriators of yesterday and the hording bourgeoisie of today.

Miserable human being! You should kiss the Black hand that has been the source of inexhaustible richness, instead you lash out with those horrible words that so degrade us and enrage us.

Those of you who have a conscience and know civics, answer: what has been the rewards for blacks for their labor, either today or in the past?

Absolutely none! If we are to talk of those tragic and horrific times of marketing human flesh; if we are to speak of those inquisitional acts, in which the poor Black man, wearing nothing, but a pair of light shorts, with their ebony-color backs exposed to the elements of nature, having the hot sun rays reverberating of their backs, and subjugated by the infamous whip, was forced to perform in inhuman labor conditions; if we are to remember the crimes committed against Blacks who were not to lift their face to face the punisher, boss, manager, patron because it would make his blood boil and maybe even seek revenge.

Yesterday Anduza, another miserable creature like many other whites, requested the whip ... for Puerto Rico, today Ramón de Castro Rivera requests the governor to get all Blacks out of the country, because they are no longer needed! What depravity have we reached! Maybe Anduza, as Castro Rivera, and all the white criminals, enslavers of Blacks, do not remember that their elders and maybe even themselves while taking all the wealth and delighting themselves in orgies, also prostituted black women, then sold their own children to the human trade. Blacks lived in dirty quarters and were forced to eat roots and fungi. To add to the vast inequity, basic education was denied to the Black people. And as a sublime rewarding law, a venerable black teacher, Rafael Cordero taught a group of white children who became luminaries in science and humanities.

Black Puerto Ricans know that yesterday Anduza requested the whip law and today Castro Rivera asserts that Black Puerto Ricans are no longer needed. Blacks must not emigrate: Puerto Rico belongs to them. Let the thieves emigrate. Comrades, defend yourselves!

Ramón Romero Rosa
March 27, 1901

Source: *Sources for the Study of Puerto Rican Migration, 1879–1930*. History Task Force/Centro de Estudios Puertorriqueños Research Foundation of the City University of New York, 1982, pp. 30–33. Translated by Guadalupe Compeán.

134. Excerpts from a Petition from Puerto Rican Workers at the Plantation Paauilo to the Governor of Puerto Rico, 1902

The Treaty of Paris, signed in 1898, stipulated that U.S. industrialists would take over most of Puerto Rico's industries. Further, under U.S. rule the commercialization of agriculture accelerated, uprooting subsistence farmers who then were forced to eke out a living in the factories and sweatshops.

Conditions worsened as Hurricane San Ciriaco (1899) ripped through the island, and 28 days of continuous rain destroyed farms, leaving 3,400 dead and thousands of people displaced. The destruction of Caribbean sugar increased the demand for sugar. In response to the demand, Hawaiian plantation owners put more land into production. They looked to Puerto Rico where there was a large unemployed labor pool. The first group of Puerto Ricans left for Hawaii in November 1900, followed within a year by over 5,000 Puerto Rican men, women, and children. They were distributed to plantations on four Hawaiian islands where they were often mistreated. The following excerpts, written from Hawaii to the governor of Puerto Rico, describe the workers' suffering and their wishes for the governor to arrange their return to their beloved Puerto Rico.

Hon. Sir:

We, the Puerto Ricans at the Plantation of Paauilo, with the greatest respect, petition and beg you for protection as well as bringing to your attention what is happening to us in this plantation. We, Puerto Ricans, that happen to be here, find ourselves abused to the point of wishing we were dead, we are like slaves, and we beg you out of your goodness to return us to our country because we do not deserve this treatment; they treat us like prisoners … we left our beloved Borinquen to seek our prosperity and have met our perdition in the territories of Oceania.

And for those reasons we turn to you to end servitude to the sugar companies and compel them to send us back in order to prevent trouble between the Puerto Ricans and the associates of the companies. The said gentlemen wish that want us to work like animals and whether right or wrong, sick or well, they want no one to remain in his house. We are no more than slaves here and we can no longer endure the savagery that is inflicted on every one of us Puerto Ricans; every day they are inflicting more barbarities on us. The first complaint is that the pay is low; it is not what they agreed to pay us before we left Puerto Rico; the second is that the company store charges us half of our day's wage; the result is that were are left with nothing. For these reasons, we, the undersigned, ask for your Honor's protection and place ourselves at your command.

Source: "Manifestación," Fondo Fortaleza. *Archivo General de Puerto Rico 14 de julio de 1902*, Sources for the Study of Puerto Rican Migration, 1879–1930. History Task Force/Centro de Estudios Puertorriqueños, Research Foundation of the City University of New York, 1982, pp. 52–53. Literal translation by Guadalupe Compean.

135. Rudyard Kipling, "The White Man's Burden," 1899

In February 1899, British novelist and poet Rudyard Kipling wrote the poem "The White Man's Burden: The United States and The Philippine Islands." Like American poet Walt Whitman (1819–1892) who supported the War against Mexico and the acquisition of half its nation, in the 1840s, Kipling laid the justification for U.S. imperialism on racial and moral superiority. "The White Man's Burden" was published in *McClure's Magazine* in February 1899, at a pivotal point in the U.S. debate over imperialism. The Treaty of Paris (1898) gave the United States control of Puerto Rico and the Philippines. Kipling's poem urged the United States to take up the burden of "civilizing" the former Spanish colonies; a thankless task, but a noble undertaking. Beginning in 1899, native Filipinos revolted against U.S. dominance, and began an insurgency lasting into 1902. Most Latin Americans resented the notion that they had to be civilized as well as Christianized, pointing to the fact that most were Catholics, hence they already were Christians.

THE WHITE MAN'S BURDEN

Take up the White Man's burden—
Send forth the best ye breed—
Go send your sons to exile
To serve your captives' need
To wait in heavy harness
On fluttered folk and wild—
Your new-caught, sullen peoples,
Half devil and half child.

Take up the White Man's burden
In patience to abide
To veil the threat of terror
And check the show of pride;
By open speech and simple
An hundred times made plain
To seek another's profit
And work another's gain....

Take up the White Man's burden—
And reap his old reward:
The blame of those ye better
The hate of those ye guard—
The cry of hosts ye humour
(Ah slowly) to the light:
"Why brought ye us from bondage,
"Our loved Egyptian night?"...

Take up the White Man's burden—
Have done with childish days—
The lightly proffered laurel,
The easy, ungrudged praise.
Comes now, to search your manhood
Through all the thankless years,
Cold-edged with dear-bought wisdom,
The judgment of your peers!

Source: Rudyard Kipling, "The White Man's Burden," *McClure's Magazine* 12 (February 1899).

136. "Revolution in Colombia," 1902

The construction of an inter-ocean canal through Yucatán, Mexico, Nicaragua, or Panama was discussed by the Spaniards as the early sixteenth century. The United States became interested in the late 1700s, as trade in the Pacific Northwest increased. Later, as U.S. interest in the Pacific Rim grew, so did the desire for a shortened all-water route to connect both oceans. In 1846, the U.S. negotiated a treaty with New Granada (present-day Panama and Colombia). New Granada granted the United States transit rights across the Isthmus of Panama in return for the United States guaranteeing its sovereignty. In 1855, U.S. investor Cornelius Vanderbilt built a railroad across Panama. However, the United States, Britain, and France wanted an all-water route. In 1878, the French gained a concession to build a sea-level canal in Panama. But, this venture went bankrupt in 1889. U.S. interest was high in obtaining the rights from the French, but a U.S. commission recommended a canal through Nicaragua in 1901. The Panama route had strong support among U.S. politicos and the French reduced their asking price. After heavy lobbying, the commission reversed its findings and recommended the Panama route, which Congress rapidly authorized. The United States and Colombia signed the Hay-Herrán Treaty (1903) that gave the United States a strip of land across the Isthmus of Panama. But the Colombian senate hesitated ratifying it. In November 1903, Panamanians revolted against Colombia and, within days, the United States and Panama signed the Hay-Bunau-Varilla Treaty giving the United States the terms that it wanted. The following article describes "the revolution."

REVOLUTION IN COLOMBIA

Bocas del Toro Threatened with Bombardment—Revolutionists Seize American Company's Property

COLON, Columbia, April 16—A launch belonging to the Panama Canal Company returned here this morning from Bocas del Toro, bringing reports that the situation there is growing more serious. Liberal troops under Gen. Buendia have reached Old Bank, a settlement on an island near the entrance to Bocas del Toro. Gen. Buendia notified the Government Commander at Bocas yesterday that fourteen hours would be given him to surrender the town, and that his non-compilance with this ultimatum would result in immediate attack. The launch left Bocas for Colon before the fourteen hours had expired.

The revolutionists at Bocas have already seized steam launches, barges, &c., belonging to the United Fruit Company. Bocas del Toro is entirely devoted to the banana business, and American interests there are almost supreme. The seizure of the property is receiving the attention of the United States gunboat *Machias*, which is now the only warship at Bocas.

It is believed that the Colombian Government is sending a commission from Honda, on the Magdalena, consisting of three prominent foreigners, which has full authority to arrange terms and treat for peace with the revolutionists.

Besides the Government victory at Soacha Feb. 23, and the defeats of Gen. Uribe-Uribe in the Department of Tolima, news received here from Barranquilla today says Government Gen. Rivera recently defeated insurgent Gen. Marin at Ibague and Chicoral, In the same department. Gen. Marin has expressed a desire to lay down his arms if his life and the lives of his troops be guaranteed by the Government.

Source: New York Times, April 17, 1902, p. 2.

137. "By Treaty or by War," 1902

Central America is an isthmus. It is a narrow piece of land dividing two great oceans. Consequently, it was of great interest to the United States and Western Europe. The U.S. and Great Britain competed fiercely in the early 1850s. American banker Cornelius Vanderbilt built the Panama Railway across the isthmus, which opened in 1855. This railroad greatly facilitated trade. Plans for an all-water route between the oceans were revived after the success of Ferdinand de Lesseps (1805–1894) in the construction of the Suez Canal, which linked the Mediterranean Sea to the Indian Ocean in 1869. Without proper financial backing, the French began construction of a Panama canal in the 1880s. However, the venture was plagued with financial difficulties as well as malaria and yellow fever. The French abandoned the project in 1893, after a great deal of work. The United States, under Theodore Roosevelt (1858–1919), bought out the French equipment and excavations in 1902, and began work in 1904 after encountering minor opposition. The following article says that Colombian opposition to the canal would be an act of war and expressed the intention of the United States to take Panama whether the Colombians wanted it or not.

BY TREATY OR BY WAR

It is incredible that the Washington dispatches correctly report Sen. [Shelby] Cullom when they represent him as intimating that the United States will have full authority to dig and operate a canal through the territory of Colombia as soon as it has taken title to the property and concessions of the New Panama Canal Company. Sen. Cullom is Chairman of the Senate Committee on Foreign Relations, and of course would be careful to make no statement of that nature unless it were amply warranted by the facts. If there were warrant for such a statement, it would be found in the terms of the concession to the New Panama Canal Company. It is not found there, but, on the contrary, the theory attributed to Sen. Cullom is expressly excluded by the language of the concession.

The Republic of Colombia granted a concession to the Panama Railroad Company, giving it exclusive privileges on the Isthmus, and by subsequent modifications this concession was made to continue for ninety-nine years from Aug. 16, 1806. The Wise concession for the Panama Canal Company required it to come to an understanding with the railroad company, which it did by purchasing a majority of its stock. The canal concession runs for ninety-nine years from the date when it shall be opened to ships. This date originally was Oct. 31, 1904. It has been extended to Oct. 31, 1910. The failure of the concession would still leave the New Panama Canal Company, through its ownership of the Panama Railroad, in legal control of the territory through which the canal is to be built. As to the power of the canal company to transfer its concessions, and thereby to give the right to enter upon the work of construction, regardless of the attitude of the Colombian Government at the time, we quote from the repost of the Isthmian Canal Commission of June 10, 1899:

The canal company is absolutely prohibited to cede or mortgage its rights, under any consideration whatever, to any nation or foreign Government, under penalty of forfeiture. The contract with the railroad company contains a like prohibition and declares further that the pain of forfeiture will be incurred by the mere act of attempting to cede or transfer its privilege to a foreign Government, and such an act is declared absolutely null and of no value or effect. There concessions, if acquired by the United States, would not give to the Government the control and ownership evidently contemplated by the law—that is, an absolute ownership in perpetuity. The right under the contract with the railroad company is designated as the "use and possession" of the property for ninety-nine years, and it is provided that "at the expiration of the term of the privilege," and by the sole fact of the expiration, the Government of Colombia shall be substituted in all the rights of the company, and shall immediately enter into the enjoyment of the line of communication, its fixtures, dependencies, and all its products. The right of the canal company is substantially of the same character. Its concession expressly provides that five years previous to the expiration of the ninety-nine years of the "privileges," the executive power shall appoint a Commissioner to examine the condition of the Canal and annexes, and make an official report describing the condition of the property in every detail. This report is to establish the condition in which the canal and its dependencies are to be delivered to the National Government on the day of the expiration of the privilege. There is no provision for an extension of either concession beyond the period mentioned, and the entire property in each case passes from the company without compensation. This being the situation, it was manifest that, even if the privileges of the companies could be purchased by, and transferred to, the United States, they were incumbered with charges and conditions that would not permit this Government to exercise all the rights of complete ownership over a canal constructed by it at the Panama route. A new arrangement is necessary if the United States is to undertake the work. The situation is peculiar, as there are three parties in interest. The United States can obtain from Columbia no concession that does not have the approval of the company, and its concessions do not permit the company to transfer or attempt to transfer its rights to a foreign Government.

Any attempt on our part to enter into possession of the property and rights of the New Panama Canal Company without first securing by treaty the sanction of the Colombian Government to the transfer would be resisted by Colombia as an act of war. It has been understood everywhere and by everybody since the negotiations with the Frenchmen began that a new treaty between Colombia and the United States was indispensable to the construction of a canal by the United States Government on the Panama route. War is the alternative of a treaty.

The situation is complicated, and it is not growing less so. Its most mysterious feature, of course, is the attitude of Señor Concha, the Minister of Colombia at Washington. The report that he does not faithfully represent his Government, that the officials at Bogota earnestly wish to make a treaty with us, while he takes an attitude which makes a treaty impossible, rests either upon idle gossip or impudent assumption. Until the contrary fact is officially proclaimed, it must always be assumed that a Minister knows what his Government wants. The Secretary of State is now, or soon will be, in a position to advise President Roosevelt whether a satisfactory title to property and control of territory in Colombia can be acquired. If title and control cannot be acquired, it is then the duty of the president under the Spooner Amendment to enter into negotiations with Costa Rica and Nicaragua for the construction of a canal on the Nicaragua route. The President and his Administration, the Republican Party, the Democratic Party, both houses of Congress, and the

American people are committed to a policy of Isthmian canal construction. There is another party not political, not openly organized, that is committed to a policy of canal obstruction and defeat. The beet-sugar interests defeated the President in his attempt to make a reciprocity treaty with Cuba. Whether the enemies of the canal will defeat him is a question of high interest and importance. We do not imagine that he will shrink from the encounter.

Source: New York Times, December 1, 1902, p. 8.

138. Excerpts from Theodore Roosevelt's Annual Message to Congress, December 6, 1904

President Theodore Roosevelt, Jr., (1858–1919), known as T. R. or Teddy, is revered in the United States and hated in Latin America until this day. As U.S. president from 1901 to 1909, he personified the "cowboy" persona. He gained popularity in the United States as the leader of the Rough Riders, a volunteer cavalry regiment that fought in Cuba during the Spanish-American War. He referred to Latin Americans as "our Little Brown brothers," had a policy that said, "speak softly and carry a big stick," believed in a strong Navy, and looked upon Caribbean bases as U.S. fueling depots. Roosevelt tied his foreign policy to the Monroe Doctrine. According to most U.S. historians, the Monroe Doctrine was used as a justification for the United States becoming an "international police power" in the Western Hemisphere in order "to see the neighboring countries stable, orderly, and prosperous." The following excerpt is known as the Roosevelt Corollary to the Monroe Doctrine. In 1823, the Monroe Doctrine was allegedly used to prevent European intervention in the Western Hemisphere. In 1904, Roosevelt expanded the doctrine to justify American intervention throughout the Western Hemisphere. To this day, some Americans claim that the United States has the right to intervene in Latin American nations to protect its interests.

In treating of our foreign policy and of the attitude that this great Nation should assume in the world at large, it is absolutely necessary to consider the Army and the Navy, and the Congress, through which the thought of the Nation finds its expression, should keep ever vividly in mind the fundamental fact that it is impossible to treat our foreign policy, whether this policy takes shape in the effort to secure justice for others or justice for ourselves, save as conditioned upon the attitude we are willing to take toward our Army, and especially toward our Navy. It is not merely unwise, it is contemptible, for a nation, as for an individual, to use high-sounding language to proclaim its purposes, or to take positions which are ridiculous if unsupported by potential force, and then to refuse to provide this force. If there is no intention of providing and keeping the force necessary to back up a strong attitude, then it is far better not to assume such an attitude.

The steady aim of this Nation, as of all enlightened nations, should be to strive to bring ever nearer the day when there shall prevail throughout the world the peace of justice. There are kinds of peace which are highly undesirable, which are in the long run as destructive as any war. Tyrants and oppressors have many times made a wilderness and called it peace. Many times peoples who were slothful or timid or shortsighted, who had been enervated by ease or by luxury, or misled by false teachings, have shrunk in unmanly fashion from doing duty that was stern and that needed self-sacrifice, and have sought to hide from their own minds their shortcomings, their ignoble motives, by calling them love of peace. The peace of tyrannous terror, the peace of craven weakness, the peace of injustice, all these should be shunned as we shun unrighteous war. The goal to set before us as a nation, the goal which should be set before all mankind, is the attainment of the peace of justice, of the peace which comes when each nation is not merely safeguarded in its own rights, but scrupulously recognizes and performs its duty toward others. Generally peace tells for righteousness; but if there is conflict between the two, then our fealty is due first to the cause of righteousness. Unrighteous wars are common, and unrighteous peace is rare; but both should be shunned. The right of freedom and the responsibility for the exercise of that right can not be divorced. One of our great poets has well and finely said that freedom is not a gift that tarries long in the hands of cowards. Neither does it tarry long in the hands of those too slothful, too dishonest, or too unintelligent to exercise it. The eternal vigilance which is the price of liberty must be exercised, sometimes to guard against outside foes; although of course far more often to guard against our own selfish or thoughtless shortcomings.

If these self-evident truths are kept before us, and only if they are so kept before us, we shall have a clear idea of what our foreign policy in its larger aspects should be. It is our duty to remember that a nation has no more right to do injustice to another nation, strong or weak, than an individual has to do injustice to another individual; that the same moral law applies in one case as in the other. But we must also remember that it is as much the duty of the Nation to guard its own rights and its own interests as it is the duty of the individual so to do. Within the Nation the individual has now delegated this right to the State, that is, to the representative of all the individuals, and it is a maxim of the law that for every wrong there is a remedy. But in international law we have not advanced by any means as far as we have advanced in municipal law. There is as yet no judicial way of enforcing a right in international law. When one nation wrongs another or wrongs many others, there is no tribunal before which the wrongdoer can be brought. Either it is necessary supinely to acquiesce in the wrong, and thus put a premium upon brutality and aggression, or else it is necessary for the aggrieved nation valiantly to stand up for its rights. Until some method is devised by which there shall be a degree of international control over offending nations, it would be a wicked thing for the most civilized powers, for those with most sense of international obligations and with keenest and most generous appreciation of the difference between right and wrong, to disarm. If the great civilized nations of the present day should completely disarm, the result would mean an immediate recrudescence of barbarism in one form or another. Under any circumstances, a sufficient armament would have to be kept up to serve the purposes of international police; and until international cohesion and the sense of international duties and rights are far more advanced than at present, a nation desirous both of securing respect for itself and of doing good to others must have a force adequate for the work which it feels is allotted to it as its part of the general world duty. Therefore it follows that a self-respecting, just, and far-seeing nation should on the one hand endeavor by every means to aid in the development of the various movements which tend to provide substitutes for war, which tend to render nations in their actions toward one another, and indeed toward their own peoples, more responsive to the general sentiment of humane and civilized mankind; and on the other hand that it should keep prepared, while scrupulously avoiding wrong-doing itself, to repel any wrong, and in exceptional cases to take action which in a more advanced stage of international relations would come under the head of the exercise of the international police. A great free people owes it to itself and to all mankind not to sink into helplessness before the powers of evil.

We are in every way endeavoring to help on, with cordial good will, every movement which will tend to bring us into more friendly relations with the rest of mankind. In pursuance of this policy I shall shortly lay before the Senate treaties of arbitration with all powers which are willing to enter into these treaties with us. It is not possible at this period of the world's development to agree to arbitrate all matters, but there are many matters of possible difference between us and other nations which can be thus arbitrated. Furthermore, at the request of the Inter Parliamentary Union, an eminent body composed of practical statesmen from all countries, I have asked the Powers to join with this Government in a second Hague conference, at which it is hoped that the work already so happily begun at The Hague may be carried some steps further toward completion. This carries out the desire expressed by the first Hague conference itself.

It is not true that the United States feels any land hunger or entertains any projects as regards the other nations of the Western Hemisphere save such as are for their welfare. All that this country desires is to see the neighboring countries stable, orderly, and prosperous. Any country whose people conduct themselves well can count upon our hearty friendship. If a nation shows that it knows how to act with reasonable efficiency and decency in social and political matters, if it keeps order and pays its obligations, it need fear no interference from the United States. Chronic wrongdoing, or an impotence which results in a general loosening of the ties of civilized society, may in America, as elsewhere, ultimately require intervention by some civilized nation, and in the Western Hemisphere the adherence of the United States to the Monroe Doctrine may force the United States, however reluctantly, in flagrant cases of such wrongdoing or impotence, to the exercise of an international police power. If every country washed by the Caribbean Sea would show the progress in stable and just civilization which with the aid of the Platt Amendment Cuba has shown since our troops left the island, and which so many of the republics in both Americas are constantly and brilliantly showing, all question of interference by this Nation with their affairs would be at an end. Our interests and those of our southern neighbors are in reality identical. They have great natural riches, and if within their borders the reign of law and justice obtains, prosperity is sure to come to them. While they thus obey the primary laws of civilized society they may rest assured that they will be treated by us in a spirit o cordial and helpful sympathy. We would interfere with them only in the last resort, and then only if it became evident that their inability or unwillingness to do justice at home and abroad had violated the rights of the United States or had invited foreign aggression to the detriment of the entire body of American nations. It is a mere truism to say that every nation, whether in America or anywhere else, which desires to maintain its freedom, its independence, must ultimately realize that the right of such independence can not be separated from the responsibility of making good use of it.

In asserting the Monroe Doctrine, in taking such steps as we have taken in regard to Cuba, Venezuela, and Panama, and in endeavoring to circumscribe the theater of war in the Far East, and to secure the open door in China, we have acted in our own interest as well as in the interest of humanity at large. There are, however, cases in which, while our own interests are not greatly involved, strong appeal is made to our sympathies. Ordinarily it is very much wiser and more useful for us to concern ourselves with striving for our own moral and material betterment here at home than to concern ourselves with trying to better the condition of things in other nations. We have plenty of sins of our own to war against, and under ordinary circumstances we can do more for the general uplifting of humanity by striving with heart and soul to put a stop to civic corruption, to brutal lawlessness, and violent race prejudices here at home than by passing resolutions and wrongdoing elsewhere. Nevertheless there are occasional crimes committed on so vast a scale and of such peculiar horror as to make us doubt whether this [is] not our manifest duty to endeavor at least to show our disapproval of the deed and our sympathy with those who have suffered by it. The cases must be extreme in which such a course is justifiable. There must be no effort made to remove the mote from our brother's eye if we refuse to remove the beam from our own. But in extreme cases, action may be justifiable and proper. What form the action shall take must depend upon the circumstances of the case; that is, upon the degree of the atrocity and upon our power to remedy it. The cases in which we could interfere by force of arms as we interfered to put a stop to intolerable conditions in Cuba are necessarily very few. Yet it is not to be expected that a people like ours, which in spite of certain very obvious shortcomings, nevertheless as a whole shows by its consistent practice its belief in the principles of civil and religious liberty and of orderly freedom, a people among whom even the worst crime, like the crime of lynching, is never more than sporadic, so that individuals and not classes are molested in their fundamental rights—it is inevitable that such a nation should desire eagerly to give expression to its horror on an occasion like that of the massacre of the Jews in Kishinev, or when it witnesses such systematic and long-extended cruelty and oppression as the cruelty and oppression of which the Armenians have been the victims, and which have won for them the indignant pity of the civilized world.

Source: Historical Documents, http://www.historicaldocuments.com/TheodoreRooseveltscorollary totheMonroeDoctrine.htm.

139. The Platt Amendment, 1903

The Platt Amendment was a rider to the Army Appropriations Act, passed on March 2, 1901, that—for all intents and purposes—made Cuba a vassal of the United States. The United States would not evacuate its forces until Cuba stipulated that Cuba would not make a treaty or enter into debt with a foreign nation without the approval of the United States. Connecticut Republican Sen. Orville H. Platt (1827–1905) offered the amendment, which was similar to the Teller Amendment in the 1898 U.S. resolution on the Recognition of the Independence of Cuba, in which the U.S. resolved to go to war with Spain over Cuba. Like the Teller Amendment (1898), the Platt Amendment said that the United Stated had no intention of annexing Cuba and would leave the country in the hands of the Cuban people. A critical difference between both amendments is that the Platt Amendment forced Cuba to lease Guantánamo Bay to the United States in perpetuity and gave the United States the right to intervene in Cuban affairs.

Article I. The Government of Cuba shall never enter into any treaty or other compact with any foreign power or powers which will impair or tend to impair the independence of Cuba, nor in any manner authorize or permit any foreign power or powers to obtain by colonization or for military or naval purposes, or otherwise, lodgment in or control over any portion of said island.

Article II. The Government of Cuba shall not assume or contract any public debt to pay the interest upon which, and to make reasonable sinking-fund provision for the ultimate discharge of which, the ordinary revenues of the Island of Cuba, after defraying the current expenses of the Government, shall be inadequate.

Article III. The Government of Cuba consents that the United States may exercise the right to intervene for the preservation of Cuban independence, the maintenance of a government adequate for the protection of life, property, and individual liberty, and for discharging the obligations with respect to Cuba imposed by the Treaty of Paris on the United States, now to be assumed and undertaken by the Government of Cuba.

...

Article V. The Government of Cuba will execute, and, as far as necessary, extend the plans already devised, or other plans to be mutually agreed upon, for the sanitation of the cities of the island, to the end that a recurrence of epidemic and infectious diseases may be prevented, thereby assuring protection to the people and commerce of Cuba, as well as to the commerce of the Southern ports of the United States and the people residing therein.

...

Article VII. To enable the United States to maintain the independence of Cuba, and to protect the people thereof, as well as for its own defense, the Government of Cuba will sell or lease to the United States lands necessary for coaling or naval stations, at certain specified points, to be agreed upon with the President of the United States.

Source: Vincent Ferraro, Mount Holyoke College, and the William and Flora Hewlett Foundation, http://www.mtholyoke.edu/acad/intrel/platt.htm.

140. Rubén Darío, "To Roosevelt" (Poem to President Theodore Roosevelt), 1904

Nicaraguan Rubén Darío (1867–1916) was one of the most admired poets in Latin America. He was the father of Latin American modernism and wielded enormous influence with Latino intellectuals and literary folk. His poetry was widely published. Darío was considered to be apolitical, but like other Latin Americans, he feared and resented the bullying of the United States. President Theodore Roosevelt (1858–1919) supported a 1903 revolution in Panama that resulted in the annexation of the Panama Canal and, in 1904, a corollary to the Monroe Doctrine justifying intervention in Latin America. The following Darío poem expresses how Latin America feared the United States and its intentions to dominate the region through force.

TO ROOSEVELT

It is with the voice of the Bible, or the verse of Walt Whitman,
that I should come to you, Hunter,
primitive and modern, simple and complicated,

with something of Washington and more of Nimrod.

You are the United States,
you are the future invader
of the naive America that has Indian blood,
that still prays to Jesus Christ and still speaks Spanish.

You are the proud and strong exemplar of your race;
you are cultured, you are skillful; you oppose Tolstoy.

And breaking horses, or murdering tigers,
you are an Alexander-Nebuchadnezzar.
(You are a professor of Energy
as today's madmen say.)

You think that life is fire,
that progress is eruption,
that wherever you shoot
you hit the future.

No.

The United States is potent and great.
When you shake there is a deep tremblor
that passes through the enormous vertebrae of the Andes.
If you clamor, it is heard like the roaring of a lion.
Hugo already said it to Grant: The stars are yours.
(The Argentine sun, ascending, barely shines,
and the Chilean star rises ...) You are rich.
You join the cult of Hercules to the cult of Mammon,
and illuminating the road of easy conquest,
Liberty raises its torch in New York.

But our America, that has had poets
since the ancient times of Netzahualcoyotl,
that has walked in the footprints of great Bacchus
who learned Pan's alphabet at once;
that consulted the stars, that knew Atlantis
whose resounding name comes to us from Plato,
that since the remote times of its life
has lived on light, on fire, on perfume, on love,
America of the great Montezuma, of the Inca,
the fragrant America of Christopher Columbus,
Catholic America, Spanish America,
the America in which noble Cuauhtemoc said:
"I'm not in a bed of roses"; that America
that trembles in hurricanes and lives on love,
it lives, you men of Saxon eyes and barbarous soul.
And it dreams. And it loves, and it vibrates, and it is the daughter of the Sun.
Be careful. Viva Spanish America!
There are a thousand cubs loosed from the Spanish lion.
Roosevelt, one would have to be, through God himself,

the-fearful Rifleman and strong Hunter,
to manage to grab us in your iron claws.

And, although you count on everything, you lack one thing:
God!

[Málaga, 1904]

Source: 1904 World Policy Institute, http://www.worldpolicy.org/globalrights/nicaragua/1904-Dar%C3%ADo-english.html.

141. "Roosevelt Boasts of Canal," 1911

In 1911, after the completion of the Panama Canal, former U.S. President Theodore Roosevelt boasted of taking the canal from Columbia in 1903, during his presidency. Colombia had hesitated signing a treaty that would have given the United States complete control over its Panamanian territory, so Panamanian friends of the United States revolted against Colombia, declared its independence and, within days, signed a treaty with the United States. The following article confirms what most knew but the United States denied—that the United States started the Panamanian war of independence and seized the canal from Colombia at the instigation of Roosevelt. In his "the end justifies the means" address in the article below he rationalized his actions.

ROOSEVELT BOASTS OF CANAL

Took It, He Says, without Giving Congress a Chance to Debate

BERKELEY, Cal., March 23—Speaking at the annual Charter Day exercises in the Greek Theatre at the University of California to-day, Col. Theodore Roosevelt made a plea for higher education and told how he started the Panama Canal.

"I am interested in the Panama Canal," he said, "because I started it. If I had followed traditional, conservative methods I would have submitted a dignified State paper of probably 200 pages to Congress and the debates on it would have been going on yet; but I took the Canal Zone and let Congress debate: and while the debate goes on the Canal does also.

After speaking at a student rally in Harmon Gymnasium to-night and attending a smoker given by the Faculty Club, Col. Roosevelt crossed the bay to San Francisco to spend the night at the home of his son, Theodore Roosevelt, Jr.

Source: *New York Times*, March 24, 1911, p. 1.

142. "Porto Rican Labor for Panama Canal," Letter to the Editor of the *New York Times*, 1904

Puerto Ricans continued their diaspora after the U.S. occupation. U.S. industry followed the flag, and the presence of U.S. corporations accelerated the commercialization of land and the uprooting of the small subsistence farmer. These displaced Puerto Ricans migrated to the cities where there was limited work. At the same time, employment contractors heavily recruited Puerto Rican labor to work in Mexico, Hawaii, California, and Panama. The following letter to the editor of the *New York Times* responds to the constant harping of American officials and citizens that Puerto Ricans should be grateful to the United States for liberating them and suggests that the people of Puerto Rico were in better financial condition under Spanish rule than U.S. occupation.

PORTO RICAN LABOR FOR PANAMA CANAL

To the Editor of the New York Times:

The suggestion made to employ Porto Ricans for work on the Panama Canal has so much to recommend it that it is to be hoped that it will receive the consideration it merits.

Up to date the people of Porto Rico have little to be grateful for to the people of the United States. Having ceased to be Spaniards they expected to become Americans, yet this has not been granted to them.

The island appears to be less prosperous now than it was under the Spanish flag, and it would seem to be a duty to assist its people in every way possible. It is to our own interest to give employment to these people, as they will doubtless return with their earnings, in part at least, so that this money will serve to help develop our "Island Paradise." All things being equal, preference should be given to those under our own flag.

Citizen
Orange, N, J., Dec. 28, 1904

Source: New York Times, December 30, 1904, p. 8.

143. "Taft to Porto Ricans," 1907

In 1907, while visiting Puerto Rico, U.S. Secretary of War William Howard Taft, who would later become president of the United States from 1909 to 1913, told the Puerto Rican people that they should be grateful to be a part of the United States. This remark was made in response to the Chief Justice of Puerto Rico's statement that it was his hope that Puerto Rican children would someday be American citizens—which at that time they were not. Taft replied that Puerto Ricans should be grateful that they had free trade with the United States but begged the question of citizenship, which he said should be left up to Congress. This was a thorny issue. The status of Puerto Ricans was left in the air. They were part of the United States but lacked the rights of American citizens. It was little consolation to have unlimited access to U.S. markets, because those same markets were commercializing agriculture and driving Puerto Ricans from the island.

TAFT TO PORTO RICANS

Tells Them Difficulties Stand in Way of American Citizenship

SAN JUAN, Porto Rico, April 15—Secretary of War Taft, who arrived here yesterday on board the Government yacht *Mayflower*, spent the day in consultation with various heads of departments inquiring minutely as to details in an effort to ascertain the reasons for the grievances of the people. Among others, he conferred with Surgeon General Robert M. O'Reilly relative to the building now being used as a military hospital.

The Supreme Court and the Executive Council entertained the Secretary at luncheon. In a speech of welcome Chief Justice Quinones expressed the hope that the Porto Rican children now growing up would receive from the United States the great honor of American citizenship.

Secretary Taft made a brief reply, in which he said Porto Rico was free from many of the difficulties existing in the Philippines and Cuba, and he called attention to the fact that trade with the United States had brought prosperity and contentment to the island. Referring to citizenship, he said:

"I beg of you to think of those things which you do have; let me call your attention to them. You have what is desired by the Philippines and Cuba, namely, the unsurpassed markets of the United States. What I am saying is not intended to oppose citizenship, but there are difficulties in the way of securing the passage of such laws through Congress."

Source: *New York Times*, April 16, 1907, p. 5.

144. Letter on Women's Roles from Luisa Capetillo to Dr. Paul Vigne, 1910

Puerto Rican feminist Luisa Capetillo (1879–1922) was a committed anarchist and activist. Capetillo's book *Mi opinión acerca de las libertades, derechos y deberes de la mujer* (*My Opinion about the Liberties, Rights and Duties of Women*) was published in 1911 and reprinted in 1913. Born out of wedlock in the northern town of Arecibo, Puerto Rico, on October 28, 1879, to working class parents, she rebelled by wearing trousers. Capetillo was highly political and tied the misery of Puerto Ricans to low pay and poor working conditions. She championed workers' rights, especially livable wages, and was an early advocate of gender rights. In the following letter, she discusses the role of women historically, particularly with regard to women entering the field of medicine as physicians.

(From L'Avenir Médical of Paris)

The legislative elections, which have just been held, have not been favorable to feminism. One or another female candidate has run, but none has been able to sustain a true struggle until the end. But this doesn't mean despair for those apostles of women's causes. All countries will continue to heed their aspirations, either under a timid veneer as in France, or in tumultuous abundance, as in England or in the Americas.

In fact, the feminist cause has had many important partisans among the strong sex. In 1877, Victor Hugo heatedly defended feminism in a letter to Leon Richer: "Women," wrote the poet, "are seen as lesser beings civically and as slaves, morally. Her [woman's] upbringing suffers from this double sense of inferiority; and from this all the suffering that man inflicts on her, which is unjust. Men have tipped the scales of the law, in whose equilibrium human consciousness is invested, putting all of the rights on their own little plates, and all the duties on the woman's. From this, the profound upheaval, from this, the slavery of woman. We need reform and this reform will be achieved for the benefit of civilization, of society, of light." The eminent philosopher, John Stuart Mill has written: "All of the egotistical inclinations, the cult of oneself, the injustice of self preference that dominates humanity, has its origin and roots in the way that current relations between men and women take place, and it is from these relations that such egotisms derive their principal force. Consider the vanity of the young man who when he becomes a man, is convinced that, without merit, without having done a thing on his own, and even if he is among the most frivolous and incapable of men, just by having been born a man, feels that he is superior to half of humanity without exception, when in that half one can find people whose superiority is capable of weighing over him every day and at every moment. By giving women the freedom to use their faculties, letting them freely choose the manner in which they want to exercise those faculties, by opening up the same work opportunities, and offering the same stimuli as those available to men, one of the principle benefits of such an endeavor would be to duplicate the total of intellectual faculties that humanity would have at its service."

But perhaps we should not follow these authors so far along this road, and instead, to return to what concerns our profession. We can agree that various women have undertaken this profession with great success.

Even in remote times, we have seen woman become interested in our art. In France, Diana of Poitiers and Marguerite of Valois are known for having practiced the art of medicine from antiquity.

Madame Necker, wife of the renowned minister of Louis XVI, was responsible for the reorganization of French hospitals.

In Germany, women doctors were numerous during the Middle ages, and even more so in the fourteenth and fifteenth centuries.

And in our times there are many women who have devoted themselves to medicine. Miss Elisabeth Blackwell, who had been a primary school teacher, is the first in the United States to become a doctor, at Boston University in 1847, also having studied in Geneva and Paris. Only eight years after Boston, the University of Philadelphia began to admit women to medical school, and this example was quickly imitated by other universities. In 1874, for the first time, Madame Putnam-Jacobi became a professor at Mount Sinai's teaching hospital. Later, there have been women doctors in the Army and one could cite the example of Madame MacGee, who was appointed military surgeon in Puerto Rico, with the rank of lieutenant. Miss María Walcher had a similar position in the Union Army during the Civil War.

Without trying to make this brief analysis something more extensive, and even if we didn't recognize that women have the same aptitude as men to undertake study as arduous as that of medicine, we can safely conclude from the previously cited examples, that women, by force of will and energy, are quite capable of doing certain jobs that they previously had been denied. This theory is constantly disputed by those who claim women's inferiority due to sexual difference, which, it is said, seems to be an immutable law of nature. But there is nothing more false than to attempt in this way to uphold the permanent superiority of men. There are numerous animal species for whom this rule has been broken. Elephants, for example, when they migrate and are about to cross into rough terrain, send the females ahead, because they are considered more apt to find the safest road.

Among birds it is often the female that is dominant in the couple. The female sparrow is not bashful about harshly reprimanding the male; and the female tosses the male sparrow out of the nest when there isn't sufficient food for the both of them. The female pigeon makes the male sit on the eggs and guard the nest from ten to four every day, while she goes off and gets some fresh air.

Among birds of prey, the female is more ferocious than the male, a fact that is well known to falconers, who prefer the females. She is so unaffectionate that, when made prisoner, she will kill her male companion.

Even among insects, a husband's fate is frequently of a most humiliating nature. The queen bee has many suitors. Forced to dash after her, the most agile male catches up with her and is accepted; but the joy of this husband is ephemeral because of course he dies. The destiny of the rivals he overcame is more enticing. These wellfed and non-working bees take on the leisurely pace of a lord, but then one fine morning, the female worker bees realize that they are feeding lazy and useless beings, and massacre the males.

But the true epitome of female triumph in the animal realm is reached in the spider. In this species, the female is much heavier and much stronger than the male, which is why the male is reduced to slavery, immediately and until the moment of fertilization. Once mating is finished and there is no more need for his services, he is simply devoured.

An elegant solution to conjugal problems! But we trust that the amiable members of the female sex have yet tended toward such a solution, in spite of overwhelming us everywhere with their vindications, and in spite of the fact that they already greet in the figure of a liberated Eve—according to the phrase coined by Miss Odette Laguerre—the engenderer of a more worthy humanity.

Source: "Doctor Paul Vigne, Paris, 1910" is reprinted with permission of the publisher of Luisa Capetillo's *A Nation of Women: An Early Feminist Speaks Out*, Edited by Fekix V. Natos Rodriguez. Houston: Arte Público Press—University of Houston © 2005. pp. 42–45. Translated by Alan West-Duran.

145. Letter on Socialism from Luisa Capetillo to Manuel Ugarte, 1911

Puerto Rican feminist Luisa Capetillo (1879–1922) was a committed anarchist and activist. In addition to her focus on gender issues, she was involved in the political and labor struggles of the working class. She condemned the exploitation of workers by political parties, religious institutions, and capitalism. She defines the kind of socialist she was in the following letter.

I am a socialist because I want all the advances, discoveries, and inventions to belong to everyone, that their socialization be achieved without privilege. Some understand this to mean that the State regulate this socialization, I see it without government. That does not mean that I will oppose a government that regulates and controls wealth, as it needs to do, but I maintain my position in being decidedly against government per se: Socialist anarchism.

What I solemnly declare here is that to be a socialist it is necessary to have analyzed and understood psychology.

It is a mistake to think oneself as a socialist and accept the fanatical dogmas, rites, and practices of religion because Socialism is truth and imposed religions are erroneous.

Equally wrong is to think oneself a socialist and be an atheist, a skeptic, and a materialist. Socialism is not a negation, nor violence, nor a utopia. It is a real and tangible truth. Under socialism there isn't room for the cunning (no!) to live comfortably from the work of others. There is no deceit, nor the imposition or imperialism over the weak or ignorant. Socialism persuades with truth, it does not wound. In socialism we find pure reason, the harmony between all, sweetness of demeanor, equality in everything. It is truth not lies, sincerity not intrigue. Now I have said sweetness of demeanor, isn't that what religions preach? Let us analyze this further. Reason is a straight path, serene, peaceful, and impassive. Jesus was a rationalist. A person whose norms follow reason does not violate himself, does not run away, does not make fun of nor express joy at the evil of his enemy or adversary.

So a reasonable person does not have enemies, and should he have them he does not hate them. What are the results of this? If they are insulted or struck by a hand, or with hurtful remarks, and respond in kind, what do they get out of it? (I cannot accept that someone be struck or mistreated without motive). Well, you'll say, what about getting even, vengeance? But reason is serene, self-controlled, it is not vengeful or injurious, and a socialist, for the good and emancipation of humankind should be reasonable. Whoever has reason is in control of themselves, and is not the instrument of vengeance and its consequences: crime, violence, and all sorts of brutal passions.

Socialism is found within the luminous Christianity that shook the foundations of Roman power, because of its notion of fraternity. And universal brotherhood will be the implementation of socialism, which is selflessness, sweetness, modesty, temperance: "All for one and one for all." These are sure steps that lead us to human perfection, toward the freedom and the still undefined spiritual progress of a plurality of superior worlds.

Let us enlighten and purify ourselves, let us educate our wills to do good, and let us consume the fire of our passions under guiding reason, in an offering to human emancipation to achieve spiritual progress.

Source: "My Profession of Faith to Manuel Ugarte" is reprinted with permission of the publisher of Luisa Capetillo's *A Nation of Women: An Early Feminist Speaks Out*, Edited by Fekix V. Natos Rodriguez. Houston: Arte Público Press—University of Houston © 2005, pp. 110–111. Translated by Alan West-Duran.